MW01224301

WITHDRAWN
From Heritage University Library

Gift of the Estate of
Robert (1938-2013)
and Gay Zieger (1938-2013)
October 2013

Heritage University Library
3240 Fort Road
Toppenish, WA 98948

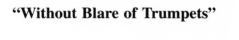

"Without Blare of Trumpets"

"Without Blare of Trumpets"

Walter Drew, the National Erectors'
Association, and the Open Shop
Movement, 1903–57

SIDNEY FINE

Ann Arbor

THE UNIVERSITY OF MICHIGAN PRESS

Copyright © by the University of Michigan 1995
All rights reserved
Published in the United States of America by
The University of Michigan Press
Manufactured in the United States of America
♾ Printed on acid-free paper

1998 1997 1996 1995   4 3 2 1

A CIP catalogue record for this book is available from the British Library.

Library of Congress Cataloging-in-Publication Data

Fine, Sidney, 1920–
    "Without blare of trumpets" : Walter Drew, the National Erectors'
Association, and the open shop movement, 1903–57 / Sidney Fine.
        p.   cm.
    Includes bibliographical references and index.
    ISBN 0-472-10576-0 (acid-free paper)
    1. National Erectors' Association—History. 2. Employers'
associations—United States—History. 3. Construction industry—
United States—Societies, etc.—History. 4. Steel industry and
trade—United States—Societies, etc.—History. 5. Trade-unions—
Construction workers—United States—History. 6. Trade-unions—
Iron and steel workers—United States—History. 7. Labor disputes—
United States—History—20th century. 8. Open and closed shop—
United States—History. 9. Drew, Walter, 1873–1961. I. Title.
HD6947.B92U63   1995
331.88'1241821'0973—dc20   94-35335
                                                        CIP

To the memory of Sophie and Isadore Schechter

Preface

Committed to what it characterized as the open shop, the National Erectors' Association (NEA) has been appraised as "the most class-conscious and belligerent national [employer] association" in the United States. From 1906 until the New Deal, it was, most conspicuously, the implacable foe of the union of the structural iron workers. The NEA continued to exist until 1957, but its role as a defender of the open shop dwindled to insignificance after the United States Supreme Court, in 1937, upheld the constitutionality of the National Labor Relations Act. A second National Erectors' Association was formed in 1969, but it was the polar opposite of the original NEA, the membership of the new association being limited to firms that recognized and dealt with the International Association of Bridge, Structural and Ornamental Iron Workers (IABSOIW).

Although the first NEA's stated concern was the erection of structural iron and steel for bridges and buildings, its principal members were fabricators as well as erectors of structural steel. The NEA, consequently, was as much involved with the steel industry as with the construction industry, a point that has received insufficient attention in the historical literature. As the only belligerent national employer association in the building industry, the NEA was interested in spreading the open shop beyond structural steel erection to the building trades as a whole, a major area of union strength; but it also saw itself as the front line of defense of the open shop in the steel industry. Should the IABSOIW succeed in organizing structural steel erection, the NEA argument ran, the union would refuse to handle steel fabricated in nonunion shops and mills. The fact that the IABSOIW claimed jurisdiction over the steel fabrication shops appeared to lend force to this argument. Since the principal member of the NEA, moreover, was the American Bridge Company, a subsidiary of United States Steel, the link between the association and the steel industry was apparent.

The commissioner of the NEA from 1906 to 1957 was Walter Drew. What has been insufficiently understood is that Drew was not just a defender of the open shop in the structural steel erection industry but that he also played a major role in seeking to spread the open shop in various communities to the building trades as a whole and, beyond that, to other unionized sectors of the economy as well. Until the New Deal changed the rules of the game in labor-management relations, there was no more influential protagonist of the open shop in the nation than Walter Drew.

It is a pleasure to acknowledge the assistance that I received in my research for this book. My efforts were facilitated by Francis Blouin, Nancy Bartlett, Ann Flowers, Christine Weideman, and the staff of the Bentley Historical Library; Michael H. Nash and Marjorie M. McNinch of the Hagley Museum and Library; Bill Creech, Tab Lewis, James Cassedy, Angie Spicer, Elizabeth K. Lockwood, and Steven A. Tilley of the National Archives and Records Administration; Francesca Pitaro of the New York Public Library; Martha Hodges of the M. P. Catherwood Library of Cornell University; Carol Alexander of the Department of Labor Library; Richard H. Harms of the Grand Rapids Public Library and Mike Johnson of Grand Rapids; Ralph A. Pugh of the Chicago Historical Society; Laura A. Endicott of the University of Virginia Library; Raymond Teichman of the Franklin D. Roosevelt Library; Peter Blodgett of The Huntington; Tamsen M. Hernandez of the Conference Board; and the late H. M. Gitelman.

Geoffrey Cowan generously provided me with copies of some documents in his possession. Bernard F. McTigue, the curator of special collections at the University of Oregon Library, was kind enough to serve briefly as my "research assistant" and to answer my questions concerning the unpublished autobiography of James B. McNamara. Despite repeated efforts and the assistance of Stuart Kaufman, director of the George Meany Memorial Archives, I was unable to gain access to the records in the possession of the IABSOIW. Fortunately, however, the Walter Drew Papers, which contain copies of the relevant union records for the critical period before 1913; the Frank P. Walsh Papers; the W. Jett Lauck Papers; the Records of the American Federation of Labor: The Samuel Gompers Era, which contain pertinent IABSOIW correspondence even for the years after Gompers's death; various record groups in the National Archives and Records Administration; other manuscript and published sources; and the union's official publication, the *Bridgemen's Magazine,* provide abundant information on the union's reaction to the open shop policy of the NEA and its members.

I owe a special debt to Dallas L. Jones, who was responsible for the deposit of the Walter Drew Papers in the Bentley Historical Library and who made summaries of interviews he had conducted available to me. My wife, Jean Fine, was my indispensable partner throughout my work on the book. I am grateful to Julia Routson for the expert typing of the manuscript.

I first dealt with some of the issues treated in this book in "The National Erectors' Association and the Dynamiters," *Labor History* 32 (Winter 1991): 5–41. I have received permission from *Labor History* to use passages from the article. The National Association of Manufacturers and the Conference Board have granted me permission to quote certain items in their records deposited in the Hagley Museum and Library. The photographs reproduced in the text were generously made available to me by the Bentley Historical Library.

Contents

CHAPTER 1

The "Organized Revolt" of Employers

American industrial relations, Sanford Jacoby has pointed out, have been characterized by an employer opposition to trade unionism "more extreme" than that of employers in other industrial countries.[1] It is hardly surprising, therefore, that the rapid growth in trade union membership at the turn of the twentieth century led to a vigorous employer reaction and a counteroffensive against unionism at both the national and local levels.

In his first message to Congress, President Theodore Roosevelt characterized the labor question as "the most vital problem with which this country or, for that matter, the whole civilized world has to deal." Three years later, in 1904, the muckraker Ray Stannard Baker concluded that this same labor question had been "the distinctive national problem" of the preceding five years. What gave substance to these remarks was the more than sixfold increase in trade union membership between 1897 and 1904, from 264,825 to 1,676,200, the increase in strikes for recognition from 13.4 percent to 41.3 percent of the total number of strikes, and the employer reaction to these developments.[2] The National Civic Federation, which had been formed in 1900, sought to preserve industrial peace by mediation and conciliation, and it viewed trade agreements as the means to improve labor-management relations.[3] More typical, however, was the employer counteroffensive against unionism and union growth.

The "organized revolt" of the employers began in 1900 with the formation of a strongly antiunion employers' association in Dayton, Ohio. Soon, an array of organizations, the American Anti-Boycott Association, the National Metal Trades Association, the National Founders' Association, and the National Association of Manufacturers joined the open shop ranks. Of special relevance for the story of the National Erectors' Association, the United States Steel Company began immediately after its formation in 1901 to move in an antiunion direction. And in the building trades, the vital center of closed shop unionism in the nation, contractors in Chicago and New York, although not prepared to break with the building trades unions, including the union of structural iron workers, sought to curb their power. There was much talk during the early years of the century, and not just by employers, about "the tyranny of unions," "the dangerous aggressions of organized labor," "the excesses of labor unions and the abuses of their power," "the coercive and brutal methods commonly employed by labor unions," union reductions of output, and union violation of contracts.[4]

"Today," John Keith announced in *Harper's Weekly* at the beginning of 1904, "capital is organizing and preparing for a mortal combat which shall forever decide the existence or at least the authority of organized labor." Whether it reflected "underlying economic conditions" in particular industries resulting from technological developments and changes in market structures, a downturn in the condition of the economy and a desire by employers to free their businesses of union rules that management believed increased costs, an employer view of his prerogatives that did not necessarily relate to a hard-headed appraisal of costs, or some combination of these factors, employers organized to confront their union opponents.

In combating unionism, employers generally insisted that they were not opposed to unions as such but only to the way unions behaved and their alleged insistence on the closed shop, the shop closed to all but union members. In point of fact, however, employer organizations could find few union practices of which they approved. They claimed that they favored the open shop, which they were apt to define in the terms used in the influential 1903 arbitration award by the Anthracite Coal Strike Commission: "no person shall be refused employment, or in any way discriminated against, on account of membership or non-membership in any labor organization, and . . . there shall be no discrimination against, or interference with, any employee who is not a member of any labor organization by members of such organizations." Workers, the commission stated, were "free to work upon what terms and at what time and for whom it may please them to do so." What employers claimed was an open shop was, however, sometimes actually a nonunion shop, a shop closed to union members, just as the so-called union shop might actually be closed to nonunion members.[5]

Dayton, Ohio, as of 1900, was regarded as "the banner town of organized labor." With John Kirby taking the lead, business interests in the city organized the Employers' Association of Dayton, with thirty-eight charter members. The association was soon able to recruit new members to combat a machinists' strike; and, following a citywide lockout the next year, Dayton became "the first 'completely open-shop city' of any appreciable size in the United States." Seeking to replicate the Dayton experience, Kirby helped to organize employer associations in other midwestern cities, for which the Dayton association served as a model. Kirby himself would go on to become president of the National Association of Manufacturers from 1909 to 1913 and "to wage war upon organized labor."[6]

Discovering "an overwhelming sentiment in favor of an antiunion legal service," the Bridgeport attorney Daniel Davenport took the initiative in the formation in 1902 of the American Anti-Boycott Association (AABA). The association appealed particularly to owners of middle-sized businesses in such competitive industries as metal fabricating and hatting that were concerned about American Federation of Labor (AFL) strikes and boycotts against goods produced by nonunion firms, picketing of struck plants, intimidation by unionists of strike replacements, and the closed shop. In the celebrated 1908 Danbury Hatters' case (*Loewe v. Lawlor*), the United States Supreme Court agreed with the AABA that the Sherman Antitrust Act applied to combinations of employees that obstructed the free flow of interstate commerce and that individual union members were liable for actions taken by their elected officers "within the scope of their employment."[7]

By the time of the *Loewe v. Lawlor* decision, the National Founders' Association (NFA), established in 1898 and composed of firms employing molders and coremakers and producing heavy machinery and iron castings, and the National Metal Trades Association (NMTA), formed in 1899 by firms that manufactured metal products, had joined the antiunion campaign. Following the lead of the NFA, which had concluded a national arbitration agreement in 1899 with the Iron Molders' Union, the NMTA negotiated an agreement with the International Association of Machinists in 1900 that involved recognition of the union but did not concede the closed shop. Alleging that the Machinists had broken the agreement by pressing for a closed shop, seeking to limit production, and striking in violation of the contract, the NMTA voided the agreement in 1901 and thereafter became "militantly opposed to the principle of collective bargaining." Three years later the NFA, dissatisfied with its relations with the Molders' Union, transformed itself from a "negotiatory" employer association into a "belligerent" antiunion association.[8]

Arguably "the most important convert to the militant open shop" movement was the National Association of Manufacturers (NAM). In 1902 David McLean Parry, president of the Parry Manufacturing Company of Indianapolis, the nation's largest carriage manufacturer, was elected president of the NAM. At its 1902 convention the NAM, which to that time had been primarily concerned with enlarging the export market for American manufactured goods and protecting the home market, adopted a resolution condemning the efforts of organized labor to secure federal legislation requiring the eight-hour day for federal employees. At the NAM's next convention, in April 1903, Parry reported that the association had succeeded in defeating the AFL effort "to engraft upon the statute books its sprigs of socialism, legalizing the denials of individual right which it had heretofore sought to enjoin by force."[9]

Parry's central concern was not organized labor's effort to secure favorable legislation but the power he believed unions exercised in the marketplace. Conceding that the "fight against organized labor" was, "in a measure, a departure" for the NAM from its "former conservative policy respecting labor," Parry asserted in his 1903 presidential address that labor's "growing power" demanded "counter-organization strong enough to resist its encroachments." He viewed organized labor as "dominating to a dangerous degree the whole social, political and governmental systems [*sic*] of the Nation." He noted in this regard the hundreds of strikes during the previous year and labor's "many acts of aggression and ruthless violation of principles." Organized labor, he alarmingly declared, "knows but one law, and that is the law of physical force—the law of the Huns and the Vandals, the law of the savages." As Parry saw it, unionism was "in all of its essential features, a mob power, knowing no master except its own will." Its leaders were "agitators and demagogues," it sought to force men into its ranks by "intimidation," and the "rule" it sought to establish was that of the "least intelligent portion of labor."

Parry, Kirby, and a few others at the 1903 convention would have liked the NAM to adopt a resolution condemning unions per se. Somewhat more moderate members at the convention, however, were troubled by Parry's "inflammatory" speech and were not prepared to go as far as he in committing the NAM to an all-out war against organized labor. In the end, the second of nine principles regarding the relations of employer and employee that convention delegates adopted stated that the NAM was not opposed to organized labor but was "unalterably opposed to boycotts, blacklists and other illegal acts of interference with the personal liberty of employer or employee." Conspicuous among the other principles was the open shop language of the Anthracite Coal Strike Commission, which was repeated verbatim. In addition, the principles called for "fair dealing" between employer and employee, the right of the employee to quit his job as he saw fit, the right of the employer to discharge employees ("with due regard to contracts"), the right of the employer to engage workers at such wages as were "mutually satisfactory" without "interference or dictation" by those not party to the arrangement, the right of employers to be "unmolested and unhampered in the management of their business," no limitation on the opportunity of an individual to learn a trade, and disapproval of strikes and lockouts not in accord with the nine principles. The words *open shop* and *closed shop* did not appear in the principles, but at its next convention the NAM added a principle declaring its "unconditional antagonism to the closed shop."[10]

Parry argued at the 1903 NAM convention that an organization "separate and distinct" from the NAM was required to "counter" organized labor. This, he said, was because the NAM included only manufacturers among its members whereas what was needed was an organization "enlisting under its banner employers of all classes." Agreeing with Parry, the delegates resolved that the president and the secretary of the NAM should cooperate with officers of other employer associations "to form a permanent central organization" that would serve as "a clearing house for ideas and provide means for cooperation on matters of common interest." A preliminary conference on September 29, 1903, attended by representatives of the NAM and several employer associations in response to the convention decision, was followed by a conference of representatives of more than three hundred national, state, and local employer organizations and citizens' alliances in Chicago on October 30 that launched the Citizens' Industrial Association of America (CIAA).[11]

The 1903 Chicago meeting was characterized by a trade journal as "the most important . . . ever called in the country for the discussion of relations between employers and wage earners." Parry was elected president of the new organization, and a constitution was adopted subject to ratification at an adjourned meeting of the convention that was held in Indianapolis in February 1904. Believing themselves on the "defensive," the delegates in Chicago viewed the industrial situation in the nation in the wildly exaggerated terms expressed by Parry at the 1903 NAM convention. A convention resolution referred to "the strained relations between employer and employee as rapidly reducing the business conditions of the country into a state of chaos and anarchy" and appraised "the forces of socialism" as "assuming control of the situation." The delegates characterized themselves not as opposing the right of workers to organize but as "carrying on a firm and uncompromising contest with the abuses of unions as now constituted and conducted." As their objectives, they listed promotion of "harmonious relations between employers and employees upon a basis of equal justice to both," assistance to both labor and management in maintaining "industrial peace," and the creation and direction of "a public sentiment in opposition to all forms of violence, coercion and intimidation."[12]

Men like Parry and Kirby thought it necessary for employers to carry on a campaign of education because they believed that the public, which in their view was being flooded with socialist and anarchist literature, was "prone to sympathize with the labor unions." As they saw it, it was necessary also to educate the political parties and especially public officials, guilty as the latter allegedly were of a "cringing attitude toward the unions." Convinced of the correctness of their own position, the leaders of the CIAA believed that "the erroneous ideas" of the trade unions could not survive "public discussion" of the matter.[13]

The nearly five hundred delegates who gathered in Indianapolis in February, most of them representing small and medium-sized business and citizen groups, voted to admit to CIAA membership all citizens who believed in the enforcement of laws to protect individuals who wished to earn a living without interference by any organization or person. "We stand for the open shop," the CIAA delegates declared. They cheered when Parry stated in his address that if unions insisted on the closed shop, it became "the duty of employers to discriminate against union labor." In addition to opposition to the closed shop, the CIAA principles included "no restriction as to the use of tools, machinery or materials" unless they were unsafe, no "limitation of output," no restriction on the number of apprentices or helpers of the proper age, no boycotts or sympathetic strikes, "no sacrifice of independent workmen to the labor union," and "no compulsory use of the union label."[14]

Following another CIAA convention in November 1904, Parry concluded that he did not have the time to continue as the organization's head. He was succeeded by C. W. Post, a member of the CIAA's executive committee, who remained the organization's president for the remainder of its existence. A Battle Creek, Michigan, entrepreneur, Post had developed Postum in the early 1890s as a substitute for coffee and then had begun producing a variety of cereal products, including Grape Nuts and Post Toasties. His first important brush with unions came in 1901, when the International Typographical Union, which was boycotting the *Los Angeles Times,* requested Post and other advertisers to withhold future advertisements. Post, "one of the greatest business advertisers of his time," refused, and when the union then listed his company as "unfair," Post bought space in newspapers across the country denouncing the union. Newspapers that did not print what he called his "educational material" lost Postum Cereal Company ads. Post organized a citizens' alliance in Battle Creek that in 1904 began to publicize Battle Creek as an open shop city.[15]

The change of CIAA presidents from Parry to Post involved more than a change of personalities. Parry had really wanted to create a national association of antiunion employers, but Post was committed to an organization in which not only organized employers but the unorganized, the citizenry, would be represented. "My idea" of the CIAA, he informed a correspondent, is that "it should stand as the national organization of the big third party, the common people, whose interests are being trespassed by the interference of labor unions with the common affairs of life." He hoped "to mass the citizens together in the various cities and villages, and through the local organizations, supported when necessary by the national organization, to prevent strikes, lockouts, boycotts and any interference with the industries and interests of the country."[16]

As Post saw it, the unions had established a "labor trust" in response to the earlier establishment of capital trusts. The labor trust, he contended, was "the largest and most oppressive trust in existence." It was "a combination to sell labor" that used "threats of violence to force people to buy its commodity." It raised prices, limited opportunity, broke contracts, and protected criminals. If it were allowed to increase its power, it would in the end dominate American life. Unlike the capital trust, which was "tangible and financially responsible" and hence was the lesser of the two trust evils, the labor trust, Post asserted, avoided legal responsibility "in every way possible" and had broken the law so frequently as to become "an insufferable menace to the people" and a threat to "the stability of the Government."

What the CIAA was trying to do, Post explained, was to protect the unorganized when organized labor and organized capital got "to scrapping between themselves." Although the two types of trusts, in Post's estimation, represented at most 20 percent of the people, he insisted that they "largely control[led]" the unorganized 80 percent. Thanks to the CIAA, however, which, Post asserted, aimed to make the trusts of capital and labor "behave," the unorganized were "beginning to wake up to the fact that they are in the majority, and that they have every right to rule." The CIAA, its secretary declared, is "the counter organization of the citizen."[17]

By January 1906 the CIAA was claiming the existence of 437 local associations, state federations under various names, and a representation of more than three million people. It sent organizers into the field to establish associations where they did not exist. It urged the prosecution of "criminal" combinations of labor in restraint of interstate trade, the combating of "class legislation," support for trade schools to train workers, and, above all, "a great education campaign" to form "a sound public opinion on the labor question." It encouraged employers to hire workers through association employment bureaus since it believed that "the chief coercive force of unionism" was "exerted through the business agent acting as an exclusive employment bureau. Employers were urged to ascertain a man's record before hiring him and not to employ the "agitator, striker, stone thrower or law breaker."[18]

The CIAA credited itself by 1906 with having had a great deal to do with "moulding public opinion particularly in the East." It sent out a staggering amount of literature, 150 million pieces in two years, and claimed that it had popularized the phrase *open shop,* a little-used term in the first years of the century. Through its secretary and the NAM's general counsel, James A. Emery, it lobbied Congress in behalf of the open shop and against the demands of the "Labor Trust," and it believed that it had increased the influence of the open shop cause in the nation. Two years of effort by the CIAA, a Denver correspondent reported early in 1905, had ended picketing and boycotting in the city and made it "practically an open shop" community except for the building trades.[19]

Increasingly, the chief interest of organizations affiliated with the CIAA, like the NAM, came to be the frustration of efforts to secure legislation favorable to labor, particularly at the national level. As Emery explained, unions were seeking to make the national and state governments their "allies" in securing legislation to shorten the workday and legalize union tactics the courts were proscribing, such as sympathetic or "malicious" strikes, boycotts, picketing, and restraints of interstate trade. In combating "these extreme demands," however, the NAM leadership believed that the various employer organizations were proceeding in a "haphazard" manner that lessened the effectiveness of their efforts.[20]

The NAM board of directors adopted a resolution on May 14, 1906, calling for the establishment of a council as "a means of harmonizing the various national organizations of employers and citizens and to unite them in a vigorous campaign against the growing social discontent in the United States." The resolution led to a July meeting of four or five national organizations at which they decided to form a secret council of industrial organizations. The proposal, however, died aborning, probably because the NAM decided that the "day had gone for any kind of secret work." At the 1907 NAM convention, the delegates approved a resolution instructing the NAM's officers to create and fund a council for the purpose of "harmonizing and federating" the various national and state organizations of "citizens, merchants and employers" and to conduct "a vigorous educational campaign for the interest of industrial peace and mutual goodwill."[21]

The decision of the NAM convention led its president, James W. Van Cleave, who was also a CIAA vice president and head of the Buck Stove and Range Company, to convene a meeting of national associations on August 19, 1907. Those present saw themselves as beleaguered, under siege, and facing a flood of labor and socialistic bills fostered by a labor "enemy" that, Van Cleave maintained, "has not been, is not[,] and will not be asleep." "It is a frequent statement," he told the delegates, "that there are tons of union and socialistic literature sent through its mails every day, and we don't send enough to wad a gun." It would have shocked the employers present to learn that American historians at a later time would view the Progressive Era as a time of rather modest reforms and one in which managerial prerogatives were not seriously challenged by organized labor.

Although the organizations represented at the 1907 convention differed on many issues, they were agreed on the centrality of the labor question. They unanimously approved a recommendation to their respective organizations providing for the creation of a "central council" on which each would be represented and whose functions would be limited to "the consideration of and action upon all questions arising from the relations between employers and employees" and that would be empowered to set up a legislative bureau, a legal bureau, and a bureau of publicity and education. If the organizations involved failed to federate, Van Cleave wrote Post, "the Unions will eat us up." They did federate, forming the National Council for Industrial Defense (NCID) in late 1907, with a constitution pledging the organization "To preserve and promote the principles of individual freedom for employers and employes in commerce and industry," to defend these principles against hostile legislation or attacks on the "legal remedies" that protected them, and to oppose "class legislation in whatever form."[22]

Since the CIAA viewed itself as the proper umbrella organization for any coalition of employer groups desiring to speak with one voice, the NAM decision to create a council that would in effect be a front for the NAM led to a bitter fight between the CIAA and the NAM that was largely shielded from public view. Although the NAM's board of directors subscribed $1,000 for the CIAA's educational work in February 1907, the contribution masked a growing discord between the two organizations, stemming in part from their lobbying efforts in Washington and perhaps because the CIAA believed that the NAM had "rebuffed" CIAA efforts to increase its membership. Whereas the NAM wished to keep affairs of the new council in its own hands, Post believed that if what was intended was to secure public support for opposition to "socialism, labor unionism and all such disintegrated [*sic*] elements," an organization like the CIAA, which, unlike the NAM, included more than employers, was the proper agency to play that role. What the CIAA clearly desired was to be "in the saddle at Washington, backed up by all these National Employer Associations."[23]

In seeking to make the CIAA the spokesman for the employer associations and interested citizens, Post was arguing from a position of weakness. Despite CIAA claims of success in producing "a wonderful change in public opinion" regarding the labor question, Post found himself carrying on the CIAA's affairs at his own expense. By March 1908 the CIAA owed Post $83,000, and the debt was increasing at the rate of $2,500 per month. The "chief revenue producer" for the CIAA was its journal, *Square Deal,* which began publishing in August 1905, but the magazine had never been "a paying proposition." The local associations that made up the CIAA were supposed to pay dues of fifty cents per year per member, but less than thirty had paid any dues as of April 1908; and even those that did pay did not do so every year, the aggregate amount received from them to that time being only $2,000. Appeals to the public and particularly to business organizations to replenish the CIAA's dwindling treasury proved to be dismal failures, Post concluding that business people were "the most selfish, pigheaded and shortsighted men and women in the country." The CIAA was also unable to attract worker support because, it decided, workers would not accept "anything which did not bear the Gompers imprimatur or the union label." On October 30, 1908, the balance in the CIAA account was $200, and before the month was out, the CIAA, alleging that it had merged with the NCID, ceased to exist as an organization. Contrary to the judgment of one scholar, however, that fact, as we shall see, hardly marked "the end of the vitality of the open shop movement" in the pre–World War I era.[24]

Reflecting his opposition to a union tactic that he ranked at or near the top of the sins he attributed to organized labor but also, it would seem, his desire to take revenge on Van Cleave, who had rejected Post's efforts to make the CIAA the controlling force in the NCID or to merge the two organizations into a "national Association of Manufacturers and Employers,"[25] Post involved him-self in 1908 in what became the celebrated case of *Gompers* v. *Buck Stove and Range Company.* Because of Buck Stove's dispute with the International Brotherhood of Foundry Employees, the AFL had initiated a boycott against the company and placed it on the Federation's published "unfair list." In a suit brought on its behalf by the AABA in the Supreme Court of the District of Columbia, the company secured a preliminary injunction in December 1907 against the AFL, restraining it from prosecuting the boycott. When the AFL defied the court order, the AABA, in January 1908, initiated contempt-of-court proceedings against Gompers, AFL secretary Frank Morrison, and AFL vice president John Mitchell. The trial court found the three guilty and sentenced them to prison terms. The AFL appealed the injunction and contempt case to the Supreme Court, which in January 1911 dismissed the injunction case as moot and ruled that the trial court should not have treated the contempt as a civil matter since a contempt proceeding was a criminal affair.[26]

Citing his own successful experience in defeating boycotts, Post had urged Van Cleave, Buck's president, to advertise in the communities where his product was being boycotted. Post offered Van Cleave more than advice. Some time before May 1908, while the case was being litigated, Post invested $60,000 in Buck Stove to prevent a large stockholder who favored "surrender" from acquiring a controlling interest in the firm. Post extracted a promise from Van Cleave for coming to his aid: Van Cleave agreed that he would leave the NAM's presidency at the end of the year to devote his full time to the company. Post wanted Emery, the CIAA's secretary, to be made president of the NAM, thinking that this would facilitate the CIAA-NCID merger Post was seeking.

Van Cleave retired as the NAM president in May 1909, but the CIAA by then had ceased to exist.[27]

The NCID was really a "creature" of the NAM, largely financed by it and controlled by its legislative committee, whose chairman was also the NCID chairman. As of December 1909, the NCID, serving as "a legislative pressure group," represented more than two hundred national, state, and local industrial and commercial associations and more than 145,000 business concerns. These organizations, however, provided the NCID with little more than their names, permitting whoever was lobbying for it to claim that he was speaking not just for the NAM but for so large a group of employers. That, it was assumed, would cause "the average politician to take notice." The chief spokesman for the NCID in Washington was James Emery, whom the organization authorized in January 1908 to represent it in legislative matters and who became its counsel in November. In addition to its Washington work, the NCID responded to calls to appear before state legislative committees in opposition to "proposed vicious class legislation," as the NAM put it.[28]

When the Sixty-first Congress adjourned on June 25, 1908, the NCID claimed victory on the legislative front "all along the line" in what it viewed as a "remarkable demonstration" of its strength. It took credit for the failure of the "labor lobby" and its friends to secure the enactment of an anti-injunction law, a bill that would have exempted unions from the Sherman Act, and a federal eight-hour bill. The NCID also played a prominent role in defeating efforts to insert Sherman Act and anti-injunction planks in the 1908 Republican party platform. Satisfied with the results, the NAM continued to support the NCID, which became the National Industrial Council in 1919.[29]

Although United States Steel became a member of the National Civic Federation, the company from its outset shared the antiunion bias of the CIAA and the NAM. United States Steel's executive committee turned its attention to labor policy "almost immediately" after the corporation had been formed in late February 1901. Aware of the strength of the Amalgamated Association of Iron, Steel and Tin Workers in the plants of American Tin Plate, American Sheet Steel, and American Steel Hoop and desirous of avoiding a strike at so unfavorable a time for the corporation, the committee instructed the corporation's subsidiaries, including the American Bridge Company, to sign agreements for unionized mills but to oppose any extension of unions to nonunion mills. The committee also agreed to a policy of shutting down mills where the union was then recognized.

The Amalgamated struck American Tin Plate, American Sheet Steel, and American Steel Hoop in July 1901 and then declared a general strike against United States Steel the next month. The strike, which ended on September 14, was a disaster for the Amalgamated. It was forced to agree to a settlement that cost it fourteen previously unionized mills, and of the twenty mills it retained, many were inefficient and were eventually abandoned by the corporation. The Amalgamated was left with twelve "active" mills, of which only eight were "first class," and United States Steel was well on its way to ousting the Amalgamated from all of its plants, which occurred in June 1909.[30]

The National Erectors' Association was concerned with both the fabrication of structural iron and steel, which tied it to the steel industry, and the erection of that steel, which linked it to the construction industry. Steel began to replace wood and stone in the erection of bridges and buildings in the 1880s. It was structural steel that "made the skyscraper possible," first in Chicago in the 1880s and then on a much larger scale in New York in the beginning years of the twentieth century. Steel was required for a building more than four stories high, and, as one general contractor put it, it became "the bridge on which everything hangs," since the steel frame for a building had to be erected before the brick and masonry work on the structure could proceed. Steel construction and the skeleton frame "reached maturity" while the use of reinforced concrete was "in its infancy." Reinforced concrete, however, became increasingly popular in building in the first quarter of the twentieth century, as the increasing consumption of portland cement, from 8.4 million barrels in 1904 to 149.3 million barrels in 1924, indicates.[31]

The steel that was fabricated for erection was produced in the steel mills, primarily of United States Steel and the Bethlehem Steel Company, in the form of plates, bars, and shapes. The steel was then transported to the shops of the fabricators, where it was fabricated for a particular erection job in accordance with the erection diagram, drawing, or design. It would be cut, punched, and drilled so as to receive the rivets that would hold it in place in the structure, and the various pieces would be put together in preparation for their erection. The fabrication of structural steel was primarily in the hands of large companies, 68 percent of the total tonnage being fabricated by 4 percent of the approximately 460 fabricating concerns in the years 1928–32. Of the 2,807,000 tons fabricated annually on the average during the years 1928–31, 29.7 percent was erected by owners, mostly railroad companies; 10.9 percent by general contractors; 16 percent by independent erectors who did no fabricating; and 43.5 percent by fabricators who did their own erecting. The independent erectors generally erected the steel in place for the owner or general contractor, who had purchased the steel from the fabricator.[32]

The development of structural steel erection brought with it a new type of worker and a new union. The bridge carpenter now became a bridgeman, and the blacksmith became a housesmith, that is, an ironworker who worked on buildings or an ornamental iron worker, "primarily an assembler," who erected stairways, balustrades, elevator enclosures, balconies, iron window guards, and gates. The terms *bridgeman* and *housesmith* were often interchanged, and although primarily a riveter, a bridgeman had other responsibilities as well. He was described in a 1905 union agreement as "competent to perform such work as the erection of structural steel and iron and ornamental metal work; the rigging and handling of travelers and other important mechanical appliances used in the erection of work; the erecting in place and connecting of members entering permanently into a structure, and the driving of field rivets." The housesmiths worked in gangs on the steel towers as long riveters, derrickmen, connectors, and planers.[33]

Structural steel and iron work was a less skilled occupation than most of the other building trades. "There is not so much mechanical ability to it," a union organizer for the trade noted in 1914. It took "probably three to four months to learn how to heat and drive rivets, and the balance" was "to become accustomed to going up high and not falling off." Union agreements required an apprentice in the trade to work six to eighteen months, as compared to three to four years for apprentices in the more skilled building trades. The union for structural steel workers did not have a training program for its members until 1948. The ironworker was "more noted for strength and physical courage than for trained skill and intelligence." The occupation, one observer noted, called for "daring and steady nerves and the sort of skill that enables one to walk around, assembling and bolting parts, on the narrow beams of the tenth story of a rising skyscraper." The Progressive Era writer Ernest Poole dubbed the ironworkers the "Cowboys of the Skies."[34]

The distinguishing characteristic of the housesmiths' trade was "great physical risk." "They work far up on dizzying structures," an investigator for the Commission on Industrial Relations reported. "They ride far out in the air on great steel girders, swung far out into the air while the pulley heads it up, up, up hundreds of feet. They creep to and fro on narrow iron beams so far up in the air that the people down below look like little ants. They toss red hot rivets to each other, catching them in buckets three or four stories below, when the failure to catch them may mean swift death to some fellow worker." Death or injury for the workers resulted from the dropping of a tool or a rivet, the "breaking of a boom" or a line, the overloading of derricks and travelers, poor rigging, and misinterpretation of signals. A union worker with forty years of experience who observed in 1925, "You got to be tough to handle steel," claimed that he had "seen forty men take the plunge. . . . No fault of their own," he remarked, "just the luck of the trade."[35]

In the years 1910–14, according to a study by the United States Bureau of Labor Statistics, structural steel workers suffered twelve deaths per one thousand workers and 353.2 accidents involving permanent (11.1) or temporary disability. "[T]he erection of structural steel," the authors of the study concluded, "must be recognized as one of the most, if not the most, hazardous industrial operations." Work-related death was no stranger to the union of structural iron workers. In the nineteen years ending June 30, 1923, the union suffered one death by accident for every 199 members. If deaths resulting from exposure while working and from heart attacks attributable to exertion are included, the death rate, according to the union, came to one per 159 members.[36]

Accident insurance rates for ironworkers in the middle 1920s were 25–50 percent higher than for workers in other trades. According to a 1931 report by the National Safety Council, for every one million man-hours of exposure, structural iron workers suffered 108.35 accidents, compared to 48.15 for general construction workers and 57.24 for coal miners. The rate of severity for accidents (number of days lost per one thousand hours of exposure) was 31.25 for structural iron workers, 5.14 for construction workers in general, and 9.44 for coal workers. For the entire period 1915–31, the frequency rate of accidents for structural iron workers averaged 90.51 and the severity rate, 22.27. The union sought to deal with the matter in the pre–workmen's compensation era by providing partial compensation for injured members and death benefits for the families of those killed. [37]

Structural iron workers not only suffered higher rates of death and accidents than other construction workers, but also, as outside workers, they worked fewer days per year. According to a report of the Committee on Elimination of Waste in Industry of the American Engineering Council, of a possible 273 working days in 1920, structural iron workers worked 150 days, as compared to an average of 189 days for building trades workers in general.[38]

For some of the perhaps fifty thousand structural iron and related workers in the early years of the twentieth century, according to a CIAA estimate, their union became "a haven of refuge." The international union of structural iron workers traces its origins to the Bridge Builders' Mutual Association founded in Chicago in the early 1880s as a mutual aid society for its twenty members. In response to the growing demand for structural iron workers, the association became a trade union in 1890 as the Bridge and Construction Men's Union. It came into conflict with another group of ironworkers who in that year formed the Architectural Iron Workers, but the two merged in 1892, taking the name Bridge and Structural Iron Workers. The organization later became Local No. 1 of the international union. New York housesmiths traced their origin to an 1864 organization. Reorganized in 1884, the organization collapsed following a failed strike, reorganized once again in 1894, and entered the international as Housesmiths' and Bridgemen's Local No. 2.[39]

Delegates from Chicago, New York, Boston, Buffalo, Pittsburgh, and possibly Cleveland were present for the founding convention of the International Association of Bridge and Structural Iron Workers (IABSIW) in 1896. As Luke Grant pointed out in his study of the union for the Commission on Industrial Relations, the international was little more than a paper organization at its outset. Locals were largely autonomous, and the union had no headquarters office, no salaried officers, and no official journal. At its 1899 convention it made plans to secure control of all ironwork and also decided to apply for an AFL charter. The charter was granted but returned the next year after "heated discussion" at the union convention. The union reaffiliated with the AFL in 1903 but with a somewhat diminished jurisdiction.

In 1901 the IABSIW became "an active national union" with twenty-seven locals and a membership of six thousand. The next year it made its president and secretary full-time salaried officers, made the *Bridgemen's Magazine,* which had been operating as a private venture, its official journal in

1903, and began talking about organizing the workers in the fabrication shops, a number that before long would reach fifty thousand.[40]

The structural steel erection trade was but one of as many as fifty crafts in the building trades. Primarily because of the economic structure of the construction industry, the building trades unions constituted the largest element in the AFL in the pre–World War I era, making up 17.7 percent of the membership in 1900 and 21 percent in 1914, when the membership of building trades unions was 555,300. In the 1890s the building trades unions in many cities joined to form building trades councils, which became "one of the most powerful institutions in the trade union world." Although building trades workers were strongly organized before the nineteenth century came to a close, their employers were not. The trade journal *Iron Age* referred to the building industry in 1903 as "the main line of fortifications of organized labor" and predicted that "the great decisive struggle" between employers and employees would occur in this sector of the economy.[41] Whatever the limitations of this prediction as a generalization, it at least applied to the structural steel erection industry.

Cooperation among the various building trades unions sometimes took the form of the sympathetic strike. This reflected not only the sense of unity among workers in the same industry and the close association of workers of different crafts on the same job site but also "the peculiar effectiveness" of this type of strike in the building industry. In many local trade agreements, the building trades unions were able to secure the inclusion of a clause providing that a sympathetic strike ordered by the building trades council did not constitute a violation of the agreement's no-strike clause. The sympathetic strike was "the most important weapon" of the building trades unions in enforcing demands on their employers.[42]

If the sympathetic strike provided evidence of the sense of unity among building trades workers, the jurisdictional strike, conversely, reflected the differences among them. Nowhere in the economy did jurisdictional strikes occur more frequently than in the construction industry. This was the result of the craft form of organization, minute subdivision of labor, "radical changes" in the materials used in construction and in methods of construction, and weak international union control over their locals.[43]

The building trades unions were able to secure employer approval of "a maze of working rules" that was indicative of the relative strength of employer and employee in collective bargaining in the industry at the turn of the century. These rules regulated the supply of labor, protected a particular craft's jurisdiction, limited the output of workers per working day, restricted the use of labor-saving devices, prohibited the employer from working on the job, specified the number of workers to perform a particular task, specified the number of apprentices and helpers who could be hired relative to the number of journeymen, limited the employer's right to hire and fire, required general contractors to sublet work only to contractors using union labor, and sometimes prohibited a contractor from using material produced in nonunion shops.[44]

The union rules of the building trades were generally enforced by the local's walking delegate or business agent, as the walking delegate came to be known. The walking delegate appeared in the industry in the 1880s as the "chief executive officer" of building trades locals. He was the person through whom the contractor might have to secure the labor he needed, and he often had the power to call strikes. He visited the job to ensure that only union members were at work and to see that the wage scale and union rules were being observed, and he settled disputes arising on the job. He became, in effect, "a practical third party to a closed shop building contract."[45]

What gave the building trades unions and their business agents so much power was the nature of the industry in which they operated and its extreme vulnerability to strikes. The owner had almost certainly borrowed money on the assumption that the building he was having constructed would be completed and occupied by a certain date. Not wishing to incur additional interest as the result of delay, he sought to protect himself by the contractual arrangements he was apt to make with the general contractor for the structure. The latter was commonly a "broker" who might sublet the work on a single building to as many as thirty subcontractors. With the advent of steel construction, however, a few very large construction companies operating in several cities were "fully equipped to render a complete service, from architectural design to decorating and finishing." Companies of this sort might use their own labor force to do a great deal of work on a building.

However the work was to be performed, either the contractor had to provide a bond to complete the work by a certain date, or the contract might provide that the contractor would be subject to a fine for late completion of the job. The contractor, consequently, wished to avoid labor trouble that would delay completion of the structure. If the contract, moreover, was of the cost-plus type, which was common, the contractor could pass on to the owner the cost of any wage increase the contractor might grant to avoid labor difficulties. If he did not have his own workforce, and few did, the contractor was likely dependent on the unions to supply him with competent mechanics, and good relations with the unions could ensure that. The fact, also, that the local building trades unions enforced the same wage scale for their workers in a particular jurisdiction meant the equalization of competition in that jurisdiction, which removed a troubling element of uncertainty for the contractor in figuring his bids.

Some contractors were willing to agree to hire union labor exclusively in return for a union commitment not to provide workers for a contractor who was not a member of the relevant contractors' association or who was outside the particular trade jurisdiction. General contractors who operated in more than one city had to take into account the possibility that if they operated on a nonunion basis in one city, they might face strikes on their jobs in other cities where the building trades unions were strong. As for the subcontractor, his bid for the work he was seeking was generally based on the assumption that he would not experience any labor trouble in performing the work.[46]

The imbalance of power between the building contractor and the business agent was an invitation to bribery and graft. This became a problem in many big cities in the 1890s, notably, as we shall see, in Chicago and New York. The business agent, for instance, might insist on the payment of "strike insurance," a bribe, by the contractor to avoid strikes, or the delegate might exact a payment to call off a strike. To be sure, for bribery to take place, there had to be a briber. The contractor might bribe a business agent to overlook a violation of union working rules or not to supply workers to a competitor. This represented, as Ray Stannard Baker put it, "a sort of balanced venality."[47]

As in other sectors of the economy, employers in the construction trades, having permitted the unions to get a head start in organizing, sought at the turn of the century to counter the power of the organized workers by forming multitrade organizations of their own. At the local level, these associations, although more effective than single-trade associations, tended to be "negotiatory" organizations designed to place limits on union power rather than "belligerent" organizations seeking to drive the building trades unions from the field. The employers learned that although they might be able to defeat the building trades unions for a time, they would have to repeat their victory "regularly and at high cost" if they continued to battle their union adversaries. The employers generally concluded that, rather than fighting the unions, if they joined with them in seeking control of the local labor market, they "could bring order and predictability to their businesses without undue risk to profits or to the authority of employers."[48]

The two most notable early efforts to form local multitrade employer associations in the building industry to counter the power of the unions occurred in the two most important centers of the construction industry, Chicago and New York. In Chicago, the building trades unions formed the Chicago Building Trades Council in 1890, but the "real power" on the union side was wielded by the leader among the union business agents, Martin B. ("Skinny") Madden, a "brilliant" but corrupt labor leader. "He got his influence," it was said, "from having eight or ten two-fisted followers who would punch on the nose anybody that wouldn't do what they wanted." The decade of the 1890s in the Chicago building trades has been described as "a period of union domination with the attendant evils of graft, petty grievances, frequent [work] stoppages, jurisdictional disputes and a type of collective bargaining decidedly dictatorial." Contractors commonly had to add the cost of strike insurance in figuring their bids. "Everybody pays, who puts up a building in Chicago," the head of one of the nation's largest construction companies was told.[49]

Reacting to the dismal state of labor relations in the building trades and especially to a plague of sympathetic strikes, the Chicago building contractors, in 1899, formed the Building Contractors' Council (BCC), "the first central group of exclusively contractors' units formed in the United States." In November of that year the BCC announced that beginning in January 1900 its affiliates would insist that foremen be the agents of the employer and that there be no limitations on the amount of work performed by a worker during the workday, no restriction on the use of tools or machinery, no restriction on the use of any raw or manufactured material except for prison-made goods, no limitation on the number of apprentices, and no interference with workmen during working hours. The BCC soon added to these six "Cardinal Principles" the principles that workers could work for whomever they saw fit and the employers could hire and fire as they saw fit. Efforts of the BCC to draw up an agreement with the Building Trades Council (BTC) embodying these principles as well as to provide for arbitration proved unavailing. This led to a BCC lockout of the building trades unions early in 1900 and a demand that they withdraw from the BTC.

Deploying two hundred to three hundred paid "sluggers," the building trades unions responded to the lockout with violence against the nonunion workers whom the employers had engaged. The press reported 250 assaults against nonunion workers resulting in five deaths, two of them of union members, and numerous injuries. Since they received very little police protection, the employers hired five hundred private guards to protect their jobs. Beginning in June, some of the unions broke away from the Building Trades Council and signed agreements embodying the Cardinal Principles, and the council itself was dissolved in April 1901, giving the employers "a sweeping victory." The power of the building trades unions declined for a time, but the employers soon began to lose interest in the BCC. The unions created a new Building Trades Council in 1903 and were able to negotiate new contracts that eliminated the ban on their joining the council. The various employer associations began to withdraw from the BCC, and the "chaotic conditions" of the 1890s returned to the Chicago construction industry.[50]

New York was indisputably "the most important building center" in the United States and the most advanced in building techniques at the beginning of the twentieth century. Until 1903 its building trades workers were far more effectively organized than their employers were. In 1884 the walking delegates of four unions organized the Board of Delegates, and it had become "dominant in the building trades" by 1890. The board split in 1894, when a faction representing the "inside trades" formed the Building Trades Council. The two boards, however, joined in 1902 to create the United Board of Building Trades, which represented an estimated sixty thousand workers in thirty-four unions and was allegedly "the strongest labor organization in the United States." It was "a Board of Bosses," the power on the board being held by the walking delegates of the constituent unions, who had the "absolute power" to call strikes. Thanks to the unprecedented building activity in the city in the early years of the new century, the United Board was able to force up wages in the building trades, the wages of housesmiths, for example, increasing from $2.50 to $4.00 a day between 1899 and 1903.[51]

The contractors in New York, many of them belonging to associations of their own trade, had organized a central Building Trades Club in 1899. Renamed the Building Trades Association in 1900, the organization was "purely social in character" and was no match for the United Board. As sometimes happened in the building trades under these circumstances, the New York building industry between 1900 and 1903 witnessed a degree of "collusion and racketeering . . . unmatched in any other city."[52]

The United Board was dominated by Samuel J. Parks, a housesmith who had been a foreman in Chicago for the George A. Fuller Construction Company, which brought him to New York in 1896, when it began operating there. It was "common talk" in New York construction circles that Parks remained on the Fuller payroll in the city, keeping that firm, the largest construction company in New York, strike free while calling strikes on its competitors. Parks took the lead in revitalizing the New York housesmiths union, which had lapsed into "a completely demoralized condition" following a failed strike in 1886. Viewing Parks as their "Moses," union members gave him credit for the increase in their wages and the decrease in their working hours that followed his appearance on the scene. The union grew to a membership of between 4,200 and 4,500 by 1903.

A "half-illiterate swaggering bully" who claimed that he "preferred 'fightin' to eatin'," Parks used his euphemistically named "entertainment committee," "a group of plug-uglies paid out of the union treasury," to promote the union cause and to keep dissenters from his leadership in line. "Some [housesmiths] did not believe unions would be good for them," Parks remarked, "and I gave them a belt on the jaw. That changed their minds."

Under Parks's leadership, the United Board became "a machine for corruption." Parks extorted money from employers, calling off strikes for a price and telling the strikers that it was "waiting money" for them. On a salary of $48 a week, he was able to deposit $11,000 in the bank in 1903. He allegedly told an employer from whom he had requested $2,000 to call off a strike, "I don't give a damn for the union, the president of the union, or the laws of the country. You can go back to work when you pay Sam Parks $2000." The sum was paid, and the strikers returned to their jobs. The ironworkers, for the most part, were not troubled by Parks's behavior. As they saw it, if he was a grafter, it was "the boss" from whom he grafted. Parks may have "made a bunch of money," one ironworker asserted, but "he did not get it out of us."[53]

The imbalance in power between employer and employee in New York's building industry was redressed in 1903. Early in May the Building Material Drivers Union, a member of the United Board, became involved in a dispute with the Material Dealers' Association and the Lumber Dealers' Association, which claimed that the Drivers Union should not have been accorded membership in the United Board. After the Drivers, supported by the United Board, went out on strike, the Material Dealers responded by closing all the material yards in the city, thus virtually shutting down the New York construction industry and idling tens of thousands of workers. Encouraged by antiunion employers, the two employer associations announced that the lockout would continue until the United Board withdrew its support from the Drivers.[54]

It was the dispute between the Material Dealers and the Drivers that triggered the formation of the Building Trades Employers' Association of New

York. Soon after the strike began, the electrical contractor Charles L. Eidlitz moved into a new office in a building whose completion the strike had delayed. A jurisdictional dispute quickly developed between the housesmiths and the carpenters as to which trade should fasten a low iron railing to the door in front of Eidlitz's office. A disgusted Eidlitz completed the job himself and then summoned the members of the Building Trades Association to a meeting, apparently on May 15, 1903, to consider their future. The "most influential general and special contractors" attended the meeting, and they declared "war" on unions seeking to "dictate terms of employment" and denounced the "intolerable rule" of the walking delegates. After Eidlitz pointed out that the building trades unions had formed a central body while the contractors dealt with the trades individually, those present resolved that the Board of Governors of the Building Trades Association should arrange with the individual contractor associations to form "a central body of employers."⁵⁵

During the next few weeks the New York builders agreed to establish the Building Trades Employers' Association (BTEA), with a governing board made up of representatives from each of the thirty-five affiliated associations and with Eidlitz as president. "[T]o enforce discipline," the members bonded themselves at from $500 to $2,500. Although the employers stated that they stood for "unionism" in the city, the BTEA declared its opposition to the sympathetic strike and extortion and bribery and called for the peaceful adjustment of jurisdictional disputes. Members agreed not to purchase lumber or other building materials from nonassociation members as long as the conflict with the unions continued.⁵⁶

The BTEA quickly devised an arbitration plan that denied any role to business agents in the plan's operation. With Parks taking the lead, the United Board voted nineteen to sixteen against accepting the arbitration plan. The dissenters, who had favored expelling the Drivers from the board, as the BTEA had insisted, now began seceding from the board and, after conferring with the BTEA, agreed to form a new board. The BTEA thereupon agreed to reopen the material yards, the purpose being to facilitate the resumption of work by unions agreeing to the arbitration plan. A recalcitrant Parks, reelected as bargaining agent of his union, responded by persuading the United Board to call a nationwide strike against BTEA members as well as a strike on numerous New York building jobs. When the BTEA on July 3 came to terms with eighteen unions, Parks had the unions involved that were still members expelled from the United Board, and his entertainment committee slugged three members of one defecting union and the president of another. At a riotous meeting of the Housesmiths' Union, at which detectives appeared to serve court papers, Parks himself slugged an opponent.⁵⁷

Seeing the Housesmiths' Union, the most important of the holdouts against the arbitration plan, as blocking the "effective resumption of work," the BTEA decided to force the issue with the union. It advised the Iron League, the local association of the structural steel employers, to resume work with whatever housesmiths were willing to take jobs. The Iron League formed these workers into a dual union, which, claiming a membership of two thousand, adopted the arbitration plan. In the following months individual housesmiths began returning to work "in great numbers."[58]

Parks eventually capitulated, but this was because the law had finally caught up with him. The contractors had been urging New York's district attorney to prosecute the "blackmailers" and had collected evidence to support a criminal proceeding. Parks was arrested on July 14, 1903, on an extortion charge, followed shortly thereafter by an assault charge and four additional extortion charges. He was found guilty on the assault charge and then indicted on five new extortion charges. He was sentenced on August 26, 1903, to from thirty to forty-two months imprisonment on the assault charge and sent to Sing Sing. His local voted unanimously to continue his salary while he was in prison. Released after a brief prison stay on "a certificate of reasonable doubt," Parks returned in triumph to head the Labor Day parade of the United Board. He succeeded in having the local's president, who had opposed him, removed from office, and Housesmiths' Local No. 2 members who did not participate in the Labor Day Parks "vindication parade" were fined $10. Parks's triumph proved to be short-lived. He was convicted at the end of October on an extortion charge and was once again sent off to Sing Sing, to be joined by several of his associates. He resigned from the union on the day of his sentencing, November 6. According to a writer in *Harper's Weekly,* Parks gave up the fight knowing that BTEA detectives had collected evidence that he had conspired to murder the president of the IABSIW, with whom, as we shall see, he was feuding.[59]

Unrepentant, Local No. 2 extended its strike to forty additional buildings and even to the Fuller Company, one of the few concerns with which it still had an agreement, because the firm had sublet work to an Iron League member. The strike took a violent turn in the middle of December, when two buildings that were involved in a dispute between Local No. 2 and the dual union were dynamited. Two weeks later Eidlitz made public a report indicating that the BTEA in its long conflict with Local No. 2 had found it necessary to maintain a force of detectives sometimes numbering as many as two hundred in order to thwart union plans that involved dynamiting, "derangement" of machinery in steel structures, and even murder. The detectives claimed that a group of seventy Parks loyalists known as "the 'wrecking crew'" had been responsible for ninety assaults on workers. Its members were reportedly paid $10 per day and $10 per assault. Only "constant care," Eidlitz claimed, had saved the life of Parks's chief rival in Local No. 2 and had frustrated the alleged plot to murder the IABSIW president.[60]

By the time Eidlitz made his sensational report public, the BTEA had clearly defeated the troublesome Local No. 2. In February 1904 the international union arranged a settlement of the strike with the BTEA, and the two parties also agreed to the merging of the two housesmiths' unions into four new locals, two of them in Manhattan, one of which was a finishers local, one in Brooklyn, and one in Jersey City. The BTEA, for the time being, had gained the upper hand in its struggle with the New York building trades unions. It had been "a pretty severe fight," a general contractor later remarked, "and it strained everybody pretty much." The conflict, however, had not caused the BTEA to abandon its belief in building trades unionism as long as the unions behaved in a responsible manner, as the employers, of course, defined responsibility. That, however, was not how the organized ironworkers chose to behave.[61]

Unlike what occurred at the local level, the effort to establish a national multitrade organization of building trades employers that could challenge the power of the building trades unions failed to secure that result. Reacting to the development of the closed shop in the building trades, the sympathetic strike, and the power of walking delegates, local builders' exchanges and general contractors formed the National Association of Builders in 1887. The association, in which general contractors had "a dominant voice," claimed a membership of thirty-five hundred firms in 1892, but it was left in a very weakened condition by the depression that began the next year, and it passed from the scene in 1902.[62]

In December 1903, in another effort to establish a national organization of building associations, delegates from 123 building trades employer associations in seventy-one cities met in Chicago to form the National Building Trades Employers' Association. Because the association "practically" committed itself to the open shop, the delegates from New York, Chicago, and Washington, D.C., refused to pledge it their adherence. Lacking proper funding and widespread support, the association died aborning.[63] In the same year, however, that the National Building Trades Employers' Association was formed, a single-trade national employers' association in the structural steel industry was established that not only committed itself to the open shop but was able to maintain that position with a high degree of success until the New Deal radically altered the nature of industrial relations in the United States.

CHAPTER 2

"We Will Conduct Our Work on the 'Open Shop' Plan"

The organization that became the National Erectors' Association (NEA), like the National Metal Trades Association and the National Founders' Association, began its history as a negotiatory organization before becoming the nation's first successful national belligerent organization in the building industry. As a subsidiary of the United States Steel Company, the American Bridge Company, the NEA's principal member, was determined from the time the steel company was formed in February 1901, and consistent with its labor policy, not to permit the existence of unions in its fabricating plants, responsible for an average of about 35 percent of the steel fabricated in the United States from 1905 to 1913. It did not initially follow a similar policy regarding the company's erection of this steel, which constituted somewhat less than 25 percent of the steel it fabricated.[1] It soon took the lead, however, in committing the association of structural steel erectors to proclaim its adherence to the open shop. The association followed this action by appointing Walter Drew as its commissioner.

After he was elected president of the International Association of Bridge and Structural Iron Workers (IABSIW) in September 1901, Frank Buchanan sought to negotiate a nationwide agreement with American Bridge. He succeeded in January 1902 in concluding a tentative agreement with S. P. Mitchell, the company's chief construction engineer, and H. F. Lofland, the erection manager of its Eastern Division. Although the agreement protected the company's interest in such matters as the amount of work to be performed by the employees, it was an unusually favorable agreement from the union's point of view. It committed the company to the closed shop and, in effect, although not in precise language, extended the agreement's provisions to the company's subcontractors. It was, however, subject to the approval of the union's locals, and the large locals foolishly rejected it, killing the agreement. Sam Parks was the major culprit in this action. A later business agent of the New York local that Parks had dominated recalled that the local had not given the agreement "one minute's consideration," Parks saying that "it should be thrown in the waste basket."[2]

On May 1, 1902, the Philadelphia local of the IABSIW went out on strike after American Bridge rejected its demand for an eight-hour day and a wage increase. Buchanan responded by calling out all the company's erection workers, and after several weeks of the strike, the company capitulated. The union's magazine appraised the result as "the grandest victory in the history of the organization." American Bridge then worked out a series of agreements with IABSIW locals, including the key New York local.[3]

By the end of 1902 American Bridge was becoming concerned about the increasing strength of the IABSIW and the consequent implications for the structural steel industry. Although the union had only 1,731 members in 1900, that number had increased to 11,000 in 1902 and 16,000 in 1903. Deciding that it was time for the industry to organize for its "self-protection," American Bridge's Mitchell convened a meeting on February 25, 1903, of eight major firms that employed structural iron and steel workers. He noted that the union had submitted new demands that called for additional restrictions on employers and, more ominous, that it was trying to organize shop workers, beginning with American Bridge, which had already experienced some shop strikes. If the others would join it, he stated, the company was prepared "to take aggressive measures" to prevent the organizing of the shop workers and would also reject union demands on behalf of the "outside men," that is, the erection workers. No doubt reflecting the view of general contractors, S. P. McConnell, president of the George A. Fuller Company, responded that his firm would join in resisting "increased demands" by the union but would not participate in any movement for "wiping out" the IABSIW.

After Mitchell failed to secure approval for a proposal that the firms represented at the meeting return unsigned the demands the union had submitted, the conferees agreed not to sign with the union without first notifying Mitchell. They also decided that Mitchell, H. H. McClintic, vice president and general manager of the McClintic-Marshall Construction Company, second only to American Bridge in the fabrication and erection of structural steel, and J. M. Cornell, who represented the New York contractors, should serve as a committee "to draft a definite plan of action."[4]

When the structural steel fabricators and erectors met again on March 3, they agreed to establish a permanent organization to be known as the National Association of Manufacturers and Erectors of Structural Steel and Iron Work—"Manufacturers" was dropped from the name before the year was out. Stating that the object of the association was "to create and preserve equitable conditions" in the relations between members and their employees, the conferees adopted a set of principles to govern the employment of structural steel and iron workers for the year 1903. These included no change in wages; the eight-hour day where it was the custom and the eight- or nine-hour day as agreed upon with the workers elsewhere; time and a half for overtime; no restriction by workers in handling materials used in construction; no limit on the amount of work performed by a worker during working hours; no restriction on the use of machinery or tools; no person, unless authorized by the employer, to interfere with workers during working hours; the right of the employer to hire and fire but without discrimination against workers because of their union membership; the stipulation that foremen who were union members were not to be subject to union rules; the right of the employer to hire one apprentice for every six bridgemen; the right of the employer to hire as many laborers as he saw fit and to use laborers, rather than skilled workers, to distribute material and for other "laborers' work"; a ban on sympathetic strikes; obligation of any local that entered into a local agreement with an employer to furnish him with as many "experienced bridgemen" as he required and, if the union could not do so, the right of the employer to engage such workers as he saw fit; the arbitration of all disputes; and a ban on strikes and lockouts pending arbitration.[5] The principles provided a clear indication of the employer view of the proper character of employer-employee relations in the erection part of the industry as of 1903.

Two days after the new association adopted its principles to govern employment relations, Buchanan declared a general strike against American Bridge. Claiming that the company had been "looking for trouble for some time," the IABSIW president pointed to what he alleged were company violations of agreements with some of the union's locals. What was involved actually were violations of custom, not of written agreements, and the grievances appear to have been "more or less trivial" in character.[6]

The strike began on March 12, after Buchanan had sought in vain to confer with American Bridge officials in an effort to avert the walkout. On March 25 the union's executive board voted to expand the strike to all work sublet by American Bridge but postponed immediate implementation of this decision. Buchanan at the same time made clear the union's interest in organizing shop workers, not just outside workers. The company responded to the strike by engaging nonunion workers and let it be known that if the union was insisting that the company employ only union members, it was "carrying matters too far." The hard-line policy regarding the ironworkers' union that American Bridge was pursuing was probably determined by United States Steel, which responded to the economic slump of 1903–04 by deciding "to pick off union outposts" in its domain as a step leading, as we shall see, to the ousting of the Amalgamated Association of Iron, Steel and Tin Workers from its plants in 1909.[7]

At the March 18 meeting of the Temporary General Executive Committee of the National Association of Manufacturers and Erectors, by which time fifty-three firms had become members, those present agreed that members should have "'no communication whatever'" with the IABSIW but should instead refer all labor matters to the committee of the association in the particular locality. It was also "the sense of the [March 18] meeting" that members should avoid signing any agreement with labor unions.[8]

Accompanied by the secretary of the New York Civic Federation, Buchanan approached J. P. Morgan at the end of March in an effort to settle the American Bridge strike and to secure an agreement with the company. Morgan assured the IABSIW president that he would secure a "fair" settlement from the company, but when Buchanan complained that the company had broken existing agreements by hiring nonunion men, Morgan retorted that he would break any agreement requiring him to employ only union members. Aided by the National Civic Federation, the IABSIW was able to arrange a meeting between American Bridge and local union representatives that resulted in a series of agreements between the company and union locals.[9]

Other than wage adjustments for particular localities, the various local agreements concluded between the union and American Bridge and other association members, which were to run from May 1, 1903, to January 1, 1905, really constituted a single, uniform national agreement. The agreements largely followed the principles the association had agreed to on March 3, but no longer was there any reference to the union's supplying a firm with its skilled workers. As the principles required, the agreements included a general arbitration clause, and they did not subject subcontractors to their terms. Eight firms withdrew from the National Association because they were unwilling to agree to the contract terms it had accepted.[10]

Both sides, initially, largely observed the terms of their agreements except in New York, where the strike and later the local agreement became involved in a bitter fight between Local No. 2 and the Building Trades Employers' Association (BTEA) as well as in a personal feud between Sam Parks and Frank Buchanan. Because of differences between the international union and the local regarding the strike and the local's refusal to accept the BTEA's arbitration agreement, Buchanan attended a meeting of the local on April 10, 1903, to ask the members to stand by the international. It turned out to be a rather "stormy meeting," with "repeated quarrels" between followers of Parks and of Buchanan. Fistfights broke out, chairs were thrown, a score of members had to be ejected, and some left the meeting with "blood running from their noses, black eyes, and other facial disfigurements."[11]

When Parks sought to spread the aforementioned Local No. 2 strike against the BTEA outside New York, Buchanan repudiated the action. He suspended the local on September 11 and annulled its charter for calling strikes in violation of the May 1, 1903, agreement and its arbitration clause, seeking to involve the locals of the IABSIW in strikes outside New York in violation of the international constitution, and for not living up to the local's constitution in the conduct of local strikes. Buchanan's letter announcing the suspension was tabled at a union meeting controlled by Parks and his men that Buchanan attended. Arriving with a half dozen "husky" members of his entertainment committee, Parks called Buchanan "the meanest kind of scab." When the international president emerged from the meeting, he had a lump on his jaw, the result of a blow from one of Parks's henchmen. Entertainment committee members also allegedly knocked down and kicked members of the local's anti-Parks faction.[12]

The fight between Parks and Buchanan was transferred from New York to Kansas City, where the IABSIW met in convention late in September and early in October 1903. Despite Buchanan's suspension of the New York local and despite the numerous legal offenses with which Parks had been charged by that time, the convention delegates voted overwhelmingly to seat the Parks delegation rather than a rival Local No. 2 delegation of Parks opponents, a decision that in effect overturned the local's suspension. The delegates followed this action by pledging their full support to the Parks local and voting it a loan of $1,000. Parks "dominated" the convention proceedings on many important issues, and his candidate for the presidency lost to Buchanan by the narrow margin of forty to forty-three.[13]

The structural steel firms and especially American Bridge were more than a little troubled by the success Parks enjoyed at the IABSIW convention. They feared that this portended strikes all over the nation, and they may have wondered about the reliability of an international union that was so willing to embrace a man like Sam Parks. The convention's welcoming of shop workers to the union also undoubtedly troubled those firms that both fabricated and erected structural steel. The *New York Times* reported that the structural steel firms were in "a sort of panic" as the result of the convention and were ready to take "more drastic measures" to combat the union.[14]

When Parks was convicted and then imprisoned a few weeks after the 1903 convention, Buchanan told Local No. 2 to give up its "losing fight" against the BTEA arbitration agreement, contending that the local had become "a laughing stock to organized labor all over the country." Finally, as previously noted, Buchanan in early February 1904 merged the two rival New York locals into four separate locals with a claimed membership of sixty-five hundred—a fifth local was later added—and settled the New York strike.[15]

Although Luke Grant claimed in his study of the IABSIW that the union made "steady progress" and increased its membership in 1904 following the New York settlement, the reverse is the fact. The union's membership declined from 16,000 in 1903 to 11,500 in 1904, and the balance in the union's treasury was also reduced. The condition of the membership was so poor that the international's 1904 fall convention agreed to permit delinquent locals to remain in good standing by paying only one-quarter of their per capita tax plus $15.[16]

In December 1904, when what had been treated as a national agreement was about to expire, the IABSIW's executive board invited the employers to meet with it to devise a new national agreement, but the National Association of Erectors of Structural Steel and Iron Work (as it was now called) refused. Individual locals then sought renewals for themselves from the association or American Bridge. The New York locals, for example, were able to work out an agreement expiring on January 1, 1906, with the Eastern District Committee of the National Association that largely repeated the 1903 agreement except that hourly wages were increased from fifty cents to fifty-six and one-quarter cents. The District Council of the United Housesmiths' and Bridgemen's Union of New York and Vicinity, the central body of the five New York district locals, then signed a closed shop agreement with the Iron League Erectors' Association (ILEA), the Employers' Association of Architectural Iron Workers, and the Ornamental Bronze and Iron Masters that continued until January 1, 1906, and incorporated the provisions of the BTEA's arbitration plan. The unions thus committed themselves not to strike until after a grievance had been submitted to arbitration and an arbitral decision rendered. Committed in principle to the open shop, the members of the Iron League had formed the ILEA as the body to join the BTEA and to implement the closed shop agreement but with the understanding that the open shop would continue to prevail in the fabrication plants. The Iron League survived but only for purposes of consultation among members on matters not pertaining to labor.[17]

The Philadelphia IABSIW local and others worked out agreements with American Bridge, which, like the Erectors' Association, was willing to sign the right kind of agreement from its point of view with erection locals in large cities.[18] One IABSIW local with which American Bridge refused to sign an agreement was the New Haven local (Local No. 15). This state of affairs precipitated a series of ill-advised actions by the IABSIW that caused the major iron and steel erection companies to commit themselves to the maintenance of the open shop in their industry. The trouble in New Haven developed at a time when several IABSIW locals were complaining about American Bridge's behavior. Believing that the situation was deteriorating, the IABSIW executive board instructed President Buchanan in May 1905 to adjust outstanding union grievances against the company and, failing that, to strike the company when the time seemed "opportune."[19]

In July 1905 American Bridge contracted with the New York, New Haven and Hartford Railroad for the erection of a railroad bridge involving the use of three thousand tons of structural steel. American Bridge sublet the erection to the Boston Bridge Company, a consistently "unfair" employer from the union's point of view. The New Haven local, which had been vainly seeking for months to secure recognition from American Bridge, demanded that the company compel Boston Bridge to employ union labor under union conditions. Since American Bridge did not have an agreement with Local 15 and since none of the local contracts that it had signed constrained it from subletting work to nonunion firms, it was under no contractual obligation whatsoever to comply with Local 15's demands. Promised international union support to "the fullest extent" by Secretary-Treasurer John J. McNamara if it got into trouble with American Bridge, the New Haven local struck American Bridge on July 25, 1905.

What support to "the fullest extent" meant, Buchanan made clear, was a national IABSIW strike against American Bridge if it refused to yield and if the international's executive board approved the action. When Buchanan then failed to persuade the company to meet with him to resolve the dispute, the board approved a strike beginning August 10 against all jobs for which American Bridge had "the first contract for erection" even if the work was then sublet to firms that recognized the union and observed union conditions.[20]

Most building trades unions at that time permitted their members to work for a "fair" subcontractor even if the primary contractor was deemed "unfair." Since American Bridge, however, erected only a portion of the structural steel that it fabricated and since it operated across the nation and could vary its policy regarding the union depending on the union's strength in different local markets, the IABSIW concluded that it could bring the company to terms and prevent it from destroying the union only if it struck all erection work in which American Bridge was involved either directly or indirectly. This meant not only antagonizing erection firms that dealt fairly with the union but also enlarging a strike the union did not have the strength to win. The strike, furthermore, was a violation of arbitration clauses in various local contracts the union had concluded with American Bridge. The union's leadership recognized what was at stake, Buchanan correctly describing the walkout as "probably the most important in the union's history."[21]

The strike initially caused American Bridge "considerable annoyance," compelling it to give up several contracts. These contracts, however, were nevertheless completed by nonunion labor. The company charged that the IABSIW was, in effect, asking it to join with the union in unionizing nonunion firms with which the company did business and not to sell structural steel to firms that did not agree with the union.[22]

The IABSIW made its task of coming to terms with American Bridge even more difficult by action taken at the union's convention in September 1905. The convention delegates not only endorsed the strike but also resolved that it was not to be called off "until every existing grievance" was "settled satisfactory to all . . . affiliated locals in the erection branch" of the union. The most important grievance to which this resolution applied involved an American Bridge contract to fabricate and deliver structural steel to the National Tube Company, another United States Steel subsidiary, for the erection of a $15 million building for its own use at McKeesport, Pennsylvania. The Pittsburgh local of the union demanded that American Bridge refuse to deliver the steel unless National Tube agreed to erect the building with union labor rather than with its own nonunion force. At that time, the Illinois Steel Company, still another United States Steel subsidiary, was the only steel company in the nation that employed union workers for erection work in and around its plants. For American Bridge and United States Steel itself, the McKeesport demand was evidence of a union intention to extend its domain beyond structural steel erection to the fabrication shops and the mills themselves, an extension to which the steel companies were unalterably opposed.[23]

The IABSIW decided to strike American Bridge at a time when the union's treasury hardly justified so formidable an undertaking. As Frank M. Ryan, the new IABSIW president elected at the September 1905 convention to replace Buchanan, later noted, the union at the time had $1,013.64 in its treasury but had death claims of $1,400 as well as other unpaid expenses so that it was about $2,000 "worse off than nothing." Its constitution made no provision for the payment of strike benefits—it did not create a fund for this purpose until a few months after the strike began—and yet it had placed itself in the position of striking unless "every existing grievance" had been adjusted to the satisfaction of all its locals.[24] This was a condition the union's leadership was unable to meet and one to which it never should have agreed.

Following the union's September convention, Ryan and the union's executive board conferred with American Bridge's Mitchell, who apparently offered the union a verbal agreement covering all company erection work whether directly or indirectly performed but not meeting all the union's demands, including the McKeesport demand. Ryan, McNamara, and a union board member then met with Mitchell and August Ziesing, the new American Bridge president, and later with W. P. Corey, the president of United States Steel, and Elbert Gary, the chairman of the corporation's board. It became clear to union officials that although Corey and Gary were willing to meet the union's subcontractor demand, there would be no agreement if the union insisted on a signed contract. Also, the steel company officials refused to extend American Bridge contracts beyond their existing January 1, 1906, expiration date, rejected the McKeesport demand, and refused to alter provisions in existing agreements regarding apprentices, foremen, the erection of false work, and the type of jobs to be performed by laborers rather than skilled workers.

Following their meeting with the United States Steel officials, the union negotiators decided to break off talks with management representatives unless, in addition to concessions already made, they agreed that the union was to erect all structural steel in the many plants of United States Steel and also that an unsigned memorandum be exchanged between Ryan and Ziesing embodying the terms of the agreement. United States Steel and American Bridge would not agree to the steel mill demand, which involved an extension of the McKeesport demand to all United States Steel plants. The union thereupon withdrew from the discussions with management.

Ziesing later claimed that union negotiators had asserted that the union intended to organize American Bridge's fabrication shops as well as the mills that supplied rolled steel to the fabrication shops by refusing to handle any steel coming from unfair shops. This was a major fear of the steel magnates, but it does not appear to have been an explicit issue in the failed negotiations. The real stumbling block was the demand of the Pittsburgh local to unionize the erection of the National Tube Company mill. Ryan attempted to persuade the local to yield on this issue and to hope that the matter could be adjusted satisfactorily at a later time, a reasonable enough request under the circumstances. When the local remained adamant, however, Ryan felt himself "condemned," as he later put it, to continue the strike, since not all outstanding grievances had been adjusted, as the convention had ordered. Although this was almost certainly an unwise decision on Ryan's part, there is no certainty— indeed, it appears unlikely—that American Bridge would have been willing to conclude a new agreement with the union after January 1, 1906, even if the union had yielded on the nettlesome McKeesport issue.[25]

With the strike on, the union refused to work for "fair" American Bridge

Company subcontractors in some localities even though they promised that, if permitted to complete existing contracts, they would not in the future accept subcontracts from nonunion firms. This simply antagonized contractors that dealt fairly with the union, as, Ryan conceded, most subcontractors did. Sometimes the union acted on "nothing more than a suspicion" that American Bridge had been the original contractor. The international went so far as to suspend the important Cleveland local for continuing to work on an American Bridge subcontract.[26] The major union misstep regarding which firms to strike involved Post and McCord, the largest steel erector in the biggest structural steel market in the nation, the city of New York and its vicinity.

At issue in the union's decision to strike Post and McCord was whether the firm was part of American Bridge, as the union claimed and the company denied. There was, to be sure, a very close connection between the two companies, but it does not appear that the union claim was correct. The ties between the two firms went back to 1900, when William H. McCord became vice president in charge of erection of the newly formed American Bridge Company. A few years later McCord resigned his position and joined with a member of the Post family to form Post and McCord. The new firm sold its fabricating plant in New York to American Bridge and confined itself to the erection business. The two companies drew up a contract in January 1904 by which Post and McCord agreed to buy its structural steel, iron, and ornamental iron and bronze and brass work from American Bridge, and the latter promised to give Post and McCord "the most favorable price" available to any of its customers as well as a rebate of $1.50 a ton if Post and McCord provided it with the shop details for the shop drawings for the material American Bridge sold Post and McCord. American Bridge also agreed to discontinue its own erection contracting in the New York area for the class of work covered by the agreement, namely, the erection of buildings. Post and McCord soon became American Bridge's "very best customer."[27]

It was Ryan himself who decided that the union should strike Post and McCord even though the business agent of the key New York local thought it would be "a losing fight." Ryan claimed that he had concluded that Post and McCord was "part and parcel" of American Bridge only after seeing a copy of the *Iron and Steel Directory* that allegedly confirmed the point. Although Post and McCord insisted that the two firms were separately incorporated, Ryan retorted that this was simply "a trick to fool the union" so that American Bridge could continue to operate nonunion while Post and McCord joined the closed shop regime of the New York building trades. Ryan presented his evidence to the District Council of the United Housesmiths' and Bridgemen's Union, and at his request, Local 40, the major New York structural steel erection local, ordered a strike against Post and McCord to begin on November 4, 1905. The company at that time had 250 men at work on eighteen different jobs.[28]

The Local 40 strike of Post and McCord was a clear-cut violation of the BTEA arbitration clause in the agreement between the New York District Council and the ILEA, the Employers' Association of Architectural Iron

Workers, and the Ornamental Bronze and Iron Masters as well as the more general arbitration clause in the agreement between the several IABSIW locals and the Eastern District Committee of the National Association of Erectors of Structural Steel and Iron Work. A representative group of New York building trades employers and unions ordered the Post and McCord strikers on November 3 back to work, but they refused to comply. This led to a November 16 meeting of the General Arbitration Board provided for in the BTEA's Joint Arbitration Plan at which all the forty-six employer representatives present and thirty-two of the forty-two labor union representatives agreed to a resolution ordering the strikers once again to return to work and to submit the question of the relationship of Post and McCord and American Bridge to a special board for determination. Ryan rejected the proposal, which led to the local's suspension from the General Arbitration Board. Ryan understood that this meant "a nasty fight for the boys" in New York since they would now have to face the "combined" opposition of the Allied Iron Associations (AIA), as the three employer groups were collectively known, and American Bridge. He was also aware that the strike would receive no assistance from the other building trades unions in New York even if the erection employers engaged nonunion workers, since the unions were parties to the arbitration agreement the ironworkers had violated.[29]

At an AIA meeting of November 21 the employers adopted a resolution calling for a lockout of all union men employed on outside work in the area covered by the arbitration agreement as soon as American Bridge provided assurance that it would cooperate with the AIA in establishing "permanent and satisfactory conditions in the Trade." The employers also agreed not to conclude any new agreement with the IABSIW or the District Council unless all three constituent groups of the AIA agreed. A special AIA committee met a few days later with American Bridge's president, who provided the assurances the AIA was seeking. The association then agreed that Post and McCord would thereafter employ such workers as the AIA could obtain and that BTEA members who employed housesmiths should inform them that the union's agents and stewards would no longer be recognized. The AIA also created a Permanent Strike Committee composed of representatives of the three affiliates and the BTEA, and it levied an assessment on all its members. The BTEA, however, did not order the general lockout of all unionized workers engaged in outside work that the AIA had desired. This may explain why the AIA resigned from the General Arbitration Board, although it attributed its action to the District Council's having violated the arbitration agreement and thus having "broken faith" with the employers.[30]

While striking Post and McCord, union ironworkers in the New York district continued to work for firms other than Post and McCord that were willing to employ them. This state of affairs, however, came to an end at the beginning of 1906. As the January 1, 1906, expiration date for the existing contract approached, the unionized New York ironworkers and particularly the large Local 40 demanded a wage increase for first-class bridgemen from $4.50

to $5.00 a day. When the principal iron trade employers rejected this demand, the District Council, ignoring Ryan's advice, decided to strike all but the few small firms that had granted the increase. One of a series of blunders by the organized workers during this critical period, this action produced a vigorous reaction by the National Association of Erectors of Structural Steel and antagonized those New York contractors who had remained friendly to the union despite its violation of the 1905 contract and its ill-advised strike against Post and McCord. Within a few days of the beginning of the new strike, Local 40's business agent realized that the union had followed a "poor strategy" and had simply added to the ranks of its enemies.[31]

When the AIA met on January 3 to consider the general strike of New York's unionized ironworkers, the members agreed to maintain the $4.50 per day maximum rate for ironworkers other than foremen and pushers. The AIA also urged the National Association of Erectors to join the New York iron firms in adopting an open shop policy.[32] This, indeed, was the subject for discussion when the executive committee of the National Association met on January 16. H. H. McClintic asserted that he would have "preferred" the continuation of agreements with individual locals but would go along with the majority if it favored the open shop. J. V. Reynders of the Pennsylvania Steel Company thought an open shop policy was "likely to cause trouble" for all of them but that the steady increase of the union's demands and its failure to observe agreements meant that the employers would have "to adopt a policy and stick to it." Speaking for American Bridge, S. P. Mitchell reported that about 85 percent of the company's workers were already on the open shop plan and that the company had agreed "to stand by" the New York firms in establishing the open shop. If the association opted for making agreements with the union, Mitchell stated, some members, and it was obvious that number included American Bridge, might have to quit the association. The committee in the end decided to withhold a final decision on the open shop question pending a meeting of the entire association with AIA members and some large non-AIA New York district contractors.[33]

On January 19 representatives of eighteen National Association of Erectors firms met with representatives of the AIA, the BTEA, and Snare and Triest, a major New York iron firm. Expressing a common concern, the representative of the ILEA noted that the cost of structural steel had risen from $4 to $6 per ton in 1898 to $15 to $18 per ton and that wages of steel erection workers had risen 50 to 80 percent during the same period. It became evident at the meeting that Chicago contractors would not join in a national open shop policy. C. L. Strobel of the Strobel Steel Construction Company told those present that even though he believed the open shop was the "correct principle," conditions in Chicago were "entirely different" than in New York. The Chicago IABSIW local, he observed, was better than other IABSIW locals, and he also noted that the agreement between the Chicago Iron League and the local did not expire until May 1, 1906. This led a member to remark that the Chicago league was run by "a lot of Old Women."

Speaking for the George A. Fuller Company, a major general contractor, Paul Starrett indicated that although he too personally favored the open shop, the "interests" of his firm in localities other than New York, including Chicago, "hindered" it from joining in an association commitment to observe the open shop.[34] Like Paul Starrett, W. Starrett of the Thompson-Starrett Company, another large general contractor, questioned if this was the proper time to adopt an open shop policy. This led the BTEA's chairman, C. L. Eidlitz, to remark that the union had "used" concerns like Thompson-Starrett "to try their bluffs and generally succeeded." Although some of those present had expressed reservations, the consensus was that the time had come for the employers to take a stand in favor of the open shop. The choice before them, one employer stated, was "either FIGHT, or GIVE IN."[35]

After the AIA representatives withdrew, the National Association members unanimously agreed to a resolution proclaiming the association's commitment to "the 'OPEN SHOP' principle." The next day the association put its stand in the form of a "Declaration of Principles." "[W]e will conduct our work on the 'Open Shop' plan," the members declared. They pledged themselves to carry out existing contracts until they expired, announced that they would accord "every man the right to work," but disavowed any intention to discriminate against union members. Since the employers, the principles stated, were "responsible for the safe and satisfactory execution" of the work performed by their employees, management had to have "full discretion" to determine who was "competent to perform the work" as well as the conditions under which it was to be performed. Wages and hours, it was stated, were to be "satisfactorily arranged to suit local conditions." The association decided at the same meeting to simplify its name to National Erectors' Association (NEA).[36]

In explaining why he thought the time had come for the NEA to adopt the open shop, Fred Cohen, the engineer of erection of the Pennsylvania Steel Company, asserted that the decision was correct from both "a financial and business point of view" and "the moral point of view." There is no doubt that structural steel employers believed that the cost of doing business was rising too rapidly because of union demands, union limitations of output, union restrictions on the number of apprentices that could be hired, and union requirements that first-class bridgemen be employed to perform jobs that management believed could be performed by laborers at half the cost.

In the judgment of the NEA's first permanent commissioner, when the association declared for the open shop, the structural steel business was being "crippled and hindered" because of union "control." Wages, he asserted, were going up, and efficiency was going down, and because of "intolerable and oftentimes petty restrictions, conditions and limitations in connection with the work," costs were becoming "almost prohibitive." The year after the NEA declared for the open shop, it claimed that, as a result, the industry had experienced "constant decreases in costs" even though employers had neither decreased wages nor increased the hours of work. It attributed the reduction of costs to greater work efficiency, the ability of the employer to grade his men and to have work performed by the proper person, freedom from petty union restrictions, absence of jurisdictional strikes, and the end of grafting business agents.[37]

Cohen did not explain what he meant by "moral" reasons for the open shop, but as the NEA's Declaration of Principles indicated, he was undoubtedly referring to employer beliefs concerning the worker's right to work without regard to whether or not he was a union member and the employer's right to manage without any need to bargain with a union about working conditions. This, after all, was the bias of nearly all American employers, and it did not so much involve a careful appraisal of the costs of doing business with or without unions as it reflected a sense of self. As a major New York iron contractor put it at the time regarding the open shop, "a personal control of business is the result aimed at."[38]

Having committed itself to the open shop, the NEA turned its attention to perfecting its organization and selecting a commissioner. Because of his "experience in labor matters," the NEA's General Executive Committee sought the advice of James Emery, secretary of the Citizens' Industrial Association of America (CIAA). Attending the January 30 meeting of the committee, Emery agreed to serve as commissioner until a permanent commissioner could be found. That task was assigned to S. P. Mitchell, the committee's chairman. The CIAA was exultant about Emery's association with the NEA, the editor of the *Square Deal* writing C. W. Post, "The work that he [Emery] is doing with the Structural Iron and Steel men . . . will prove to be the entering wedge in the disintegration of the closed shop ranks."[39]

Following the January 30 meeting, the NEA, claiming that it represented 80 percent of the large contractors engaged in steel construction, made its Declaration of Principles public for the first time and decided to post the statement in the shops of the large concerns. Hailing the news, the official publication of the National Association of Manufacturers appraised the declaration as the "final revolt" of the structural steel industry against the union that had developed by "slow degrees" following the 1903 housesmiths' strike. The CIAA's official journal greeted the action as "one of the most important events in the history of the struggle between the open shop and the closed shop armies."[40]

The NEA found it difficult originally to resolve its organizational problems. Although it agreed to assess its members $1 per person employed in erection work, it could not agree on a constitution or by-laws; some members, notably the general contractors, apparently did not seem ready to abide by the Declaration of Principles; and the association's first choice for commissioner changed his mind about the position after first accepting it. More than a little annoyed at this turn of events, H. H. McClintic asked at the NEA's February 23 meeting, "Do we want an Association or not?" The answer was clearly "yes," and by the end of March Walter Drew had been appointed commissioner for a three-month trial period.[41] From that point forward, Drew and the NEA became synonymous, and he would remain the association's commissioner as long as it continued to exist.

Walter Drew was born in Williamston, Michigan, on September 13, 1873. He traced his paternal ancestry to Morrill N. Drew, who arrived in the United States from England in 1660. Walter's father, a lawyer and an inventor, invented the Bissel carpet sweeper. Walter was educated in the public schools of Grand Rapids, Michigan, and then went on to the University of Michigan, where he received his B.A. in 1894 and his LL.B. in 1896. Admitted to the Michigan bar in 1896, he became a member of a Grand Rapids law firm and then formed the law partnership of Drew and Heald in 1904 and Drew and Campau in 1906.

Drew married Georgie Virgin, whom he had met in college, in 1902, but she died the next year from blood poisoning following an operation. Stricken by the loss, Drew remained devoted to his wife's memory. He had a painting made of her from photographs and an artist's sketch of a model who resembled her that he hung in his apartment. He remained a widower until 1931, when he married Nell Corneal. Both marriages were childless.

Drew, whose brother was an artist, became a collector of painting and mezzotint. He was a reader of history, philosophy, and science and apparently had some interest in music and the theater. He was a "firm believer" in astrology and after his second marriage became a student of Christian Science, which was his wife's faith.

Drew handled some labor cases as a fledgling attorney, helped to organize the Citizens Alliance of Grand Rapids in 1904, and became the organization's counsel and secretary as well as the counsel of the Employers' Association of Grand Rapids. He also served for a time as chairman of the Industrial Committee of the Grand Rapids Board of Trade.[42]

It was in Grand Rapids in the few years before he became the NEA's commissioner that Drew received his schooling in the labor question and formed the ideas on that subject that he was to advocate and seek to implement for the rest of his active life. He characterized the Citizens Alliance in a May 1904 report as its secretary as "the organized liberty-loving public" and as an organization that aimed to secure "the enforcement of law, the preservation of order, the free and unrestricted right to employ and to labor, and fair wages, fair prices and fair methods on the part of both employer and employe." It opposed "violence, co-ercion [*sic*], the 'closed shop,' the sympathetic strike, the boycott, and the union label" but also "the black list and the sympathetic lockout." Drew had referred a bit earlier to the closed shop and the union label as "the last two links in the chain of union slavery."[43]

The Alliance, Drew stated, as he was to do both for the NEA and himself again and again in later years, was not opposed to "unions as such," unions that were "properly organized" and that employed "lawful and proper methods." It was "the prevalent union methods," he claimed, to which the Citizens Alliance took exception. These included the closed shop, reduction of output, limitation of the number of apprentices, and "thuggery and violence," and the CIAA had been the result. "It was a revolt against unionism," Drew said. "Not unionism in principle, but unionism in fact." The trouble, Drew argued, was that unions did not want to be reformed, and so the "elimination of [the] evils" of unionism had come to mean "war" against unions.[44]

The great labor event of 1904 in Grand Rapids and "the first test" of the new Citizens Alliance of Grand Rapids was a teamsters' strike. The year before, the teamsters' local had secured a closed shop contract following a victorious strike that had even included the boycotting of a Grand Rapids undertaker, which, Drew claimed, gave him, as the undertaker's attorney, his "first good view into the workings of the boycott." Seeing the issue of the 1904 strike as the open shop versus the closed shop, the team owners presented a solid front against the strikers, enjoyed the support of the Citizens Alliance and the city's business community, and emerged victorious. This victory, Drew observed, changed the industrial climate in Grand Rapids, and he was delighted to report that when the CIAA met in national convention at the end of 1904, Grand Rapids was spoken of as "the banner open shop town." This reputation, Drew claimed in later years, had persuaded capital to invest in the city despite its disadvantages in location and in terms of freight rates. He further claimed that he had learned as chairman of the Industrial Committee of the city's Board of Trade that the first question outside capital asked when considering whether to enter a city was, "What are your labor conditions? Do the unions control your town?"[45]

Drew was frequently called upon by Alliance members in Grand Rapids as well as local employer associations for legal opinions and legal advice. This led him to make a careful study of the law as it applied to such labor matters as the boycott, the closed shop, and the blacklist and led to his publication of three pieces that helped to build his reputation as something of an expert in this field: "The Law Relating to the Closed Shop Contract"; "The Union and the Law: Some Legal Phases of the Labor Question," a paper originally read before the Michigan Judges Association and then reprinted in the *Square Deal;* and "The Open Shop: An Economic Discussion."

"The most important industrial questions of the present day," Drew contended, "arise out of the combination of labor." Drew maintained that other than statutes that were in any event largely declaratory of the common law, "the principles involved in labor controversies" were "those of the old common law of conspiracy," which condemned "a combination to do an unlawful act or to do any act by unlawful means." Citing New York and Illinois cases in support, Drew argued that a closed shop "to establish or foster a monopoly of the labor market" was contrary to public policy and hence void. It was also "settled by the great weight of authority," he maintained, "that malice on the part of a combination—the intent wantonly to inflict injury on others"—was "unlawful" and "a combination with such a motive" constituted "a conspiracy." If the purpose of the combination was unlawful, he pointed out, any means to further that purpose was similarly unlawful.

As acts by a combination deemed unlawful, Drew listed "violence or threats of violence to person or property, fraud, falsehood, and misrepresentation, and the intimidation, oppression or coercion of an individual or his employees or those who deal with him." A closed shop contract that sought to compel a nonunion worker to join a union or prevent him from securing employment or the coercion of an employer into signing such a contract, as Drew understood it, became part of "an unlawful conspiracy." A government body, moreover, could not legally agree to a closed shop contract since that partook of the nature of class legislation. To the question, then, as to whether it was possible to have a valid closed shop contract, Drew at this stage of his career responded that whatever might be possible theoretically, the "practical answer" was no.

At the same time as he challenged the legality of the typical closed shop contract, Drew defended managerial prerogatives. Anything that lessened the "authority and control" of the captains of industry, he contended, tended to lessen production, decreased profits, and reduced wages, and was consequently to be condemned.[46] It goes without saying that Drew's views regarding unions, the closed shop, and the captains of industry could only have been pleasing to the NEA's leaders.

Over the years Drew became absolutely "obsessed with the 'labor question.'" A stubborn and "inflexible" person who was certain of the rectitude of his own views and cared little for the contrary opinion of others, Drew made the labor question and the open shop his favorite, indeed, almost his only, subjects of conversation.[47]

It was Emery who recommended Drew to the NEA. Employer associations were inclined to hire lawyers to provide them with legal advice on labor matters, and Drew was coming to be known as "a bright young man who had made a specialty of labor laws." Drew also had played an active role in the deliberations of the CIAA's 1905 convention, which no doubt brought him to Emery's attention. It was probably Emery who asked Drew to come to Washington in the spring of 1906 to argue before the House Judiciary Committee against an anti-injunction bill that the AFL was pressing, and during that visit Drew met some of the NEA's "big men."[48]

As the NEA's new commissioner, Drew had to deal with the strike of the IABSIW that had been initiated against American Bridge in August 1905 and then had spread to just about all of New York's structural steel erectors at the beginning of 1906. The strike had not developed to the union's satisfaction either nationally or in New York, but there were also some defections from the employers' ranks. Ryan complained to McNamara in December 1905 that he was concerned about the "readiness" with which American Bridge had been able to man its jobs as well as the "indifference" shown by some of the unionists in responding to the strike. Four months later the IABSIW president told the union's executive board that "only a small per cent" of the American Bridge jobs originally struck were still "tied up" and that, despite the union's "efforts," the company had been able to complete every job it had taken over from a struck subcontractor.

The union centered its efforts in New York, but it was unable to cut off the flow of manpower to the erection contractors. Post and McCord had some difficulty for a time manning its jobs, but it was increasingly able to secure the strike replacements—"snakes," the union called them—that it needed. As the strike continued, the major firms became strengthened in their resolve to maintain the open shop in the steel erection industry. There was no point making agreements with the union, one of them said, because it would "break them anyway." The issue, as William C. Post bluntly expressed it, was "breaking the union or breaking themselves," and it was the union the employers were determined to break.[49]

After the union struck for higher wages at the beginning of January 1906, the AIA specified that no housesmith was to be employed unless he had a valid card from the association's employment bureau. The AIA advertised for men outside New York, the strike committee agreeing to pay the railroad fare for workers who traveled to the city to fill the jobs of strikers. The association also enlarged the labor supply for its jobs by providing for the training of new ironworkers.

In establishing its employment bureau and in recruiting strike replacements, the AIA was aided by the labor bureau managers of the National Metal Trades Association. By March 7 the New York firms had imported 650 workers, and New York unionists had begun to return to work "by the wholesale." By March 11 the employment bureau had registered 3,399 workers, more than enough to replace all the strikers. Also, with less fanfare than in the 1903 strike, the AIA created a dual union among the housesmiths who replaced strikers, but it dealt with these workers as individuals, not as members of the new union.[50]

Not all iron contractors, to be sure, observed the AIA's wage policy or its employment bureau requirement. In February 1906 five firms, including the two major general contractors, George A. Fuller and Thompson-Starrett, reached a compromise agreement with the union, rehiring five hundred unionists at $4.80 a day, but only as individuals and without recognizing the union. Only Fuller among the five, however, was an AIA member. Two additional firms would have joined the five had the union been willing to yield on the apprentice issue. It is possible also, as Ryan charged, that United States Steel, presumably through American Bridge, kept other employers from making any concessions to the union by threatening to withhold steel from them if they deviated from the AIA's strike policy.[51]

Seeking to put additional pressure on New York employers, Ryan sought to persuade the city's Central Federated Union to declare a sympathy strike against AIA contractors. The Federated Union refused but adopted a resolution on February 24 requesting the AFL to try to settle the dispute. Acting on the resolution, Samuel Gompers sought a meeting with the AIA but without success. Although refusing to meet with Gompers, the AIA strike committee did meet on March 16 with a committee of labor representatives from the General Arbitration Board who, although conceding that the housesmiths' union had been "in error" in its behavior, sought a "basis of settlement" by which the union could be recognized and reinstated on the board. The employers rejected the overture, asserting that they had been deceived when they had previously agreed to recognize the union and admit it to the board. It had been their understanding, the employers stated, that when the old Parks local had been merged with the dual union the employers had created in the 1903 strike, the "objectionable elements" in Local No. 2 would be eradicated. That, the employers maintained, had not occurred, and not only had the old "criminal element" resumed its control of the union, but the men who had formed the dual union had been "driven out," and there had been "more or less trouble" ever since. The employers made it clear that their open shop policy was not subject to change.[52]

Frustrated by their inability to settle either the national strike against American Bridge or the New York strike and seeing the jobs of union members being increasingly filled by strikebreakers, the IABSIW, with the blessing of its national leadership, reacted with violence. The violence, mostly slugging but also the damaging of property and some dynamiting, was largely confined to the key New York district, but there were a few violent episodes elsewhere as well.

In New York, the end of the Parks regime did not mean the end of Local 40's entertainment committee or its practice, as a character in Leroy Scott's novel phrased it, of "transmittin unionism to the brain by the fist." A member of the committee who had participated in a couple of its 1905 assaults recalled that the committee consisted of twelve to fifteen members and some volunteers and was under the direction of the local's business agent. In addition to their daily pay, they received $150, he recalled, for beating up and hospitalizing a foreman on an open shop job.[53]

"[W]e have been doing business at the risk of life and limb," William C. Post publicly stated in March 1906. He was referring to "the continuous crimes against person and property" that the AIA attributed to union action. The first violence occurred with the cutting of the guy ropes of a derrick on a Post and McCord job. A few days later three men shot, stabbed, and beat a guard on the same job, an assault that resulted in three convictions. The AIA listed forty-four cases of assault by July 11, 1906, some of them involving more than one person. Workers seeking to register at the AIA's employment bureau were sometimes "intimidated," allegedly by unionists, and damage was sustained by derricks and other machinery of firms operating with nonunion labor.

The AIA claimed that sixty-eight nonunion workers had been hospitalized by March 1. One strikebreaker died as the result of a blow on the head, another was thrown into the Hudson River, and a man on roller skates threw ammonia at a Post and McCord foreman, "painfully" burning his face. Other strike replacements were able to defend themselves against their attackers, and AIA attorneys conceded that in some instances the nonunion men "invited the altercation." A great majority of the assailants escaped apprehension because many assaults occurred from behind and identification proved to be impossible, but the assaults resulting in severe injury generally led to arrests and convictions. In one assault case, the secretary-treasurer of the District Council of the United Housesmiths' and Bridgemen's Union informed the international that the council had used $1,000 sent it by the international to support the strike to settle a bail bond of an accused member who had skipped town as "the cheapest way out of trouble and [to] protect the organization from being placed in a very compromising position."[54]

More ominous and a portent of things to come for the erection industry were several dynamitings in New York. The AIA's employment bureau office was dynamited without loss of life on December 19, and there were two additional dynamitings and two attempted dynamitings in January and February 1906. The Bliss Building, under construction by Post and McCord, suffered some dynamite damage on January 8, and then toward the end of February detectives frustrated an apparent effort to dynamite the building a second time. It turned out that one of the three men involved in the latter attempt was a police informer who said that he had "wormed himself into the confidence" of the union and become a member of its "inner circle" and had tipped off Post and McCord as to what was to occur. One of the two arrestees was a member of one of the locals making up the District Council. He confessed to the crime, and his partner and he were convicted and sentenced.[55]

The AIA responded to the violence by hiring guards to protect the jobs of members, detectives to track down the culprits, and lawyers to seek their indictment and prosecution. The association allegedly had a force of sixty-four detectives at work by January 14 and had employed 140 guards by January 22; and by March 7 its attorneys had secured the indictment of fourteen alleged perpetrators of violence, with the BTEA meeting half of the expenses involved. Early in March, with violence mounting, a Post and McCord executive suggested that the AIA needed "a man on the inside" to secure information on the union and suggested the employment for this purpose of the Corporations Auxiliary Company, a detective service that Post and McCord was already using. The AIA shortly thereafter authorized its secretary to sign a contract with the detective agency.

Although the AIA could not stop all the violence, it was highly successful in combating the strike itself. Ryan informed the union's board members in April that the situation in New York was growing "more critical from day to day" and that it was costing the United Housesmiths and Bridgemen, as the unionized erectors were known, $2,000 a week "to take care of the distress cases alone." In another month the New York locals were offering "almost any terms" to secure recognition and their reinstatement on the General Arbitration Board.[56]

The violence outside New York, directed against American Bridge, was sporadic and widely scattered. "[B]eginning to get hostile" because of strike replacements the company had shipped from Boston to man a job in Egypt, Pennsylvania, members of the Pittsburgh local "drove one gang of snakes out," George Hagerty, the local's secretary, informed McNamara in December 1905. When Hagerty then asked for "a few good strong arm men to go and clean [up] this job," McNamara responded that "some such move . . . should be taken." In February Hagerty informed McNamara that two of the Boston men had been hurt, adding, "to[o] damn bad they werent [*sic*] killed." He also noted that machinery worth $15,000 had been damaged at the plant that was being erected.

There was some union violence in Cleveland and New Orleans, where a union member was shot and killed in a fight between unionists and strike replacements. In heavily unionized San Francisco, the international's first vice president reported that only one contractor had refused to hire union members, but, the union official observed, "we will get him." Neither Ryan nor McNamara appeared to object to violent acts directed against "unfair jobs" or "snakes." Regarding one job that Ryan had reported was filled with strike-breakers, McNamara rather nonchalantly replied that one of these workers was dead, another had been "knocked over board" and was "done for," and two others had been sent to the hospital.[57]

There was at least one attempted dynamiting outside New York before Drew became the NEA's commissioner. On December 8, 1905, a fuse that had been lighted became extinguished before igniting thirteen sticks of dynamite, thus preventing the wrecking of a bridge at Miller Falls, Massachusetts, for whose construction American Bridge was the main contractor. At the beginning of April 1906 three sticks of dynamite were discovered by a watchman under a hoisting engine at a new Cleveland structure, but the union was innocent in this instance. The watchman himself, "a man of very little intelligence," soon confessed to the deed, claiming that he had acted as he did because the company supervising the job had discharged several night watchmen and he wanted to demonstrate that night watchmen were needed on the job.[58]

By the time he became the NEA's commissioner, Walter Drew had come to some conclusions as to how employers were to "handle" strikes, views that over the years he sought to implement. Acknowledging the right to strike and conceding that one of the "chief causes" for industrial disputes was "the mean and unprincipled employer," Drew nevertheless believed that strikes were all too often called to establish and/or maintain "vicious, uneconomic and un-American principles" like the closed shop or the limitation of output and were fought without regard to the "moral and legal rights of others." As Drew saw it, "every contest against such a strike" was "right morally and economically." In combating strikes of this sort, and Drew was thinking particularly of the building trades, he thought that the first and most important requirement was for all the employers in the affected industry in the locality to "get together and keep together." If this occurred, he believed, the outcome was "inevitable" because capital could "live together longer without producing" than labor could.

The next requirement in Drew's strike battle plan was for the struck firms to gain the "sympathy, encouragement, and even active support" of employers in other industries with which the employers being struck had dealings as either buyers or sellers. Since Drew believed that it was "largely true" that "public sentiment" was "the most powerful factor in labor troubles," he recommended that employers fighting for principle in a strike should take their case to the people of the community.

It was important in a strike, Drew contended, for employers to protect the "new men" engaged to replace strikers. He stressed the importance of establishing an employment bureau to maintain the open shop since this made it possible to hire new workers without their joining a union. He thought that injunctions against strike activity should be sought only as a last resort, since he saw the injunction as "to some extent a sign of weakness" and a legal action that led workers to believe that they were not equal to employers before the law, which, he maintained, was "the seed of socialism." Drew recognized that, in the absence of police protection, private guards might be needed to protect strike property, but he cautioned that these guards must be "carefully selected" and watched because they sometimes provoked trouble where none existed and that many companies that supplied guards were "thoroughly rotten" and increased rather than lessened trouble.

The "most important thing" for the employer to do, in Drew's estimation, came after the strike. He had to be loyal to the men he had hired even if they were less efficient than the strikers they had replaced lest he throw away "the fruits of victory" and cause the workers to believe that they needed a union for job security. The employer, finally, Drew advised, should not take advantage of the strikers' defeat to cut wages, increase working hours, or make working conditions "more burdensome," since this would only serve to stimulate union organization and lead to another strike.[59]

During the brief trial period for which the NEA had engaged him, Drew convinced his employers that he was, indeed, the right man for the commissioner's job. Much of his effort was devoted to Chicago, where the closed shop was entrenched in the erection industry, and New York, the center of the strike and of the NEA's business interests. The effort of the relatively unknown Drew at this time to preach the open shop in the building trades in unionized Chicago was lampooned in the Chicago press by the labor writer Luke Grant, who portrayed Drew as saying that the open shop had been established in Grand Rapids, Kalamazoo, "Podunk and several other flourishing centers," and so why not in Chicago. "He is a young man and quite enthusiastic," Grant wrote, "and probably does not fully realize the extent of the project he has undertaken. The building trades workmen are not looking for the open shop and they are not losing sleep over Mr. Drew's visit. It is a good guess Mr. Drew will be considerably older before he succeeds in his project."[60]

Drew presented quite a different picture to his employers of the results of his initial efforts in Chicago. He told the NEA's executive committee on April 4 that after he had spoken to the Chicago Iron League, its members were "gradually beginning to recognize conditions tending to the 'Open Shop.'" Writing his parents, Drew exulted that his "fondest hopes" had been "realized" in that the Chicago Iron League had "stood out" against the local's demands regarding a new contract and had even pressed for an open shop agreement. A strike had resulted, Drew noting that after he had met with the Building Contractors' Council, of which the league was a member, it had endorsed the league position. All this had occurred, he proudly wrote, even though the NEA thought he "could do nothing" in Chicago.

Drew thought that, at the very least, since the Chicago local was engaged in a strike, it would no longer be able to provide funds to the IABSIW to aid the strike of the ironworkers in other localities. Also, American Bridge by early May was planning to arrange for the construction of Chicago's South Side Elevated Railway on an open shop basis after displacing a firm to which it had sublet the contract but that proposed to operate with union members. It seemed to Drew that "the last Union stronghold [Chicago] would be carried," and he could "see no other result than the destruction" of the IABSIW. In the end, however, the Chicago Iron League signed a contract with Local 1, but Drew contended that the terms were less onerous from the employers' point of view than they would have been had not the NEA and its commissioner bucked up the Chicago league.[61]

Drew began his work in New York by meeting with three of the iron firms that had agreed to pay their workers $4.80 a day, and he received their assurances that they would not agree to a closed shop and would cooperate with the AIA. Since the NEA believed that it needed an employment bureau of its own in New York, Drew arranged with the AIA to use half of the space of the AIA's bureau but as an entirely separate operation. As he studied the New York situation, Drew concluded that the NEA and AIA should be run by the same person although preserving their "separate identity." This idea appealed to and was approved by both organizations, the AIA agreeing to pay one-third of Drew's salary and with the details, including the merger of the two employment bureaus, left to Drew.[62]

A major problem that Drew had to address in New York was the construction of the Blackwell's Island Bridge spanning the Harlem River, a $4 million job for which the Pennsylvania Steel Company, an NEA member, was the contractor. The New York housesmiths' union had been able for several months to shut off the supply of skilled workers the company needed to complete the job. Meeting with the NEA's executive committee and the AIA on April 30, Pennsylvania Steel's Thomas Earle reported that his company was being pressed by New York's mayor to resume work on the bridge by a date certain and that the company might consequently be compelled to employ union labor for the job. The NEA executive committee decided that Drew should take charge of the matter and should arrange with the various nonunion iron contractors to provide Pennsylvania Steel with the labor it needed for the job. Appearing before the AIA's strike committee on May 9, Drew urged members to supply ironworkers to Pennsylvania Steel "even at some discomfort to themselves."[63]

Work on the bridge resumed about May 10, Drew having arranged for a complement of forty to fifty workers, who passed through streets on their way to work lined with pickets and union sympathizers. The number of workers eventually reached five hundred, and Pennsylvania Steel was able to proceed with the construction to its conclusion. To protect its workers, the company had to employ twenty to thirty guards for a two-year period at a cost of $35,000 and to devise "a very elaborate system" to ensure that only workers with proper identification could get onto the bridge. There were attempts to wreck the travelers used for the job, and there were several assaults on workers, one of them involving Local 40's business agent, who was arrested and fined.[64]

The inability of the IABSIW to prevent the resumption of work on the Blackwell's Island Bridge was illustrative of its inability to pressure the NEA to negotiate a new agreement to replace the agreement that had expired on January 1, 1906. At its April 17, 1906, meeting the association adopted a set of "Principles and Working Rules" to govern its relations with its workers that largely preserved the status quo regarding wages and working conditions and pretty much repeated the terms of the agreement that had previously been negotiated with several IABSIW locals. The terms, however, were not subject to negotiation with the union, nor did they include any management commitment to hire union labor.[65]

In a public statement on May 9, Drew announced for the NEA that relations between the association and the union had been so unsatisfactory that renewal of those relations, at least with the union as then constituted, was "out of the question." The NEA concerns, he stated, would conduct their operations on an open shop basis without discriminating against workers because of their union affiliation or lack of same. Indicating that the NEA Principles and Working Rules would be posted at NEA jobs, he asserted that since fair wages, hours, and working conditions were guaranteed to workers, they had no reason to join a union. He noted, furthermore, that the wage scale the NEA had adopted was the minimum its members would pay and that "better men" now had the opportunity to earn more. Revealing that NEA employment bureaus had been opened in New York, Pittsburgh, and, temporarily, in Cincinnati, Drew sought to assure workers who registered at these bureaus that they would be protected. He informed NEA members the next day that strike conditions were "most encouraging and could scarcely be better," that, except for Chicago, IABSIW locals were "demoralized" and out of funds, and that "better men" among union members were ready to return to work.[66]

Despite Drew's picture of a "demoralized" union and despite the failure of the AFL to levy an assessment on its members to aid the IABSIW—an AFL appeal to its affiliates for voluntary contributions netted only $201.30—the union was not about to give up its fight against the erection firms and the open shop. The Cleveland local, over McNamara's objection, decided at the end of

April to strike for a pay raise and was soon, as he put it, "into the fight with a vengence [*sic*]." Asked by President Ryan on May 8 to vote on a proposal to strike all NEA members seeking to operate on an open shop basis, the union's executive board responded in the affirmative without dissent.[67]

Undoubtedly impressed with how Drew had performed in dealing with the strike of the iron workers, the NEA's executive committee decided on May 25 to engage his services for one year beginning on July 1, 1906, at a salary of $6,000. The AIA's strike committee subsequently agreed to pay $2,400 of this sum. The headquarters of the NEA were to be in New York. Drew was confident of the future and what he could accomplish. "I have big visions here in New York," he wrote his parents. "With the iron business back of me, I am in a position to be a powerful influence in the building trades. . . . I shall be in the fight when it comes and shall try to work out some ideas of my own when the smoke clears away." It was Drew's "nature," he correctly said of himself at a later time, "to go ahead with zeal and enthusiasm in any cause" in which he believed. The open shop, as he assumed his commissionership, was a "cause" in which he passionately believed, and he was to devote himself to it with the "zeal and enthusiasm" of a crusader. His efforts quickly gained him a national reputation. "Few men in the country," a Louisville newspaper said of Drew in the first year of his commissionership, "are so well-qualified to speak on modern unionism as Mr. Drew. A man of culture and a deep student, he combines with these qualities a long [*sic*] practical experience in handling . . . strikes and negotiations with labor unions."[68]

CHAPTER 3

National Erectors' Association.
What It Is. What It Does.

As the constitution that it finally adopted in 1909 specified, membership in the National Erectors' Association (NEA) was open to "[a]ny individual, firm or corporation engaged wholly or in part in the erection of iron and steel bridges, buildings or other structural iron and steel work" that subscribed to the association's principles. Eschewing any concern about trade practices or the pricing of its work and limiting itself to labor matters, the organization had only one objective, "the institution and maintenance of the open shop principle." By this principle, the NEA explained in its 1907 booklet, *National Erectors' Association. What It Is. What It Does.*, it meant the employment of workers "irrespective of membership in any organization, and without discrimination." Its single-mindedness distinguished the NEA from other employer associations in the building trades and accounted at least in part for its long-term success. It was classified by Clarence E. Bonnett in his study of employer associations as "the most class-conscious and belligerent" of the various national employer associations."[1]

The NEA in the pre–New Deal era employed a variety of means to ward off unionism in its members' plants. Walter Drew, as the association's commissioner, implemented its open shop policy, but he also placed his own stamp on that policy. He sought at the same time to strengthen the open shop in structural steel erection in those cities where it already existed and to extend it elsewhere.

The number of NEA members varied over time. The association, for example, had twenty-seven members in 1914, fifty in 1917, and fifty-five in 1920. Some firms, believing that they benefited from the NEA's open shop policy, contributed to the association without becoming members. The NEA also had "a close working agreement" with the three iron associations in New York that had formed the Allied Iron Associations (AIA), most of whose members were not NEA members. The association also often worked "in harmony" with local builders' exchanges and employer associations.[2]

The NEA was governed by an executive committee, initially composed of seven members and later of ten, elected by the membership. Its commissioner, Walter Drew, was the association's executive officer. He conducted the NEA's business and executed its policies under the executive committee's direction, and he provided the members with legal advice. At Drew's suggestion, the executive committee in 1906 appointed a finance committee of three members that included Drew. The NEA operated outside New York City, which was its headquarters, through district and field managers. It established employment bureaus in several cities and arranged with local employer associations to use their bureaus in other cities.[3]

The funds to support the NEA were derived from assessments determined by its executive committee. The initial assessment set by the committee in February 1906 was based on the daily average of the number of employees engaged in erection by each member in the preceding six months, the sum in the years 1906–08 ranging from twenty-five cents to one dollar per employee. At the end of November 1906 the executive committee decided that when the monthly balance in the association's treasury fell below $3,500, the larger concerns in the organization should make up the difference. The sum paid by individual members determined their voting power in the election of executive committee members, each member being entitled to one vote for every $100 dues or majority fraction thereof that it paid annually. Each member, however, was entitled to at least one vote, and the committee was to include no more than one member from any particular firm.[4]

The NEA's dominant member was the American Bridge Company. As Drew asserted in writing to United States Steel's counsel, the NEA "in the first instance was organized largely through the efforts of the Bridge Company." When Drew became commissioner, American Bridge's counsel requested that all proceedings of the NEA's executive committee be submitted to him before being put into effect. Aware, however, of the labor claim that the NEA was the tool of the steel trust, Drew responded that the NEA had to be an independent organization, he would take direction only from its executive committee, and he would resign if the American Bridge counsel had his way. The counsel then agreed that American Bridge would not seek any kind of oversight of the NEA. The company undoubtedly understood that it did not have to do so in order to make its influence felt in the association. Accounting for slightly more than 50 percent of the total tonnage of structural steel both fabricated and erected by NEA members in 1913 and 1914 combined, American Bridge spoke with considerable authority in the NEA. After American Bridge, the two most important NEA members were the McClintic-Marshall Construction Company, which accounted for about 12 percent of the NEA total of fabricated and erected structural steel in 1913–14 and which became a Bethlehem Steel subsidiary in 1931, and the Pennsylvania Steel Company, which accounted for about 8 percent of the NEA total in 1913–14.[5]

Although named an erectors' association, the principal NEA members were primarily fabricators rather than erectors of structural steel. In 1913, for example, NEA members fabricated twice as much steel as they erected. American Bridge, as we have seen, erected only about 25 percent of the steel that it fabricated. Indeed, it regarded erection as "only incidental" compared to fabrication and maintained an erection force to ensure the erection of at least some of its steel should general contractors or independent erectors refuse to erect its steel for one reason or another, possibly because it was an open shop company.[6]

It may seem anomalous that firms more interested in steel fabrication than in its erection should have created an association devoted to the open shop in erection. The reason, however, is clear: the fabricators of structural steel, as Drew stressed, saw its erection as "the front line trenches" of the steel industry that had to be held against a union drive to organize the shops. "[T]he chief reason for our whole Open Shop movement," Drew wrote American Bridge's manager of erection, "is fundamentally to protect the Shop." The concern of the fabricators was that the International Association of Bridge and Structural Iron Workers (IABSIW), once strongly entrenched in the erection branch of the industry, would be able to organize the shops, over which it claimed jurisdiction, by not permitting its members to handle any structural steel fabricated in nonunion shops. This, after all, was the practice of such building trades unions as the carpenters, the stonecutters, and the marble workers regarding the products on which their members worked. Indeed, if the IABSIW succeeded in bringing the closed shop to the erection of structural steel, the fear was that it might be able to extend its domain not only to the fabricating shops but to the steel mills that rolled the steel that ended up in bridges and buildings. The "dream" of the AFL, Drew warned United States Steel, was "to use the Iron Workers' Union as an entering wedge for the closed shop in the steel industry." This is why Drew claimed that the labor policy of the iron and steel erectors was "more largely and directly a matter concerned with the steel industry than with the building industry."[7]

The obvious importance to the NEA of the fabrication end of the structural steel industry led the association eventually to alter the method by which its members were assessed to meet the NEA's expenses. Rather than assessing members on the basis only of the number of employees engaged in erection, the NEA's executive committee decided at its meeting of April 5, 1912, that members thereafter should pay their dues on the basis of five cents per ton of material fabricated and five cents per ton of steel erected during the preceding month. This method of assessment, which obviously produced more revenue for the NEA,[8] more nearly reflected the relative economic strength of NEA members than the previous assessment method had. When American Bridge and McClintic-Marshall, although agreeing in general with the new arrangement, complained that it was unfair because, as American Bridge's manager of erection put it, the company's fabrication work did not come "within the reach of labor unions and such disturbing elements," Drew reminded them that they owed this state of affairs to the NEA's holding the line against the unionization of the steel erection industry. He noted, moreover, that contractors who erected but did not fabricate steel did not have the same motive as the fabricators to maintain "a fixed and permanent labor policy" and were inclined to deal with unions if that meant "avoiding trouble." Over the life of the NEA, American

Bridge contributed 39 percent of the NEA's income; Bethlehem Steel and its subsidiaries, including McClintic-Marshall, contributed 33.9 percent.[9]

Although United States Steel was not itself an NEA member, two of its subsidiaries, American Bridge and the Illinois Steel Company, were; and the steel corporation itself served as a looming presence insofar as the NEA was concerned. Drew's appointment as NEA commissioner thus apparently enjoyed "the encouragement and approval" of Elbert H. Gary, the chairman of United States Steel's board of directors. At a meeting of December 14, 1916, the NEA's executive committee, after deciding to raise wages for first-class bridgemen to match a raise by United States Steel that affected American Bridge, resolved that a committee that included Drew should confer with United States Steel officials to urge the corporation to notify the NEA about changes in wage rates it intended to make, since that inevitably affected NEA wage policy. Drew told the NEA's secretary that in writing up the committee's minutes, he should simply refer to the decision to raise NEA wages without mentioning the proposed NEA–United States Steel conference. When the NEA at a later time incurred a substantial legal debt in a labor case, United States Steel helped out with a large contribution. There was "every reason to believe," Drew wrote the head of McClintic-Marshall in 1917, that United States Steel was "convinced of the importance of the work of the [National Erectors'] Association as an assistance to it in carrying out its general labor policy."[10]

The NEA sought to strengthen the open shop among its members and to aid them when in trouble. It encouraged NEA members to deal with their workers in a uniform manner, as with wages, and it served as "a clearinghouse" for members. Through its employment bureaus, it provided workers for members and even nonmembers seeking to maintain the open shop, and it sometimes organized a guard service for members requiring that kind of protection. The NEA commissioner sought to deal with deviations by members from the association's open shop policy, attempted to enlarge the membership of the NEA, and became a key figure in spreading the open shop beyond structural steel erection to the building trades in particular and to industrial America in general.[11]

Throughout his long tenure as NEA commissioner, Drew served as spokesman not only for the NEA but also for the principle of the open shop. He spoke and wrote with regularity about unions, the virtues of the open shop, and the evils of the closed shop. As he told an NEA member, he regarded the education of public opinion as "one of the most important features" of the open shop movement. "The general labor problem in this material age," he asserted in 1906, "is the problem of the century." He recognized, he stated, that it was "the age of combination" and that no one could stop workingmen from organizing into unions; and he conceded that trade union growth was largely due to "the hard and unequal conditions forced upon the workingman in the past by his master." Rhetorically, he professed to believe that it was entirely proper for management to deal with "good unions and good union men," unions that were free of corruption and whose members gave a fair day's work for a fair day's pay. Save for the Brotherhood of Locomotive Engineers, however, such unions existed only in theory for Drew, not in fact.[12]

Unlike someone like C. W. Post, Drew, aware of the NEA's ties to United States Steel, attacked the behavior of combinations of union men but not of business combinations. As Drew viewed the matter, unions chose not to follow the "path of constructive service" but rather to rely on force, of which, he maintained, the closed shop was "the concrete expression." He therefore regarded it as a mistake for an employer to recognize even a union that agreed to the open shop principle, because an agreement on these terms, he feared, would serve as "an entering wedge to force a complete closed shop sooner or later." Indeed, Drew contended that the "absolute non-union shop was justified" since the closed shop, he insisted, was the "fundamental principle" at least of the AFL unions and one that they would not submit to arbitration.[13]

For Drew, the term *union* and the term *closed shop*, "that great economic crime of our modern industrial system," were virtually synonymous. "The main purpose of labor unionism," he argued, was "to secure a monopoly to itself of the labor market and having secured a monopoly, to exact such conditions as may be desired." There was no real bargaining under these conditions, he declared, but only "a demand and a surrender." Once it was strong enough, moreover, a union would restrict membership in its ranks, limit output by one means or another, and by "coercion and intimidation" seek to countermand the law of supply and demand. For the sake of discipline, also, as Drew construed it, unions sought to keep all workers "on the same plane"; and, with wages fixed for the workforce, there was no incentive for the individual to do good work, and the standard set by "the incompetent and shiftless" became the standard for all. When unions went out on strike, Drew charged, they sought to coerce nonunion workers from replacing strikers by "social ostracism, threats, intimidation, violence, and even death."[14]

"[T]he first great legal fact" regarding trade unions, Drew told the Commission on Industrial Relations in 1915, was that they were not legally responsible for their actions and the injury they inflicted on others. This legal "irresponsibility," he maintained, was "a constant temptation to arbitrary, selfish and reckless action."[15]

Fearing all unions, Drew was not inclined to distinguish between the AFL brand of unionism and that of the Industrial Workers of the World (IWW). Indeed, he saw the AFL as posing the greater danger of the two. "The I.W.W. and similar movements," he wrote, "caused a great deal of local and temporary trouble" but did not "contain the elements of danger to be found in the A.F. of L. brand of unionism." Behind the "respectable front" of the Federation, he insisted, "exactly the same kind of thing goes on as with the I.W.W. In the last analysis, they both have the common doctrine of 'rule or ruin.'" They had "the same class-consciousness, the same hostility toward the rest of society." It was easier, however, as he saw it, to combat the IWW because it operated "in the open," whereas "the closed shop unionism" of the AFL worked "in the dark, through intrigue and politics and breach of faith." The "methods" of the AFL were thus, in the end, "more effective and more dangerous" than those of the IWW.[16]

Drew, understandably, was especially concerned about unionism in the construction industry, an industry in which the cost of labor constituted about one half of the total building cost, not including labor involved in producing building materials and in transporting and handling them. Drew pointed out that unionism not only had "a stronger foothold" in this industry than in almost any other but also that the unionized building trades were "the backbone of the closed shop" in cities around the country. When Drew spoke of the alleged evils of unionism and the closed shop, he most commonly had building trades unionism in mind.[17]

In dealing with the building trades unions, Drew focused on graft and corruption, sympathetic and jurisdictional strikes, contract violations, and increased building costs and the consequences thereof. The walking delegates of the building trades unions, Drew complained, gained "control and authority" over the job and, as a result, became "a practical third party to a closed shop building contract." All too often, moreover, Drew maintained, the delegate was corrupt. Pointing to Sam Parks and examples in Chicago and San Francisco, Drew said of the walking delegate, "He levies blackmail, he calls strikes for money and calls them off for more money."[18]

Over time, Drew became increasingly concerned about the sympathetic strike as a weapon of building trades unionism. He claimed in a 1922 address that the sympathetic strike was "the most important weapon" of the building trades unions and the one on which their "autocratic power" mainly rested. The employer who signed a closed shop agreement assumed, Drew asserted, that he would be free of jurisdictional strikes, but the fact of the matter was that the closed shop brought "insecurity," not "security," and "a turmoil of labor trouble from start to finish." Drew's favorite example to support this sweeping generalization was the 140 days of strikes that a closed shop contractor had had to deal with in the building of the Statler Hotel in Detroit. In a study of twenty-two large closed shop building jobs in Pittsburgh between 1924 and 1930 that totaled $35 million, Drew found that seventeen had experienced forty-four strikes, thirty-eight of them resulting from jurisdictional strikes and twenty-eight of them involving the IABSIW. [19]

The chief objection to the closed shop in the building trades, Drew increasingly argued, was the "abnormal and uneconomic increase in the cost of production." Drew attributed this mainly to union restrictions on output, "unreasonable union regulations," lack of incentive for the workers resulting from a uniform wage scale, restrictions on the supply of labor, and graft. Sometimes the NEA commissioner offered the higher wages of closed shop workers as compared to open shop mechanics as a cause for rising costs, but at other times he denied that the closed shop unionist necessarily received higher pay than his open shop counterpart.[20]

Drew contended that because of inflated building costs resulting from closed shop contracts, construction was impeded in cities where the building trades were closed as compared to those where the open shop prevailed. He cited statistical evidence from 1909 and 1910 to support this generalization, although conceding, as he rarely did, that local factors were "sometimes" more important than such considerations as excessive building costs in explaining the disparity. Drew claimed, moreover, that with the exception of New York, which, he asserted in 1910, could "bear the burden of the uneconomic cost of the closed shop," capital tended to shun cities where construction costs were excessive, placing those cities at a competitive disadvantage with open shop cities. Ignoring a host of other explanations and assuming that unionization or the lack of same was the controlling factor, Drew pointed out that the number of wage earners in open shop Los Angeles had increased from 5,173 to 31,352 between 1899 and 1914, whereas the number in closed shop San Francisco had fallen from 32,555 to 31,758 during the same years despite the "natural advantages" enjoyed by the bay city. Drew made a similar comparison between closed shop Cleveland and open shop Detroit from 1914 to 1927. "[N]othing is more harmful to a city than a bad building situation," he contended, and he therefore urged that building costs be viewed as "a community problem."[21]

Among the building trades unions, Drew, understandably, was especially critical of the IABSIW. The structural iron workers, he wrote a general contractor in 1909, were "the hardest class in the building trades to handle." Wherever they were able to secure an agreement from their employers, he charged, they used their strength "to make continuous trouble, to establish a system of graft, and to soldier on the work." They were almost always, he claimed, "at the head" of the trouble in the building trades in large cities. The union's resort to violence, as we shall see, confirmed for Drew what a contemptible organization the IABSIW was.[22]

The open shop, Drew maintained, reduced the cost of structural steel erection. This was because output was not affected by union restrictions and also because the open shop left employers free to grade their workers and to pay them accordingly and to assign common laborers at much lower wages than first-class bridgemen to perform such tasks as erecting false work or unloading material, the latter, according to the president of one construction company, constituting about 10 percent of the work at the job site. As reinforced concrete came into greater use, the IABSIW insisted that union members be assigned the task of setting the rods in the concrete, a task that Drew pointed out was performed on nonunion jobs by laborers at one-half the wage paid skilled bridgemen.[23]

Drew claimed in 1913 that because of savings resulting from open shop construction, structural steel erection costs had been reduced anywhere from 20 to 35 percent since the open shop had been introduced in the industry. In his study of the NEA, however, Luke Grant contradicted Drew's assertions about the cost savings resulting from open shop construction. On the basis of interviews with members of some "large structural iron firms" that had replaced union men with nonunion workers, Grant concluded that there was "little foundation for the claim that union men are less efficient than open shop men" and that, if anything, union housesmiths were the superior workers. Grant cited no cost figures to support his conclusion, nor did he deal specifically with the cost savings to which Drew had referred.[24]

The American Bridge Company's manager of erection informed Drew in September 1907 that, thanks to his company's adoption of the open shop, it had saved $5.00 per ton as compared to previous years in the erection of industrial buildings, fifty cents or $1.00 per ton in erecting tiered or office buildings, $2.25 per ton in erecting railroad viaducts, and about $1.50 per ton in erecting "three pin connected spans." He attributed the greater savings in erecting railroad viaducts than other structures to the fact that the company could more readily employ new and inexperienced workers for these jobs than for the others, since the work was "lighter and less dangerous." Drew claimed the next year that structural iron workers were driving two hundred to four hundred rivets per day under open shop conditions as compared to seventy-five to one hundred per day when jobs were closed.[25]

Structural iron work, it should be noted, required less skill than other building trades, and, over time, open shop erectors were able to train new men for erection jobs. Drew undoubtedly exaggerated the cost advantages of open shop construction, but freedom from union rules regarding such matters as apprenticeship, grading of labor, and the like probably permitted at least some open shop structural steel firms to reduce their costs. American Bridge's manager of erection, after all, had no reason to deceive Drew about this matter in a private letter.

Although the NEA consistently defined its open shop policy as meaning the employment of workers "irrespective of membership in any organization, and without discrimination," that did not mean that the association was passive about the existence of unionism among ironworkers. Indeed, the NEA employed a variety of tactics throughout its history to discourage unionization of its members' employees. "Union substitution," to use Sanford Jacoby's phraseology for the employer effort to provide wages and working conditions that matched union standards, was one such tactic. "Why should we sit idly by while agitators organize the workmen without making some counter-move to offset their efforts?" Drew asked. Since workers joined unions to secure better working conditions, the "first move" of the employer, Drew advised, was to examine the working conditions of his labor force to see if he could do anything to bring standards to "a proper level" if they were not already there. As Drew saw it, fair treatment of employees was "one of the highest and most vital functions of an employers' organization," and this meant not cutting wages, lengthening hours, or imposing working conditions that would not obtain were the closed shop in effect.[26]

The principal condition of work affecting the open shop about which Drew was concerned throughout his long commissionership was wages. If a worker received the same wage under open shop conditions as under the closed shop, Drew believed, he would have no reason to join a union. The NEA had no "hard and fast rule" regarding the wages of member firm employees. What its executive committee did was to recommend from time to time a wage scale for particular localities so as to place members in each locality on an equal basis. These recommendations or suggestions were without "coercive power" and were not always followed by members, but Drew contended that the observance of the recommended rates would be "of great value as a stabilizing factor in the industry." Wage uniformity, "stability of wage rates" in a locality, was the goal because, Drew maintained, if wages and other working conditions were entirely left to the discretion of individual employers, some would take advantage of the open shop "to drive a better bargain with their men" than they thought their competitors would. This, Drew stated, not only meant unfair competition, but it would bring "reproach upon the open shop" and stimulate union organization. Drew also feared that if employers took advantage of the open shop to pay their structural iron workers less than mechanics received in comparable jobs in other building trades, this would increase support for the ironworkers among the other building trades. More, as a result, he believed, would be lost "in the long run" than any temporary gain resulting from the lower wage.[27]

Drew was inclined to view all wage issues in terms of their bearing on the open shop. Thus, when a key NEA member objected in 1929 to an executive committee recommendation to increase wages and reduce hours in the New York district lest to do otherwise would give "a decided black eye" to the open shop stand of the erectors, Drew replied, "To my mind, the question of wages and hours, while of course important, does not compare with that of maintaining and increasing the strength of our open shop position and avoiding the disorganization, inefficiency and exorbitant costs of the closed shop operation."[28]

When the erection business was slack or even "almost at a standstill" and there was talk among employers of reducing wages, as toward the end of 1907, during the recession of 1920–21, or the slump in building in 1927, Drew's advice was always for NEA members to let the wage cutting begin with the unionized building trades, not with open shop erectors. If NEA members were the first to act rather than the last, he cautioned, unionists would say that the open shop meant lower wages. Drew advised, however, that NEA members could take advantage of hard times to "weed out the poor men and the trouble makers and build up a good force of high-grade, industrious and loyal open-shop workers" and, by so doing, could maintain or even increase existing wages.[29]

Drew's position regarding wage increases was that they should appear to be "the voluntary act" of the employer rather than a concession forced by union demands. As open shop employers, he told the Minimum Wage Commission of the National Civic Federation, NEA members raised wages because it was the "fair" thing to do, members could afford it, and, if not, "the people on the other side would get together, and we would have a fight." In June 1916 the NEA's executive committee specifically recommended a wage increase because "trouble" was likely to ensue otherwise and, for the first time, specifically recommended that workers be graded and paid according to their "worth." Grading was designed, in part, to discourage unionism by dividing the workforce.[30]

Not all NEA members shared Drew's view that immediate economic considerations should be subordinated to long-term open shop considerations in the setting of wages. Wages should rise and fall according to "general conditions" and should not be determined by the union rate, declared the president of the Wisconsin Bridge and Iron Company. Raising wages before workers actually demanded same had no appeal, similarly, for McClintic-Marshall's erection manager. Pittsburgh members of the NEA agreed, believing that wages should be set to keep men at work and for no other reason. The general manager of the Phoenix Bridge Company rejected the argument that, to preserve the open shop, erectors had to raise wages before other employers did as "a false principle" ; and he thought it "somewhat naive" to believe that the open shop would become more popular with the men if employers increased their wages.[31]

Drew sometimes called NEA members and even nonmembers to account if they "abused" the open shop principle by reducing wages or lengthening hours. He chided even the division erection manager of American Bridge in 1932 about paying lower wages in New York than other contractors did, noting that wage cutting in the city might prove "disastrous" to the open shop in the iron trade. He told the secretary of Hartford's Open Shop Builders' Trade Exchange that the NEA could not supply the city with ironworkers at the rates the secretary had mentioned since NEA members paid more than that.[32]

Although the presence of the IABSIW was a critical factor in the determination of NEA wage policy, a point that even Drew conceded, that did not mean that union and open shop rates in the structural steel erection industry were identical. There were rare occasions when open shop employers paid a higher wage than closed shop workers were receiving in the same locality, but the union scale, more commonly, was above the open shop rate in most communities. In his 1915 study, Luke Grant reported that NEA wages in the association's New York "stronghold" were below the union scale and below wages paid most building tradesmen in the city. The union scale in New York was, indeed, a few cents per hour higher than the NEA rate at the time, a difference that the NEA soon eliminated, and the NEA paid no higher wage elsewhere, but open shop steel erection wages compared favorably with those of many of the unionized building trades even though the ironworkers' trade required less skill than most other building trades did. In New York, as of July 1915 for example, ironworkers received higher wages per hour than painters and as much as carpenters and sheet metal workers but less than bricklayers, plasterers, plumbers, steam fitters, and gas fitters. Also, from 1906, when the NEA declared for the open shop, to 1914, NEA wages increased by 11.2 percent as compared to an average of 10 percent for the other building trades in New York. Although NEA wages at the time appear to have been below the union scale in most cities outside New York, Drew thought this an unfair comparison because NEA members outside the New York metropolitan area worked mainly on bridges and viaducts rather than buildings, and working conditions on the two types of structures were quite dissimilar.[33]

As of April 1917, union and NEA rates were identical in New York, Kansas City, Newark, and Jersey City, and the union rate was only one-quarter of a cent higher per hour in Chicago and one and one-quarter cents per hour higher in Cleveland and Indianapolis. Five years later union and NEA rates were the same in New York, Chicago, Philadelphia, and Pittsburgh, but the union scale was higher in Detroit, Kansas City, and Minneapolis. In July 1932 the union and the NEA scales were identical in New York and San Francisco, but the union scale was higher in other large cities. Even if wages paid by NEA members were below the union scale, as was common, nonunion workers, as the IABSIW conceded, nevertheless tended to earn more than their nonunion counterparts since they enjoyed steadier work.[34] All in all, it seems that the wages NEA members paid their open shop workers did not constitute an important spur to unionism.

As Drew saw it, an employment bureau that both workers and their employers "patronized" was "the best and surest way of maintaining the open shop" since it assured the open shop employer "a steady and normal supply of men." By the beginning of 1915 the NEA had such bureaus in New York, Pittsburgh, Buffalo, Cleveland, and Kansas City. Sometimes the bureaus in several cities cooperated in supplying men needed by a particular contractor. It was NEA policy, also, for its employment bureaus "to keep in touch with the local situation" wherever a bureau was located and to cooperate in open shop fights in that community.

Each worker registered at a bureau was given a card to take to the foreman on the job. The manager of the New York bureau, however, claimed in 1920 that registrants were not asked about their union status, which strains credulity in view of Drew's characterization of the employment bureaus as "Open shop" bureaus. It was no doubt more than a coincidence that the key New York bureau was managed for several years by a detective who had worked for an agency that specialized in labor espionage.[35]

NEA employment bureaus not only supplied workers for open shop steel erectors in nonstrike situations but also assisted such employers in manning their jobs when their employees went out on strike. If there was "serious trouble" in a locality where there was no bureau, the NEA dispatched the manager of one of its bureaus to the community to assist not only in securing men but in "taking care of different phases of the situation" that might develop. Drew insisted that the NEA did not actually provide strikebreakers but simply men to do open shop work, a distinction without a difference. Workers supplied by a bureau in a strike generally had to sign a statement that defined the terms of their employment and testified to their knowledge that the job to which they were being sent was being struck. The NEA preference was that these workers be guaranteed against discharge once the strike was settled.[36]

Since the "common practice" in the building trades was for workers to seek jobs at the work site, it is perhaps not surprising that the NEA's open shop members, contrary to Drew's hopes, secured less than 50 percent of their men through an NEA employment bureau. In line with National Founders' Association practice, Drew would have liked to develop a "preferred list of men of special merit and industry" who would be available to employers as needed, but except for a time in New York, as will become evident, the NEA did not develop such a list.[37]

If structural steel erection firms were expected to turn to the NEA's employment bureaus for their workers, they had to be assured that competent open shop workers would be made available to them. The NEA, unlike some other employer associations, did not establish training schools to provide workers with the equivalence of the union apprenticeship. Some inexperienced workers were trained on the job, but many of the men supplied by the employment bureaus were skilled structural iron workers who had given up their union cards to seek employment or were union members willing to work under open shop conditions. Drew, indeed, maintained in 1933 that from the time the NEA had been established, "a preponderance" of the mechanics on open shop jobs had been union members who had been hired as individuals. In any event, firms committed to the open shop were generally able to obtain a sufficient number of workers even though there is some dispute as to how efficient these workers were.[38]

In addition to providing workers for open shop employers, the NEA, "in time of acute trouble," secured guards for members who needed them to protect nonunion workers or the job itself. When this was done, the individual employers paid for the guards. Proper guarding became a major concern for the NEA once open shop erection jobs began to fall prey to vandalism and dynamiting.[39]

The NEA and Drew saw foremen as critical to the maintenance of the open shop in the erection industry. The NEA was wary of foremen since many of them had come up through the union ranks and sometimes remained union members while serving as foremen. The danger, in Drew's view, was that foremen on open shop jobs, because of "timidity or sympathy," might give preference to union members in hiring and thus effectively unionize the job. Drew urged contractors to keep an eye on their foremen and to remind them who paid their wages and that the firm's policy was the open shop. He thought it entirely proper for employers to require their foremen to state in writing that they were not union members. When the erection business slumped in 1907, Drew asked NEA members to send him the names of any foremen who were being laid off so that he could help them find work and thus demonstrate that the NEA was "looking out for them under open shop conditions."[40]

During the 1903 ironworkers' strike in New York, the New York open shop erectors organized a club of nonunion foremen. The agreement worked out between the employers and the foremen's organization provided that the employers were to give the foremen members preference in employment, and they in turn were to have no affiliation with any labor organization. In 1916 the Iron League Erectors' Association (ILEA) reached a similar agreement with the foremen's organization, which by then had the name United Supervising Iron and Steel Erectors' Association of America. Drew urged NEA firms to support the organization, and he informed its members that he took "a personal interest" in them and would "stand back of them in every emergency."[41]

The NEA did not hesitate to use coercive tactics in its efforts to enforce the open shop policy. From the start, the association adopted the policy of having members insert a clause in contracts with subcontractors requiring them to operate on an open shop basis. Sometimes a member went so far as to require a cash bond of a subcontractor as a way of enforcing this contract clause, and members sometimes canceled contracts when the open shop requirement was not observed. In an effort to implement the NEA's subcontractor policy, Drew drew up a contract clause specifying that an NEA agent could visit the job in question and enforce the open shop policy by hiring and firing workers. After it was discovered that the Strobel Steel Construction Company of Chicago was violating the open shop clause in contracts it had received from American Bridge, Drew took up the matter with the Strobel firm, which then resigned from the NEA. The next year American Bridge told a subcontractor in Salt Lake City that it would give him all of the company's work in the locality if he operated open shop but that otherwise he would get none at all.[42]

NEA members, to be sure, sometimes ignored the association's sub-contract policy when they saw it to their business advantage to do so. Even American Bridge and the Pennsylvania Steel Company both did so during the early years of the open shop fight. The chief engineer of the Missouri Valley Bridge and Iron Company informed Drew in 1928 that it was "perfectly proper and in fact desirable to permit occasional subletting of work by members . . . to union concerns" because, he rationalized, this enabled members to "enlarge their field of action" and might in this way enlarge the reach of the NEA as well.[43]

Drew conceded that it was sometimes necessary for subcontractors to employ union ironworkers in order to avoid trouble with other building trades. He did not, however, hesitate to remind members of their obligations regarding subcontractors, as the NEA's executive committee instructed him to do. He thus informed the Phoenix Bridge Company in 1907, "I think a little pressure brought to bear on some of these subcontractors will cause them to come over to our side." In dealing with one recalcitrant, the Shoemaker Bridge Company, Drew reported, "I brought every influence I know of to bear through different channels, to no avail."[44]

Another way the NEA could coerce subcontractors was for its members to deny them steel if they did not observe an open shop policy. As Drew noted, the steel fabricator "occupies a strong position. He controls the material." The practice of denying steel, as we shall see, became the subject after World War I of a major state legislative investigation and a probe by both the Department of Justice and the Federal Trade Commission. The NEA at that time insisted that the policy had been adopted to meet a particular situation at a particular time, but it appears that the practice was not as time specific as the NEA claimed. The IABSIW complained as early as 1906 that American Bridge was denying steel to contractors whose workforce was unionized, and in 1908 the union's secretary-treasurer cited the specific instance of McClintic-Marshall's denying steel to the Syracuse Bridge Company because it planned to operate with union labor. A union organizer told the Commission on Industrial Relations in 1914 that some large contractors had said that they were reluctant to do business with the union because they feared what United States Steel "might do to them in restricting deliveries [of steel], etc." Two years later the Lackawanna Bridge Company told a Department of Labor representative that NEA members would deny the company steel if it operated on a closed shop basis.[45]

Despite the NEA's repeated assertion that its policy was to employ workers without regard to whether or not they were union members, it did not hesitate to discriminate against IABSIW members. "[I]n every so[-]called Open Shop," the IABSIW secretary-treasurer declared in 1911, "rank discrimination against [the] union is practiced, first, last and all the time." A New Jersey local informed the international in 1910 that the Phoenix Bridge Company had discharged all of its union workers on a New Jersey job "for the crime of joining the union." Members who secured jobs in New York, the union's president complained in 1915, had to hide their union membership and were discharged if employers discovered that fact. John W. Johnson, head of New York's Local 40, told the Commission on Industrial Relations in 1914 that NEA members did not discriminate against union members when their labor was needed, but when it was not, "they [employers] like to laugh at our men walking the street and [they] put the other fellow on that they can get along with."[46]

Scholarly appraisal of the NEA's behavior regarding the employment of union workers has ranged from the assertion of an economist in a major study of the building industry that the association observed a "genuine open shop" policy to the conclusion of a historian in a study of industrial violence that the NEA made use of "microscopic blacklists" in combating the IABSIW. As a characterization of overall NEA policy in the three decades before the New Deal, neither of these generalizations is correct. Much closer to the reality was the Johnson characterization of NEA policy offered to the Commission on Industrial Relations. That policy is best described as one of preference for nonunion workers, which, depending on the local demand for labor and the local supply of union and nonunion workers, could result in a shop from which union workers were barred or one in which a substantial number of union members might be employed as individuals but without the employer's recognizing their union status in any way.[47]

The NEA–New York ILEA policy of preference for nonunion workers was formulated by Drew against the backdrop of the ironworkers' strike during which the NEA had proclaimed its commitment to the open shop. The NEA commissioner recognized during the business slump in the spring of 1907 that since hundreds of ironworkers were without jobs, employers might be tempted to hire union members to replace the "not quite so good" nonunion workers then manning jobs. He told the employers that it would be "poor business" to do so since the union men would in the end gain control of the jobs and the employers would then have to deal with the same kind of union behavior that had led to the break with the IABSIW in the first place. The "loyalty" of the nonunion worker who had worked during the strike, Drew asserted, was "worth even more than his ability," and so the employer should give him job preference even if he was not as competent a worker as a union replacement would be. Drew also suggested that employers make individual contracts— "yellow dog" contracts—with "high-grade, loyal, open-shop men" for a fixed period of time stipulating that they were not to join the union or strike during the period of the contract. The NEA soon thereafter announced as its official policy that "loyal independent workers" who had accepted employment during the strike were to receive "preference in employment."[48]

As he explained in 1916 to New York's ILEA, whose counsel he was, Drew believed that it was essential in an open shop concern that about 60 percent of the workers on a job should be nonunion. The ILEA then specifically resolved to instruct foremen to give preference in hiring to nonunion workers. The secretary of both the ILEA and NEA testified at a later time that the minutes of the relevant ILEA meeting actually stated that foremen were not to employ "card [union] men" and that the open shop meant that no union men were to be employed. The secretary surmised that a field agent of the aforementioned United Supervising Iron and Steel Erectors' Association, for whom the ILEA provided support for a six-month period beginning on April 1, 1917, was to visit jobs in the New York district to ensure that the ILEA policy regarding card men was being observed.[49]

The ILEA policy adopted in 1916 appears to have been only a temporary one. In late 1919 the ILEA, instead of barring all union workers from its jobs, resolved that all new jobs be started with "a substantial [but unspecified] percentage" of nonunion workers unless a preexisting contract clause forbade that. What this meant in practice was that nonunion workers were the first hired, and when business was slack, this could mean that all the workers on a particular job might be nonunion.[50]

In 1924, when faced again with the possibility of the return of the closed shop to iron erection in the NEA's New York stronghold, Drew and the New York open shop iron contractors drew up a "preferred list" of "first-class reliable men irrespective of union membership" who were to be given preference in employment, even over existing job holders. The assumption, or at least the hope, was that those on the list would look to their employer, not to the union, for security of employment and would not want to jeopardize their job status by striking.[51]

What happened in the important New York district regarding the employment of union and nonunion workers did not, to be sure, determine what NEA members did elsewhere. Practice actually varied from company to company and time to time. Drew conceded in 1908 that "a good many [NEA] concerns" were employing union men "entirely or to a very large extent." The Phoenix Bridge Company informed Drew in 1924 that it did not think it "wise or right" to discharge union workers without cause but that, in Rochester, at least, it did not intend to hire any more of them and would discharge them first in any reduction of force. NEA members were supposed to observe the association's open shop policy, but Drew did not chide them for defining the open shop as a closed nonunion shop.[52] In any event, discrimination against union members was one means by which the NEA sought to combat the IABSIW, particularly in New York at certain times.

The NEA conceded that it had engaged in labor espionage in "the early years of the open shop fight," justifying this because of union attacks on the industry's open shop workers and especially on the property of NEA firms. In 1921 Drew wrote a United States Senate Committee that since 1912 and the big federal dynamite trial, which will be considered in a later chapter, the NEA had "employed only two secret service operatives for a few weeks only and at widely separated periods." The next year Drew wrote Clarence E. Bonnett, who was gathering information for his book on employer associations, that the NEA had not for several years maintained "anything in the nature of a secret service."[53]

The NEA, as we shall see, did indeed step up its espionage activity during the period when the property of its members was being dynamited and its open shop workers assaulted, including even some limited espionage directed against the Industrial Workers of the World (IWW). It is also true that Drew soured on the established private detective agencies after the NEA had engaged the services of several of them. What one could expect from such agencies, he noted, was "high bills, padded expense accounts, reports that . . . were many times 'faked'; work continued when the operatives knew that there was nothing to work upon." He described the well-known Corporations Auxiliary Company as one of many agencies that "capitalize on the differences between labor and capital and which render little in the way of real service—in fact, such concerns often make trouble where none existed previously."[54]

If it is then possible to find a small element of truth in Drew's statements to the Senate committee and Bonnett, the fact of the matter is that the statements were misleading, to put the matter as gently as possible. The NEA engaged in labor espionage before slugging and dynamiting became a major concern of the association, and it continued to spy on the union and to use "inside" men to do so after violence had ceased to be a major problem for NEA members.

The NEA and American Bridge engaged in labor espionage from the very beginning of Drew's commissionership. The purpose at the outset was not to anticipate acts of violence but rather to ferret out union members who might be in the employ of open shop concerns, to check on the attitude of foremen, and to anticipate and counteract union organizing efforts. "I dog the new . . . [members] with spies and provide detectives and yank them on the carpet,"

Drew wrote his parents. He told NEA members in 1907 that they should let him know if they wanted any job investigated. The IABSIW, which itself resorted to the use of "inside men" in open shop firms so as to keep itself informed of employer plans, discovered in 1908 that the recording secretary of its key New York Local 40 was associated with what the international characterized as "a strike-breaking detective agency."

Attempting to counter efforts to unionize fabrication shops in Boston in 1913, Drew sought the aid of American Bridge's chief espionage agent. Shortly thereafter Drew wrote the secretary of Cleveland's Builders' Exchange, "I have sources of information high up in the Union, and at different times have had inside sources in Cleveland." The NEA had a "special man" in Memphis in 1915 providing information to the Pennsylvania Steel Company, and the association's district manager in Pittsburgh informed Drew in 1916 that he had three or four "good men" working inside the Pittsburgh local. After the big dynamite trial, Drew's favorite detective, Robert J. Foster, rented an office from the NEA in New York that adjoined Drew's office, and the NEA continued to pay Foster for detective services. Drew wrote an NEA member in 1919 that Foster had a half dozen operatives who were IABSIW members.[55]

Drew saw espionage as a critical element in the establishment and maintenance of the open shop. Advising the American Erectors' Association, whose counsel he became, on how to establish the open shop among plate fabricators and erectors, Drew stressed the importance of using a detective service before trouble from workers developed. "I find," he observed in the fall of 1914, "that after a fight really starts, it is very hard for a detective to work himself into any big valuable sources of information. If he is already established on the ground, he is in much better position to anticipate and prevent lawlessness." After seeking to conciliate a New York ironworkers' strike in 1920, James J. Barrett, a United States Department of Labor commissioner of conciliation, concluded that the NEA and the allied ILEA maintained the open shop by a "spy system" and that the NEA had "a large number of so-called 'under cover' representatives or spies."[56]

Whether NEA labor espionage was as effective in deterring union organization as Barrett asserted is hard to say. Luke Grant in his 1915 study stressed the "suspicion" that "pervaded every [IABSIW] local" and concluded that the effect of espionage on the union had been "utterly demoralizing." After learning in 1909 that several New York union members had been tried by the union for furnishing information to the NEA, Drew informed association members that "the whole [union] organization" appeared to be "infested with mutual suspicion, distrust and weakness."[57] In any event, Drew thought espionage of sufficient importance in combating the IABSIW to make use of labor spies from the beginning of his commissionership and to continue the practice for many years after he claimed that it had all but been abandoned.

Like United States Steel and other employers in the Progressive Era, the NEA saw welfare capitalism—"paternalism," to use Jacoby's word—as still another way to discourage unionism. United States Steel by 1912 was spending

$5 million a year on welfare programs that included some aid for workers injured on the job and the families of workers who suffered job-related fatal accidents, accident prevention programs, pensions for long-term employees, sanitation work, and such "welfare items" as playgrounds and lunchrooms. United States Steel employees were also able to purchase the corporation's preferred stock at below market prices. In 1908 McClintic-Marshall adopted profit-sharing and disability compensation plans for the workers at its Pittsburgh plant.[58]

Because of the extremely hazardous nature of the ironworker's job, Drew saw accident insurance as a welfare program of particular importance for NEA members. After Drew first broached the idea at an executive committee meeting in September 1908, the committee authorized him to sign a contract with an insurance firm along the lines he had suggested. The contract Drew concluded in September 1909 with the United States Health and Accident Insurance Company specified that employees covered by the plan were to pay a $3 entrance fee and then $1 per month and provided benefits not only for accidents but for sickness as well. The plan was a modest one that involved no employer contribution, but Drew estimated that it would yield covered employees 25 percent more in benefits at the same cost than if they had purchased similar insurance individually.[59]

The NEA's accident-sickness insurance plan was not available to union members, which reveals its real purpose, and individual policies were to be voided if they fell into the hands of union men. Foremen were instructed to "use every precaution necessary in selecting applicants for the insurance," each of whom was to receive a card from an NEA employment bureau certifying his eligibility. "The object of the proposition," Drew told the NEA, "is entirely to build up a strong and efficient organization, which will be independent of any union or the control of any set of men. . . . A little reflection," he remarked, "will suggest to you the many ways the value that a strong loyal following of open shop men, whose identity is known through some such arrangement as this, who are in constant touch with our bureaus, will be in maintaining our [open shop] policies." Claiming that the New York ironworkers were "enthusiastic" about the plan, Drew thought that it would remove the incentive for NEA workers to join the union and might even cause unionists to quit the IABSIW so that they could "come in on the plan."[60]

It is doubtful that the NEA's modest insurance plan was of more than marginal effect as a means of strengthening the NEA's open shop policy. It was, in any event, soon upstaged by the enactment of workmen's compensation plans in the various states that did not require any contribution by workers and that were not limited to nonunion workers. The NEA now shifted its attention from its own insurance plan to the legislative effort to deal with job-related accidents, and Drew, as we shall see, actively sought to influence the shape of the state compensation laws.

Drew's concern about providing NEA workers with accident insurance reflected a growing belief on his part that "progressive open-shop employers" had to do more than provide their workers with fair wages and decent working conditions if the employers were to dissuade their workers from joining unions. It was "better," he believed, "to head off trouble than to fight it," and the way for employers to do that was to adopt schemes of welfare capitalism. He came to regard group insurance as "one of the most effective of these measures" and as aiding employers in securing "steady workers" and thus reducing the high cost of turnover.[61]

By the time the United States entered World War I, Drew had decided that if employers were to resist unionization, they would have to provide their workers not only with schemes of welfare capitalism but also with some kind of machinery that would enable them to vent and gain consideration for their grievances. When he first became the NEA's commissioner, Drew was less concerned about what NEA employees had to say to their employers than about the reverse. In order to counter alleged union misstatements, he thought it wise for iron contractors, from time to time, to enclose brief statements in the pay envelopes of their employees. This, he optimistically assumed, would help to convince the workers that there was a strong organization behind them as long as they eschewed unionism. In addition to rebutting union claims, the NEA notices "to our Men," as in New York, generally informed the workers that the steel erection firms would not under any circumstances retreat from the open shop.[62]

Insofar as NEA members and their New York allies played some role in creating dual unions of open shop employees to counter the IABSIW, they were, in theory anyhow, establishing a mechanism through which employees could air their grievances and seek improved working conditions. This, it will be recalled, was a tactic to which the Allied Iron Associations (AIA) had resorted in both 1903 and 1906. McClintic-Marshall formed the "Independent Iron Workers" in Pittsburgh in 1907, but the IABSIW local there soon reported that the dual union had been "all shot to H——" and had been brought under local union "control."

In the fall of 1914 open shop workers in New York received a state charter for the Housesmiths and Structural Iron Workers of New York and Vicinity, Incorporated. When representatives of the new union met with Drew in the fall of 1915 to seek a wage increase, the NEA commissioner responded that there were "no economic reasons" to justify an increase. The union meekly accepted Drew's reasoning, informing him that the organization was "duly impressed" with his argument and that its leadership had unanimously agreed to defer the wage demand for the time being. Explaining what had happened to the NEA and noting that the dual union had a "considerable membership," Drew stated that he was always ready "to discuss labor questions informally" with NEA workers "in the endeavor to show them the reciprocity of interest [of employer and employee] and enable them to look at labor questions from a broad viewpoint," which, of course, meant Drew's "viewpoint."[63]

Hard-line NEA members objected to Drew's dealing with the dual New York housesmiths' union. B. L. Worden, president of the Lackawanna Bridge

Company, complained that what Drew was doing was contrary to the NEA's open shop policy. "[I]f we are fostering a rival union," Worden explained, "we are merely breeding a serpent to sting us." He thought that NEA members should deal with their employees only as "individuals" rather than what he construed as discriminating "between two unions instead of dealing with one." Drew responded that he was not "fostering a local union" and that the "most effective way" to increase membership in the IABSIW was "to begin to fight it and to persecute it." If the NEA, Drew asserted, discriminated against the dual union's members, who, he said, had been "of real assistance in acting as a sort of balance-wheel" in the workforce, it would push them into the IABSIW or cause them to line up against their employers.[64]

The difference between Drew and some NEA members regarding contact with nonunion NEA workers became evident once again in the Pittsburgh-Youngstown district in May 1916, when a committee claiming to represent two hundred unorganized structural steel workers sought a wage increase. McClintic-Marshall responded by discharging the activists among the nonunion group. Drew, on the other hand, was prepared to talk to the workers and to explain to them why a wage increase was not justified at that time. He did not doubt that the employers could "fight through a strike," but he believed that the more important consideration was not to cause the workers involved to believe that they had to join a union to gain consideration of their demands. When a strike did develop in the district, four major NEA members, including American Bridge and McClintic-Marshall, resolved neither to grant the wage increase nor to negotiate with the strikers. While seeking strike replacements through the NEA's employment bureaus, Drew sought to convince the strikers of the "friendship and good faith" of NEA members. He advised the employers at the same time that a small increase was justified. The strikers, who kept the IABSIW at arm's length, returned to their jobs after about two weeks, having received the promise of a modest wage increase. Drew chose to see all this as a "vindication" of the NEA's open shop policy.[65]

By the time the United States entered World War I, Drew had decided that employers should provide their workers with some form of employee representation in order to stave off the unionization of their labor force. "This is the age of combination," he wrote the secretary of the Manufacturers' Association of Wilmington. "Organized effort is a common thought with the workers. If this interest and tendency is not recognized by giving them some form of collective action, the probability that they will accept what is offered to them from the outside is greatly increased." He concluded that a committee representing the employees that could present grievances to the management would be of great value to the employer, separated from his employees as he commonly was by superintendents or foremen. Drew's advice was that employers should confer only with committees made up of their own employees and whose membership was at least 50 percent nonunion.[66] Drew, as the United States went to war, was prepared to go somewhat further in placating the NEA's workers than many of the association's members were.

■

In the years following his assumption of the NEA's commissionership and before the United States entry into World War I, Drew sought to strengthen the NEA position in those cities where the open shop had been introduced and to extend the NEA's domain to other cities as well. New York, as always, was at the very center of Drew's concerns about the NEA and its open shop policy.

In New York, the NEA was eventually able to claim victory in the strike that was under way when Drew became the NEA's commissioner. Unable to weaken the resistance of the employers and with individual union members filtering back to work, the ironworkers' union in the city, whose strike, as we have seen, was already weakening, suffered a severe blow when it appeared to be implicated in a major accident on July 11, 1906, that resulted in the death of one person and injury to two others. The scene of the accident was the Plaza Hotel, then under construction. The general contractor for the structure, the George A. Fuller Company, although employing union men itself, had subcontracted some finishing work on stairways to Winslow Brothers, which employed nonunion workers. After structural iron workers had dropped red-hot rivets, iron and steel bars, and heavy tools on the nonunion men who worked below the union workers, Fuller engaged private guards to protect the nonunionists.

The story that initially appeared in the press about the accident was that union men, armed with sledgehammers, heavy wrenches, and iron bars, had thrown three guards from the eighth floor of the structure through the framework to the fifth floor, resulting in the death from a fractured skull of one guard and injury to the two others. Seven unionists were arrested for the incident, the *New York Times* referring to the union in a caption as "The Murderous Housesmiths." As Drew advised NEA members, the Plaza affair increased the "odium" of the New York union and "materially changed" the situation in the strike in the employers' favor. Even employers in the other building trades now concluded that the AIA could not be expected to deal with "a body of murderers." A coroner's jury, however, concluded that the deaths had been accidental, and the coroner, without any evidence to support the charge, claimed that the accident had resulted from the effort of the AIA and the Fuller Company, which was not an AIA member, to "discredit" the United Housesmiths so that the union would not be reinstated on the General Arbitration Board. Despite the verdict of the coroner's jury, the state tried five workers for the assault on one of the three guards, but the jury failed to reach a verdict. One defendant, however, who had fled the jurisdiction before the case could be retried, later pleaded guilty to a felonious assault charge and was sentenced to three years in prison.[67]

On July 22, 1906, the United Housesmiths, over the objections of IABSIW president Frank Ryan, voted to return to work as individuals for local New York structural steel contractors at the old $4.50 rate per day but to continue the strike against the few members of the ILEA who were also NEA members, notably the key Post and McCord Company. As the secretary of the District Council, who deplored the decision, informed union headquarters, the union housesmiths had no alternative since, as he put it, "we were fast losing our men." When Fuller, following the July 11 incident, discharged the union mechanics working for the company on the Plaza building, Drew informed NEA members that "substantially no large employer of iron workers" in New York was using union members any longer.[68]

Drew interpreted the United Housesmiths' decision as a "clever move" designed to cause a "split" between NEA members and nonmember New York iron firms. "As a counter move," Drew, who was serving both the NEA and AIA and saw to it that they "worked in close harmony," persuaded the AIA on July 23 to instruct its members to refuse to take back union members unless the United Housesmiths agreed to return to NEA as well as AIA jobs. There was a scarcity of ironworkers at the time, however, and AIA members were consequently willing to take back "limited numbers" of unionists as individuals. The AIA, at the same time, informed its employees that member firms would be "loyal" to those who had worked during the strike.[69]

Drew had "a strenuous time" preventing New York iron employers from "throwing away the fruits of victory" by hiring union members in violation of the AIA's July 23 decision. "I found they could not be trusted," Drew said of the New York firms, and "that their word as to what they were doing could not be relied upon." Drew, who attributed "nine out of ten labor problems" to the "apathy and indifference of employers," thought that it was the habit of employers to believe that labor matters would take care of themselves once a strike was over. He warned the New York employers that union members agreeing to return as individuals were simply "playing one card in the game, their aim being to get as many men on the job as possible and [then] to drive off" the nonunion workers. If it appeared that the drift was once again toward unionism, he feared, nonunion workers on AIA jobs would decide that they had to join the union to keep their jobs. To forestall this, Drew suggested that the employers offer "yearly contracts" to "the best of the men" hired during the strike.[70]

Drew did not content himself with the suggestion of yearly contracts to prevent the unionization of AIA jobs. He also employed "several private detectives" to keep himself "constantly informed" regarding the composition of the work force of AIA members. When the AIA adopted its July 23 resolution, Drew informed his parents, association representatives had asked him how he would enforce it. "I laughed," he wrote, "and said I would find a way," and that as long as he was commissioner, "they would toe the mark" or would have to fire him.[71]

Drew and the AIA used the information gathered by detectives to notify employers about union men on their jobs and to remind the employers that they were to hire only through the AIA's employment bureau and were to employ only those union men who had worked during the strike. Sometimes the employers themselves asked Drew to check on their labor force. Drew agreed to send AIA members a list of men who had worked during the strike, accompanied by remarks on their qualifications, so that they could be placed on a "preferred list" and could serve as a nucleus of "loyal men" in any particular firm. The NEA also assured the AIA that it would aid the New York firms in maintaining the open shop.[72]

Although Drew, the NEA, and the AIA were not able to persuade all the New York iron contractors to limit their hiring of union members to those who had worked during the strike, the NEA commissioner and the two organizations were almost entirely successful as 1906 drew to a close in keeping New York's structural steel erection industry on an open shop basis. When the IABSIW met in convention in September 1906, there was "strong sentiment" among delegates from New York and eastern locals to settle the Post and McCord strike, and the union's executive board met in New York after the convention in a futile effort to achieve that result.[73]

By the beginning of 1907, a year in which the NEA took "direct control" of the AIA's employment bureau, Drew reported that "careful investigation" had revealed that less than half of the IABSIW's New York members were employed, many of them not as ironworkers. Large numbers of unionized ironworkers, he noted, had left the city to seek work elsewhere, and many workers were coming to New York from Pittsburgh, Cleveland, and elsewhere to work on an open shop basis. The few iron contractors who employed union members did not observe union rules, and by April all New York contractors were paying workers the AIA-NEA rate of $4.50 per day. The United Housesmiths were reportedly "demoralized" and suffering from "desertions," internal dissension, and lack of funds. The District Council did not call off the strike against NEA members, but Local 40 decided to permit its members to work for Post and McCord, an action that the international union sanctioned.[74]

When the IABSIW sought in October 1907 to break the New York "monotony" by extending to New York a Newark strike against an NEA member who operated in both cities, the NEA was quickly able to man the struck job, and the strike proved to be a dismal failure for the union. Frank Webb, an IABSIW board member who was based in New York, reported to international union headquarters that the constant refrain among unionized ironworkers in New York was, "Why don't the Int. [*sic*] let us go to work as well as the scabs?" The unemployment resulting from the hard times beginning in late 1907 and extending through 1908 did not, of course, make things any easier for New York's unionized ironworkers. Surrendering to the inevitable, the IABSIW in 1908 authorized the New York locals to permit union members to work for all the open shop firms in the city.[75]

Between 1908 and the United States entry into World War I in 1917, the ten ILEA firms experienced little difficulty in maintaining the open shop. The Employers' Association of Architectural Iron Workers, made up almost entirely of small firms operating ornamental iron shops and engaging in tenement house work, would actually have granted the union recognition, but the AIA used its position as a member of the Building Trades Employers' Association to stop this. When there was a shop strike in 1911, the NEA "took charge of the fight," and the AIA pressured the union by locking out the outside workers who supported the inside strike. The IABSIW was weakened further in the same year when it was suspended from the New York Board of Delegates because of a jurisdictional dispute with the Metal Lathers, which, Drew maintained, made the IABSIW "even more of an outlaw" in New York. When there was fear early in 1916 that the union might be making inroads in some firms, the local iron contractors instructed their foremen to replace union workers with nonunion mechanics, and Drew advised that the number of open shop men not fall below 60 percent of the total number of workers in a firm. The NEA and the ILEA at the same time increased the wages of ironworkers to counter any desire for unionism at a time when there was "a very substantial increase" in the amount of work in the structural steel erection business.[76]

When the United States went to war in April 1917, New York was a closed shop city in the building trades with the sole exception of the structural iron workers' trade. Although some building trades employers who operated closed shop sought for a time to pressure the ILEA to come to terms with the iron-workers, believing that they had been "punished enough," employers in the closed shop building trades, according to Drew, had come to recognize that the NEA acted "as a balance wheel in the general labor situation." Actually, by April 1917 only two ILEA members, Post and McCord and Levering and Garrigues, both major firms, were also NEA members. Although other local contractors had given up their NEA membership and the ILEA no longer contributed to the NEA, the two associations had the same address, the New York erection firms used the NEA's New York employment bureau, and Drew, as NEA commissioner and counsel for the ILEA, successfully coordinated the labor policies of the two organizations.[77]

The NEA added Buffalo to the open shop territory in iron work in 1914–15. When the unionized ironworkers in that city went out on strike on a job because the contractor was using nonunion carpenters, the erection contractors decided to place their work on an open shop basis, a decision that led to the extension of the strike to other construction jobs. Drew quickly came to the assistance of the iron firms, providing them with strikebreakers and assigning the NEA's man in Cleveland to aid the local firms. All of Buffalo's fabricators and erectors of structural steel joined the NEA, and they were able to place their work on an open shop basis. In Pittsburgh, where the IABSIW local had been ready to abandon the strike against the NEA by the end of 1906, the city's iron and steel erection firms soon joined the NEA and declared for the open shop; and the ironworkers' local permitted its members to work for these firms on that basis. Philadelphia and northern New Jersey in the East, however, remained largely closed to the NEA before 1917. Drew, nevertheless, advised the Erectors' Association of Philadelphia in 1912 how it might go about implementing an open shop policy, which is what it did after World War I.[78]

In Cleveland, the building trades unions, including the IABSIW, were strongly organized when Drew became NEA commissioner. Since the open shop was "not a normal condition" in erection work in Cleveland, Drew informed the NEA that he would "take strenuous measures" there, including the opening of an employment bureau. The NEA, however, was unable during the pre–World War I era to make much headway in Cleveland. Ever the optimist where the NEA's fortunes were concerned, Drew, however, saw some "hopeful signs" in Cleveland in 1909 because the city's Employers' Association had initiated a "strenuous open shop campaign," the Builders' Exchange was urging members to patronize open shop contractors, and especially because of a dispute that developed concerning the construction of a grandstand and two pavilions for the Cleveland Baseball Club.[79]

When McClintic-Marshall learned that the bidding for the ballpark construction had been limited to concerns employing union labor, it urged Drew to "get after the Owners of this work" and to persuade them to accept bids from open shop companies. Seeking to enlist the aid of the National Association of Manufacturers (NAM) in doing precisely this, Drew explained that since the Cleveland club claimed that, as a member of the League of Baseball Clubs, it had to follow league policy to use only union labor in construction, what was at stake was a matter of "national importance" and provided an opportunity to bring the open shop issue "into the limelight." If the NEA, the NAM, and Cleveland employers were to "go after" the league in this matter, Drew wrote, "there ought to be some fireworks somewhere that somebody could see." As for himself, Drew remarked, "I have my toe on the mark ready to start whenever you [NAM] want to enter the lists."[80]

After representatives of the NEA, the NAM, and Cleveland employer associations, whose aid Drew had enlisted, visited the president of the Cleveland Baseball Club, the club reopened the bidding so as to permit open shop firms to submit bids. The new bids, the club conceded, were thousands of dollars below the original bids from closed shop contractors. The contract for the structural steel and iron work had apparently already been let to a closed shop concern, Forest City Steel and Iron Company, but the general contract was now let to a company that employed nonunion labor. This led Cleveland's Local 17 of the IABSIW, at the request of the city's Building Trades Council, to strike the ballpark job. The council further decided to conduct "systematic boycotts" of the Cleveland Baseball Club wherever the Cleveland team played. By this time, however, the middle of September, the 1909 baseball season was drawing to a close. After a strike that lasted only a day and a half, Local 17 members returned to work, agreeing to work alongside nonunion workers.[81]

When the 1910 baseball season began in April, the Cleveland Building Trades Council resumed its boycott of the Cleveland team. Seeking to "crystallize some open shop sentiment," Drew, who urged the city's Employers' Association to take legal action against the boycott, stated that the NEA was willing to involve itself in the Cleveland matter in any way necessary, "personal, financial or otherwise." Despite the appearance of union pickets with cameras and notebooks outside the ballpark at the beginning of the baseball season, attendance was unaffected. The secretary of the Builders' Exchange wrote to builders' associations in all American League cities requesting owners of the teams in those cities to disregard any request to cooperate in the boycott when the Cleveland team visited. The boycott proved to be a failure, but the Cleveland Baseball Club and the building trades unions nevertheless came to an understanding about future construction work that spelled defeat for Drew and the NEA.[82]

In June 1911 Drew wrote an NEA member that Cleveland was "one of the worst places we have dealt with." Unlike the NEA's employment bureaus in places like New York and Pittsburgh, the Cleveland bureau, he noted, was rarely called upon to supply workers and was kept in the city only for its "moral effect." Local iron contractors refused to join the NEA, and when "outside" NEA members did work in the city, they brought their own work gangs with them. In 1913 Drew, belatedly taking action on an NEA Executive Committee decision, closed the Cleveland bureau, transferred the NEA's Cleveland secretary, and added Cleveland to the responsibilities of the association's Central District manager in Pittsburgh.[83]

When Local 17 arranged in 1913 with the Hoisting Engineers and the Bricklayers to gain exclusive control for itself over the setting of iron rods in reinforced concrete, Drew, as with the construction at the baseball park, thought this was an issue the NEA could exploit since the setting of rods was usually performed by common labor at about half the wages of skilled housesmiths. He immediately came to the assistance of Cleveland's General Contractors' Association when it organized to resist the arrangement, and he provided for the NEA's H. R. Brady to take charge of the Protective Association that the contractors had established. Once again, however, Drew was disappointed since the contractors dispensed with Brady's services after some months and then "surrendered" to Local 17 in the spring of 1915.[84]

The agreement between the contractors and the Cleveland Building Trades Council covering reinforced concrete was followed by a series of agreements between contractors and building trades unions applying to individual trades. The business agent of the council subsequently announced that the unions making up the council would not work on any building that was to be occupied by "unfair" firms or individuals. This announcement, Drew stated, revealed the danger and the evils of the closed shop in the construction industry. Cleveland business interests came to the same conclusion, and by the time the United States entered World War I, the Cleveland Chamber of Commerce had decided that the time had come for the city's businesses to curb the power of the city's building trades unions, including Local 17 of the IABSIW.[85]

Although Drew failed in his determined effort to establish the open shop in structural steel erection in Cleveland, he enjoyed success west of the city in Gary, Indiana, Milwaukee, and Kansas City. Drew's greatest early victory as NEA commissioner was his success in persuading Illinois Steel to build its sprawling Gary plant on an open shop basis. Since Illinois Steel, according to the president of Chicago's Local 1 of the IABSIW, the union's most powerful local, had always treated the union "fair[ly]," the local looked forward to the building of the huge plant, whose construction required about seventy-five thousand tons of structural steel. Seeing the Gary job as "vital" to the NEA,

Drew traveled to Chicago in early April 1906 to confer with Illinois Steel officials and to urge the erection of the Gary plant on an open shop basis. Since Illinois Steel was a United States Steel subsidiary, Drew's task could not have been too difficult. Illinois Steel proposed that the job be declared open shop but that the company, at least at the start, engage union workers for the plant's construction. Drew responded that that would make the job "practically a union job" but that if nonunion men were hired at the outset, it would become "a real open shop job" even if union workers were employed at a later time.

Local 1 offered to agree to almost any working conditions at Gary if the job was declared closed. Illinois Steel, however, rejected the local's overtures and announced that the plant would be constructed on an open shop basis. This led Local 1 on October 31 to declare a strike on Illinois Steel at its South Works in Chicago, in Joliet, and elsewhere. Illinois Steel sought Drew's help in securing ironworkers, and he was able to supply one hundred men within two weeks at a saving to Illinois Steel, he pointed out, of twenty cents per hour per worker as compared to the cost of union labor. With the strike soon "well in hand," Illinois Steel decided that it would not reemploy the union strikers, Drew informing the NEA's executive committee that this was "the severest blow dealt the union in the west."[86]

The decision of Illinois Steel to adopt the open shop was one of a series of acts leading to the virtual elimination of unionism in the plants of United States Steel and its subsidiaries. The final blow was struck when American Sheet and Tin Plate announced on June 1, 1909, that it would not renew its contracts with the Amalgamated Association of Iron, Steel and Tin Workers when they expired on June 30. A failed strike followed that reduced the Amalgamated to impotence, with a membership in 1911 of only forty-three hundred, and left the IABSIW as the only union of any significance in the steel industry and its subsidiary trades.[87]

In Milwaukee, all the structural steel erection firms joined the NEA in 1907, but most soon returned to their union ways. In 1914 the city's two major steel erection firms, the Worden-Allen Company and the Milwaukee Bridge Company, in an action the IABSIW attributed to Drew's machinations, fought off a union demand for a wage increase and opted for the open shop. The city's other erection firms followed suit, which led the NEA to open an employment bureau in the city.[88]

Since Kansas City was "a natural recruiting point for bridgemen" in the West, Drew sought for years to enroll the city's structural steel firms in the NEA. He succeeded with a few contractors during the NEA's early years, but most thought it "impossible . . . to break loose [from the unions] at once." By April 1917, however, there was an NEA employment bureau in the city, and the open shop was firmly established among the structural steel firms. Drew was willing to make concessions to enroll Kansas City contractors in the NEA. When the head of the A. M. Blodgett concern inquired of the NEA commissioner as to whether the company would be obligated if it joined the NEA not to employ union workers even if some "special job" required it, Drew replied that the NEA had "no fixed rules that would work a hardship" on a member if it proved "extremely difficult or costly" for it to work on an open shop basis. "All we ask from a member," Drew wrote, "is that he be thoroughly in sympathy with the open shop and willing to make every reasonable effort to operate on that basis." This satisfied Blodgett, who joined the NEA.[89]

The NEA decided that it was essential for the association to open an office in Kansas City or some other western city. Structural steel work was becoming important enough in that region by that time so that Drew and the NEA thought it "a matter of common business judgment" to bring the west under the NEA's wing, something that could perhaps be done by establishing an employment bureau there rather than, as Drew put it, simply relying on "hot air." The NEA considered both Kansas City and St. Louis as possible locations for a western office but decided on the former, since there were no bridge concerns in St. Louis, whereas Kansas City had several, and the St. Louis contractors, unlike their Kansas City counterparts, expressed little desire to break off relations with the city's well-organized building trades unions.[90]

After some delay, Drew transferred J. W. Poushey from the NEA's Pittsburgh office to open an NEA office in Kansas City but then replaced him with J. A. G. Badorf, another trusted NEA aide. No sooner had the association opened its office than the Kansas City Terminal Railway Company presented it with what Drew saw as a possible disaster in terms of the open shop policy the NEA was seeking to establish in the city. The company appeared to be yielding to the threat of a general strike by the building trades unions if it let the contract for the erection of a bridge to the low bidder, the Missouri Valley Bridge and Iron Company, an NEA member and an open shop concern. Drew remonstrated with H. H. Adams, Kansas City Terminal's president, stating that in giving the job to a firm employing IABSIW members, he would raise the cost of the work by 20–35 percent, would be dealing with a union discredited, as we shall see, by its association with dynamiting, and would be encouraging other firms to follow suit.[91]

Drew did not rely on the force of his argument alone to win over Adams. The NEA commissioner started what he described as "a sort of flank movement" among Kansas City general contractors to get them to declare for the open shop, which, he assumed, would give the local building trades unions planning to strike Kansas City Terminal in support of the ironworkers "something to think about without bothering" the NEA and its members. He advised the contractors that it was time for them to take "rightful control of their industry" and to rid themselves of such evils as jurisdictional and sympathetic strikes, the boycott of building materials, and the use of high-priced labor to perform tasks as readily performed by common labor. He informed them that when he had spoken to the city's leading businessmen on a visit to Kansas City, they had understood when he explained how the "arbitrary and unreasonable practices" of the closed shop, particularly in the building trades unions, had adversely affected the city's industrial development. If the contractors joined together, Drew said, they could deprive the unions of "nine-tenths" of their strength, and the NEA, he informed them, was prepared to aid the effort.[92]

With the NEA's Badorf taking the lead, the contractors formed the Building Construction Employers' Association, and they made Badorf its secretary. Apparently yielding to Drew's importunities and his "flank movement," Adams awarded the bridge contract to Missouri Valley, and the building trades unions remained on the job. The Rock Island Railroad Company, which had let a contract to a Kansas City construction firm to perform some work for the railroad on a union basis, also now reversed itself. Although the NEA thus attracted some of Kansas City's major structural steel contractors to its ranks and helped to influence the labor policy of two of the railroads in the area, it was disappointed in the behavior of the Building Construction Employers' Association. There was a lack of cooperation between general contractors and subcontractors, many contractors refused to join the association, and it proved difficult for Badorf to appeal to members on the basis of "principle" as distinguished from dollars and cents. The "ethics" of the contracting business, he wrote Drew, would "almost be a disgrace to Hell itself."[93]

In the pre–World War I era Drew regularly pointed to Chicago and San Francisco as the "closed shop citadels" that were most resistant to the open shop principle in the structural steel industry. Although the closed shop prevailed in the Chicago building trades, that did not mean that NEA members from outside Chicago did not occasionally erect steel in the city with nonunion labor. In a notable instance in 1906, the Pittsburgh Steel Construction Company, as an American Bridge subcontractor, erected the steel for the South Side Elevated Railway on an open shop basis. Drew devoted several weeks to this job and, because Chicago's Local 1, as Drew put it, was "very ugly" about the matter, arranged for "a complex system of guards." He converted two large houses along the right of way into a boardinghouse for workers, which enabled them to proceed to and from their jobs on privately owned property.[94]

Although Drew failed to persuade Chicago's iron contractors, joined together in the Chicago Iron League, to commit themselves to the open shop, he could point to a few positive developments in Chicago from the NEA point of view. As in New York, the conviction of Chicago building trades labor leaders for extortion provided Drew with ammunition with which to attack the alleged consequences of the closed shop. In 1909 three Chicago labor leaders, including Martin B. "Skinny" Madden, president of the Associated Building Trades, were found guilty of extortion, Drew declaring that "graft and corruption seem inevitable under closed shop conditions." In April 1915, following a ten-month probe, a special federal grand jury inquiring into agreements between contractors and unions to bar outside contractors and building materials from the Chicago market handed down one hundred indictments. The president of the Chicago Building Trades Council was among the eighteen labor leaders and forty-one contractors indicted.[95]

Drew took some comfort from the fact that the powerful Chicago local of the IABSIW, unlike Cleveland's Local 17, was unable to gain control over reinforced concrete work. On April 30, 1915, the Chicago local struck the jobs of all contractors who refused to yield it jurisdiction over this task. After a strike of more than nine weeks, the union settled for a three-year closed shop contract that did not concede it the reinforced concrete jurisdiction it had sought. Although "strong sentiment" developed among Chicago Iron League members during the strike to commit themselves to the open shop, a Chicago iron contractor advised Drew that the league had been unable to resist the "pressure" to settle on a closed shop basis exerted by material dealers, general contractors, and the Building Trades Council. The terms of the agreement did, however, permit Chicago contractors to operate on an open shop basis outside the city.[96]

Following the 1915 strike, some Chicago contractors wanted to join the NEA, but Drew informed them that they could not do so as long as they operated on a closed shop basis. He did, however, offer to assist their effort to operate open shop outside the city, an offer one or two of them accepted. Chicago, for the time being, remained a closed shop city for structural steel erection, but Drew thought that conditions had been "greatly bettered" by the 1915 agreement since it incorporated the aforementioned Cardinal Principles that the Building Contractors' Council had formulated in 1900, principles that became the basis for a uniform agreement in 1915 between Chicago's Building Construction Employers' Association, which succeeded the Building Contractors' Council in 1911, and the Building Trades Council.[97]

Testifying before the Commission on Industrial Relations in September 1914, Grant Fee, president of the San Francisco Building Trades Employers' Association, reported that building trades employers in the city had to "submit to union rule." He noted, moreover, that there was no real collective bargaining in the building trades: the unions, instead, adopted "a so-called law" regarding wages, hours, and working conditions that went into effect as far as they were concerned once approved by the city's Building Trades Council. As Michael Kazin has pointed out, San Francisco had the strongest labor movement in the nation in the Progressive Era, and the Building Trades Council was "the epitome" of that strength.[98]

When the San Francisco contractors formed the Building Trades Employers' Association in 1912 in order to restrain union power, the iron contractors turned to the NEA for advice as to how to conduct the fight. Following a successful employer confrontation with the Hoisting Engineers, the secretary of the Erectors' Association of California informed Drew late in 1913 that he thought the building trades employers were at last "finding [their] feet." It was not, however, until 1916 that the city's business community mounted a major challenge to union power in the city.[99]

The triggering event that galvanized San Francisco employers was a waterfront strike by the San Francisco Waterfront Employees' Union that began on June 1, 1916. The strike, which violated a contract signed in the presence of a commissioner of conciliation of the Department of Labor, was attended by a considerable amount of violence perpetrated by both sides, tied up about $2.5 million in merchandise, and "absolutely paralyzed" shipping into and out of the port of San Francisco. To heighten the anger of businessmen resulting from the loss of business, the strikers permitted freight to be hauled through the picket lines to customers friendly to the union.

On June 10 the San Francisco Chamber of Commerce authorized a committee headed by its president, Frederick J. Koster, to raise funds to deal with the waterfront strike and "any other 'intolerable' harassments of local business." After Mayor James Rolph refused to assign additional police to the waterfront, Koster convened a mass meeting of businessmen on July 10 that approved a resolution endorsing the open shop and authorizing Koster to appoint a Law and Order Committee. Within a week the committee had raised $600,000 to prosecute the fight, and by the fall the sum had reached $4 million, and the Chamber of Commerce had added five thousand members and had become the largest such chamber in the nation.

On July 22 a bomb killed ten people in a San Francisco Preparedness Day parade, followed by the arrest five days later of six "radical labor activists," the most prominent of whom were Tom Mooney and Warren Billings. For the Law and Order Committee, the bombing provided dramatic evidence of the danger posed by the San Francisco brand of unionism, and it helped the committee to break the longshoremen's strike.[100]

Quite apart from the longshoremen's strike, additional strikes by Bay Area River Steamboatmen and culinary workers heightened tension in San Francisco. More important, however, was a strike by the city's eight hundred or so structural and ornamental iron workers. Their local, which Drew claimed had become so powerful that it had "practically destroyed" the San Francisco shop industry, had set July 10, 1916, as the deadline for shop employers to grant the ironworkers the eight-hour day. Fifty-four of sixty-four shop firms complied, but ten shops, accounting for 90 percent of the structural steel fabricated in San Francisco, agreed to stand together in resisting the union and bonded themselves as an earnest of their intention to cooperate. The resisting shop owners received the support of the Building Trades Employers' Association and the Law and Order Committee, which supplied the firms with guards to protect the strike replacements they had employed, enabling them to resume operations on an open shop basis. Four of the ten firms yielded to the union in October, which led to a law suit against them by the remaining six.

Dyer Brothers, one of the holdout firms, was the low bidder to erect the structural steel for the tuberculosis wing of the city-owned hospital. The Law and Order Committee provided armed guards for the job, but on December 1 the head of the city's Bureau of Public Works ordered the guards off the premises, which led the strikebreakers to quit their jobs. After Dyer Brothers failed to meet a bureau deadline to complete the job in three days, the bureau canceled the contract and finished the job itself. The Law and Order Committee now withheld support from the six holdouts, and by the end of January 1917, they had all met the union's eight-hour demand. The defeat led to the dissolution of the Building Trades Employers' Association, and although the Law and Order Committee maintained its existence until 1919, its power was ebbing by the late spring of 1917.[101]

Drew, who had supplied the Law and Order Committee with data concerning the wages and hours of structural iron workers around the nation, had exulted for a time about developments in San Francisco. "I consider no single happening in recent industrial history," he wrote while the shop strike was underway, "as so significant and important as the movement in San Francisco to throw off the shackles of closed-shop union domination."[102] The strike, to be sure, ended in defeat for the open shop forces, but it was the prelude to a successful effort led by Koster and others after the war to curb the power of the San Francisco building trades unions.

Drew and the NEA, along with other open shop organizations, won a minor victory over the San Francisco building trades unions regarding the erection of facilities for the Panama-Pacific International Exposition, which opened in San Francisco in 1913. Drew, as he put it, "started a movement" all over the United States for open shop firms and contractors to be guaranteed that they could install exhibits at the exposition and erect buildings with open shop workers "free from the domination and exactions of the San Francisco unions." Drew was able to inform NEA members at the beginning of 1913 that the committee in charge of the exposition had agreed that construction contractors could employ such labor as they saw fit in erecting exhibits. The San Francisco building trades unions agreed with respect to any exhibit construction in which they were engaged not to restrict output, stage jurisdictional strikes, or object to the use of building materials fabricated by nonunion labor.[103]

How successful was the NEA in establishing and maintaining the open shop in the structural steel industry before 1917? The association certainly succeeded in achieving its principal objectives in combating the IABSIW, prevention of the spread of unionism from the erection of structural steel to the shops that fabricated the steel and, secondly, the maintenance of the open shop in the New York district, the most important location in the nation for the erection of structural steel. Also, although Drew complained that not all NEA members complied with the association's open shop policy and that too many NEA employees were union members, the NEA was more than holding its own in its fight with the IABSIW as the nation became a belligerent in World War I in April 1917.[104]

The NEA and the American Bridge Company "seem to be securing all or nearly all of the future work," the union's secretary-treasurer lamented in writing to an IABSIW local official in January 1908. In New York, a prominent union official informed headquarters a few months later that the "cry all around" among IABSIW members was "what is to be gained by sticking?" Even most of "the Old Timers," a union officer reported, had left or were leaving the union.

When the union met in convention in the fall of 1908, delegate after delegate rose to attack the union's ban on working for NEA members, especially American Bridge. Contending that banned firms were meeting union wage and hour standards or at least offering to do so and that the fight against the NEA had been lost, delegates pressed for a policy of local option that would permit each local to decide for itself whether its members should be allowed to work for proscribed open shop firms. They were "getting tired of seeing big jobs go up without their help," one delegate declared. The union's national leadership, which had rejected the request of delegates from New York, Brooklyn, and Philadelphia as early as 1907 to adopt a local option policy, threw its full weight against the local option proposal, Ryan remonstrating that what had been proposed would lead to the union's dissolution. In the end, the delegates rejected the local option resolution by a vote of 12–40. At the union's 1913 convention, however, the delegates granted the locals authority to work for open shop firms that met union conditions of employment and, in so doing, to work alongside nonunion mechanics.[105]

If the NEA goal was the actual destruction of the IABSIW, it conspicuously failed to achieve that objective. The union's membership dropped from 11,600 in 1907 to 9,600 in 1909, but then rose to 13,200 in 1914 and 16,000 in 1917. The increase, however, was partly the result of the expansion of the structural steel erection industry and, of greater importance, the addition to the union's membership of ornamental iron workers, pile drivers, and machinery movers and riggers. In 1916, for example, half of the union's membership consisted of workers in these categories, few of whom were employed by NEA members. The census of occupations, indeed, classified only 18,836 workers as structural iron workers in 1920.[106]

The NEA was particularly concerned, as has been noted, to maintain the open shop in the New York district, which accounted for about one-third of the steel tonnage annually erected in the United States. Although NEA members and allied firms hired union members as individuals, the NEA was able to keep structural steel erection in the New York district on an open shop basis even though all the other building trades in the city were unionized. Outside New York, the NEA enjoyed success in such places as Pittsburgh, Hartford, Buffalo, and Milwaukee, but Chicago, St. Louis, San Francisco, and increasingly Cleveland were union strongholds in the pre–World War I era. Drew in 1915 placed the tonnage fabricated by NEA members at 80 percent of the total and claimed that members erected somewhat more than 50 percent of the tonnage erected, which seems about correct. As Drew noted, moreover, the major NEA members were less concerned about the erection of buildings than with the construction of bridges and viaducts, and here the open shop prevailed without serious challenge. In this branch of the industry, unlike the erection of city buildings, the IABSIW could not look to the support of the other building trades in seeking recognition from NEA members.[107]

In seeking to ascertain why unionism was able to establish itself in the British steel industry during the years 1880–1914 but not in the same industry in the United States, historian James Holt concluded that "the most striking difference between the two situations" was not the behavior of employees but rather the behavior of employers. "The most important reason" for the failure of steel unionism in the United States during the pre–World War I years, he judged, was the opposition of the employers.[108] This generalization not only applies to the steel mills but also explains why the IABSIW was unable to match the success of other building trades unions in its efforts to unionize the structural steel erection industry and to penetrate the shops where structural steel was fabricated. Whatever the union's lack of success, however, it was at least strong enough to serve as a deterrent to employer behavior with regard to wages and working conditions. The same might very well have been true of other nonunionized industries in which unions were present in at least some strength in the pre–New Deal era.

When Drew reported to NEA members on the state of the association as of the spring of 1917, he called attention to the strong position of the NEA. Its membership, he noted, had increased from twenty-seven to fifty since 1914, steel buildings were being erected on an open shop basis in cities like Milwaukee and Buffalo that had only recently been closed shop communities, fewer cities than in recent years were exclusively closed shop in the building industry, most work outside city districts, notably bridges, continued to be performed on an open shop basis, and railroad construction, whether undertaken by the roads themselves or by contractors, was "quite generally" open shop work.[109] Drew did not mention that the NEA had helped to keep the shops of American Bridge, McClintic-Marshall, and the other steel fabricators free of unions. He could also have noted that the era of slugging and dynamiting in the structural steel industry had come to an end.

CHAPTER 4

Slugging and Dynamiting

In prosecuting its strike against the American Bridge Company and the National Erectors' Association (NEA) that began in August 1905 and in seeking recognition for the union, the International Association of Bridge and Structural Iron Workers (IABSIW) resorted to violence, the slugging of nonunion foremen and workers, and the destruction of the structures of open shop contractors. The NEA, in response, adopted a series of measures to protect its open shop workers and the structures it was erecting. Although the dynamiting of steel structures and of the *Los Angeles Times* building in particular understandably attracted far more attention at the time and since than assaults on nonunion workers and strike replacements, union-sanctioned slugging, which was at its height before the dynamiting campaign really got under way, continued while the dynamiting was occurring and did not altogether cease after the dynamiting came to an end. Violence was a troubling characteristic of employer-employee relations in the structural steel erection industry during the pre–World War 1 era.[1]

Insofar as they had lost their jobs to strikebreakers, unionized iron-workers, like other workers, saw the "scabs" as "enemies" who were depriving the unionists of their livelihood. The assaults on strike replacements, other open shop workers, and watchmen were, however, less the result of impetuous action by frustrated individual workers than they were premeditated encounters organized under the direction of the local leadership of the IABSIW. Unlike New York Local 40's infamous entertainment committee, some locals appear to have established "slugging gangs" on an ad hoc rather than a regular basis. Although some building trades unions at the time engaged "professional sluggers" who were not union members, the slugging in the structural steel erection industry appears to have been done entirely by union members.[2]

IABSIW locals and the international union itself met the legal expenses of sluggers who were arrested and tried and paid the forfeited bonds when they skipped bail as "the cheapest way out of trouble." They also supported sluggers while incarcerated and after they had fled arrest. The international on occasion changed the names of sluggers in the union's records in an effort to conceal their identity. The hope of the union in encouraging and countenancing slugging was that by making "trouble" for open shop contractors and raising their costs, they would be forced to deal with the union lest their contracts be taken away from them.[3]

Drew recorded ninety-six assaults occurring between December 20, 1905, and January 13, 1912, but this is almost certainly an underestimate. Wielding wrenches, hammers, coupling pins, blackjacks, and pipes wrapped in paper, and sometimes armed with guns, the sluggers fractured skulls and jaws, broke arms and noses, and beat their victims into unconsciousness. The assaults led to four deaths, one of them a slugger, and fourteen convictions.[4]

The Pittsburgh local of the IABSIW, which noted that it was "dispensing money for entertainment purposes," informed the international in March 1907 regarding one job, "We have the open shop all shot to hell." The foremen on the job, the writer reported, were "all in the hospital," and the scabs had quit their jobs after the local had "decided to go after the bunch of stiffs here." After an assault on twenty strikebreakers in Salt Lake City, two of whom were "brutally beaten and severely injured," the Minneapolis Steel Machinery Company surrendered its erection contract, and the general contractor then let the work to a unionized firm. If the "snakes" working for the York Bridge Company in Scranton did not get "a damn good trimming" and were permitted to work "unmolested," it was "a cinch," the Scranton local leadership believed, that the company would not deal with the union.[5]

P. A. Cooley, the dominant figure in the IABSIW's New Orleans local and a member of the IABSIW's executive board, was arrested for assault and battery in the fall of 1910 after knocking down a nonunion contractor who suffered a severe head wound when he struck a post. After Cooley had first "hired" two witnesses to testify that the victim had struck the first blow, the union official decided to plead guilty to a single assault charge. "I don't think he will scab for a while," Cooley said of the victim, who had required the insertion of a steel plate in his head. Leading "a gang of thugs," Tom Dorsey, business agent of New York City's ornamental iron workers local, hit a nonunion worker in the face with an eight-pound hammer, knocking out his teeth and breaking his jaw. Dorsey, in the end, pleaded guilty and went to jail. According to a former official of the Indianapolis local, the IABSIW's secretary-treasurer, John J. McNamara, told him regarding a nonunion foreman "to put him out of business, or put him in the hospital."[6]

Thomas Slattery, a former Sam Parks lieutenant and the business agent of the IABSIW's Brooklyn local, had a record of assaults that began in December 1905 and continued for almost a decade. Allegedly "the presiding genius of the paid plug-uglies" in New York, he was arrested again and again on assault charges, but he managed by one means or another to escape conviction except for a $10 fine in a 1911 case. "Slattery," a disgusted NEA official remarked in 1912, "must be one of the best citizens of Brooklyn and evidently has no trouble in obtaining friends to testify to this fact in court."[7]

Drew paid special attention to two assault cases, both involving the Cleveland IABSIW local. Drew described the first of these, perpetrated by John Bordan and Robert Elsemore, to a subcommittee of the Senate Judiciary Committee in 1912 as part of his indictment of the IABSIW. The NEA commissioner was especially anxious to press the case because it had originated while Frank Buchanan was the union's president, and Buchanan in 1912 was a congressman and, as Drew saw it, was seeking the enactment of "vicious labor legislation." In 1905 Buchanan had authorized J. E. McClory of the Cleveland local and a later IABSIW president "to do some missionary work" in Toledo. McClory hired four men for the assignment, including Bordan and Elsemore, and paid them $150, the check being issued by McNamara. The "missionary work" took the form of an assault on July 17, 1905, on an employee of an open shop firm that was erecting structural steel in Toledo. Bordan and Elsemore were subsequently arrested in Cleveland, pleaded guilty, and were sentenced to six months in prison. They were paroled after five months, during which they had each received payments of more than $300 from the union, which also paid their legal expenses. When the IABSIW refused them additional compensation after their release, they sued the international but settled out of court for $60 each. Drew cited the case as providing evidence of the complicity of the international union in the slugging of nonunion workers and to show that Buchanan was also tarred with the violence brush even though he insisted that the two sluggers had "nothing" on him.[8]

The second Cleveland slugging episode that Drew emphasized resulted from the effort in 1907 of the Pittsburgh Steel Construction Company, an NEA member, to erect an ore bridge over the right-of-way of the Pennsylvania Railroad in Ashtabula, Ohio. Strongly unionized Ashtabula was within the jurisdiction of Cleveland's Local 17, which "stirred up the whole town" against the company. After a "mob" had driven Pittsburgh Steel's open shop workers from the city and a nonunion foreman had been shot, Local 17 offered the company generous terms if it would recognize the union. When this tactic as well as the union's effort to persuade the Pennsylvania Railroad Company to transfer the contract to a unionized firm both failed and Pittsburgh Steel resumed work on the bridge, Local 17, on February 6, 1907, resorted to force. Armed with gas pipes, blackjacks, and other weapons, seven union members assaulted George W. Ryle, the foreman on the job. Beaten to the ground, Ryle pulled out a revolver and shot and killed one of his assailants. Three of the sluggers, John O'Brien, Stephen Davern, and "Rube" Shane, were arrested and then released on $500 bail each. The three jumped bail, the union paying their forfeited bonds. O'Brien was rearrested and sentenced to from three to thirty years imprisonment after the brother of the deceased unionist testified that Charles Smith, Local 17's secretary, had paid the deceased $100 "to go down there and do this job."[9]

Drew and the NEA's district manager in Cleveland actively aided the county prosecutor in the prosecution of the Ashtabula case, and the NEA paid the legal costs incurred by the Pittsburgh Steel Company. Drew not only fought union efforts to secure O'Brien's parole but relentlessly pursued Shane and Davern for the next several years. Davern fled to New Orleans and then to San Francisco, where he was kept under cover by an IABSIW vice president.

Thwarted in his prolonged efforts to secure additional compensation from the union, a "badly crippled" Davern turned to the NEA for assistance, offering in return to provide evidence on the assault. Drew tentatively took up the offer, hoping to use the information in a pending dynamite case, but when the prosecution saw no need for Davern's testimony, Drew decided not to pay him.[10]

The Cleveland ironworkers, Drew noted in 1911, made "more trouble than all the other unions [locals] put together." According to two reports prepared by the Committee on Labor Disputes of the Cleveland Chamber of Commerce, Local 17 sluggers were involved in forty-nine different assaults from the beginning of 1906 to the end of 1915, but this understated the matter judging from information sent to NEA headquarters by the association's district manager in Cleveland and open shop erection firms working in the city. Led generally by Peter J. Smith, a one-time business agent of the local whom American Bridge's erection manager described as "an instigator" of violence and "a procurer of others to do the work," the assault teams, made up of fifteen or so men, went after the "very best [open shop] men." These assaults, often occurring "off the work on the principal streets of the city," led to numerous injuries and two deaths. The high command of the IABSIW had only praise for the Cleveland sluggers, the union's secretary-treasurer writing members of the executive board that "the only way" to deal with recalcitrant firms was "to go after them the way Cleveland does." Local 17, its business agent reported at the IABSIW's 1910 convention, "makes it as unpleasant as possible for those doing . . . [open shop work] and as costly as they can." He claimed that "some very large contracts" had been transferred from open shop to unionized firms as a result.[11]

The NEA believed that the problem of dealing with assaults in Cleveland was especially difficult because of a lack of cooperation by police authorities, partly because the labor unions in the city were "so mixed up with politics." After speaking to a Cleveland police inspector who, he thought, "leaned toward Unions," a Pennsylvania Steel official wrote his superior, "we are not only bucking against the Union, but against the whole police force." The majority of the assault cases in the city did not lead to convictions, sometimes because of failure to arrest or to prosecute, sometimes because witnesses were unwilling to testify. When convictions were obtained, the sentences were often lenient and were frequently suspended. Of 161 assailants between 1906 and July 31, 1911, only 8 were arrested, 4 of whom were convicted. Three of the 4 received minimal sentences, and 1 was paroled.

In one case illustrative of the state of affairs about which the NEA complained, Tim Murphy of Local 17 was convicted in 1906 for an assault on an American Bridge timekeeper, fined $1, sentenced to sixty days in the workhouse, and paroled after eleven days. At the end of the next year he was appointed a city bridge inspector and stationed at a bridge being erected by an open shop concern. In 1908 he was arrested for receiving stolen property and jumped bail. He was rearrested in March 1909, pleaded guilty, and was sentenced to two years imprisonment but was promptly paroled. He was subsequently elected president of the local.[12]

The NEA and the open shop firms used a variety of tactics to counter assaults on open shop workers in Cleveland. Individual firms guarded their jobs, and although it was not the normal NEA practice, the association arranged for some guarding at its own expense. The Van Dorn Iron Works Company took its workers to and from their jobs in a bus that had a "field piece over the end board," and Pennsylvania Steel guarded its men even on the city's trolley cars. The NEA also sought to deal with the problem by the use of espionage in the hopes of nipping planned assaults in the bud. Although it was able to plant spies "high up in the union," the tactic proved to be of minimal value. The "inside men" reported mainly on what transpired at meetings of the local, but slugging jobs were not discussed at meetings. In addition to espionage, the NEA stood ready to provide workers for firms resisting the union, and it advised lawsuits against Cleveland authorities for failure to provide open shop jobs with "full protection."[13]

The NEA turned to the Cleveland Chamber of Commerce for assistance in dealing with slugging in the city. Agreeing with Drew about the harmful effect of violence on the city's business climate, the chamber interceded with the police and city authorities in a successful effort to encourage a stronger police response to incidents of violence. With the NEA commissioner's aid, the chamber's Committee on Labor Disputes also prepared a report on violence in the city that appeared in June 1915 and was supplemented by a second report in January 1916.[14]

So serious did violence and the threat of violence in Cleveland appear to the NEA that its executive committee decided in 1912 to hire Gavin's Detective Agency of Philadelphia "to clean up the whole situation . . . by the use of summary methods." What the NEA had in mind was for "outside people" to come into the city and, in a few days, to "rid Cleveland" of its "vicious element" by using "tactics similar to their own." The NEA's assistant commissioner, J. A. G. Badorf, was prepared to bring as many as fifty men into Cleveland to "make a desert of the town so far as strong arm men working for and in the pay of Pete Smith are concerned." When other commitments prevented the Gavin Agency from undertaking the assignment, Drew turned to the Thiel Detective Agency, but in the end the NEA's drastic plan of meeting force with force was not implemented.[15]

Local 17 persisted in its use of violence because the tactic appeared to be meeting with success with regard to both local firms like Van Dorn and even such major national concerns as the Pennsylvania Steel Company. Van Dorn found its men so "intimidated by union tactics" that it could not afford to take on small jobs with any confidence of earning a profit. After fighting Local 17 for four years and after four of its best men had been assaulted and hospitalized, the company resigned from the NEA in October 1911. "We have gone the limit and spared no expense in the fight," T. B. Van Dorn, the company's head, reported, but he had concluded that it was "a losing game." The company, he said, had gone "the whole route[,] including guards, guns, dogs, busses, police, high wages, etc.," and even doing its erecting work at night, but all to no avail.[16]

The erection engineer of Pennsylvania Steel informed Drew in June 1911 that the company had lost "a large part of . . . [its] gang through fear." He concluded that slugging was "more to be dreaded" than dynamiting because although it was possible, to some degree, "to control the policies" of individual companies, the "feelings" of open shop workers, fearing and experiencing assaults, could not be controlled. The fear of violence, indeed, made it difficult for even the largest NEA concerns to recruit nonunion workers outside the city for Cleveland jobs, McClintic-Marshall reporting that it had lost three Cleveland jobs for this reason.[17]

However much the NEA was concerned about the threat posed to the open shop by slugging, it was far more troubled by the dynamiting of structures erected or being erected by nonunion labor. There were "scattered and isolated cases" of dynamitings and attempted dynamitings in 1905, 1906, and 1907, but it was during the next four years that dynamiting became more common than slugging as a union tactic. All in all, from the summer of 1905 to the end of September 1911, eighty-six structural steel jobs were dynamited or damaged in some other way, and there were an additional fifteen attempts to inflict damage on open shop jobs. Sixty-six of these attacks were on the jobs of NEA members, and thirty-five involved structures and shops of open shop concerns that were not NEA members. The contractors for almost half of the NEA structures that were attacked were the association's two principal members, American Bridge (seventeen structures) and McClintic-Marshall (fourteen structures). Bridges and viaducts of various sorts, especially railroad bridges, were the favorite targets, but damage was also inflicted on material on railroad cars or in railroad yards, construction equipment (derricks, cranes, hoisting engines), buildings, and shops.[18]

Dynamiting in the structural steel industry was initially directed at partially erected structures being put up by the principal NEA members. Toward the end of the dynamiting period, however, the structures and shops of non-association members increasingly became the targets. The damage from most of the dynamitings was rather modest, ranging from $25 to $5,000, but there were exceptions. The dynamiting on November 4, 1909, of a crane and surrounding material in Cleveland resulted in damage of $40,000; a dynamiting in February 1911 damaged a $1 million plant; and dynamitings the next month resulted in total damage of $145,000.[19]

Initially, the dynamiters used dynamite with a fulminating cap and about a fifty-foot long fuse attached that exploded in about thirty minutes. Starting in the summer of 1909, they began to use the so-called infernal machine, an alarm clock operated by dry-cell batteries attached to a board connected by a wire and a fulminating cap to the explosive material. The perpetrators set the alarm for a time when they would be far away from the scene of the explosion. Nitroglycerin eventually replaced dynamite as the favorite explosive substance, although one of the principal dynamiters thought that nitroglycerin was "too quick" and that dynamite produced "a better result."

Usually twenty pounds of dynamite or ten pounds of nitroglycerin were used to set off an explosion, and generally two charges were ignited. The dynamite and nitroglycerin used for explosions, some purchased, some stolen, were stored in different places in Ohio, Pennsylvania, and in Indianapolis, including the American Central Life Building in that city, the headquarters of the IABSIW. The explosives were transported to the job to be destroyed in suitcases carried on passenger trains, checked in railway stations, and taken into hotels. It was estimated that over the years between three hundred to four hundred pounds of nitroglycerin and two thousand pounds of dynamite were carried from place to place to set off explosions. Thanks to good fortune, no loss of life resulted from the dynamitings until the *Los Angeles Times* building was dynamited on October 1, 1910. A watchman, however, was shot and killed when he discovered an attempt to damage the job he was guarding, and several watchmen were seriously injured in confrontations with prospective or actual dynamiters.[20]

Unlike the physical assaults on open shop foremen and workers, which originated at the local level and proceeded from "no general plan of action," the dynamite campaign was directed from IABSIW headquarters, although local leaders, on occasion, took the initiative, aided by the support of the international union. The IABSIW was clearly not driven to the use of dynamite because of despair resulting from miserable working conditions. As the record demonstrates and as writer John Fitch noted at the time, the housesmiths were not "some sweated, underpaid group of workers." What was involved was what the union perceived as a threat to its very existence posed by the NEA, which would neither recognize nor deal with the union and that seemed determined to operate on an open shop basis. The IABSIW was convinced that the NEA was simply "another name for the Steel Trust," which, the union believed, was using the NEA to extirpate the last vestige of unionism in the steel industry. Were that to occur, as the union saw it, union workers would be completely "under the foot" of their employers, and working conditions would then deteriorate. "The most virulent form of industrial violence," Philip Taft and Philip Ross concluded in their study of the history of labor violence in the United States, "occurred in situations in which efforts were made to destroy a functioning union or to deny to a union recognition." As they also noted, "the outstanding example of a campaign of force" by a union was that directed by the IABSIW against the NEA.[21]

In addition to what the union perceived as a threat to its existence, the nature of the job of the ironworker has been suggested as a possible reason for the IABSIW's dynamite campaign. Occupations that involved "great physical risk," Inis Weed concluded in a study for the Commission on Industrial Relations, produced "greater violence in a period of struggle" than occupations without such risks. "Men who fearlessly swing out into space 100 or 200 feet above ground and sit astride high beams tossing hot rivets to each other," a journalist noted at the time of the dynamitings, "have within them an element of recklessness that does not belong to all men."[22]

It will be recalled that the IABSIW strike against the NEA and American Bridge appeared to be on the verge of collapse when the union met in convention in September 1908. A Brooklyn delegate urged the international to take "more drastic and radical action" in conducting the strike or permit union members to return to work "indiscriminately throughout the country." The international was unwilling to permit members to return to work, but it began to employ "more drastic and radical" tactics, namely, dynamiting. If "smashing their [strikebreakers] faces or killing their guards" did not cause open shop firms to deal with the union, the next step, as one writer put it, was to destroy the jobs themselves.

The use of dynamite was obviously designed to induce owners and contractors to award jobs to unionized firms lest the jobs be destroyed or their completion materially delayed. At the very least, the union thought, dynamiting would increase the costs of nonunion firms and place them at a competitive disadvantage with unionized firms by requiring them to institute expensive guarding systems to protect their jobs from destruction. Insofar as dynamiting was directed at the railroads, the intention, union officials privately averred, was to discourage the roads, the major purchasers of structural steel, from buying or transporting structural steel produced in nonunion fabricating shops.[23]

Dynamiting did indeed add to the costs of open shop erectors for both guarding and espionage. As Drew told a Senate subcommittee, NEA jobs, as the result of dynamiting, had "gone up like a fort under siege in time of war." The NEA commissioner in 1909 described for a journalist a Cleveland viaduct job that was well-lighted, surrounded by barbed wire, guarded by watchmen armed with rifles at either end of the structure, and patrolled by half a dozen dogs. He noted that the "same general system, with variations," was being used on other jobs.[24]

Pennsylvania Steel, as we have seen, used twenty to thirty guards for two years at a cost of $35,000 to guard its Blackwell's Island Bridge job. McClintic-Marshall somewhat later spent $28,000 guarding a bridge that it was erecting in Cleveland. Quite apart from the costs for guarding, the NEA expended at least $50,000 for espionage services over and above expenses for detectives incurred by individual NEA firms like American Bridge. The large NEA firms took out insurance against dynamiting, but although Drew from the start thought that the NEA itself should insure its members against losses resulting from dynamiting, the association did not follow his advice.[25]

As Drew acknowledged, open shop erection contractors sometimes were refused contracts even though they were the low bidder because owners or general contractors feared the job would be subject to "delay" or "trouble." The IABSIW specifically stressed this matter in dealing with contractors, McNamara thus advising a local union officer in 1909 to say that the reason a company erecting steel for a bridge across the Missouri River should unionize its workforce was the difficulties open shop concerns had experienced in completing large contracts.[26]

After Albert Von Spreckelsen refused to agree to the complete unionization of his labor force at work on the Murat Temple in Indianapolis, the workers, including ironworkers, went out on strike. Two or three days after a visitor told an assistant foreman on the job, "if you don't [unionize], the whole damn business is going to get blowed up," Von Spreckelsen, on October 25, 1910, "got a surprise party" when three other buildings he was erecting as well as the garage and barn at the rear of his residence were all dynamited at about the same time. Unable to secure other contracts as a result, he also had to give up the Murat Temple contract, since he refused to unionize the job.[27]

R. D. Jones, an American Bridge Company subcontractor, was compelled in 1910 to surrender two erection contracts in Salt Lake City, one of them for the Utah Hotel, after the hotel structure was dynamited—the local IABSIW leader had told the international in advance that he was "pretty sure" Jones would "never erect that 'Particular Job.' " The general manager of the Peoria and Pekin Union Railway, which had let the steel contract for the erection of a bridge across the Illinois River to McClintic-Marshall, was told by IABSIW officers in early 1910 that unless the steel work was erected by union workers, there "would be hell to pay," or "something was going to happen," or words to that effect. Two girders of the bridge were dynamited on June 4, 1910, and two carloads of material used in the bridge's construction were dynamited on September 4, 1910.[28]

After Jesse D. Smith, the manager of the Pan-American Bridge Company, rejected the request of an IABSIW official, who happened to be the paymaster of the dynamiters, that the company unionize a job in Peoria, the company's plant in Newcastle, Indiana, was dynamited on April 5, 1910. Pan-American then agreed to unionize and was assured by the union official that it no longer needed to guard its jobs. In March 1911, the same official, "in a fit of rage," told George W. Caldwell of the Caldwell-Drake Iron Works, which was erecting the county courthouse building in Omaha on an open shop basis and refused to unionize, "Well, we will get even with you yet." The next night the courthouse and the company's plant in Columbus, Indiana, were dynamited a few minutes apart. "[I]ntimidated" by the explosions, told by the Bank of Omaha that it could not afford to extend the firm any more credit, and its bonding company having become "nervous," Caldwell-Drake decided to unionize. "We wore him out," the Omaha local informed McNamara. Wallace Marshall, president of the Lafayette Engineering Company, referred to the IABSIW as "dynamiting thugs" in refusing the demand of a drunken union representative to unionize an addition to the French Lick Hotel that the Lafayette Bridge Works was erecting. Two weeks later, on March 20, 1911, the addition was dynamited, which led the hotel proprietor to discharge all nonunion workers on the job.[29]

After Caldwell-Drake capitulated to the union, John J. McNamara told the individual who had dynamited the Omaha courthouse, "We have got the little fellows lined up now, and by God, we are going after the big fellows." The "big fellows," however, did not yield to the dynamite threat. Although some "little fellows" did agree to unionize as the result of dynamitings and although the union's membership increased during the dynamiting campaign (from 10,400 in 1908 to 12,280 in 1911), as did the union's treasury balance (from $24,689 in 1908–9 to $51,191 in 1910–11), the dynamitings only strengthened the NEA's determination to resist the union, did not reduce the association's share of the erection business, and probably increased "open shop sentiment" in the business community at large. In the end, the dynamiting campaign led to the arrest, conviction, and jailing of the entire leadership of the IABSIW and the discrediting of the union itself.[30]

The IABSIW understandably sought to conceal its expenditures for dynamiting and similar purposes. The union constitution required that there be a monthly report in the union's official journal, the *Bridgemen's Magazine,* of receipts and expenditures. The IABSIW Executive Board, however, issued an official notice on February 3, 1906, that because of the strike against American Bridge, the monthly statement thereafter would include receipts only and would exclude expenditures and "recapitulation." The board authorized funds for "Organization Purposes" that were funneled to "Certain Officials" primarily for dynamiting and were reported, but not accurately, in the union's magazine. According to a Department of Justice accountant, from October 22, 1907, to April 11, 1911, $22,811.87 was withdrawn from the union's treasury for "Organization Purposes." After McNamara complained that the union's "enemies and knockers" could "draw all sorts of conclusions" from the sums advanced to various officials, the executive board decided in 1909 or 1910 to set aside $1,000 each month for deposit in McNamara's personal account without any accounting at all. It was McNamara, it should be noted, who dispensed the union's funds for dynamiting. Union correspondence strongly indicates that during the latter half of 1907, the IABSIW Executive Board agreed on a policy of allocating $200 for the effort to "cripple" an open shop job by dynamiting or some other means.[31]

Although the IABSIW sought to conceal its expenditures for dynamiting, it nevertheless preserved correspondence that implicated the union in numerous explosions, generally by inference but sometimes directly. McNamara wrote a local IABSIW officer shortly before the secretary-treasurer's arrest, "the Lord only knows who reads all the letters that come into this office as well as all that leave it." As it turned out, the NEA shortly thereafter became a reader of "all the letters," which helped to convict the union's leadership. Oddly enough, although McNamara, himself an attorney, preserved the incriminating union correspondence pertaining to dynamiting, he paid his private secretary from April 1907 to January 1910, who knew "too much," $400 after she threatened to expose "certain doings" of the union; and the IABSIW secretary-treasurer and his brother James apparently even considered the possibility of having a Cincinnati acquaintance of theirs "blow up" the former secretary.[32]

Local IABSIW leaders and McNamara, to whom local officers addressed their union letters, ofttimes indicated in their correspondence that it was best not to incriminate themselves in their letters regarding actual or potential dynamitings. "There may be several items that [it] would not do to put in writing," the secretary of the Cincinnati local wrote McNamara in February 1908. After a Salt Lake City union official wrote McNamara in November 1909 that the union could not "afford to let" an open shop contractor "put . . . up" a particular building, McNamara replied, "the less we write about matters of this kind, the better it will be for all concerned."[33]

In their union correspondence, President Ryan and McNamara never specifically instructed their correspondents to dynamite a particular structure, but what they did write could certainly be interpreted in that way. McNamara thus wrote a Kansas City local leader that no restraints would be placed on the local "from doing everything possible to delay and make unprofitable the contracts of unfair firms." When Frank Webb, a New York union leader and sometimes executive board member, indicated that he did not know what to recommend regarding some unfair jobs since he did not know the "workings" of the international and "how far some one wants to go," Ryan sent him $200 each for two unfair jobs, the usual fee for a dynamiting, and stated, "I am disposed to be liberal where effective organization work can be accomplished." Ryan similarly informed a Philadelphia union official that the money advanced to him to deal with unfair jobs was "to be used . . . in any manner found to be most effective in delaying or adding to the cost of the work." The union president stated that he did not wish to be told how the money had been spent, but, he added, "if results or showing" was made with the money already provided, "the prospects for additional aid" would be "brighter."[34]

As McNamara had instructed, local leaders enclosed clippings describing dynamitings in their jurisdiction with the letters they sent to headquarters. Union leaders, tongue in cheek, sometimes described dynamitings as resulting from such atmospheric conditions as high winds and heavy rains. Even the *Bridgemen's Magazine,* available for all to read, provided a description of this sort following the aforementioned April 5, 1910, dynamiting of the Pan-American plant in Newcastle and the subsequent unionization of the company's Peoria job. "Halley's comet," the business agent of the Peoria local reported, "passed through here on time and found about thirty of our members working for the Pan-American Bridge Company. . . . This was a scab job to start with, but this company had to be shown that Union men were the cheaper."[35]

Some union letters referred to property destruction without blaming what had occurred on the weather. There are references in the letters to McNamara from local officials about wanting "to cripple a job," "to ditch the balance" of a job after a traveler had been overturned, or expecting "to do a little job," and the like. Saying he was too "well known" in the city to buy explosives, a Cincinnati unionist, who later confessed to a dynamiting, specifically asked McNamara to send him what was required so that the local could "go after" an unfair job "in the right way." A few months later a job of the concern in question was dynamited. In the least guarded of the union letters regarding dynamiting, the business agent of the Duluth local wrote McNamara following an August 1–2, 1910, dynamiting in Superior, Wisconsin, "We have had some real Dynamiters here[,] not the kind we had a year ago but the real thing was done." And if a document in the Drew papers is genuine, and it appears to be, the slugger Thomas Slattery, no doubt expecting to produce laughter, introduced or contemplated introducing a resolution at the union's 1910 convention that does not, to be sure, appear in the published convention proceedings, stating "[t]hat no more bombs or explosives of any kind be exploded while this convention is in session."[36]

The principal dynamiters were Ortie McManigal, George E. Davis, and James B. McNamara. Born in Bloomville, Ohio, and having worked in nearby Tiffin in the stone quarries, where he became familiar with dynamite, McManigal became a structural iron worker in 1903, when he was apparently twenty-nine years old. While working for the Oscar Daniels Company in Detroit in May 1907, McManigal was approached by Herbert S. Hockin, the business agent of the IABSIW Detroit local, who knew about McManigal's familiarity with dynamite, and was urged to secure dynamite for a Detroit job. In the early morning of June 25 McManigal dynamited the Detroit City Gas Company building, which was being erected by the nonunion Russel Wheel and Foundry Company, the target of a failed structural ironworkers' strike in 1903. He received $75 for the job, apparently provided by the Detroit local. The money was placed in an envelope with the note "Compliments of the Executive Board. More to follow." This was the first of what would be a series of explosive charges set off by McManigal. Hockin, who was detained by the Detroit police following the dynamiting but quickly released, told McManigal shortly afterward that the open shop erectors had gotten the "upper hand" but that the union was "going to put" them and the NEA "out of business."[37]

Before McManigal dynamited a second job, another ironworker, George E. Davis, had begun his career as a dynamiter. An ironworker since 1900 who had become familiar with the use of dynamite as the result of experience in the mining and construction industries, Davis was approached by Frank Webb of the IABSIW in late December 1907 about blowing up a railroad bridge over the Newark branch of the Erie Railroad near Harrison, New Jersey. Webb, who had received $200 from the international for the job, became Davis's paymaster for a series of dynamitings. Ryan reposed a great deal of confidence in Webb, no doubt because, as he had written the IABSIW president, "I never did believe in talking to [*sic*] much, and in cases of this kind [I] know nothing." After Davis had set off a dynamite charge on December 23, 1907, that damaged a girder and floor of the railroad bridge, Webb asked him if he wished to continue doing work of this sort. When Davis replied in the affirmative, Webb told him that this would require the approval of the IABSIW executive board. "I got what I was after," Webb subsequently informed Davis.[38]

According to Davis, John J. McNamara had authorized $950 for blowing up the Blackwell's Island Bridge, a key IABSIW target. Davis recalled that he asked $1,500 for the job, which Webb said he could get for him. After surveying the site, Davis raised the price to $2,500 but then decided that the assignment was too difficult and was likely, allegedly, to lead to too many deaths.

From February 3 to May 22, 1908, Davis was responsible for the damaging of eight nonunion jobs, seven of them by dynamite in New York, New Jersey, Maryland, and Pennsylvania. The most important of these was the Scherzer Drawbridge over Eastchester Bay in Pelham, New York. Aided by two other men, Davis removed the clamps on four guys of the draw, causing it to roll forward into the bay and resulting in damage of between $5,000 and $10,000. In seeking funds from New York's Local 40 to pay for the job, an official of the local told its recording secretary, "Well, you know it costs something to get the wind to blow the right way."[39]

After Davis dynamited and destroyed a traveler used in erecting a railroad bridge in North Bradshaw, Maryland, Ryan, meeting the dynamiter in New York, allegedly told him, "If you keep on doing that kind of work, you can call on me any old time for money." Ryan also told Davis a bit later that he was to pretend not to recognize the union president if he encountered him on the street. Late in May, after Davis had successfully dynamited six nonunion jobs in less than two months, Ryan, according to Davis, told the dynamiter, "you must be a wizard to do so many jobs and not get caught at it." Davis's luck, however, was about to run out. After dynamiting material in the storage yard used for the construction of the Taunton River Bridge in Somerset, Massachusetts, on June 15, 1908, Davis, who had been using the name George O'Donnell, boarded a streetcar that went to nearby Fall River. Suspicious of his passenger, the conductor phoned the authorities when the car arrived at the car barns en route. Questioned by a constable, Davis pulled a revolver and apparently assaulted the policeman. He was arrested, convicted on a charge of "assault with a dangerous weapon," and sentenced to three years in prison. The IABSIW provided him with an attorney, and Webb, under an assumed name, visited the prisoner. The NEA, as we shall see, was on Davis's trail at the time and came close to breaking the dynamite plot at this point.[40]

While Davis languished in prison, McManigal continued in his role as a dynamiter. Working in Chicago in February 1908, he was again contacted by Hockin, by then an IABSIW organizer, to undertake a dynamiting job in Clinton, Iowa. McManigal accepted the assignment and was also responsible for two additional dynamitings in 1908, two in 1909, and twelve in 1910, Hockin serving as his paymaster. McManigal was searched but let go shortly after he set the charge that damaged a railroad bridge in Buffalo on July 1, 1908. In July 1909 Hockin told McManigal that he, Hockin, had another man working for him who was using the alarm-clock device to blow up jobs, its first use having been to dynamite a railroad bridge in Steubenville, Ohio, on June 21, 1909. The other man turned out to be James B. McNamara, the younger brother of the union's secretary-treasurer, John J. McNamara. Described as "an anemic, chain-smoking ne'er-do-well" who was fond of women, liquor, and gambling, James was a printer by trade who found it difficult to hold a job. After James lost his job in 1907, Hockin, with the support of John J. McNamara, enlisted the younger McNamara's services as a dynamiter, the two joining on May 9, 1909, in the dynamiting of a railroad bridge in Cincinnati. McManigal met James as J. B. Brice before McNamara revealed his true identity. McNamara described the clock device to McManigal and also indicated that he had been using nitroglycerin rather than dynamite.[41]

McManigal was a full-time ironworker and a part-time dynamiter until the spring of 1910, when Hockin told McManigal that he had "enough work to keep . . . [him] busy all the time." From that point forward until his arrest, McManigal's role was exclusively that of a dynamiter. In late June 1910 he learned from James McNamara that although Hockin had generally been paying McManigal $125 for a dynamite job, the set union price for a dynamiting was $200. Aware now that he had been "double crossed," McManigal, when he was next in Indianapolis, complained to John J. McNamara, who now discovered that Hockin, characterized by the union's secretary-treasurer as a "crooked son of a bitch," had been cheating the union and McManigal. When the matter was brought to Ryan's attention, he decided that John McNamara should be McManigal's paymaster thereafter. Sometime after this Ryan told McManigal that he did not want him to come to the union's office in Indianapolis and that he should "change . . . his appearance" more often.[42]

On or about July 15, 1910, James McNamara informed McManigal that he was on his way to the West Coast. It was this trip that culminated in the dynamiting of the *Los Angeles Times* building on October 1, 1910. Los Angeles was described in 1910 by an IABSIW organizer working there as "the great stronghold and citadel of the organized enemies of organized labor." The city's opposition to unionism was personified by Harrison Gray Otis, the owner and publisher of the *Times,* whom some saw as "the most notorious, most persistent and most unfair enemy of trade unionism on the North American continent." A contemporary writer referred to Los Angeles as the "Otistown of the Open Shop."[43]

A printers' strike in 1890 initiated what the *Los Angeles Times* viewed as the "beginning" of Los Angeles's "war . . . for the open shop." Although other city newspapers met the Typographical Union's demands, the *Times,* of which Otis had assumed control in 1882, refused to do so. This led to a bitter fight between the union and the newspaper and a prolonged union boycott of the *Times*'s advertisers and subscribers that eventually took on nationwide proportions. The boycott was taken up after a few years by the city's Council of Labor (later Central Labor Council), and the *Times*'s opposition to unionism became part of a citywide employer movement for the open shop.

The "chief reliance" of the Los Angeles employer interests in combating unionism was the city's Merchants' and Manufacturers' Association (MMA). Formed in 1896, the MMA took up the open shop fight in January 1903 and soon thereafter "consummated its partnership with Otis and other antiunion employers." A variety of employer organizations operated in conjunction with the MMA, one of the most important being the Founders' and Employers' Association, which became the unyielding defendant of the open shop in the metal trades, including the structural steel industry.[44]

The IABSIW had formed a local (No. 51) in Los Angeles in 1903, but in the spring of 1910 it had only sixty-five members, most of them involved in erecting ornamental iron for firms outside the city. The local's jurisdiction, however, extended not only to the erection of structural steel but also to the steel fabrication shops. The union scale was $3.50 for eight hours of work, but Los Angeles ironworkers as of 1910 were actually receiving between $1.75 and $2.25 for ten hours of work. To secure jobs, ironworkers, like other metal trades workers in the city, had to be screened by the employment agency of the Founders' Association, which used a card index system to separate union and nonunion workers. "[W]henever a man working for any of the local firms would signify any intention of joining our organization, or would come down to a meeting . . . ," an IABSIW organizer later declared, "the next morning he was instantly discharged from the job." Although resolutely opposed to any dealings with the IABSIW, none of the Founders' Association firms was an NEA member.[45]

In its first-ever move to support the union effort in a single city, the AFL in 1907 assessed its membership to assist the Los Angeles unions. Despite the AFL action, the labor movement in the city languished during the next year or so, but it began to revive beginning in the late summer of 1909. In March 1910 the IABSIW Executive Board informed the Los Angeles Building Trades Council that the ironworkers' union was willing to bear its share of the expenses involved in a general organizing campaign. The board subsequently gave E. A. Clancy, the IABSIW's first vice president and a West Coast resident, the "full power" to involve Local 51 in any "concerted organization scheme" inaugurated in Los Angeles.

The most important effort to unionize Los Angeles in the history of the city to that time was launched on June 1, 1910, largely as the result of the initiative of the San Francisco labor movement. Employers in the Bay Area had informed the San Francisco Metal Trades Council that they would not renew contracts with the metal trades that were due to expire on June 1, 1910, unless the San Francisco unions could equalize hours and wages in southern California with those in the San Francisco area. That meant bringing San Francisco's eight-hour day and wage scale to Los Angeles, where the ten-hour day and a considerably lower wage scale prevailed in the metal trades. The San Francisco employers extended the union contracts in that city until August 1, 1910, to await the effects of their ultimatum.[46]

The San Francisco unions dispatched organizers representing the city's ten metal trades unions to assist the fight in Los Angeles. Their aid proved unavailing, however, and when the Los Angeles employers rejected the union wage and hour demands, the city's metal trades unions, including Local 51, went out on strike. The strike was financed and directed by the state's labor organizations, led by the San Francisco unions. They formed a General Campaign Strike Committee, chaired by O. A. Tveitmoe, the secretary of the San Francisco Building Trades Council. "We intend to carry on this fight until Los Angeles is unionized," Tveitmoe wrote the IABSIW, "whether it takes one month or one year or ten years."[47]

"[T]hey have started the greatest strike any part of the country had for a long time," Clancy informed the IABSIW on June 3. J. E. Timmons, the IABSIW organizer in Los Angeles, thought that his union had "more to gain" in the conflict than any of the other metal trades unions, since it was the weakest among them. "We must win this fight or unionism [in Los Angeles] is doomed for years to come," he reported, a view shared by E. J. Hendricks, Local 51's business agent, who asserted that the strike meant "either the making or breaking" of the local. Responding to assertions of this sort, the IABSIW contributed $1,000 in August to sustain the strike, appealed to its locals to aid Local 51, and indicated that it was "ready, willing and anxious" to do what it could to aid the strike.[48]

With "a great deal of steel work" about to be started by Los Angeles open shop firms, Hendricks had written McNamara in December 1909, "If you have a good live one back there (not a kid glove man) that you could send us here in the early part of next year I believe he could accomplish a great deal of good." When the strike began, "the live one" Clancy asked to be sent was none other than the organizer of dynamitings, Hockin. Ryan, however, initially urged that Clancy find someone in the area for the assignment. This did not materialize, and, as already noted, the individual whom the union, in the end, dispatched to the West Coast was the dynamiter James McNamara. It should come as no surprise that it was he who dynamited the *Los Angeles Times* building.[49]

"It was war from the jump," the *Los Angeles Times* commented in its history of the strike. "Both sides called every resource into play." The employers brought in strikebreakers from around the country and engaged in extensive espionage, the NEA reportedly assisting the Founders' Association in this regard. The MMA was "instrumental" in securing the adoption by the Los Angeles Common Council of a drastic antipicketing ordinance that even prohibited "loud or unusual noises or verbal proclamations in the streets of Los Angeles" and led eventually to 442 arrests. "We are having lots of trouble," the IABSIW organizer in Los Angeles informed the international on September 3, "but the other fellow is having a great deal more." Local 51 "kept a full line of pickets out everyday," and its members, as "the toughest fighters" among the city's unionists, became conspicuously involved in the "street fighting" that was one of the strike's features. They sought to dissuade imported strikebreakers from taking jobs or working and, as was the union's wont, did not hesitate to use physical force for this purpose. In a major fight of September 2 that led to the arrest of several Local 51 members, the union's sluggers sent twenty-five nonstrikers to the hospital. There were strikebreakers "everywhere with cracked heads and broken noses," Timmons reported to the IABSIW. On September 24 C. L. Marrs, the local's president, Charles F. Stevens, a member of its executive board, and C. F. Grow, the business agent of the International

Association of Machinists in the city, were arrested on a charge of assault with intent to kill a badly beaten strikebreaker. All three were subsequently convicted and sent to prison.[50]

Initially, the strike appeared to be going well for the metal trades in general and Local 51 in particular. Timmons reported that the strikers quickly got workers to leave the metal shops and were able to pull the structural steel workers off some of the buildings on which they were working. Tveitmoe claimed on July 26 that nine shops had conceded the eight-hour day and agreed to unionize and that three large buildings were being erected by union workers.[51]

Although the unions probably exaggerated their success, the outlook for them appeared rather promising when on October 1, 1910, the *Los Angeles Times* building was dynamited with a loss of twenty lives. The charge destroyed the first floor walk on one side of the building and set the entire structure on fire. The cost of the damage came to $509,900, offset for the *Times* by $264,069 in insurance and $49,000 saved in the form of salvaged presses. "[A]ll we were trying to do was to educate a lot of finks down there," James McNamara, who had set the charge, later told a detective. "I was trying to get Otis," McManigal claimed that James had told him when James returned from Los Angeles. Seizing on the fact that there had been employee complaints about gas leaks in the building, the Los Angeles unions, disputing the *Times*'s claim that a "Unionist Bomb" had wrecked the building, blamed the disaster on "faulty gas fixtures and inadequate escape facilities."[52]

It became evident on the afternoon of October 1 that, quite apart from the *Times* building, someone—it was, indeed, James B. McNamara—had sought to dynamite the homes of Felix J. Zeehandelaar, the secretary of the MMA, and Harrison Gray Otis. A box containing dynamite and an "infernal machine" that had failed to explode was found outside Zeehandelaar's home, and soon thereafter the police discovered a similar box outside Otis's home that exploded without injury to the police as they were examining it. The unexploded dynamite at the Zeehandelaar home was traced to its purchasers, J. B. Brice, J. B. Leonard, and William Morris, aliases for James McNamara, Matthew Schmidt, and David Caplan, respectively. They were indicted for the *Los Angeles Times* bombing on January 5, 1911.[53]

When Schmidt emerged from prison after his conviction for his part in the *Los Angeles Times* bombing, he stated that it was not the IABSIW that had given the order to dynamite the *Times* building. It is probable, although not absolutely certain, that it was, indeed, the San Francisco unionists who had ordered the dynamiting. In his study of the San Francisco building trades, Michael Kazin came to a rather cautious conclusion about this matter, stating that Tveitmoe and "some others" in San Francisco "at least knew of the McNamaras' plans and may have participated in their formation." In his confession, McManigal claimed James McNamara had told him that the San Francisco people "wanted the Times put out of business," and McManigal reported John McNamara as saying, "That wild San Francisco bunch did this."

Drew and the federal government came to the same conclusion. Drew noted, however, that although the dynamiting of the *Times* building was "not a part of the general fight of the iron workers for a closed shop," there was "a natural relation" between the two since the action was an incident in a strike aimed at unionizing Los Angeles in which the ironworkers were major participants. That was why, as Drew saw it, the IABSIW had loaned James McNamara to the San Francisco strike leaders.[54]

When James McNamara had expressed a desire for McManigal to accompany him to the coast, brother John had demurred, saying he had jobs for McManigal elsewhere in the country. Also, if one of the two dynamiters was apprehended, John asserted, "he would have the other man loose, so he could keep up the noise; and so that when there would be an explosion in the west, there would be an echo in the east; and when an explosion happened in the east, there would be an echo in the west; so as to keep them guessing as to who it was." Providing an "echo in the east," McManigal dynamited two bridges in Worcester, Massachusetts, on October 10, 1910.

On December 8 John McNamara instructed McManigal to go to Los Angeles to "damage or destroy" the Llewellyn Iron Works, the Baker Iron Works, the *Times* auxiliary plant, and two buildings under construction, the Alexandria Hotel annex and the Hall of Records. These explosions, McNamara told McManigal, were to be the Christmas present he had promised Tveitmoe. From its perspective, the IABSIW had good reason for selecting the five targets assigned to McManigal. An IABSIW local official had described the Llewellyn Iron Works as "the biggest snake firm in the country," and it was one that, in McNamara's view, had "caused us [IABSIW] lots of trouble in Los Angeles and vicinity." The head of the Baker Iron Works was one of "the hardest and most unyielding of fighters" in defense of the open shop. After the dynamiting of the *Times* building, the publication of the newspaper had been switched to the auxiliary plant. As for the Alexandria Hotel annex and the Hall of Records, they were not only two of the largest construction jobs in the city, but the Llewellyn Iron Works had supplied the steel for both of them. Because he claimed that he could not locate the Alexandria Hotel annex and the Hall of Records, which seems improbable, and the *Times* plant and the Baker Iron Works were both well guarded and well lit, McManigal dynamited only one of his five targets, the Llewellyn Iron Works. He set a charge that exploded on Christmas day, destroyed the office and part of the foundry, and provided Tveitmoe with his Christmas present.[55]

Before he was arrested on April 11, 1911, McManigal was responsible for at least four more dynamitings, in one of which he was joined by James McNamara. McManigal's first job was the dynamiting of the Municipal Building in Springfield, Massachusetts, on April 4, 1911. When the dynamiter George Davis ended his prison term about that time, Webb told him regarding the Springfield explosion, "I was just giving you a little send off." Davis was to be responsible for one more dynamiting, an American Bridge Company viaduct in Mt. Vernon, New York, but if McManigal and he are to be believed, the

IABSIW was contemplating a much stepped-up dynamiting effort when the authorities apprehended the dynamiters and the union's leadership.

McManigal testified that John McNamara talked to him in March 1911 about a plan to organize "a gang of about eight or ten good fellows" who would be dispersed about the country and would use "signals" to have jobs come off at the same time and, by so doing, "to keep them guessing." Along the same lines, Davis claimed that Webb had told him that the union intended to put him "on the road and in charge of a bunch of men" whom he would select, the plan being that they would dynamite several jobs on the same night in different parts of the country. McNamara, McManigal also testified, had discussed with him a scheme "to fix up some express packages" that would be sent to NEA members, who would be blown up when they opened the packages, and also to send similar packages as Christmas presents to "State Officials and some other people." The union's secretary-treasurer, according to McManigal, had also discussed with him a wild plan to set fires in different parts of Los Angeles at the same time, cause some explosions, blow up the water mains, and "burn the city off the map." McManigal, furthermore, claimed that McNamara wanted him to go to Panama to blow up the locks of the Panama Canal since McClintic-Marshall had the contract for some of the steel work. According to the dynamiter, McNamara also spoke about stealing the gate receipts of the Indianapolis Speedway. There is no corroboration of either the McManigal or the Davis allegations.[56]

The dynamiting of open shop jobs, needless to say, was a major concern of the NEA, and by April 15, 1908, Drew was describing dynamiting as "the most serious problem" the association had "faced." The NEA reacted to the matter for the first time in October 1906, when its executive committee, responding to the request of the association's Pittsburgh district committee, approved a $5,000 grant to the committee to apprehend whoever had dynamited a bridge in Cleveland. The NEA consensus at that time was that the pursuit of dynamiters should be the responsibility of individual NEA members. Eventually, however, the NEA decided that it had to take "a leading hand" in dealing with the problem. In February 1908 the NEA instructed J. A. G. Badorf, its assistant commissioner, to devote his full time to investigating the union connection with the dynamiting of association jobs. Two months later the NEA's executive committee created a three-person Committee on Dynamiting, of which Drew as a member, and imposed a special assessment on its members and the affiliated New York organizations to establish a fund for the investigation and prosecution of the perpetrators of dynamitings and other "outrages."[57]

The NEA Executive Committee had authorized Drew in March and April 1907 to appoint "a special man," a euphemism for a detective or detective agency, when in his judgment this could lead to "beneficial results." Although the committee had slugging primarily in mind at this time, the authorization and the increase in dynamitings led Drew, who reported himself as being "kept constantly in tension" by the vandalism, to arrange from time to time for the services of four different detective agencies. American Bridge had its own detectives, with whom Drew kept in touch, and detectives of some of the railroad companies, "stirred up" by the dynamiting of their property, also provided the NEA with assistance on occasion.[58]

It appears that NEA-employed detectives were shadowing McManigal "night and day" as early as March 1908, and Drew and his agents were definitely on Hockin's trail by June 1, 1908. The Committee on Dynamiting informed the executive committee on June 19, 1908, that "efforts [at apprehending the dynamiters] were gradually nearing a point . . . [where] somebody would be caught." As evidence, the dynamiting committee cited the arrest of George O'Donnell (Davis) following the aforementioned dynamiting a few days earlier of structural iron material for the Taunton River Bridge in Somerset, Massachusetts.[59]

The NEA, indeed, came close to linking the IABSIW to the dynamiting in the Davis case. A Thiel Detective Agency operative had trailed Davis following his dynamiting of the Slade's Ferry Bridge at Fall River, Massachusetts, on April 26, 1908. Once Davis had been arrested, Drew sent Badorf to Somerset to investigate, and the NEA commissioner offered the Fall River police inspector the aid of a Pinkerton detective in the effort to connect Davis to the Somerset dynamiting. Drew's purpose was "to get at the man higher up" who, he believed, was providing the funding for dynamiting and to "use the . . . [Davis] case as an opening wedge into the whole conspiracy." This was in accord with the consensus in the NEA that "special efforts should be made towards implicating and apprehending the leaders of the International rather than giving too much attention to . . . trying to find out the perpetrators after the dynamiting." The link to Davis was IABSIW board member Frank Webb, and NEA detectives had discovered a few clues that Drew thought led "conclusively" from one man to the other. Drew provided Fall River authorities with this information, and he even paid the expenses of a "boy" hired by the city's police inspector to do undercover work on Davis. Since the NEA information proved to be "purely circumstantial," however, the Massachusetts authorities were unable to charge Davis with a dynamiting offense, but they did secure his conviction, as we have seen, on the charge of assault with a dangerous weapon.[60]

Not only was the NEA unable to capitalize on its investigation of Davis, but espionage efforts that should have implicated the IABSIW leadership and brought the dynamite campaign to a halt failed to do so. Drew not only had agents shadowing McManigal and Hockin, but in the same month that Davis was arrested, the NEA commissioner had two agents trailing John J. McNamara, the central figure in the dynamite campaign. In addition, the operative of one of the agencies Drew had employed had by that time secured a position as janitor in the American Central Life Building, where the IABSIW headquarters was located, and he had been able to secure a key to McNamara's desk and to go through his papers "systematically." In a letter to the head of an NEA firm that he understandably asked to be destroyed, Drew revealed that one of the

NEA's spies at the time was actually "a Union iron worker in high standing" who had been president of one of the IABSIW's largest locals. NEA detectives had also shadowed several men in the East who, the association thought, handled the money "for these things," and Drew claimed that one NEA spy was actually "a member of the gang who does these things." The NEA commissioner, indeed, reported that there had been "two different jobs framed up" that would have enabled the NEA to catch "the [dynamite] crowd red-handed" had not the jobs been "called off for one reason or another."[61]

Since the NEA had to "cut down expenses," Drew decided in June 1908 to stop the shadowing of Hockin and to discontinue the use of one of his two Indianapolis operatives since, at least regarding the latter espionage effort, he doubted that the "game" was "worth the candle." At its July 24, 1908, meeting the executive committee decided to meet the NEA's cash shortage by assessing the organization's five largest members $1 per employee. This action apparently failed to solve the NEA's financial problems, since Drew, by the end of August, had dispensed with the services of his single remaining Indianapolis operative, who had provided the commissioner with "no information of value," and had eliminated all but two of the detectives in the NEA's employ. On September 11, 1908, the NEA decided to discontinue secret service activity entirely after December 1.[62]

It is hard to know why NEA espionage aimed at the right targets yielded so little in the way of proof about the IABSIW's involvement in the dynamiting. Drew, to be sure, claimed that he knew who the guilty parties were for just about all the dynamitings but that the NEA lacked the "legal proof . . . to take [the perpetrators] in." Perhaps Drew, who had serious doubts about the integrity of private detective agencies, did not believe what they were telling him, or perhaps the detectives the NEA employed were simply incompetent. In any event, the NEA decided on July 9, 1909, to develop a secret service organization of its own as likely to achieve better results than relying on one or another of the private detective agencies. The association agreed to raise $10,000, soon cut to $5,000, by subscription and $1,000 per month by assessment for this purpose. Drew put Badorf in charge of the new service, and the policy was to employ "good men" gradually.

Drew thought that if the NEA's secret service organization proved effective, it would repay "many times over" the cost individual members were incurring in guarding their jobs. The sum agreed upon by the NEA executive committee, however, was not forthcoming, and the association's financial woes continued. By the end of August 1910 Drew had only two men "constantly at work," but he noted, perhaps whistling in the dark, that he had "several good sources of information in addition," that some of the larger NEA members "practically looked after matters . . . of this kind" on their own, and that he had arranged—he did not say by whom—for the shadowing of those suspected of planning and carrying out the dynamiting. The dynamiting continued, however, despite these claimed efforts and despite the information a member of the Indianapolis local of the IABSIW had given Indianapolis police in 1909 that they would find the dynamiters if they followed John McNamara and Hockin.[63]

In late June 1910 Herbert Hockin, by then a member of the IABSIW executive board, decided to turn informer. He claimed that his motive was to forestall union plans for "wholesale murder," but it is more likely that he was concerned about his status in the union since John McNamara, as noted, had discovered that Hockin was not paying McManigal the $200 due him for each dynamiting job. In any event, Hockin approached Lindsay L. Jewell, the head of McClintic-Marshall's steel erection department, and, pledging Jewell to protect his informer's identity, which Jewell did, began providing the executive with information. On September 1 Hockin warned Jewell about plans to dynamite the railroad bridge his company was erecting for the Peoria and Pekin Union Railway in Peoria. Although Jewell passed the warning on to the manager of the railroad company, that did not forestall the dynamiting of the bridge on the night of September 4. The Lucas Bridge and Iron Company plant in the same city was also dynamited that same night, an explosion that badly damaged not only the plant but also six adjacent buildings and "seriously injured" a night watchman. An infernal machine attached to a ten-quart can of nitroglycerin that had failed to explode was found at the site of the Peoria and Pekin explosion, and it helped forge "the claim of evidence" that led to the apprehension of the men accused of dynamiting the *Los Angeles Times* building.

Jewell did not see Hockin again until ten days to two weeks after the *Times* explosion, at which time he reported that James McNamara was Brice and had been aided by the two men later revealed to be Schmidt and Caplan. Hockin named the two McNamaras and McManigal as "the active factors in the work [dynamiting]." When Jewell, still concealing his source from the NEA and Drew, contacted the United States Secret Service to relay this information, he was advised to take the matter up with William J. Burns, head of the Burns National Detective Agency, who had been retained by the mayor of Los Angeles to investigate the *Times* explosion. Jewell then gave "the whole story" to Raymond J. Burns, William's son and the secretary and treasurer of the Burns Agency. Leaving for Panama to head a construction company, Jewell advised Hockin to deal directly with William Burns thereafter.

Hockin told the younger Burns on November 2, 1910, not only that Brice was James McNamara but that J. W. McGraw, who the Burns Agency had correctly concluded was responsible for the Peoria and Pekin bombing, was McManigal. Without sharing this information with Drew, the Burns Agency arranged to shadow McManigal and James McNamara, and yet the two were responsible for eight additional dynamitings before being arrested on April 11, 1911. Quite independently of the Burns Agency, the NEA, which had compiled a list of dynamiting suspects, informed Los Angeles authorities that Brice was James McNamara once it received a description of the three men indicted for the dynamiting of the *Times* building.[64]

Until the end of the great dynamite trial in December 1912, the enigmatic Hockin remained in the IABSIW's good graces and appears, indeed, to have been involved in at least one additional dynamiting. He continued at the same time to supply Burns with information but without revealing everything and, according to Burns, without always telling the truth. As a United States attorney who prosecuted Hockin later stated, he was "working both ends against the middle." After serving a prison term following the trial and conviction of the IABSIW leadership, Hockin, interestingly enough, went to work for the Burns Agency and boasted to Drew in 1918 that he had placed "secret operatives" in different plants.[65]

CHAPTER 5

"The Largest Criminal Conspiracy Trial"

Walter Drew's immediate reaction to the dynamiting of the *Los Angeles Times* building was to announce that he would submit the evidence the National Erectors' Association (NEA) had gathered about the dynamiting of open shop erection jobs to the Los Angeles authorities investigating the *Times* affair. Going beyond this, the NEA in the interval between October 1, 1910, and the arrest of the principal suspects in April 1911 developed a three-pronged strategy to put a halt to the dynamiting: enlisting the assistance of nonmembers in "a general movement" against the dynamiting campaign; attempting to use the Sherman Antitrust Act against the International Association of Bridge and Structural Iron Workers (IABSIW); and intensifying detective work to apprehend the dynamiters.[1] In the end, the NEA played a very large part in the prosecution of the guilty parties and in the great federal trial that led to the conviction of the union's leadership.

Drew favored a national movement of employer associations to deal with the dynamiting problem. At the NEA's executive committee meeting of October 25, 1910, he reported that he had conferred with representatives of the National Association of Manufacturers (NAM), the National Metal Trades Association, and the National Founders' Association, all committed to the open shop, with a view to developing a collective effort to gather and disseminate information about the dynamiting of open shop work. The committee authorized Drew on January 9, 1911, to meet with NAM president John W. Kirby, Jr., presidents of the nation's employer associations, and G. L. Peck, general manager of Pennsylvania Lines West, to devise a cooperative plan to run down the dynamiters and to raise funds for that purpose. Drew found that Kirby and Peck agreed on the need for "some general action," and the three men decided that a small committee should be formed for this purpose but should be kept "thoroughly quiet."[2]

At the request of his two confederates, Drew prepared a lengthy statement reviewing the dynamiting campaign that was presumably to be used to enlist support for the "general action." He warned that the "dynamiting habit" was "becoming acquired" and, if not halted, would become "thoroughly entrenched as an incident of labor troubles." As remedies for the problem, Drew suggested the development and proper use of "a large secret service organization," invoking the Sherman Act against the IABSIW, "strict laws" regulating the sale and use of explosives, a "campaign of publicity" focusing on the source of the dynamiting, and the letting of work to open shop erectors.[3]

As the dynamiting continued in the first three months of 1911,[4] Drew expressed concern about the implications of what was happening for the open shop. Railroad companies, he noted, were becoming hesitant about letting contracts to NEA members, an action, the NEA commissioner warned, that imperiled the association's open shop policy. How, he asked, could one expect "the smaller interests" to stand by the open shop if the big railroad companies did not do so? He indicated that the NAM stood with the NEA on the dynamiting issue, and he asserted that if the railroads also took an "unequivocal stand" on the matter and refused to contract for work with closed shop concerns as long as the dynamiting continued, the problem would be "nine-tenths solved." Making clear his priorities, Drew wrote Peck, "I am in hopes of making the whole thing rebound to a great increase in open shop conditions everywhere." As he informed NEA members at about the same time, Drew believed that the dynamiting, in the end, was likely to increase open shop support among employers, and he was doing his best "to bring this about and to crystallize the resentment into tangible support and co-operation."[5]

The NEA decided that it could not wait until it was able to line up the support of outside interests in order to step up its own efforts to deal with the dynamiting problem. Acting on a resolution presented by the executive committee, the NEA's membership voted at a general meeting on March 28, 1911, to assess member firms five cents per ton on all metal work fabricated and five cents per ton on metal work erected and to secure similar contributions from nonmember fabricators and erectors as well as contributions from other employers. The money so raised was to be used to put an end to the dynamiting of jobs of NEA members and other contributors primarily by organizing "an effective secret service" as well as by other means.[6]

At the NEA's October 25, 1910, executive committee meeting Drew asserted that the evidence demonstrated that the IABSIW was a conspiracy in restraint of interstate trade and hence in violation of the Sherman Act. He not only urged the federal government to prosecute the union but also tried to persuade individual NEA members to seek triple damages for injuries they had suffered at the union's hands and, by so doing, to "take away their money." Drew's argument for Sherman Act prosecution, which relied on the precedent of the Danbury Hatters case, was that the union's "general and controlling purpose" was "to prevent the securing or performing of contracts for the erection of structural steel by so-called 'unfair' firms," such contracts generally involving fabrication in one state and erection of the product in another state. When an NEA committee discussed the matter with Attorney General George W. Wickersham, he "tacitly agreed" with the Drew position, but the deputy to whom Wickersham referred the committee forestalled action by insisting on "a perfect case" before he would be willing to proceed.[7]

In seeking to encourage private suits to recover damages from the IABSIW, Drew turned to the NEA's two largest members, American Bridge and McClintic-Marshall. They were unwilling, however, to initiate suits on their own although ready to proceed as part of the NEA as a whole, which Drew believed could not be justified in terms of the law. Once again indicating its importance for the NEA, United States Steel thought it inadvisable for American Bridge or the NEA itself to act in the matter lest this prejudice passage of amendments to the Sherman Act the steel company was then seeking.[8]

Believing that the dynamiting originated in the union's "inner circle," NEA members thought it advisable "to cover completely" the movements of the IABSIW's executive board members and possibly "to secure the information" sent out from John McNamara's office. With this in mind, the NEA's executive committee, on January 9, 1911, authorized a three-person committee that included Drew to contract with the Burns Detective Agency on a "trial" basis for two to three months of service at a sum not to exceed $15,000. Burns, however, was unwilling to undertake an investigation limited in both "time and expense." It is doubtful that this was displeasing to Drew, who, as we have seen, had a poor opinion of private detective agencies in general and thought that the Burns Agency, in particular, had done a poor job in investigating the aforementioned Peoria and Pekin Union Railway explosion.[9]

Before any of the post–*Los Angeles Times* dynamiting initiatives of the NEA could proceed very far, the status of its antidynamiting plans was altered by the arrest of James McNamara and Ortie McManigal on April 11, 1911, the securing by Burns of McManigal's confession on April 13 and 14, and the arrest on April 22 of John McNamara. Drew played no part in the arrest of McManigal and James McNamara, but he was conspicuously involved in the arrest of John McNamara and the search of IABSIW headquarters in Indianapolis that followed. Advised by the Burns Agency that McManigal and James McNamara were under arrest, Drew went to Chicago, where he met W. Joseph Ford, the assistant district attorney of Los Angeles County, who was armed with an extradition request for John McNamara from the governor of California. Along with Ford and Martin S. Hyland, the Indianapolis superintendent of police, Drew presented the extradition papers to Governor Thomas Marshall of Indiana and secured from him a warrant for McNamara's arrest. Two police officers then picked up the union official, who was in the midst of a meeting of the IABSIW's executive board, and took him before a municipal court judge, James A. Collins, who held the brief hearing required by Indiana law to determine if McNamara was indeed the person named in the extradition papers. Collins then turned McNamara over to James Hossick, a Los Angeles detective sergeant, and Burns, who promptly took the union official, "manacled head and foot," out of the state in an automobile. Although he had been extradited primarily on the basis of a murder charge, McNamara was indicted in Los Angeles on May 5, 1911, not on that charge but as a coconspirator in the bombing of the Llewellyn Iron Works.[10]

IABSIW and AFL officials immediately charged that Drew, Burns, and their coadjutors had "kidnapped" McNamara just as Idaho and Colorado officials had connived in the abduction of William D. Haywood, Charles Moyer, and George Pettibone following the assassination in 1905 of Idaho Governor Frank Steunenberg. The AFL charged that United States Steel and its alleged minions in the NEA, having failed to destroy the IABSIW by the tactics the steel trust had employed to destroy other unions, were seeking to fasten the "horrible . . . crime" of dynamiting on the IABSIW as the means of destroying that union. The Chicago Federation of Labor thought it significant that "the hired legal assassin" of the NEA, Walter Drew, was present when John McNamara was seized. Perhaps, some union officials thought, the dynamiting was all a frame-up, "the work of spies hired by the steel employers," as the IABSIW and some historians were still speculating many years later. Had not a disgruntled watchman, after all, confessed that it was not the union but he who had placed the dynamite that was discovered on the roof of the Taylor Arcade in Cleveland in March 1906? And was it not a remarkable coincidence, doubters of the IABSIW's responsibility for the *Times* bombing asked, that bombs were "conveniently discovered" at the same time at the homes of Harrison Gray Otis and F. J. Zeehandelaar? Perhaps, also, some in the IABSIW knew about the two aborted dynamitings that Drew, as we have seen, reported as having been "framed up."[11]

"[W]e did unravel some red tape in a rather sudden manner," Drew wrote his mother regarding the extradition of McNamara, but the matter was not as simple as all that. Indiana law required that an individual whose extradition had been requested was to be taken before the state circuit, superior, or criminal court "nearest or most convenient of access to the place" where the arrest was made. McNamara had been taken before a municipal court judge, but Drew insisted that Hyland had indicated that this was common practice in Indianapolis. Although McNamara was denied counsel by Judge Collins and given no time to put his affairs in order, this was not a violation of Indiana's extradition law, and the union's attorney, although objecting to the denial of counsel, did not claim otherwise. The state's law, however, specified that the individual to be extradited must have been in the state to which he was to be taken at the time the alleged offense for which he was being extradited had occurred, which was simply not true of McNamara. Under California law, moreover, the governor of that state was to request extradition only for an alleged fugitive who was under arrest in another state. On the basis of a wire from Burns dated April 15 in which he falsely stated that he had arrested and was holding John McNamara, the Los Angeles County district attorney that same day submitted a sworn affidavit to California's governor asserting that McNamara was under arrest in Indianapolis, and it was on the basis of this affidavit that the governor had requested the extradition.

Although Drew told the Commission on Industrial Relations that there was "no question but what the extradition papers were all right," he seems to have known that McNamara had not been removed from Indiana legally. Burns, however, rushed the union official out of the state to avoid a grant of habeas corpus by which McNamara could have forestalled extradition. "This was done in the interests of justice," Drew remarked three years later, "and personally I would do it over again."[12]

Drew, Ford, and Frank Fox, the driver of the car that took McNamara out of Indiana, were arrested on April 24 and 25. Along with Burns, Hossick, and J. A. G. Badorf, they were bound over to the Marion County (Indianapolis) grand jury on a kidnapping charge. Drew, who was briefly unable to post his $10,000 bond, allegedly sought to resist the constable assigned to take him to jail. A day later the NEA commissioner allegedly attacked a constable who came to the hotel where Drew was staying in a vain effort to arrest Burns, who was "hiding" in Drew's room. The constable swore out an assault and battery charge against Drew, and Judge Collins then fined him $1 and costs. A few days later, however, the judge suspended the payment, much to the anger of the unions headquartered in Indianapolis, which, Drew claimed, had persuaded the constable to swear out the charge against the NEA commissioner even though he was innocent.[13]

Determined to secure the conviction of Drew, Burns, and the others, the officers of the international unions in Indianapolis engaged counsel to prosecute the case and hired detectives who shadowed Drew and Badorf "constantly." Drew thought that his shadows were "most friendly" and even gave him "a grin once in a while." He talked to them sometimes and told them where he was going "to save them trouble." If he was amused, however, the union leaders in the city were not. They warned Frank C. Baker, the county prosecutor, and Judge Joseph T. Markey, who was presiding over the grand jury investigating the McNamara extradition, that organized labor would not let the matter drop if the grand jury did not return an indictment for kidnapping; and they also complained to the governor of Indiana and the mayor of Indianapolis about what had occurred. "Really alarmed" about the union pressure being brought on public officials, Drew arranged for employer associations and businessmen all over the nation to send telegrams and resolutions to the Indiana governor, Baker, and the police to "offset" the union efforts.[14]

The Marion County grand jury refused to indict Drew, Badorf, and Fox but returned indictments against Burns and Hossick. The indictments, however, were later dismissed in criminal court, apparently because the applicable Indiana statute had by then been declared unconstitutional. A resolution by Congressman Victor Berger calling for a congressional investigation of the alleged McNamara kidnapping was rejected by the House Committee on Rules.[15]

After John McNamara's arrest, Drew, Badorf, Burns, Hyland, and Captain of Detectives William H. Holtz arrived at IABSIW headquarters, Hyland having secured search warrants from Judge Collins authorizing searches for "explosives or dangerous articles." Burns and Holtz searched McNamara's desk, and Drew, until stopped by President Frank Ryan, began looking at the contents of file cases. Drew and Burns then proceeded from the union offices on the fourth floor of the American Central Life Building to the fifth floor to search a vault for which McManigal had supplied Burns the combination. According to Burns, they found nothing of particular interest. The building superintendent then informed the search party of a vault in the basement that John McNamara had had built in February 1911 and to which he had brought various items from time to time. The vault was padlocked, and union attorney Leo M. Rappaport, whom Ryan had summoned, forbade the searchers to break in without a warrant, telling Hyland, surprisingly, "You are getting into something that is a bigger affair than you think it is." Drew, Hyland, and Burns thereupon secured the necessary warrant from Judge Collins. Inside the vault they found books and letter files on top of eighty-six sticks of dynamite, alarm clocks, fulminating caps, dry-cell batteries, a fuse, and a case to carry nitroglycerin.

Returning to the fourth floor, Drew told Ryan that there was "enough dynamite and high explosives in the cellar to blow up this entire building." Ryan professed ignorance of a basement vault and even of a basement. The search party now wanted to open the safe in the union offices, but the executive board members present claimed not to know the combination. A locksmith was sent for who drilled the safe open in the early morning hours of April 23. No member of the search party still present had the keys to open the inner doors of the safe, but Badorf and Burns knew that Drew, who had returned to his hotel, had come into possession of the keys when they had been taken from McNamara following his arrest. After Drew was summoned, the inner doors were opened, and the NEA commissioner, advised by Badorf, the NEA official most knowledgeable about the dynamitings, told Hyland to seize six or seven books of check stubs and receipts, hoping apparently to find receipts for money paid to McManigal and James McNamara. Although the search party had "left untouched" the bulk of the records in the union offices, they had obviously confined neither their search nor their seizure to "explosives or dangerous articles."[16]

Before the search of the American Central Life Building had been completed, Drew, Burns, and some of the others went out to the Dan Jones farm just west of Indianapolis, where John McNamara had rented a barn that McManigal had informed Burns was being used to store dynamite. Inside a piano box in the barn, the searchers found seventeen sticks of dynamite and two quarts of nitroglycerin. The McManigal confession also led Badorf and Burns to journey to Tiffin, Ohio, where, in what was described as "a depot or distributing station for the 'dynamite squad,'" they found 541 one-pound sticks of dynamite in a shed on the farm of McManigal's father. Some incriminating correspondence between the two McNamara brothers, finally, was discovered in a search of the family home in Cincinnati. Drew himself remained in Indianapolis "to dig up evidence" against the IABSIW members. "And you can guess," the widower

Drew wrote his mother, "that I am quite happy with a fight downtown [about the kidnapping charge] and a country club and lots of girls as a side issue."[17]

The arrest of the McNamaras and the seizure of the apparently incriminating evidence that followed led to intense activity by the NEA to secure the successful prosecution of the arrestees. The association sought to raise funds for the Los Angeles prosecution, and it significantly aided the Los Angeles district attorney, John D. Fredericks, in preparing the case for trial. Although determined to see the dynamite affair through to a successful conclusion whether or not it received contributions from outside sources, the NEA turned to the railroads, United States Steel, independent steel producers, and local employer associations in a renewed effort to raise adequate funds. The AFL Executive Council, convinced of the innocence of the McNamaras, was raising money for their defense—it eventually raised $236,105—and Drew was determined that the prosecution not be lacking in funds.[18]

Drew and the NEA focused much of their fund-raising on the railroads. In contacting railroad interests, Drew stressed the extent to which dynamiting had been directed at railroad bridges and material carried in railroad cars, including two dynamitings of railroad property on March 16 and March 25, 1911, that involved losses of $50,000 in each instance. The NEA was understandably concerned about railroad support because the bulk of the association's erection work was for railroad companies. Drew thought that, quite apart from the fact that railroad property had been singled out for dynamiting, the railroad companies should support the NEA because they saved money thanks to the economies resulting from the open shop erection of their work, for which the NEA was responsible.[19]

"While the iron is hot," Drew told prospective donors, "every effort should be made to clean up the whole situation thoroughly and in all of its ramifications." If the arrestees were allowed to go free, he warned, it would mean that "the use of dynamite in industrial troubles" could not be "prevented or punished" and "the closed shop, militant unionism," which he asserted had "thrown in its lot with these people," would "receive a tremendous impetus to its already arrogant dominion and power and a new spirit of contempt for law."[20]

The NEA was quite successful in supplementing its own funds for the prosecution of the dynamiters with funds from non-NEA sources. United States Steel, independent steel companies, and the railroad companies were responsive to Drew's appeal, several railroad companies contributing $5,000 each. Responding to Drew's urgings, the Indianapolis Employers' Association raised $10,000 to carry on the investigation of dynamiting in Marion County. Following a meeting with Drew, NAM president Kirby and former NAM president and Indianapolis resident David M. Parry sent out an appeal for funds in early September to "a selected number of men." Enclosed with the appeal was a confidential statement about the dynamite cases that Drew had prepared. Although it is not certain how much money the NEA was able to raise from nonmember contributors, Drew informed the association in September 1913 that the NEA had a surplus of $50,000 on hand that remained from the money collected from "outside sources."[21]

Although the Los Angeles prosecution received substantial funding from the city and county of Los Angeles and the city's Merchants' and Manufacturers' Association, Fredericks regarded the money provided him by local public and private sources as insufficient to meet the expenses of "a frightfully expensive case." In addition to its normal expenses, the prosecution had to protect witnesses from alleged attempts at bribery and intimidation by the defense, scattering them "in the mountains and various places for safety," an expenditure for which public funds could not be used. Also, since Fredericks agreed with the NEA that the "most effective prosecution" required "going into the whole series of outrages before and after" the dynamiting of the *Times* building and the Llewellyn Iron Works, "showing the connection of them all," the prosecution had to bring about two hundred witnesses from outside California to testify. The NEA's executive committee decided on July 18, 1911, to send $25,000 to Fredericks, and by early October 1911, when the McNamaras' trial began, he had received $50,000 from sources outside California.[22]

Following the arrest of the McNamaras and McManigal, the NEA turned once again to the Burns Agency and this time contracted with it to deal with "all Eastern cases," meaning cases outside California. Wary of Burns, Drew did not close down his own secret service operation despite the association's arrangement with the detective. Drew informed the executive committee in October 1911 that he had "a good man" of his own working in Indianapolis as well as "six or seven operatives . . . doing shadow work and guard service." Unhappy with the information Burns was providing, Drew decided in late November to dispense with the detective's services.[23]

Since the NEA assumed that much of the evidence the prosecution would introduce in the McNamara trial would seek to link the *Times* bombing with the dynamiting of NEA jobs, it made overtures, supported by Otis, to be represented in Los Angeles by its own counsel. When the press got wind of this, however, Fredericks solicited a letter from Drew to the effect that there was no basis for the allegation that the NEA would provide attorneys to aid the prosecution. Drew now sought publicly to distance the NEA from the prosecution beyond expressing a willingness to make information available to serve the ends of justice. Fredericks eventually appointed Oscar Lawler, a former United States assistant attorney general and former Los Angeles county district attorney, to assist the prosecution, an appointment that was entirely acceptable to the NEA.[24]

Although the NEA in the end did not appoint its own counsel to collaborate with Fredericks, it rendered him invaluable assistance in preparing his case. Since, as noted, the plan of the prosecution was "to open up the whole series of dynamitings all over the county," Drew provided Fredericks with "a mass of evidence" that the NEA had gathered and was gathering about the numerous dynamitings. In August Drew dispatched Badorf, who had been collecting witness statements in Indianapolis, to Los Angeles to assist the prosecution as it prepared for trial. Seeking to conceal his identity in conformity with the NEA's desire to remain in the "background" so as to counter union claims that the "steel interests" were engaged in a "campaign of persecution" against the IABSIW, Badorf aided Assistant District Attorney Ford to "line up matters in each case" and in charting the movements of McManigal and James McNamara. Badorf also examined and reacted to the information McManigal was providing the prosecution—he supplied "new things almost every day," Badorf reported.[25]

The private detective Robert J. Foster, whom Drew employed just after the *Times* bombing, established contact with B. John Cooke, who had been McNamara's bookkeeper and stenographer from July 1910 to February 1911, a period during which some of the "worst" dynamitings had occurred. Cooke had revealed little if anything when called before the Marion County grand jury, but he proved to be "a mine of information" once taken in tow by the NEA, revealing, for example, what appeared to have been union payments for dynamiting jobs. Fredericks wanted Cooke to come to Los Angeles as a witness, and Drew stood ready to pay for the transportation of Cooke and his wife. Drew also uncovered a potential witness who had sold John McNamara 220 quarts of nitroglycerin. Drew and Foster took "unusual precautions" to keep potential prosecution witnesses "under cover" and away from the defense and to provide them with financial assistance as well. Drew also prepared "a detailed statement or brief" of the case that was to be used in the Los Angeles trial.[26]

While seeking to aid the prosecution in Los Angeles, Drew and the NEA were also very much involved in protecting the evidence seized in Indianapolis following the arrest of John McNamara, attempting to arrange for the transfer of the relevant records to Los Angeles, and seeking the local prosecution of IABSIW officials. The police turned over the evidence they had seized in the American Central Life Building to the Marion County grand jury, and the county prosecutor, following John McNamara's arrest, subpoenaed additional union records.[27] The seized evidence became a major source of contention between employers and unionists in Indianapolis.

Labor and management were arrayed against one another in dramatic fashion in Indianapolis. The headquarters city of nine international unions, Indianapolis was "a stronghold of organized labor." Prosecutor Baker and Judge Markey were both "in sympathy with . . . the union element," and Baker was allegedly on "intimate terms" with IABSIW attorneys Rappaport and Henry Seyfried. Indianapolis, however, was not only a union center; its Employers' Association, formed in 1904, was reputedly "one of the most successful" open shop organizations in the nation.[28]

Both the union and the employer forces in Indianapolis sought to bring pressure on Baker to influence his handling of the IABSIW case. "The labor people," McClintic-Marshall's manager of erection informed the company's head on May 2, were "beginning to make things pretty warm for any officials connected with this affair who are dependent upon votes for their office." Drew, for his part, mobilized the Indianapolis Employers' Association to work in "thorough harmony" with the NEA and to influence the prosecuting authorities in a "quiet" but "persistent manner." Although urging the Employers' Association to act, Drew, in a letter to its secretary that Drew told him to destroy, asserted that "one of the worst things that could happen" was "for the charge to be made that the Erectors' Association" was "trying to control the local authorities, which, of course," Drew wrote, "we are not doing," but which, of course, it was attempting to do. Drew wanted whatever was done to look like "the voluntary and spontaneous action of the local business interests," not an effort by the "'steel interests' . . . to coerce or influence official action."[29]

Drew's objective was to secure the indictment of as many IABSIW board members as possible, while the union forces, as noted, were intent upon the prosecution of the alleged kidnappers. Responding to the conflicting pressures on him, Baker, who had stated publicly that McNamara had been removed from Indianapolis in an illegal manner, appointed as assistant prosecutors to aid him both IABSIW attorney Seyfried, whose concern was to be the kidnapping case, and Employers' Association attorney C. C. Shirley, who worked closely with Drew and Badorf in the effort to secure the prosecution of union officials.[30]

Aware of an Indiana statute that made it a felony not only deliberately to damage property in the state but also to conspire in Indiana to damage property in other states, Badorf, aided by Foster, lined up witnesses who could provide testimony about a few major dynamiting cases in Indiana and nearby states, such as the key Peoria case. Drew, Badorf, and Shirley also sought to develop a conspiracy case that involved IABSIW board members—"practically everything I did here," Badorf wrote Drew, had that as its object. Badorf also persuaded Baker on May 17 to employ two accountants, C. E. Freeman and J. E. Talbot, to inventory and arrange the seized records; and since the prosecutor was short of funds, it was the NEA, in a revealing mixture of public and private, that paid the two men the $30 a day they received for their services. At the request of union attorneys, Judge Markey ruled that the union records that had been seized could be examined only by the prosecutor, the grand jury, and union officials, and the two accountants were not to discuss the records they examined with anyone but Baker. Although both Baker and Shirley stated that the accountants complied with this order, it is certain that Freeman eventually informed Foster, who enjoyed the accountant's "full confidence," that the records included correspondence that incriminated the union's leadership and corroborated McManigal's confession.[31]

Shirley prepared an elaborate brief of the evidence that he presented to the Marion County grand jury. On June 17, 1911, the grand jury not only indicted Burns and Hossick, as already noted, but also returned indictments against John McNamara that Shirley helped Baker prepare and that Badorf contended he had "practically forced." The IABSIW secretary-treasurer was charged with storing dynamite in the American Central Life Building as well as conspiring to destroy the property of the Peoria and Pekin Union Railway. Seeing this action as only a first step, the NEA pressed for additional indictments of union officers by the new grand jury that convened in July. It was unable, however, to push Baker to act on the McNamara indictments or to seek additional indictments, even though Drew thought that there was "evidence before the Grand Jury . . . sufficient to place the majority, if not all, of the members of the Executive Board under grave and serious suspicion of crime." Since Baker would not act as Drew desired, the NEA commissioner increasingly saw federal prosecution as the means of "getting the Executive Board."[32]

The NEA, from the start, had feared that the evidence seized in Indianapolis would be returned to the union or, at least, would become unavailable for prosecutorial purposes in either Los Angeles or Indianapolis. Friendly to the union, Baker permitted Rappaport and Herbert Hockin, who, interestingly enough, had replaced John McNamara as the IABSIW secretary-treasurer, to remove items from the seized material; and the prosecutor also provided the union attorneys with transcripts of the daily proceedings of the Marion County grand jury. On one notable occasion, Baker permitted Rappaport, who was on his way to visit the jailed John McNamara, to take along some of the latter's bank records, including the stubs of checks drawn on his personal account that McNamara had written McManigal. On McNamara's advice, Rappaport, as he later admitted, destroyed a key checkbook as well as a bankbook and some canceled checks.[33]

That the bulk of the seized records were not returned to the IABSIW was due to the efforts of Robert Foster, working under Drew's direction. When Foster came to Indianapolis on April 30, Drew told him to keep an eye on Baker and the union attorneys and to protect the seized evidence. "I have to take care of the Arsenal," the detective wrote, "and see that none of our ammunition is taken as we will need it all when we make the advance on the Enemy Strong Hold." Foster arranged for the guarding of the grand jury room in the courthouse, where the records were kept, with the Employers' Association of Indianapolis paying for the guards. He also "fixed things" with the deputy sheriff assigned to Baker's office, where the two accountants worked, not to respond to demands by Baker or Markey for removal of documents on the grounds that the deputy did not recognize their signatures, which at least delayed removals. In the latter part of June the accountants expressed concern about the records because some "tough-looking customers" were hanging around the courthouse. When Foster relayed this information to Drew, he suggested that Freeman get Baker's permission, which the accountant did, to place the important documents in a vault in the Indiana Trust Company in Freeman's name. Foster then advised Freeman regarding which records should be placed in the vault.[34]

Fredericks visited Indianapolis in June 1911, met with Baker in Drew's presence, and they agreed that the proper prosecutorial strategy was to try the Los Angeles case, "the primary and important matter," before trying any Indianapolis case. They agreed, furthermore, that the evidence in the possession of the Marion County Criminal Court would be sent to Los Angeles for the McNamara trial, with the understanding that it would be returned to Indianapolis and that McManigal would be brought there to testify after the California trial had been concluded. In the end, however, Baker resisted efforts both to transfer the records to Los Angeles or to permit the photographing of the documents for use in the McNamara trial.[35]

Advised by Shirley that the seized records would "hang" John McNamara and concluding, no doubt because of information coming from Freeman via Foster that the evidence "went far to establish the general conspiracy to commit these outrages," Drew became increasingly concerned about the safety of the records. When he learned in early October that Baker intended to return "a wagonload of records" to the union attorneys, the NEA commissioner had Ferdinand Winter, a prominent Indianapolis attorney who had been engaged to represent Fredericks in the matter,[36] file a motion on the latter's behalf for transfer of the records to Los Angeles. Advised by Rappaport and Seyfried during oral argument on the motion, Baker filed a countermotion requesting that the judge order the retention of the records in the county, presumably because they were required there for possible prosecution, which, as Drew pointed out, Baker had no intention of undertaking. Undoubtedly "influenced" by Baker, Markey rejected the Winter motion.[37]

Drew was now more and more convinced that federal action was the only way to extract the seized evidence from the grip of the Marion County authorities. In the meantime, however, he had Winter move in court to have the records photographed, hoping that they could then be transferred in that form. Markey took the matter under advisement and then permitted union counsel to secure a delay of any decision on one pretext or another. The Indianapolis Employers' Association, however, through the cooperation of the owners of the American Central Life Building, was able to arrange for the surreptitious photographing of the documents that the Los Angeles prosecutor desired and for which Drew paid. Both sides, in the meantime, used detectives to shadow their adversaries.[38]

On October 25, while Markey was still delaying a decision on the motion to photograph, Charles W. Miller, the United States attorney in Indianapolis, filed an application in the Marion County Criminal Court for delivery to the federal government of the records stored in the Indiana Trust Company. On Saturday, November 4, Freeman advised Foster that Baker was planning, apparently that day, to turn over the records to the union attorneys. Told by Drew that it was his responsibility to safeguard the records, Foster tried to persuade Miller to subpoena the records at once, but since the grand jury was not scheduled to convene until the following Tuesday, the federal attorney, according to Foster's recollection, claimed he could do nothing to protect the records. Foster then went to the Indiana Trust Company and told the individual in charge that he, Foster, was speaking for the federal government and that there appeared to be a conspiracy under way to remove evidence that incriminated the IABSIW and that the federal government was about to seize. Failing to reach the bank's attorney by phone, the official was puzzled as to what to do. Foster, however, told him that if he delivered the evidence to anyone other than a representative of the United States government, it would be "bad" for him. The official thereupon agreed not to surrender the evidence over the weekend. As Foster recalled the event, Baker entered the bank just after the detective had left. When a "red-faced" Baker emerged from the bank, he came up to Foster, who had been waiting outside, and shoving his fist toward the detective's face, said, "I'll get you yet."[39]

On Tuesday, November 7, the day the federal grand jury convened, Miller arranged for the issuance of federal subpoenas for the seized union records. When the subpoenas were not immediately complied with, United States District Court Judge Albert Anderson sent a marshal after the records, which were then placed in the Federal Building. According to Drew, Miller was "astounded" at the nature of the evidence and was now "thoroughly aroused" about the need for action.[40]

Hockin had kept the jailed John McNamara informed about the fate of the union records that the NEA had done so much to protect as well as the fact that witnesses who could provide testimony damaging to McNamara were being made available to Fredericks by the NEA. Quite apart from other factors that have drawn most of the attention of historians, this information may very well have helped to induce the McNamara brothers to plead guilty. It is noteworthy that as the final negotiations were taking place in Los Angeles that led to the guilty pleas of the McNamara brothers, Clarence Darrow, their principal attorney, sent Rappaport a cipher telegram authorizing him, as he had requested, to spend $1,000 to secure the seized union evidence and to keep the records in Indianapolis. Would the McNamaras have admitted guilt, a prominent member of the Indianapolis Employers' Association asked, if their "direct and 'indirect' representatives" in Indianapolis "had succeeded in making a getaway of the Indianapolis evidence?" The question is particularly pertinent with regard to John J. McNamara, for whose role in the dynamiting the Indianapolis evidence was absolutely indispensable.[41]

Seeking Drew's advice, Fredericks wired him on November 25 that the McNamara defense was offering to plead James guilty and that he was willing to "take the limit" if the case against his brother, who, unlike James, was a prominent union official, was dismissed. Drew responded that this arrangement, which was not acceptable to Fredericks, should be agreed to only in return for a full confession by the brothers that would "expose" not only IABSIW operations and "the parties involved" but also "the connection with other organizations," by which Drew almost certainly meant the leadership of the AFL. In any event, Drew noted, although he had "no great desire to pursue the defendants" if "all the ramifications of the conspiracy" could be revealed, there was no need for concessions in view of the evidence available in Indianapolis and the "perfect cases" against IABSIW Executive Board members that federal attorneys were presenting to the grand jury there. Before "a roomful of astonished spectators," the McNamaras pleaded guilty on December 1,

1911, James to the dynamiting of the *Times* building, John to his role in the Llewellyn dynamiting. They did not then or later, however, provide the "complete statement" Drew would have liked.

Drew wired Fredericks on December 4 that the NEA did not "join in the demand for the death penalty" for James McNamara, believing him "the weak, paid tool of the others." The next day, more or less in accordance with arrangements worked out between the defense and the prosecutor, who was not, as has been charged, "under pressure" from the NEA to act as he did, Judge Walter Bordwell sentenced James McNamara to life imprisonment and John McNamara to a fifteen-year term. On the witness stand more than a year later, Fredericks, misrepresenting the facts, denied consulting with Drew about the disposition of the case and denied receiving a message from him about the death penalty.[42]

The guilty pleas of the McNamaras doomed the strike of the metal workers in Los Angeles that had been going so well for the IABSIW and the other unions. The prolonged strike was finally called off at the end of January 1912. The open shop forces thought that what had occurred provided them with a grand "educational opportunity" to convince the public of the evil character of organized labor and of the AFL. The NAM's James Emery, who professed himself to be "saturated with this matter," wrote C. W. Post after the guilty pleas of the McNamaras that the dynamite crimes were "not individual but representative, the acts of agents executing the policy of an organization, not the offences [*sic*] of embittered individuals expressing their private hate." The "moral responsibility" for the deeds, he believed, could be placed on the AFL, and he thought that its "legal culpability" could likewise be established. "I shall not be satisfied," he wrote, "until this whole criminal campaign is brought home . . . to the doors of the American Federation of Labor." It is not surprising under the circumstances that the NAM's John Kirby and David Parry paid for an effort to collect evidence against Samuel Gompers.[43]

Drew's reaction to the guilty pleas of the McNamaras and their conviction was that this was "only the beginning" in the task of convicting "every other person concerned in this hideous conspiracy," including those "behind" the brothers. Like Emery, Drew contended that the "real conspirators" were "men high in the councils of labor." The McNamaras, he asserted, were merely "tools of a coterie of men" seeking to force the closed shop on the structural steel industry. Describing the McNamara trial now as "a side show," Drew viewed the prospective federal trial in Indianapolis as the means of reaching the principals in the dynamite conspiracy.[44]

Drew based his justification for a federal trial on Sections 232 and 235 of the United States Criminal Code, which made it a felony to carry explosives on interstate carriers, and also on the conspiracy section of the code. After Drew, in person, delivered cipher messages of September 21, 1911, to Attorney General Wickersham from Fredericks and Lawler urging a federal probe, Wickersham wired A. I. McCormick, the United States attorney for the Southern District of California, to present the evidence to a grand jury if the evidence warranted that.[45]

Assistant Attorney General W. R. Harr opposed a federal prosecution because he thought, incorrectly, that the evidence for same rested entirely on the "alleged confession" of McManigal. Also, both McCormick and he saw federal prosecution as being only "a tool in aid of State prosecution," which, indeed, had been the principal motive of Drew and the others at the outset. Harr and McCormick, furthermore, feared that, given "public feeling" at that juncture of the Progressive Era, federal intervention would inject a class spirit in the case. These arguments appeared persuasive to Wickersham, but when Drew informed the attorney general that he had an "abundance of evidence" to support a federal prosecution, Wickersham invited the NEA commissioner to present his case to the Justice Department in Washington. In a memorandum that he took along with him for a meeting with Wickersham early in October, Drew stressed that the crime he was asking federal authorities to investigate was "not cognizable in the State Courts." What had happened in Los Angeles, he asserted, was "part of a national conspiracy" involving about one hundred dynamite explosions in different parts of the country and could be dealt with only by the federal government. The attorney general responded to Drew's presentation by instructing Miller to pursue the subject with Drew.[46]

When Miller subsequently asked Drew for a "full, complete, detailed statement" of the evidence of violation of federal law, the NEA commissioner, in a "Destroy this" letter to Foster, wrote that he believed Freeman could show Miller in five minutes enough documents to force federal action. Drew realized, however, that Freeman would be held in contempt of court if he revealed what he had learned from the seized evidence. Drew told Miller that much of the evidence the NEA had itself developed had been sent to Los Angeles and urged him to obtain the records in possession of the Marion County grand jury that Drew knew were incriminating. Although still urging a federal probe in Los Angeles, Drew by this time was arguing that Indianapolis, as the headquarters of the alleged national conspiracy, was the more important place for federal action.[47]

Some writers have attributed the decision of the federal government to initiate an investigation of dynamiting wholly or at least in part to a conversation on that subject that Lawler and Otis had with President William Howard Taft in Los Angeles on October 16 or 17. Herbert Shapiro has suggested that the two Californians may have supplied "a powerful emotional edge" to their argument for federal intervention by focusing the president's attention on a failed attempt to dynamite a bridge twenty miles north of Santa Barbara over which the train taking Taft to Los Angeles was to pass and which had been delayed for hours as a result. The press reported that thirty-nine sticks of dynamite had been found under the bridge and that a Southern Pacific Railroad Company watchman had frightened off two suspects before the fuse could be lit to explode the dynamite. Although Shapiro has expressed doubt that what the press reported had actually occurred, Lawler informed Wickersham on October 23 that "railroad secret service men" were "convinced" that the reported dynamiting attempt was the work of "persons connected with the conspiracy, having their headquarters on the Pacific Coast."[48]

Whether or not the train episode was a pseudoevent designed to influence the president's judgment, Louis Adamic's assertion that Taft, when he returned to Washington, "ordered the Department of Justice to make a full investigation" of the dynamitings is almost certainly inaccurate. Lawler, to be sure, stated in the October 23 message to Wickersham in which he referred to the dynamiting attempt that he had told the president that McCormick had authorized him to say that the federal attorney was "willing to institute [grand jury] proceedings" but wished the president's sanction. Although Taft seemed to favor federal action, it appears from Lawler's letter that the president left the decision to Wickersham.

It is all but certain that the Lawler letter had not even been read in Washington when Miller on October 25 initiated the federal government's effort to gain possession of the seized union records, and Wickersham did not bother to reply to the letter until November 18. Also, what Lawler was pressing for was a federal grand jury investigation in Los Angeles, and he specifically argued against making Indianapolis the site of the probe. By the time Wickersham responded to Lawler, however, a federal grand jury was already examining the evidence in Indianapolis. Wickersham did not order a federal investigation in Los Angeles until November 17, and he made it clear that the proceedings there were to be subordinated to the Indianapolis probe, which would be the "primary one." The attorney general subsequently appointed Lawler to serve as special assistant to the attorney general to investigate possible federal law violations, an action Drew had urged. Lawler's target, however, was the San Francisco labor leaders who were believed involved in the *Times* bombing rather than the IABSIW leaders, Drew's target. The federal grand jury in Los Angeles eventually returned indictments against six unionists, but the cases were subsequently dismissed.[49]

It was Drew rather than anyone else who prevailed upon the federal government to initiate its investigation of dynamiting. Drew, who had persuaded Wickersham to discuss a federal probe with Taft even before he left for Los Angeles, conversed with Harr on October 17, and the assistant attorney general now agreed that a federal investigation of the dynamiting was required. Two days later Harr stated specifically that the decision to investigate had been reached in a conference among Miller, the attorney general, and himself in which they concluded that the information Drew had presented to Wickersham regarding the transportation of explosives on interstate carriers required "careful investigation." On October 21 Drew presented Miller with a detailed summary of the evidence supporting the purported violation of federal law in the dynamitings. Miller also met with Winter, Shirley, some of Burns's agents, and, most important of all, with Freeeman, who apparently told Miller "indirectly" what the evidence in the Indiana Trust Company revealed. The Burns men and Burns himself, despite their access to Hockin, had little to offer Miller, who thought he had been "treated shabbily" by the Burns Agency; but the others, all in one way or another associated with Drew, led Miller to subpoena the seized union records. Wickersham stated specifically to McCormick on November 17 that the federal government's decision to undertake the grand jury investigation of the dynamitings was based on information supplied by Drew. As the NEA commissioner accurately stated, his efforts to secure federal action in the dynamite matter had "culminated satisfactorily."[50]

From the time the seized union records came into the hands of the federal government until the conclusion of the great dynamite trial at the end of 1912, the NEA was closely associated with the United States attorneys in the preparation and prosecution of the case. Once again, the private and public spheres became intertwined. Miller later conceded that although he had hoped to make the Indianapolis case the "case of the Government" and not to avail himself of the NEA's services, it became necessary for him as the case "progressed" to turn to the NEA for help.[51]

Anxious to push the case "as hard and fast" as he could, Drew summoned Badorf from Los Angeles to work with Miller and to "facilitate the prosecution," advising Badorf, typically, to "keep under cover all you can." Drew loaned his secretary, Bessie L. Crocker, to the government because of her familiarity with the case, and the NEA commissioner also loaned Foster to Miller. Drew himself supplied Miller with data, some of it newly discovered; he arranged for the shadowing of a McNamara secretary who had typed his "incriminating letters" and who later testified regarding the IABSIW's dual system of bookkeeping that was designed to conceal payments for dynamiting; he agreed to pay a potential witness who had information on dynamiting in Cleveland; and he paid some of the federal government's expenses in preparing the case for the grand jury until the government, on November 21, assumed full financial responsibility for the case.[52]

Badorf, so knowledgeable about the dynamite cases, proved to be an invaluable ally of the prosecution. He examined the thousands of letters already in the government's hands or soon to come into its possession and was able to arrange the correspondence so as to relate particular dynamite cases to particular violations of federal law. At Miller's request, Badorf prepared a detailed statement of the case, and he had to "practically teach the case" and its "many ramifications" to the federal attorneys. Department of Justice field men, Badorf informed Drew, went over "practically everything in order to give the matter a strictly government color."[53]

Although Drew learned from the bookkeeper Cooke that evidence of an incriminating sort remained in the union's possession, Miller was reluctant to subpoena the material. Foster, consequently, "cultivated" Hockin, who had offered to help the NEA, and he began supplying the NEA detective with "piecemeal evidence" but "not the real dope." Once the McNamaras pleaded guilty, however, Hockin became more cooperative and arranged for Foster to pick up the union's records.

Foster, Freeman, and Talbot visited the union offices on the night of December 6, 1911, and picked up a key checkbook and four receipt books. They returned the next night and took away twelve suitcases full of letters and "old papers" that constituted "the entire contents" of the union's fourth-floor offices. On December 9 Hockin gave Foster some documents when the two were in the Federal Building, and that night, while Drew waited in "a darkened door" across the street from the American Central Life Building, Foster, Badorf, Freeman, and two others removed all the records in the vault McNamara had used on the floor above the union offices, which Hockin had left open for them. The documents seized, which filled three automobiles, were promptly turned over to Miller. They contained "a good deal of very important stuff" bearing on the preceding two years, a critical period for the government's case. "I guess we have all we need here," Miller reportedly said. Quite apart from the documents that were taken, Foster later testified that Hockin had told him just after the December 9 raid that he would make "a clean breast of everything to Miller," which, Hockin claimed, he then did.[54]

Foster next arranged with Hockin to place a dictograph in IABSIW President Frank Ryan's office. Drew was hoping that, with the dictograph in place, Hockin would "lead Ryan and the others in conversations about the various [dynamiting] jobs" and that evidence might also be obtained to link Gompers with the dynamitings. "I don't want to be the only goat in this case," Hockin told Drew. "When you get me you can get the whole bunch." Foster installed the dictograph on New Year's day, 1912, drilling through a concrete floor to pass the wire to the floor below.

The dictograph was discovered on January 27, 1912. Foster claimed that it had yielded "practically nothing," since Hockin, "double crossing again," had steered conversations away from Ryan's office. Although Miller stated in his closing argument in the trial that eventually ensued that he had not used any dictograph evidence in the trial, Drew claimed that "a great quantity of evidence" secured from the dictograph had been used. Since, unsurprisingly, there was no direct reference to dictograph evidence in the trial, it is difficult to know whether such evidence played any part in the development of the government's case. As for Gompers, Drew never discovered any "tangible evidence" that the AFL president had prior knowledge of any of the dynamitings.[55]

After receiving reports from Hockin and an associate of Darrow that labor leaders, including Ryan, had allegedly arranged for a Chicago "gangster" to assault or assassinate Drew, Foster sought out the IABSIW president on January 27, 1912, to warn him not to harm the NEA commissioner. As Ryan told the story, when Foster refused to leave the union president's office, Ryan sought to push him out. Foster thereupon struck him, and after the two had exchanged blows, Foster, saying, "I will get you, you s——," drew a revolver and hit Ryan with it before Hockin and others could restrain the detective. Foster claimed that Ryan had grabbed and choked him before he struck the union president on the skull with a revolver, drawing blood and blinding Ryan temporarily, and then pulled out a second gun to hold off other unionists who were approaching him. Foster was arrested and charged with five offenses, including assault with intent to commit murder. He was later convicted on a single count of carrying a concealed weapon.[56]

On February 6, 1912, the federal grand jury in Indianapolis returned thirty-two indictments against fifty-four unionists, fifty-one of whom were IABSIW members, including the union's top leadership and local officers and business agents. They were charged with carrying dynamite and nitroglycerin aboard passenger trains engaged in interstate commerce and with conspiring "to commit an offense against the United States." The theory of the government was that those who hired the dynamiters or had "guilty knowledge" of their actions were guilty of "aiding and abetting," which made them principals according to the law. The indictments were limited to conveying offenses beginning in 1910 since the applicable statute did not include a penalty clause before that date. Of those indicted, forty-five actually went to trial on October 1. The bonds for the arrestees came to $340,000, which Ryan saw as related to Drew's threat to "break us [the union] financially."[57]

It is possible that a plot was hatched to do away with Drew during the period between the February 6 indictments and the start of the Indianapolis trial. Edward J. Brennan, a special agent of the federal government's Bureau of Investigation who had come to Indianapolis late in 1911 to investigate the dynamite cases, testified at the trial that Hockin had informed him in May 1912 that on a Hockin visit to San Quentin John McNamara had told him, "I would like to see them get Burns and Drew." A San Francisco labor leader had then told Hockin, he reported, that on his return to Indianapolis, he would be visited by someone who would say, "My name is Arrow, not Darrow." Hockin told Brennan that a person introduced himself in Indianapolis with these code words and subsequently gave Hockin a package that he then turned over to Walter Davis, an ironworker brother of the dynamiter George Davis. Walter Davis shortly thereafter gave Hockin a ticket for the package, which had been checked in the parcel room of the Union Station in the city. When Fred Sherman, the business agent of the IABSIW's Indianapolis local and a defendant in the federal trial, asked Hockin for the ticket, he told him that it had been lost. Hockin turned the ticket over to a United States marshal, who testified that when the package was opened, it was found to contain a fuse, fulminating caps, and an alarm clock wrapped in a copy of the *San Francisco Chronicle* of April 13, 1912.

Although the package was real enough, we have only Hockin's word for the purpose to which it was to be put, and Miller, at least, did not believe the Hockin story. In his confession, however, the dynamiter George Davis stated that Frank Webb, his paymaster, had told him that "a price had been fixed" of $5,000 each for the assassination of Drew and Burns and $3,000 for the slaying of Badorf. Webb, Davis claimed, had sounded him out about his "getting Burns." Drew, his second wife later noted, began to carry a gun at the time because of concern that his life was endangered.[58]

The NEA did not remain idle during the nine-month interval between the return of the indictments and the beginning of the Indianapolis trial. As Drew informed a prominent NEA member, "not even the Government" had "the same motive" as the NEA did in seeing the federal case through "to a finish." Drew, for one thing, employed a number of operatives so as to have "an inside group" at work on the various dynamiting cases. Badorf, for his part, continued to advise the federal attorneys in preparing the government's case for trial, and he helped draft the government's brief for the case.[59]

Characterized by the contemporary writer John Fitch as "one of the most amazing cases ever tried in an American court" and reportedly "the largest criminal conspiracy trial" in American history to that time, the Indianapolis trial began on October 1 and went to the jury on December 26. The government called 499 witnesses, the defense, 188. The record ran to twenty-one thousand pages of testimony and about five thousand pages of documentary exhibits, and the batteries, clocks, fulminating caps, tools, and guns used by the dynamiters, as well as parts of the "infernal machines" discovered where explosions had occurred, were all exhibited to the jury. In a critical decision, the judge ruled that evidence regarding explosions was admissible as "tending to establish a larger conspiracy to destroy and injure open-shop work, of which the lesser conspiracy to transport explosives on trains was a necessary and incidental part." Although the prosecution charged only twenty-five direct violations of United States laws constituting one "continuing conspiracy," it offered evidence of ninety explosions, sixty-one of them on jobs of NEA members. The defense, on the other hand, was not permitted to provide evidence regarding employer behavior that might have been claimed as "provocation" for union behavior. Ortie McManigal was the key prosecution witness in the trial. The defense was unable to shake his testimony in cross-examination, and, in any event, it was corroborated by hotel registers, bank records, correspondence, physical evidence, and eyewitnesses.[60]

Foster and Badorf continued to assist the government during the course of the Indianapolis trial. In his able summary of the trial for *Survey,* John Fitch noted that the address given him for Badorf turned out to be the office of the United States attorney in the Federal Building in Indianapolis. Badorf took Fitch into a guarded room in the building to which the NEA assistant commissioner had "easy access" and where he showed Fitch the government's exhibits. Drew, for his part, availed himself of a "special agent" working for American Bridge in an effort to secure information concerning defense witnesses so that the prosecution could "discredit" their testimony. Foster, similarly, informed Drew that Miller wanted the detective "to stick close" to two of the defense attorneys, which Foster did.[61]

In his closing argument for the government, Miller stated that "the real 'Crime of the Century'" was not the bombing of the *Times* building but rather "this damnable 'conspiracy' which contemplated the nation-wide destruction of life and property." The defense, on the other hand, denied the existence of a conspiracy among the defendants to transport explosives. Much of the defense testimony took the form of "character evidence."

Two defendants pleaded guilty in the Indianapolis trial, McManigal and the Cincinnati local's Ed Clark, who confessed to a single dynamiting and, like McManigal, testified for the government. Of the forty defendants whose cases went to the jury, thirty-eight, including Ryan, all but two members of the IABSIW executive board, former board members, and local leaders across the nation, were found guilty. Five defendants received suspended sentences, and the judge sentenced the others to terms ranging from one year to seven years. In pronouncing sentence, Judge Albert Anderson specifically linked the dynamitings and the trial to the union's reaction to the NEA's effort to enforce the open shop in the structural steel industry. "This system of destruction," he declared, "was not carried out for revenge or in obedience to any other human passion, but for the deliberate purpose, by a veritable reign of terror, to enforce compliance with the demands of the iron workers upon the open and closed shop question."[62]

"Perhaps there never has been a trial of such magnitude in which the prosecution was so thoroughly prepared," remarked Newton W. Harding, the principal defense attorney. Quite apart from the efforts of the United States attorneys who prosecuted the case, the NEA deserved a major share of the credit for this compliment. In a hyperbolic appraisal of what had occurred, United States Circuit Court Judge William L. Putnam wrote the attorney general, "the preparation of those trials and the conduct of them, combined with the result, constitute the most monumental exhibition of the enforcement of the criminal law, and the most profound event in the triumph of law and justice ever exhibited wherever the Anglo-Saxon race has governed." Drew's concern, typically, was less the "punishment for the individual defendants" than it was "the moral effect of the verdict upon the public conscience and in the future development of organized labor."[63]

The thirty-three defendants sentenced to prison terms arrived at Leavenworth on January 1, 1913, accompanied by forty-four guards and five newsmen on a train the prisoners named "the 'Hockin' special." They were released after a few days on bonds totaling $2,140,000. Thirty defendants appealed their conviction to the Circuit Court of Appeals for the Seventh Circuit, which upheld the original decision for twenty-four defendants, including Ryan, but reversed the lower court for the six others, remanding their cases for new trials. Only one of the six was later convicted. The United States Supreme Court denied certiorari for the twenty-four defendants whose sentences had been upheld.[64]

Following the trial, the NEA provided McManigal with "quite a substantial sum of money" and also contributed to Clark's support until his death in 1919. As Drew saw it, if witnesses who aided the NEA were not assisted when in need, they would be "a walking example" of the perils of turning state's evidence, and others would be reluctant to "come across" if there was trouble in the future.[65]

Drew returned to the idea of individual damage suits against the IABSIW once the Indianapolis trial had come to a close and the evidence of numerous dynamitings had been spread on the record. He favored this tactic as a means of reaching the union's funds, which he estimated as between $75,000 and $100,000, and as a way of "bringing home to the unions and their members some sense of responsibility, some recognition of the fact that if they do certain things, they have got to pay the price." The executive committee authorized Drew to ascertain whether legal action was indeed practicable, but the matter was dropped when the attorney to whom Drew turned for advice concluded that a suit in the union's name would not be advisable even in states whose laws permitted such suits, because the courts had held the relevant statutes applicable only to individual union members in these states. A similar fate befell Drew's effort to secure federal and/or state prosecution of Pete Smith and one other Cleveland unionist, since, the NEA commissioner claimed, the evidence provided in the Indianapolis trial proved their guilt. Drew also failed in his attempt to have the widows and children of those killed in the dynamiting of the *Times* building sue for damages.[66]

Persistent in his relentless pursuit of the IABSIW, Drew after the Indianapolis trial sought once again to induce the federal government to prosecute the union under the Sherman Act. Writing to Attorney General James C. McReynolds in February 1914, Drew contended that the Indianapolis trial had proved that the IABSIW was a combination in violation of the Sherman Act and was, indeed, "one of the greatest criminal conspiracies in industrial history." The Antitrust Division of the Justice Department was not persuaded by Drew's reasoning, taking the position that contracts to erect structural steel and iron were "ordinary building agreements" that did not involve interstate commerce.[67]

Although the federal grand jury probe in Los Angeles did not lead to a federal trial, the *Times* bombing did lead to state trials in California of Clarence Darrow, Matthew Schmidt, and David Caplan, in all of which the NEA became involved to some degree. Darrow was tried beginning in May 1912, before the Indianapolis trial began, for the alleged bribery of a venireman for the McNamara trial and then a second time in January 1913 for the alleged bribery of an actual juror. Interestingly enough, soon after he entered the McNamara case, Darrow had written Gompers, "It [the case] is filled only with trouble for me," and he indicated that if he could withdraw from the case, he would sacrifice his fee and the $10,000 he had already received from the AFL.[68]

Drew revealed that the NEA helped to finance the first Darrow case, and the association, once again, played a part in gathering evidence for the prosecution. The biographers of Earl Rogers, Darrow's lawyer in the first bribery trial, assert that the NEA involved itself in the case because "the forces behind the open shop were determined to place him [Darrow] behind prison bars." No doubt the NEA would have been pleased to see the defender of the McNamaras and other unionists "behind prison bars," but Drew's interest in the Darrow case was less Darrow than Darrow as a possible means to a desired end. Drew hoped that information could be obtained in a Darrow trial that would bear on the dynamitings in various cities, information that could then be used in the forthcoming Indianapolis trial. Since the AFL had financed Darrow's defense of the McNamaras and since Hockin had told Foster that Ryan and John McNamara had "assured him [Hockin] Gompers knew everything that was going on," Drew was also looking for evidence that might tie the AFL president to the dynamitings in some way. When it appeared that Darrow was prepared to plead guilty and to pay a fine of $10,000 but to escape jail provided that he told all he knew about the dynamitings, possibly implicating Gompers, Drew favored the arrangement. Badorf, however, although writing Drew that he supposed that Gompers was "the party desired," opposed the projected plea bargain and, in any event, thought that it would be difficult to convict Gompers on the basis of Darrow's testimony alone.[69]

No sooner had Darrow been indicted on January 29, 1912, than Lawler, who was assisting Fredericks in the case, asked Drew for Foster's services. Drew authorized this, placing Foster under Lawler's "direction and control" and instructing the detective to remain under cover. Lawler knew that Foster had been in touch with John Harrington, a lawyer and the chief investigator for Darrow in the McNamara case, who had been providing the NEA with information either because, as Darrow charged, he had refused Harrington a substantial pay increase for his services or, as Foster informed Drew, because Harrington feared that he would be linked to Darrow in the bribery case. Harrington, who had earlier told Foster about alleged plans to assassinate Drew, now fed the detective information about a series of alleged Darrow misdeeds and law violations as the McNamaras' defense counsel.[70]

At least with Drew's knowledge and possibly on his instruction, Foster arranged with Harrington in early February to place a dictograph in his Los Angeles hotel room. Harrington was supposed to steer Darrow to this room and to engage him in conversation along lines suggested by Lawler. The dictograph was first discovered by a hotel maid, whom Foster apparently persuaded not to report the fact, and then by a bellhop, who had it removed on March 12. Although Foster later recalled that streetcar and radiator noise made the words difficult to decipher, Drew claimed that the evidence the dictograph provided was "greatly beneficial" to the Indianapolis trial, and it became a cause célèbre in the first Darrow trial. On May 27, 1912, during the course of the trial, the *Los Angeles Examiner* quoted Foster as saying that the dictograph evidence would "convict" Darrow. The defense charged that Foster had tried to smuggle the newspaper into the jury room, which led to the initiation of contempt proceedings against the NEA detective. The case was transferred to the court of another judge, who dismissed the charge, asserting that it was "a trumped-up affair."[71]

Dictograph evidence at the time of the first Darrow trial had never been used in a Los Angeles courtroom. Although failing in repeated efforts to introduce the dictograph evidence, the prosecutor asked "a series of impeaching questions" in cross-examining Darrow that were supposedly based on that evidence. In his plea to the jury, Darrow accused Harrington of having plotted with the NEA to convict the defendant, insisted that the prosecution had learned nothing from the dictograph, and argued that if the NEA had attempted to entrap him in that way, it could also have been guilty of plotting his "ruin" by staging the alleged bribery to make it appear that he was the guilty party. Even though Darrow's own chief attorney in the case concluded that his client was guilty, an opinion shared by "nearly everyone" familiar with the case, the jury acquitted Darrow after a mere thirty-four minutes of deliberation. Darrow also escaped conviction in a second trial the next year, following the Indianapolis trial, but this time the jury voted eight to four for his conviction.[72]

Matthew Schmidt and David Caplan, it will be recalled, had been indicted on January 5, 1911, along with James McNamara, for the murder of those who perished in the *Times* building. They escaped arrest until February 1915, when both were apprehended within five days of one another.[73] By that time the NEA had received the confession of the dynamiter George Davis, which strengthened the association's case against the IABSIW, a case that figured prominently in the trials of Schmidt and Caplan. On September 6, 1913, Davis wrote Drew, "I know lots of things you may want to know." Asserting that he had "done their [the union's] dirty work for them for a long time" but that the IABSIW now wanted him "done away with," Davis, who was "practically 'broke,'" turned to the NEA in the hope of "getting money" or a job. Foster met with Davis in a Pittsburgh hotel, convinced him that the detective knew "all about" him, and then accompanied Davis to New York, where on September 12 and 13 he dictated a confession in the presence of Drew, Foster, and Crocker.[74]

Union correspondence appeared to corroborate the Davis story, and an ironworker named Rudolph Tonnings, who assisted Davis in several dynamitings, later corroborated Davis, in part, in a signed confession. "He tells a marvelous story," Miller remarked after reading the Davis confession, and "paints some of the leaders still blacker than the first coats they received." Miller came to New York for Davis's arrest on October 2, and the confession was then released to the press, both Miller and Drew appreciating that "the great importance of this matter" was "the publicity end of it." Davis was taken to Indianapolis, where he pleaded guilty and received a suspended sentence. He was not disappointed in his hope for financial assistance from the NEA: by June 1915 he had received $1,121, and the NEA was still contributing to his support six months before his death in early 1924.[75]

In preparing for the Schmidt trial, James W. Noel, who had served as a special assistant to Miller in the Indianapolis trial and was now serving as special counsel for the Schmidt trial, advised Drew that he not only wanted Davis to testify but also wanted the same kind of cooperation from the NEA that the federal government had received in the Indianapolis trial. Drew informed Noel that the NEA had "no particular interest" in the prosecution of the two men other than the fear that their acquittal might "cast doubt" on "the good work" already achieved in the dynamite cases and might support claims of "a mere frame-up" by Burns, then in especially bad repute.[76]

Since the argument of the state in the Schmidt trial was that the criminal acts with which he was charged were part of "a nation-wide conspiracy," his trial, to some degree, was a reprise of the Indianapolis trial. The evidence the

NEA had so materially helped to compile for the Indianapolis trial was offered once again, and many of the same witnesses, including McManigal and Drew, repeated their testimony. The principal new witness was Davis, the "McManigal of the East," and his testimony strengthened the prosecution's claim of a nationwide dynamite conspiracy. It took the jury less than thirty minutes to find Schmidt guilty of murder in the first degree, and he was sentenced to life imprisonment on January 12, 1916.[77]

"The last chapter of 'The Crime of the Century'" began on April 5, 1916, with the start of the Caplan trial. It was actually the Schmidt trial all over again, but the outcome was different, the jury dividing seven to five in favor of conviction. In a second trial that concluded in December 1916, Caplan was found guilty of manslaughter in the second degree and sentenced to ten years of imprisonment.[78]

The NEA's long campaign against the dynamiters came to an end with the second Caplan trial, but Drew was altogether displeased with the reaction of the AFL and the IABSIW to what had occurred. Attending the February–March 1913 convention of the IABSIW, Gompers declared, "I am not your accuser." Ryan, just having been released on bail from Leavenworth, was reelected the union's president. In November 1919 Drew unhappily observed that eleven of the men convicted in Indianapolis held office in the union, including President P. J. Morrin. Ryan, at the time, his seven-year sentence having been commuted by President Woodrow Wilson on April 6, 1918, was serving as a member of the national committee the AFL had appointed to organize the steel industry. After being released from prison in the spring of 1921, John McNamara became the business agent of the IABSIW's Indianapolis local, only to run afoul of the law once again and eventually to be ejected from the union.[79]

Although disappointed at the union's reinstatement of its convicted officers, Drew was able to use the guilty pleas of the McNamaras, the later convictions in federal court of the IABSIW leadership, and the evidence the dynamite trials provided as a powerful weapon to wield against the IABSIW and in favor of the open shop. Drew's first important use of this tactic, even before the Indianapolis trial began, was in testimony he gave to a subcommittee of the Senate Committee on the Judiciary in a successful effort to derail an anti-injunction measure that had passed the House. In remarks that were reprinted and circulated by the NAM, Drew reviewed the history of the dynamiting of NEA and open shop jobs and noted that the union responsible for same and that remained an affiliate in good standing of the AFL was urging the legislation the committee was considering. Did Congress, he asked, propose to protect from the injunction process persons who belonged to a union of that kind?[80] This argument and Drew's efforts to forestall legislation sought by union forces and opposed by employers were illustrative of the role Drew played in promoting the open shop and combating unionism not just in the structural steel industry but, as the next chapter will indicate, in the economy as a whole.

CHAPTER 6

"The Most Successful Open Shop Producer"

What has generally been ignored in the relatively brief mention made of Walter Drew in histories of American industrial relations is the large role he played in spreading the open shop beyond the structural steel industry at both the local and national levels. Contemporaries were aware of the fact, however. "Walter Drew," the editor of the journal of the Citizens' Industrial Association of America (CIAA) declared, is "the most successful open shop producer . . . that we have any record of."[1] Although Drew's activities as an "open shop producer" were not confined to the period before the United States entered World War I, the subject of this chapter, they were very much in evidence during those years.

"It is my constant effort," Drew wrote a National Erectors' Association (NEA) member in 1910, "to increase the efficiency and standing of the Association and its radius of influence, both local and national, . . . with a minimum of expenditure." Not only was he active on the legislative front, state and national, but as NEA commissioner Drew sought "to organize and crystallize open shop sentiment in different cities." In soliciting NEA membership, Drew made the point that the association sought to facilitate the open shop movement in other trades as well as in the structural steel industry. As the only national employers' association in the building industry committed to the open shop, the NEA, Drew observed, was "looked to more and more as a leader and an ally in local open shop movements." Whenever nonunion contractors in the building trades wanted to rid themselves of unionism, they were likely to turn to the NEA, which provided such assistance as it could "on the theory that it all . . . [helped] the common cause." Drew did not exaggerate when he wrote a construction company in 1913, "We are recognized throughout the country as the leading open-shop influence in the building trades."[2]

Given his role as commissioner of an organization of structural steel erectors, it is hardly surprising that Drew's particular focus in extending the open shop was the building trades. As Drew saw it, the building industry was "the most important of all industries," and conditions in the industry had "a more wide-spread influence in our national industrial life than conditions in any other industry." Also, the building industry, as we have seen, was peculiarly vulnerable to unionization and the closed shop. If the open shop could be established in the building trades, Drew maintained, "there would be little trouble about working open shop in other lines." His efforts, indeed, to bring the open shop to the building trades in a particular community sometimes became a campaign to place all business and industry in that community on an open shop basis. "As a practical matter," Drew asserted in 1913, "it is easier to put a whole town on an open-shop basis and keep it there, than it is to maintain an open shop in a single industry."[3]

It was Drew's contention from the start that the mere existence of the NEA as a successful open shop organization served as a deterrent to union behavior in the building trades in general. Claiming with some exaggeration in the early months of his commissionership that NEA members were erecting 90 percent of the nation's structural steel, Drew remarked that "a great wedge, a wedge of steel and iron," had been "driven into the very heart of the closed shop system in the building trades." He noted that some large nonmember construction firms, such as the George A. Fuller Company, contributed to the NEA because the open shop in the structural steel erection industry was "a constant warning to the building trades unions" as to what could happen to them and, consequently, "in some degree," made even "closed-shop dealing more equitable."[4]

If Drew saw the open shop in steel erection as having an effect on labor relations in the other building trades, he also understood that the behavior of the other building trades had an effect on the ability of the NEA to maintain the open shop in its trade. By initiating "a general open shop campaign in all the building trades," the NEA, Drew hoped, was sending a message to them that support of the ironworkers, as by sympathetic strikes, was "more trouble than it . . . [was] worth."[5]

Drew's concern about preventing other trades from threatening the open shop in structural steel erection explains his interest from the very beginning of his commissionership in the formation of some kind of general contractors' association. He saw the general contractor as "the weak link in the open shop chain as far as raising steel [was] concerned." The remedy in Drew's view for the "weak position" of the general contractor in dealing with unions was a national general contractors' association. Working with the NEA, whose members' structural steel had "serious implications upon the whole work," such an association, Drew believed, would not be at the mercy of local conditions in the building industry and could "dictate" the terms of building contracts. Drew did not assume that a general contractors' association would necessarily commit itself to the open shop, but he thought that it could at least take a stand against the sympathetic strike and could refuse to deal with "corrupt or unfair" unions.[6]

The closest Drew came to the realization of his desire for the formation of the right kind of national general contractors' association was the establishment in February 1912 of the National Association of Building Trades Employers (NABTE). Since the association appeared to be committed to opposing the sympathetic and the jurisdictional strike, which Drew was certain would result in "a great increase in open-shop operations," he solicited funds for the NABTE from national employer associations, offered advice on labor policy to the NABTE's secretary and dominant figure, I. H. Scates, and sought to persuade general contractors to join the organization. The NABTE, however, failed to take the kind of stand on the labor question for which Drew had hoped.[7]

Since he could not persuade general contractors to form the kind of national association that would be of aid to the open shop, Drew, lowering his sights, campaigned against clauses in building contracts requiring the use of union labor. To include such a contract clause, Drew contended, was to do an "injustice" to the large majority of nonunion building trades workers. Under "unrestricted conditions," moreover, Drew claimed, the general contractor could get both the "best prices and best work." When public authorities limited construction to firms employing union labor, Drew advised the parties adversely affected by such contracts that they were "void" and that the issuing authority was subject to suit.[8]

The degree of Drew's involvement in open shop campaigns across the country varied from place to place and time to time. Sometimes, as in the instances of Spokane, Washington, and Birmingham, Alabama, Drew supplied data helpful to the open shop cause that local activists had requested. Recognized by employers as an expert in the area of labor law, Drew sometimes provided requested legal advice, responding to inquiries regarding such matters as strikes and boycotts.[9]

Drew played an especially important role in counseling the Business Men's Association of Omaha (BMA). Founded in 1903 after a "serious strike and lockout" in the building trades, the BMA had converted Omaha into an open shop city. Since Omaha was free of labor trouble for many years after 1903, employers, "little by little," began once again to deal with unions, with the result that the city, after a time, was on the way to becoming a closed shop community. When the BMA in 1916 and early 1917 began considering agreements with the building trades unions designed to exclude outside contractors from working in Omaha, the news set off alarm bells in the NEA. Drew warned the BMA that if it went the union route, Omaha would be "at a serious and even ruinous disadvantage in competition" with open shop cities, and J. A. G. Badorf, then the NEA's district manager in the area, struck up a relationship with the BMA's secretary, Alvin T. Johnson. Learning that Johnson had expressed a favorable interest in some kind of arbitration agreement with the unions to do away with strikes, Drew bombarded the secretary with information concerning the fate of such plans in New York, Chicago, and San Francisco. After Badorf "made a very good impression" in a speech at a BMA meeting at the end of March 1917, the association reaffirmed its allegiance to the open shop, and it then turned to Drew for advice regarding the maintenance of that policy. He counseled against leaving decisions regarding wages and

working conditions to individual employers lest this lead to "unfair competition" and brought "reproach upon the open shop." He suggested that some
machinery be established that would permit employees to air their
grievances.[10]

In Pittsburgh, Columbus, Ohio, and Buffalo, Drew or one of his aides
played some part either in the decision of an employer group to commit itself to
the open shop or in the creation of an employer association that took that stand.
After he spoke to Pittsburgh's master builders in behalf of the open shop in the
fall of 1906, the city's Builders' League unanimously approved an open shop
resolution that it successfully implemented. In Columbus, where employers
had asked Drew as early as 1907 to advise and assist them in their desire "to get
out of the closed shop woods," it was Drew's aide, H. R. Brady, who in 1915
was instrumental in the organization of an association that included all employers engaged in the manufacture or erection of building materials and that
committed itself to the open shop. Drew sought to encourage the new organization, and the NEA assisted it in securing workers to replace strikers.[11]

In Buffalo, Brady followed the aforementioned successful NEA effort in
placing structural steel erection on an open shop basis in late 1914 and early
1915 by helping to organize a citywide employers' association. Working with
this organization and the city's Builders' Exchange, the NEA succeeded in
making Buffalo "practically an open-shop town in the building industry." Even
in New York, a closed shop city in the building trades except for structural steel
erection, when the marble employers ran into trouble with the union in their
trade, they not only declared for the open shop but offered Drew a retainer to
help them deal with a strike and attendant legal matters. Although "gratified"
that he had been approached by a group that had been "most strongly opposed"
to the NEA, Drew was unable to accept the offer. He did, however, agree to
assist the employers.[12]

Drew was instrumental in stimulating and assisting open shop efforts in
New England. Following a building trades strike in 1910 in Hartford, Connecticut, a strongly unionized city, Drew made several trips there to speak to
manufacturers and businessmen. James Emery supplemented Drew's efforts—
the two men were "in a class by [themselves]," according to a leading manufacturer in the city—and the result was the formation of a strong employers'
association representing the city's various business interests. The open shop
made steady gains in Hartford in the next several years and was firmly established there when the United States went to war in April 1917. As part of "a
general open-shop movement" in New England that he was "helping to push
along," Drew spoke to the Springfield (Massachusetts) Employers' Association in 1916 and found the organization "determined to accomplish something"
regarding the open shop.[13]

Drew gained such a formidable reputation as someone who could bring
the open shop to a community that wished to move in that direction that he
could not accept all the offers that came his way to help launch or assist such
efforts. That reputation was formed in 1907 as the result primarily of the large

part Drew played in bringing the open shop to Washington, D.C., and Duluth, Minnesota. In May 1907 the Employers' Association of the Building Trades of the District of Columbia invited Drew to come to the nation's capital to "take over a big fight in the Building Trades." Thinking that this would be "a lively and interesting job" because Washington was the headquarters of the AFL and building was its "one great industry," Drew accepted the offer and was retained as counsel and advisor to the Employers' Association and the Master Builders.[14]

Disturbed by the increase in building costs and the decline in construction in Washington, the Employers' Association attributed this state of affairs to the closed shop and the attendant union restrictive practices that had prevailed in the building industry in the District for some years. Because of the allegedly "abnormal costs" for building labor and building materials, the federal government in 1907 was considering a halt in building in the District except for what was "absolutely necessary."

What specifically triggered the employer invitation to Drew to come to Washington was a dispute between master plumbers and journeymen, who were not completely unionized, regarding the right of the former to employ nonunion plumbers. The dispute was twice submitted to arbitration, the master plumbers being upheld on each occasion. After the second arbitration decision, the Federated Trade Unions of the city threatened a strike unless all nonunion plumbers were discharged, which led to a third arbitration at the end of May 1907. This time the arbitrators not only ruled, as before, that master plumbers could employ nonunion plumbers but also that other trades must not strike to secure the discharge of the nonunionists. When some ironworkers went out on strike despite this, the Employers' Association on June 6 ordered a lockout of all trades refusing to work with the nonunion plumbers.[15]

With Drew energetically directing strategy, the builders replaced all unionists who struck in violation of the award and replaced them with resident nonunion workers or workers brought to the city from New York, Philadelphia, and Boston in groups of anywhere from ten to one hundred. The open shop was declared at the same time in each of the trades in which union members refused to work alongside nonunionists. Drew, typically, advised the employers to grant the strikebreakers assurance of "permanent employment" and not to reduce their wages but to insist on a fair day's work for a fair day's pay. He also mounted a campaign of "publicity and education" directed particularly at the District's owners, bankers, and businessmen, telling them that they were "the real parties" in the fight because they paid the difference in cost between closed shop and open shop operation. The city's business interests came out "solidly in favor of the open shop" and rendered the cause, as Drew put it, "much quiet but effective assistance." Drew, indeed, saw this as "the most significant feature" of the dispute. The officers of the international unions in the building trades, assembled in Washington in September 1907, sought to meet with the Employers' Association to resolve the dispute, but the employers, who had the upper hand by then, refused.

To counter the heavy picketing in the strike by the bricklayers, Drew filed an injunction suit in federal court that had an immediately quieting effect and that the court eventually granted. By the late spring of 1908 the open shop had been "firmly established" in Washington. The CIAA's *Square Deal* lauded Drew's efforts, asserting that "no one" had "rendered more valuable service" in promoting the open shop than he.[16]

Drew's success in Washington led to an invitation to him from Duluth to direct a similar effort there. As in Washington, the closed shop had become the norm in the building industry in Duluth, with the result that wage scales in the building trades in the city were higher even than in New York. The dispute in Duluth that led to the call to Drew stemmed from the decision of a large local general contractor who had been the successful bidder for the erection of a large building in the city to award the subcontract for the steel erection to the American Bridge Company. When the NEA firm began the job with open shop workers, the city's Structural Building Trades Alliance, in violation of its contract, initiated a sympathetic strike to compel the discharge of the nonunion workers. The general contractor thereupon offered to pay American Bridge the full contract price if it would permit the general contractor to arrange for the steel erection on a closed shop basis. When American Bridge refused the offer, the city's contractors, "aroused" by the strike, issued a declaration on November 28, 1907, favoring the open shop.[17]

Arriving in Duluth at the beginning of December, Drew addressed several meetings a day during the next few days and started what he characterized as "a landslide" in favor of the open shop. The city's Builders' Exchange, the Real Estate Exchange Board, the Commercial Club, and city architects all endorsed the open shop. A mass meeting of citizens on December 4 approved a resolution that was apparently Drew's handiwork condemning the closed shop in the strongest possible terms and claiming that it had "seriously handicapped" Duluth's economic growth "in competition with other cities." The resolution proclaimed support for the adoption of the open shop in "every branch of business industry and enterprise" in the city and urged the Duluth Commercial Club to appoint an open shop committee to take charge of the fight against the unions. A Citizens' Association was quickly formed in response to the resolution to raise such funds as were needed to conduct the struggle.

Drew had hoped "to get them started" in Duluth so that they could "run it themselves," and he succeeded in doing just that. Workers were brought in from outside Duluth to man the jobs left vacant by the strikers and were joined by strikers returning to their jobs. The secretary of the Builders' Exchange later reported that the Structural Building Trades Alliance had been outmaneuvered in the dispute and simply "went to pieces." Some unions surrendered and advised their members to return to work, some started "co-operative shops" to sustain their members, and some continued the struggle. Within a few months, the fight was over, and the open shop had become the rule in Duluth.[18]

Despite the economic slump in the nation, Duluth experienced a "building boom" following the city's introduction of the open shop. "The men are getting disgusted," an International Association of Bridge and Structural Iron Workers (IABSIW) official reported to John McNamara in July 1910, "for it seems as though every unfair company in the country are [*sic*] doing some work here." Although these had been efforts to form some kind of central union body in the city, "the locals," the official remarked, "seem[ed] to remember Drew" and refused to sign a charter. Drew, from whom the Duluth employers continued to seek advice, regarded Duluth as one of his greatest successes as an open shop advocate.[19]

The successful implementation of the open shop in Washington and Duluth made Drew a commanding figure in the fight against unionism in the years before World War I. The CIAA, one of its leaders declared regarding the success of the NEA commissioner in promoting the open shop, had come to rely on Drew as "the practical man who can secure practical results in the quickest and easiest way." The IABSIW, for different reasons, was inclined to agree. Drew, its official journal remarked in April 1908, "seems to have the power to hypnotize a community (otherwise sane) into the belief that the way to bring prosperity is to align businessmen against the laboring man in an effort to reduce his purchasing power."[20]

It was Drew's published account of his success in Duluth that led the Gary Commercial Club, concerned about high building costs in that city, to enlist the aid of the NEA commissioner at the beginning of 1911. Although Gary's Contractors and Material Men's Association had already declared for the open shop, the Commercial Club was not ready "to show an open hand." Drew, however, advised that it was "a serious mistake" for the club not to make its position known. The club followed Drew's advice and, having done so, its secretary wrote Drew, "Tell us how to proceed."

The major labor dispute once Gary's business leaders had declared for the open shop involved the building trades. As Drew saw it, the principal problem facing the contractors was "to get men" to replace strikers. Drew arranged to have workers brought in from outside Gary, and these mechanics, as well as the willingness of some Gary unionists to work alongside nonunion men, enabled the contractors to keep their jobs manned during the strike. "[T]he whole town was stirred up," and the fight was soon won. "GARY is an absolutely OPEN SHOP TOWN," the Commercial Club's secretary wrote Drew before the year was out. "[W]e have forgotten there ever was a thing called UNIONISM. [E]very man now controls his own Business." At the end of the next year, the club claimed that even though contractors had not cut wages, lengthened hours, or altered working conditions, building costs had been reduced 12 percent in the city since the open shop had been introduced.[21]

Wilmington, Delaware, was the last city Drew aided in adopting the open shop before the United States entered World War I. He was invited there, it is not clear by whom, in the spring of 1916 when the city faced a threatened strike by the building trades unions for the closed shop. He quickly organized an Employers' Association consisting of 150 of "the best concerns" as charter members. Since it had been his experience that building contractors, who, as he regularly noted, were just the "agents" of the owners, could not be held in line "without the pressure of some outside force," he arranged for a committee of manufacturers and representatives of other business interests to visit the contractors to deliver an open shop message, which caused them to see the "light." With the city's business interests united behind the contractors on the open shop issue, the threatened general strike dissipated on May 1 into a walkout of fifteen electricians, whose places were promptly filled. This was pretty much "the end of the matter," leaving building in Wilmington "practically on an open-shop basis."[22]

Drew continued to advise the Wilmington Employers' Association on the procedures it should follow once the open shop had been established in the city. When there was a move in June 1916 to organize the city's textile workers, the association asked Drew for a detective, which he promptly supplied. Believing that it was "better" for employers "to head off trouble than to fight it," Drew advised management to bring working conditions to "a proper level" if they were not already there and to adopt some form of employee representation as well as schemes of welfare capitalism. He counseled the city's Manufacturers' Association on the drawing up of yellow-dog contracts but advised against resort to blacklists. The Manufacturers' Association continued to seek Drew's advice after the war.[23]

Quite apart from his effort to spread the open shop to the building trades and various communities, Drew became involved in the battle to establish the open shop by firms that erected oil and gas tanks, particularly in Oklahoma and Texas. The seven largest plate contractors, who were responsible for about 80–90 percent of the tank work in the nation, decided in the fall of 1914 to break off relations with the Brotherhood of Boilermakers, Iron Shipbuilders and Helpers of America because of behavior by the union membership that the union's leadership itself later condemned. Living in small towns near where they worked in the oil fields, the tank workers were prone to drunkenness and occasionally bizarre behavior. "They tear up sheets and blankets and break up lights in the camp and demand" that they be replaced, an NEA official reported to Drew, and "they shoot a man same as a dog here and no questions asked." They were apt to strike over "foolish grievances," as the union leadership conceded, and sometimes in violation of contract. Drew was especially exercised about the permit system the Boilermakers' Union used in the fields. Although unable to supply anywhere near enough workers to the contractors, the union nevertheless refused to admit new members and instead permitted nonunion workers to take available jobs on the condition that they turn over 10 percent of their wages to the union.[24]

Seeking assistance in dealing with their labor troubles, the plate contractors turned to Drew, who sent one of his aides, John W. Poushey, to the Oklahoma fields to examine the situation. "The time is ripe for an open shop fight there," Poushey soon reported to Drew. Drew offered to aid the plate contractors and even to serve as their counsel, an offer that was accepted.

In November 1914 the seven plate contractors formed themselves into the

American Erectors' Association (AEA). The association's object, its constitution declared, was the "institution and maintenance of the Open Shop principle in the employment of labor in the erection of steel tanks, oil refinery work, and other plate and steel iron work." Along with his NEA duties, Poushey served as the AEA's secretary. Informed that the new organization anticipated trouble from the union, Drew advised the NEA's district manager in Kansas City, where union headquarters were located, to place a man "inside of the union there" and also to send someone to Oklahoma to gather information.[25]

The Boilermakers called a strike against the plate contractors on January 18, 1915, after the latter made it clear that they would not recognize the union or permit any union stewards on the job. About one thousand men were involved in the strike in the Oklahoma oil fields, and there were additional strikes in Texas. Poushey and the NEA helped supply the contractors with strike replacements, and Drew provided advice regarding their protection, expressing his usual caution about the use of private guards in labor disputes. He also counseled the contractors regarding the prosecution of strikers believed guilty of violence. AEA members had all the workers they needed by the end of March, and the contractors claimed that their employees were doing "much better work" than had been possible under union conditions. By the middle of April the strike was over, and the union had been defeated.[26]

Following the strike, the AEA accepted Drew's advice to appoint the NEA's H. R. Brady as a field man. As the AEA's counsel, Drew offered the plate contractors advice on how best to maintain the open shop, particularly stressing the importance of foremen in that regard. Drew advised the AEA that, other things being equal, it should give preference in employment to nonunion workers and that at least 50 percent of a company's skilled workers should be nonunion mechanics. He advised the employers to consider all demands and grievances presented by committees of their workers provided that at least 50 percent of the committee members were nonunion workers and all members were employees of the particular contractor. He did advise, however, that workers should not be discriminated against for protesting working conditions. The AEA continued to refuse to deal with the Boilermakers, but about half of its workers were union members as of March 1917, presumably having been engaged as individuals.[27]

Because of the NEA's and his own experience in dealing with the problem of dynamiting, Drew came to play a behind-the-scenes part on the management side in the great railroad shopmen's strike on the Harriman lines that began on September 30, 1911. The principal cause of the dispute was the refusal of the railroad management to negotiate with the System Federation of the Harriman lines, a coalition of the shopcraft unions on the eight Harriman roads, even though the management was willing to meet with the individual unions. Julius Kruttschnitt, director of maintenance and operations of the Union Pacific and Southern Pacific and the effective operating head of the Harriman lines, claimed that the Harriman system was being asked to "deliver itself practically bound hand and foot into the power" of the unions that made up the Federation.

The strike was accompanied by some "widely scattered violence" as well as the sabotage of railroad property. The railroad management dismissed the strikers and secured replacements and was able by January 1, 1912, to operate successfully without its former employees. The strike then "became a gruelling endurance test for the men," with defeat "inevitable," although the prolonged dispute was not officially called off until June 28, 1915.[28]

On March 18, 1912, a locomotive boiler exploded in the Southern Pacific railroad yards in San Antonio, resulting ultimately in thirty-two deaths, mostly strikebreakers. Expert opinion was divided as to whether the locomotive had been dynamited or had exploded because of excessive steam pressure. When the "army of detectives" the Harriman management had employed failed to discover the "foul play" that Kruttschnitt suspected had caused the explosion, the railroad executive, whom Drew had already contacted for financial assistance in seeking to apprehend the dynamiters of open shop work, turned to the NEA commissioner for advice and assistance. Drew was willing to accept the assignment, he later told Kruttschnitt, because of "a certain community of interest . . . among all employers" but, more likely, because he feared that if unionists could "get away" with this first big explosion since the McNamara guilty pleas, the NEA's "whole work" in that case was "likely to be of no benefit."[29]

Although Drew relied on more than one detective "to find some sources of information" about the San Antonio explosion, the "one good man" he hoped could break the case was the NEA commissioner's favorite detective, Robert J. Foster. Drew instructed Foster to gain the confidence of John Scott, the secretary-treasurer of the Harriman System Federation, whom Drew envisioned as playing the role of John J. McNamara in the San Antonio case. Drew advised Foster to see if he could possibly "work a dictograph" on Scott, as he had on Frank Ryan and Clarence Darrow. Foster first went to San Antonio, where his espionage efforts convinced him that the locomotive had been dynamited. After proceeding to San Francisco, Foster, who had disguised his identity and posed as "a crank of socialism," and his wife developed a friendship with Scott and his wife. Foster was soon aiding Scott in putting out the System Federation's news bulletin, and the detective also handled Scott's incoming mail.

Foster was able after some months to have his operatives go through Scott's records. Scott, however, the detective reported, had "burned a lot of letters," and no evidence was discovered to link the System Federation with the San Antonio explosion. Foster did, however, discover that the Federation used "inside men," unionists who had remained at work during the strike so as to provide information about their employer and who had committed acts of sabotage against railroad property. Foster provided Kruttschnitt with a list of such men, which presumably led to their dismissal. Foster was also able to establish a relationship with Scott that paved the way for the NEA's later involvement in the great railroad shopmen's strike of 1921–22. For a few years after the failed Drew-Foster effort to discover the cause of the San Antonio explosion, "a virtual open shop" prevailed in the shops of the Union Pacific and some other Harriman roads, a result that could only have pleased Drew.[30]

Drew's central position as a promoter of the open shop was further evidenced by his role in such "peak associations" as the CIAA, the National Council for Industrial Defense (NCID), and the National Association of Manufacturers (NAM). When the major employer associations decided that they needed someone to represent them before the Commission on Industrial Relations, they selected Drew. He was also one of the organizers of the National Industrial Conference Board (NICB).

Drew was of particular importance to the CIAA, with which, as previously noted, he had been closely associated in Grand Rapids even before he became the NEA's commissioner. He addressed its 1906 convention on "The Closed Shop in the Building Industry," served on several of its committees, and was an important contributor to its journal, the *Square Deal.* He was, above all, the person on whom the CIAA called when it was requested to assist an open shop effort in one community or another.[31]

Drew was among those present at the meeting of the National Trades Associations on August 19, 1907, that launched the NCID. Fresh from his victory in Washington, Drew made it clear that the NEA's involvement in the new organization being contemplated would have to be limited to the open shop, an issue he urged the gathering to address. A member of the committee of seven the delegates selected to take action on the issues raised at the meeting, Drew actively participated in the committee sessions following the August conclave that worked out the details of organization for what became the NCID. Having said at the August 19 meeting that the proposed new organization, by showing that it had "the good[s]," could secure the financial assistance of the railroads and the trusts, Drew was made chairman of the NCID's finance committee. As we shall see, he also aided the NCID's legislative lobbying in Washington and elsewhere.[32]

Associated with the NAM in the launching of the NCID, Drew forged even closer ties between the NEA and the manufacturers' association, and the two organizations agreed in 1910 to establish and fund the National Open Shop Publicity Bureau, with Drew as the bureau's manager. The purpose of the bureau was to secure "recognition and patronage" for open shop contractors and to eliminate the closed shop, which meant that Drew's purpose had become the bureau's purpose. "Patronize the Open Shop Contractor in Your Building Operations" was the bureau's slogan. The focus on the building industry reflected Drew's reiterated view of the centrality of that industry and its importance to all businessmen, including manufacturers.[33]

The Open Shop Publicity Bureau issued a series of bulletins such as Drew's *The Story of Duluth, A Letter to the Architect,* and *Labor Unions and the Law.* Initially, according to Drew, never one to underestimate his success, the bureau met with "a tremendous response." It developed a mailing list of two hundred and received fifteen thousand requests for its first bulletin as well as a large number of letters from owners, builders, and architects. By 1915, however, the NAM had ended its support of the bureau, which led to its demise. Drew's ties to the NAM, however, were not limited to his role as the manager of the Open Shop Publicity Bureau. He was associated with the NAM in the NCID, he drew up several of the resolutions at the NAM's 1911 convention, and the NAM circulated his 1912 Senate testimony in opposition to anti-injunction legislation. After World War I, as will become evident, Drew was conspicuously involved in the NAM's efforts to promote the open shop in the nation.[34]

Not only was Drew interested in cooperation between the NEA and the NAM, but he also favored the formation of some kind of "joint council" of national employer associations interested in labor matters to provide for cooperation among them and to exchange ideas. At a meeting of Drew, the general manager of the NAM, and the commissioner of the National Metal Trades Associations (NMTA) to consider the formation of a National Federation of Organizations, the three agreed that Drew should call a preliminary meeting for this purpose. Responding to Drew's invitation, representatives of eight employer associations met on October 19, 1912, but the idea of a national federation died aborning.[35] It was, however, a precursor in a sense of the Joint Committee of Associated Employers that was formed in 1914.

The guilty pleas of the McNamara brothers following the dynamiting of the *Los Angeles Times* building, as Allen Davis has remarked, were "almost a personal tragedy" for some progressive reformers. Fearing that their efforts to improve working conditions would be "overshadowed by the sensational headlines about strikes and violence," a group of these reformers, consequently, petitioned President William Howard Taft in late December 1911 to establish a federal commission on industrial relations. The first item on the list of subjects the petitioners wished such a commission to investigate was "conditions of labor during the last six years in the structural iron trade." As Drew saw it, "certain social reformers and apologists for union violence," supported by organized labor, wanted a government study that would yield "a purely partisan report" that would "justify or at least condone" labor's use of violence by blaming it on "employer oppression" of the workingman.[36]

The recommendation of the reformers bore fruit when President Taft on August 23, 1912, signed into law a bill providing for the creation of the Commission on Industrial Relations. The commission was to consist of nine presidentially appointed members, three to represent management; three, labor; and three, the public. A Democratic Senate blocked Taft's selections for the commission, which left the choice to the incoming president, Woodrow Wilson. As the employer members, Wilson selected Harris Weinstock, who operated a closed shop, Thruston Ballard, "a paternalistic and highly progressive employer," and Frederick Delano, president of the Wabash Railroad. The Taft appointees to the commission had included the NAM's Ferdinand C. Schwedtman, who, in effect, represented the open shop employers, and as the committee's chairman, Taft had appointed the conservative Senator George B. Sutherland. Wilson did not name Schwedtman or any other open shop representative to the commission, and as the commission's chairman, drawn from the public members, he appointed Frank P. Walsh, a prolabor attorney.

Drew did not think that the commission Wilson appointed was "a safe one." He complained that the president had appointed the three labor representatives to the commission only after administration consultation with organized labor but that the employer associations had had no say in the choice of the employer members. As Drew saw it, moreover, the three representatives of the public on the commission, Walsh, Mrs. J. Borden Harriman, and Professor John R. Commons, were all committed to the protection of organized labor. As the work of the commission proceeded, however, Drew came to a rather favorable view of Commons, whom he characterized as the "one ray of hope" on the commission because of his "apparent honesty of purpose and desire for constructive results."[37]

Because of their distrust of the commission and its membership, the open shop employer associations initially made no collective effort to present their view of the labor question to the commission. The employers also complained about the "favoritism for organized labor" displayed by the commission at its public hearings in Washington, New York, and Philadelphia, Drew protesting that employer witnesses had been "subjected to sarcastic and, in some cases, rude treatment." When representatives of several employer associations conferred about the matter at the NAM's annual convention in May 1914, they decided that they had erred in distancing themselves from the commission's work, since that would enable the commission to say that it was not the commission's fault if the employers had chosen not to avail themselves of the opportunity to present their views. James Emery thereupon inquired of Walsh whether the commission would consider the "continuing formal presentation" before it by the employers through "counsel of standing, experience and capacity." Walsh indicated that he did not object to the proposal.[38]

Meeting on July 24, 1914, representatives of the national employer associations "chiefly known for their open shop principle," the NMTA, the National Founders' Association (NFA), the NAM, the NCID, and the NEA, agreed to constitute themselves as the Joint Committee of Associated Employers with the aim of securing proper representation of employer interests in the investigations and at the hearings of the Commission on Industrial Relations. They selected Drew as their counsel, not only, we can safely assume, because of the relationship of the dynamiting of NEA structures to the creation of the commission, but also because they were simply ratifying an established fact: Drew had become the foremost exponent of the open shop principle in American industry. When Drew discussed his role with Walsh, the commission chairman told him that the commission would call any witnesses whom Drew proposed, ask the questions Drew had submitted, provide him the special reports investigators had prepared before the commission took final action on them, and permit him to submit statements in rebuttal of purported statements of fact.[39]

While helping to gather information for what turned out to be Luke Grant's study for the commission of the structural iron industry, Drew began to act on his presumption that the work of the commission presented "a greater opportunity" to the employers than to the unions because the employers, in Drew's estimation, were rarely able to gain public attention for their views. The plan Drew worked out was to secure an outline of the commission's plans for hearings in a particular city, visit the city to interview employers, select "strong" employer witnesses, and have them testify as to why they operated on an open shop basis. Drew himself attended the hearings or sent substitutes and submitted questions to witnesses through the commission's counsel. The plan worked to Drew's satisfaction when put into effect at the commission's Chicago hearings. As Drew noted, the employer side was "forcibly presented" and received a good deal of press attention. This was the "first time," Drew insisted, that the "evils" of organized labor had been brought to public attention.[40]

Drew regarded the Los Angeles and San Francisco hearings as "most important" because of "the high industrial tension" on the West Coast. The Chicago success, from Drew's perspective, was repeated on the West Coast. In Los Angeles, the city's conspicuous foes of organized labor, Harrison Gray Otis, F. J. Zeehandelaar, and Fred Baker, were provided with a forum to expound their views on the evils of unionism. Among others, Grant Fee, the president of the San Francisco Building Trades Employers' Association, played a similar role in the Bay city.[41]

Drew suggested to the commission that, quite apart from its hearings in individual cities, it should conduct a series of hearings focusing on "certain great national industries" at which evidence could be provided in a "systematic, consecutive and comprehensive manner." According to Drew, Walsh approved the suggestion, but it never came to fruition. It is surprising, indeed, that although it assigned one of its investigators to study the structural iron industry, the commission did not conduct public hearings on labor relations in that industry given the relationship of that subject to the creation of the commission itself. When Drew testified before the commission, it was as part of a session not on the structural iron industry but rather on labor and the law. Drew, typically, complained that unions could not legally be sued. He insisted that "the chief primary aim" of unionism was "the establishment of the closed shop" and that the closed shop led "naturally to force as a method." He attacked efforts to curb the use of injunctions in labor disputes and defended himself against the charge of having participated in the "kidnapping" of John McNamara.[42]

The head of the commission's Research Division, Charles V. McCarthy, and commission member Commons sought to bring to the commission something resembling the "Wisconsin Idea," the gathering of facts by an agency like Wisconsin's Legislative Reference Bureau as the basis for drawing up legislative measures. They proposed the creation of an advisory committee made up of representatives of the employers and organized labor to which legislative proposals being considered by the commission, along with supporting factual information, could be submitted before the commission took formal action on them. The Joint Committee of Associated Employers agreed to the idea when Commons and McCarthy proposed it to them, Drew considering the plan "an epoch-making step." Several meetings followed at which Joint Committee members and AFL representatives discussed unemployment, industrial safety and sanitation, and vocational education. The conferences were "most friendly," Drew reported, and "practical agreement" was reached on "a number of fundamentals" relating to legislation dealing with the subjects under discussion. It was Commons's plan to proceed from "the least disputatious issues," like those noted, to far more contentious matters such as collective bargaining and the closed and open shop.[43]

Frank Walsh was much less than enthusiastic about the Commons-McCarthy plan. He complained to an acquaintance that what was taking place was "little short of espionage on our work by the representatives of those forces in the country [the open shop employers] which a great majority of the workers, at least, believe to be the principal despoilers of their rights and the most notorious exploiters of their kind." Because of budget problems, Walsh in late February 1915 sharply reduced the funding for the Research Division, and McCarthy was shortly thereafter replaced by Basil Manly as the division's director. Some weeks later Walsh let it be known that the conferences were not to be resumed.[44]

Unable to agree, the commission issued three reports in August 1915, a report prepared by Manly and endorsed by Walsh and the three labor members, a report by the three employer representatives, and a report by Commons and Mrs. Harriman that the three employer members also endorsed. The Manly report, which was anathema to Drew, was viewed by the public as the "official" report because it appeared first when the commission's *Final Report* was transmitted to Congress. As Drew correctly pointed out, however, only the Commons-Harriman report among the three commanded a commission majority.[45]

Manly noted that although the vast majority of employer representatives who came before the commission maintained what they called an open shop, they would not, "as a rule, willingly or knowingly employ union men." Employer statements that they were willing to deal with their own employees but not with an outside organization, Manly claimed, had been "generally found to be specious." The Manly report recommended that the right of workers to organize for their "individual and collective interests" be guaranteed by the Constitution and protected by legislation. It recommended further that the Federal Trade Commission be empowered to investigate "the unfair treatment of labor in all respects."

Although the three employer representatives maintained that workers were justified in organizing to protect themselves against "exploitation and oppression," they concluded that the unions had "not come into court with clean hands." The employers asserted their belief in collective bargaining "when fairly and properly conducted" but noted at the same time that employers who attributed their refusal to bargain to the behavior of the unions had "good cause" for this stance. The reasons they cited for the refusal of employers to deal with unions were the reasons Drew regularly noted in defending the open shop.

In their report, Commons and Harriman recommended the establishment of state and federal industrial commissions to administer all labor laws. The federal commission was to seek the advice of an "advisory representative council" composed of employer and labor members as well as the secretaries of commerce and of labor. This was, in effect, a refurbishing of the Commons-McCarthy scheme that Drew had found workable but that Walsh had torpedoed.[46]

As for the Luke Grant report on the NEA and the IABSIW that the commission had authorized, Drew thought it significant that although Grant was himself a union member, he had found "no wrongs or oppressions under the open shop" to justify the IABSIW's dynamiting campaign. Although he disputed Grant's assertions regarding the wages paid by NEA members, Drew regarded the report as "in the main fair" and as refuting the assumption of the reformers who had urged the establishment of the commission.[47]

Drew's experience as counsel for the Joint Committee of Associated Employers led to his involvement in the founding of the National Industrial Conference Board (now the Conference Board). After the Joint Committee's activity came to an end, four of its members, Drew, Emery, Magnus W. Alexander, employment manager at General Electric's West Lynn, Massachusetts, plant, and William H. Barr, president of the NFA, remained in "close contact." Alexander, who had written Drew in the fall of 1913 about the need to initiate a national education campaign to create "a more just opinion of the industrial problem . . . and of the true position of the employer in relation to his employees," suggested to the NEA commissioner the next year that employer representatives should meet quietly to discuss "the industrial problem." This led to the first of the Yama Conferences in New York State beginning on June 5, 1915.[48]

The purpose of the first Yama Conference, attended by twenty-three employers and representatives of employer associations, was to discuss the increasing strife between labor and capital and "the effect of the rapidly multiplying amount of restrictive labor and social legislation on the conduct of business." Reacting in exaggerated fashion to the reforms of the Progressive Era and especially to Woodrow Wilson's New Freedom, those present saw business at the time as operating in a "hostile atmosphere." It fell to Drew at the meeting, in familiar fashion and to warm applause, to attack the closed shop in the building industry and to note the alleged cost benefits of construction under open shop conditions. Taking a position that Drew had long advocated, those present warned that the open shop alone would not make for "general improvement" unless employers behaved responsibly toward their employees and that attacks on labor unions "as such" were unwise and improper.[49]

Following a second Yama Conference in September 1915, representatives of twelve national employer associations met on May 5, 1916, to establish the

National Industrial Conference Board. Its membership was open to all "national associations of industrial employers." Its purposes, the NICB soon announced, were to (1) stimulate the study and the "equitable solution of economic issues in industry"; (2) foster "harmonious relations" between employer and employee; (3) assist in the formulation of "sound and constructive economic legislation"; (4) foster cooperation between government and industry; (5) present facts to the public regarding industry; (6) "stimulate the employer to maintain good conditions of work," to "provide fair treatment for his workers and to take personal interest in them"; and (7) "develop among the employees a reasonable attitude toward manufactures and other industry, to inspire a sense of fair play, efficiency and loyalty." As of early 1917 the NICB was made up of two delegates from twelve different national associations and had a "staff of experts" to investigate industrial problems.[50]

Drew, who predicted that the NICB would be attacked by "the unions, the Socialists, the uplifters, and even well-intentioned, scientific, meddling university theorists," informed Walter Lippmann that the board was "not a fighting organization" and that its focus would be on "careful research and constructive work." Writing the president of the National City Bank, Drew commented regarding the NICB, "We want to make it a supreme court on industrial matters, the officially-recognized voice of the business man and employer, its conclusions and recommendations accepted and followed because of the deliberative method by which they have been reached and the reason and proof upon which they are based." Drew, of course, hoped to make that "officially-recognized voice" speak in behalf of his concept of the open shop, and after World War I he made a determined effort to achieve that result.[51]

Like so many big employers and representatives of employer organizations at the time the NICB was formed, Drew was concerned about "a growing distrust of business" that he believed had resulted in "a flood of restrictive legislation." From the beginning of his commissionership, Drew had interpreted his responsibilities as including the effort to combat federal and state legislation that he believed adversely affected employer interests in general and the interests of NEA members and the open shop in particular. Emery and he, Drew wrote his parents in June 1906, "call ourselves the bulwarks of defense for the Nation's rights. You would be surprised," he asserted, "at all the fool things proposed to be passed as laws." In soliciting NEA membership, Drew noted the association's role in fighting "pernicious labor legislation in Washington." Robert H. Wiebe has asserted that "by 1910 every employer association had placed politics first on its agenda." This, as a matter of fact, was not true of the NEA, but it did attach considerable importance to the subject.[52]

Drew was especially concerned about efforts to enact federal anti-injunction and eight-hour-day legislation and the growing support in the states for employer liability and workmen's compensation legislation. Unions sought legislative curbs on the use of the injunction, Drew maintained, because courts of equity issued the writ to halt union boycotts, sympathetic strikes, and "the organized intimidation and violence of the picket line and other familiar forms of coercion common to union warfare." If anti-injunction laws such as the AFL was seeking were enacted, Drew contended, it would remove an "obstacle" to the Federation's securing a monopoly of the labor market and the closed shop. Labor, Drew charged, was seeking "special immunity and privileges" for one class that was "openly and avowedly engaged in warfare with another class." Drew called on NEA members to oppose the Pearre anti-injunction bill, which Congress considered in 1907 and 1908 but which did not pass; and, in the name of the NEA, he joined in the successful NCID campaign in 1908 to prevent the Republican party from inserting an anti-injunction plank in its 1908 platform.[53]

At the request of the NCID, Drew testified against the Clayton anti-injunction bill in 1912. When the Senate rejected the bill, Drew gave himself some of the credit, attributing the result, in part, to his recital of "the long record of crimes in the iron erection industry." When another version of the measure was enacted in 1914, Drew correctly stated that it was "simply declaratory of existing law in those particulars where it can be said to be of benefit to the unions." He had been especially concerned in opposing the 1912 bill about its providing for jury trials in contempt cases. Although the 1914 Clayton Act did provide for jury trials, it severely limited the application of contempt procedures.[54]

Drew professed to be no more disturbed by the Clayton Act's provisions regarding unions and the antitrust law than about its anti-injunction provisions. Like the CIAA, he had been denouncing union efforts to seek exemption for themselves from the antitrust legislation as "radical and vicious class legislation." The Clayton Act provided such an exemption, but only when unions were "lawfully" pursuing "legitimate objectives," which Drew correctly understood as essentially reaffirming existing law.[55]

Drew played a prominent role in organizing employer opposition to a federal eight-hour bill that organized labor was urging in 1908. The measure specified the eight-hour-day standard for government construction and subjected contractors and subcontractors to penalty for violations. Passage of the bill, Drew pointed out to NEA members, would mean that no structural steel could be used in government buildings that came from shops working more than eight hours a day, as the shops then were. Since it was a "practical impossibility," Drew insisted, to run the same shop on a different schedule of hours for those workers fabricating steel for government buildings and for other workers, the effect of the bill would be to prevent the steel shops from bidding on government work unless they adopted the eight-hour day for all their workers. He insisted, also, that the measure was not intended to limit hours of work but rather to provide "a unit by which to measure wages."[56]

Emery, for the NCID, was in charge of the employer effort to defeat the eight-hour bill, with Drew serving as his key ally. As he informed his parents in February 1908, Drew was "burning the wires" to NEA members, urging them to testify against the bill before the House Labor Committee. For two days the NEA commissioner himself questioned employer witnesses appearing before the committee and elicited testimony from them that the measure would "hamper" work on government buildings and "materially increase" costs and that it was really a wage, not an hours, bill. Not only did the CIAA praise Drew's efforts in opposing the bill, but the chairman of the House Labor Committee told the NEA commissioner that the evidence against the measure presented by NEA members had been "the most vital and important" brought to the committee's attention to that time. Congress adjourned in June 1908 without having passed the bill.[57]

New York State had an eight-hour law that, like the defeated federal bill, applied to public construction and the "material used thereon." Drew, who had opposed the measure, was pleased when the Appellate Division of New York's Supreme Court, subsequently upheld by the New York Court of Appeals, ruled that the law did not apply to material fabricated away from the job but only to work actually done at the job site. The same New York law required contractors to pay the prevailing wage on public work. New York's Local 40 charged in 1908 that the McClintic-Marshall Company was violating the law by using common laborers rather than skilled bridgemen at a higher wage to deliver steel for the erection of some of the Chelsea piers. The union also alleged that its business agent had rejected a bribe offer from McClintic-Marshall to withdraw the union complaint. Representing the company, which denied the bribe charge, Drew secured the dismissal of the union complaint by the Comptroller's Department on the grounds that the law did not apply to the case at issue.[58]

No legislative subject occupied more of Drew's attention between 1909 and 1915 than workmen's compensation. Given the salience of the subject in the Progressive Era and, more particularly, the high rate of accident among structural steel erection workers, it is hardly surprising that Drew regarded workmen's compensation as "one of the most important . . . industrial issues of the time." At least one NEA member thought workmen's compensation "foreign to the open shop movement," but Drew never took that position. Although he asserted that no one "seriously objects" to the principle of workmen's compensation, he preferred voluntary compensation plans, such as the plans put into effect in 1911 by United States Steel and International Harvester, or "permissive laws" to legislatively mandated compensation.[59]

Understanding that the movement for workmen's compensation legislation could not be successfully resisted, Drew, speaking to the NAM convention in 1911, urged business interests to "take charge" of the matter lest "this vital, fundamental issue . . . be determined by the radical in his own way." And the radical goal, Drew claimed, was "unlimited liability coupled with unlimited damages." He advised the NEA membership to seek "sane, fair and uniform methods of compensation" suitable to the structural steel industry. He was especially concerned that the state liability and compensation laws be uniform in character, provide for employee compensation as "fully and fairly as possible," eliminate employee litigation, and not result in the "crippling of industry."[60]

Drew involved himself on the legislative front in seeking to shape workmen's compensation laws in the manner he thought proper. He had done "quite a little active work chiefly on the firing line" in opposing "radical" employer liability measures, Drew wrote in the spring of 1910. Just before that, in February 1910, Drew represented the NEA and the NAM before the New Jersey State Senate in opposition to what he characterized as "the most drastic [employer liability] law of all." "I was able to riddle it so effectively," he wrote an NEA member, "that they did not dare report it without another hearing." By the time that hearing was held, Drew and his allies had been able "to marshall enough forces" to get the bill bottled up in committee. The "elective" and largely ineffective bill that finally passed in 1911 had the support of United States Steel and other employers, although Drew thought that even that measure had "some very serious defects."[61]

Drew was concerned about workmen's compensation legislation in New York State because of the critical importance of New York City to the NEA. In 1910 New York passed both an Employers' Liability Act applying to all occupations and a Compensation Act covering eight "dangerous employments," among which was any industry requiring iron or steel frame work. In the trades covered by the Compensation Act, injured workers could pursue their claims under that statute or under the Liability Act. Since employer defenses in liability suits were substantially reduced by the Liability Act, injured workers were inclined to select that alternative, with the result that the Compensation Act became "practically a dead letter." Employers in the hazardous trades, however, Drew complained, had to carry insurance to meet employee claims under both statutes. The New York Court of Appeals came to the rescue, declaring the Compensation Act unconstitutional in 1911.[62]

New York passed a new compensation measure, effective on July 1, 1914, that had been advocated by organized labor and that Drew denounced as "vicious in nature" even though he claimed that he had been able to have it amended before its passage. The law, which survived a constitutional test, specified a number of occupations for which compensation was compulsory, including structural steel and iron erection; made employers liable for worker injuries regardless of cause, except for "employee's willful intent or intoxication"; and provided for payments up to two-thirds of the injured worker's wage for a specified period of weeks, as compared to 50 percent in most states. The law, Drew told NEA members, placed New York employers at a disadvantage as compared to competitors in other states. New York's superintendent of insurance, Drew thus reported, estimated the insurance cost for New York employers at 268 percent the cost for insurance of employers in Massachusetts.[63]

Drew would have disagreed with historian Roy Lubove's judgment many years later that "[b]usiness imperatives proved more influential in shaping workmen's compensation than considerations of equity and social expediency." Drew complained about "the chaotic condition" created by the various state compensation and liability laws and also about the cost they imposed on employers. What had been needed, he maintained in 1916, was "a fixed, stable and uniform system," but the fact was that no two states as of that time had identical laws, similar provisions in different state laws had been differently interpreted, and different rules had been prescribed for different employers depending on the hazards of particular occupations. As for cost, Drew noted that one large NEA member had seen its insurance cost for work accidents increase ninefold between 1910 and 1912, and another large member, which carried its own insurance, had experienced a 50 percent cost increase during the same years.[64]

Although Drew conceded that compensation legislation had provided "a greater measure of justice" for the worker than had previously prevailed, he believed that this had been achieved "at the expense of an unequal and ill-distributed burden laid upon industry generally." He saw this as "a serious indictment" of the "national intelligence" and as a lesson to be learned in dealing with the old-age insurance, then also under consideration. To be sure, he did not view workmen's compensation as a form of social insurance and as a precedent in this area of reform, since, as he construed the matter, it was not based on a concept of social obligation but rather on the obligation of the employer to be just to his employees.[65]

Although Drew could claim some success both in his efforts to spread the open shop and in opposing legislation that he believed inimical to the interests of the NEA and the larger business community as well, he could hardly have been pleased with the growth of trade union membership in general and building trades unionism in particular in the decade preceding United States entry into World War I. During the first ten years of his commissionership, the total membership of American trade unions grew by more than 43 percent (from 1,958,700 in 1906 to 2,808,000 in 1916), and membership in building trades unions by about 42 percent (from 389,000 to 552,900).[66] Even more alarming from the perspective of open shop employers was the remarkable gain in union membership, partly as the result of government support, once the United States became a belligerent in World War I. Drew, as we shall see, was hardly a passive observer of this development.

CHAPTER 7

World War I

As the war in Europe began to stimulate the American economy, Drew expressed concern that "war rush orders" not serve as a reason for changes in the condition of labor that would then become permanent. Although he saw some justice in worker demands to share in the prosperity engendered by war production, he was not prepared to give any ground in the defense of the open shop in American industry.[1] He was sometimes successful in his efforts to resist union demands, but the drift of wartime labor policy was in a direction altogether displeasing to Drew and the open shop forces.

During the period of American neutrality in World War I Drew was especially concerned that a strike by the International Association of Bridge and Structural Iron Workers (IABSIW) against the Remington Arms Company of Bridgeport, Connecticut, might serve as a precedent for loosening the grip of the open shop on the structural iron industry. About thirty structural iron workers walked out of a Remington small arms plant and then a munitions plant on July 12 and 13, 1915, as the result of a jurisdictional dispute with millwrights and carpenters. The union also threatened to strike twenty-one establishments with Remington subcontracts, which would have tied up practically all the machine shops in Bridgeport, a major producer of small arms and ammunition for the Allies. The company blamed the strike on German sympathizers, a contention on which Drew seized, linking the Remington strike to an earlier union threat of sympathetic strikes against the Crucible Steel Company for subcontracting the structural steel erection of a munitions plant in Newark to the American Bridge Company.

Drew advised the Remington firm that "the quickest way" to end its strike was for the company to take over all contracts in Bridgeport shops where trouble developed and to place the work involved on an open shop basis. He promised the aid of the open shop employer associations in helping Remington deal with any consequent labor difficulties. Drew also sent the detective Robert Foster to Sir Cecil Spring-Rice, the British ambassador to the United States, to discuss "the increasing indications" that the difficulties manufacturers of war materials for the Allies were facing were the result of "an organized and systematic effort." Taking credit for outlining "a course of action" for Crucible Steel that, he claimed, had enabled it to cope with its Newark problem, Drew proposed to Spring-Rice that concerns that were manufacturing war supplies should organize some kind of association to protect their "mutual interests." Such an association, he indicated, would be able to meet any labor troubles that might develop by introducing the open shop in the affected plants, and it would enjoy the support of the national employer associations and their labor bureaus in doing so.[2]

When the press reported that banking interests might use their influence to induce Remington to bow to union demands, Drew urged the United States Steel Company to head off the bankers. The president of Hartford's Employers' Association declared shortly after the Remington strike began that it was "a grand failure," but to avert a threatened strike of machinists in sympathy with the ironworkers as well as for wage and hour concessions, Remington granted the machinists the eight-hour day and a pay increase.[3]

Drew not only sought to promote the open shop by his vain effort to persuade firms producing war materials to join together to resist union demands, but he also sought to derive an antiunion lesson from the industrial experience of the warring nations. Whereas trade union restrictions, Drew claimed, had brought Great Britain "to the verge of industrial disaster and military defeat," the early success of German arms demonstrated the "vital connection between military efficiency and industrial efficiency." Drawing the parallel, Drew pointed to the restrictive practices of the building trades unions in the United States and the AFL's opposition to scientific management practices as warning signs for the nation. Once the United States itself became a belligerent, Drew regularly pointed out that England had been compelled to abandon the restrictive practices of the nation's trade unions and to adopt the "open shop in all its essential principles" in order to harness its industrial strength for Britain's war effort.[4]

On April 7, 1917, a few days after the United States entered World War I, the Council of National Defense (CND) and its Advisory Commission[5] adopted a declaration drafted by the Executive Committee of the Committee on Labor of the commission, headed by Samuel Gompers, that, as modified a bit later, stated that employers and employees in private industry were not "to take advantage of the existing abnormal conditions to change the standards which they were unable to change under normal conditions." Specifically, the amplifying statement declared that there should be no "arbitrary changes in wages" by labor or management and no strikes or lockouts without providing opportunity for "established agencies" to adjust matters without a work stoppage.

Although the secretary of labor stated that employers in the emergency had no right to interfere with union efforts to organize workers, the no-change-in-standards pronouncement seemed to imply that a union like the IABSIW that had failed to organize steel fabrication shops before the war was not to attempt to do so during the war. This was a point that Drew regularly made during the war, and he was not alone in this judgment. As Valerie Conner noted in her study of the National War Labor Board, not only employers but "significant elements of the labor movement . . . read the statement as an acquiescence in the open shop."[6]

Just after the United States entered the war, Drew wrote his friend James Emery that the AFL commitment to support the war effort "should be met by our own." The employers, Drew thought, should not "interject any note of hostility or discord" in their response but should stress "in a quiet way" that "the real backbone of industry lies in the open-shop establishments of the country." To deal with any threat to the "open shop forces" that the war might bring, Drew suggested the possible revival of the Joint Committee of Associated Employers that had dealt with the Commission on Industrial Relations. Nothing came of this proposal, but the National Industrial Conference Board (NICB) did appoint a committee of five to keep "in constant touch" with the CND's Advisory Commission and to acquaint the commission with the "practical problems" of manufacturers in connection with the defense program and to facilitate cooperation with the government.[7]

Drew was also concerned that although organized labor had gained representation on such bodies as the Committee on Labor and the Cantonment Adjustment Commission, set up to implement the agreement between the War Department and the AFL regarding the building of cantonments, it was "a practical impossibility" to provide similar representation for the 90 percent of the workers in the civilian labor force who were unorganized. Increasingly, moreover, he became convinced that agents of the War, Navy, and Labor Departments were assisting the efforts of organized labor to extend the closed shop. He informed NEA members in October 1917 that there was "a growing concern among manufacturers and contractors doing war work" that a "large percentage" of government agents involved in the war effort were "strongly pro-union" and were using their influence accordingly. He advised members to challenge the authority of any government agent who took that position.[8]

During the war the shipbuilding industry replaced the general construction industry as the focus of attention of the open shop forces in the nation. In April 1917 the United States Shipping Board created the Emergency Fleet Corporation (EFC) to expand existing shipbuilding plants and to construct new ones, build merchant vessels, operate commandeered yards, supervise the completion of requisitioned vessels, and adjust questions affecting labor in the shipbuilding industry. The most important part of the government's massive shipbuilding program, and, as Drew put it, "one of the great essentials of the Government's war program," was the fabrication and assembling of standardized steel ships. The material for the ships was fabricated, in the main, in the plants of NEA members.[9]

When the United States entered the war, the nation's shipbuilding industry was in a sorry state. The industry was unprofitable, shipyards were in poor physical condition, wages were relatively low, workers were hired and fired in a "haphazard way," and employers "paid little attention to the safety and comfort" of their employees. Securing a labor supply, especially a supply of skilled labor, became the EFC's "most urgent problem" as it sought to meet the nation's wartime shipping requirements. The number of workers in the shipyards rose from 44,962 in 63 shipyards in 1916 to 375,000 in 210 yards on October 1, 1918.[10]

In seeking shipyard workers, employers could look to the United States Employment Service (USES), the United States Public Service Reserve, the labor bureaus of employer associations, and workers seeking jobs on their own. The USES was established by the Department of Labor in 1914 as part of the Division of Information of the Bureau of Immigration. Other public employment agencies were merged with it during the war, and it was reorganized and became "a distinct and separate employment service" on January 3, 1918. Using traveling field agents to enroll workers, it cooperated with the EFC in seeking to locate skilled workers for the shipyards. After August 1, 1918, the shipyards had to obtain unskilled workers through the USES. The secretary of labor created the Public Service Reserve, described as "the recruiting arm" of the USES, in June 1917 to register citizens volunteering their services for war work. In still another effort to recruit labor, the Shipping Board and the Department of Labor formed the United States Shipyard Volunteers, which enrolled 280,000 persons, but they were not, in the end, called to work.[11]

As the labor needs of the shipyards mounted, employers decided that it was unwise to rely on government agencies to recruit workers for the yards lest this pose a threat to the open shop in an increasingly important part of the wartime economy. This became an immediate concern of the Steel Fabricators of the United States, which was formed on November 27, 1917, to work with the government in meeting the nation's defense needs. Its members represented about 90 percent of the structural steel and bridge steel plants in the nation and produced most of the structural steel material for the shipyards. Walter Drew served as the organization's counsel. Lewis D. Rights, the secretary-treasurer of the Fabricators' War Service Committee, wrote Drew soon after the organization was formed, expressing its interest in providing open shop workers for the construction of the steel ships.[12]

Reacting to what Rights had written him, Drew urged NEA members to contribute workers to the shipyards from their own labor force. He instructed the NEA's labor bureaus to register men for the yards and to get in touch with NEA members in their districts with this in mind. He sent questionnaires to members to gather data regarding the available supply of workers, and the commissioner's office, which kept in touch with the various shipyards, served as "a clearing house."

Drew eventually advised NEA members to take on new workers and to train them for shipyard work, thus supplementing the training schools of such firms as the Submarine Boat Corporation. He was anxious to see that NEA workers, open shop men, were placed before the 250,000 persons the Public Service Reserve had registered for shipyard work by late July 1918 began their "general rush" to the yards. He informed a Connecticut manufacturer in March

1918 that the NEA's recruitment effort had been so successful that its members were no longer "bothered with the problem of the attitude of federal agents."[13]

What may very well have been on Drew's mind when he wrote about the "attitude" of federal agents was information he had received at the beginning of 1918 that the USES office opened in St. Paul to recruit workers for the Seattle shipyards had advertised in a Minneapolis newspaper that it would send only union members to the West Coast yards. Drew's response to this news was to assert that the federal government could not legally act in this way and to advise open shop employer associations to work with the USES and the Public Service Reserve if "properly run" but to "expose" and "fight" them insofar as they made themselves "part of the machinery for extending the closed shop." Reacting to Drew's criticism, J. B. Densmore, the director of the USES, pointed out that since the Seattle shipyards were operated on a closed shop basis, it was "useless" to send nonunion workers there.[14]

Convinced that what had occurred in Minneapolis was not unique and that "a large percentage" of USES agents were influenced by the union point of view, Drew played a prominent role in 1918 and in the early postwar period in the campaign by employer organizations to discredit the USES as "incompetent," "extravagant," and "a tool of organized labor's business agents or some welfare folks," and hence as not deserving of further federal support. There was, to be sure, some justice to the employer complaints. The service was "inefficient," the Department of Labor had appointed many union officers to USES positions, and the AFL had been "able to influence, if not fully control, the service." Once the war was over, Congress sharply reduced the funding for the USES, and on October 10, 1919, all its offices were either closed or transferred to state and local governments.[15]

Unsurprisingly in view of the enormous expansion of the shipbuilding industry in World War I, most yards and shipbuilding plants were run by inexperienced managers and manned by inexperienced workmen. There was much "idling" and absenteeism by the workers, a good deal of labor turnover reflecting different wage rates in different yards and in public and private employment, poor relations between labor and management, and a marked decline of efficiency as compared to before the war. Former structural iron-workers, several thousand of whom took jobs in the shipyards, were among the discontented members of the labor force in the industry. Structural iron work, as such, was not recognized as a branch of shipbuilding work, the IABSIW having conceded jurisdiction over such work to the Brotherhood of Boiler-makers, Iron Shipbuilders and Helpers of America. The IABSIW, which once war came sought in vain to secure a classification for shipyard ironworkers as a "basic" trade, viewed with considerable disapproval the conditions of work in the yards and especially the open shop status of shipbuilding labor in the East Coast yards. The union's leadership consequently concluded that its members had "no business [working] on steel ships." As the union's president informed Samuel Gompers, IABSIW rules forbade the union from supplying workers for jobs employing nonunion workers, and the union apparently sometimes fined members who ignored its rules and took shipyard positions.[16]

As the result of shipyard strikes and threatened strikes, Louis B. Wehle, counsel to the EFC, proposed to the AFL the establishment of machinery to settle disputes in shipyards having contracts with the Navy and the EFC. On August 20, 1917, Wehle and the officers of the AFL's Metal Trades Department reached an agreement to set up the Shipbuilding Labor Adjustment Board (SLAB). It was given jurisdiction over disputes regarding "wages, hours or conditions of labor in the construction or repair of shipbuilding plants or ships in shipyards" of the EFC, the Shipping Board, or under contract to the EFC. The SLAB was to consist of three members, one representing the public and appointed by the president of the United States, a second selected by the EFC, and a third designated by the president of the AFL. A revised shipbuilding agreement of December 8, 1917, specified that disputes thereafter were to be referred to a tripartite adjustment board, provided for a board of review and appeal, and changed the wage standard that the SLAB was to follow. The "recognition of the international unions and collective bargaining" involved in the establishment of the SLAB was "a blow" to open shoppers like Drew. The SLAB, indeed, encouraged collective bargaining in resolving disputes, continued closed shop arrangements where they already existed, and authorized the establishment of shop committees where union arrangements were absent.[17]

Drew's reaction to the SLAB was that although it had been established to deal with demands for change in wages, hours, and working conditions, the closed shop was not one of these conditions. That the government should operate or sanction a closed shop in war work, he stated in October 1917, was "unthinkable" and would lead to "practical chaos," as it had in wartime England until the British unions agreed to the open shop. Drew sought to persuade the Shipping Board to issue a statement that its policy was to adhere to the status quo insofar as the closed shop–open shop issue was concerned. Despite Drew's concern about the unionization of shipyard workers, only 17 of 527 shipbuilding and marine equipment plants were unionized as of September 1917.[18]

The NEA resistance to union demands for the closed shop in shipbuilding centered on Port Newark, where the Lackawanna Bridge Company, an NEA member, had a subcontract from the Submarine Boat Corporation, acting as an EFC agent, to erect and equip "the most efficient and advanced" of the steel shipbuilding plants in the nation. The building trades of Newark, which were unionized, sought to unionize the Lackawanna job. The company, which was "uncompromisingly open shop," borrowed Drew's assistant, H. R. Brady, to serve as its employment and welfare commissioner, and Drew himself kept in "close touch" with Brady and with the Lackawanna firm.

Despite IABSIW policy, some of its members sought employment with Lackawanna, and the union, apparently, did not discourage them from doing so. In October 1917 the IABSIW, supported by other unions, threatened to strike Lackawanna, claiming that the company had denied its members employment. Drew, in response, sought to persuade the Shipping Board to resist the IABSIW demands. He characterized the union for the board as "the most quarrelsome and troublesome of the trades," noted that it had been suspended from the AFL—the result of a jurisdictional dispute with the carpenters—reminded the board that the AFL had committed itself to maintain existing standards of employment, and warned that union success in this instance would plunge the structural steel industry into "turmoil and strife" at a time when the government was seeking "full efficiency and capacity."[19]

On October 28, 1917, the Newark Building Trades Council ordered a general strike against Lackawanna for recognition and to secure the prevailing wage for the building trades in the area. The strike was a fiasco, Drew claiming that of the one thousand men then working for Lackawanna, only one skilled worker and ninety laborers had walked out. That, however, did not end the matter. On October 29 the Newark Board of Business Agents informed the Shipping Board that working conditions at the Port Newark Terminal were unfair to organized labor and that the Newark unions would strike all federal government work there, work that involved thirty thousand mechanics and laborers, unless the government remedied the situation. The Newark unionists claimed that Lackawanna was the only unfair concern working on a government contract at the Port Newark Terminal, attributing this state of affairs to the malign influence of the NEA. The Conciliation Service of the Department of Labor responded to the strike threat by sending Commissioner E. E. Greenawalt to Newark, and he persuaded the unions to defer the strike pending negotiations with Lackawanna.[20]

Greenawalt arranged for representatives of the Newark building trades and P. W. Petersen, the superintendent of the Lackawanna job, to meet with him on November 1, but the conference failed to resolve the dispute. Claiming that Lackawanna was already paying some trades above the union scale, Petersen indicated that the company did not object to the prevailing wage demand, and he stated that the company would not discriminate against union workers even though it appeared from the record that it might have done so previously. He made it clear, however, that the company would not allow union stewards on the job since that, he claimed, led to "a whole lot of friction," nor would it hire workers through the union, which Greenawalt had said was the way for Lackawanna to secure the services of the best mechanics. Precisely the kind of government agent to whom Drew objected, Greenawalt also urged the company to bargain with the union. It was better for the company, he advised, "to have men who are bound together and deal collectively" than "to deal with a promiscuous gathering of men," some of whom were union, some of whom were not, since the union organization would then be responsible for all the men on the job. Petersen responded that if the company employed only union men, it would not be able to secure the material, presumably fabricated steel, that it needed to operate.[21]

Greenawalt secured a second postponement of the strike until November 7 pending another conference, this one arranged by the Newark Board of Public Works. The participants in the second Lackawanna conference, held on November 5, included the commissioners of the Board of Public Works; union representatives, including the president of the New Jersey Federation of Labor; B. L. Worden, president of Lackawanna and general manager of the Submarine Boat Corporation; the EFC's Wehle; and Walter Drew. Returning to an issue raised at the first conference, the IABSIW representative at the meeting claimed that Worden had told the union that if he granted the "strictly closed shop" it had demanded, the NEA would deny him steel, a contention that Worden denied. "This is a Union City and a Union State," the president of the New Jersey Federation of Labor declared, "and we intend that it shall remain that way."

When union representatives agreed with Drew that the unions were proposing to strike all government work in the area in order to force the government to order Lackawanna to discharge the nonunion workers in its employ, the NEA commissioner responded that the government, under the law, could not discriminate between union and nonunion workers. He noted that when a general building trades strike had been called to compel the New England Structural Iron Company to discharge its nonunion workers at the Watertown Arsenal, Colonel F. C. Dickson brought in federal troops to break the strike and stated that the federal government could not tell a contractor whom to hire. The conference ended, according to Wehle, "under conditions of considerable hostility" and without a union commitment not to strike. The EFC counsel attributed this outcome to Greenawalt's behavior at the conference.[22]

After a brief delay, the Newark building trades unions ordered a strike beginning on November 12 on all federal government work in their jurisdiction in order to force the unionization of the Lackawanna job. Drew saw this as "a test case on the closed-shop question," with Newark having been selected for the "test" because the building trades there were "more strongly unionized" than the similar trades in other cities in the East where ships were being built. Strikers walked off their jobs at two shipyards, a supply depot for the Corps of Engineers, and a supply depot for the Quartermasters Corps, Greenawalt estimating the total number of strikers as nine thousand. The next day, however, the AFL leadership ordered the strikers back to work, perhaps at the behest of President Woodrow Wilson, who spoke to the AFL convention in Buffalo, the first president to do so, perhaps because the Building Trades Department had agreed to press the Newark case in Washington, perhaps because Secretary of War Newton D. Baker had reportedly threatened "drastic action" otherwise. "I believe the closed-shop issue has been met and passed," Drew wrote Worden a few weeks later.[23]

The labor force of the Submarine Boat Corporation grew as the war continued, the NEA's labor bureaus assisting the corporation in securing needed workers. Drew characterized Submarine Boat at war's end as open shop "in the best sense of the word," since union men were employed alongside nonunion men as long as their work was satisfactory. The SLAB thought otherwise, however, reinstating with back pay five unionists who had complained in October that they had been dismissed because of their union affiliation, not, as the company claimed, because of their proselytizing for the union during working hours.[24]

Drew was pleased not only at the outcome of the Port Newark strike but also at the failure of a brief strike that had begun on October 31, 1917, at the Fore River plant of the Bethlehem Shipbuilding Corporation in Quincy, Massachusetts, and that enjoyed the support of the Building Trades Council of Greater Boston and Quincy. When the SLAB on February 14, 1918, announced its award for the shipyards of the Delaware Shipbuilding District, the award contained the kind of statement Drew had been seeking from the board: "the Board will not tolerate any discrimination either on the part of employers or employees between union and non-union men."[25]

Fearful that the prounion forces would capitalize on the war to push the closed shop, Drew, from the war's beginning, had wanted the federal government to commit itself to a policy of neutrality regarding the open and closed shop issue. He saw the NICB as the private agency that could help to move government policy in this direction. As he wrote a fellow employer association executive, Drew envisioned "the possibility of making" the NICB "a big thing."[26]

As it turned out, the NICB sought to perform the role Drew had envisioned for it. Late in the summer of 1917 the CND asked the committee of five that the board, it will be recalled, had established to keep in touch with the CND's Advisory Commission for its views regarding the means to ensure the uninterrupted flow of goods in wartime. The NICB thereupon convened a meeting on August 29, 1917, of member associations and the executive officers of unaffiliated associations of manufacturers and of individual companies at which "labor problems" were "discussed at length." A preliminary statement was drawn up as the result of the session that was then revised by the NICB's executive committee and submitted in the form of recommendations to the CND on September 6, 1917. The statement called on the government, as its "guiding principle," to reassert the aforementioned open shop doctrine pronounced by the Anthracite Coal Strike Commission in March 1903.

To implement the CND's no-change-in-standards policy, the NICB proposed that there be no change in legislatively mandated safety and health requirements except upon the CND's recommendation; that wage demands be tested by the prevailing local standard of the establishment as of the beginning of the war, adjusted to meet advances in the cost of living; that hours standards be what was required by law or prevailed in the particular establishment at the beginning of the war unless the CND decided otherwise in order to meet "the requirements of the Government"; and that there be no change in the status of shops that were union or open at the beginning of the war. The NICB also proposed the creation of a tripartite government board to adjust labor disputes for the duration of the war on the basis of the standards proposed and that its decisions be binding on parties to the dispute. The NICB, finally, urged that there be no strikes or lockouts for the duration and that the CND call a conference of labor representatives to join in the pledge of support made in behalf of the employers.[27]

The NICB statement was fully in accord with the policies favored by Drew and the other open shop advocates, and the NEA commissioner joined other NICB representatives in securing the endorsement of the statement by the United States Chamber of Commerce. He was prepared to entrust the adjustment of disputes during the war to "outside parties," but only if they accepted "the fundamental principles" approved by the NICB, especially the "status quo ante" principle regarding the closed shop and open shop question. For Drew, as always, and now in wartime, "the question of the closed shop" was "the most important single question" facing American industry. If it were to be extended, he warned, it would give more power to "the radical, the mercenary and the unpatriotic elements of labor, with no corresponding added control or responsibility."[28]

The AFL denounced the NICB proposals at its November 1917 convention. The Federation wanted wages adjusted for "equity" before cost-of-living adjustments were made, it urged that there be no restrictions on the right of workers to bargain through their chosen representatives, and it sought to reserve the right to strike as a last resort. On January 28, 1918, the secretary of labor, to whom the president had entrusted the responsibility of "formulating and administering . . . a national labor program" for the war, invited the NICB and the AFL each to designate five persons to confer with a view to reaching an agreement regarding wartime employment relations. Each group was to select a sixth person to represent the public. The five NICB representatives included two NEA members, Worden and C. E. Michael, president of the Virginia Bridge and Iron Company. The employer group picked William Howard Taft as its choice for public representative; the AFL selected Frank Walsh.[29]

Designated as the War Labor Conference Board, the twelve conferees presented their recommendations to the secretary of labor on March 29, 1918. Their statement was more supportive of the trade union position than the NICB proposal was. It called for the creation of a national war labor board to adjust disputes affecting war production, its membership paralleling the membership of the War Labor Conference Board. As for the principles to govern employment relations in war industries, the March 29 statement specified that there were to be no strikes or lockouts for the duration; "recognized and affirmed" "the right of workers to organize in trade unions and to bargain collectively, through chosen representatives," a right that was "not [to] be denied, abridged, or interfered with by employers in any manner whatsoever"; forbade employers to discharge workers because they were union members or because of "legitimate trade-union activities"; forbade workers in exercising their right to organize to use "coercive methods of any kind" to induce other workers to join a union or to induce employers to bargain with a union; provided for the continuation of the union shop where it already existed as well as union standards of wages, hours, and conditions of work; provided similarly for the status quo where union and nonunion employees worked together and where the employer met only with their own employees, but without, at the same time, denying the right of workers in such establishments to form or to join unions or to be discouraged from doing so and without preventing the labor board or an umpire from granting an improvement in working conditions; recognized the "basic eight-hour day" as applying wherever the law required same and the determination of hours in other instances "with due regard to governmental necessities and the welfare, health, and proper comfort of the workers"; called for "maximum production" in all war industries and frowned upon "methods of work and operation" by employers or workers that limited production; recommended that "regard" be had for existing labor standards in a locality in the fixing of hours, wages, and working conditions; and proclaimed the right of workers to a "living wage," defined as a minimum rate that would "ensure the subsistence of the worker and his family in health and reasonable comfort."[30]

Taft wrote his daughter that he had had "to read the riot act" to the employers "once or twice" to get them to vote for the War Labor Conference Board statement. If Drew, however, was disappointed in the statement, a compromise agreement to be sure, he did not say so. The agreement, after all, incorporated the status quo provision regarding the closed and open shop for which he had been pressing, and as he understood what had been agreed to, open shop employers did not have to "recognize or deal with the union in any way." In theory, Drew had never denied the right of workers to organize as long as unionists did not coerce nonunionists, and the agreement met that condition. He had been urging maximum production from the start, and, in his view, it was primarily union restrictions that diminished output. Drew hailed the agreement as "the most important happening in the industrial world," and he undoubtedly believed that when he said it.[31]

Acting on the recommendation of the War Labor Conference Board, President Wilson on April 8, 1918, approved the formation of the National War Labor Board (NWLB). The board's membership was the same as that of the War Labor Conference Board, Taft and Walsh serving as cochairmen, and the principles the board was to follow were those spelled out by the Conference Board. In dealing with local controversies, two board members, one an employer member, one a union member, were to serve as a section to adjust the dispute. When the board through a section or some other means was unable to adjust a jointly submitted dispute, the board as a whole sat as "a board of arbitration" to resolve the matter. If it could not do so by unanimous vote, it was to appoint an umpire to decide the case. The board was not to deal with labor controversies in "any field of industrial or other activity" governed by other agreements, as in shipbuilding, or where federal law provided a means of settlement that had not been invoked.[32]

Drew hoped that if employers supported the NWLB, it would become "a stabilizing influence and a rock of refuge" for them even if it did some things that they would have done "differently." As it became evident, however, that the board was tilting in the direction of organized labor, employers became increasingly hostile to it. It was the board's promotion and encouragement of collective bargaining that particularly troubled employers. They were thus concerned about its decision to set up shop committees in plants that had not been unionized, to provide for the selection of these committees without employer interference, and to require employers to recognize and deal with such committees once constituted. The board forbade employers to blacklist union members, contract with individual employees not to join a union, compel workers to join a company union, or object to the wearing of union buttons by employees. Open shop employers were "beginning to lose faith" in the board, *Iron Age* noted in early September 1918. The next month the NICB, which had played such a large part in the creation of the board, complained that labor organizations had "gained an undue strength in the industrial employment relationship."[33]

Drew, after some initial hesitation, joined the ranks of the employer critics of the board and, indeed, became one of their principal spokesmen. As he saw it, the NWLB simply misinterpreted the principles it was supposed to observe. What constituted "the right to organize" that the NWLB was required to protect lay at the heart of Drew's objections to the board. What the principle connoted, according to Drew's interpretation, was the right of "workers" to organize, not of a "union" to do so. It also meant, he said, that workers had an equal right not to organize. They were entitled to a "free choice" in this matter, Drew contended, and that meant that they were to have knowledge of the facts involved. Employers, Drew believed, had to provide workers with information to offset the "vicious misrepresentation" of the facts by labor organizers. Not only could such employer action not be construed as employer interference with the right to organize, but employers had "just ground of complaint" to the board about any organizing campaign accompanied by false statements, "intimidation," and efforts to induce a strike in "a peaceful establishment." Drew thought that in dealing with employment relations, the board should conform to the practice of nonunion establishments and localities and that the imposition of any shop committees, for example, under these circumstances constituted "the introduction of an unusual, foreign and disturbing condition" that could not "fail to affect the morale, discipline and efficiency" that had been "built up under existing methods and policies of management." To avoid the imposition on him of a shop committee, the employer, Drew advised, could "assist his workers in developing a simple system of representation" in the plant.

Drew insisted that the right to organize did not sanction an "organized and systematic campaign" of a union to unionize a nonunion shop where there was no employment controversy. To lend board support to such a campaign, he charged, would transform the board into "an instrument for the extension of unionism rather than for the adjustment of controversies in the interest of the nation's maximum war effort." The NWLB's charter, to be sure, provided that employees were not to be discharged for "legitimate union activity," but Drew did not regard the effort of a union to organize an open shop plant as "legitimate." Drew prepared a notice for open shop employers to post in their plants stating that, as open shop employers, they could not be required to recognize or deal with a union in any way. Employers, he thought, could "afford, through the medium of the War Labor Board, to give up a good deal" if they could "preserve this one basic policy inviolable." He turned on the board when it became evident that open shop employers could not keep that "one basic policy inviolable." He no doubt saw Frank Walsh as the cause for the NWLB's failure to construe its role regarding unionism as the NEA commissioner would have wished. Thinking back to their relationship when Walsh was chairman of the Commission on Industrial Relations, Drew remarked, "I spent a long time in close association with Mr. Walsh."[34]

Drew's construction of the right to organize became especially salient for him when the officers of fifteen AFL international unions, at a conference on August 1, 1918, formed the National Committee for Organizing Iron and Steel Workers. Drew professed to be outraged at this development. "A campaign of this kind directed at a great peaceful industry engaged upon essential war work," he wrote an employer association executive, "cannot have anything but a demoralizing effect and [would] be most prejudicial to war production."[35]

Speaking for the Steel Fabricators, the NEA, and the Bridge Builders' and Structural Society and asking the secretaries of national and local employer associations to join him, Drew protested the steel organizing drive to the NWLB. He claimed that the unions were invoking the board's sanction to institute "an aggressive and systematic campaign" to unionize the structural steel shops of the country even though they were operating "on terms of peace and harmony" with their employees. He asserted that the steel fabricators were not questioning the right of workers to organize, but that right, he insisted, and the right of a national union "to institute a country-wide attack in war time on peaceful establishments" whose operations were "essential" to the war effort were not the same. Drew could not resist informing the board that one of the unions involved in the steel organizing drive, the IABSIW, had been associated with dynamiting, had never called off its strike against NEA firms, and fined its members for working in shipyards, calling them "scabs" and "yellow dogs." In addition to protesting to the NWLB, the NEA recommended that its members inform their employees that it was federal government policy not to discriminate between union and nonunion employees on work done for the government and that employers who had conducted their business on an open shop basis before the war could not be required to deal with a union if their employees became members.[36]

Some effort was made by the IABSIW to organize the steel fabrication shops in Pittsburgh, Buffalo, and elsewhere. Although the union claimed in September 1918 that it had organized eight shop locals with two thousand members, its organizing efforts, which met employer opposition, achieved only modest results, and the shop locals that were established proved to be very weak.[37]

The major wartime dispute involving structural steel erection employers and the IABSIW actually concerned wages rather than the right to organize.

Following the lead of the American Bridge Company, the members of New York's Iron League Erectors' Association (ILEA) raised wartime wages on three occasions until they reached eighty cents an hour for first-class bridgemen on April 15, 1918. The New York IABSIW structural steel locals, however, had announced early in April that the union scale would be eighty-seven and one-half cents beginning on May 1. Explaining to the ILEA as its counsel why it should not agree to the union wage demand, Drew pointed out that ironworkers were needed in the shipyards and that the SLAB on April 6, 1918, had set the rate in Atlantic Coast yards for pneumatic riveters, the position ironworkers normally filled, at seventy cents. To set wages in nonessential industries above the rate for government work, Drew charged, would place the latter at a disadvantage and would be "impractical and contrary to the nation's interests." Drew, moreover, informed the ILEA that Felix Frankfurter, the head of the War Labor Policies Board, had warned that if private, nonessential industries behaved in this way, the War Industries Board would cut off their supply of material. Drew also asserted that since workers were available at the eighty-cent rate, the union was seeking to take advantage of "emergency conditions" to force an "artificial and arbitrary rate" for its members.[38]

At a meeting of the ILEA attended by Drew and a representative of the Submarine Boat Corporation, the association appointed a committee to meet with the proper government agency about the wage demand, leaving the necessary arrangements in Drew's hands. The New York ironworkers' locals responded to the employer failure to meet the union's wage demand by going out on strike. In behalf of the ILEA, Drew thereupon requested the NWLB to assume jurisdiction since "the disaffection" was spreading to war work. Frankfurter commended Drew's action, stating, "The problem you are raising [the relationship of wages in private industry and in government work] is one of the most complicated and all-pervading . . . industrial questions raised by the war."[39]

The New York IABSIW locals (35 and 40) agreed to return to work at the two government jobs affected by the strike pending a NWLB decision. At a conference on June 18 a NWLB examiner proposed to Drew, representing the employers, and D. A. Coyle, representing the union, that the union members return to all the struck work, public and private, and that the eighty-cent rate be maintained pending an NWLB decision. If the board decided on a rate lower than eighty cents, the examiner proposed, the union would make "proper refunds" to the employers; and if the board set a higher rate, it would have retroactive effect. Drew accepted the proposal, but when Coyle submitted it to the union, it rejected the arrangement.[40]

At an NWLB hearing in New York on July 8 conducted by a two-member section, the union representatives stated that the union would not accept an award applying to "private" employment. They asserted, moreover, that there was "nothing to adjust" since, they claimed, 90 percent of the employers were already paying the higher rate. "They want our men now," one union representative declared, "but they don't recognize Union conditions, and they want to use the Government as a whip and the war as a club to force us to put our men to work" at a lower wage.[41]

Although the section in its preliminary report advised that the case be "continued until final action by [the] section," the unwillingness of the union to submit the dispute to the board left it little alternative given NWLB rules but to drop the case from its docket for lack of jurisdiction. Drew now contended that the refusal of the IABSIW to submit the wage controversy to the NWLB placed it in "practical contempt" of the board, and it should therefore not be permitted to avail itself of board services and protection when it suited the union to do so. He conferred with Taft about the matter and reported that the NWLB cochairman thought this position "just and practicable," but Taft did not quite remember the conversation in that way. In any event, following American Bridge's lead, NEA members now raised bridgemen's wages to eighty-seven and one-half cents, and the SLAB, unable to secure workers at the seventy-cent rate it had decreed, set an eighty-cent rate for skilled shipyard workers in all yards.[42]

Other than the right to organize, the wartime labor question that most concerned Drew and the NEA was that of hours. In executive orders of March 27 and April 28, 1917, President Wilson, as authorized by the Naval Appropriations Act of March 1917, suspended the federal eight-hour law of June 19, 1912, insofar as it applied to the type of work performed on government contracts for the military or for defense purposes. Workers exempted from the law were to receive time-and-one-half pay for hours worked above eight in any day. This action converted the "actual" eight-hour day into a "basic" eight-hour day for the workers to whom it applied. Drew informed NEA members that the president's order did not affect their production, since the chief of ordnance had ruled in February 1917 that fabricated structural steel came within the class of "Supplies" purchased on the open market "an appreciable portion" of which was not regularly manufactured by the federal government and hence was exempted from the eight-hour law. Drew was consequently perturbed when federal department heads reversed "long-established interpretations of the law" to include work that had been considered exempt from its terms. This practice, Drew complained, introduced "an unsettling and disorganizing factor into private industry" and was "the meanest kind of a hold-up for increased wage[s]."[43]

An opponent of the eight-hour law in peacetime, as we have seen, Drew was especially critical of the penalty overtime rate in wartime. As before the war, he noted that what was called an hours law was really a wages law, and he insisted that, as a practical matter, manufacturers who operated their plants on a nine- or ten-hour basis would have to pay all their workers the penalty rate even if only a portion of them were engaged in war work. The available evidence, he claimed, did not support the argument that reducing the hours of work would increase efficiency. He cited British evidence that workers achieved more in efficiency without experiencing fatigue or injury working for nine or ten hours or even more as compared to working fewer hours. Workers, he charged, were prolonging the workday to secure the overtime rate, and if they received double time for Sunday work, they might absent themselves from work on Monday. Since, in his view, there was no "universal economic day common to all industry," Drew believed the question of hours was best left to be decided by agreement between employer and employee or as the result of expert investigation of different classes of work to determine the proper number of hours that would produce an efficient result with due regard for employee health.[44]

In a major eight-hour NWLB case involving a structural steel firm, the employer concerned turned to Drew to argue the company's case before the board. The contestants were the Fort Pitt Bridge Works of Cannonsburg, Pennsylvania, which produced boat sections for Submarine Boat and material used in building airplane hangars and airplane repair shops and in steel buildings for the Ordnance Department, and an IABSIW local formed in the plant after the war began that enjoyed the support of the International Association of Machinists local in the plant. About eight hundred workers were involved. The ironworkers, who worked a nine-hour day, wanted to secure nine hours pay for eight hours of work and time and a half for hours above eight. After threatening a strike to gain its demands, the local joined the company in submitting the dispute to the NWLB. At the first hearing before a board section on July 24, 1918, the company insisted that the eight-hour law did not apply to fabricated steel and noted that all of its competitors in the Pittsburgh area worked a basic nine-hour day.[45]

In a brief prepared for a resumed hearing on August 14, Drew argued that since the New York locals of the IABSIW were "in contempt" of the board, it should not consider the case of any other IABSIW local. Stressing another of his favorite themes, Drew contended that although the fabrication of steel ships was "the most important [wartime] work" of the government, the IABSIW was "greatly hostile" to shipbuilding work for its members, which, Drew suggested, demonstrated its "general attitude" toward government work. Although he reiterated his view that the law did not apply to the work in question, Drew contended that even if it did, the reduction of the workday in the plant would limit production at a time when maximum production was required and that, in any event, the workers had not claimed that they wanted the shorter day because of "governmental necessity" or for health reasons. A wage increase, he insisted, would not be in accord with the prevailing wage standard for structural steel shops in the area but would, rather, place Fort Pitt at a "ruinous disadvantage" in competition with other shops.[46]

Before the NWLB could render a decision in the case, United States Steel on September 22, 1918, adopted the eight-hour day, and Fort Pitt followed suit on October 1. The board subsequently dismissed the Fort Pitt case "without prejudice, for lack of prosecution." Drew claimed that the board had thrown out the case because of his contention that the IABSIW had defied it elsewhere and that he had been able to "defeat" a union demand for the eight-hour day in the only case in which the NWLB had not granted the demand.[47] This, however, was an inaccurate rendering of what had occurred.

Drew realized that the NEA, in which American Bridge played so prominent a role, would have no choice but to follow United States Steel in adopting the eight-hour day. Drew thought, however, that the steel corporation could avoid "the detrimental effect of the [eight-hour day] action" by applying the overtime rate only for hours in excess of forty-eight per week, a principle that the NWLB had agreed to consider. United States Steel, however, thought the Drew proposal "impractical," believing that it had committed itself to the basic eight-hour day as usually understood. In serving as counsel for a non-NEA firm, Drew in October 1918 urged the board to follow the forty-eight hour rule, and the NWLB did indeed apply that criterion in deciding that and several other hours cases that month but conditioned on the employers granting the workers affected a minimum number of working hours per week—forty-four in the case Drew argued—if they were employed on the first day of the week.[48]

Drew's efforts to promote the open shop and defend employer interests during World War I were not confined to the NEA. As counsel for the American Erectors' Association (AEA), he continued, primarily through his subordinates, to direct its fight against the Boilermakers' Union.[49] The United Engineering and Foundry Company of Youngstown, the Wheeling Mold and Foundry Company, and the Rochester Founders all engaged Drew rather than an attorney from the ranks of the Founders' Association to argue their cases before the NWLB.[50]

The Steel Fabricators Association relied on Drew as its counsel, as one member indicated, because of his "knowledge and experience" at a time when the labor question had become so "urgent." The association arranged with the NEA to use its labor bureaus to secure nonunion labor, and its executive committee looked to Drew to protest the AFL effort to organize the fabrication shops.[51]

Bridgeport, Connecticut, employers availed themselves of the services of Drew, along with the American Anti-Boycott Association's Walter Gordon Merritt, in dealing with what became one of the most important disputes to come before the NWLB. The skilled machinists in Bridgeport's factories, so important to the nation's arms production, underwent a deskilling process during the war years. Not only did employers hire more unskilled workers, but as production tasks were increasingly subdivided, skilled machinists were placed in "multiple occupational categories," with each classification having "a hierarchy of grades and wage rates." Employers in the open shop firms of the city defended the complex classification scheme as the means by which they could reward individual merit appropriately, but, as Jeffrey Haydu has noted, the classifications served as a "pretext" for wage reductions and, in any event, subverted union wage standards and undermined "craft power." The machinists union demanded that jobs of toolroom machinists be assigned to a few categories, each of which was to receive a minimum rate. Strikes to achieve this goal led to War Department intervention and an award on June 8, 1918, that gave the machinists at least part of what they wanted. The award antagonized many Bridgeport employers, who voted not to comply. This led Secretary of War Baker to set aside the award and to transfer the case to the NWLB.

The manufacturers summoned Drew to Bridgeport, and after "several stormy sessions" he persuaded manufacturers representing 90 percent of the city's employment to seek an NWLB ruling on the wages of all trades, not just the wages of machinists and toolmakers. Drew understood that if the board had to decide the wages of all the city's workers, it was likely to consider only the adequacy of the minimum rates paid for each classification in terms of the cost of living and would not attempt to enforce "any standard classifications" or to interfere with the "individual system" of classification used by open shop employers in each shop. Drew thought that it would be "a precedent of great value" if the board left existing classification schemes intact.

When the NWLB proved unable to resolve the Bridgeport dispute, the case was referred to an umpire, who, as Drew and the employers had hoped, rejected the union demand and established minimum hourly wages geared to existing rates, with the largest increases going to the lowest-paid workers, who were largely nonunion. The employees won the basic eight-hour day, which was already in effect in most Bridgeport plants, and provision was made for shop committees, but the wage award led to the only prearmistice strike against an NWLB decision. President Wilson ordered the strikers back to work, warning them that he would otherwise remove their draft exemptions and would bar them from working for one year in a defense-related job. The machinists thereupon returned to work. As for the shop committee plan, the NWLB examiner appointed to supervise the award later pronounced the plan a failure in the smaller city plants because of the "passive resistance" of management. The larger city firms saw the shop committees as serving to stave off the unionization of their workers.[52]

Believing that conditions in their highly unionized industry had become "unsupportable" and that it might be necessary "to establish a new regime," the American Men's and Boys' Clothing Manufacturers' Association engaged Drew to serve as its counsel in dealing with the Amalgamated Clothing Workers. The union was seeking in the summer of 1918 to reduce the weekly hours of work in the boys' clothing branch of the industry from forty-eight to forty-four and also was demanding a 20 percent wage increase. The clothing manufacturers were willing to increase wages, but they were determined not to reduce hours, and they complained about union practices that they claimed restricted output in violation of the existing contract. In accepting the clothing assignment, Drew did not encourage the employers to think that he would attempt to bring the open shop to their industry. He did not do so, he wrote Frankfurter, because "it meant a bitter and prolonged strife in an industry where all parties are brought into peculiarly close and intimate relationships in a very restricted area." He advised the employers to "make a supreme effort in the fullest good faith" to conduct the industry in accordance with the existing closed shop agreement. If that failed, then, he stated, they "could talk about handling the situation along other lines."[53]

Speaking for the employers, Drew argued that if the forty-four hour demand were granted, the shorter hours would spread to the entire industry and would affect the production of uniforms for the military. The employers took up the dispute with William Z. Ripley, the War Department's administrator of labor standards for army clothing, and offered to take the matter to the NWLB, but the union was not disposed to go this route and to back away from its demand. On October 28 fifteen thousand workers struck 250 boys' clothing shops, and the walkout eventually spread to the men's clothing shops as well, with fifty-five thousand workers leaving their jobs.[54]

The union charged that the employers were trying to destroy the union and to reinstate the "irresponsible regime of the sweat-shop period." Although it must have galled him to say so, Drew responded that the employers recognized the need for the "full and complete organization" of the workers in the industry and did not regard the closed shop that prevailed as "arbitrable." He noted, however, that the employers did wish to submit to arbitration certain union practices that they believed "detrimental" to the industry. Eventually, the two sides agreed to submit their dispute to an Advisory Board consisting of Frankfurter, Louis Marshall, and Ripley as impartial chairman. The subjects to be considered by the board were the hours and wages questions and allegedly restrictive union practices that the employers charged undermined shop discipline, specifically the union's effective control of hiring and firing. Drew claimed that Frankfurter had committed himself in advance to the forty-four hour demand and hence was not "impartial."[55]

In a preliminary report of January 22, 1919, the Advisory Board granted the union its hours demand, deferred a decision on wages but later granted an increase, and agreed to study the "formation of principles and establishment of machinery" that would lead to improved efficiency, production, and discipline. Drew stressed to the board as it studied the latter question the need to establish "a proper balance of power between the parties" regarding hiring and firing. In an intermediate report submitted on February 14, 1919, the board recommended a procedure for settling disputes between the employers and the union, stated that the employers had "the power of discipline and discharge" subject to some limitations, and advised that the exercise of that power be vested in an employment manager appointed by the employers subject to the approval of the impartial chairman.[56]

It is interesting to note that the employers and Drew decided that the employment manager should be Drew's man, J. A. G. Badorf. Badorf, however, did not get the job, because the union was concerned about his "former connections" and the Advisory Board thought the position should go to someone more familiar with the industry. Drew's last word to the American Men's and Boys' Clothing Manufacturers' Association was that it should "keep in touch" with "employers generally" and should seek to understand the problems they faced in dealing with unions. Drew realized that he could not dislodge the union in the boys' and men's clothing industry, but he probably derived some comfort from the fact that he had helped for the moment to strengthen management somewhat in its dealings with the union on the shop floor.[57]

The war did not deter Drew from seeking to spread the open shop to communities where it did not already exist or to strengthen it where it did. He continued to give "advice and assistance" to the Business Men's Association of Omaha, he attempted to stimulate "open shop sentiment" in Newark by meeting with employer organizations, and he assisted employers in combating unionism in Kansas City and Danbury, Connecticut. In Kansas City, where, despite some gains for the NEA in the prewar era, as already noted, the secretary general of the city's Contractors' Association reported that organized labor had "swooped down upon . . . [the] city to make it the Organized City of America," the employers appeared "helpless" as to "how to proceed in the matter." Baffled as they faced what became almost a general strike, the employers asked Drew and the NEA for help. Asserting that it had put Drew's recommendations into effect—just what those recommendations were is unclear—the city's Employers' Association soon reported that it "gave organized labor the most genteel dressing down they have encountered for many years" and declared that it was "prepared to repeat the dose if necessary." When the American Bridge Company began to erect a $2 million power plant for the Kansas City Light and Power Company in late October 1918, the city's building trades union struck the firm. Drew quickly offered the aid of one of his assistants, but the company gained the upper hand in the dispute before help arrived. As the war drew to a close, the secretary of the Employers' Association described the labor situation in Kansas City as "thoroughly in hand."[58]

Industrial relations in Danbury had attracted attention primarily because the United States Supreme Court had held in 1908 that a secondary interstate boycott that the United Hatters of North America had conducted to bring Danbury hat manufacturer Dietrich Loewe to terms constituted an unlawful conspiracy in violation of the Sherman Antitrust Act. Following the decision, the American Anti-Boycott Association successfully brought suit against individual members of the United Hatters on the ground that they were liable for the actions of the union's leadership, resulting in a prolonged struggle that finally ended in July 1917 with the payment to Loewe by the AFL of $234,192.[59] It was at about this point, where the story normally ends, that Drew came into the picture.

Danbury's hat manufacturers, having provoked a strike of the United Hatters in May 1917 and having adopted the open shop, retained Drew as their counsel and advisor for a few weeks in the fall of 1917 to help them keep their industry and the city itself on an open shop basis. Seeing his "missionary work" as "the final climax" to the *Loewe* case, Drew persuaded the city's leading banking interests to sign a public statement endorsing the open shop stand of the hat manufacturers. He advised the manufacturers to improve working conditions, hire a labor agent to secure workers, advertise for apprentices, train new workers, stress that jobs offered were permanent, perhaps adopt a system of individual employee contracts, and mention the open shop in all their advertisements. Drew himself used the press to counter union claims, and he enlisted the support of Hartford's open shop manufacturers. A few weeks after he came to Danbury, Drew wrote C. E. Whitney, the head of the Hartford Manufacturers' Association, that he feared his part in Danbury had not been "particularly helpful." Whitney, who was himself probably the single most influential figure in bringing the open shop to Danbury, responded that the NEA commissioner's efforts in the city were "the most important part of the work to free Danbury" from the closed shop. In paying Drew for his services in February 1918, the hat manufacturers reported that the open shop movement in the city was "getting along as well as can be expected." The hatters' strike continued until January 1922 and ended in the utter defeat of the union, leaving Danbury an open shop community.[60]

Because of the great importance of the labor question in World War I, George Creel, the head of the federal government's Committee on Public Information, thought it advisable for the committee to publish statements in defense of the closed shop by a union spokesman and of the open shop by a spokesman for that position. He asked Gompers to speak for the closed shop, and it is no surprise that he requested Drew to provide the open shop statement. The proposal came to naught because Gompers would not join in the effort, but what occurred is another indication of Drew's central place in the open shop movement.[61]

Although the structural steel industry was largely able to resist unionization during World War I, the union movement grew apace during the war years. Total union membership increased 29 percent from 1914 to 1918 (from 2,687,000 to 3,467,000), membership in the International Association of Bridge, Structural and Ornamental Iron Workers—Ornamental was added to the name in 1916—by about the same percentage (from 13,200 to 18,600), and building trades union membership by 26 percent (from 555,300 to 700,000). As union membership continued to escalate in the early postwar period,[62] Drew and the NEA joined in the employer offensive to halt the union advance and to force the labor movement into retreat.

CHAPTER 8

"The Shadow of a Greater Contest": Steel and the Open Shop, 1919–20

The National Erectors' Association (NEA) from its inception had seen itself not only as the defender of the open shop in the erection of structural steel but also as the first line of defense against unionization of the steel fabrication shops and, ultimately, the steel mills themselves. If the International Association of Bridge, Structural and Ornamental Iron Workers (IABSOIW), the argument went, secured a closed shop in the erection of structural steel, it would refuse to handle fabricated steel produced in nonunion shops. That is why, as we have seen, Drew insisted that the labor policy of the NEA was "more largely and directly . . . connected with the steel industry than with the building industry."[1] The NEA consequently joined with the steel companies and the steel fabricators in resisting the AFL effort initiated in World War I to organize the steel industry. The association centered its action in New York and, to a lesser extent, Philadelphia, where it sought to prevent the delivery of structural steel to contractors who would erect it with union labor.

Encouraged by government support of unionism in World War I, the IABSOIW made a more determined effort at the time than ever before to organize the steel fabrication shops. The steel mills themselves, as already noted, also became a major object of union attention once the National Committee for Organizing Iron and Steel Workers was formed on August 1, 1918, with the IABSOIW, the largest union in the steel industry, an active member. For Drew and the NEA, the threat to the open shop in steel posed by this action was brought into sharp focus late in 1919 when the Building Trades Employers' Association (BTEA) and the Building Trades Council (BTC) in New York, the NEA's vital center, concluded what amounted to a closed shop agreement that appeared to be directed at the only open shop stronghold in the city's building trades, structural steel erection. The possible impact of this development was not lost on either the fabrication shops or the major steel producers, since it coincided with the AFL's steel organizing campaign.

Although the IABSOIW had long claimed jurisdiction over the fabrication shops, it was not until December 1918 that the union constitution was amended, effective January 1, 1919, to make it explicit that the union's jurisdiction extended to the fabrication of structural steel and cast iron as well as their erection. At the union's September 1918 convention, moreover, the delegates unanimously referred a resolution to the union's executive board providing that whenever 50 percent or more of the shop workers were organized, IABSOIW members would be forbidden to erect any material fabricated by nonunion workers.[2]

The IABSOIW campaign to organize the fabrication shops, as already noted, had not proceeded very far as of the end of World War I, but the effort was stepped up after the war. Also, what the steel fabricators feared came to pass in St. Louis in the early spring of 1919, when the city's BTC supported a strike by the IABSOIW shop local by ordering a boycott against the steel fabricated in the city's five fabrication shops.[3]

When a constituent union of the National Committee for Organizing Iron and Steel Workers sought in May 1919 to confer with Judge Elbert H. Gary, the chairman of the board of United States Steel, he responded, "As you know, we do not confer, negotiate with, or combat labor unions as such. We stand for the open shop." Gary the next month ignored a request from Samuel Gompers to confer with the committee. Unable to negotiate with the most important of the steel companies, the committee called for a work stoppage beginning on September 22 against the steel firms. If the strike succeeded and the IABSOIW as a result were able to enroll the workers properly within its jurisdiction, the union's president asserted, its membership would increase about fivefold, to one hundred thousand. "[E]very available man we have or can possibly spare," he reported in November, "is engaged on the steel campaign." The union also contributed "a large amount of money" to the effort.[4]

The "prime conspirators," to use the phrase of a Federal Trade Commission (FTC) examiner, in the employer effort to prevent the unionization of the structural steel shops and structural steel erection as part of the general AFL effort to organize the steel industry were Walter Drew and Thomas Earle, by then vice president of the Bethlehem Steel Bridge Corporation, the Bethlehem Steel Company's erection subsidiary and an NEA member. Writing to Earle on June 25, 1919, Drew indicated how the steel employers could combat union efforts to use control of erection to unionize the shops. One method, he asserted, was for the fabricators to sell their product only on an erected basis, which meant that the seller erected the steel himself or arranged for its erection, rather than on an f.o.b. (cars) delivered basis, which left the buyer free to arrange for the erection of the product. Steel contractors, Drew also suggested, could become general contractors themselves and, by so doing, be in a position to enforce the open shop in the building trades working under a particular contract. Drew noted that he had had "very favorable talks" along these lines with both Gary and August Ziesing, the American Bridge president.[5]

Concerned about what he assumed was a closed shop erection contract in Buffalo, Drew informed the Lackawanna Bridge Company in August 1919 that the steel mills, at the time, were "very much concerned with the Union question" and that erection firms could secure the cooperation of the mills in resisting unionization of erection jobs. "Where does he get his steel?" Drew asked about the Buffalo company involved. Two weeks later Drew reported to the NEA's executive committee that he had visited Gary, J. A. Farrell, the president of United States Steel, and Eugene G. Grace, the president of Bethlehem Steel, and that they had made evident their "positive intention to prevent unionizing of [steel] shops."[6]

Once the steel strike began the next month, the NEA joined with other open shop employer organizations to "back up" Gary's hard-line antiunion position. Although an NEA district manager reported that 50 percent of the shop workers in one McClintic-Marshall plant had joined the strike at its outset, he also indicated that most shops were fully manned, with the "main trouble caused by foreigners in [the] Chicago district." There was, in any event, no likelihood that the major fabrication firms would tolerate the unionization of their shops. After the strike had been under way for several weeks, Drew repored that the NEA, in individual instances, had been "of very material assistance" in dealing with the shop troubles.[7]

In Chicago, a major center of the steel strike, workers in the fabrication shops joined workers in the mills on strike. IABSOIW business agents ordered union erection workers not to erect steel from unfair shops in the city, and the Chicago Teamsters' local supported the strike by refusing to haul steel from unfair shops in the city. Drew offered the Chicago fabricators "all possible assistance," and he appealed to fabricators outside the city to support the effort to prevent the unionization of the Chicago shops. When contractors who had arranged to purchase steel from the American Bridge Company yielded to union demands and sought to be released from their contracts so that they could erect the steel with union labor, the company refused and in four instances erected the steel itself without trouble. "The unions have laid down when they found that they were up against the American Bridge Company," its president informed the president of United States Steel.

Combating the strike, the Chicago Iron League protested that the walkout violated the joint arbitration agreement between the Building Construction Employers' Association and the Building Trades Council. The dispute was submitted to an arbitrator, who ruled against the union. The Building Trades Council thereupon ordered the strikers back to work, but the IABSOIW countermanded the order. The strike, however, petered out without the ironworkers having gained the recognition they sought.[8]

The general steel strike was called off on January 8, 1920, months before the Chicago strike ended. The IABSOIW conceded that it had lost five thousand members as a result. Its average paid-up membership, however, was 27,700 as of June 30, 1920, compared to 18,607 on June 30, 1918, and 24,000 on June 30, 1919. The number of the union's shop locals had increased from eight to thirty during the two years, but the union's membership remained concentrated outside these shops.[9]

An organizational tactic that the IABSOIW used during the steel strike and that it continued to employ afterward was to place workers in the shops, but not only in the shops, in "open shop locals" that eventually came to be known collectively as the "Red, White and Blue Union." Members of this "union" paid a $3 initiation fee rather than the usual $25 or $50 and were permitted to work in open shop firms alongside nonunion workers. The plan was to have them remain in that status until enough of them had been organized to confront their employers and to be transferred to one of the regular locals. A large number of ironworkers joined the new locals in several localities but especially in Pittsburgh during the period from October 1919 to April 1920.

NEA members and New York's Iron League Erectors' Association (ILEA) responded to the formation of the open shop locals by informing their employees that the new locals were simply the IABSOIW in another guise, "the same wolf in sheep's clothing." They made it clear, furthermore, that they would not recognize or deal with these locals. The IABSOIW's principal organizer during the steel drive organized an open shop local among shop workers in Pittsburgh, but the union's journal reported a few months later that the local's members were being "fired in bunches" for refusing to support NEA policies. It is unlikely that this was an isolated example of employer reaction to the formation of the open shop locals.[10]

The NEA and the steel firms were especially concerned as trouble loomed in the steel industry about the impact of simultaneous labor developments in the key New York district. After the ironworkers' union had been suspended from New York's General Arbitration Board in the fall of 1905, the ILEA, although committed to the open shop, remained a member of the BTEA. After the arbitration plan lapsed in 1910, the general agreement between the BTEA and the BTC was replaced by individual agreements between the employer association in a particular trade and the union in that trade. There was, of course, no such agreement in the structural iron and steel industry.

As of 1919, the ILEA, composed of most of the large local concerns as well as of some "outside" firms, erected about 75–80 percent of the structural steel in the New York metropolitan area. Most of its members both fabricated and erected structural steel, but some were erectors only, notably the Post and McCord Company. The member firms performed their work as subcontractors under general contractors or under the direct control of owners, architects, or engineers. Over time, the general contractors, who operated on a closed shop basis, did less and less erecting themselves; by the end of World War I only the Thompson-Starrett firm erected any significant tonnage of structural steel in New York.[11]

The ILEA was linked to both the NEA and the steel companies. The New York organization shared an office with the NEA and helped defray the cost of its New York labor bureau. Five ILEA members, including McClintic-Marshall, the second largest steel fabricating company in the nation, were also NEA members as of 1919. Post and McCord, one of the "moving spirits" in the ILEA and also an NEA member, was, as we have seen, the "best customer" of

American Bridge, the "fabricating, selling and erecting subsidiary" of United States Steel. American Bridge did no erecting in New York City, leaving that task to Post and McCord. Levering and Garrigues, an NEA member, and Hay Foundry and Iron Works, two of the more prominent ILEA members, had "always been considered in the trade as natural outlets for a large portion of the Bethlehem Steel Company's plain material." McClintic-Marshall was considered to be a "Mellon interest," and it would eventually be absorbed by Bethlehem.[12]

After the general arbitration plan lapsed in New York, the business agents of the individual building trades unions began to regain much of the power they had lost under the plan, and the BTC was weakened. This state of affairs began to change after the war with the emergence of Robert P. Brindell as the dominant figure on the labor scene in the building trades. A "semi-literate Canadian" who arrived in New York in 1905, Brindell worked initially as a dock builder's helper, the first step in a career that was to make him, according to a 1970 study of union corruption, "the most successful extortionist the building trades were ever to know." He joined the Independent Dock Union, which received an AFL charter in 1907, and became its business agent five years later. Eventually chartered as a Brotherhood of Carpenters local, Brindell's union won a jurisdictional fight with a rival New York dock builders' union that had become an IABSOIW local, an action that led to the aforementioned temporary suspension of the IABSOIW from the AFL.

The outbreak of war in Europe in 1914 and the subsequent increase in the foreign trade of the United States proved to be a boon for New York's dockworkers. Brindell's influence in the Board of Business Agents of the building trades unions began to grow, and by war's end he had become the "czar of the New York building trades." Exacting fifty cents per worker per month from the dockworkers, a total of about $30,500 per year, Brindell in 1918 was "the highest-paid trade union leader in the country." In the second half of 1919 Brindell's efforts to secure a "stronger affiliation" among the building trades unions and the use of the sympathetic strike dovetailed with a BTEA desire to stabilize the increasingly unsettled labor conditions in the booming building trades and led to a BTEA-BTC agreement that threatened the open shop status of structural steel erection and fabrication in New York. With labor scarce and the demand for it increasing, the building trades unions were able to force up wages. One trade would strike to secure a wage increase, generally in violation of contract, and when it succeeded, other trades, by "outlaw" strikes, would "force through proportionate increases." This state of affairs led to several months of "a general chaotic condition," made it difficult for contractors to figure the labor cost for jobs, and created uncertainty about their ability to complete their contracts.[13]

On August 8, 1919, the Board of Governors of the BTEA appointed a special committee to develop a policy "to regulate the conditions prevailing in the [building] industry." The committee recommended two weeks later that another committee be appointed to negotiate an agreement with the unions "to maintain peace and a stable wage" for 1920. During the course of the committee's negotiations with the Board of Business Agents, the AFL, in October 1919, replaced the board with a new Building Trades Council composed of the building trades unions in New York affiliated with the Federation and with Brindell as chairman. The BTC insisted as a condition for an agreement that all the building trades be included, which the BTEA negotiators understood meant, in effect, the likely effort to unionize the ironworkers. Knowing that this would be anathema to the ILEA, the BTEA negotiators sought to dissuade the union representatives from pressing the demand, but the employers yielded when the BTC negotiators made it plain that the inclusion of the ironworkers was the sine qua non for the kind of agreement the BTEA believed was "absolutely essential" to stabilize the building industry.[14]

The BTEA-BTC agreement was concluded on November 20 and approved by the Board of Governors on December 19, 1919. It applied to thirty-three unions and upwards of one hundred thousand workers, thirty BTEA member associations, and some one thousand individual employers and was to be in effect until the end of 1921. In addition to its provisions regarding wages and hours, the contract provided that the unions, individually and collectively, were not to strike a BTEA member, nor was a BTEA member to lock out any of his employees. A Board of Arbitration was established to which disputes were to be submitted, and its decisions were to be binding on the parties. Of special importance to the ILEA and employer interests in the steel industry was the contract provision that it was not to be considered a violation of the agreement for any member union to strike a job on which nonunion workers were employed, a condition that, the contract specified, was to be confirmed by the Board of Arbitration before a strike could be undertaken.[15]

It was the fear that the BTEA would feel itself obliged to conclude the kind of agreement it did conclude that had led Drew as early as June 1919 to propose that the fabrication shops sell their product on an erected basis only and that the steel companies take on the role of general contractor. Drew and the president of the ILEA had "a most satisfactory talk" on this subject with Eugene Grace, and he assured them of his "fullest cooperation," as did other major steel firms. Listing in a September letter several iron firms in the New York district that were operating closed shop, Drew specifically asked for Grace's help in dealing with the matter. What Drew obviously had in mind was the denial of steel to such firms. As he had stated years before the crisis of 1919–20, the supplier of material was "in a position to exercise a beneficial influence" on the recipient.[16]

The ILEA informed the BTEA that it would be pleased to cooperate with other members in the matter of wages but would not agree to any arrangements affecting the open shop policy of ILEA members. Taking defensive action at a special meeting of October 26, 1919, before the BTEA-BTC agreement was concluded, the ILEA adopted a resolution providing that its members were to insert a clause in all new contracts for the erection of structural steel providing that the seller had the right to select the employees involved irrespective of their membership in any labor organization in accordance with the "established customs and rules" of the BTEA, which meant that structural steel was to be provided on an erected basis only. The ILEA at the same time reaffirmed its commitment to the open shop principle.[17]

Once the BTC-BTEA agreement had been approved by the negotiators, Drew and the ILEA insisted that it not only would lead to a closed shop in steel erection but would also be harmful to the community. The association pointed out that the iron trade had been the only one among the building trades to enjoy labor peace for the preceding thirteen years and claimed that the open shop had reduced erection costs by 25 percent even though the open shop erection firms paid wages at least equivalent to the union scale. Given the high building demand of the time and the existing shortage of labor, Drew and the ILEA further contended that the closed shop and the restriction of the labor market to union members would make it impossible for contractors to secure an adequate number of workers, which would further raise construction costs to the public's detriment. The union that would be erecting the steel under closed shop conditions, moreover, Drew and the ILEA pointedly noted, was "a notorious trouble maker" about one-third of whose incumbent officers had been convicted in the great dynamite trial.

It was not only the public about which the open shop erectors and fabricators were concerned. A major fear on their part was that if the BTC proved able to add structural steel erection to the closed shop trades, the general contractors, who had largely surrendered structural steel erection to open shop firms, would begin to purchase steel on f.o.b. contracts, erect it with closed shop workers, and drive the open shop firms from the field. The general contractors, indeed, began to act precisely as Drew and the ILEA had assumed they would, but Drew and the ILEA had prepared a defense in depth.[18]

Insisting that the BTEA negotiators had yielded to the BTC threat of sympathetic strikes directed against open shop and ILEA jobs, the erection firms contended that the BTEA and the BTC were engaged in an illegal conspiracy. On November 26 the ILEA addressed a letter to all architects, owners, and prospective builders in the New York metropolitan area stating that the BTEA-BTC agreement was designed to compel the ILEA to adopt "the un-American policy of the closed shop." If the effort were successful, the ILEA claimed, the result would be decreasing efficiency of workers, limitation of the supply of labor, strikes and other delays, and higher building costs. The addressees were asked to insert an open shop clause in all contracts similar to the clause to which ILEA members, as noted, had already agreed. ILEA members also sent notices to their employees with their payroll slips stating that the association's open shop policy would remain unchanged and repudiating "false and misleading statements" to the contrary. Seeking to ensure the adherence of their own number to the open shop policy, the ILEA agreed on November 26 that any member who violated the open shop policy in erecting steel and iron in the Greater New York and Long Island area was to pay $500 in "liquidated damages" to each member who had observed the agreement. Since there were thirty-six signers, this amounted to a prospective penalty of $17,500.[19]

Although the ILEA defined the open shop as meaning the hiring of workers without regard to their union membership, the association resolved at a December 11 meeting to employ "a substantial percentage of non-union workers" on all new erection jobs unless contract terms prevented this. "Substantial" was not defined in the resolution, but the policy agreed to implied a check on a worker's possible union affiliation when he was hired, a task left to the Industrial Committee that the ILEA created on the same day. The committee was empowered to devise means to carry out ILEA policy, employ assistance (detectives?) as needed, and incur any expense deemed necessary. The committee asked Drew to consider placing an "outside man on the job" to make sure that superintendents were "handling it [the job] properly."[20]

When the BTEA's Board of Governors signed the BTEA-BTC agreement on December 19, the ILEA took one additional step to strengthen its hand. It decided at the end of the month that any f.o.b. quotation or "bid" should state that it was being made "subject to agreement by buyer to have the steel erected by an *experienced* erector of buyer's own choosing, but who shall be satisfactory to the seller." All quotations above twenty-five tons were to be referred to the Industrial Committee.[21]

By December the ILEA had increased its membership to include almost all the firms that fabricated and erected steel and iron work in the New York district. It also had received assurances of "cooperation" from the few non-members in the district. The association, furthermore, enjoyed the unqualified support of the NEA. Drew thought that it was additionally necessary for the ILEA to gain the cooperation of the large "outside" steel firms with access to the New York market. Taking his customary position that structural steel erection was the first line of defense for the maintenance of the open shop in the steel industry as a whole, Drew sought this outside support even before BTEA and BTC negotiators had concluded their agreement. He thus appealed to the mill owners and large fabricators to send representatives to a November 5 dinner of the New York iron contractors at which the means of implementing the ILEA's open shop policy were to be considered. Bethlehem Steel was represented at the meeting, Grace assuring Drew, "[A]s manufacturers of steel we recognize but one labor policy, that is the Open Shop." A United States Steel official thought that Drew's motive at this stage in wanting firms like the steel corporation present at the meeting was "to put some backbone on the movement and stir up the lukewarm contractors." Whatever Drew's motive, those attending the November 5 dinner reaffirmed the ILEA's open shop decision of October 21.[22]

The association of steel fabricators left no doubt that it too was committed to the open shop principle. Meeting in Pittsburgh on November 20, 1919, with Thomas Earle presiding, the fabricators organized the National Steel Fabricators Association (NSFA) to replace the wartime Steel Fabricators of the United States, Drew remaining as counsel. The eighty-six firms making up the association, many of them among the NEA's fifty-four members at the time, accounted for 60 percent of all the structural steel produced in the United States

Walter Drew

Dynamited Utah hotel, April 19, 1910

Structural iron workers

Walter Drew at eighty-six

Dynamited Hoboken viaduct, March 31, 1909

James Emery

Frank Ryan

H. S. Hockin

Ortie McManigal

James B. McNamara

John J. McNamara

and 90–95 percent when the production of American Bridge, which had been a member of the Steel Fabricators but did not join the new organization, was added.

The principal subject of discussion at the November 20, 1919, meeting, coming on the very day that the BTEA-BTC agreement was concluded in New York, was the "labor situation." Asserting that the open shop was "an American Institution beneficial to the Employee, Employer and the Public" and that "organized efforts" were being made to unionize the steel fabricating industry, the NSFA went "on record as being unreservedly and entirely in favor of the 'Open Shop' in all the fabricating plants." In furtherance of this commitment, those present recommended that it be the "policy" of the members "to adjust their businesses so that the steel fabricated by them is erected 'Open Shop.'" The association's executive committee, on which both the NEA and AEA were represented, was "instructed to use all the influence in its power [to this end] with mills, fabricators, contractors and business associations."[23] Early in January the NSFA distributed a letter prepared by Drew indicating that the "important thing" for the fabrication shops was to sell steel in the New York market on an erected basis or with knowledge that the erector would be an open shop concern.[24]

The NSFA proved to be a rather "inactive" body, "a mere paper organization," Drew called it. It held only two membership meetings, and its central office did little more than distribute information of interest to the association's members. It does not appear that the NSFA, as an organization, "used any influence" to coordinate or enforce the policy regarding steel sales that it had adopted, which was the steel industry's defense against charges of collusion. There is every reason to believe, however, that most members faithfully adhered to the steel sales policy.[25]

Among the "outside" concerns supplying the New York market with steel, Bethlehem Steel was the most outspoken in its support of the ILEA. Bethlehem, however, was not prepared to lose sales to competitors that might not insist on the sale of their steel on an erected basis only. The ILEA's president, however, assured Grace on this score, advising him that the ILEA had "the most practical evidence possible" of United States Steel's adherence to the steel sales policy. When Earle somewhat later questioned Drew about an f.o.b. sale of steel in New York by American Bridge, Drew replied that this was due to an "inadvertence" and that steps were being taken "to straighten it up." That, indeed, is precisely what happened, and American Bridge promptly withdrew the bid Earle had questioned.[26]

By the time the BTEA-BTC agreement went into effect on January 1, 1920, Drew and his allies had arranged for the all but complete ban on the sale of structural steel in New York for anything but open shop erection. The fact that the threat to the open shop erection of structural steel in the New York district coincided with the great steel strike of 1919–20 made it easier for United States Steel, independents like Bethlehem, and outside fabricators to view what was happening in New York as an effort by the unions in the steel industry to gain "leverage" over steel manufacturing itself, the point that Drew had insistently made from the start. "Back of the New York battle," declared an FTC member, was "the shadow of a greater contest."[27]

When the BTEA-BTC agreement went into effect, the BTC initiated a sympathetic strike against jobs on which nonunion ironworkers were employed. Strikes were called in January and the early part of February against five jobs, the most important of which was the Metropolitan Life annex, but the general sympathetic strike that the BTC had threatened against all ILEA jobs did not materialize. The strikes failed to halt the work of the ILEA firms, which were able to man the struck jobs with open shop workers. The ILEA received the backing of the city's Chamber of Commerce and Board of Trade and Transportation as well as the owners of the struck buildings. Following the lead of American Bridge, which had announced a 10 percent wage increase for its shop workers beginning on February 1, the ILEA decided on February 7 to increase the pay of open shop housesmiths by the same percentage as of May 1, which meant that nonunion workers would receive a wage 10 percent above the union scale. The new ILEA rate, apparently, went into effect almost immediately, which no doubt strengthened the association's position with nonstriking open shop workers.[28]

The 1908 New York case of *McCord* v. *Thompson-Starrett* appeared to provide legal support for Drew's contention that the BTEA-BTC agreement, viewed as an agreement to force the unionization of the ironworkers, was illegal. The New York Supreme Court, upheld by the New York Court of Appeals, had ruled in the case that although an individual employer could lawfully agree with a union to employ its members exclusively, "such an agreement when participated in by all or by a large proportion of employers in any community becomes oppressive and contrary to public policy." Drew also pointed to a decision handed down by the Court of Chancery in New Jersey in August 1920 that held a closed shop agreement "designed to unionize an entire industry" in Hudson County to be illegal.[29]

By early March 1920 Drew was pronouncing the BTC strike a failure, and the BTEA's leadership admitted as much. The unionized trades, other than the IABSOIW, began returning to work on open shop jobs in May, the BTC called off the strike at the end of the month, and union workers, now including IABSOIW members, once again worked alongside nonunion ironworkers just as they had before January 1, 1920. In April, as the strike was ebbing, the BTC successfully pressed the BTEA for a wage increase of one dollar a day to match the increase received by the ironworkers and the bricklayers, who had not been a party to the BTEA-BTC argeement.[30]

The end of the BTC strike also brought an end to the ILEA's membership in the BTEA. Since the BTEA constitution required a ninety-day notice in writing before a withdrawal could occur, ILEA members simply resigned from the ILEA itself, and, if not already members, joined the Iron League, which, "although dormant [since 1903], was a properly organized association." The ILEA, in effect, thus became the Iron League, a non-BTEA member.[31]

As Drew informed NEA members, the ILEA victory in New York could not have been achieved without the cooperation of the "outside companies." There is no question that in late 1919 and during the course of the building trades strike in the first several months of 1920, steel was simply unavailable to closed shop erectors in New York. Insofar as steel companies pretended to be willing to provide steel on an f.o.b. basis, their practice was to tell the prospective purchasers that the steel could not be delivered until some time after the contractor needed the material.[32]

Seeing the BTEA-BTC agreement as "part of this general plan" to organize the steel industry, the manager of Bethlehem Steel's structural steel department instructed the Bethlehem Steel Bridge Corporation not to accept contracts for steel that called for erection by union workers. Grace instructed the manager of all Bethlehem units to do nothing to "embarrass" the corporation's labor policy. When questioned about American Bridge's policy with respect to providing steel for New York, Joshua Hatfield, the company's vice president who was in charge of sales, responded, "I never talk labor." He claimed that although the company's own erection force was nonunion, it had "never . . . emphasized" the open shop in selling steel. American Bridge, of course, did not have to do so insofar as the New York market was concerned since the company's fabricated steel was erected in that market by Post and McCord, an open shop ILEA firm. McClintic-Marshall was less guarded than its rival in indicating how it had reacted to the BTEA-BTC agreement: its president stated that the company had adopted a policy of no f.o.b. sales of its steel.[33]

As Drew had anticipated, once the BTEA and the BTC came to an agreement, New York's general contractors, notably the two most important, Thompson-Starrett, "the greatest building construction company" in the nation, and George A. Fuller Company, sought to purchase structural steel to be erected by union workers. Their position was that, given the BTEA-BTC agreement, that was the only way steel could be erected in New York without a strike.[34]

When Louis J. Horowitz, Thompson-Starrett's president, approached Hatfield about buying steel for a large Park Avenue building, the American Bridge vice president, contrary to his later testimony, set a prohibitively late delivery date because, according to Horowitz, Hatfield wanted the steel erected open shop. After a call to United States Steel also failed to yield any steel, Horowitz turned to Bethlehem, of which Thompson-Starrett was "an old customer," although its last contract with Bethlehem had been in 1915. Not inclined, as he put it, "to aggravate the labor situation," G. H. Blakeley, manager of Bethlehem's structural steel department and president of the Bethlehem Steel Bridge Corporation, told Horowitz that Bethlehem would sell steel only if it was to be erected under open shop conditions. "We have to protect ourselves," Grace similarly told Horowitz in rejecting his request for steel. When Horowitz, seeking to allay Grace's concern that unionization of erection would lead to the unionization of the steel shops, stated that he had an "understanding" with the union that it would not refuse to handle steel coming from nonunion shops, the Bethlehem president replied that he lacked "confidence" in such promises. Horowitz testified in December 1920 that the last f.o.b. sale his company had been able to arrange with any supplier of steel had been in October 1919, just as the controversy between the ILEA and BTEA was coming to a head. Although it owned about $100,000 in erecting equipment, Thompson-Starrett had to buy steel for the time being erected in place and to arrange for its erection by an ILEA member.[35]

Finding it difficult to obtain steel on an f.o.b. basis toward the end of 1919, Fuller's president, Paul Starrett, proposed to Bethlehem, with which Fuller had not previously had a contractual relationship, to place an annual order with the steel firm of fifty thousand tons of structural steel, which was about 70 percent of Bethlehem's yearly output of the material. Grace's reply was that Bethlehem's order books were full and that it had to give preference to its regular customers. "Don't you imagine for a moment," Grace told Starrett, "that we are going to let you fellows build up an organization of union men who can refuse to erect our steel and force union conditions on our shops." Starrett then suggested to Grace and Charles Schwab, Bethlehem's chairman of the board, that Fuller would be interested in building a fabricating plant of its own in the Bethlehem, Pennsylvania, area, something it could not realistically do unless Bethlehem were willing to supply it with plain steel. Schwab said that the company would take the matter under consideration, which was the last Starrett heard about the proposal. Schwab's statement to Starrett that Bethlehem had been putting up a fight to maintain the open shop and did not intend to have "the fruits of their labor taken from it" no doubt explains Bethlehem's silence.

Fuller, to be sure, had not erected any steel in New York with its own labor force since before World War I. Although it now wished to do so because of the BTEA-BTC agreement, it found that it was blocked by Bethlehem from taking the step. Fuller consequently disposed of its New York erecting equipment, valued at about $250,000, selling some of it and shipping the rest to other locations.[36]

Structural steel erection firms in northern New Jersey, the location of many ILEA fabrication plants, had as much trouble as contractors in neighboring New York City in obtaining steel for anything but open shop erection. According to an affidavit supplied by the bargaining agent of a New Jersey IABSOIW local, Louis Hay of the Hay Foundry and Iron Works told him that if the firm did not comply with NEA and ILEA wishes as to how steel was to be erected, "he might just as well put a lock and key on his plant and close down." The owner of a small shop in Newark similarly told a Department of Labor conciliator that the ILEA had notified him that he would be denied steel if he recognized the union.[37]

Putting aside the fact that they received their plain steel from open shop firms, it should be noted that there were many other reasons why open shop fabricators of structural steel might have wanted to erect their product themselves. Some companies had their own erection forces that they wanted to keep occupied. If they did their own erecting, moreover, they would be able to "control the operation better" than if the erection were sublet. They could also in this way avoid "back charges" by the contractor or erector because of some alleged error in fabrication that caused additional work by the erector. None of these factors, however, was as large a consideration for steel fabricators as was the objective of forestalling the unionization of their industry. As American Bridge's president put it to the president of United States Steel in May 1920, "We have to fight this out where we stand or we will be gradually driven to the wall."[38] The failure of the strike against open shop steel erection in New York demonstrated that the steel firms had successfully stood their ground and checked the feared unionization of the industry.

The BTC's abandonment of the strike on open shop jobs in New York had "a very demoralizing and discouraging effect" on the ironworkers' key New York Local 40. P. J. Morrin, the IABSOIW president, attributed the strike's failure, in part, to the lack of full support given the ironworkers by the BTC but also, understandably, to the refusal of the big steel firms to supply steel for unionized erection. Morrin met with Frank Walsh, who had become the union's general counsel in 1918, to see what could be done about the alleged discrimination by the steel interests against "fair" contractors. Their decision was to turn to the federal government for assistance.[39]

Writing on June 20, 1920, to the AFL's secretary-treasurer, Frank Morrison, and claiming that the NEA was using "every possible method" of discrimination against union employees, Morrin requested the Federation's aid in persuading the federal government to investigate the NEA's behavior in New York. Supplementing Morrin's own appeal to Washington, Morrison discussed the matter with Secretary of Labor William B. Wilson, who instructed Commissioner of Conciliation James J. Barrett to "take up [the] New York Steel strike situation." Unable to bring the two sides together, Barrett, who estimated the number of workers involved at about six thousand, observed in his final report to the director of conciliation that "a large number of contractors" had been "absolutely cut off from carrying on their business" and had been forced to sublet their work to open shop erectors who were members of the Iron League. Barrett gathered his information in collaboration with Patrick F. Duffy, an AFL organizer whom the Federation had assigned to assist the IABSOIW in the New York strike.[40]

Other than the greater New York area, the only large city where the steel producers sought to control the erection of their product to combat the threat of unionism was Philadelphia.[41] And here, as in New York, Walter Drew was the key player. As of the spring of 1919 steel was being erected in Philadelphia on both a closed shop and an open shop basis. The iron trade in the city was organized differently than in New York. For jobs of less than one hundred tons of steel in Philadelphia, an iron dealer or "broker" purchased the structural steel that he then sublet to a general contractor or owner to be erected. For large jobs, general contractors usually purchased their steel f.o.b. cars and did their own erecting. What led the steel producers in the spring of 1919 to favor the sale of steel on an erected basis only was an agreement to resolve labor disputes negotiated on April 23 by an advisory board of the employer associations in the building trades affiliated with the Master Builders' Exchange and the Allied Council of Associated Building Trades representing the unions. Believing that the agreement "strongly favored the unions" and would prevent the iron trade from operating on an open shop basis, members of the trade who thought that the Builders' Exchange did not adequately represent them decided to organize to resist the application of the agreement to the iron business. To assist in forming an iron league, W. Nelson Mayhew, a partner in the Montgomery Iron and Steel Company and a leading figure in the city's iron trade, turned to Walter Drew, who, as Mayhew put it, was "known to be an ardent open shop advocate and [was] legally experienced in fostering associations to further such policy." The Philadelphia general contractor John R. Wiggins, who had "fathered" the April 23 agreement, thought, however, that it was the "big steel people" who had requested Drew to deal with the Philadelphia situation.[42]

Drew immediately set about to organize the iron firms into an association and to point it in what he saw as the right direction. He appeared at May meetings of what became the Iron League of Philadelphia, which appointed him its counsel, at which he stressed the virtues of the open shop and recited his usual arguments about the linkage between closed shop structural steel erection and the unionization of the steel shops. His advice, that the purpose of the Iron League, composed of brokers, fabricators, and erectors, should be the maintenance of the open shop in both erection and manufacturing, was accepted unanimously, and those present then approved another motion not to execute any contract that stipulated the kind of labor to be used in erecting steel. This meant, of course, that the steel was to be erected only on a nonunion basis. Iron brokers and fabricators then began to tell erectors who operated closed shops that the outside mills and fabricators would not supply them with steel unless they agreed to erect it on an open shop basis. Some general contractors, however, continued to solicit and to receive f.o.b. bids and to erect steel with union labor. Noting that the NEA was "solidly back" of the Iron League, Drew appealed to general contractors, bankers, manufacturers, and other business interests in Philadelphia to support the Iron League and the open shop.[43]

Beginning in March 1920 Drew sought to arrange for the same sort of denial of steel for closed shop erection in Philadelphia as already prevailed in New York. Although successful to some degree, Drew was unable to secure the same kind of cooperation from outside concerns selling steel for erection in Philadelphia as in providing steel for New York because of the lack of unity among members of the Philadelphia Iron League.[44]

In July 1920 Drew asked A. S. Roberts, a New York Iron League counsel who was assisting the NEA commissioner in Philadelphia, to help implement a policy, as in New York, of requiring that all bids for more than twenty-five tons of steel be on an erected basis only. Roberts secured such an agreement, but not all the fabricators were willing to sign it. Frank McCord urged American Bridge to sell steel only on an erected basis in Philadelphia, and Levering and

Garrigues and Hay Foundry and Iron Works "put it up" to Bethlehem to do the same. The secretary of the Philadelphia Iron League thought that the results were "pretty good" from an open shop point of view, several Philadelphia contractors finding themselves unable to secure steel unless it was to be erected by open shop workers. One Philadelphia erector later told an FTC examiner that the erected-only sales policy had been extended in August 1920 to cover bids of even less than twenty-five tons and that he, at least, had then laid off all the union members working for him. Some Philadelphia contractors, nevertheless, continued to be able to purchase steel on an f.o.b. basis and to erect it with such labor as they chose. As a McClintic-Marshall official stated in May 1921, his company had sought to pursue the same policy as regards the sale of steel in Philadelphia as it had in New York, but things had "not been lined up so well" in Philadelphia.[45]

The steel boycott in New York became the subject of a state legislative probe as well as a United States Department of Justice inquiry, and the FTC examined what had occurred in both New York and Philadelphia to determine if a violation of federal law was involved. The New York legislature established a Joint Legislative Committee on Housing on April 18, 1919, to investigate the causes for the lack of construction of new buildings and apartments as well as for the increase in rents in the state's cities but especially in New York City. The committee began taking testimony immediately, but it was not until December 1920 that it began hearing witnesses with regard to the steel delivery matter.

When the committee's mandate was enlarged in September 1920, it accepted the offer of Samuel Untermeyer, who had served as counsel of the Pujo Committee in 1912, to serve as its counsel without compensation. Chaired by Senator Charles C. Lockwood and popularly referred to by his name, the committee elicited information that was very damaging to the BTC and, especially, its head, Robert P. Brindell, as well as numerous employer associations affiliated with the BTEA. It also provided an airing of the efforts of the ILEA, the fabrication shops, and the steel mills to deny steel to open shop erectors in New York.[46]

At a very early stage of its inquiry, the Lockwood Committee discovered that nearly all the building trades unions in New York were under "the absolute dominion of one man," Brindell. Brindell and his "piratical crew," the committee reported, had used their union positions to engage in "a vast campaign of extorting money from builders and building contractors." When the city's house-wrecking union, the so-called Zaranko Union, refused to join the BTC, Brindell organized his own wreckers' union. If a contractor then used the Zaranko rather than the Brindell union, Brindell would deny him workers to erect a new building on the site or might compel the "offender" to pay tribute to avoid a strike or to be permitted to build on the site. Brindell also charged wrecking contractors to have their names placed on an approved list of contractors whom it was safe for an owner or general contractor to employ without incurring a strike. When the Zaranko Union was destroyed by these tactics, Brindell made its former members pay a permit fee to obtain work.

Sometimes, Brindell made contractors pay him "tribute" in order to employ nonunion workers. On several occasions, he exacted substantial sums from contractors either for not initiating a strike or for calling off a strike. This became a special problem for contractors employing nonunion ironworkers, which is what they had to do to obtain steel. In a period of about ten to eleven months, Brindell was able to exact more than $1 million from contractors. When one contractor offered him $2,000 to continue a job without a strike, the labor leader asked, "Do you think I am a piker?" Brindell was indicted on several counts of extortion in November 1920, found guilty in February 1921, and sentenced to five to ten years imprisonment.[47]

When the Lockwood Committee resumed its hearings in December 1921, it exposed rules and practices of the building trades unions that, it charged, "destroy efficiency, delay operations and increase expenses." These were, for the most part, practices that Drew had consistently condemned as characteristic of the building trades unions, such as limiting the number of apprentices, limiting the amount of work per day, requiring skilled mechanics to perform laborers' work, prohibiting the use of labor-saving devices, requiring that work be done at the job site rather than more economically in the shop, and closing the union books to new members but permitting nonmembers to work for a fee.[48]

The Lockwood Committee revealed that many of the constituent employer associations of the BTEA restricted competition by bid rigging, "trade strangulation," price fixing, profiteering, and other "abuses" that resulted in "the exaction of tribute from owners, builders and contractors." Much of this was made possible by collusive agreements between the BTEA and the BTC providing that the relevant unions were to refuse to supply labor to any person or firm that was not a member of the BTEA or a constituent employer association if a member employer required the services of union workers. Just about "every article entering into building construction," a contemporary writer summarized, "has been shown to be under the control of merciless, gouging, monopolistic combines." State trials that ensued resulted in the jailing of sixty defendants and the payment of $254,000 in fines, and federal trials led to the imprisonment of forty-four defendants and the payment of $213,500 in fines.[49]

The IABSOIW and especially its general counsel Frank Walsh, aided by his old associate Basil Manly, "butted into the Building Material controversy," as Walsh put it, and played a critical role in preparing the Lockwood Committee and Untermeyer for the conduct of the iron and steel trade phase of the committee's hearings. "Our job," Walsh asserted, "is to get them [Lockwood] to go after the Steel Trust and the National Erectors' Association, which, we claim, are the head devils in the whole enterprise." Morrin and Walsh claimed to have persuaded the committee to seize the minutes of both the NEA and the ILEA as well as some of their correspondence. Drew, however, reported later that the New York office of the NEA had been broken into and ransacked at the time. In any event, copies of the NEA and ILEA minutes ended up in the Walsh Papers, not the Drew Papers. Untermeyer, who, although a major Bethlehem stockholder, allegedly had "an ancient grudge against the steel industry" and was a critic of United States Steel's labor policy, authorized Manly "to put on" an "examiner" who was to be paid by the committee. The examiner Manly selected was Samuel Evans, a member of Walsh's staff. Walsh prepared a complaint for the committee that was based on material his office and the IABSOIW had compiled but also included the aforementioned material that Barrett and Duffy had gathered in investigating the New York strike.[50]

Beginning on December 14, 1920, and continuing to December 17, the Lockwood Committee heard testimony about the manner in which fabricators supplied structural steel for erection and also the labor policy of the steel industry. Paul Starrett explained that "the entire construction operation" depended on the erection of the steel frame of the building, and Louis Horowitz and he provided information on the inability of unionized firms to obtain steel on an f.o.b. basis or on time to meet building requirements. Starrett claimed that a "good" union gang could erect steel 25–35 percent more cheaply than a nonunion gang could, and Horowitz agreed that union members had "the best talent and skill." Frank McCord, however, rebutted this testimony, noting that it hardly squared with the fact that the Fuller Company had sublet many erection jobs to Post and McCord, an open shop firm, for five years before steel had become unavailable for closed shop erection.

C. E. Cheney, the secretary of both the NEA and the ILEA, agreed for all practical purposes with Untermeyer's judgment that an open shop really meant a shop without any union members. Grace, for his part, told the committee that Bethlehem would not recognize a union even if it represented 95 percent of the company's employees.[51]

When the private detective Robert Foster appeared before the committee, he disputed as "false and malicious" a summary of his career Untermeyer presented that included a dishonorable discharge from the army and a record as a Louisville police officer of drunkenness, disorderly conduct, assault and battery, and conduct unbecoming an officer. "An aggressive and defiant witness," Foster stated that forty to forty-five operatives worked for him, eight of them in the steel industry and six others inside unions. Although he agreed that he might have in his possession as many as five hundred reports to the NEA and the AEA, he claimed that since the Indianapolis dynamite trial and his founding of Foster's Industrial and Detective Bureau, Drew had employed him only on one occasion, about eighteen months previously. Cheney, however, was later questioned about $3,093.47 in NEA checks to Foster in 1916, 1917, and 1919 that seemed to contradict the detective's testimony about his limited service for the NEA since 1912. The committee found Foster in contempt for refusing to produce operative reports that it had subpoenaed.

Stating, "I'll go to hell before I tell anything of my relations with my clients," Foster, whom Gompers characterized as "the chief detective of the steel people," was arrested on December 17 and indicted both for "wilfully refusing to testify" and for "wilfully refusing to produce material." He was fined $500 and sentenced to thirty days in prison early in 1922, but the sentence was later set aside by the New York Court of Appeals on the grounds that the questions the Lockwood Committee had asked Foster and the material sought from him were not relevant to the purposes of the committee. Foster by then had served his prison term, but the $500 fine he had paid was returned to him. On March 30, 1921, he instituted a $100,000 libel suit against Untermeyer for allegedly making false statements about the detective's career. The suit was later dismissed with the consent of both parties after Untermeyer admitted some inaccuracies in the Foster career summary.[52]

Drew was ejected from the Lockwood Committee hearings and hissed by the audience on December 16 when he did not remain silent despite being instructed by Untermeyer to do so. When Drew encountered Untermeyer the next day and sought to explain that he had meant no discourtesy to the committee's counsel, Untermeyer shot back, "[Y]ou had better disband the National Erectors' League [Association], the Iron League, and the National Association of Steel Fabricators. Otherwise," he said, "you are all likely to be indicted."[53]

After Cheney concluded his testimony on December 17, the Lockwood Committee accepted Untermeyer's recommendation that the testimony of the steel fabricators and erectors and the accompanying exhibits be sent to the special grand jury then sitting in New York County and also to the United States attorney in the district because of what appeared to be "a series of flagrant violations" of both state and federal law. The committee later concluded that "the so-called 'Open Shop' as enforced by the Steel Companies in all their ramifications is neither more nor less than a non-Union shop." It accused the steel companies of maintaining "a vast spying system" and of blacklisting union members. In the committee's opinion, it was because of the ability of the steel industry to enforce its open shop policy that Brindell had been able "to blackmail" builders in New York and that builders who did not subscribe to the open shop were unable to purchase steel. The IABSOIW agreed, claiming that the Lockwood hearings had revealed "a conspiracy to break the only effective [labor] organization in the steel industry."[54] This, needless to say, was hardly how Drew saw matters. In providing briefs for government officials, in statements to the press, and in correspondence with one person or another, he defended the structural steel firms from the charges levied against them in the Lockwood Committee hearings and by the committee itself. Drew maintained that the BTEA-BTC agreement of 1919, aimed, in the NEA commissioner's view, at achieving "an absolutely complete monopoly of the entire building industry in New York City," constituted "an illegal combination" in violation of the Sherman Antitrust Act, since it sought by the joint action of employer associations and unions and by sympathetic strikes to destroy the interstate trade of iron concerns that took contracts to fabricate, transport, and erect structural steel and because it sought to place iron and steel erection in the hands of a union committed to the kind of illegal secondary boycott condemned in *Duplex Printing Press Company* v. *Deering*.

If, for the sake of argument, Drew contended, one assumed that a combination of fabricators had been organized that refused to sell steel on an f.o.b.

basis in order to combat the Brindell combination, it was a reasonable action, limited to the emergency it faced, "commensurate" only with it, and that ceased when the emergency ceased. Its "dominant purpose," he maintained, "was not to restrain trade but to protect business, not from lawful competition, but from an illegal combination." The iron firms, he insisted, had employed appropriate "defensive tactics," and no more, to keep the channels of trade open.[55]

Quite apart from the allegedly defensive nature of the restrictions imposed on f.o.b. sales of steel, Drew asserted that most fabricators of structural steel erected their steel themselves and that only "a negligible amount of fabricated material" was sold for others to erect. It would, moreover, have been "business suicide," he declared, for the iron firms, given the character of the BTEA-BTC agreement, to have sold their steel to members of the "combine," who were committed to having it erected on a closed shop basis and who, in any event, were involved in an illegal combination.[56]

It is not certain, despite Drew's argument, that the practice of denying steel for closed shop erection ceased when the New York strike came to an end. At its May 20, 1920, meeting, by which time Local 40 had authorized its members to return to work, the Iron League, it is true, authorized its members to make f.o.b. sales, but only for twenty-five tons or less, and to use "utmost care" even in doing this so as to ensure the open shop erection of the steel. McClintic-Marshall informed an FTC examiner in May 1921 that the Iron League had changed its policy at the beginning of 1921 and that members since then were selling steel without regard to the method of its erection. The secretary of Hay Foundry and Iron Works, an Iron League member, told the FTC at about the same time, however, that the league policy had not changed and that general contractors who said otherwise were "liars." He was probably referring to Horowitz and Starrett, both of whom had stated by then that there had indeed been "a real change of policy" and that their firms were securing steel on an f.o.b. basis, Starrett reporting that he had received such bids from "practically all the steel companies."

What seems evident is that steel had become available on an f.o.b. basis in New York by the end of 1921 or shortly thereafter but not in Philadelphia. Untermeyer was convinced at the end of 1921 that the steel "people" were "up to their old practices," but when Walsh, at Morrin's suggestion, assigned a special investigator to ascertain the truth of the matter, the union counsel learned that the "old practices" had indeed been abandoned. As late as 1933, however, Walsh and Morrin were still complaining that although the open shop steel companies were using methods less "open and crude" than at the time of the Lockwood Committee hearings, they continued to "make the life of the independent [unionized] erector hazardous." The charge was that the steel firms, for example, delayed deliveries to unionized contractors and charged independents more for steel than they charged their own erection subsidiaries. The Morrin-Walsh allegations were echoed by the Labor Advisory Board of the National Recovery Administration (NRA), which reported in 1934 that "a considerable body of evidence" had been presented to the NRA revealing "discrimination" by steel fabricators against erectors and general contractors employing union labor.[57]

Although Drew, to make a point, had assumed the existence of a combination to prevent the sale of steel for erection on a closed shop basis, he sought to combat the view that a combination in any real sense had actually been formed. He thus argued that the ILEA's twenty-five-ton decision did "not control the final act of any member." Straining credulity, he claimed that he "did not entirely approve" of the action. He noted that when he learned of the similar agreement of the Philadelphia Iron League, he advised that all copies thereof be destroyed, which, of course, contradicted his assertion about the innocuous nature of such an agreement and revealed his concern about its possible illegality. He insisted that the NSFA advice to its members to adjust their steel sales so as to ensure its erection by open shop workers was just a recommendation and not a policy commitment and was also "very ill-advised." As for the NEA, Drew claimed that it had never taken any action regarding steel sales and was, in any event, only "sort of an advisory body." Each company interested in the market for steel, Drew maintained, had a right to know the facts, and so he kept them advised of the situation. And if, given the circumstances, individual companies refused to sell steel for its erection on a closed shop basis, they did so, Drew insisted, for "self-preservation."[58] Drew's role, however, was less passive than these assertions indicated.

Drew rejected the charge that the iron firms blacklisted union members, asserting, as he always did, that the open shop meant the employment of workers without regard to their affiliation with any organization. He pointed out in this regard that the IABSOIW had stated in its journal that almost all of its New York members were at work, which meant that most of them were almost certainly working for open shop firms. Drew claimed that neither the NEA nor the Iron League had a "spy system." Foster, he said, had done "a little work" for the two organizations since the dynamite trial and had had some operatives in steel plants for a few months but only one or two in NEA shops, which left unexplained the NEA checks Foster had received in 1916, 1917, and 1919.[59]

Citing the "general graft and corruption" that the Lockwood Committee had exposed, Drew made a telling point in observing that the iron contractors were the only employer group in the New York building trades not charged with "price fixing, exploitation or corruption of any kind." Had they joined the effort to establish "a complete monopoly of labor" in the building trades, he asserted, they would have been acting against "the public welfare."[60]

The evidence gathered by the Lockwood Committee concerning steel fabrication and erection was first examined for possible legal action by the New York County district attorney. As B. L. Shinn, an FTC attorney and the examiner in charge of its New York office, indicated, "every possible influence of organized labor was brought to bear on the District Attorney" to force him to prosecute the New York Iron League but without success. This was probably because New York's courts had held that combinations limiting the sale of material in the state were legal.[61]

Without the state government having rendered any decision, the Department of Justice stepped in and directed that the steel matter be presented to a federal grand jury in the Southern District of New York. The attorney general of the United States appointed William Rand, "one of the ablest lawyers" in New York City, and Isadore Kreisel as special assistants to the attorney general to take charge of the proceedings and to decide whether there had been a conspiracy to restrain the interstate sale of structural steel. Aided by other attorneys and by investigators, the two special attorneys conducted a six-week investigation beginning in January 1921. In addition to the evidence provided by the Lockwood Committee and gathered by the federal officials, the NEA and the Iron League voluntarily submitted pertinent records, and Drew, Iron League members, and representatives of some outside concerns voluntarily appeared as witnesses before the grand jury and waived their immunity.

The federal grand jury decided in the middle of February not to indict the Iron League or any other organization or person, Morrin later claiming that Untermeyer had learned that a single changed vote would have altered the outcome. Untermeyer attributed the failure to indict to what he claimed was the unprecedented action of the grand jury in permitting the defendants to testify without the knowledge of the complainants. Drew, however, maintained that what had happened was within the discretion of the grand jury and was "perfectly proper." Because of criticism directed at the failure of the grand jury to indict, Attorney General Harry Daugherty ordered another investigation of the same matter, this time extending beyond New York to other large cities. Whatever the nature of this investigation, it did not result in any indictments.[62]

Rand told the chairman of the FTC that the grand jury decision not to indict had been "fully justified" and that it would have done more harm than good for it to have decided otherwise. Drew, however, revealed at a later time that Rand, presumably at an early stage of the proceedings, had suggested that the defendants accept a consent decree in an equity proceeding that would have joined the NEA, the Iron League, United States Steel, and others from seeking to control the sale of steel. The NEA commissioner claimed that he had opposed acceptance of the decree even though the lawyer representing the Iron League in the case had been willing to go along.[63]

"Failing in every other quarter," the IABSOIW, Shinn reported, turned to the FTC for redress. Actually, however, the union had filed a complaint with the FTC in late November 1920, but the commission did not act on it until the spring and summer of 1921, when it made an extensive investigation of the steel sale issue that included an examination of the evidence gathered by the Department of Justice. The union complaint alleged that the NEA and ILEA were guilty of "unfair practices" that suppressed competition and created an "unlawful monopoly" in violation of the Clayton Antitrust Act and "irreparably injured" the union by denying its members the opportunity to work to which they were legally entitled. Drew presented the ILEA's defense in a lengthy statement to the FTC.[64]

The FTC investigation became linked in a curious way with the dynamite trials, to which Drew regularly referred in seeking to discredit the NEA's union opponent. Walsh in the early stages of the investigation had agreed to travel to San Francisco with IABSOIW president Morrin to be on hand when John J. McNamara was released from San Quentin. Morrin wanted Walsh to be available "in case of an emergency out there" that might result from the still outstanding Indianapolis indictment against McNamara. Walsh, however, decided in late April 1921 that it would be "a grave mistake" for him to meet McNamara at a time when the IABSOIW counsel was in charge of "the legal end" of the union's fight against the NEA and the Iron League. These two organizations, Walsh wrote Morrin, recognized that "they are in a death battle with your organization, that is, if we beat them here, it may result in their dissolution absolutely; that if they beat us, they will, at least, make giant headway in their fight to destroy your organization." If the FTC, Walsh asserted, decided to hold a public hearing, as he anticipated, he would have to argue the union's case against Drew, whose defense of "these illegal organizations," Walsh maintained, was based "almost solely" on the allegation that the IABSOIW was itself an illegal organization whose power was based on "intimidation and violence." If he went to San Francisco, Walsh explained, it would be "impossible" to separate the McNamara case from the FTC investigation, and if Drew could associate the union with the McNamara case, it would "give him the vantage ground" he was "always seeking." As it turned out, McNamara was released from prison without incident and without Walsh being present.[65]

Frank B. Lent, the FTC's principal examiner in the steel case, concluded in his final report in late July 1921 that there had been a conspiracy among Iron League members and at least Bethlehem Steel among the outside fabricators from December 1919 to at least the end of April 1920 that restrained interstate trade by preventing general contractors in New York from purchasing fabricated steel from both in-state and out-of-state fabricators. Since some of the conspirators competed with the general contractors in the erection of structural steel, the conspiracy, Lent contended, constituted "unfair competition." He maintained, however, that the conspiracy had "entirely ceased" in New York, which is problematic, and although noting that this was not in itself "a defense," he thought that it demonstrated, taking all the circumstances into account, that the conspiracy had been "entered into for the purpose of enabling its members to keep from being forced into another extremely vicious conspiracy, and to defend themselves from the purposes of such other conspiracy, which was aimed at the very existence of their businesses." Like Drew, Lent saw the action by the ILEA, with the cooperation of the outside fabricators, as "a purely defensive measure—a conspiracy to keep out of a more gigantic conspiracy" and one "vastly more injurious to the general public." This, Lent thought, made "the justification . . . full and complete, and the defense sufficient."

Lent saw the same justification "from both a moral and a legal standpoint" for the Philadelphia "conspiracy" as he saw for the New York action. There was no evidence, he indicated, that the Philadelphia conspiracy had come to an end, but since the action, in his view, was warranted and, in any event, was "rather ineffective," he did not believe that the public interest justified a proceeding against it. Although Lent believed that there had been "technical violations" in the steel case of both the Sherman Act and the Federal Trade Commission Act, he recommended dismissal of the IABSOIW application.[66]

Concurring in Lent's conclusion, his superior, B. L. Shinn, noted that the only complainant in the case was a labor union and, as such, was neither in competition with any of the indicated defendants nor was it "engaged in commerce." He also remarked, correctly, that Thompson-Starrett and the Fuller Company, which had provided the principal evidence about an alleged conspiracy, were dependent on union labor to operate their businesses and that their officers had testified before the Lockwood Committee "only because of pressure brought to bear on them by the unions." Neither they nor any fabricators, Shinn noted, had complained to the FTC. He pointed out, furthermore, that the application of the IABSOIW did not so much relate to competition between the respondents and the general contractors as it did to the question of labor relations, which was not within the FTC's purview.[67]

The FTC's Board of Review agreed with Shinn that the case did not involve "the question of competition in commerce" but rather that of the open shop versus the closed shop. The board did not agree with Lent that there had been any restraint of trade or conspiracy in the case, since, in the board's opinion, the erection of buildings was a matter "wholly intrastate" and did not constitute commerce.[68]

The most liberal FTC member, Victor Murdock, viewed the steel case, quite properly, as opening "the door to the whole scene, a gigantic struggle between the steel industry and the unionized steel workers," with the union's application serving as "an echo of that struggle." He concluded that the evidence in the record revealed "a dangerous tendency . . . to unduly hinder competition" and that Bethlehem's refusal to sell steel to Thompson-Starrett was "an unfair method of competition." Given the attendant circumstances, however, and "the unusual post-war conditions" surrounding the case, Murdock did not believe that this "single concrete bit of evidence" warranted the commission's "hanging a proceeding in the public interest upon it." Murdock consequently voted with the other commissioners on July 23, 1923, to order the dismissal of the case.[69]

The FTC's dismissal of the union's case against the NEA and the ILEA brought to an end the investigations by public authorities regarding the sale of structural steel, particularly in the New York market. Without providing any details, Drew, however, informed NEA members that there had been an almost successful effort, presumably instigated by the IABSOIW, to have a United States Senate committee investigate the matter. As he looked back upon almost three years of union effort to restrain or even dissolve the NEA and the ILEA, Drew correctly judged that "the real object of the attack was the open shop policy of the steel industry."[70] The IABSOIW would have agreed, although it would have changed "open shop policy" to "nonunion shop policy." The victors were clearly the NEA, the ILEA and its Iron League successor, and the steel companies.

Although the NEA and the ILEA were subjected to neither state nor federal prosecution as the result of the Lockwood Committee hearings, Untermeyer himself continued to engage in "frequent and public attacks" on both organizations. Drew charged Untermeyer with bias against the open shop and also with having failed, as the Lockwood Committee's counsel, to seek the kind of labor reforms the committee's hearings indicated were needed and that Drew thought necessary.

Denouncing the NEA and the Iron League as comprising "the most vicious form of a criminal conspiracy," Untermeyer wrote, "I shall never stop until this vicious effort [to deny steel to unionized firms] is exposed and punished." He dismissed the open shop as "not a possible thing," characterized United States Steel as "the greatest enemy" of "industrial peace," and singled out Drew as being "in active charge of the 'so-called "open shop" or anti-union crusade of the steel companies.' " He charged that the ILEA had been "mainly responsible" for Brindell, giving him "the pretext to demand tribute." Untermeyer, at the same time, attacked the BTEA as "a more vicious organization" than the BTC and claimed that his "greatest difficulty" had been "to secure equal justice as between the criminals in the labor movement and the much more subtle, persistent and unregenerate criminals among the employers in the financial world." He repeated his criticisms of the NEA, the Iron League, and the steel companies before a Senate committee in 1921 of which, probably not coincidentally, Walsh was the counsel, and, like Walsh, he eventually became an IABSOIW counsel himself.[71]

Never one to ignore criticism, Drew responded in kind to Untermeyer. "[U]nder cover of the authority of the state," Untermeyer, Drew charged, was engaged in a personal vendetta against the steel fabricators and erectors. He complained that Untermeyer had used the Lockwood Committee "to further and to maintain closed-shop control of the building industry," the worst of sins as far as Drew was concerned.[72]

The Lockwood Committee and Untermeyer recommended a series of reforms that they wished the building trades unions to adopt, such as the abandonment of restrictions on the number of apprentices and on union membership and the elimination of rules prohibiting the use of "approved machinery and improved methods."[73] Although Drew could hardly have quarreled with recommendations of this sort, they fell far short of what he believed necessary. He protested that Untermeyer wanted the government to prosecute the NEA and the ILEA but had not sought state legislation to make illegal the kinds of agreements between unions and employer associations in the "Brindell combine" that kept non-union-made building materials out of the New York market, nor had he sought to have the BTEA-BTC agreement dissolved. "I believe," Untermeyer had said on this point, "that there's evidence of criminal conspiracy between the Council and the Association, but it would be a herculean task to conduct that prosecution. By the time it is over, the present contract with the Council will have ended and the law of supply and demand in the labor market will have solved the problem." Drew noted in response that this was not the position Untermeyer had taken with regard to the ILEA. Drew was also displeased that the Lockwood Committee had not sought to outlaw the sympathetic strike, which Drew thought would have been taking "a long step toward cleaning up the building situation."[74]

No doubt because of the Lockwood Committee revelations, the BTEA-BTC agreement was not renewed when it expired at the end of 1921. On October 22, 1922, however, the BTEA and BTC did agree to a set of principles to govern agreements between individual unions and the corresponding employer association and also to the reestablishment of a central arbitration board. The AFL revoked the BTC's charter in March 1922 and organized a new BTC in New York City a year later. The reforms resulting from the Lockwood Committee both with regard to the employers and the building trades unions proved to be quite "limited," and the abuses the committee had exposed continued to plague New York's building industry.[75] Much of Drew's time after 1921 continued to be taken up with labor problems in New York.

CHAPTER 9

"The Dominant Industrial Relations Philosophy in the 1920's"

"The open shop," Allen Wakstein noted in his study of the subject, was "the dominant industrial relations philosophy in the 1920's." A recrudescence of a movement that, with conspicuous exceptions like the National Erectors' Association (NEA), had begun to ebb before World War I and had been largely dormant during the war itself, the antiunionism of the 1920s was a response to both the impressive union gains during the war years and the militant unionism of postarmistice America culminating in the great steel strike of 1919–20.[1] As before World War I, Drew served as a principal spokesman for the open shop position, and he was involved in efforts at both the national and local levels to promote the open shop cause.

Total trade union membership grew from 2,687,100 in 1914 to 5,047,800 in 1920, an 88 percent increase. It was the alleged behavior of organized labor, however, not only the sheer increase in the number of union members, that troubled so many employers. What stimulated the open shop movement of the early 1920s, according to *Iron Age,* was "the overbearing manner of trade unionists," which the journal attributed to wartime conditions and the support the federal government had accorded organized labor. The strikes in 1919, a year in which more than four million workers engaged in work stoppages, a number not again reached until 1937, especially aroused employers. Notable among the 3,630 strikes in 1919 were a brief general strike in Seattle in support of a strike by shipyard workers, a police strike in Boston, a coal strike in defiance of a United States government injunction, and the steel strike. Other than "local abuses," it was to these strikes that the National Association of Manufacturers (NAM) attributed the open shop movement of the 1920s.[2]

The Seattle general strike triggered the formation in March 1919 of the Associated Industries of Seattle, which denounced the closed shop and proclaimed its support for the open shop "American Plan." Beginning in Texas soon thereafter, community after community embraced the principle of the open shop. Single-trade and multitrade national employer organizations, including the open shop associations of the pre–World War I era, the NEA, the National Metal Trades Association (NMTA), the National Founders' Association (NFA), and the NAM, added their strength to the local open shop organizations. A survey of September 1920 revealed that there were at that time 540 open shop organizations of one sort or another in 247 cities in 44 states, a number that included 23 national trade and industrial associations. The movement was especially strong at the local level in the west–south central region of the nation.[3]

Attempts to achieve a national federation of open shop associations in the 1920s proved to be unavailing. The first important effort along these lines was initiated by A. J. Allen, the ambitious secretary of the Associated Employers of Indianapolis, a city that had gained a reputation as "The Graveyard of Union Aspirations." After surveying the numerous open shop organizations, Allen concluded that there was interest in some kind of federation to coordinate their activities. He consequently invited more than one thousand organizations to send representatives to a convention that was to meet in Indianapolis in December 1920. The convention was never held, however, the principal opposition to the Allen proposal having come from the national employer and trade organizations. One of the outspoken critics of the idea was Walter Drew, who it will be recalled, had favored some sort of "joint council" of national employer associations before the war but who thought the Allen proposal "neither wise nor practical." He advised Allen that the federation he was contemplating would be interpreted as "a national organized movement" to crush labor unions, and the reaction to such efforts in the past, Drew remarked, had always been "most injurious to the efforts of those who were out on the firing line doing the real fighting for the open shop." The NAM and the NMTA joined Drew in opposition to the Allen proposal.[4]

In January 1921 the Illinois Manufacturers' Association convened a national conference of state manufacturers' associations in Chicago that resolved to support the open shop, but no new umbrella organization resulted from the meeting. In a little-known effort in December 1921 Herbert George, the president of the Employers' Association of Denver, proposed the creation of an American Federation of Employers to challenge the American Federation of Labor. Viewing the proposal once again as aiming at an employers' "war" on unions "on a national scale," Drew told George that the federation he contemplated would "emphasize the class-conscious nature of the whole labor movement and give a new impetus to the organization of workers along class-conscious lines." The employers were better advised, Drew remarked, to involve themselves in the "proper orientation" of their businesses to improve the manner in which they dealt with their workers. Persuaded to abandon his proposal, George reported that local employer associations had favored the idea but that the "big National associations . . . [were] not inclined to take on any more responsibilities in the way of expense," which was hardly the basis for Drew's objection.[5]

The closest the open shop forces came to launching a national federation of open shop organizations was the American Plan–Open Shop Conference launched in Salt Lake City in April 1922 at a meeting of executives of open shop associations in twenty-nine cities that had been arranged by the Utah Associated Industries. Meeting semiannually initially and then annually until 1933, the conference in its early years enlisted the interest primarily of open shop associations in the western part of the nation, but it attracted a national representation beginning in 1926. It was throughout its life, however, nothing more than "an informal gathering of open-shop association executives."[6]

The open shop movement in an organizational sense was at its height during the years 1920–23, trade union membership declining 28.2 percent during those years, from 5,047,800 to 3,622,000. The movement gained strength from the recession of 1920–21, which stimulated employers to cut costs and weakened union resistance. It became less aggressive after 1923, reflecting the successes already achieved by employers, economic prosperity, and the shift of the AFL, as Irving Bernstein has phrased it, "from militancy to respectability." In a 1928 study, the NAM's Open Shop Department concluded that 81.3 percent of workers in manufacturing plants worked in open shops, 11.3 percent in nonunion shops that discriminated against union members, and 7.4 percent in closed shops. These figures, however, excluded building, transportation, and mining, areas of the economy where union strength was well above the average for American industry. Trade union membership declined at a slower rate after 1923 until the end of the 1920s as compared to 1920–23, total membership falling by 5 percent between 1923 and 1929 (to 3,442,600). The unions suffered an additional 13.6 percent decline by 1933 (to 2,973,000).

The building trades unions fared better than trade unions as a whole during the 1920s. The membership of the building trades unions declined by 11 percent from 1920 to 1923 (from 887,900 to 789,500) but increased by 16.4 percent in the next six years (to 919,000) as building construction boomed. The collapse of that boom, however, led to a 36.5 percent decline in building trades union membership between 1929 and 1933 (to 582,000). The membership of the building trades unions constituted 17.6 percent of total union membership in the nation in 1920, 26.7 percent in 1929, and 19.6 percent in 1933.[7]

Like Drew and the open shop advocates of the pre–World War I era, the open shop organizations in the 1920s generally directed their fire not at trade unionism as such but rather at trade union practices, most conspicuously the closed shop, which they were prone to equate with trade unionism itself. Employer spokesmen characterized the open shop as the embodiment of American principles—the very phrase "American Plan" became associated with the movement. The open shop, employer spokesmen contended, comported with American ideals of independence and the freedom of the individual. It was alleged to provide "equal opportunity for all and special privileges for none," whereas closed shop unionism, by contrast, was said to contravene American ideals. Sounding a note that Drew had regularly sounded before the war, the open shop advocates also insisted that the economic prosperity of a community was enhanced by the open shop and threatened by the closed shop. Some employers meant what they said in describing the open shop as the employment of workers without regard to their organizational affiliation; others, while embracing the open shop rhetorically, discriminated against union members in one way or another and in practice operated closed nonunion shops.[8]

Few spoke or wrote with greater authority about the open shop during its heyday in the 1920s than Walter Drew. Like others, Drew attributed the growing popularity of the movement to union abuse of the power it had gained during and just after the war. The high wages workers had received during the war, Drew maintained, had been accompanied by a 30 percent decline in worker efficiency, and he contrasted the thousands of strikes initiated by organized labor in the early postwar period with the "minimum of friction" in open shop establishments. Reacting in highly exaggerated fashion to what had happened in Seattle and to the Plumb Plan advanced by the Railroad Brotherhoods that called for the operation of the railroads by the federal government, Drew contended in the summer of 1919 that the extension of union power would lead to "further radical demands looking toward the socialization and nationalization of industry."

The unions have "helped us a whole lot lately," Drew wrote James Emery in September 1919. The public had received an "education" in trade unionism that employers could not have provided by the expenditure of millions of dollars, Drew commented at about the same time. "The selfish greed and lust for power which constitute the inner spirit of organized labor," the NEA commissioner claimed, "have been shown up in all their ugliness and the people have learned that the real issue is not between the unions and the employer but between the unions and society as a whole."[9]

As he interpreted what was happening, Drew thought it especially important that the open shop movement was being "staged" not by particular groups of employers but by "the general business interests of the communities." The business interests, he believed, could achieve what "no group of employers fighting their partisan fight" could accomplish. They could win press and public support and could see to it that employers did not misbehave in dealing with their workers. Drew was also pleased with the increasing use of the term "American Plan," since, he maintained, it avoided "the controversial and technical atmosphere that surrounded the term 'open shop.'"

As before the war, Drew did not rhetorically dispute the right of workers to organize and to join a union, but he insisted that this right presumed the equal right of workers not to join a union. Significantly narrowing his acceptance of the right to organize, Drew argued that it rested on the right of workers to bargain individually, which the right to organize could not supersede, and did not include the "right to undertake a deliberate and systematic campaign" to organize establishments in an industry in which employment relations were "peaceful and satisfactory." In any event, he contended, the right of a union to undertake a campaign of that sort was "no greater or more sacred than the right of the employer to use legitimate and proper methods in maintaining his existing relations with his employees." Drew did not spell out what these "methods" might be, but it is not difficult to fill in the blanks.[10]

Drew in the 1920s conceded that the closed shop could be legally established in a single establishment by the voluntary agreement of employer and employee although not by "force or coercion." At the same time, however, since he contended that the closed shop was "the concrete embodiment of the doctrine of force," he believed that there could be no real bargaining under closed shop conditions but only, as we have seen Drew put it, a pattern of "a demand and a surrender." Rejecting the closed shop in reality and hostile to independent unionism, Drew for a time thought that the employee representation schemes and the shop committees that became so common in American industry in the 1920s could succeed if established in good faith by both parties. When the secretary of the Wilmington Manufacturers Association sent him a copy of an employee representation plan in 1919, Drew advised that the employer should discuss the plan informally with the leaders of the employees in the plant to ascertain what they thought about the matter rather than presenting it as a "cut and dried scheme" in which employees were supposed to participate. Several months later, however, Drew told an NMTA convention that employee representation plans had worked well in some places, poorly in others, but that it was simply "unreasonable" to believe that machinery of this sort could resolve "the fundamental underlying issues in industry." He was concerned as a matter of fact that employers would ignore their plans once introduced and that they would then "naturally drift into labor control."[11]

Perhaps responding to some of the overtones of prewar progressivism, Drew asserted in the early 1920s, as did other open shop advocates, that the employer was not in business just to make a profit but was rather "a trustee for the beneficial use of the forces of industry that he controlled" and was consequently responsible to both his workers and the consuming public. As always, Drew believed that the proper policy for the employer was to strengthen his position with his workers by treating them fairly and dealing with such matters as plant safety and sanitation and workmen's compensation and, perhaps in response to War Labor Board principles and the advent of women suffrage, providing women workers with equal pay for equal work. He thought that workers would be less likely to turn to unionism if they believed that their interests were "fully protected" by their employers.

"This is the time," Drew wrote an employers' association secretary in the fall of 1920, "to consolidate our position, to make sure of keeping the ground that is daily being won. Our worst enemy at this time," he added, "is not the agitator, but the employer who attempts to take advantage of the reaction against the unions in order to return to the old methods of exploitation and unfairness." The employer who behaved in that manner, who took "unfair advantage" of open shop conditions, Drew stated, brought discredit on the open shop. "I have found," Drew wrote the president of the Citizens' Alliance of Minneapolis at the end of 1921, "that my chief work through many years of activity has consisted not in fighting unions, but in holding employers in line on right principles." Drew made it clear that he did not mean by his criticism of irresponsible employers that management should fail to oppose "the evils of unionism" wherever and whenever they manifested themselves.[12]

A true believer, Drew contended that it was literally the "patriotic duty" of employers to maintain the open shop. "Will you pardon me," he wrote the president of the American Bridge Company in 1926, "if I say that I believe the open shop in our industries is something more than a mere business policy. I believe that it is so vitally connected with the stability and future success of the nation as to make its maintenance a matter of duty and serious responsibility on the part of those who occupy positions of industrial leadership."[13]

Drew just after World War I thought that the United States needed a national labor policy, and he played a large part in the employer effort to achieve that result through the National Industrial Conference Board (NICB). The drafting of some kind of national labor policies program by the NICB went back to January 24, 1918, when Drew and L. F. Loree, the president of the Delaware and Hudson Railroad Company, asserting that the education of the public in "fundamental economic principles . . . must inevitably lead to greater conservatism on their part" and to a better relationship between employer and employee, proposed to the board that these principles be expressed in "terse and concise language" and then disseminated. The NICB appointed a Committee on Principles of four members that included Drew to implement the Drew-Loree proposal. Little was accomplished by the committee before the war ended, but the NICB left no doubt that one of the "fundamental economic principles" to which it was committed was the open shop. At the Ninth Yama Conference in October 1918 the conferees unanimously agreed that the open shop, both in war and peace, was "essential to American industry and the prosperity of the country" and that it "expressed" the nation's "democratic principle," a judgment that the board's executive committee reaffirmed in December.[14]

It appears to have been Drew's intent as the key draftsman for the Committee on Labor Policies, as the Committee on Principles was renamed in April 1919, to avoid the kind of "controversial utterance" appropriate for "militant groups" like the NEA and to devise a statement of "the broad, underlying legal and economic principles" that left "no room for argument or criticism." In accordance with the Drew position, early drafts of the "Labor Policies Program" avoided specific reference to the open shop and dealt in general terms with such matters as freedom of contract, the right of association, the rights and obligations of the individual and of management, the obligation to secure production, "opportunity and reward for effort," hours and wages, the settlement of disputes, and the legal responsibility of combinations of employers and employees. To be sure, concepts such as "freedom of the individual" were defined so as to proscribe the closed shop and leave management free to refuse to bargain with union representatives.[15]

The Labor Policies Committee was still in the drafting stage when President Wilson on September 3, 1919, invited the NICB to select five of the fifteen employer representatives to take part in a Washington conference of employers, employees, and representatives of the general public designed, if possible, to achieve "some common ground of agreement and action with regard to the future conduct of industry." Drew thought that the employer group should deal with "questions of fundamental principle" and avoid spelling out "a concrete program" lest this place them "in the position of obstructionists" should the conference fail to come to any agreement.[16]

The Labor Policies Committee agreed upon a statement at a September 30 meeting that was "taken as a sort of basis in preparing the statement of the employer group" at the Washington conference. When the employers presented their statement on October 10 at what came to be known as the President's Industrial Conference, it did indeed resemble the Labor Policies Committee's draft in many respects, but it had a more militant and propagandistic character than Drew had wished. It was a statement, he thought, more appropriate for militant open shop organizations like the NEA, the NMTA, and the NFA than for the more broadly based NICB. Unlike the Labor Policies Committee draft, the employer statement specifically endorsed the open shop and accepted the right of an employer and his workers to agree voluntarily to a "closed union shop" or a "closed nonunion shop" but asserted that no employer could be required to deal with individuals or groups who were not his own employees or had not been chosen from among them. In the end, the refusal of the employer representatives to agree to any statement that would require them to bargain with worker representatives who were not their employees proved to be the obstacle to any agreement at the conference on an industrial relations policy. For the employer representatives to have accepted unions and collective bargaining without at the same time insisting on their right to refuse to deal with outside union representatives, Drew remarked, would have been to invite the kind of disruptive union organizing campaigns that the War Labor Board had decided were permitted by the principles governing its operation.[17]

Magnus Alexander, the NICB's managing director, advised the Labor Policies Committee to adopt the Industrial Conference's employer statement either verbatim or in modified form as the NICB statement of labor principles. Since the five United States Chamber of Commerce representatives present at the conference had joined with the other employer representatives in subscribing to the statement, Alexander hoped that the Chamber of Commerce would then also endorse the statement. Drew, however, took exception to this advice, and so the NICB committee, which had been "inclined" to support Alexander, decided to continue working on its own draft and to let the board choose between what it devised and the employer statement at the Washington conference.[18]

A Drew draft of January 17, 1920, but with two significant additions, became the basis for "A Statement of Principles Underlying the Employment Relation" that was agreed to on February 2, 1920, at a joint meeting of the Labor Policies Committee and the Committee on Industrial Relations of the United States Chamber of Commerce. Drew and the NICB committee agreed to add to Drew's draft principles dealing with the open shop and employee representation. The Statement of Principles asserted that open shop operation, defined as "the right of employer and employee to enter into, and determine the conditions of employment relations with each other, without reference to the affiliation or non-affiliation of either with any organization, was an essential part of the individual right of contract possessed by each of the parties." The representation statement proclaimed that when employer and employees, rather than dealing with each other individually, agreed by "mutual consent" for either party to negotiate through representatives, the other party could ask that these representatives "not be chosen or controlled by, or in any degree represent, any outside group or interest in the questions at issue." Following Drew's draft, other principles in the statement provided that employers, in effect, could refuse to bargain with employee representatives; specified that combinations of workers as well as of employers must be legally responsible for the conduct of their agents; asserted that it was "the duty of management" to assist workers to secure "regular employment" for which they were suited and to provide them with "proper safeguards" for their "health and safety" and with the "incentive and opportunity" to improve themselves; rejected the setting of a universal workday in favor of the determination of working hours industry by industry; and called for a ban on strikes by public employees and for state regulation to assure "continuous and unimpaired operation of public utility service."[19]

Drew, surprisingly, regarded the principles in the statement dealing with the open shop and employer and employee relations as "a matter of policy" rather than of "principle," to which he would have preferred to confine the statement. He informed United States Steel's Judge Gary, however, that "a strong sentiment" had developed to include the two items. Drew explained that the open shop principle of the statement "tried not to condemn even by implication" employers who operated nonunion shops, but that assertion is belied by the statement's characterization of nondiscriminatory hiring as "an essential part of the individual right of contract." Drew was correct, however, in asserting that the representation principle of the statement enabled the employer to ignore the presence of a union in dealing with his employees.[20]

The United States Chamber of Commerce, which had not previously taken a stand on labor matters, submitted the Statement of Principles to its affiliated organizations to secure their reaction. The results, made public at the end of July 1920, indicated overwhelming support for the statement's key principles, the open shop definition by a vote of 1,665 to 4, the limitation of worker representatives to one's own employees by a vote of 1,568 to 54, and the principle that unions be held legally responsible for their actions by a vote of 1,671 to 4. At its 1921 convention, accordingly, the Chamber of Commerce officially endorsed the open shop. Drew, who had worked with the chamber's Committee on Industrial Relations in preparing the document, also became a member of the chamber's Committee on American Ideals. When the four-person committee reported in September 1920, it attacked the "unsound philosophy" of the trade union movement as contributing to the respectability of "the doctrines of . . . radical and revolutionary organizations."[21]

The NICB, although adhering to the "fundamental proposition" of the

Labor Policies program, did not immediately approve the February 2 statement. Before acting, it wished to have its Labor Policies Committee's reaction to a preliminary report of the Committee on Labor Relations of the Cleveland Chamber of Commerce and the report of the President's Second Industrial Conference. Drew, whom the NICB apparently requested to examine the Cleveland report, characterized it as an effort to arrive at a "compromise between the traditional views of the employer and the principles and program of organized labor." Since the report, among other things, permitted employees to select an "advisor or advocate" to aid them in bargaining with their employer, provided for multiplant bargaining, denied the employer the right to discriminate in hiring or discharging workers even if this were necessary to protect against the closed shop, and did not ban strikes in government service or public utilities, it is not surprising that Drew was highly critical of the document, and it did not cause the Labor Policies Committee to alter the February 2 Statement of Principles.[22]

The Wilson administration selected the membership for the President's Second Industrial Conference, which was convened on December 1, 1919, and reported on April 14, 1920, without regard to their organizational affiliation, and it altogether ignored the "aggressive anti-union employers." The conference's report endorsed collective bargaining between employers and employees and specifically approved the shop-committee approach to employee representation. The major focus of the conference was on the settlement of industrial disputes, for which the conferees recommended the establishment of regional boards of adjustment and a National Industrial Board to which decisions at the regional level could be appealed.[23]

The NICB's managing director expressed concern that the principal proposal of the Second Industrial Conference, if put into effect, would lead to "concentration of control, essentially political in character." Even "more important," he thought, was the lack of any "well defined body of principles" in the proposal to guide the national and regional boards in reaching decisions in labor disputes. Drew, for his part, was troubled that the conferees had taken "the narrow view of the industrial problem as a mere squabble between employer and employee" and had ignored the kinds of issues dealt with in the February 2 Statement of Principles. If there were to be a national industrial tribunal, Drew thought, it would have to deal with "the great matters of fundamental principle" in industry. When the NEA commissioner discussed the conference report with United States Steel's Judge Gary, he asserted that the dispute-settlement idea was "a dangerous proposition." He expressed his "approval," however, of the Labor Policies Committee's Statement of Principles.[24]

The Second Industrial Conference report led to no significant result and did not cause the Labor Policies Committee to alter its February 2 statement. Acting on the advice of the committee, the NICB decided on November 18, 1920, to discharge the committee and not to issue the Statement of Principles, which it had already approved, but rather to place it on file for such use as the board might decide advisable at a later time. Since the United States Chamber of Commerce had already adopted the statement and other employer associations had "applied" its principles, the board decided that publication of the statement "might weaken" the NICB's "standing" in the eyes of the public. This probably reflected the increasing inclination of the NICB, with its varied business membership, to serve primarily as an objective "economic research" organization whose reports would not be seen by the public as serving a partisan purpose. In February 1925 the NEA, consequently, withdrew from the board. The chief purpose of the NEA, Drew explained, was "to stand for the open shop . . . and to do this in a militant and forceful manner when defense of the principles of the open shop require[d] such action," a position, he thought, that had become an "embarrassment" to the NICB.[25]

The principal draftsman of the statement on labor relations of both the NICB and the Chamber of Commerce, Drew also played a critically important role in the effort of the NAM to promote the open shop in the 1920s. Following the recommendation of James Emery that the NAM must become "the recognized national authority and medium for open shop propaganda," the NAM's president, as authorized by its board of directors, appointed the members of an Open Shop Committee on July 7, 1920, "to take up active work and propaganda for the open shop" and to promote the open shop in local communities. President Stephen C. Mason appointed Drew and Emery, among others, as members of the committee, and the two men also served as the committee's cocounsel.[26]

Appointed at the committee's first meeting on September 17, 1920, to a subcommittee to draft a statement suggesting the purposes of the committee, Drew at the next meeting reported that he thought the committee's "chief function" should be to furnish material for the use of those advocating open shop principles. He also favored interesting women in the open shop movement. The committee recommended the creation of an Open Shop Department under the committee's direction that would collect and disseminate information regarding the open shop and its relationship to "our national ideals and institutions and to industrial stability, productivity and national program [progress?]," initiate and encourage local open shop movements, and cooperate with local and national organizations committed to the open shop. The first of these objectives, as Drew had advised, proved to be the major activity of the Open Shop Department. The NAM engaged Noel Sargent to head the department.[27]

When the Open Shop Committee suggested at an early meeting the possibility of designating an NAM field agent for New England to ascertain if the purchasing agents of member firms took into account "the stand of sellers on the open shop question," Drew, always concerned about anything that might damage the open shop cause, successfully advised against the proposal since it smacked of a "boycott." Drew thought that the committee should issue pamphlets that provided facts "and *only* facts." The committee chairman thereupon appointed Drew to head the Subcommittee on Bulletins, which were to be issued regularly. Taking a position to which he consistently returned, Drew advised that employers should forthwith "clean house and . . . improve conditions in their plants" that were less than "satisfactory." Following Drew's suggestion, the committee a few weeks later resolved that its educational or publicity effort should stress "the broad fundamental principles of the open shop" but should be kept free of "specific controversies" and that efforts should be made "to stimulate a wider appreciation among employers of their obligation with respect to the human factor in industry and of their duty to take the initiative in securing and maintaining their relations with their employees on a basis of fair dealing and efficiency, through an understanding of their mutuality of interest." The committee subsequently designated Drew to draw up a "definite program of operations" based on this resolution.[28]

When the NAM on October 9–10, 1922, hosted a meeting of the presidents and managers of open shop organizations, Drew stressed the two points he thought essential to the success of the open shop movement, the importance of public opinion and, since he believed that the "real fate" of the open shop depended on the behavior of management, educating employers regarding their "obligations and duties" with respect to both their workers and the public. The conferees, following Drew's lead, approved a resolution calling for a stepped-up effort by the Open Shop Department to educate employers, employees, and the public regarding "right relations in industry and the mutual rights, duties and obligations" of each of the three and to impress upon employers "the need for the most enlightened, progressive and statesmanlike conduct of their activities." The NAM itself, similarly, adopted a resolution at its 1923 convention stressing the employer's obligation to the workers and the public. Also, in accord with Drew's advice, the Open Shop Department tried, in meeting its educational responsibilities, to make its investigations as "scientific" as possible. The department submitted all its educational material regarding the open shop to Drew for suggestions and approval.[29]

The NAM's concern about the responsibility of employers to improve employer-employee relations reflected the view not just of individuals like Drew but also of the association's Employment Relations Committee. Explaining that the public, which viewed the NAM as "primarily a Union Smashing Organization," unfortunately understood the phrase "open shop" to mean "Let's Fight," whereas the committee thought the phrase "Industrial Relations" was understood to mean "Get Together," it wished the NAM to coordinate and harmonize the two approaches. The minutes of the Open Shop Committee leave no doubt that it did not dissent from this view.[30]

In September 1926 the Open Shop and Employment Relations committees prepared a preliminary revision of the NAM's Declaration of Principles that provided their joint view of the proper employment relationship. The interests of employer and employee, they agreed, could "best be promoted by free discussion of employment problems and by cooperative effort." They believed that there should be "adequate provision" in each plant for "the administration of justice, the discussion of employment problems and the promotion of cooperative effort." They wished the NAM to reiterate that it was "not opposed to organized labor as such" but was opposed to strikes, lockouts, and boycotts and to "restrictive measures" that limited production and raised costs. The committees at the same time proposed that the NAM go on record as approving all "well-considered plans" to promote the education, health, and safety of workers as well as their "continuity of employment." They endorsed the open shop policy as "the only policy consistent with the American ideal of individual liberty." The joint statement reiterated some of the assertions in the NAM's 1903 Declaration of Principles but went beyond that statement in its assertions regarding joint employer-employee discussion of problems and its emphasis on employer obligations and not just employer rights. The NAM's board of directors, for which the revised statement had been prepared, accordingly changed the name of the Open Shop Department at the beginning of 1926 to Industrial Relations Department as being "more comprehensive and more descriptive" of the department's activities. The NAM, however, did not alter its long-standing Declaration of Principles to include the main elements of the Joint Committee report, and it continued to designate the department by its original title despite the name change.[31]

Within a few years of its establishment, the Open Shop Department was issuing a flood of literature to promote the open shop. The department distributed its publications primarily to college teachers in the social sciences, seeing them as important molders of opinion, and to the clergy, which it regarded as having gained additional influence as the result of the introduction of women suffrage. The department noted in 1923 that three state universities were distributing its open shop literature throughout their states through the "Package Loan Library." It conceded that it had failed to win over the Roman Catholic clergy, but it reported some success with Protestant clergymen and in persuading the Federal Council of the Churches of Christ to modify its support of the closed shop.[32]

The Open Shop Department supplied information in the early 1920s to fifteen hundred high school and college debaters, the NAM noting in 1930 that the open shop side had defeated the closed shop supporters in two-thirds of the debates on the subject. The *Open Shop Encyclopedia for Debaters* that the department published in 1921 has been characterized as "the best single source" for the NAM's position on the open shop. Sargent informed Open Shop Committee members that Drew and one other member had provided "valuable advice and assistance" in the preparation of the volume, which included some of Drew's statements on the subject. The NAM in 1923, with some justice, described the Open Shop Department as "the nationally recognized clearing house for accurate and reliable open shop information." The department also offered guidance to state and local industrial and trade associations.[33]

In addition to the significant role he played with regard to the publications of the Open Shop Department, Drew, clearly the Open Shop Committee's most influential member, served the committee in other ways. He helped Sargent prepare the department's reports; he was designated to write a letter to NAM members to secure special funds for the open shop drive; Emery and he drafted the letter to members during the 1923 coal strike advising them to purchase their coal from companies that were operating despite the strike; and Sargent and he prepared a statement urging open shop employers to patronize other open shop employers, an idea specifically endorsed by the NAM's board of directors. It was Drew, also, who took the lead in appealing to the board for more funding for the Open Shop Department's "statistical effort." Following a suggestion Drew had made soon after the Open Shop Committee had been established, it decided in 1927 to hire someone to present the open shop point of view to women's clubs.[34]

The Open Shop Department's statistical publications were particularly concerned with the open shop and the closed shop in the building industry. The department viewed construction as the most important industry in the nation and "the best single barometer of industrial conditions." Sargent noted that 50 percent of all securities issued in 1920 were for some form of construction and that construction was second only to agriculture in terms of the number of persons to whom it gave employment. The industry was also of major concern to the numerous community open shop organizations because of the practices of the building trades unions that allegedly drove up building costs and negatively affected the economic well-being of the community. The Open Shop Department, moreover, was painfully aware that the construction industry was the most difficult industry in which to establish open shop conditions. The committee's expert on the industry, needless to say, was Walter Drew. Informing the chairman of the NEA's executive committee in 1927 that the building trades unions, unlike other unions, were not only holding their own in terms of membership but were also serving as "an entering wedge" into all those industries that supplied material for construction, Drew reported that he was working through the Open Shop Department to combat these unions.[35]

The statistics the Open Shop Department released in the first half of the 1920s favorably compared construction in open shop cities with construction in closed shop cities. In 1923, for example, the department reported that there were 41 percent more building permits per capita in cities where building was at least 75 percent open than where it was closed. In 1924, according to the department, the cost per cubic foot in the construction of school buildings was 38 percent higher under closed shop than under open shop conditions". The percentage of total construction performed on an open shop basis, the Open Shop Department happily reported, rose from 10 percent in 1920 to 40 percent in 1925, but the construction statistics after that date told a different story, falling to 28 percent for open shop cities in 1928 and remaining at that figure for the rest of the decade. Sargent was especially discouraged that large national chains, hotels for example, and large general contractors, fearing strikes against construction in closed shop cities, were opting for closed shop construction everywhere.[36]

Quite apart from his role as a member of the NAM's Open Shop Committee, Drew, of course, had a special interest as NEA commissioner in the construction industry. Because of the industry's critical importance to the economy as a whole, Drew viewed construction as "affected with a public interest" and as approaching the status of a public utility. In a reprise of views he had expressed before the war, he charged that construction was in "the grip of unionism of a radical and irresponsible character" that not only drove up building costs but also, where it was strong, sought to extend its control to other industries by refusing to work on material fabricated by nonunion labor.

Unlike the manufacturer, who produced at his own risk and had to sell his product in a competitive market, the building contractor, operating on a cost plus contract and serving as "a mere broker or agent" for the owner, was inclined, Drew noted, to capitulate to union demands and simply passed on the resulting higher cost to the owner and, in effect, to the community. As in New York, Drew pointed out, the builder might be inclined to deal with closed shop unions as the means of excluding outside competition.

From long experience, Drew was convinced that the building trades would never "set their own house in order" unless "pushed and pulled by someone else." This required the action of some "organized and forceful group," and the logical "group," as Drew saw it, was the general business interests of the community. The "general public" could not be counted on to deal with the problem, Drew believed, because it was "more or less of a myth" when it came to action even though it was more directly affected by the construction industry than by any other.

What he was calling for, Drew insisted, was not a war on the building trades unions but rather a campaign for certain "fundamental principles" such as freedom of contract, the sanctity of trade agreements, respect for the rights of others, a ban on sympathetic strikes, on which he believed the "autocratic power" of the building trades unions mainly rested, and the maintenance of law and order. Whatever he might have said about a war against the building trades unions, however, Drew actually wanted to break the power of these critically important unions. "The situation in the building trades," he declared in 1926, "is the one great canker sore of our industrial system. It is the great menace to the open shop in our manufacturing industries and to those factors and conditions which are responsible for the nation's industrial efficiency and prosperity."[37]

San Francisco and Chicago, two cities with powerful building trades unions in the pre–World War I era, served as models, in effect, for the Drew prescription as to how a city should deal with its building problems and its building trades unions. "Not a hammer was lifted, or a brick laid, or a pipe fitted, or a wall plastered or painted or papered without the sanction of the unions," one writer noted regarding pre–World War I San Francisco. "The walking delegate roved the town in state, issuing orders and imposing penalties." The war, however, "demoralized" the city's building industry, with as many as one-half of the ironworkers, plumbers, painters, and carpenters taking jobs in the shipbuilding industry. The industry was slow to recover at war's end, and employers began to complain about the restrictive practices of the building trades unions that raised costs.[38]

When twenty-seven San Francisco building trades unions demanded wage increases in February 1920, employer resistance led to some strikes. In July the Builders' Exchange, its ranks but recently augmented by antiunion producers and suppliers of building materials, announced its support for the open shop. A few trades went out on strike, but the head of the Building Trades Council, Patrick McCarthy, favored arbitration, as did the Industrial Relations Committee of the Chamber of Commerce, which had succeeded the Law and Order Committee. The result was the establishment in January 1921 of a three-person arbitration board to rule on the pay demands of seventeen crafts. Its decision, handed down on March 31 in the midst of a business recession, provided for a wage cut of 7.5 percent to take effect on May 9 and to be revised in six months in accordance with changes in the cost of living. The painters promptly went out on strike, and the Building Trades Council subsequently rejected the award. The general contractors retaliated by locking out the union mechanics working on nine downtown buildings. The San Francisco Chamber of Commerce announced its support of the lockout, and a Citizens' Committee was formed that quickly raised $1 million from manufacturers and bankers to lend additional assistance.[39]

The Builders' Exchange announced on June 2 that its affiliates would begin operating on an open shop basis after twelve days. Sensing the ebbing of its power, the Building Trades Council was now willing to permit its members to work alongside nonunion mechanics, but in a July 7 referendum only four locals agreed with this position. With a large-scale building strike looming, the city's Chamber of Commerce established the Industrial Association on July 25 to direct the fight for the American Plan. Representing a spectrum of San Francisco business interests rather than primarily building contractors or material men, the association liked to think of itself as "a community organization" rather than as an employers' association. The anticipated strike, which began on August 4, ended on August 27, with the union forces in full retreat.[40]

The Industrial Association for the remainder of the 1920s and into the 1930s served as the defender of the open shop and "the active directing force behind all labor problems" in San Francisco. Although its "most important relations" were with the Builders' Exchange and its more than one thousand building contractors and dealers, practically all of San Francisco's important businesses embraced the open shop in the 1920s. In dealing with the building trades unions, the Industrial Association employed a variety of means to enforce the open shop. It abolished jurisdictional lines among the trades and, in what has been characterized as its "most significant innovation," established training schools for some trades as a substitute for the unions' apprenticeship system. It also introduced a plan of group insurance for building trades workers. Seeking to maintain a fifty-fifty ratio of union and nonunion mechanics, it operated an employment agency that funneled nonunion workers to jobs—it had placed sixty-four thousand workers by 1928—and also advertised for nonunion workers outside San Francisco. It established an "inspection and protection department" to guard American Plan jobs.

The permit system the Industrial Association introduced during the May 1920 lockout proved to be a particularly effective device to combat the building trades unions. Contractors had to secure a permit from the Builders' Exchange before they could receive material from manufacturers and material dealers, and permits were granted only if the contractor operated open shop and paid Builders' Exchange wages. These wages were set by four Impartial Wage Boards, which fixed rates below the levels prevailing in cities where the building trades were unionized. The permit system survived both state and federal court tests.[41]

As the Industrial Association asserted its dominance, the San Francisco building trades unions experienced "a progressive decline." The International Association of Bridge, Structural and Ornamental Iron Workers (IABSOIW) was in an especially bad way in the city, the union's international president complaining in 1929 that "no union in San Francisco . . . [had] felt the iron heel of the Industrial Association more than the Iron Workers' Union."[42]

Drew, of course, welcomed the introduction of the open shop in San Francisco's construction industry. When the city's Builders' Exchange informed the NEA in late June 1921 that the city needed first-class erection gangs to work on the American Plan, Drew and the NEA promptly responded. The same was true the next month when the Contractors Association of San Francisco made a similar request. The ability of the NEA to maintain the open shop in the structural steel industry was also important to the Industrial Association. "[I]t has always been our feeling," the association's managing director wrote Drew in 1930, "that control of the structural steel was of paramount importance in the maintenance of our whole program."[43]

Developments in the construction industry in Chicago following World War I paralleled those in San Francisco. In 1920 some contractors less friendly to unions than the Building Construction Employers' Association was and believing that wage increases for the building trades unions since the war had hindered construction in the city formed the rival Associated Builders of Chicago. At the beginning of 1921, a time of recession and heavy unemployment in the building trades, the two employer associations sought to cut the wages of skilled workers by 20 percent and of laborers by 30 percent, which led to a general building trades strike. The parties agreed to arbitrate the wage dispute, but the unions rejected the agreement in a referendum. This led to a general lockout by the employers and a second arbitration agreement, the two sides in June 1921 selecting Judge Kenesaw Mountain Landis, the commissioner of major league baseball, as the arbitrator.[44]

The Landis arbitration was influenced by a concurrent state investigation of the Chicago building industry. The Illinois state legislature adopted a joint resolution on March 21, 1921, providing for a legislative commission to investigate combinations and agreements among builders, material men, and workers that were believed to have affected building costs in Chicago. Popularly known as the Dailey Commission after its chairman, State Senator John Dailey, the commission held hearings in Chicago from March 25 to June 30, after which the newly created Illinois Building Investigation Commission, with the same personnel but with added powers, took up the task. The commission hearings, very much like the Lockwood Committee hearings in New York, revealed that "Chicago's building industry had been strangled by a criminal alliance between crooked contractors and dishonest labor leaders." The commission exposed a series of price-fixing combinations as well as a variety of union working rules that lessened productivity and provided an opportunity for unscrupulous business agents.

The Dailey Commission's inquiry led to the impaneling of a Cook County grand jury to investigate the Chicago building situation. By the time the commission reported on December 15, 1922, forty "bombers, conspirators, jury bribers, and perjurers" had been convicted in state trials, and indictments were pending against 218 additional individuals. In addition, six indictments had been returned in federal court involving 121 corporations and 135 individuals, six contractor associations, and twenty-one union members.[45]

Because of the Dailey Commission revelations, Landis claimed that the public interest demanded that he consider not only the wage dispute submitted to him but also union working rules. In the award he handed down on September 7, 1921, he referred to "a maze of rules artificially created to give the parties a monopoly and . . . rules designed to produce waste for the sake of waste." The award required the adoption of a new uniform contract for the building trades and a revision of union rules. Landis also slashed wage rates by anywhere from 10 to 25 percent, and whereas existing wage schedules provided uniform minimum wage rates, the rates Landis set varied from trade to trade and were to be the maximum rates. The award, moreover, applied even to trades that had not agreed to submit to arbitration. Several trades asked for a rehearing, to which Landis agreed provided the trades concerned returned to work and removed the working rules to which he had objected. He set a somewhat higher wage for two trades in a supplementary award in December.[46]

A series of strikes by seven trades that had not joined the arbitration and six that had followed the Landis Award. The Chicago Building Trades Council, however, ratified the award on October 1, the carpenters, who adamantly opposed the arbitration and the award, claiming that union leaders who had accepted the award were "looking for an immunity bath to clear themselves of past deeds." In an effort to place construction in Chicago on a "100 percent Landis" basis, the Citizens' Committee to Enforce the Landis Award was formed in November under the auspices of Chicago's Association of Commerce. The committee's chairman, T. E. Donnelley, headed the largest open shop printing plant in the city.

When the Citizens' Committee sent letters to two hundred Chicago businessmen inviting them to join the committee, 150 agreed in three days. The 176 members who eventually made up the committee represented the major business interests of Chicago, but persons directly connected with the construction industry were excluded from membership. The Chicago Federation of Labor approved a resolution introduced by the city's IABSOIW local protesting the name of "citizens' committee" for "a committee representing 'privileged interests' and 'big business' in their worst form."[47]

The Citizens' Committee announced that it would support contractors and unions abiding by the Landis Award. If a particular unionized trade refused to accept the award, it was declared an "outlaw," and the trade was to be operated thereafter on an open shop basis with a maximum of 50 percent of the workers to be union members. As of the beginning of September 1922, thirteen trades had been declared "outlaw," and seventeen were operating on a closed shop basis.

The committee took over the employment office that the contractors had established, set up branch offices in twenty-three cities, and advertised for nonunion workers outside Chicago. In the first five years of its operation the committee placed 127,549 workers in Landis Award jobs. It established a trade school to train building trades mechanics, set up a "protection department" of 741 persons to protect Landis Award jobs, and hired detectives and inspectors to visit jobs to ensure that Landis Award terms were being observed. In an unusual action, it took out a "mammoth" insurance policy that eventually rose to $120 million and that provided for the reimbursement of Landis Award contractors whose property had been damaged by union "wrecking crews."[48]

A strike against the Landis Award that began on January 4, 1922, proved to be "a lamentable failure" and was called off on January 8. The Chicago Federation of Labor resolved on March 19 to place all major league baseball clubs on its "unfair" list unless they dismissed Landis. The slugging of nonunion workers and the vandalization and bombing of Landis Award jobs that followed the award culminated on May 9, 1922, in the death of two policemen and retaliatory raids by the police on Building Trades Council headquarters and other union offices and the arrest of four hundred unionists. Eight unionists were indicted for murder, but none was convicted on that charge.[49]

Initially, a claimed 85 percent of the city's contractors and builders agreed to observe Landis Award conditions, and five hundred architects pledged to limit their work to Landis Award jobs. When the award expired in May 1923, it was renewed for three years, but the working rules originally imposed were no longer to be considered obligatory. In September 1923 some large general contractors quit the Citizens' Committee, claiming they faced strikes against their jobs in cities other than Chicago. The building boom in Chicago also attracted new construction firms that did not abide by the terms of the Landis Award. Landis Award jobs no longer commanded the field once the initial award expired, although the Citizens' Committee was by no means ready to surrender to the unions. When the 1923 contract expired on May 31, 1926, the Building Trades Council, unwilling to renew the award, announced that union members would be called off any job on which Landis Award workers were employed. Accepting the challenge, the Citizens' Committee completed several large buildings with open shop workers that year and the next, but it went "out of business" in 1929 following an adverse Illinois Supreme Court decision in a case against some of its practices that was initiated by the Carpenters' Union. The committee was replaced by the Landis Award Employers' Association, but the new group controlled only about 10 percent of the city's construction jobs, and the closed shop prevailed once again in the Chicago building trades.[50]

Drew, who followed the Chicago story with "tremendous interest," promised the Citizens' Committee his help if needed, and he kept his promise. In May 1922 Pierce E. Wright, the secretary of the Associated Building Employers of Detroit, complained to Drew that the recruitment of workers in Detroit by the Citizens' Committee was "disrupting local conditions," might force Detroit builders to raise wages, and might even lead to some sort of Detroit retaliatory action against Chicago. Successfully calming Wright, Drew responded that the importance of victory in Chicago was "so great" that "it should largely control all other considerations." When Donnelley advised Drew in June 1923 that the situation in Chicago was becoming "pretty critical" because of the defection of several general contractors, Drew sought to persuade three of the contractors to support the Citizens' Committee.[51]

When in August and September 1926 Chicago's unionized ironworkers and several other trades struck two Chicago buildings, Drew and the NEA promptly supplied open shop erectors from outside Chicago. The jobs were successfully completed, and the Citizens' Committee, for the first time, placed the structural steel erection trade on an open shop basis, the Chicago IABSOIW local having abided by the Landis Award to that time.

At the behest of the Building Trades Council, the ironworkers and several other trades, in April 1927, struck the Mather Building, Chicago's tallest at the time. With the help of the NEA, which promptly answered the Citizens' Committee's appeal for assistance, the committee was able to complete the building with open shop workers. The NEA similarly assisted the committee that same year in seeing to it that steel was erected by open shop workers on the Chicago Club Building and other buildings in the Loop district. The NEA also contributed a modest sum to the committee. The committee thanked Drew and the NEA for their "splendid cooperation" and expressed regret that other open shop employer associations had not been equally supportive over the years.[52]

Drew's effort to support the open shop at the local level was not confined to Chicago and San Francisco. When a contractor in April 1920 asked the NICB to help the Dallas Chamber of Commerce to establish "stable open shop conditions" in the city, Magnus Alexander turned the request over to Drew, who promptly offered the NEA's cooperation and advice. Drew not only aided the Associated Building Employers in Detroit in preventing some closed shop construction in the city in 1924, but the NEA also contributed to the support of its employment office, since the NEA did not have an employment office of its own in Detroit, allegedly "the most open of the open shop cities." The NEA had a similar arrangement with the American Plan Association in Cleveland.

"We are 'going after' the building trades situation here [Indianapolis] this spring," A. J. Allen wrote Drew at the end of 1921, "and you can be of very great assistance to us." Drew, who had been advising Allen how to proceed in seeking to bring the open shop to the city's building trades, spoke to the Associated Employers of Indianapolis and guests early in 1922 on "Buildings and the Public," a speech that was then distributed by the NAM's Open Shop Department. When the association decided a few years later that it needed a private detective to deal with "vandalism" in the city's building industry, Allen turned to Drew, who suggested his favorite detective, Robert J. Foster, for the role.[53]

Drew's involvement with the Philadelphia Chamber of Commerce and its efforts to establish the open shop in Philadelphia appears to have resulted from his aforementioned association with the Philadelphia Iron League. An investigator whom Frank Walsh had probably employed provided the Federal Trade Commission, however, with quite a different version of what had occurred. According to the investigator's account, for which corroboration is lacking, Edward T. Stotesbury of the important Drexel Company and Alba Johnson, the former president of the Baldwin Locomotive Works, visited J. P. Morgan, apparently during the steel strike, and the investment banker allegedly told them that United States Steel had decided to launch an open shop movement throughout the nation through chambers of commerce and boards of trade. It was Morgan, according to this account, who put the two Philadelphia businessmen in touch with Drew, and he then worked with them on plans for a citywide open shop campaign.[54]

What is certain is that Drew met in May 1920 with the Executive Committee of the Philadelphia Chamber of Commerce and, at its request, drew up a platform of principles for an open shop movement in the city. The document was vintage Drew, including such principles as the sanctity of agreements, "full legal responsibility" for unions, the right not to organize, a ban on sympathetic strikes and strikes by government workers, the need for uninterrupted utility service, and a condemnation of "intentional" restrictions of production to create "an artificial scarcity." The Industrial Relations Committee of the chamber largely adopted Drew's draft on June 10, and Drew became the committee's advisor.

When Philadelphia longshoremen went out on strike at the end of June and demanded a closed shop, the Industrial Relations Committee announced that it would seek to apply the open shop to every industry in the city. After being approached by Drew, the city's banks and insurance companies appointed a committee to cooperate with the Industrial Relations Committee. Drew was pleased that the open shop campaign in Philadelphia met his criterion for such a movement, one directed by businessmen from various sectors of the economy rather than just by "partisan" employers.[55]

An investigator who had attended a secret meeting of the Industrial Relations Committee reported that Drew had told the members "how to act to keep within the law." The investigator indicated that the committee, which planned "to do a lot of educational work to keep the men away from the American Federation of Labor," feared labor violence and was gathering weapons to meet the threat. The committee's "first overt action" was against the building trades unions, typical of local open shop movements. By 1923, according to the secretary of the Philadelphia Builders' Exchange and Employers' Association, 60 to 65 percent of the city's building trades employees worked under open shop conditions, whereas the building trades had been almost completely closed shop in 1919. Drew's direct connection with the Industrial Relations Committee, however, seems to have ended soon after the open shop movement in the city had been successfully launched.[56]

Drew would have liked to protect the open shop in the building trades wherever it had been adopted after World War I by the establishment of a general contractors' association that would adapt to the prevailing labor policy of any particular locality. Since local chambers of commerce and business groups in so many cities were leading movements to challenge the closed shop in the building trades, Drew thought that he could appeal to general contractors by suggesting that they would find it difficult to secure building contracts in these cities unless they agreed to operate in accordance with local conditions and opposed the sympathetic strike.[57]

Unable to persuade the general contractors to take the initiative he wished, Drew thought that another approach to the national building situation would be to work out some kind of cooperative arrangement among the numerous local open shop associations concerned about building conditions. He would have liked these associations to adopt a national code of principles for the construction industry and to establish machinery to enforce the code. He also favored the training of "new mechanics upon a large scale" both locally and nationally in order to break the hold of the building trades unions on the skilled trades. He believed, furthermore, that the jurisdictional lines among the trades could be simplified by the development of eight to ten basic trades to do all the necessary work on a building rather than the thirty or forty trades to which the unions had allocated the work. One of "the bright spots" Drew saw in the construction industry was the incorporation in 1927 of the Industrial Construction Company by the American Plan Association of Cleveland and a citizens' committee to erect structures on an open shop basis in competition with the city's contractors, who were linked to the city's closed shop building trades unions. The company, however, although it had completed fifty-nine buildings by early 1930, was "not a complete success," and it was liquidated in January 1933.[58]

The NEA did not participate in the one organization that was designed to fashion "a code of constructive principles" for the building industry on a national basis, the American Construction Council (ACC). The council was established in 1922 with Franklin D. Roosevelt as its president "to bring together all elements in the building business on the Closed Shop basis." Roosevelt's purpose was to coordinate the various branches of the construction industry to deal with such industry problems as seasonal unemployment and to improve the image of an industry that had been rocked by scandals. When R. C.

Marshall, Jr., the chairman of the Temporary Operating Committee for the council, invited the NEA to join the organization, Drew responded that he doubted that the building business could be reformed as long as closed shop unionism in the industry was "recognized" and remained "unregulated and irresponsible."[59]

At Roosevelt's invitation, Drew and a few others met with the future president at his Hyde Park home in May 1922 to discuss plans for the ACC. Drew, however, heard nothing at the meeting that changed his mind about the council. He nevertheless thought that the open shop forces, without endorsing the ACC, should seek to influence it to agree to "certain fundamental principles" such as "trade autonomy." If each trade were permitted to pursue its own labor policy on a national basis without hindrance from closed shop trades, the open shop structural steel erectors, for example, would no longer have to face the threat of sympathetic strikes by closed shop unions in other trades in one community or another. Drew also thought that a group representing the public rather than the builders and the unions should occupy the "predominating position" in the ACC.[60]

Drew was invited to preside and to speak at the opening meeting of the ACC on June 19, 1922, but he declined the offer since he did not wish to commit the NEA to the new organization. Despite the NEA's refusal to join the ACC, Roosevelt continued to try to involve Drew in council affairs, Marshall visited Drew on several occasions to discuss council matters, and Drew gave him the names of persons who could help in drawing up the kind of code of ethics for the industry that the NEA commissioner favored. Nothing much came, however, from Drew's suggestions or from the ACC itself, which turned out to be "little more than a paper organization."[61]

In addition to his efforts to promote and support the open shop in private construction, Drew sought to do the same for public construction. He thus saw "a great deal of good" in the suggestion that an open shop clause be inserted in building contracts for public work, since public authorities, as he understood it, could not legally discriminate against workers on the basis of their membership or nonmembership in any organization. Emery, however, persuaded Drew that it would be a mistake to pursue this proposal since it might boomerang. Should the federal government reject the suggestion, Emery observed, it would appear that it had rejected the open shop principle as well.[62]

The issue of government building contracts arose in another guise in 1929 when NEA members began to complain that the federal government was accepting bids for public construction only from general contractors. The general contractors then proceeded to let the subcontracts only to firms that operated on a closed shop basis, thus excluding NEA firms. Drew appreciated the seriousness of this matter for the NEA, especially at a time when private construction was on the wane. As he understood it, although general contractors had not in the past been "in the habit of taking the steel contract" themselves, they were doing so more and more by 1929 and were having the steel for their jobs erected by closed shop firms to avoid labor trouble in closed shop communities. If this continued, he feared, it would increase the power of the "trouble-making and contract-breaking" IABSOIW on government work and would drive up its cost. The solution for the problem, Drew believed, was for the government to let the steel contract for a building separately from the rest of the contract.[63]

After the NAM had taken up the contract matter with the Supervising Architect's office of the Treasury Department, which was in charge of the federal government's building program, Drew discussed the issue with Assistant Secretary of the Treasury Ferry Heath. In addition to stressing the cost factor and the alleged untrustworthiness of the IABSOIW, Drew contended that by letting contracts for government buildings to general contractors, the federal government was, in effect, doing indirectly what it could not legally do directly, that is, discriminating against one kind of labor, the labor employed by open shop steel erectors, who, Drew claimed, were responsible for 80 percent of the structural steel then being erected in the nation. Heath responded that the government let its building contracts to the lowest bidder without specifying the use of any kind of labor and, rebutting allegations to the contrary, stated that the government had been letting "lump-sum contracts" for at least twenty-five years in order to expedite production. Were the government to let the steel contract separately, he maintained, the result would be both delay and labor trouble.[64]

When the Fort Pitt Bridge Works in 1932 received a contract for eighty-seven hundred tons of steel for the Post Office Building in Washington, D.C., the general contractor told the company that it would have to erect the steel with union labor. Responding to the assertion of the American Bridge Company's general manager of erection that the government's policy of letting contracts for government buildings only to general contractors was correct, Drew suggested that perhaps NEA members could subsidize a contractor who was "hardup" to bid on government contracts and who would then erect the steel on an open shop basis if his bid was accepted. Another possibility was to follow a Treasury suggestion that NEA members should themselves function as general contractors if they wished to "control the [labor] policy," but no NEA member seriously considered either of the two suggested ways of coping with the federal government's contract policy for public construction.[65]

Drew's concern that federal government policy favored the closed shop in the construction of public buildings was heightened by a labor dispute involving the construction of a post office building in Pittsburgh in 1932. The general contractor for the building's superstructure let the contract for the delivery of sand and gravel for the project to an open shop firm, the Pittsburgh Gravel Company. This led to a strike idling two hundred workers on the building by the Hoisting Engineers' Union, which refused to handle the material for a company that employed nonunion engineers lest this violate the union's contract with the Pittsburgh Building Trades Employers' Association. A Department of Labor conciliator agreed with the union's interpretation of the contract.

The conciliator's "decision" incensed Drew, who claimed that the federal government had no legal right to force the closed shop under the guise of mediation. If, moreover, he declared, workers on a public building could use their union status "as a lever to force the closed shop in the production and transportation of building materials," the public works program of the federal government would be faced with "continual warfare." He urged the head of Pittsburgh Gravel to involve local business organizations in its support, advised the company to seek an injunction against "coercion" if the general contractor canceled the subcontract, and sent along a "memorandum of law" on this point. The Pittsburgh Chamber of Commerce did inject itself into the affair, but the dispute was in the end settled in Washington to the union's satisfaction. The rights of the open shop gravel men, Drew protested, had been "thrown into the discard" in what amounted to "a conspiracy against the open shop."[66]

Drew's commitment to the open shop extended in the 1920s to the domain of transportation at both the local and national levels. He became a member of New York's Citizens' Transportation Committee, and he came to the aid of the railroads in their efforts to stave off the unionization of their shops.

In settling a longshoremen's strike in October 1919, the National Adjustment Commission, the wartime federal adjustment agency for the longshore industry, maintained a wage differential in favor of longshoremen on deep-sea piers as compared to those on coastwise piers because the coastwise lines were operating at a loss. The longshoremen accepted the award, but the coastwise longshoremen on coastwise piers in New York struck in March 1920 for a wage increase. After not operating for several weeks, the coastwise firms engaged strike replacements, which led the Transportation Trades Council of New York and Vicinity to resolve not to transport goods to or from any coastwise piers that were on strike and also not to transport nonunion merchandise to coastwise vessels. An organization of about one hundred thousand members, the Transportation Trades Council was a federation of teamsters and chauffeurs and various branches of the longshore trades. The strike and the boycott that followed tied up the coastwise transportation of merchandise between New York and the South Atlantic states and, according to the city's Merchants' Association, cost the city $1 million a day and seriously affected industrial plants that were denied needed raw materials.[67]

The various commercial organizations of New York, led by the Merchants' Association, formed a Committee for the Protection of the Rights of the Public in the Transportation of Goods in order to resolve the dispute, but without success. The committee decided to fight the teamsters even if this required establishing the committee's own trucking service. The bargaining agents of sixteen teamster locals with forty-four thousand members responded that they would "accept the challenge." The Protection Committee gave way on May 14 to the Citizens' Transportation Committee (CTC), composed of executives of the city's commercial organizations and the chairman and vice-chairman of the committees its predecessor had already formed. In its Declaration of Principles, the new committee asserted that "all classes of people and merchandise should be served by transportation and trucking facilities without discrimination."[68]

Drew accepted an invitation to join the CTC, becoming the chairman of both its Publicity Committee and its Subcommittee on Outside Cooperation and a member of its Law Committee. The assignments made good sense, since no one on the CTC had more experience than he in publicizing the importance of the nondiscriminatory handling of goods, no one was in a better position to coordinate the efforts of the committee with similar committees and organizations elsewhere, which was the responsibility of Drew's subcommittee, and he was, of course, an experienced labor lawyer. For Drew, the CTC was protecting "the great open-shop industry of the nation . . . against a very serious menace." As he noted, tactics such as those employed by the Transportation Trades Council had been employed to exclude non-union-made material in many of the building trades in large cities, a problem never far from Drew's mind as NEA commissioner.[69]

The CTC successfully fought the union boycott on both the legal and the economic fronts. The Law Committee, even before the CTC had been formed, had initiated injunction proceedings against the Transportation Trades Council; and, in a suit in which Burgess Brothers, a lumber company, was the plaintiff, the committee secured a ruling from the New York Supreme Court on June 9, 1920, which was upheld on appeal, that the union effort "to exclude open-shop merchandise from the channels of trade and markets of the nation" was "a conspiracy against the public welfare" in violation of federal law. The day after the decision, the CTC, which had raised funds to create its own open shop trucking service, dispatched its trucks for the first time to the four struck piers. When the Old Dominion Transportation Company bowed to a longshoremen threat to strike any steamship line accepting merchandise delivered by the CTC, the Law Committee secured an injunction restraining unions from threatening strikes against Old Dominion for receiving CTC-delivered merchandise. After the injunction had initially been set aside, it was upheld on appeal.[70]

"This is a movement for the open shop," the CTC's chairman, William Fellows Morgan, publicly announced. Drew, a few days later, however, wrote a railroad executive that the committee was "not engaged in a crusade to establish the open shop" but was seeking rather to prevent public transportation from being interrupted by sympathetic strikes and boycotts. Service that did not discriminate between union- and non-union-made goods, like employers who did not discriminate between union and nonunion workmen, fully accorded, however, with Drew's definition of what constituted an open shop. As he noted, moreover, had the union boycott succeeded, it would have compelled the unionization of all firms receiving or shipping goods through the port of New York. Unable to stop the movement of the CTC's trucks, the teamsters first, on August 11, and the longshoremen the next week decided to return to work, ending "one of the longest strikes in the history" of New York harbor.[71]

The great railroad shopmen's strike that began on July 1, 1922, has been described as "the first national strike by nonoperating railroad workers that directly threatened the country's economic and social lifeline." Since the railroads bought between 40 to 50 percent of all iron and steel produced in the United States at war's end and since the railroad shops became a major battleground in the conflict in the 1920s between open shop advocates and the union forces, it is hardly surprising that Drew involved himself in the employer effort to roll back the unionization of the shops that had occurred during the war. Drew, indeed, had expressed concern about the shops soon after the United States entered the war and one month before the federal government took over the railroads.[72]

The 434,000 shopcraft workers, machinists, blacksmiths, boilermakers, sheet metal workers, electrical workers, and carmen, constituted about 19.5 percent of the workers in the railroad industry as of World War I. Somewhere between 20 to 30 percent of the shopcraft workers were organized into AFL unions when the federal government assumed control of the railroads at the end of 1917. Federal operation of the railroads proved to be a "tremendous impetus" to the organization of the shopcrafts, and by the time the government returned the roads to their owners, the percentage of organized workers had soared to about 80 percent of those employed in the railroad shops.[73]

The Director General of the Railroad Administration forbade (General Order No. 8, February 21, 1918) discrimination in "the employment, retention, or conditions of employment" of railroad workers because of their membership or nonmembership in any organization. At the end of May 1918 the Railroad Administration created Railroad Board of Adjustment No. 2,[74] composed of an equal number of railroad management and shop union representatives, to deal with shopcraft controversies that could not be settled by the parties to the dispute. Deadlocked cases were to be referred to the Director General. The Railroad Administration raised shopcraft wages; established the basic eight-hour day with time and a half for overtime, Sundays, and legal holidays; accorded the shopcraft workers seniority; abolished piecework; and provided detailed classifications for each craft and grade of work. Before government operation of the roads, the wages, hours, and working conditions of shopcraft employees had varied from road to road, but "standardization and uniformity" now became the rule. The wartime orders and their supplements regarding working conditions in the industry were embodied in a National Agreement concluded between the shopcraft unions and the Railroad Administration on September 30, 1919, one of five such agreements with the various railroad unions.[75]

The Transportation Act of 1920, which ended federal control of the roads as of March 1, 1920, established a Railroad Labor Board (RLB) of nine members, three each representing labor, management, and the public. The board was to hear and decide disputes involving grievances, rules, and working conditions that an adjustment board had been unable to resolve. Once the roads had been transferred to private hands, the Association of Railway Executives was determined to restore employment relations in the shopcraft industry to the status prevailing before the federal government had so markedly altered those relations. No railroad executive was more outspoken on this matter than W. W. Atterbury, the vice president in charge of operations of the Pennsylvania Railroad System, in whose shops the open shop had prevailed before the war. If the railroads failed to push the shopcraft unions into retreat, that, he warned, would break the solid front presented by the "forces of the 'American plan.'"

The railroad executives wanted to do away with both Board of Adjustment No. 2 and the National Agreement for shop workers. With economic recession affecting railroad revenues in 1920–21, the executives also wanted to reduce wages. Although the various adjustment boards had performed a useful function and had operated in a creditable manner, the carriers complained that they had had an adverse effect on discipline and had impaired efficiency because they lessened the ability of local railroad management to deal with problems on the spot. The railroad executives also objected to the National Agreement for the shopcrafts and its rules and regulations dealing with such matters as punitive overtime, restrictions on the right of management to hire and fire, and employee classifications. They complained that the agreement had been drawn up without employer involvement, ignored local conditions, and led to the closed shop in the industry.[76]

The issue posed by the conflict between the carriers and the shopcraft unions, Drew advised NEA members in September 1920, was "the most important that . . . [had] arisen in the industrial field since the war." Were the shopcraft unions to succeed in their effort to "perpetuate" what they had won under federal control and to "unionize and standardize" railway labor, he warned, it would be "an immeasurable calamity to American industry and the public welfare."[77]

Drew took the position that the issue of labor relations in the shopcraft industry was a matter not just for railroad management and railroad labor to decide. It had been "the plain intent" of Congress in enacting the Transportation Act of 1920, he contended, "to make the paramount interest of the public in transportation a prime and controlling factor in future settlements of railroad labor questions." The public, Drew maintained, was interested in "uninterrupted[,] efficient and economical [railroad] service," and since higher operating costs were likely to be reflected in higher rates, the public was necessarily concerned about labor questions in the industry. He thought it essential, consequently, not only for the NEA and similar organizations to encourage railroad executives not to yield to union demands but also for interested parties to present their views to the RLB.[78]

Drew opposed the union demand to retain Board of Adjustment No. 2 and the National Agreement for the shopcrafts. The board and the agreement, he maintained, had centralized control of railway labor in the hands of union leaders, deprived nonunionists of representation, led to standardization of shopcraft working conditions across the land despite regional, railroad, and system differences, and resulted in a 50 percent decline in efficiency. His preference was for each road to handle its own labor affairs, with an appeal to the RLB available for an aggrieved party, which coincided with the employer position.[79]

The Transportation Act provided that boards of adjustment "may be established," but it left to the parties the decision as to whether there should be boards for individual roads, for groups of roads, or for the roads as a whole. Faced with labor's desire for national boards and employer opposition to this, the RLB concluded that it had no jurisdiction in the matter. The various national agreements supposedly had expired when federal control of the roads ended, but the RLB decided on July 20, 1920, to permit the continuation of the agreements for the time being. Drew thought that the board lacked the authority to make any such decision.[80]

Drew sought to marshal support among employer and commercial organizations for the position of the railroad executives regarding their relations with the shop unions. He urged these organizations to communicate with the RLB, to seek to appear before it, and to urge railway executives not to bow to union demands. In communicating with employer groups, Drew stressed the danger that a "national closed shop" in the railroad field would pose for efforts to maintain the open shop elsewhere. As chairman of the CTC's Publicity Committee, Drew communicated with two thousand commercial and business organizations, many of which, like the employer groups, expressed their views to the RLB. Drew believed that his efforts had "stiffened" the railroad executives even though some of them were inclined to agree with the unions.[81]

Whether or not the RLB was affected to any degree by the appeals of employers and business groups is unclear. In any event, after hearings that began on January 10, 1921, the board decided (Decision No. 119) that the national agreements should expire on July 1, 1921. It called in the same decision for the carriers and the union system organizations on the various roads to confer regarding working rules and working conditions. It listed sixteen principles to guide the parties in these negotiations. Principle No. 15, the critical one from the point of view of both the unions and the open shop advocates, provided that the majority of any craft or class of employees had the right to determine which organization should represent that craft or class. Organizations that were thus selected had the right, according to the decision, to make agreements applying to all employees in the particular class or craft, without however infringing the right of nonmembers to present grievances personally or through selected representatives.[82]

Decision No. 119 brought the RLB and the shop unions into conflict with the Pennsylvania Railroad, which was intent on negotiating only with its own employees. On June 6, 1921, the company held an election among its shopcraft employees to select representatives from among themselves to deal with management. The ballot did not permit a vote for an organization, which violated Principle No. 15. System Federation No. 90, which claimed to represent 75 percent of Pennsylvania Railroad's shop employees and with which the company had negotiated during the period of government operation, advised shopcraft employees to boycott the company election and held an election of its own that called for a yes or no vote as to whether the workers wished to be represented by No. 90 but made no provision for voting for an individual. Of the 33,104 employees eligible to vote in the company-held election, only 5,236 voted, and since 1,757 of these votes were invalid, the total valid vote was only 3,479. Excluding the votes cast by workers whom the company had laid off, System Federation No. 90 received 26,055 of the 26,062 votes cast in its election.[83]

Ignoring the results of the union election, the Pennsylvania management proceeded to negotiate an agreement with the shopcraft employees selected in its balloting. System No. 90 protested to the RLB, which, after a hearing, ruled (Decision No. 218) both elections invalid and set forth rules for another election that permitted employees to vote for System Federation No. 90, any other organization, or an individual. Refusing to abide by the decision, the Pennsylvania Railroad sought to have the RLB set it aside on the ground that the board lacked the authority to prescribe election terms. When the RLB refused to rescind the decision, the railway company secured a temporary injunction from Judge Kenesaw Mountain Landis restraining the board from enforcing Decision No. 218. The injunction was upheld in federal district court on May 4, 1922, Judge George T. Page restraining the RLB from ruling that the company had violated the law. The RLB appealed to the United States Supreme Court, which on June 12, 1923, upheld the authority of the board to have rendered Decision No. 218 but stated that its "only sanction" was "the force of public opinion." The RLB thereupon found the Pennsylvania in violation of Decision No. 218, but the company continued to negotiate with its company union, and System Federation No. 90's effort to block this in federal court proved unavailing.[84]

Delighted when the Pennsylvania Railroad challenged the RLB's jurisdiction in the election matter, Drew promised the company business support "to the limit." For him, the issue was whether a company would be able to deal only with its own employees or only with union representatives, which, he thought, would lead to the closed shop. He thought that public representation was required at board hearings on the Pennsylvania case because of its "encroaching decisions," which was Emery's position as well. The NAM, the NEA, and the NFA consequently petitioned the RLB on July 23, 1921, to permit them to appear before the board to present "vital facts and considerations" regarding the Pennsylvania case that would enable the board to reach "a conclusion with respect to the superior public interest involved." The RLB rejected the petition, asserting that to have done otherwise would have resulted in "such delay and embarrassment" as to hinder the work of the board. Drew concluded from this that the board was "not a fit body to protect the public interest in railroad labor matters."[85]

On July 21, 1922, an estimated four hundred thousand shopcraft employees went out on strike, the workers having approved strike ballots dealing with contracting out (a practice by which railroad companies sublet repair work to open shop firms that did not observe union wages, hours, and working conditions), the RLB's authorization of piecework, and a wage cut the RLB had ordered. System Federation No. 90 had previously received authorization from its members to strike the Pennsylvania on the representation issue.[86]

The shopmen strike proved to be "an unmitigated disaster" for the shopcraft unionists. On September 11, 1922, the strike leadership authorized strikers to return to their jobs with companies that recognized their seniority, which became a major issue after the strike began, and that dropped legal proceedings against strikers. By early 1925 the strike had been called off on all the roads except the Pennsylvania and the Long Island Railroads, where the strike continued until September 10, 1928. By 1929 only about 25 to 30 percent of the shopcraft workers were union members, and a sizable majority of the shop employees were in company, not independent, unions.[87]

In the early spring of 1925 a Pennsylvania Railroad passenger car experienced "serious" mechanical trouble in New Jersey that suggested the possibility of vandalism. Robert Foster, the detective who worked so closely with the NEA, suggested to a Pennsylvania Railroad vice president he knew that the matter should be investigated, and Foster received the assignment. Learning that John Scott, whom, it will be recalled, Foster had befriended during the Harriman strike, was the secretary of the AFL's Railway Employees' Department (RED), of which the shopcraft unions were members, Foster reestablished contact with the union official. According to Foster's uncorroborated account, he discovered that some members of the RED's executive committee had inflicted "great wrong" on the Scott family that had led to the death of one of the two Scott daughters. Convinced, apparently, that he had been mistreated by his union associates and unhappy with the way the strike had developed, Scott turned over to Foster "file after file" of what the detective characterized as "incriminating documents" demonstrating that strike leaders had "engaged in a gigantic criminal conspiracy against the railroads" that had resulted in deaths, injuries, and the destruction of railroad property. The documentation, as might have been expected, ended up in the Drew Papers.[88]

On April 25, 1927, Foster, accompanied by Harry Chandler, Harrison Gray Otis's successor as publisher of the *Los Angeles Times,* presented Attorney General John G. Sargent a lengthy fifty-nine page bill of particulars directed against the RED. It is a reasonable guess that Drew had participated in the drafting of the document. The damage to person and property in the strike, the document alleged, had been perpetrated mainly by "inside men," as in the Harriman strike. Foster also claimed that the record showed that some members of the Interstate Commerce Commission had used their position to further the RED's purposes. The Foster brief included a sampling of the documents the detective had received from Scott to support the Foster allegations—the documents were actually more suggestive than conclusive—and also stated that Scott was willing to assist the government in prosecuting the alleged conspirators.[89]

Sargent arranged for Foster to go over the brief with J. Edgar Hoover, and Foster thought that the Federal Bureau of Investigation director had "appeared to be impressed" by what he saw. Assistant Attorney General C. R. Luhring, however, advised Foster that the statute of limitations prevented the government from taking action in the case. Unable to persuade the Department of Justice to act, Foster turned to the president. In a letter to President Herbert Hoover that had probably been written by Drew, Foster sought to counter the Department of Justice's arguments and suggested the government's filing a bill of equity to dissolve the RED. The White House referred the matter to Luhring, who found Foster's arguments defective. And there the matter rested.[90]

As before World War I, Drew's concern about the open shop extended to the area of politics and legislation insofar as they might affect the open shop cause. This became evident in the 1928 presidential election when he learned that Republican candidate Herbert Hoover had instructed that all printing for the Republican National Committee must carry the union label. Drew thought that since Hoover wanted business support and since, in the NEA commissioner's estimation, the nation's prosperity rested entirely on open shop firms, the union label decision demanded the "organized protest" of open shop businessmen. If Hoover, who Drew believed lacked "any scruples in this matter," did not favor the open shop while a candidate, what, Drew wondered, could be expected of him were he to be elected president? "[T]he chief threat to business and to continued prosperity," Drew wrote a trade association executive, "lies in the political field and in the tendency of the two parties to compromise on fundamentals." He thought that the World War I experience had demonstrated how quickly the unions could "extend their control" if they could say that the federal government favored them.

The NAM's Open Shop Department, which took charge of the union label fight, Drew, San Francisco's Frederick J. Koster, W. W. Atterbury, and the militant open shop organizations all sought to persuade the Republican National Committee as well as the Democratic party to open up the bidding for its printing to all printing firms, with the contract going to the lowest bidder. Hoover denied that he had issued instructions to confine party printing to union firms, but both parties, as had become their custom, followed that policy in the 1928 presidential campaign.[91]

The union label matter was one of the issues on Drew's mind when he drafted a piece on "The Politicians and the Labor Question" during the 1928 campaign. He found the political situation to be "most disturbing" from an open shop point of view. He was troubled that both parties were promising legislation to deal with what they claimed were the abuses of the injunction in the labor field even though Drew believed that the allegations of abuse had been "repeatedly disproved." He was also concerned that both parties had pledged their support for collective bargaining in their platforms. Although asserting, as he always did, that workers had the right to bargain, he feared that the inclusion of the principle in the party platforms in response to the request of organized labor would be taken to mean that the two parties favored collective bargaining as the unions construed that phrase, which, as Drew chose to believe, meant "bargaining with the unions on a closed shop basis." Drew was especially displeased with Hoover, not only because of the union label issue but also because Drew had learned that Hoover, as secretary of commerce, had silently supported the request of the AFL's Building Trades Department that the United States Chamber of Commerce building in Washington, D.C., be erected by a union contractor even though chamber affiliates had voted "almost unanimously" to have it erected on an open shop basis.[92]

The enactment of the Davis-Bacon Act in 1931 and the Norris–La Guardia Act in 1932 did nothing to assuage Drew's concern that "the preservation of fundamental Americanism in industry . . . [had] become a major political issue." Passed over Hoover's veto, the Davis-Bacon Act provided that work on federal buildings must be compensated at "the prevailing rate of wages for work of a similar nature" in the area where the building was being constructed. When the measure was under consideration in Congress, Drew worked with the NAM and the General Contractors' Association to have "some sound and proper clauses" included in the bill, but their intervention was unavailing. The NEA, actually, did not take part in this effort "openly and actively" lest doing so jeopardize the lobbying of the steel industry at the time to secure favorable tariff schedules, indicating once again the ties between the NEA and United States Steel in particular.

When a prominent NEA member complained that the Davis-Bacon Act, as enforced, discriminated in favor of organized labor, Drew responded that he had been "constantly working" on the matter, providing information to the press, the Chamber of Commerce, and employer organizations. He complained that the law was proving to be a "serious handicap" in the construction of public buildings and that the building trades unions were keeping their wage scales artificially high despite the depressed state of the economy so as to compel the payment of similarly high wages on public construction.[93]

When the Norris–La Guardia anti-injunction bill was before the United States Senate, Drew protested in the name of the NEA that the bill was "class legislation in favor of a militant, strongly organized group which already . . . [enjoyed] a large measure of legal privilege and immunity." Pointing to the behavior of the building trades unions in various cities, he predicted that, if passed, the measure would invite "the collusive agreement and the racket." Drew's recurring concern from the outset of his NEA commissionership was that the building trades unions would be able to boycott building materials produced in nonunion or open shops. Since he saw the injunction as the chief defense against this tactic, he believed that the enactment of the Norris–La Guardia Act had "limited or destroyed" a weapon critical to the defense of the open shop.[94] Drew was clearly troubled about the drift of public policy in the nation even before Franklin D. Roosevelt became president.

Drew's wide-ranging efforts to promote and defend the open shop, efforts that went well beyond his immediate responsibilities as NEA commissioner, have attracted relatively little attention from historians. In a letter to an NEA member in 1926, Drew, in a sense, provided his own explanation for this fact. After recounting all that he was doing in addition to his NEA activities to promote the open shop on both the local and national levels, he commented, "All of this work has been done quietly and without blare of trumpets."[95]

CHAPTER 10

"The Most Belligerent National Association": The NEA, 1920–33

The National Erectors' Association (NEA) as of 1920 had a membership of fifty-five companies, and it had labor bureaus and branch offices in New York, Pittsburgh, Philadelphia, Buffalo, Cleveland, Milwaukee, and Kansas City. The structural steel for bridges continued to be erected on an open shop basis, but the NEA and the International Association of Bridge, Structural and Ornamental Iron Workers (IABSOIW) were more evenly matched in the area of residential and commercial building, the open shop predominating in some major cities, the closed shop in others.[1] The NEA, expectedly, waged its most important battle to preserve the open shop in the 1920–33 period in New York City. It also made a determined effort to bring down Theodore Brandle, the czar of the structural steel industry in unionized New Jersey.

When Clarence E. Bonnett in his 1922 book dealing with employer associations categorized the NEA, as already noted, as "the most class-conscious and belligerent national association" in the nation, Walter Drew protested to the author. There was a difference, he asserted, between defending oneself against union aggression and seeking to destroy unions. "[T]he portrayal of the industrial situation in the light merely of a battle between two class-conscious forces seeking to destroy each other," the NEA commissioner wrote Bonnett, "is not only fundamentally unsound but outlines the problem in the public mind in a most unfortunate and unhealthy way." Drew's objections notwithstanding, "belligerent" correctly describes the NEA insofar as the maintenance of its conception of the open shop was concerned. In his study of the open shop movement of the 1919–33 period, historian Allen Wakstein agreed with Bonnett that the NEA was in the early 1920s "undoubtedly the most belligerent national association in the United States."[2]

In the 1920s the NEA continued to use the tactics it had employed before World War I to prevent unionism from establishing itself in its members' firms. As always, Drew in the 1920s stressed that the open shop policy was "worthless" if the employer relied on "a weak foreman" or one with "closed shop leanings." He advised employers to check on their foremen from time to time and to let them know in no uncertain terms that their employer was committed to the open shop. To help ensure the loyalty of their foremen, the New York Iron League established a "Thrift Fund" to which each foreman and his employer contributed two dollars a week. The foreman could borrow from the fund under certain circumstances and could draw out the entire sum after ten years.[3]

NEA members after World War I were generally willing to employ union workers as individuals as long as their employment did not appear to threaten unionization of the job. When the open shop appeared to be at risk, however, as in New York in 1920, the NEA and its allies made it a matter of policy to restrict the number of union members whom they would employ. Drew, also, did not hesitate to provide employers with a so-called yellow-dog contract in which the employer stated that he would not knowingly employ union members and the individual hired stated that he was not a union member and would not become one as long as he held that job.[4]

As already noted, the open shop movement of the 1920s lost momentum after the first few years of the decade. Conforming to this pattern, the NEA appeared to be losing strength in the second half of the decade,[5] but some of its key members seemed to be weakening in their commitment to the open shop cause even before that. The NEA received a particularly hard blow when the American Bridge Company, the association's most important member, decided at the end of 1920 to resign from the organization. Although the company's general manager of erection put it that way, American Bridge was actually surrendering only its membership on the NEA's executive committee, not in the NEA itself. Drew was almost certainly correct in his assumption that this action, which was in line with United States Steel policy regarding similar memberships, was designed to avoid "giving color" to the oft-made union charge that the steel corporation dominated the NEA and that it was "a mere tool" of the steel interests.[6]

It became evident in the 1920s that important NEA members, faced at a time of high demand with a choice between selling steel tonnage and fighting for the open shop, were inclined to decide that "business is business." The NEA, Drew observed in January 1926, had had "a harder time to preserve the open shop" in the industry in the preceding five years than "even during the dynamite regime." NEA membership had dropped to forty-eight by early 1926, some resignations occurring because members did not wish to observe the NEA wage scale. Drew feared that even the largest NEA firms that supplied fabricated steel for erection purposes appeared to have forgotten that the open shop was the steel industry's "corner-stone." Whereas the IABSOIW had been waging a "determined and energetic campaign to get back the closed shop in the industry," the NEA, in Drew's estimation, seemed to be in "a process of disintegration." "[V]ery much discouraged," he tendered his resignation as NEA commissioner in May or June 1926 but was persuaded by his superiors to remain at his post.[7]

When the Shoemaker Bridge Company sublet steel for closed shop erection in New York in 1926, Drew hesitated to seek the Shoemaker firm's expulsion from the NEA because, the NEA commissioner remarked, if members were to be expelled for acting as Shoemaker had, it would have cost the NEA its "strongest members," notably American Bridge and McClintic-Marshall, both of which had provided steel for closed shop erection in Chicago, Philadelphia, New England, and elsewhere. Even the percentage of steel erected in New York on an open shop basis began to decline in the 1920s. In 1928 Shoemaker resigned from the NEA, its president explaining that the firm dealt with general contractors all over the nation who operated on a closed shop basis, which meant that Shoemaker either had to forgo the business available to it or agree to closed shop erection.[8]

As the Shoemaker firm indicated, the problem for the NEA was the old nemesis of the open shop in the building trades, the general contractor. What was happening in the 1920s was that the large steel fabricators, unlike what had occurred in New York in 1919–20, were increasingly selling steel to general contractors on an f.o.b. basis, and, fearing strikes in one city if they permitted open shop erection in another city, the contractors arranged for the erection on a closed shop basis of all the steel they purchased. This not only made it extremely difficult to erect steel with open shop workers, but local NEA firms that fabricated structural steel to be erected by open shop workers found it difficult to compete with general contractors who obtained their steel from major steel fabricators like American Bridge or McClintic-Marshall.[9]

As of 1930, structural steel was being erected on a predominantly closed shop basis in Chicago, Detroit, St. Louis, Cleveland, Pittsburgh, Baltimore, Kansas City, Boston, and Jersey City but largely on an open shop basis in New York, Buffalo, Philadelphia, Minneapolis, St. Paul, Milwaukee, San Francisco, Los Angeles, Seattle, and Dallas. The open shop continued to prevail throughout the nation in the erection of bridges and in the fabrication shops and the steel mills. Drew estimated in 1930 that about 80 percent of the structural steel erected in the nation for all purposes was erected on an open shop basis. The IABSOIW journal put the figure for the 1926–29 period at two-thirds of the total.[10]

The center of the fight to maintain the open shop in structural steel erection, as had been true from the NEA's beginning, was New York City. About 35 percent of the structural steel erected in the nation in the mid-1920s was erected in New York State, most of it in New York City. This was more than three times as much steel as was erected in any other state. From 1919 until the New Deal, the IABSOIW centered its organizing efforts on New York City. The union and Drew agreed that the fate of the open shop in structural steel erection in the nation rested on the outcome of the battle between the union and the open shop iron firms in that city.[11]

The IABSOIW had seen its membership fall from a high of 27,560 in 1919–20 to a low of 15,113 in 1921–22 as the result, primarily, of the failed steel strike and the severe decline in the building industry that set in toward the end of 1920 and continued for about eighteen months thereafter. President P. J. Morrin reported at the beginning of November 1921 that only about 20 percent of the union's members were then working. With conditions in the building industry, however, very much on the upswing in 1923, the union launched a vigorous organizing campaign, using sixteen special organizers to supplement the efforts of local organizers and the union's vice presidents. The union made "good progress" in the next several months, its membership numbering 22,399 as of January 1924. Of that total, 5,778 were enrolled in structural steel and other locals in the New York district, where the organizing campaign had centered. Under Morrin's leadership, also, the international strengthened its organizational structure, abandoning the "rather loose and slip-shod" practices that had permitted the locals to ignore the international's leadership. Local agreements now required the international's approval, as did local strikes.[12]

Once the Building Trades Employers' Association–Building Trades Council agreement came to an end in New York on January 1, 1922, the Iron League, as we have seen, did not hesitate to employ union members, but as individuals only. By the spring of 1924 the IABSOIW was claiming that 98 percent of the New York district's ironworkers had been enrolled in the union's ranks, and Drew, the Iron League's counsel, agreed. Preparing for trouble, the league began devising a "preferred list" of first-class reliable men regardless of their union status to whom preference was to be given in employment even to the extent of their displacing workers not on the list. It will be recalled that the Iron League hoped that those on the list would look to their employers for security of employment and would not wish to jeopardize their status by striking. The league had previously appointed an "outside labor superinten-dent" who was to keep track of work "coming along" and "finishing" and who was to prepare on this basis a list of the most efficient workers as a force of "semi-permanent erection personnel" whom members might wish to favor with schemes of welfare capitalism.[13]

The expected happened on May 1, 1924, when five structural steel locals in the New York district (two of them in northern New Jersey) struck for a wage increase from $10.50 to $12.00 a day as well as a signed agreement. The Iron League rejected the demand for a signed agreement out of hand and also resisted the wage demand, Drew pointing out that the wages of New York ironworkers had kept pace with the highest in the industry and with the wages of most of the building trades as well. According to the Iron League, twelve hundred workers walked out on sixty-two jobs, predominantly those of league members. The union put the strikers at a slightly higher number, 1,359 or 1,369, or about 24 percent of the union's claimed membership in the district.[14]

As might have been expected, the Iron League turned to the NEA's labor bureaus to supply strike replacements. The league promised "competent men" regular jobs and job preference in the future, telling them that they were not strikebreakers. It paid the transportation fare of the replacements and met their room and board expenses until they began drawing pay. If they quit the job before working a full week, these costs were deducted from their pay. The league even tried to bring in some Indians from Canada to man struck jobs, apparently without success.[15]

The IABSOIW sought to checkmate the efforts of the Iron League to recruit strike replacements from outside New York. It attempted to infiltrate "some good friendly brother" into groups of workers being dispatched to New York from Pittsburgh, Detroit, and elsewhere whose role was to persuade the strikebreakers to turn back by giving them the "real facts" about the strike. Union representatives in New York met all incoming trains, boats, and ferries and sought to influence potential strike replacements not to take strikers' jobs. The union paid the fares of the recruited workers back to their homes if they agreed to return and persuaded some who remained in New York to join the union or at least not to accept work from the struck firms. The union also placed ads in the newspapers of cities in which strike replacements were being recruited warning ironworkers to remain away from New York. The union claimed that of 2,191 workers whom it exaggeratedly reported the Iron League had brought to New York by June 15, only two hundred remained at work.[16]

Union ironworkers, engaged in what Morrin characterized as "the fight of the century" against "the heart of the opposition," picketed the struck jobs and apparently followed strike replacements to and from work. The Iron League claimed that the union resorted to intimidation and violence in seeking to discourage nonstrikers from remaining at work. The league gathered one hundred affidavits to this effect, but the union, alleging that the strike was distinguished by its lack of violence and "rough stuff," charged that the affidavits had been acquired on the basis of "misrepresentations of the grossest character." The league engaged Robert Foster to provide guards to protect struck jobs and strike replacements, and it solicited the cooperation of railway companies in an effort to prevent strike replacements coming to New York from being "annoyed" by union representatives.[17]

The Iron League's strike committee assigned strike replacements as they arrived to member firms. The strike committee required foremen, who had signed contracts with league members not to join a union on a closed shop basis, to keep a record of workers using "abusive language or acting in a threatening manner to intimidate [other] workmen"; and one can assume that employees seeking to promote the union cause on the job were discharged. The league also employed private detectives for espionage purposes.[18]

The General Strike Committee that ran the strike for the union was made up of one member from the strike committee of each district local involved in the dispute plus President Morrin. All members of the IABSOIW executive board were present in New York at the beginning of the walkout, and twenty international organizers helped run the strike. IABSOIW members throughout the nation were initially assessed one day's pay and later $2 per month to support the strike, but the international failed to persuade the AFL to assess its membership for the cause. AFL general organizer Hugh Frayne did, however, provide the union with at least moral support.[19]

The Building Trades Council of Greater New York pledged the strikers its support. Among the building trades in the district, however, the real support for the strikers came from a local of the International Union of Steam and Operating Engineers, thirty of whose members began walking off their jobs on May 5 in violation of the union's contract with the Iron League.[20] Since work by ironworkers on the upper stories of a building could not proceed unless the hoisting engineers brought material to them, the strike of the engineers posed a major threat to Iron League firms. The league, however, was able at considerable expense to secure and train nonunion replacements for the engineers who struck.[21]

On June 18 the Iron League filed an injunction in the New York Supreme Court against the IABSOIW and the business agents of the Operating Engineers and some other unions. Claiming that the defendants were engaged in a conspiracy to compel the Iron League to adopt the closed shop, the plaintiffs listed a variety of alleged union actions of violence and intimidation directed against nonstrikers, foremen, potential strike replacements, and drivers bringing men and material to struck jobs. The complaint also described allegedly "vicious" picketing of the struck jobs, the offices of the plaintiffs, the places where they secured material, the homes of workers and foremen, and the employment offices where strike replacements were engaged. The complaint alleged further that the defendants had threatened general contractors with strikes if they did not cancel the subcontracts they had awarded the plaintiffs and that general contractors had complied in three instances. The plaintiffs demanded that the defendants be restrained from engaging in just about any action that would promote the strike and be required to pay the plaintiffs $5 million in damages for the injury allegedly caused their businesses by the strike.[22]

Claiming that issuance of the requested restraining order would break the strike, union attorneys, notably Frank Walsh and Samuel Untermeyer, sought to persuade the court to delay granting the writ pending a trial on the merits of the order. The union attorneys also filed a counterclaim against Iron League members designed to restrain them from allegedly seeking to destroy the IABSOIW and from allegedly discriminating against "fair" contractors through league connections with the steel companies and the consequent refusal of the latter to sell steel for union erection. The union sought $10 million in damages from Iron League members.[23]

On July 24 Judge Richard P. Lydon denied the Iron League's motion for an injunction pending a trial of the case. The papers presented to him by the two sides, the judge asserted, created doubt in his mind as to whether the defendants had overstepped their rights and whether the plaintiffs, whose complaint, the judge held, lacked "probative force," were entitled to injunctive relief. It was possible also, Lydon stated, that the defendants' claim that the league lacked standing in a court of equity since it had not come into court with clean hands might be sustained in a trial.[24]

By the time Lydon rendered his decision, the Iron League, according to Drew, had enough workers to man its jobs, and the strike, "for all practical purposes," was over. The Iron League and Drew, whom Walsh in arguing the union's case had characterized as "the notorious Walter Drew," consequently decided not to press the league's injunction case any further.[25] They sought, instead, as we shall see, to seek a new injunction on different grounds, continuing a legal battle with the union that was not to be finally resolved until 1933.

Although Drew's allegation that the strike was over at least approximated the truth, the IABSOIW did not concede the point and continued to picket Iron League jobs until restrained from doing so by another injunction in March 1925. The league by then, its jobs fully manned and the construction industry prospering, had agreed to pay the ironworkers the $12 a day they had sought months earlier. The league now sought a new injunction against the union, this time in federal court, because of what it viewed as a union attempt to secure the boycott of open shop erection jobs. Beginning in the late summer of 1924, the union arranged for the Daily Dodge Work Reports, which contained information on construction jobs from the time they were contemplated until contracts were awarded, to be sent to its New York locals and the international union representatives who were assisting them. The union used this information to contact owners, architects, and contractors in an effort to dissuade them from awarding structural steel erection contracts to nonunion firms.[26]

In the injunction they sought from the United States District Court for the Southern District of New York in February 1925, four Iron League members, two of whom were also NEA members, claimed that they would suffer irreparable damage if the defendants proceeded with their alleged boycott of nonunion firms by use of the Dodge Reports. The plaintiffs claimed that the union was conspiring to achieve the closed shop and was interfering with interstate commerce in doing so. Judge John C. Knox on March 11 granted the plaintiffs a "drastic" temporary injunction restraining the defendants from "intimidating, coercing," or "inducing" any person from refusing to work for the plaintiffs, advising or conducting a boycott against them, calling an industry sympathetic strike, or doing anything else "tending to interfere in any way" with the plaintiffs. The union effort to quash the temporary injunction failed, leaving it in effect until the court could determine whether a permanent injunction should be issued. The judge appointed a referee to adjudge the claims of the plaintiffs set forth in the pleadings as well as the union's counterclaim against the Iron League and the NEA, which was largely a reprise of the union's case before the Lockwood Committee.[27]

The Knox injunction, Morrin informed the president of the AFL some years later, "worked [sic] havoc upon our organization plans and tied our hands completely so that we were unable to do effective organization work." Not only was the strike very expensive for the union—it had expended $300,000 on the dispute by August 1924—but it also led to a secessionist movement in its big New York Local 40, headed by one of the local's former business agents, that apparently stemmed from the desire of some New York unionists to work for large open shop contractors even though the strike continued. The international responded by taking over the administration of Local 40 and one other New York local. The strike also proved to be "a very expensive thing" for the Iron League. Its strike committee estimated in November 1925 that the direct cost to members had been $1,100,000, of which $70,000 had come from league funds and most of the remainder from four or five of "the more important members," three of whom were also NEA members. League firms had also lost "a large amount of business" to competitors operating on a closed shop basis.[28]

Although the IABSOIW was restrained by the federal injunction for the rest of the 1920s, that did not mean that the Iron League faced no threat to its open shop stand. Its problem stemmed from the Bricklayers' Union and an old foe, the general contractor. In the spring of 1926 the Bricklayers' Union engaged in what Drew described as "a sort of guerilla warfare" on building jobs in the Bronx and Westchester on which nonunion ironworkers were employed. Drew and the league were able to get this action called off by talking to national officers of the Bricklayers' Union, but trouble from the same source occurred once again in the fall.

A delegation from the ironworkers' locals, accompanied by Morrin, sought to enlist the assistance of the general contractors with headquarters in New York in securing an agreement with the Iron League. At a luncheon meeting in December 1926 of the general contractors, the league executive committee, and Drew, the NEA commissioner defended the open shop, but he reported in a memorandum of the meeting that "not a single voice was raised in behalf of the Iron League or its position." Support for the open shop in structural steel erection in New York appeared to be waning, Drew informing the president of American Bridge late in 1926 that whereas 70–75 percent of the structural steel in New York had been erected a few years earlier by open shop workers, "barely 50% of the work" was then being erected on that basis.[29]

Not only did the position of the open shop iron firms appear to be weakening, but the Iron League itself was soon to disappear as an independent entity. In early 1926 steel erectors formed the Structural Steel Board of Trade (SSBT) to deal with "cooperative matters" in the industry not relating to labor. The organization, however, amended its constitution in March 1927 to include labor matters among its concerns, and it declared its support for the open shop. The Iron League was then consolidated with the SSBT as of April 1, 1927.[30]

Drew's concern about the future of the open shop in structural steel erection in New York was alleviated on October 30, 1929, when the lawyer William Cannon, the referee appointed by Judge Knox, rendered a report and decision in the federal injunction case that was "largely favorable" to the plaintiffs. Although the referee ruled against them on the question of whether structural steel erection in New York was part of interstate commerce and also did not deal directly with the question of the closed shop that they had raised, he sustained the key boycotting charge. At the conclusion of the testimony presented to the referee, Merritt Lane, the counsel for the plaintiffs, had moved for the dismissal of the union's counterclaim on the ground that evidence was lacking to support it. Conceding that the union had not "put in any proof on the counter claim," Walsh, for the union, had not objected to the motion, which the referee granted.[31]

Following the referee's decision, Federal Judge Frank A. Coleman issued a permanent injunction against the defendants in the case that recapitulated the restraints the original restraining order had placed on them. He also required them to pay court costs of $6,765 as well as $10,000 to the referee. The legal costs to the open shop erectors who had brought the two injunction suits beginning in 1924 came to $32,287. The United States Steel Company, significantly, contributed $25,000 to help meet these costs.[32]

Drew viewed the decision in the injunction case, which the union appealed, as "a notable victory" that "greatly strengthened" the open shop policy of the structural steel erectors. He did not anticipate that the SSBT would almost immediately come close to abandoning that policy altogether. The issue that provoked the radical change in the SSBT's open shop policy stemmed from the construction of the eighty-eight story Empire State Building, the tallest in the nation at the time. The general contractor for the building, Starrett Brothers and Eken, one of the largest firms of its kind in the United States, apparently had assured the IABSOIW that the building would be erected by union labor; and the union received the same assurance from the president of the Empire State Building, Alfred E. Smith, New York's former governor and the Democratic candidate for the presidency in 1928. On March 17, 1930, however, Post and McCord, an SSBT member that operated on an open shop basis, began erecting the structural steel on the Empire State Building. The IABSOIW responded by striking all Starrett Brothers and Eken jobs in the nation, idling at least seven hundred workers on a dozen jobs in New York, Newark, Chicago, and Cincinnati.[33]

Smith sought to mediate the dispute between the SSBT and the IABSOIW. "Al seems to be on our side," Walsh reported about the mediator, with whom Walsh had been associated in Democratic party politics. Smith asked Post and McCord to agree to hire union workers for the Empire State job, and when the company responded that it had provided the SSBT with a $50,000 bond that it would operate on an open shop basis, Smith offered to have the Empire State Building Company pay the $50,000 if Post and McCord agreed to forswear its open shop commitment in this instance. When it became evident that Post and McCord and the SSBT would not agree to Smith's entreaties, the former governor informed the union that there was nothing more he could do about the matter. Paul Starrett thereupon pressed the SSBT to reverse its open shop policy and to conclude an agreement with the union. If not, he said, he would "throw Post and McCord . . . off of the . . . Empire Building."[34]

The IABSOIW strike and Starrett's insistent efforts to induce the SSBT and Post and McCord to recognize the union led four SSBT firms and Drew to initiate contempt proceedings in federal court against Starrett and the union's leadership for violating the federal injunction that had been made permanent on February 14, 1930. While the matter was pending, the SSBT, importuned by Starrett and other general contractors and fearing the loss of its subcontracts to erect steel if it continued to adhere to its open shop policy, "fully authorized" its chairman, Charles R. Eidlitz, by a divided vote, to negotiate an agreement with the IABSOIW "along lines as reported by him." When he had "arrived at a satisfactory agreement," he was to present it to the SSBT for "execution." Since some SSBT members already operated closed shop and since the steel board had previously sought to persuade the union to provide workers only for SSBT members, the decision was probably less surprising than it might otherwise seem.[35]

Eidlitz, Morrin, and William J. McCain, the union's general secretary, were able to reach an agreement by May 12 except for some "disputed points" that were submitted to AFL president William Green for "final decision." The IABSOIW then ordered the strikers on Starrett Brothers and Eken jobs to return to work. After Green made his decision, Eidlitz and the union signed a contract on May 22. The agreement, including the points decided by Green, provided for a wage of $15.40 for an eight-hour day, time and a half for overtime, and double time for holidays. It gave the SSBT forty-five days "to bring about a complete change from non-union or open-shop conditions in New York, Brooklyn and vicinity to the establishment of union conditions and a collective relationship between the two organizations." There were to be no strikes or lockouts during the ten-year life of the agreement, and provision was made for the resolution of disputes. Local men were to receive at least 50 percent of the erection jobs in the New York district, but there were to be no other restrictions on the employer's right to hire and fire. Although membership in the union was to be optional for superintendents and foremen, pushers had to be union members, and the union agreed to accept into its ranks all nonunion workers employed by the SSBT. Union members were to operate all burning and welding machines, and there was to be no piecework. The union agreed not to question whether the steel its members erected had been fabricated in union or nonunion shops and also committed itself not to unionize the fabrication shops of SSBT members.[36]

For Drew, the agreement between the SSBT and the IABSOIW spelled "disaster." It would mean, he claimed, a doubling of the cost of erecting structural steel and would "greatly increase the power of the unions and the inefficiency, exploitation and racketeering in the building industry" that were preventing a return to prosperity in the nation, then in the early stages of depression. If the open shop could not be maintained in steel erection in New York City, the nation's largest market for structural steel, it would be "practically impossible," Drew contended, to maintain it anywhere in the United States. He feared that the IABSOIW success in New York would be "heralded as a tremendous victory of organized labor against the steel industry," which, he maintained, had "always been the real objective of the iron workers' fight." As he had long argued, Drew asserted that once structural steel erection was unionized, "a strong buffer" against the unionization of the steel fabrication shops and the steel mills would be removed, and the path would be open for the "progressive unionization" of the steel industry as a whole.[37]

The open shop forces around the country viewed with the gravest concern what was happening in New York and its likely impact not only on structural steel erection elsewhere but also on the building industry, the steel industry, and manufacturing in general. The secretary of Milwaukee's Employers Council was "appalled." "What takes place in a market like New York," he wrote Noel Sargent, "is going to spread over the entire country." Victory for the closed shop in New York, the general manager of the Landis Award Employers' Association feared, would be "an entering wedge for a fight on the open shop throughout the United States." Concerns of a similar nature were expressed by employer groups in Chicago, San Francisco, Philadelphia, Minneapolis, and Dallas and by the Industrial Relations (Open Shop) Department of the National Association of Manufacturers.[38]

On May 23 Eidlitz submitted to the SSBT the agreement he had concluded with the IABSOIW and characterized it as "satisfactory." The discussion that followed within the board led to a demand for some changes in the agreement that Morrin was unwilling to accept. On June 5 the agreement was referred for further consideration to the SSBT's Labor Committee, headed by Robert T. Brooks, the president of George A. Just Company, an NEA member. After additional efforts to modify the agreement and after Secretary of Labor James J. Davis had apparently urged its acceptance, the SSBT on July 1 unanimously agreed to end all negotiations with the IABSOIW.[39]

Just why the SSBT reversed itself and abandoned efforts to come to terms with the IABSOIW is not altogether certain. What is evident, however, is that the NEA, as the president of the Iron and Steel Fabricators of Milwaukee put it, was "a very vital factor" in the decision, probably working through Brooks to induce the delay that Drew believed was crucial to the outcome. The official reason the SSBT gave when it broke off negotiations with the union related to conditions in the structural steel erection trade in New Jersey. The SSBT had seen the agreement as the means of establishing "uniform labor conditions" throughout the New York metropolitan district, including northern New Jersey, closed shop territory in which the New York firms hoped the arrangement with the union would enable them to compete. During the period of delay, however, "the deplorable labor conditions" in the iron trade in New Jersey, including racketeering and collusive bidding, had been exposed in the press. The leadership of the IABSOIW had refused to deal with the problem, and the SSBT feared, it claimed, that if it approved the agreement, the same conditions would spread to New York. As will soon become evident, it was Drew who was gathering information on the "rotten conditions" in New Jersey and who was seeking federal prosecution of those involved, and it is safe to assume that he kept the SSBT and its Labor Committee apprised of the matter and its implications for them.

Drew may have influenced the SSBT decision to break off negotiations with the union in another way. The SSBT had seen the agreement as a means of reducing the f.o.b. sales of structural steel to general contractors. Drew, however, gathered data to demonstrate that when local fabricators had agreed to the closed shop, f.o.b. sales of steel, especially for large structures, had increased, not decreased, with "practically all the business" going to the large outside shops of American Bridge, McClintic-Marshall, and Bethlehem. Since nearly all SSBT members were fabricators as well as erectors, Drew stressed to them that they would be worse off, not better off, if they came to terms with the IABSOIW.[40]

What we do not know is the extent to which the big steel companies, accepting Drew's "buffer" thesis, may have influenced the SSBT decision. Since, however, there was general agreement about the importance of "the selling policy" of the big steel companies, it is likely that they played some role in persuading the SSBT to reverse itself. Eugene Grace of Bethlehem, we do know, "interjected" himself in the SSBT deliberations, but he thought that he had been ineffective. The NEA, for its part, contacted J. P. Morgan "indirectly" in an effort, apparently, "to convince the financial interests behind the corporation [United States Steel] of the folly of their attitude," and Drew was also in touch about the matter with the corporation's general counsel. United States Steel, after all, was committed to the NEA and the maintenance of the open shop in structural steel erection, and it is difficult to believe that it remained passive when it appeared as though the structural steel then being erected in New York on an open shop basis would in the future be erected by union labor.[41]

The legal battle between the IABSOIW and the New York open shop firms continued after the collapse of the negotiations between the union and the SSBT. On July 15, 1930, Federal Judge William Bondy denied the motion of the four New York iron firms to charge Morrin and Starrett with contempt for violation of Judge Coleman's injunction. The strike at issue, Bondy ruled, had been against Starrett Brothers and Eken, not against any of the plaintiffs, and Post and McCord, the firm that had the structural steel subcontract for the Empire State Building, was not one of the plaintiffs.[42]

The IABSOIW in late November 1930 filed a $3.5 million damage suit in the New York Supreme Court against the SSBT for repudiating the Eidlitz-Morrin agreement. The union demanded that the eighteen SSBT firms be enjoined from employing any but union members and that they cease inducing union members to give up their membership. Supreme Court Judge William H. Black granted the union a preliminary injunction on January 3, 1931, the first time that a state court had held a union contract to be enforceable and had granted "immediate relief." The Appellate Division of the court, however, reversed the decision the next month on the ground that the so-called contract was only a tentative agreement, as the SSBT maintained, and also that the union was not entitled to injunctive relief since it had not come into court with clean hands in view of its strike against Starrett Brothers and Eken.[43]

Defeated in seeking damages from the SSBT, the IABSOIW succeeded in its appeal against the Coleman injunction. Agreeing with the lower court that there had been no interference with interstate commerce that violated the antitrust laws ("building is not commerce"), the United States Circuit Court of Appeals for the Second Circuit based its decision on the ground that the plaintiffs had been unable to establish federal jurisdiction on the basis of diversity of citizenship since they had failed to demonstrate that no members of the defendant union were citizens of New Jersey or Pennsylvania, the domiciles of the four plaintiff firms, all of which, incidentally, had by then been acquired by McClintic-Marshall.[44]

On appeal, a unanimous United State Supreme Court, on April 10, 1933, in the case of *Levering and Garrigues et al.* v. *Morrin,* upheld the lower court. The Supreme Court dealt with only the interstate commerce aspect of the case, rejecting the iron firms' contention that union behavior regarding the erection of steel in New York interfered with the transportation of steel from outside the state. The Court held that "the sole aim" of the alleged union conspiracy was "to halt or suppress local building operations as a means of compelling the employment of union labor, not for the purpose of affecting the sale or transit of materials in interstate commerce." If in suppressing the local use of material, the union, in effect, curtailed the shipment of steel in interstate commerce, "that result," the Court held, "was incidental, indirect and remote" and, therefore, did not constitute a violation of the Sherman Antitrust Act, as the Court had previously held. The controlling precedent in the case, ironically, was *Industrial Association* v. *United States,* in which the Court had upheld the San Francisco Industrial Association's use of a permit system to maintain the open shop in that city.[45]

After the Supreme Court's decision in *Levering and Garrigues,* the complainant moved to amend its bill of complaint in an effort to conform with the Circuit Court's decision on the diversity of citizenship issue. The federal district court then directed the entering of a new decree against Morrin and three other union officials as individuals. The union, through Walsh, appealed the decision on the ground that it was in violation of the Norris–La Guardia Anti-Injunction Act of 1932. Both the Circuit Court and the Supreme Court upheld the union's appeal, Walsh informing Morrin that the Supreme Court decision was "a great precedent" for similar cases.[46] This brought to an end the protracted legal battle between the IABSOIW and New York's leading structural steel firms.

The United States Supreme Court's constricted definition of the Constitution's interstate commerce clause in the *Levering and Garrigues* case, characteristic of the pre–New Deal Court, served as an insurmountable barrier to Drew's determined efforts to secure the federal prosecution of the IABSOIW in northern New Jersey for violation of the Sherman Act. The dominant IABSOIW figure in New Jersey, Theodore M. Brandle, was, however, successfully prosecuted for income tax evasion, and his sway in the state was brought to an end.

In the spring of 1926 a new Iron League of New Jersey, composed eventually of 126 fabricators and erectors of structural steel in the four northern counties of the state, was formed to succeed an organization of the same name that had disbanded. The league reached an agreement on December 15, 1926, with the three IABSOIW locals in northern New Jersey (in Newark, Jersey City, and Perth Amboy), which had a claimed membership of about five thousand. The key person on the union side in arranging the settlement was

Brandle, vice president of the IABSOIW, business agent of Local 45 in Jersey City, president of the Iron Workers' District Council in New Jersey, president of the Building Trades Council of Hudson County, president of the Board of Business Representatives of the Allied Trades of Hudson County, president of the Building Trades Council of the state of New Jersey, general organizer for the AFL, president of the Branleygran Corporation, which handled surety bonds and insurance for contractors, president of Labor's National Bank of New Jersey, president of the Union Labor Investment Corporation, and ally of Frank Hague, the powerful mayor of Jersey City. "The brand of Brandle is on New Jersey," commented the *New York Evening Post.*[47]

In August 1927 Iron League member Simon Fein suggested the formation of a subsidiary group of the larger shops of the league to deal with the general contractors. There already was a Quality and Credit Survey Bureau of league members to "protect . . . [their] interests in the apartment house field." The larger firms were amenable to Fein's suggestion, since they believed that they had "suffered" from the practice of general contractors who sometimes took the low bid from a league member and then used it to persuade "some un-scrupulous bidder" to take the job at an even lower price. The result was the formation on August 22, 1927, of the Steel Board of Trade by fourteen league members. The Iron League and its two subsidiaries accounted for just about 100 percent of the steel fabricated in northern New Jersey and 95 percent of the steel fabricated in the state as a whole.[48]

Seeking to monopolize the fabrication of structural steel that was erected in New Jersey, the Iron League resolved at a meeting of October 17, 1927, that members should discontinue the use of "foreign [fabricated] steel" that was being imported into New Jersey for erection purposes. Deciding that it needed "a big man" to enforce this decision, to deal with problems arising among members, and to secure "protection on the job" and avoid labor trouble, the Iron League, in an extraordinary action on February 22, 1928, appointed Bran-dle its director-general at an annual salary of $10,000. His official duties were "to bring capital and labor together and create a more friendly feeling" between them and to protect "the general welfare of the Iron League."[49]

Under the leadership of Brandle and his associates, the Iron League devised a system of collusive bidding, sought to exclude foreign competition from the state in both the fabrication and erection of structural steel, pressured general contractors to confine the fabrication and erection of steel to league members, and created "labor trouble" on jobs secured by out-of-state contractors or on which out-of-state fabricated steel or other material was used. As soon as a contract was let for a new structure or to repair an existing one that required the use of structural steel or ornamental iron, the league notified all members, who were divided into four classes for bidding purposes depending on the amount of tonnage they were equipped to fabricate. Class A shops, members of the Steel Board of Trade, bid on jobs of 150 tons or more, and Class B shops, mainly those associated with the Quality and Credit Survey Bureau, bid on jobs of under 150 tons. The smaller Class C and D shops, which had no separate organization of their own, bid on jobs of very small tonnage (Class C) or repair work (Class D). Ornamental iron jobs of $15,000 or more were placed in the Class A category, and iron jobs of smaller sums were allocated to the other three classes. A small Central Committee dominated the Class A firms, which did the bulk of the fabricating in the state.

All members eligible to bid on Class A jobs "checked in" their bids on printed forms in the Board of Trade office. The Central Committee then assigned the job to one of the bidders, not necessarily the lowest bidder. All the other bidders were then required to raise their bids to a figure above that of the winning bid. If the general contractor did not let the job to the designated bidder, Brandle and his lieutenants either refused to provide the contractor with ironworkers or made sure that the job did not run "smoothly." For contracts in excess of 1,500 tons, members had to pay the treasurer 2.5 percent of the gross amount of the bid, and bids were accordingly increased to account for the fee. Of this sum, 1 percent was retained by the Board of Trade and disbursed for such matters as "entertainment" or "convention expense." The other 1.5 percent went to Brandle's lieutenant, Jack Delaney, who said of himself, "I represent . . . Brandle who owns me, body and soul, and every act that I do is the act of Theodore Brandle." The 2.5 percent contributions yielded large sums, $75,000 over one four-month period.

Brandle and his minions rendered two services for the 1.5 percent payments they received. They sought to exclude out-of-state competitors of Iron League members from supplying structural steel or ornamental iron for New Jersey jobs and from erecting the steel or iron in the state, and they took steps to ensure that general contractors both inside and outside New Jersey let contracts for the fabrication or erection of structural steel only to league members. In an October 1928 speech, Brandle thus stated, "Yes, I am trying to build a fence around it [New Jersey] so high no one can scale it and with everyone coming in passing inspection first." Brandle's motto was "Jersey work for Jersey people." The union stationed representatives at the principal entrances to the state, and they traced suspicious goods inside the state to check on possible violations. The Central Committee fined members who purchased out-of-state material or denied them jobs. Brandle boasted in October 1928 that 85 to 87 percent of the structural iron work in the state was being performed by league members, as compared to 40 percent before the new system had been adopted.[50]

Out-of-state steel contractors who received New Jersey contracts were likely, as noted, to experience labor difficulties during the Brandle era. If the relevant local provided them with any workers at all, they were apt to be what were "called 'dead ones,'" such as cripples and old men and inefficient men," so as to raise the cost of the job prohibitively and to teach the offender "a lesson." Sometimes an outside firm could receive a job if it paid "protection money," that is, a cash bribe—$15,000 in one instance—or it would be suggested that the job could go forward if the firm involved purchased stock in the Labor National Bank or invested in the Union Labor Investment Corporation.[51]

It was not only out-of-state fabricators of structural steel that encountered problems in seeking to sell their product in New Jersey. Companies providing other building materials or supplies, such as stone, brick, cement, sand, gravel, plaster, or pipe, ran into similar difficulties. New Jersey contractors were sometimes "coerced" into canceling contracts with out-of-state building supply firms or were required to buy from a "friendly" source, notably John P. Callaghan and Sons, one of whose stockholders happened to be the president of Newark's Building Trades Council. If the contractors involved refused to purchase their material as instructed, the building jobs using their products encountered labor trouble, or the trucks from out of state seeking to deliver the products in New Jersey ran into problems. The discrimination against suppliers of building materials in favor of certain New Jersey firms added substantially to building costs in the state. According to McClintic-Marshall, the cost of structural steel erection was $5-$15 per ton higher in closed shop and protectionist New Jersey than in open shop New York or Philadelphia, although the wage rates for ironworkers in the three jurisdictions were about the same.[52]

The ironworkers of northern New Jersey were almost all union members, but some union members were more equal than others. Beginning in 1923 or 1924 no ironworker in northern New Jersey could obtain a job unless he received a permit from his local's business agent, and no contractor dared employ a worker without a permit in this closed shop industry unless the contractor was prepared for labor trouble. Because of allegations of favoritism, the permit system was supplemented in January 1929 by a card-index system by which workers were to receive jobs in rotation. When a worker finished a job, his card was supposed to go to the bottom of the pile, and he was to wait his turn for another job. Some of Newark Local 11's eight hundred members charged, however, that the local's business agent, Thomas Sherlock, and other local officials shuffled the cards so as to discriminate in favor of their friends and against their enemies in the local. Opponents of the local's leadership were intimidated, and in one instance at least, in the spring of 1930, a member who complained about the system and the "strong arm methods" used to maintain it was so severely beaten by the sergeant at arms, a former prizefighter, that he had to be hospitalized.[53]

Local 11 voted 309 to 4 in May 1930 to abolish the permit and card-index systems, but the vote was ignored by the local's leadership, the District Council of Hudson County, and the IABSOIW leadership, to whom the membership complaint had been carried. In September 1930 the local voted to abandon the card-index system for ninety days, and the next month it made the same decision for the permit system, but the international's leadership ordered the restoration of both systems and suspended further meetings of the local. Four members of the local responded on October 9, 1930, by initiating a lawsuit against the local's leadership in New Jersey's Court of Chancery. They charged that Sherlock collected money from members for permission to work and from contractors to avoid labor trouble and that some contractors had suffered large losses or had been forced out of business as a result. It required a federal court order to restrain the international from trying the four who had brought the suit and other local members who had provided supporting affidavits.

The Chancery Court issued a permanent injunction on March 23, 1932, restraining Sherlock and the officers of Local 11 from suspending or expelling any member who refused to work under the card-index or permit systems. These systems, the court declared, were "part of a much larger plan having for its object the monopolization of the labor market in the building trades and the unjust enrichment of unscrupulous labor leaders at the expense of the public and the workmen under their control." Unrepentant, the international responded to the court decision by once again suspending meetings of the local. For Drew, what had transpired shed light on the question of whether the IABSOIW was "a fit and proper partner in collective bargaining."[54]

In December 1929, before the Chancery Court action, the Iron League ousted Brandle as its director-general. It is not certain whether this was because a "better element" in the league had rebelled against Brandle's racketeering behavior as director-general or whether attorneys of some league members, with a Federal Trade Commission (FTC) investigation of the league and the IABSOIW under way, had advised their clients that the league would be charged with antitrust law violations unless it changed its ways. Brandle did not go quietly. He persuaded eight of the largest Iron League firms to quit the organization and form a new Structural Steel Board of Trade of New Jersey that he organized and that operated very much as the Steel Board of Trade had, although with "greater secrecy."[55]

At some point in 1929 Drew retained Robert Foster to gather evidence regarding what the NEA commissioner thought probably constituted a restraint of interstate trade in violation of federal law by the New Jersey Iron League and the IABSOIW. Drew's concern was obvious since NEA members found themselves "practically locked out" of New Jersey, unable to sell their structural steel to New Jersey contractors and unable to erect steel in the state without the greatest of difficulty. McClintic-Marshalls's vice president thus informed Drew that although its largest fabrication plant was in Pottstown, Pennsylvania, near the New Jersey line, it could not sell its steel in New Jersey.[56]

The difficulty NEA firms faced in New Jersey derived not only from the fact that they were not domiciled there but also because the building trades unions in the northern part of the state did not permit their members to work alongside nonunion ironworkers. This became evident, for example, when the Bethlehem Steel Bridge Corporation, and the Phoenix Bridge Company, two major NEA firms, were awarded contracts in 1929 to erect two bridges over the Hackensack River for the Pennsylvania Railroad Company, a $400,000 job. The Pennsylvania found itself unable to secure a permit from the Jersey City commissioners for the river foundation work for the bridges unless it first came to terms with Brandle. The net result of union pressure was that the Pennsylvania had to shift the masonry work from an open shop to a closed shop contractor and to cancel the steel contracts with Bethlehem and Phoenix. It is noteworthy that even the Pennsylvania's hard-line foe of unionism, W. W. Atterbury, had been forced to conform to New Jersey's closed shop regime.[57]

In July 1931 the New Jersey State Highway Commission contracted with the NEA's three most prominent members as of that time, American Bridge, McClintic-Marshall, and Phoenix Bridge, to construct sections of State Highway Route 25 (the Pulaski Skyway) between Newark and Jersey City as well as bridges over the Passaic and Hackensack Rivers as part of the route. The commission had turned to open shop fabricators and erectors because the steel tonnage involved, somewhere between seventy thousand and one hundred thousand tons, was well beyond the capacity of the New Jersey shops and perhaps also because of the *Newark Evening News*'s persistent criticism of the labor scene in northern New Jersey that had aroused businessmen, bankers, and others in the area.

Brandle and the leaders of Local 11 and 45 in Jersey City and Newark respectively were determined that the erection work on Route 25 be performed exclusively by New Jersey union members, not by the open shop workers the three NEA firms employed even though they gave preference to local workers insofar as possible. The unionists resorted to massive and intimidating picketing of the jobs, followed workers on the project to and from their dwellings, and assaulted them with reinforced concrete rods, blackjacks, iron bolts, and other weapons. City officials, in Jersey City and Newark in particular, were initially at least more sympathetic to the union than to the nonunion workers and their employers. American Bridge, for example, had to secure an injunction to be able to lay track on an unused street in Jersey City.

Inadequately protected by local police forces, the three companies, on Drew's recommendation, turned to Foster's Industrial and Detective Bureau to guard their jobs. Foster provided more than one hundred guards over a ten-month period along a stretch of highway of two to three miles and also used undercover operatives to spy on the union locals. Because of the gauntlet of pickets the workers for the three companies had to run in the Jersey City streets, going to and from work, Foster hired a tugboat to take the workers between Staten Island and the Jersey City job. This proved to be ineffective, however, since pickets stationed on the bridges under which the tugboat passed pelted it with rocks. Foster thereupon chartered a Hudson River steamboat, on which the workers could be housed and fed. Most workers, however, found this uncomfortable, preferring to take their chances in the streets.

The police in Jersey City, Newark, and Kearny eventually began to supplement Foster's guards in protecting the highway job. In an altercation between guards and pickets on November 17, 1931, a Foster guard shot and seriously wounded an individual whom the press reported as being a union man but who claimed to have been "just taking a walk" in the vicinity. American Bridge eventually made a $4,000 out-of-court settlement with the man. In what was reportedly the thirty-fifth attack of the "Bridge War," thirty to forty unionists assaulted six workers on February 27, 1932, killing one of them. Twenty-one persons were indicted for murder, but all escaped conviction.[58]

Despite the difficulties they faced, the NEA firms were able to complete their jobs in about one year. The costs they incurred in guarding the work as well as for espionage came to $289,462 on a job of more than $2 million. Brandle also paid a high price for the losing battle he had fought to stop work on the Pulaski Skyway. Anxious to provide work for his constituents and to appease employers at a time of depression, Mayor Hague wanted to avoid labor trouble in Jersey City. The murder of the worker on the Skyway job was the last straw for the mayor, who ordered the Jersey City police to break the strike in the city, pressed for the conviction of whoever was guilty of the murder, severed his ties to Brandle, and began a "war" on labor "racketeering."[59]

It was not to Hague but to the federal government that Drew looked to deal with the evils of Brandleism that so directly affected the NEA and its open shop policy. The FTC began looking into alleged antitrust violations in New Jersey after a Philadelphia iron firm informed the commission in August 1929 that it could not secure a steel contract in northern New Jersey because it was located outside the state. After what appears to have been a cursory examination, an FTC examiner concluded that there was enough evidence to warrant a federal grand jury probe. A few days later, however, the FTC, with whom Drew had cooperated, bowed out of the matter and turned the case over to the Department of Justice.[60]

Drew, Foster, and Roberts B. Thomas, the New York SSBT's counsel, in a meeting of April 16, 1930, urged the Department of Justice to undertake an investigation of the alleged restraint of interstate trade in building materials by the IABSOIW and contractors in northern New Jersey. Drew described the labor situation in New Jersey for the Antitrust Division as "worse in many ways" than elsewhere in the nation. He provided the division with *Newark Evening News* clippings to supplement his contention, but it appears that the information in the clippings was largely based on information Drew and Foster had supplied the newspaper. Although division officials apparently had some reservations about Drew's importunities because of the NEA's well-known opposition to organized labor, they were persuaded to examine the FTC file in the case, which Drew, personally, helped them to secure, and to investigate the matter further.[61]

Over the next few months it was Drew and Foster who appear to have gathered the bulk of the information on New Jersey for the Justice Department, Drew pressing the department to act "while the iron . . . [was] hot." James Maxwell Fassett, the special assistant to the attorney general who was handling the case, subsequently complained that Foster was "trying to force the hand" of the department. Concerned about the inaction and lack of "seeming interest" of the Antitrust Division after it had had the case before it for several months, Drew went over the division's head, taking the matter to the attorney general, William D. Mitchell. He responded by talking to the Antitrust Division's head,

John Lord O'Brian, about the case and the desirability in dealing with antitrust matters not only to enforce the law but also to serve the public welfare. O'Brian promptly informed Drew that Fassett was ready to examine witnesses, and it was Drew and Foster who made the witnesses available.[62]

After examining the witnesses Drew and Foster had suggested, Fassett concluded that there probably was a conspiracy to keep fabricated steel and manufactured ornamental iron out of New Jersey and that "a very serious element of restraint" was evidenced by "the excessive prices uniformly charged" for erection as a result. He recommended that Drew and Foster be told that what the Antitrust Division needed was evidence of "specific acts of restraint and interference with commodities actually moving in interstate commerce or threats to prevent the performance of executed contracts which require in their performance the transportation of goods in interstate commerce." Foster supplied O'Brian with additional witness statements, but Drew disputed Fassett's conclusion that evidence of "overt acts" was lacking in the evidence Foster and he had already provided.[63]

Unlike the success he had enjoyed in persuading the federal government to prosecute in the great dynamite case, Drew was unable to prod the Antitrust Division to prosecute in the New Jersey case. O'Brian concluded at the end of March 1932 that "substantially all" the fifty incidents involving the Iron League and labor leaders in New Jersey that the Antitrust Division had examined constituted violations of state acts against extortion, bribery, assault, and the like rather than violations of the Sherman Act. The cases complained of, he judged, did not, for the most part, involve any "physical interference with interstate commerce," the indicated restraints having occurred after the material had arrived in New Jersey.

The conclusion of the Antitrust Division regarding the New Jersey case derived from several important judgments. Drew had pointed out that all the rolled steel used in New Jersey came from out of state, but the Antitrust Division view was that if a conspiracy existed, it was directed against fabricated steel and ornamental iron, not the rolled steel, since the rolled steel that was imported was fabricated in the state. Fassett, moreover, took the remarkable position that if all interstate commerce in fabricated steel and ornamental iron had indeed been wiped out because of fear of doing business in New Jersey, there was then no interstate shipment of material with which the alleged conspiracy could have interfered. This made it irrelevant, for example, that a firm like Beers and Tapman, a Bristol, Pennsylvania, fabricator and erector of structural steel that had done one-third of its business in New Jersey, had stopped seeking contracts there because of union problems it had encountered while trying to operate in the state. This contrasted with the conclusion of an FTC examiner who had worked on the case that the Beers and Tapman experience was evidence of "a direct restraint on goods moving in interstate commerce." O'Brian, to be sure, understood that there had been interference with the erection of structural steel that involved interstate commerce, but he concluded that this had not been "so widespread as to lay a burden" on that commerce, a judgment that seems in line with the *Levering and Garrigues* case. Finally, O'Brian assumed that the response of union defendants to prosecution would be that the acts complained of were intended to protect local union labor, not to interfere with interstate commerce, and he thought that this argument was likely to sway a jury in New Jersey should the case be tried.[64]

Although he chose not to prosecute, O'Brian decided to keep the New Jersey case open in the event a complaint in the future might justify prosecution. Since such a complaint did not reach the department in the next ten months, Fassett, on June 27, 1933, recommended that the docket on the case be closed. Interestingly enough, when Thurman Arnold mounted his ambitious case against the building industry in 1939, he instructed that the New Jersey file be made available to his assistant in charge of the case.[65]

Although Brandle escaped being joined in a federal antitrust suit, he did not escape federal prosecution. Brandle and his associate, Joseph H. Hurley, the sole two officers and stockholders of the Branleygran Corporation, were indicted late in 1930 for income tax evasion for the years 1926–28. After a first trial resulted in a hung jury, the two men pleaded guilty in April 1932 to defrauding the government and were required to pay $88,712.65 in back taxes, interest, and a penalty fee. The Branleygran Corporation pleaded guilty to a conspiracy charge and was fined $5,000.[66]

After Brandle pleaded guilty to income tax evasion, the AFL conducted an investigation of his record that included a failed attempt to gain access to the relevant Antitrust Division file. Prodded for months by the AFL, an "embarrassed" IABSOIW General Executive Board, after a trial and hearing, expelled Brandle and four associates from the union on June 22, 1933. By that time the courts had placed both Locals 11 and 45 in receivership, and Local 45 had voted 359 to 1 to accept Brandle's resignation as its business agent. On May 8, 1934, Brandle resigned as president of the New Jersey State Building Trades Council, and an insurgent group then seized control of the council and removed the "last vestige of the reign" of Theodore M. Brandle in New Jersey.[67]

The sordid events in the New Jersey building trades unfolded as the nation sank deeper into depression. The iron firms and their workers and the NEA itself were by no means immune to the effects of the severe business downturn. In early February 1931 New York SSBT members reported that they were employing 40 percent fewer workers than at the same time in the previous year. The decline in business as well as the merger of a number of the fabricators led the SSBT to conclude that an organization of its "broad scope and activities" was no longer needed and that what was required was "a simplified organization" like the old Iron League, which was revived at the beginning of 1933 and replaced the SSBT.

The NEA executive committee agreed in September 1931 to slash the wages of bridgemen 10 percent, and by the end of June 1932 the wages of ironworkers had fallen another 25 percent in most cities. Outside of the New York City area, the union rate at that time for ironworkers was about eleven cents per hour above the open shop rate, but the union rate was not always being paid. The index of employment in the fabrication shops fell from 107.7 in September 1929 (1926 = 100) to 37.8 in March 1933, and the per capita weekly earnings of shop employees fell from $30.93 to $13.40 during the same period. Feeling the economic pinch, the NEA in July 1932 closed its labor bureaus in Philadelphia, Buffalo, Milwaukee, Pittsburgh, and Kansas City. The New York bureau was retained, but its manager's salary was reduced by 21 percent. Drew at the same time took a voluntary 24 percent cut in his salary. He suffered a bigger loss in the stock market, losing all but $250,000 of the $5 million he was reputedly worth in 1929. Drew, however, eventually rebuilt his fortune, leaving an estate valued at between $2.5 and $3 million at his death.[68]

The IABSOIW, needless to say, was also hard hit by the depression of the pre–New Deal years, its membership dropping from 20,991 in 1927–28 to 16,559 in October 1932, a 21 percent decline. Presumably only about one-half of the members were actually structural iron workers, 28,906 gainful workers being so classified in the 1930 census. On the other hand, the sharp decrease in the depression of private construction relative to public construction, on which union labor was commonly employed, led to a considerable increase in the proportion of steel erected by union members, the IABSOIW claiming that organized labor erected 71 percent of the total steel tonnage erected in 1932, more than double the union's estimate for the 1926–29 period.[69]

The NEA in the early depression years had its differences with the Hoover administration even though it had been able to withstand the challenge posed to the open shop in the vital New York district. It was soon to face a far more formidable challenge to its open shop policy in the legislation of Franklin D. Roosevelt's New Deal.

CHAPTER 11

"New and Different Conditions": The NEA, 1933–57

The coup de grâce for the National Erectors' Association (NEA) and the open shop in the structural steel industry was delivered by the New Deal. Trouble loomed for the open shop forces when Section 7(a) was added to the National Industrial Recovery Act (NIRA) in June 1933. It soon appeared, however, that the NEA might be able to meet this threat to its existence, but the association's fortunes took a turn for the worse when the constitutionality of the National Labor Relations Act was upheld by the Supreme Court in April 1937. Drew, almost single-handedly, kept the NEA alive for another twenty years, until 1957, but it was increasingly an organization in name only.

When the Black Thirty-Hour bill passed the House in April 1933, Drew informed NEA members that if the measure were actually enacted and then survived a test of its constitutionality, "it would establish a revolutionary principle in our political and social system." Drew worked with the National Association of Manufacturers (NAM) to defeat the Black bill, and he urged NEA members to register an "emphatic protest" against the measure with members of Congress. Although he thought that "strange and unusual things" were taking place in the early New Deal, Drew took heart when the Black bill was abandoned in favor of a measure providing for the self-regulation of industry. "Voluntary agreements in industry for the purpose of stabilizing conditions to prevent any undue price and wage cutting by a temporary suspension of the anti-trust act, would be desirable," Drew wrote an employer association executive. The trouble, however, in the NEA commissioner's view, was that organized labor was "trying to get its program" incorporated in the recovery bill, and if that should occur, Drew believed, "the price might be more than the benefits were worth." Fearing a threat to open shop businesses, Drew met with a group of open shop industrialists in Washington in May 1933, and they appointed a "steering committee" that was "strongly open shop" to try to derail the provision in the recovery bill that organized labor was seeking.[1]

When Congress approved the National Industrial Recovery bill with Section 7(a) included, Drew sought to put the best face on what he actually regarded as "very bad." The right of workers to organize and to bargain collectively through representatives of their own choosing, he advised structural steel fabricators and erectors, did not mean that workers were obligated to do so, nor did it require any particular form of bargaining. Employers, he advised, could continue to bargain with their workers individually, with committees the workers designated for that purpose, or with a company union; and employers should be aware, Drew stressed, that Section 7(a) did not authorize the government to enforce the closed shop. As Drew understood the law, since unions could "only act as agents for a group of employees in a specific company," it was not necessary for an employer to conclude an agreement with a union "as such" or to refer to it by name in any agreement. On a motion by Drew, the NAM's Employment Relations Committee specifically advised the organization's board of directors to issue a statement to employers setting forth the Drew analysis of Section 7(a).[2]

Grasping at straws, Drew speculated that the NIRA might actually remove the incentive for workers to join a union. "If the Government fixed wages and hours," he asked rhetorically, "why join a union?" The unions, indeed, Drew correctly judged, were "going to be disappointed in their great hopes of organizing industry with the assistance of the Act."[3]

The International Association of Bridge, Structural and Ornamental Iron Workers (IABSOIW) saw the NIRA as providing the opportunity for it, at long last, to organize the larger fabrication and ornamental iron shops to which its jurisdiction extended. As President P. J. Morrin explained to Frank Walsh, the only way for the union to gain the benefits of the NIRA was to organize. If it failed in that task, he feared, some other union would organize the workers in the steel and iron shops and might then challenge the IABSOIW even in the erection area. Although the IABSOIW began once again to organize shop locals, it found the task difficult because of the opposition of the steel companies. The union had signed an agreement in September 1931 with the Structural Steel and Bridge Erectors' Association (SSBEA) regarding the erection of steel and reinforced concrete bridges and viaducts, ore and steel conveyors, and unloaders; and the two parties supplemented the agreement in July 1933 to include the erection of buildings and power plants. Centered in Illinois, the SSBEA, however, included few large firms and only one erection contractor in the key New York market. The IABSOIW's membership rose from 10,318 in 1932–33 to 13,220 in 1934–35, but this was hardly the great leap forward the union had anticipated when Section 7(a) became law.[4]

Like so many other employers, steel fabricators such as American Bridge sought to meet their collective bargaining obligations under Section 7(a) by establishing company unions. The determination of the steel fabricators and erectors to resist outside unionization was put to the test when the ironworkers' union went out on strike in August 1934 in an effort to organize the shops of the Worden-Allen Company, the Wisconsin Bridge and Iron Company, and the Lakeside Bridge and Steel Company, all located in Milwaukee. Drew quickly alerted NEA members to the situation, advising them to make sure that the machinery for collective bargaining in their shops was operating effectively and to provide for a full hearing of all employee grievances so that they could be disposed of before additional labor trouble developed.[5]

Reflecting the view of the three Milwaukee companies, Worden-Allen informed its employees that none of them was required to belong to any organization and that the company would meet with the freely chosen representatives of any group of employees or with individuals who so desired and would not discriminate against workers but would continue to operate on an open shop basis. Drew, who attended a meeting convened on August 16 by the Chicago Regional Labor Board in an effort to compose the Worden-Allen dispute, insisted that the closed shop the union workers were seeking was unlawful under Section 7(a), a point disputed by the Regional Labor Board representative. The employers and Drew were perturbed that the strikers were made eligible for public relief, which presumably enabled them to prolong their strike.[6]

The members of Milwaukee's Society of Iron and Steel Fabricators, J. M. Bell, the secretary-manager of the Milwaukee Employers' Council, informed Drew, thought that the "eyes of the industry, all over the country," were watching strike developments in Milwaukee. It was therefore essential, they believed, for Milwaukee fabricators to demonstrate that the union could not "break through" in the city. The fabricators also saw themselves as protectors of the open shop in the erection end of the structural steel industry, whose organization, they claimed, was the union's "ultimate objective" in the strike. Drew assured Bell that the "whole industry" was "solidly" in support of the Milwaukee fabricators.[7]

Aided by the Chicago Regional Labor Board and Department of Labor conciliators, the strikers and management came to terms at Worden-Allen in November 2, at Lakeside on November 10, and Wisconsin Bridge and Iron in early December. Worden-Allen asserted in its agreement, which was largely followed in the settlement of the other two strikes, that it would "go as far toward recognizing a union in the capacity of bargaining agent as the law requires." What this meant specifically, the agreement stated, was that the company agreed to recognize a bargaining committee composed of specific individuals as the bargaining agency for such employees as designated the committee to represent them. Employees who did not wish to be represented by the committee were free to bargain individually with management. Although the union was not mentioned by name, the agreement stated that the employees could "establish the official designation of the bargaining committee" and that the employer would recognize that designation in negotiating with the committee. The employer pledged not to discriminate against union members or strike activists, and labor and management agreed that employees were not to be "coerced or intimidated" by either party in the selection of their representatives.[8]

Drew was pleased that the union had not been recognized as such or named in the strike agreement, the bargaining agency could bargain only for those workers who specifically gave it that authority, and workers were protected from coercion from any source, including the union. "These," he stated, "are all parts of the fundamental principles we have been trying to have recognized at Washington." He happily concluded that the closed shop in the steel fabricating industry did "not appear to have made headway" in Milwaukee. Certainly the Milwaukee IABSOIW local had had to recede a good distance from its original demands.[9]

In New York, the Iron League firms did not even go as far as the Milwaukee firms did in reacting to the IABSOIW demand for recognition. Drew thought that "a new chapter" had been started in the fight of the IABSOIW to gain the closed shop in New York City when the union's two principal steel erection locals were admitted on December 4, 1933, to the city's Building Trades Council (BTC) since, under BTC rules, other trades were obliged to support IABSOIW strikes against open shop jobs. The IABSOIW locals quickly put Drew's assumption to the test when they gained support of the BTC unions for a strike against a Post and McCord job. The company, however, successfully checkmated this effort by securing an injunction against the BTC and the IABSOIW locals on the ground that they were involved in an illegal secondary boycott to gain the closed shop. A second strike in support of the ironworkers that the BTC called against a McClintic-Marshall job was called off before Drew could proceed with an injunction suit he was preparing in the company's behalf.[10]

On April 4, 1935, several New York building trades unions staged a strike in support of the IABSOIW locals on the Pier 88 construction job because McClintic-Marshall, which was erecting the steel for the job, employed non-union ironworkers. Since the pier was being readied for the docking in June of the new French liner, the *Normandie,* the city's dock commissioner persuaded the strikers to return to their jobs by promising that he would halt work then under way on Piers 90 and 92, for which McClintic-Marshall was also the steel contractor, pending an investigation of alleged "irregularities" by the contractor, particularly alleged violations of Public Works Administration (PWA) regulations. The Iron League was soon complaining that the city government had to be pushed to approve the letting of contracts for steel work to open shop firms on other jobs.[11]

In still another action in support of the IABSOIW locals, eight building trades unions struck the Downtown Post Office building on August 1, 1935, seven weeks after the NIRA had been declared unconstitutional, once again because McClintic-Marshall held the steel contract. The building, which took up almost an entire city block, was being constructed in two sections, and as soon as the foundation had been prepared for the first section, which preceded the strike, McClintic-Marshall began erecting the steel frame of the section. The strike halted work on the second section, for which the foundation had not been completed. The strike lasted for about eleven weeks, until October 14, while futile efforts, in which Department of Labor conciliators played a part, were made to bring the two sides together. McClintic-Marshall would not even agree to speak to union ironworker representatives unless they could provide documentary proof, which they could not, that they enjoyed local autonomy—the two locals involved were still being administered by the international—and had authority to make local agreements. McClintic-Marshall stood its ground regarding unionization, and in the end the BTC voted to return to work without any of the union demands having been met. New York at the end of 1935 remained open shop territory in the area of structural steel erection.[12]

Since so much of the construction once the New Deal got under way was federal-government supported, the NEA had a special interest in the labor policies of the PWA, especially its wage and hiring policies. By agreement with the AFL's Building Trades Department, the PWA on August 25, 1933, divided the United States into three geographical zones, and it set the minimum wage for both skilled and unskilled labor in each. If the prevailing wage in any community as of April 1, 1933, was above the minimum set, that became the governing rate. As it worked out, since the prevailing rate was commonly the union rate, workers on PWA projects generally received union wages, especially in the biggest cities.[13]

Since open shop rates for structural steel workers were below the union scale in most communities, PWA wage policy meant that open shop employers in the structural steel industry had to raise the wages of their workers, even though McClintic-Marshall complained that the union rate was not necessarily the going rate. Drew protested to the PWA administrator, Harold L. Ickes, that the agency's prevailing wage policy had the effect of the federal government's delegating to "a self-interested private group" the power to determine wages on public work. Drew and the open shop employers, however, were unable to secure any change in PWA wage policy.[14]

Of greater concern to the NEA and open shop employers than the PWA's wage standard was the manner in which workers on PWA projects were hired. At its outset the PWA specified that skilled labor was to be secured "in the customary ways through recognized trade union locals." This led to a protest to Ickes by a committee representing the nation's open shop organizations that included Drew. In response, the PWA modified its hiring order so that "independent" workers, that is, nonunion workers, were to be obtained through the United States Employment Service (USES). Also, employers of independent workers in a particular locality were not required to discharge those workers whom they already employed in order to hire new workers through the USES. Although Drew regarded the revision of the original PWA order as a considerable improvement, he did not like the recognition that the PWA, in effect, gave to closed shop building contracts and feared that this might prove to be "a strong incentive" for workers to join unions. Without really citing hard evidence, Drew and employers in the heavy construction industry claimed that the PWA discriminated in favor of union members in public work, a matter of great concern for a perfervid open shop advocate like Drew given the large volume of federal government construction in the depressed 1930s.[15]

The NEA effort to resist unionization in the first two years of the New Deal and to shape PWA policy so as to protect the open shop in the building industry occurred against a backdrop of the failed effort by the structural steel industry, responding to the NIRA, to devise a code for the industry that could gain Roosevelt administration approval. The code for the structural steel and iron fabricating industry was drafted by a committee of the American Institute of Steel Construction (AISC), which in 1921 had replaced the National Steel Fabricators Association and then became incorporated in 1925. The institute, which in 1933 represented 164 of the 462 firms in the industry, claimed that it had accounted for 87 percent of the total steel tonnage fabricated in the nation in 1932. It employed about twenty-five thousand workers in 1933, half the number it had employed in 1930. Its principal firms, notably NEA members American Bridge and McClintic-Marshall, engaged in the erection of structural steel as well as its fabrication.[16]

C. G. Conley, the president of the AISC and of the Mt. Vernon Bridge Company, appointed a five-person committee to draft the industry's code that included representatives of American Bridge, Bethlehem Fabricators, and McClintic-Marshall, both of the latter Bethlehem Steel subsidiaries as of 1933. The central question the code committee faced was whether to include the erection of steel as well as its fabrication in the AISC code. Although the New York Iron League's secretary and counsel, Roberts B. Thomas, drafted a possible separate code for erection, Drew advised Conley soon after the NIRA became law to include erection in the AISC code. Reflecting court decisions on the matter, Drew asserted that erection work and building trades labor had generally been categorized as "local" matters and so were not covered by the NIRA, which, as Drew understood the statute, applied only to products entirely in interstate commerce. Therefore, Drew maintained, a code governing erection alone would have to be based on a voluntary agreement among the affected parties and would then not have the authority of the NIRA back of it for enforcement purposes. He pointed out, however, that when contracts were let that included both fabrication and erection, as was common, the wages, hours, and other conditions of labor of the erection workers became "important competitive factors" that influenced the terms of the contract. Unless there were "stable and uniform competitive conditions" for such work, he consequently maintained, the success of a code for fabrication would be "seriously jeopardized." The "only way" the authority of the NIRA could "be brought to bear upon conditions in . . . erecting work," Drew concluded, was to include erection in the AISC code. Agreeing with Drew, the NEA's executive committee specifically requested on August 25, 1933, that erection be included in the fabricators' code since erection was "so intimately bound up with its fabrication."[17]

The AISC was undoubtedly predisposed to accept the advice of Drew and the NEA on the erection issue. Its key members, engaged as they were in both fabrication and erection, competed with independent erectors as well as with general contractors and owners who purchased steel and then sublet it for erection. Given these conditions, the AISC claimed that it had to include erection in its code since there was "no other way of protecting themselves against chiselers." Because of their opposition to unions, the fabricator-erectors, moreover, had no intention of permitting steel erection labor to slip from their grasp. In support of their position, they were able to point to the fact that the Federal Trade Commission had approved a voluntary code for the AISC in 1930 that included erection.[18]

The AISC marked time regarding the drafting of its code while awaiting the completion of the code for the basic steel industry. Although not a member of the AISC code committee, Drew served as a key advisor to the group on such matters as erection labor, bidding on "structures erected complete," and the competition of AISC members with general contractors and structural steel subcontractors. "We certainly are under obligations [*sic*] to you for the work you have done on this [code] and for the very fine suggestions you have . . . made as to our code," Conley wrote Drew during the code-drafting process.[19]

The AISC Board of Directors approved a draft code on August 14 that was endorsed by the membership two days later. It was submitted to the National Recovery Administration (NRA) on September 7, after the Roosevelt administration had approved the basic steel code. The AISC code did not contain the open shop clause the institute originally had contemplated including because the NRA had already eliminated such a clause from the steel code. It was obviously for the same reason that the AISC rejected a Drew suggestion that its code include a provision forbidding employees to engage in organizational activities in the shop or on the job while receiving pay. The NRA insisted on some revisions of the AISC code as submitted, which led to some redrafting of the document and delayed a public hearing on the code until October 30, 1933.[20]

The AISC code defined the structural steel and iron fabricating industry to which it applied as the fabrication of steel or iron shapes, plates, or bars, the sale of these products, and, in a crucial assertion, "the business of doing the erection work thereon . . . when the fabricating thereof and the erection work thereon are done by the same member of the Code." It provided that erectors who did not fabricate and hence were not members of the industry as defined could become code members and by so doing make the code's provisions applicable to their erection work. The voting power of code members was to be determined by the quotient obtained by dividing by one thousand the average annual tonnage a member had fabricated during the years 1928–30 and by dividing by ten thousand the average tonnage a member had erected during the same years. Each member, however, was to have at least one vote. The code was to be administered by the AISC's board of directors.

In a purported effort "to prevent unfair methods of competition in the Industry," the hours and wages provisions of the code were to apply to labor engaged in the erection of the industry's products whether or not the work was performed by a code member. Accordingly, if a member sublet erection work to a nonmember, the member was to obtain an agreement from the nonmember to apply the wages and hours provisions of the AISC code.[21]

Although the code placed erection work within its confines whether or not an erector became a code member, erectors were given little incentive to become members given the method of voting the code prescribed. Voting power was securely lodged in the hands of firms that both fabricated and erected and especially American Bridge and Bethlehem, which between them would have cast half the votes of the membership. Although there was no specific open shop provision in the code, its terms lodged effective power in the administration of the code in open shop firms that had no intention of abandoning the open shop. "We Shall Maintain the Open Shop," Bethlehem's Eugene Grace flatly declared.[22]

Like the AISC, the IABSOIW was giving thought to the kind of code that would best suit its interests. To assist it in the necessary research and statistical work and the analysis of relevant data, the union engaged W. Jett Lauck, who had been associated with Frank Walsh, the union's general counsel, in the work of the National War Labor Board in World War I. With the prospective code for the industry in mind, Morrin worked out the aforementioned agreement with the SSBEA that included the erection of buildings, and on April 29, 1933, the SSBEA submitted a code of its own to the NRA, a separate erection code, as an alternative to the AISC code. The SSBEA informed the NRA that there had been "a violent storm of protest" among independent erectors at being included in the AISC code, which, the SSBEA argued, was the code of "an entirely different industry." Insisting that the IABSOIW's membership was confined to erection workers, which was not entirely correct, Morrin, in advance of the code hearings, protested to Hugh S. Johnson, the NRA's head, that the AISC code covered "two separate and distinct industries."[23]

The central question at the hearings on the AISC code was whether fabrication and erection were to be included in the same code or dealt with in separate codes. Conley, for the AISC, contended that erection was "an integral part of the fabricating business," fabricators did "the most difficult and costly erection work," and purchasers generally insisted that fabrication and erection be part of a single contract. Offering the SSBEA code as a substitute for the AISC code insofar as erection was concerned, Edward H. Handy, the SSBEA secretary, charged that the institute was not "truly representative" of the steel erection industry and that fabricators and erectors were in the oppositional position of seller and buyer.

Morrin made the principal argument at the hearing against the inclusion of erection in the proposed code. Charging that the principal fabricators of structural steel had sought in the past to make their product available only under conditions that involved the elimination of organized labor in the industry, he portrayed the code as being the "supreme effort" by the industry to destroy the IABSOIW and independent structural steel erectors. The chief villains in this regard, Morrin asserted, were United States Steel and Bethlehem Steel, and it was these companies, he noted, that would dominate the administration of the AISC code if it was approved.[24]

Claiming that fabrication was part of the steel manufacturing industry and erection was part of the construction industry, Morrin wanted erection to be governed by the SSBEA code, whose labor provisions had been arrived at by bargaining between the SSBEA and the IABSOIW. Both AFL president William Green and Frank Walsh endorsed the view Morrin had expressed. Walsh stressed that the antiunion United States Steel and Bethlehem wanted to carry their antiunion policies into the erection area, where, he maintained, "a strong and active labor organization" existed. Walsh might have noted that the NEA had performed that role for the steel companies ever since its formation. As a report prepared in 1935 for the NRA's Board of Review indicated, the issue presented by the AISC code involved "the most dramatic story in NRA— the struggle between organized labor and open-shop employers."[25]

During the posthearing period, the question of whether there should be a single code or separate codes for fabrication and erection was "hotly debated." Almost daily conferences were held between NRA officials and boards and the AISC on the one hand and the union on the other, the code committee refusing for months to meet face-to-face with union representatives. In part, the dispute regarding whether the AISC could speak for the erection industry hinged on whether the fabricators erected more than 50 percent of the steel erected annually. The dispute hinged on whether the tonnage erected annually by owners and others, especially railroads, should be excluded from the total, as the AISC contended, or should be included, as the IABSOIW and the NRA's Division of Research and Planning maintained.[26]

In arguing for a separate erection code, the union and some independent erectors charged, and some in the NRA agreed, that the big fabricators used their power to discriminate against independent erectors by refusing in some instances to sell steel on an f.o.b. basis to erectors or general contractors who used union labor, charging excessive prices when they did sell f.o.b., or delaying or mixing up deliveries to unionized contractors. The result, these code opponents maintained, was that the fabricators, having a monopoly control of the supply of structural steel, were absorbing an increasing share of the building erection business just as they already monopolized the erection of bridges and viaducts. The AISC denied the charge, claiming that competition prevented the use of the practices indicated.[27]

Although the AISC provided redrafts of its code to meet some of the objections to the original document, it let the NRA know that unless erection was included in the institute's code, the industry preferred not to have a code at all. Morrin claimed that President Roosevelt, to whom the union president had written, prevented the AISC from having its way in January 1934, but the key factor in turning the tide within the NRA against a single code was the administration's approval of the code for the construction industry on January 31, 1934. The construction code defined the industry as including the "designing and the constructing of (and the installing and the applying, including the assembling at the site, of manufactured parts and products incorporated in and to") buildings and "fixed structures." This definition, the NRA's Legal Division concluded, covered structural steel erection.

Provisions of the construction code made it entirely predictable that the

AISC would resist any and all efforts to include structural steel erection as a division of that code. The code provided that representative associations of employers and employees might through collective bargaining determine the wages, hours, and conditions of labor of occupations or operations in each division or subdivision of the code. It also called for the establishment of a National Construction Planning and Adjustment Board consisting of ten persons selected by the NRA's Industrial Advisory Board from nominations by the Construction Code Authority, ten by the Labor Advisory Board from nominations by the building trades unions, and a twenty-first member appointed by the president of the United States on the nomination of the NRA administrator. The board was to promote "better relations" between employers and employees in the industry and to deal with differences arising regarding wages, hours, and working conditions. It did not help matters from the AISC point of view that one of the persons soon appointed to serve on the Planning and Adjustment Board was P. J. Morrin. Unlike the AISC, the IABSOIW, with its strength concentrated in the erection branch of the structural steel industry and unable to unionize the fabrication shops, obviously wished to have structural steel erection included as a division of the construction code, in whose administration organized labor was so well represented.[28]

On March 14, 1934, Hugh Johnson ordered that erection work be governed by the relevant provisions of the construction code and administered by a committee of erectors. He also instructed that representatives of organized labor were to sit in with structural steel industry representatives in dealing with questions concerning wages, hours, and working conditions. "This is a new day in which we are living," the NRA division administrator for the AISC code told the code committee, "and we have got to regard the rights of labor as well as the rights of industry." He did not think, he said, that the industrialists would be "contaminated" by speaking to union officials. Verbally chastising the committee for failing to realize that there was "opposition" to the AISC code, he threatened to recommend "an imposed code" if the committee remained "obstinate."[29]

And "obstinate" the code committee remained, although it did finally talk to IABSOIW representatives on April 20. It also submitted another draft of a code on that date that provided for two erectors to serve as associate members of the code authority and for erection to be supervised under the AISC code by a committee of the two associate members and five AISC directors whose firms engaged in erection. It was playing a "game of hide-and-seek," according to the deputy division administrator dealing with the code, while "the larger element of the industry" was "taking practically all the business" and the "smaller fabricators" were "facing annihilation." In what made the AISC code "peculiarly different" from any other code, every NRA board—the Industrial Advisory Board, the Labor Advisory Board, the Legal Division, Planning and Research, and the Review Section—disapproved of the revised AISC code of April 20.[30]

On July 11, 1934, Johnson approved the structural steel and iron fabricating industry code, but he deleted from it all provisions pertaining to erection and specified that erection work was to be governed by the relevant chapter of the construction industry code. He also revised the wage and hour provisions of the AISC code and provided further that code members were not to sell fabricated steel and/or erection work at a price below the member's cost for same, an action designed to protect the independent erector.

Meeting on July 16, the AISC code committee, which had not been consulted in advance by Johnson, refused to accept the July 11 order, and two days later the institute's board of directors unanimously came to the same conclusion. The structural steel industry was reputedly "the first major industrial group to take so vigorous a stand against NRA." The code committee accused Johnson of "an arbitrary attempt to exercise powers" not conferred by the NIRA. The committee pointed out that it was not represented on the Construction Code Authority, which, it noted, was "dominated and controlled" by purchasers of AISC products and by contractors who dealt principally in competing structural materials such as reinforced concrete. The deputy division administrator also received about one hundred messages protesting the Johnson order, all of them worded similarly. This was in addition to 224 telegrams received in May that had urged approval of the code with erection included.[31]

Responding to the AISC opposition, the NRA on July 23 stayed the operation of the AISC code until August 6 and then granted a second stay for an additional ten days. When the second stay lapsed, no further stay was granted, nor did the NRA take any steps to implement the code; but on October 9, 1934, the National Industrial Recovery Board (NIRB), which had replaced the single administrator for industrial recovery, granted a third stay retroactive to August 16 and of indefinite duration. The effort of the AISC while its code and Johnson's July 11 order were in a state of suspended animation centered on devising "some kind of Bridge" between the AISC code and the construction code, particularly the formation of some kind of joint committee of the two to deal with "overlapping problems" of the two codes but without removing erection from the AISC code.[32]

Although Conley complained that the NRA had "kicked about and mishandled" the structural steel industry because of "ignorance and lack of policy," the AISC was willing to make some concessions to satisfy NRA criticisms of its code, but it would not yield on the inclusion of erection in its code. The NRA was aware, however, that if it sought to enforce Johnson's July 11 order or to impose a code on the AISC, the steel industry would challenge the NRA in the courts, a test the NRA preferred to avoid. Conceding that it was impossible to produce a code governing the fabrication and erection of structural steel that would be acceptable to the parties concerned, the NIRB on April 16, 1935, decided for all practical purposes to let the matter drop, the AISC code never having been put into effect. The next month the NIRA itself was declared unconstitutional in the case of *Schechter Poultry Corporation* v.

United States. The case, it is worthy of note, was financed by the American Iron and Steel Institute, the code authority for the basic steel code.[33]

"The history of the negotiations of the Structural Iron and Steel Fabricating Code," wrote a government economist who served as an NRA labor advisor, "must go down in history as one of the greatest blots on NRA. It [NRA] had arrived in July, 1934, at a deliberate conclusion fully aware of its consequences, but it had not the courage to see that its convictions were carried out."[34] The history of the code negotiations must also "go down in history" as a revealing example of the uncompromising opposition to unionism of employers in the steel industry, whose first line of defense since almost the beginning of the century had been the NEA. It was, after all, the determination of the structural steel shops to protect this line of defense and the open shop that explains the failed negotiations concerning the adoption of a code for the structural steel and iron fabricating industry.

One month after the *Schechter* decision Congress approved the National Labor Relations bill, and the president signed it into law on July 5, 1935. Drew had been concerned about the adoption of a measure of this sort from the time the Wagner-Connery Labor Disputes bill, the predecessor of the National Labor Relations Act (NLRA), was being considered in Congress more than a year earlier. Writing to NEA members on March 17, 1934, and urging them to protest the bill, he characterized the measure as "drastic and revolutionary in its provisions" and as going beyond "all previous efforts to bring about by law a closed shop in American industry." He pointed to sections of the bill that gave strikers the status of employees but denied that status to strike replacements, sanctioned the closed shop, specified unfair labor practices by employers that would "discourage and make ineffective the company union," and granted the labor board for which the act provided powers that, as Drew saw it, went "far beyond any ever conferred on a court or other judicial body" in the United States. He noted that the measure failed to proscribe "unfair" practices by unions even though many unions, in Drew's view, had become "little less than organized rackets," oppressed their rank and file, made "collusive agreements" with employers, and engaged in "all sorts of vicious, anti-social practices."[35]

Drew in early April 1934 sent the Senate a "statement in opposition" to the Wagner-Connery bill that dwelled at length on the alleged evils of the closed shop and the AFL brand of unionism, especially in the building trades and especially in New York and New Jersey. He wrote the secretary of the National Founders' Association that the public attention aroused by the bill furnished "a splendid opportunity to get the real facts in the labor situation before the people." With this in mind, he arranged to have his views of the measure made available in pamphlet form and also saw to it that they were brought to the attention of President Roosevelt.[36]

The Labor Disputes bill was not enacted in 1934, and when 1935 began, Drew asserted that the open shop was "stronger in the [erection] industry than it was before." Soon, however, the NEA and its commissioner had to face the prospect of another Wagner bill, which shortly became the NLRA. Drew, once again, called for "vigorous and determined protest" by NEA members. Analyzing the bill for them, he asserted that it not only had all the defects from the point of view of the open shop employer of the 1934 bill but also included "a new and revolutionary feature," the principle of majority rule in the selection by workers of their representatives for collective bargaining purposes. Drew, however, thought that perhaps "the most mischievous" feature of the bill was the power it granted the National Labor Relations Board to determine the appropriate unit for bargaining purposes. The measure, Drew concluded, was "designed solely to control, restrict and penalize the employer." His concern was assuaged, however, by his belief, like that of so many other attorneys, that it would be held unconstitutional.[37]

Before the constitutionality of the NLRA was resolved, the Senate's La Follette Committee began to investigate the labor policies of employer associations. The National Industrial Council, as the National Council for Industrial Defense had been renamed, met in June 1936 and appointed a committee "to follow the inquiry and develop policy with respect to it." Drew was appointed the committee's chairman, once again testifying to his central place in the open shop ranks. The NEA, surprisingly, was not summoned to appear before the committee, as other employer associations were, but Drew complained that it had been "subjected to every kind of investigation," including, he claimed, the search for almost a year of its wastepaper baskets to find "some ground to attack" the association.[38]

When the Supreme Court in April 1937 in *Labor Board* v. *Jones and Laughlin* proved Drew's judgment about the NLRA's constitutionality erroneous, his initial reaction was that the NLRB would "assume control over [fabrication] shop labor relations" but that erection would be exempted from the statute because it was essentially local in character. As it turned out, however, the Supreme Court's validation of the NLRA sealed the fate of the NEA, but, unlike the NEA's principal members, Drew, who was unable mentally or emotionally to abandon his commitment to the open shop, was loath to come to that conclusion. When the chairman of the NEA's executive committee inquired of Drew following the *Jones and Laughlin* decision whether membership in the NEA was now of "any value," the NEA commissioner responded that if the association dissolved, it would be "a confession of weakness and [would] aggravate rather than lessen the efforts against our [open shop] policy." He did not believe, he asserted, that the open shop was "as hopeless as it might seem," and he thought that employers could still make agreements with individual workers and bargain only with their own employees as long as the employer avoided "influence, or interference, or coercion" in so doing.[39]

Drew was actually putting a brave face on developments that were pointing to the end of the open shop in the structural steel industry and the demise of the NEA itself. The United States Steel agreement with the Steel Workers' Organizing Committee (SWOC), consummated a month before the *Jones and Laughlin* decision, was supplemented in the following weeks by agreements between SWOC and United States Steel's subsidiaries, including American

Bridge. On April 1, 1937, the IABSOIW launched a nationwide drive to organize what it estimated, with some exaggeration, were seventy-five thousand workers in the steel fabrication shops as well as additional structural steel erectors. It sent one hundred organizers into the field, eliminated the initiation fee for shop workers, and reduced it for outside workers. It soon reported the chartering of fifty new shop locals and gains among outside workers also. In June the major structural steel firms met with President Morrin in St. Louis and reached an unsigned agreement for the shop workers that was confirmed by a "handshake." The employers committed themselves to hire their workers through the union and to follow union rules. The IABSOIW's membership rose dramatically from 17,200 in 1936 to 31,700 in 1937, 62,700 in 1941, and 100,500 in 1944.[40]

Probably even more painful for Drew to accept than the St. Louis handshake agreement was a signed, closed shop agreement in June 1937 between the resurrected New York Iron League and the Building and Construction Trades Council of Greater New York, Long Island, and Vicinity, which included the two New York IABSOIW structural steel erection locals. The agreement, which followed the enactment of New York's "little" Wagner Act, was another step leading to the dissolution of the open shop, Clyde MacCornack, the chairman of the NEA's executive committee, reminding Drew that NEA had always taken the position that if it could not "save New York as open shop territory, the open shop movement would be completely defeated throughout the country in the building trades."[41]

Once the major NEA firms came to terms with the IABSOIW in 1937, the association became "increasingly inactive," its "labor situation," as Drew put it, being "governed by new and different conditions." As of March 20, 1939, only two of the NEA's labor bureaus remained open, and by the time the United States became a belligerent in World War II, none of the association's bureaus was operating. At the end of 1938, after only fifteen members had paid their assessments for the year in full, the NEA lowered the assessments from four cents per ton fabricated and four cents per ton erected to one cent per ton for each, and, at his own request, Drew's salary was reduced. Of the twenty-nine surviving members in 1941, only twelve paid their tonnage assessment in full.[42]

The IABSOIW in the meantime became less and less like the organization that Drew had associated with all the evils of unionism. The great dynamite trial had led to a sharp decline in the union's resort to violence as a method, and recognition led it to focus on collective bargaining for bread-and-butter gains. It became, that is to say, a conventional craft union, reportedly "one of the most conservative . . . in the entire labor movement."[43]

The few NEA members who still retained any interest in the association kept it alive during World War II but only so as to see what the postwar readjustment might bring. The executive committee suspended tonnage payments in 1945 and then discontinued all assessments and dues in April 1947. Rather than liquidating the organization at that time, the committee decided to use the surplus in the NEA's treasury to enable the association to survive for the time being. As of September 1951 the NEA office in New York remained open only two days a week, and by the next year American Bridge and Bethlehem, the NEA's two most important members, had decided that the time had come to dissolve the association. If, despite this, the NEA remained alive for five additional years, it was because of Drew's dogged insistence that it could still serve a purpose.[44]

Unable to bring himself to reassess his commitment to the open shop or to revise his exaggerated appraisal of the power of organized labor, Drew continued after World War II to speak out in familiar terms about developments on the labor scene. He thus joined in the employer effort to influence the shape of what became the Taft-Hartley Act of 1947. As a matter of fact, the NAM's Employment Relations Committee, with Drew playing an active part, had urged as early as May 1937 that the NLRA be amended very much along the lines of the later Taft-Hartley Act. Late in 1946, Drew's principal advice to Congress regarding labor legislation was to equalize the bargaining power of labor and management by making unions "legally responsible for their conduct." The damage provisions of Taft-Hartley did not, however, go far enough to satisfy Drew, who complained that, despite the statute, the unions still occupied a "privileged position" in bargaining with employers because they did not have "the same legal responsibility" for their conduct that employers did. He continued also to rail against what he viewed as labor's monopoly power and its "deliberate restriction of production." He saw "big labor" as the "real monopoly in the country" and was concerned that big business appeared unable to do much about that. When President Harry S. Truman seized the steel mills in April 1952, Drew vainly sought to have United States Steel seek an injunction against the president and the Congress of Industrial Organizations for conspiring to violate the Taft-Hartley Act. Even if the suit were unsuccessful, as the steel corporation believed it would be, Drew thought that United States Steel could score a propaganda point by demonstrating that the unions controlled even the president of the United States.[45]

What was most heartening to Drew on the national labor scene following World War II was the progress of the right-to-work movement that began toward the end of the war. As Drew saw it, the open shop to which the NEA had been committed was "the same thing" as the right to work. It was "the same old fight, only in a new direction," he insisted, involving as it did the ban several states imposed on the closed shop and, generally, other union-security arrangements as well. As Drew construed the history of employer-employee relations in the United States in the twentieth century, there had been "a spontaneous movement" against the closed shop at the beginning of the century that led to the formation of citizens' alliances throughout the nation and, he might have added, the establishment of the NEA and other employer associations as well. This movement, he judged, had been "largely successful" until, as the result of World War I and federal government support, the unions again "secured a strong foothold by taking advantage of the national emergency." The result, he indicated, had been "another spontaneous uprising over the country against the labor monopoly" that was "largely successful" until the enactment of the NLRA. According to Drew's reading of the record, "the abuse of union power" resulting from the operation of the NLRA had led to "the third national uprising," culminating in the Taft-Hartley Act and right-to-work laws or constitutional amendments in eighteen states as of the spring of 1956 and "growing public recognition of the danger inherent in the rapidly growing labor monopoly."[46]

Drew kept "in constant touch and co-operate[d] with" the National Right to Work Committee, as he also continued to do with the NAM. Because of the right-to-work movement and what he believed was "a general reaction against the closed shop," Drew thought that it would be a mistake for the NEA to dissolve. That, however, was not the view of the NEA's dominant members. The chairman of its executive committee presented the group in January 1954 with the tentative draft of a plan to liquidate the association, and the committee decided a few months later to seek legal advice regarding its authority to dispose of the NEA's assets. The counsel the NEA engaged advised that since the association was not incorporated, it could not be dissolved but could be "abandoned for all practical purposes," which is what the committee agreed to do. There was approximately $150,000 in the NEA treasury as of the spring of 1956, and the committee decided to make some provision for Drew, who was eighty at the time, and NEA secretary Bessie Crocker, who was seventy-two, and to use the remainder of the sum for Walter Drew scholarships, the recipients to be selected by the AISC's Committee on Education.[47]

MacCornack had "several 'sad' meetings" with Drew about the NEA's liquidation, which Drew, a believer to the end, sought to resist. The association was officially terminated as of April 30, 1957. The sister of Robert J. Foster, who worked for Drew on occasion after the NEA's dissolution and until his death on Christmas Day 1961, recalled that he would come to his office in the late afternoon and "just sit and stare and sometimes reminisce about the past."[48]

The NEA experience reveals the centrality of employer opposition, irrespective of worker attitudes, as an explanation for the limited growth of unionism in the United States as compared to the industrialized nations of western Europe.[49] For thirty years after its founding, the NEA functioned as the nation's most belligerent national antiunion employer association. Insofar as it saw its role as checkmating unionism in structural steel erection lest it spread to the open shop fabrication shops and mills of the steel industry, it succeeded until the New Deal and the NLRA drastically changed the character of employer-employee relations in the nation and limited the weapons available to antiunion employers in combating unionism. Throughout the NEA's history the spokesman for the association and the organizer of its efforts in behalf of the open shop was Walter Drew. His role in the NEA and his less well known role in the broader open shop movement both at the national and the local levels mark him as one of the foremost advocates of the open shop in the entire history of the nation.

Drew did not live to see the weakening of unionism that he had been predicting in the last two decades of his life. "[T]he most successful attempts at union busting" after Drew's death occurred, interestingly enough, in the construction industry, the union density in the industry decreasing from more than 50 percent in 1960 to 23.5 percent in 1984. As Drew would have advised, the antiunion drive in the industry was directed not by the two major employer associations in the building trades but by the Business Roundtable, an association of the largest industrial companies in the nation that had been formed in 1969. Its first chairman, and how appropriate that would have seemed to Drew and the NEA, was Roger Blough, the former chairman of the board of United States Steel.[50]

In October 1969 independent steel erectors formed a new National Erectors' Association—sometimes referred to as the National Steel Erectors' Association—whose membership was limited to firms that recognized the IABSOIW. Since the IABSOIW's jurisdiction was being invaded by other craft unions, supported by their "counterpart contractor associations," the erector firms thought it essential to unite with the union in their trade to defend the erectors' business and the workers' jobs. Although the major structural steel fabricators, notably American Bridge and Bethlehem, initially opposed the action, they soon joined the new NEA. The relationship of the structural steel firms and the IABSOIW over a period of more than six decades had thus come full circle.[51] No one would have been more distressed at what had occurred than Walter Drew.

Abbrevations

DP	Walter Drew Papers, Bentley Historical Library, Ann Arbor, Michigan
NARA	National Archives and Records Administration, Washington, D.C.
NYT	*New York Times*
RG	Record Group

Notes

Chapter 1

1. Jacoby, "Norms and Cycles: The Dynamics of Nonunion Industrial Relations in the United States, 1897–1987," in Katharine G. Abraham and Robert McKersie, eds., *New Developments in the Labor Market* (Cambridge, Mass.: MIT Press, 1990), p. 45.

2. Baker, "Parker and Roosevelt on Labor," *McLure's Magazine* 24 (Nov. 1904): 41; Leo Wolman, *The Growth of American Trade Unions, 1880–1923* (New York: National Bureau of Economic Research, 1924), p. 33; Frank T. Stockton, *The Closed Shop in American Trade Unions* (Baltimore: Johns Hopkins University Studies, 1911), pp. 52–53.

3. See Marguerite Green, *The National Civic Federation and the American Labor Movement* (Washington: Catholic University of America Press, 1956), for a history of the National Civic Federation.

4. John Keith, "The New Union of Employers," *Harper's Weekly* 48 (Jan. 23, 1904): 130; *Iron Age* 71 (Feb. 5, 1903): 25; ibid. 73 (Jan. 4, 1904): 37; *American Industries* (Jan. 15, 1903): 1; Isaac F. Marcosson, "The Fight for the Open Shop," *World's Work* 11 (Dec. 1905): 6955, 6959; Lewis L. Lorwin, *The American Federation of Labor* (Washington: Brookings Institution, 1933), pp. 79–80.

5. Keith, "Union of Employers," p. 130; Jeffrey Haydu, "Employers, Unions, and American Exceptionalism. . . ," *International Review of Social History* 33 (1988): 26–38; David Montgomery, *Workers' Control in America* (Cambridge: Cambridge University Press, 1979), pp. 91–92; Jacoby, "Norms and Cycles," p. 26; Allen Morton Wakstein, "The Open-Shop Movement, 1919–1933" (Ph.D. diss., University of Illinois, 1961), p. 7; Stockton, *Closed Shop*, pp. 45–46; Robert H. Wiebe, *Businessmen and Reform: A Study of the Progressive Movement* (Cambridge, Mass.: Harvard University Press, 1962), pp. 161–62; Jerome L. Toner, *The Closed Shop in the American Labor Movement* (Washington: Catholic University of America Press, 1941), p. 76; *Iron Age* 71 (Mar. 26, 1903): 28; National Association of Manufacturers, Minutes of the Board of Directors, Feb. 24, 1910, Ser. V, Reel 1, Archives of the National Association of Manufacturers, Accession 1411, Hagley Museum and Library, Wilmington, Delaware; H. E. Hoagland, "Closed Shop versus Open Shop," *American Economic Review* 8 (Dec. 1918): 758–61.

6. Marcosson, "Open Shop," p. 6959; Keith, "Union of Employers," p. 130; Wakstein, "Open-Shop Movement," p. 8; Green, *National Civic Federation,* pp. 92–93; Philip S. Foner, *History of the Labor Movement in the United States* (New York:

International Publishers, 1964), 3:34; Albion Guilford Taylor, *Labor Policies of the National Association of Manufacturers* (Urbana: University of Illinois, 1928), p. 41.

7. Wiebe, *Businessmen and Reform,* p. 168; *American Industries* (Oct. 15, 1902): 1–2, (Nov. 11, 1902): 5, 7; Daniel Robinson Ernst, "The Lawyers and the Labor Trust: A History of the American Anti-Boycott Association" (Ph.D. diss., Princeton University, 1989), pp. 57–60, 106–17, 132–76; Walter Gordon Merritt, *History of the League for Industrial Rights* (New York: League for Industrial Rights, 1925), pp. 7–17, 23–31, 96–97; Foner, *Labor Movement,* 3:39–40.

8. Clarence E. Bonnett, *Employers' Associations in the United States* (New York: Macmillan Co., 1922), pp. 63–69, 98–117; Mark Perlman, *The Machinists* (Cambridge, Mass.: Harvard University Press, 1961), pp. 25–27; David Montgomery, *The Fall of the House of Labor: The Workplace, the State, and American Labor Activism, 1865–1925* (New York: Cambridge University Press, 1987), pp. 260–67; Jeffrey Haydu, *Between Craft and Class: Skilled Workers and Factory Politics in the United States and Britain* (Berkeley: University of California Press, 1988), pp. 78–84; Margaret Loomis Stecker, "The National Founders' Association," *Quarterly Journal of Economics* 30 (Feb. 1916): 352–86; *Industry* 2 (Feb. 15, 1919): 9; Senate Committee on Education and Labor, *Violations of Free Speech and Rights of Labor,* 76 Cong., 1 sess., 1939, Report No. 6, Part 4, *Labor Policies of Employers' Associations,* Part 1, p. 5; Thomas A. Klug, "The Roots of the Open Shop: Employers, Trade Unions, and Craft Labor Markets in Detroit, 1859–1907" (Ph.D. diss., Wayne State University, 1993), pp. 471–705.

9. Wiebe, *Businessmen and Reform,* pp. 25, 168; Marshall Cushing, Memorandum for All Field Men, Dec. 23, 1902, in *Confidential Correspondence Submitted to the Subcommittee of the Committee on the Judiciary, United States Senate, by the National Association of Manufacturers, under Subpoena* (Washington: Government Printing Office, 1913), 77 Cong., Reel 6, Records of the National Association of Manufacturers, Accession 1521, Hagley Museum and Library; Albert K. Steigerwalt, *The National Association of Manufacturers, 1895–1914* (Ann Arbor: Bureau of Business Research, Graduate School of Business Administration, 1964), pp. 45–102; National Association of Manufacturers, *Proceedings of the Eighth Annual Convention, April 14–17, 1903,* p. 14.

10. Parry to C. W. Post, Nov. 20, 1903, Box 1, C. W. Post Papers, Bentley Historical Library, Ann Arbor, Michigan; NAM, *Eighth Annual Convention,* pp. 14–25, 50, 133–34, 165–69, 206–7, 215, 221, 228–29, 236–37; NAM, *Proceedings of the Ninth Annual Convention, May 17–19, 1904,* p. 173.

11. Green, *National Civic Federation;* Taylor, *Labor Policies,* p. 41; NAM, *Eighth Annual Convention,* pp. 57, 62, 169, 199–221; J. W. Kirby to Parry, Dec. 23, 1904, Box 1, Post Papers.

12. Frederick W. Job to Post, Nov. 10, 1903, Kirby to Parry, Dec. 23, 1904, Box 1, Post Papers; *Iron Age* 72 (Oct. 29, 1903): 26, (Nov. 5, 1903): 22–23; Subcommittee of the Senate Committee on the Judiciary, *Maintenance of a Lobby to Influence Legislation,* 63 Cong., 1 sess.. 1913, 4:3716.

13. Kirby to Parry, Dec. 23, 1904, Box 1, Post Papers.

14. *Censor* [Apr. 21, 1904], Box 2, ibid.; *Iron Age* 73 (Mar. 3, 1904): 9; *Square Deal* 2 (Aug. 1906): 3, (Dec. 1906): 16; Selig Perlman and Philip Taft, *History of Labor in the United States, 1896–1932* (New York: Macmillan Co., 1935), pp. 136–37.

15. *Los Angeles Times,* Nov. 30, 1904, Scrapbook #4, Box 5, Post Papers; Parry to Post, Nov. 20, 1903, Dec. 27, 1904, May 24, 1905, Box 1, ibid.; "C. W. Post and the National Association of Manufacturers," undated, Box 2, ibid.; Doris McLaughlin,

"The Second Battle of Battle Creek—the Open Shop Movement in the Early Twentieth Century," *Labor History* 14 (Summer 1973): 324–25, 334.

16. [Post] to Horatio Seymour, May 24, 1905, Box 1, Post Papers; Post, "The Citizens' Industrial Association of America," *System* (Oct. 1905): 426, Scrapbook #4, Box 5, ibid.

17. Post, "Proclamation of Freedom," May 1, 1905, Box 3, ibid.; Post to James O' Hearn, Aug. 20, 1906, Box 2, ibid.; *Square Deal* 1 (Aug. 1905): 3–4, 6, (Sept. 1905): 29, (Mar. 1906): 15.

18. *Square Deal* 1 (Sept. 1905): 29, 30, (Mar. 1906): 15, (July 1906): 15; ibid. 4 (Jan. 1909): 6–7; CIAA to Dear Sir [Nov. 1905], James A. Emery to Post, Jan. 16, 1907, Post to Emery, Jan. 18, 1907, Box 1, Post Papers; "The Citizen's Industrial Association of America," Dec. 3–4, 1906, ibid.

19. [Post] to Kirby, Mar. 26, 1906, [?] to W. C. [*sic*] Post, Jan. 21, 1905, Emery to Post, May 8, 1907, Wilson Vance to Post, May 17, 1907, Vance to Harrison Gray Otis, Apr. 3, 1908, Box 1, ibid.; Meeting of National Trades Associations, Aug. 19, 1907, Reel 4, Accession 1521; *Square Deal* 2 (Jan. 1907): 9–10; ibid. 4 (Jan. 1909): 7.

20. *Maintenance of a Lobby,* 4:3720; *American Industries* 7 (June 1, 1908): 22–23; Subcommittee of Senate Committee on Education and Labor, *Violations of Free Speech and the Rights of Labor,* 75 Cong., 3 sess., 1938, Part 18, pp. 8051–52; President James W. Van Cleave to Dear Sir, June 28, 1907, Box 1, Post Papers; Wakstein, "Open-Shop Movement," p. 26.

21. Minutes NAM Board of Directors, May 14, 1906, Ser. V, Reel 1, Accession 1411; Meeting of National Trades Associations, Aug. 19, 1907, Reel 4, Accession 1521; NAM, *Proceedings of the Twelfth Annual Convention, May 20–22, 1907,* pp. 208–9; *American Industries* 5 (July 1907): 2.

22. Meeting of National Trades Associations, Aug. 19, 1907, Reel 4, Accession 1521; Van Cleave to Post, Sept. 20, 1907, Box 1, Post Papers; *Violations,* Part 18, pp. 8052–53.

23. Minutes NAM Board of Directors, Feb. 1, 1907, Ser. V, Reel 1, Accession 1411; Van Cleave to Post, June 3, 24, 1907, Vance to Emery, Oct. 29, 1907, Post to Van Cleave, Aug. 7, Nov. 13, 1907, Box 1, Post Papers; Vance to Hawk, Dec. 10, 1907, Box 4, ibid.

24. Post to Van Cleave, Jan. 18, 1908, Vance to Post, June 25, Aug. 19, 1908, Post to Vance, Aug. 28, 1908, Emery to Post, Oct. 2, 3, 8, 1908, Post to Emery, Oct. 6, 1908, Box 1, Post Papers; Post, "National Citizens' Industrial Association," Dec. 9, 1908, Box 2, ibid.; [Post] address, undated, Box 3, ibid.; Vance to Otis, Apr. 3, 1908, ibid.; *Square Deal* 4 (Jan. 1909): 1; *Maintenance of a Lobby,* 4:3748; Wakstein, "Open-Shop Movement," p. 27. Cf. Toner, *Closed Shop,* p. 126.

25. Post to Van Cleave, Mar. 14, 16, 1908, Post to Hawk, May 10, 1908, Emery to Post, Oct. 3, 1908, Box 1, Post Papers; Post to Van Cleave, Apr. 24, 1908, Box 2, ibid.

26. The case is dealt with in illuminating detail in Ernst, "Lawyers and the Labor Trust," pp. 177–213.

27. [Post] to Van Cleave, Feb. 12, 1908, Box 1, Post Papers; Post to Hawk, May 10, 1908, Box 2, ibid.; "Post and the National Association of Manufacturers," ibid. When Buck Stove following Van Cleave's death in 1911 came to an agreement with the union in its plant, Post, still a company stockholder, vainly instituted a lawsuit to block the agreement. Philip Taft, *The A. F. of L. in the Time of Gompers* (New York: Harper and Brothers, 1957), p. 270.

28. Van Cleave to Postum Cereal Co., Apr. 1, 1908, Box 1, Post Papers; President

[Kirby] to James Rawls, Dec. 20, 1909, Box 2, ibid.; Foner, *Labor Movement,* 3:40–41; *Maintenance of a Lobby,* 4:3714, 3745.

29. Vance to Otis, Apr. 15, 1908, Box 4, Post Papers; Van Cleave to Postum Cereal Co., June 10, 1908, Vance to Post, June 25, 1908, Box 1, ibid.; President to Rawls, Dec. 20, 1909, Emery to Post, Feb. 25, 1909, Box 2, ibid.; Kirby, "The National Council for Industrial Defense" [1908], ibid.; *American Industries* 7 (June 15, 1908): 18–19, 26–29; NAM, *Proceedings of the Sixteenth Annual Convention, May15–17, 1911,* pp. 83–85; Bonnett, *Employers' Associations,* p. 375; *Square Deal* 3 (July 1908): 69.

30. Wiebe, *Businessmen and Reform,* p. 166; David Brody, *Steelworkers in America: The Nonunion Era* (New York: Harper and Brothers, 1960), pp. 60–73; John A. Garraty, "The United States Steel Corporation versus Labor," *Labor History* 1 (Winter 1960): 9–14, 26–27; *Report on Conditions of Employment in the Iron and Steel Industry in the United States,* 62 Cong., 1 sess., Doc. No. 110, 1913, 3:117–135; Jesse Robinson, *The Amalgamated Association of Iron, Steel and Tin Workers* (Baltimore: Johns Hopkins Press, 1920), p. 21.

31. Melvin M. Rotsch, "Building with Steel and Concrete," in Melvin Kranzberg and Carroll W. Pursell, eds., *Technology and Western Civilization* (New York: Oxford University Press, 1967), 2:196–207; Carl W. Condit, *The Rise of the Skyscraper* (Chicago: University of Chicago Press, 1952), pp. 112–16; "The Common Welfare," *Survey* 27 (Dec. 20, 1913): 1407; *NYT,* Nov. 1, Dec. 15, 1920; William Haber, *Industrial Relations in the Building Industry* (New York: Arno and New York Times, 1971), pp. 17–18, 21–22.

32. Untitled item [June 10, 1908], Box 14, DP; George P. Alt and J. M. Fassett, Memorandum for John Lord O'Brian, Apr. 16, 1930, File 60-138-43, Records of the Department of Justice, RG 60, NARA; R. B. Thomas to O'Brian, May 1, 1930, ibid.; In Re: Investigation of Building Materials Re: Steel Investigation, Statement of Walter Gordon Merritt and Walter Drew, Jan. 13, 1921, File 1-2258-1, Records of the Federal Trade Commission, RG 122, ibid.; American Institute of Steel Construction, Code of Fair Competition . . . Memorandum. . . , Nov. 6, 1933, Box 5454, Records of the National Recovery Administration, RG 9, ibid.; Leighton H. Peebles, "History of the Code of Fair Competition for the Structural Steel and Iron Fabricating Industry," Oct. 13, 1936, pp. 102–3, Box 7639, ibid. The percentages used in the Peebles history were incorrectly calculated.

33. "An Informal History of the Iron Workers" (reprinted from the *Ironworker,* 1971), p. 2, copy in my possession; John R. Commons, "The New York Building Trades," in Commons, ed., *Trade Unionism and Labor Problems* (Boston: Ginn and Co., 1905), p. 86; Frank L. Shaw, *The Building Trades* (Cleveland: Survey Committee of the Cleveland Foundation, 1916), p. 23; Luke Grant, *The National Erectors' Association and the International Association of Bridge and Structural Ironworkers* (Washington, 1915), p. 164; *NYT,* June 7, 1908.

34. Commission on Industrial Relations, *Industrial Relations. Final Report and Testimony,* 64 Cong., 1 sess., S. Doc. No. 415, 1916, 6:5630; ibid. 2:1615; Commons, "New York Building Trades," p. 86; Haber, *Building Industry,* p. 292; Grant, *Erectors' Association,* pp. 5–6, 7–8; Shaw, *Building Trades,* p. 23; Ernest Poole, "Cowboys of the Skies," *Everybody's* 19 (Nov. 1908): 641–53; "Informal History," p. 8.

35. Inis Weed, "Preliminary Report on Violence," Part I, n.d., pp. 86–87, Records of the Commission on Industrial Relations, Department of Labor, RG 174, NARA; *Bridgemen's Magazine* 9 (Dec. 1909): 78–79; ibid. 7 (July 1907): 386–87; Shaw, *Building Trades,* pp. 23, 61; "Forty Years a Daredevil," *Literary Digest* 85 (May 30, 1925): 38.

36. Lucien W. Chaney and Hugh S. Hanna, *The Safety Movement in the Iron and Steel Industry, 1907 to 1917,* United States Bureau of Labor Statistics, Bulletin No. 234 (Washington: Government Printing Office, 1918), pp. 241–43; *Bridgemen's Magazine* 5 (June 1905): 19; ibid. 12 (July 1912): 458–59; ibid. 24 (Jan. 1924): 14.

37. Haber, *Building Industry,* p. 292; Transcript of Hearing on Code . . . of Structural Steel and Iron Fabricating Industry, Oct. 30, 1933, pp. 157–59, Appendix, pp. 126–28, Box 7241, RG 9.

38. Haber, *Building Industry,* p. 98; *Bridgemen's Magazine* 22 (Apr. 1922): 168.

39. Walter V. Woehlke, "Terrorism in America," *Outlook* 100 (Feb. 17, 1912): 361; *Square Deal* 1 (Feb. 1906): 8; Constitution and By-Laws of United Housesmiths' and Bridgemen's Union of New York and Vicinity, Local No. 40, n.d., Box 17, DP. There were eighteen thousand structural metal workers in 1910 and thirty-three thousand in 1920. U.S. Bureau of the Census, *Historical Statistics of the United States, Colonial Times to 1957* (Washington: Government Printing Office, 1960), p. 76.

40. Grant, *Erectors' Association,* pp. 5, 20, 24; *Bridgemen's Magazine* 1 (Nov. 1901): 124; ibid. 2 (Oct. 1902): 9; ibid. 9 (Aug. 1909): 463; *Bridgemen's Magazine* 19 (Nov. 1919): 555; Peebles, "Code of Fair Competition," p. 7. *Square Deal* 1 (Feb. 1906): 8, places the number in the shops at 150,000, but that is obviously an error.

41. Michael Kazin, *Barons of Labor: The San Francisco Building Trades and Union Power in the Progressive Era* (Urbana: University of Illinois Press, 1987), pp. 6, 9n; *Iron Age* 72 (July 30, 1903): 24; Perlman and Taft, *History of Labor,* p. 82; Lorwin, *American Federation of Labor,* p. 377; George E. Barnett, "Growth of Labor Organizations in the United States, 1897–1914," *Quarterly Journal of Economics* 30 (Aug. 1916): 793; Wolman, *Trade Unions,* pp. 110–11.

42. Stockton, *Closed Shop,* pp. 98–99; Solomon Blum, "Trade Union Rules in the Building Trades," in Jacob Hollander and George E. Barnett, eds., *Studies in American Trade Unionism* (New York: Henry Holt, 1907), pp. 315–16; Drew, "Building and the Public," Feb. 16, 1922, Box 29, DP.

43. Blum, "Trade Union Rules," p. 310; Royal E. Montgomery, *Industrial Relations in the Chicago Building Trades* (Chicago: University of Chicago Press, 1927), p. 119; Haber, *Building Industry,* pp. 152–53.

44. Montgomery, *Chicago Building Trades,* p. 155; Haber, *Building Industry,* pp. 197–237; Blum, "Trade Union Rules," pp. 300, 318; Stockton, *Closed Shop,* pp. 84, 92–94.

45. Haber, *Building Industry,* pp. 318–20; Blum, "Trade Union Rules," p. 297; John Hutchinson, *The Imperfect Union: A History of Corruption in American Trade Unions* (New York: E. P. Dutton and Co., 1970), pp. 25–26, 32–33; Drew, "To Build Open or Closed, Which?" *Square Deal* 6 (June 1910): 399–400.

46. Montgomery, *Chicago Building Trades,* p. 213; Haber, *Building Industry,* pp. 57–61, 238; Perlman and Taft, *History of Labor,* p. 82; Drew, "The Closed Shop in the Building Industry," Dec. 14, 1906, Box 29, DP; Drew to Gentlemen, Aug. 28, 1906, Box 15, DP; Drew to Nathan Miller, July 19, 1927, Box 12, DP; *Iron Age* 72 (July 30, 1903): 24–25; Haydu, "American Exceptionalism," p. 38; Hutchinson, *Imperfect Union,* pp. 26–27; Shaw, *Building Trades,* pp. 41–42; John R. Commons, "Causes of the Union Shop Policy," *Publications of the American Economic Association,* 3d Ser. 6 (1905): 155–56.

47. Robert A. Christie, *Empire in Wood: A History of the Carpenters' Union* (Ithaca: Cornell University Press, 1956), pp. 156–57; Haber, *Building Industry,* pp. 321–24; Perlman and Taft, *History of Labor,* pp. 82, 94; Montgomery, *Chicago Building Trades,*

pp. 213–15; Ray Stannard Baker, "Trust's New Tool—the Labor Boss," *McClure's Magazine* 22 (Nov. 1903): 38.

48. William Franklin Willoughby, "Employers' Associations for Dealing with Labor in the United States," *Quarterly Journal of Economics* 20 (Nov. 1905): 138–39; Christie, *Empire in Wood*, p. 160; Robert Max Jackson, *The Formation of Craft Labor Markets* (Orlando: Academic Press, 1984), pp. 213–14, 232–33, 239–41; Haber, *Building Industry*, pp. 238–40, 253–56, 442, 446, 458–59.

49. Eugene Staley, *History of the Illinois Federation of Labor* (Chicago: University of Chicago Press, 1930), p. 191; Haber, *Building Industry*, pp. 372–73, 396; Richard Schneirov and Thomas J. Suhrbur, *Union Brotherhood, Union Town: The History of the Carpenters' Union of Chicago, 1863–1987* (Carbondale: Southern Illinois University Press, 1988), p. 76; Louis J. Horowitz and Boyden Sparks, *The Towers of New York* (New York: Simon and Schuster, 1937), pp. 209–14; E. M. Craig, "Building Conditions in Chicago," *American Contractor* 44 (Jan. 6, 1923): 24–25.

50. Ernest Bogart, "The Chicago Building Trades Dispute," in Commons, ed., *Trade Unionism and Labor Problems*, pp. 92–93, 117–18, 126–27; Craig, "Building Conditions," Jan. 13, 1923, pp. 23–24, Jan. 27, 1923, pp. 20–22, Feb. 3, 1923, pp. 26–27, Feb. 10, 1923, pp. 26–27, Mar. 10, 1923, pp. 27–28, Mar. 24, 1923, pp. 23–24, Mar. 31, 1923, pp. 25–27, Apr. 14, 1923, pp. 23–25, May 12, 1923, pp. 4–7, May 26, 1923, pp. 22–23, July 7, 1923, pp. 23–24; Schneirov and Suhrbur, *Union Brotherhood*, pp. 76–85; Haber, *Building Industry*, pp. 374–79; Jackson, *Craft Labor Markets*, pp. 235–37; Bonnett, *Employers' Associations*, pp. 191–92.

51. Commons, "New York Building Trades," pp. 65–68; Haber, *Building Industry*, pp. 346–49; Christie, *Empire in Wood*, p. 202; Willoughby, "Employers' Associations," pp. 137–38; Baker, "Labor Boss," pp. 34–35; *NYT*, Apr. 8, 1903.

52. William English Walling, "The Building Trades Employers and the Unions," *World's Work* 6 (Aug. 1903): 3790–92; Keith, "Union of Employers," p. 130; *NYT*, May 16, 1903; Christie, *Empire in Wood*, p. 203; Haber, *Building Industry*, pp. 348–49; Bonnett, *Employers' Associations*, pp. 160–61.

53. For Parks, see Craig, "Building Conditions," Mar. 24, 1923, p. 24; Baker, "Labor Boss," pp. 31–34, 39–42; Hutchinson, *Imperfect Union*, pp. 30–31; Harold Seidman, *Labor Czars: A History of Labor Racketeering* (New York: Liveright Publishing Co., 1938), pp. 11–17; Haber, *Building Industry*, pp. 321–22; Franklin Clarkin, "The Daily Walk of the Walking Delegate," *Century Magazine* 67 (Dec. 1903): 299; Commons, "New York Building Trades," pp. 69–70; *NYT*, June 9, Sept. 6, 8, 1903; Perlman and Taft, *History of Labor*, p. 95; and Commission on Industrial Relations, *Industrial Relations*, 4:76.

54. *NYT*, May 7, 10, June 2, 4, 7, 1903; Minutes of Meeting of Emergency Committee, May 20, 1903, Marc Eidlitz and Sons Papers, New York Public Library, New York, New York; Commons, "New York Building Trades," pp. 71–72; *Bridgemen's Magazine* 3 (Jan. 1904): 11; Perlman and Taft, *History of Labor*, p. 89.

55. Keith, "Union of Employers," p. 130; *NYT*, May 16, 1903; *Iron Age* 71 (May 21, 1903): 22.

56. *NYT*, May 20, 27, June 2, 9, 10, 1903; Keith, "Union of Employers," p. 130; F. W. Hilbert, "Employers' Associations in the United States," in Hollander and Barnett, eds., *Trade Unionism*, pp. 191–92; Haber, *Building Industry*, pp. 350–51; Jackson, *Craft Labor Markets*, p. 238.

57. "Building Trades Employers' Association," June 3, 1903, Eidlitz and Sons Pa-

pers; *NYT,* June 2, 6, 7, 9, 10, 15–18, 20–23, 25, 26, 28, July 3, 4, 7, 9–11, 15, 18, 19, 21, 28, 29, 1903. There is a copy of the arbitration plan in Box 4, DP.

58. Commission on Industrial Relations, *Industrial Relations,* 2:1585–86; *NYT,* July 18, 28, 29, Aug. 1, 2, 4, 8, 10, 13, 15, 18, 29, Sept. 5, 13, 15, 1903; National Protective Association of Housesmiths and Bridgemen Local Assembly No. 3, New York, n.d., Box 8, DP; Samuel B. Donnelly to Marc Eidlitz and Sons, Nov. 15, 1904, Eidlitz and Sons Papers.

59. Walling, "Employers and the Unions," pp. 3792, 3794; *NYT,* June 9, 10, 12, 18, July 15, 21, 22, 30, 31, Aug. 5, 12, 14, 22, 23, 27–29, Sept. 1, 8, 12, 13, 17, Oct. 29–31, Nov. 7, Dec. 28, 1903; Seidman, *Labor Czars,* pp. 17–21, 22–26; Hutchinson, *Imperfect Union,* pp. 34–35; Keith, "Union of Employers," p. 133.

60. *NYT,* June 26, 30, July 1, Aug. 15, Sept. 11, 12, Nov. 10, 22, Dec. 3, 7, 14, 28, 1903; *Bridgemen's Magazine* 3 (Nov. 1903): 11–12, (Dec. 1903): 16, 18, 30–31, (Jan. 1904): 12–13.

61. *Bridgemen's Magazine* 3 (Feb. 1904): 22; Commission on Industrial Relations, *Industrial Relations,* 1:647.

62. Jackson, *Craft Labor Markets,* pp. 215–19, 233–34; Haydu, "American Exceptionalism," p. 38; Haber, *Building Industry,* pp. 448–50.

63. *Iron Age* 72 (Dec. 24, 1903): 30; Craig, "Building Conditions," May 26, 1923, p. 23; Hilbert, "Employers' Associations," pp. 205–6; Haber, *Building Industry,* p. 459.

Chapter 2

1. Luke Grant, *Erectors' Association, and the International Association of Bridge and Structural Ironworkers* (Washington, 1915), pp. 53–54. American Bridge operated twenty-four fabrication plants in 1904. Frank Ryan to John J. McNamara, Nov. 8, 1905, and enclosure, Box 22, DP.

2. Grant, *Erectors' Association,* pp. 21–23.

3. Ibid., p. 23; *Bridgemen's Magazine* 2 (Sept. 1902): 4.

4. Leo Wolman, *The Growth of American Trade Unions, 1880–1923* (New York: National Bureau of Economic Research, 1924), p. 110; *Iron Age* 71 (Mar. 12, 1903): 32; *Iron Trade Review* 36 (Mar. 26, 1903): 37; Minutes of Meeting. . . , Feb. 25, 1903, Box 37A, Frank Walsh Papers, New York Public Library, New York, New York; *Square Deal* 1 (Feb. 1906): 8.

5. Minutes of Meeting of General Committee of NEA, Mar. 3, 1903, Box 37A, Walsh Papers; General Principles and Conditions Adopted, Mar. 3, 1903, ibid.; "National Association of Erectors of Structural Steel and Iron Work," undated, Box 1, DP.

6. Grant, *Erectors' Association,* pp. 26–28; *Bridgemen's Magazine* 2 (Mar. 1903): 16, (Apr. 1903): 4–6; *Iron Age* 7 (Mar. 5, 1903): 32; *NYT,* Mar. 5, 8, 1903.

7. *NYT,* Mar. 8, 9, 13, 18, Apr. 5, 10, 1903; *Bridgemen's Magazine* 2 (Apr. 1903): 6, 10; David Montgomery, *Workers' Control in America* (Cambridge, England: Cambridge University Press, 1979), p. 92; *Iron Trade Review* 36 (Mar. 26, 1903): 37; Grant, *Erectors' Association,* p. 102; David Brody, *Steelworkers in America: The Nonunion Era* (New York: Harper and Brothers, 1960), p. 76.

8. Edwin J. Ogden to Members, Mar. 20, 1903, Box 26, DP; Minutes of Meeting of Temporary General Executive Committee of the National Association of Manufacturers and Erectors of Structural Steel and Iron Work, Mar. 18, 1903, Box 37A, Walsh Papers; *Iron Age* 71 (Mar. 26, 1903): 37.

9. *Bridgemen's Magazine* 2 (May, 1903): 4, 13; *NYT,* Mar. 29, Apr. 2, 3, 8, 15, 24, Aug. 16, 1903; Temporary General Executive Committee Minutes, Apr. 20, June 5, 1903, Box 37A, Walsh Papers; Grant, *Erectors' Association,* p. 28.

10. Temporary Executive Committee Minutes, Apr. 20, June 5, 1903, Box 37A, Walsh Papers; [Resolution], Apr. 23, 1903, Box 28, DP; Luke Grant, Preliminary Report. . . , undated, Records of Commission on Industrial Relations, in Records of Department of Labor, RG 174, NARA.

11. Temporary General Executive Committee Minutes, June 5, 1903, Box 37A, Walsh Papers; Grant, *Erectors' Association,* p. 31; Grant, Preliminary Report, RG 174; *NYT,* Apr. 3, 11, July 28, 29, Aug. 2, 11, 12, 16, Dec. 14, 1903; C. E. Cheney to S. P. Mitchell, July 10, 1903, Box 13, DP; *Bridgemen's Magazine* 3 (Jan. 1904): 11.

12. *NYT,* Sept. 5, 12, 13, 1903.

13. Ibid., Sept. 18, 22, 24, 26–28, Oct. 1, 3, 4, 1903.

14. Ibid., Sept. 24, 27, 1903.

15. Ibid., Oct. 30, 31, Nov. 7, 10, 11, 23, Dec. 14, 28, 1903, Feb. 3, 1904; *Bridgemen's Magazine* 3 (Jan. 1904): 11, 12, (Feb. 1904): 22, (Apr. 1904): 4–5.

16. Grant, *Erectors' Association,* p. 34; Wolman, *Trade Unions,* p. 110; *Bridgemen's Magazine* 4 (Oct. 1904): 17, 21–22.

17. *Bridgemen's Magazine* 4 (Feb. 1905): 4, (Mar. 1905): 18; Grant, *Erectors' Association,* pp. 34, 35, 162–76; undated document, Box 11, DP.

18. Grant, *Erectors' Association,* pp. 34–35, 177–81; *Bridgemen's Magazine* 8 (Oct. 1908): 755.

19. Buchanan to John J. McNamara, July 28, 1905, Box 22, DP; *Bridgemen's Magazine* 7 (Mar. 1907): 170; ibid. 8 (Oct. 1908): 755.

20. Buchanan to McNamara, July 6, 28, 1905, McNamara to Robert Hart, Aug. 8, 1905, Box 22, DP; McNamara Circular No. 30. . . , Aug. 9, 1905, ibid.; *Bridgemen's Magazine* 5 (Sept. 1905): 6, 55; Grant, *Erectors' Association,* pp. 35–36.

21. *Bridgemen's Magazine* 5 (Sept. 1905): 8, 47; Grant, *Erectors' Association,* p. 65.

22. *Iron Trade Review* 38 (Aug. 24, 1905): 9.

23. *Bridgemen's Magazine* 5 (Oct. 1905): 83; ibid. 6 (Oct. 1906): 53; ibid. 8 (Oct. 1908): 755–56; Buchanan to McNamara, July 28, 1905, Box 4, DP; *National Erectors' Association. What It Is. What It Does.* [Nov. 1907], Box 29, DP; Grant, *Erectors' Association,* pp. 38–39.

24. U.S. District Court, District of Indiana, United States v. Frank M. Ryan, et al., No. 3-Consolidated, No. 53 (Dec. 2, 1912): 14667, Box 35, DP; McNamara to E. J. Hendricks, June 14, 1910, Box 25, DP; *Bridgemen's Magazine* 6 (Oct. 1906): 52, 56–57.

25. For the negotiations, see McNamara to J. J. McRay, Oct. 18, 1905, Box 22, DP; *Bridgemen's Magazine* 6 (Oct. 1906): 52–53; ibid. 8 (Oct. 1908): 737–40; and Grant, *Erectors' Association,* pp. 40–45. There are differing accounts of the negotiations between the union and the steel company officials. Grant relied on the retrospective views of Ryan and Ziesing, but I have relied primarily on accounts closer to the time.

26. *Bridgemen's Magazine* 6 (Oct. 1906): 53, 54; ibid, 8 (Oct. 1908): 740; E. L. Warden et al. to Buchanan, Aug. 10, 1905, Box 4, DP; Drew, "Between Employer and Employee. . . ," *System* 116 (Feb. 1907): 115, copy in Box 29, DP; Grant, *Erectors' Association,* pp. 65–68.

27. Statement by Joshua Hatfield, Feb. 8, 1921, Exhibit File No. 3, File 1-2258-1, Records of the Federal Trade Commission, RG 122, NARA; Frank B. McCord testimony, Dec. 14, 1920, pp. 3388–98, 3402–3, 3406–8, Exhibit File No. 6, ibid.; Hatfield

testimony, Dec. 15, 1920, pp. 3695–98, ibid.; Copy of agreement. . . , Jan. 1, 1904, Exhibit File No. 1, ibid.

28. Ryan to McNamara, Nov. 5, 1905, Box 22, DP; *Bridgemen's Magazine* 5 (Dec. 1905): 27; Grant, *Erectors' Association,* p. 59; Minutes of Allied Iron Associations (AIA), Mar. 7, 1906, Box 1, DP; *NYT,* Dec. 8, 1905, Mar. 7, 17, 1906.

29. Ryan to McNamara, Nov. 5, 1905, Box 22, DP; *Bridgemen's Magazine* 5 (Jan. 1906): 28; Commission on Industrial Relations, *Industrial Relations. Final Report and Testimony,* 64 Cong., 1 sess., S. Doc. No. 415, 1916, 2:1589, 1612–13, 1617; *Iron Age* 76 (Dec. 14, 1905): 1635; Grant, *Erectors' Association,* pp. 59–60.

30. Minutes of Meeting of Iron Trade, Nov. 21, 24, 1905, Box 1, DP; Minutes of Strike Committee, Dec. 12, 1905, May 25, 1906 (enclosing Cheney to W. A. Garrigues, May 21, 1906), ibid.; Ryan to McNamara, Dec. 13, 1905, Box 22, DP.

31. J. P. Larrimer to McNamara, Jan. 11, 1906, P. F. Farrell to McNamara, Jan. 31, 1905, Box 22, DP; Ryan to Farrell, July 2, 1907, Box 23, DP; *Bridgemen's Magazine* 5 (Jan. 1906): 29; ibid. 6 (Oct. 1906): 52, 54; ibid. 8 (Oct. 1908): 740; Grant, *Erectors' Association,* p. 61.

32. AIA Minutes, Jan. 31, 1906, Box 1, DP; Commission on Industrial Relations, *Industrial Relations,* 2:1614; *NEA. What It Is.*

33. Minutes of Executive Committee of . . . Erectors. . . , Jan. 16, 1906, Box 37A, Walsh Papers.

34. Ryan claimed that Fuller officials had told him that their company had wanted to meet the $5.00 demand but had feared that the "influence" of the AIA would have been "thrown against them" had the company done so. Ryan to McNamara, Jan. 16, 1906, Box 22, DP.

35. Minutes of Meeting of National Association and Committee from New York AIA, Jan. 19, 1906, Box 37A, Walsh Papers.

36. National Association Minutes, Jan. 19, 20, 1906, ibid.; Cheney to John Sterling Deans, Jan. 20, 1906, Box 2, DP.

37. Minutes of Meeting of General Executive Committee and Western District Members, Jan. 24, 1906, Box 37A, Walsh Papers; Drew to Kansas City Structural Steel Co., July 25, 1907, Box 9, DP; *NEA. What It Is.*; H. F. Lofland to Drew, Sept. 23, 1907, Box 2, DP; Drew, "Closed Shop Unionism," *Square Deal* 3 (Jan. 1908): 38–39; Commission on Industrial Relations, *Industrial Relations,* 6:5312–13.

38. AIA Minutes, May 21, 1906, Box 1, DP; *Iron Age* 77 (Jan. 25, 1906): 375. See Sanford M. Jacoby, "Norms and Cycles: The Dynamics of Nonunion Industrial Relations in the United States, 1877–1987," in Katharine G. Abraham and Robert B. McKersie, eds., *New Developments in the Labor Market* (Cambridge, Mass.: MIT Press, 1990), p. 26.

39. General Executive Committee Minutes, Jan. 30, 1906, Box 37A, Walsh Papers; Wilson Vance to Post, Feb. 21, 1906, Box 4, C. W. Post Papers, Bentley Historical Library, Ann Arbor, Michigan.

40. NEA Release [Jan. 31, 1906], Box 15, DP; *American Industries* 4 (Feb. 1906): 4; *Iron Age* 77 (Jan. 25, 1906): 375; *Square Deal* 1 (Feb. 1906): 8; ibid. (Mar. 1906): 11.

41. Minutes of NEA General Executive Committee, Feb. 16, 1906, Box 37A, Walsh Papers; Minutes of NEA, Feb. 23, Mar. 13, 1906, ibid.; NEA Central District, Mar. 24, 1906, Box 14, DP; Cheney to General Executive Committee, Mar. 28, 1906, ibid.

42. For biographical information concerning Drew, see copy submitted for *National Cyclopedia of American Biography,* 1962, Box 28, DP; Data re Walter Drew, Jan. 22, 1954, ibid.; Dallas Jones interviews with Mrs. Walter Drew, Nov. 12, 1962, pp. 2–4, 7,

Mrs. Josephine Foster, Nov. 12, 1962, p. 7, Fred Taylor, Nov. 14, 1962, pp. 1, 4, and Mrs. Lynn Franklin, Dec. 11, 1962, pp. 3, 4, transcripts in my possession; Franklin to Jones, Dec. 30, 1962, in my possession; Citizens Alliance of Grand Rapids, Secretary's First Annual Report, Jan. 1, 1905, Grand Rapids Public Library, Grand Rapids, Michigan; Drew to Dwight Havens, June 23, 1911, Box 5, DP; and Commission on Industrial Relations, *Industrial Relations,* 11:10731–32.

43. Drew, Citizens Alliance of Grand Rapids, Special Report of Secretary, May 14, 1904, Grand Rapids Public Library; Drew, Citizens Alliance, May 23, 1904, ibid.

44. Drew, Citizens Alliance, May 23, 1904, ibid.

45. Drew, Special Report of Secretary, ibid.; Drew, First Annual Report, Jan. 1, 1905, ibid.; Drew to Havens, June 23, 1911, Feb. 26, 1913, Box 5, DP.

46. Drew, First Annual Report, Jan. 1, 1905, Grand Rapids Public Library; Drew, "The Law Relating to the Closed Shop Contract," Apr. 1, 1905, Box 29, DP; Drew, "The Open Shop: An Economic Discussion," Jan. 7, 1906, ibid.; Drew, "The Union and the Law: Some Legal Phases of the Labor Question," *Square Deal* 1 (May 1906): 21–24.

47. Jones interviews with Mrs. Drew, Nov. 14, 1962, pp. 1, 3, Mrs. Foster, Nov. 12, 1962, p. 5, Taylor, pp. 1, 3, and Noel Sargent, Nov. 15, 1912, pp. 1–2, transcripts in my possession.

48. Drew to NAM, Jan. 6, 1949, Box 22, DP; Daniel R. Ernst, "The Closed Shop, the Proprietary Capitalist, and the Law, 1877–1915," in Sanford M. Jacoby, ed., *Masters to Managers: Historical and Comparative Perspectives on American Employers* (New York: Columbia University Press, 1991), pp. 136–37; *Grand Rapids Herald,* July 10 [1906], clipping in Box 29, DP; *Square Deal* 1 (Dec. 1905): 5, 30; Commission on Industrial Relations, *Industrial Relations,* 11:10731.

49. Ryan to McNamara, Nov. 27, Dec. 7, 1905, McNamara to Ryan, Nov. 29, 1905, McCray to McNamara, Oct. 22, Dec. 21, 1905, Moulton H. Davis to McNamara, Mar. 25, 1906, Ryan to Members Executive Board, Apr. 11, 1906, Box 22, DP; [*New York World,* Dec. 11, 1905], clipping in ibid.; AIA Minutes, Dec. 14, 1905, Box 1, DP; Strike Committee Minutes, Jan. 3, 24, 1906, ibid.

50. AIA Minutes, Dec. 14, 1905, Jan. 3, Mar. 7, 14, May 21, 1906, Box 1, DP; Strike Committee Minutes, Dec. 6, 8, 1905, Jan. 22, 24, Mar. 12, Apr. 19, 1906, ibid.; B. Moore to McNamara, Dec. 17, 1905, Feb. 17, 1906, Box 22, DP; *NYT,* Jan. 10, 1906; *Iron Age* 77 (Jan. 18, 1906): 299.

51. AIA Minutes, Mar. 7, May 21, 1906, Box 1, DP; Strike Committee Minutes, Jan. 10, 17, 24, Feb. 9, Mar. 5, 7, 9, 17, Apr. 19, May 25 (enclosing Cheney to Garrigues, May 21, 1906), Box 1, DP; Ryan to McNamara, Jan. 30, Feb. 4, 6, 1906, Box 22, DP; *Iron Age* 77 (Feb. 15, 1906): 613.

52. Ryan to McNamara, Jan. 6, 1906, Box 22, DP; AIA Minutes, Jan. 31, Mar. 14, 1906, Box 1, DP; Strike Committee Minutes, Mar. 9, 14, 16, 1906, ibid.; *NYT,* Jan. 20, Feb. 25, Mar. 7, 17, 1906; *Iron Age* 77 (Feb. 1, 1906): 449.

53. Scott, *The Walking Delegate* (Upper Saddle River, N.J.: Literature House., 1969), p. 213; Statement of George E. Davis. . . , Oct. 4, 1913, pp. 9–11, 124, Box 6, DP.

54. AIA Minutes, Dec. 14, Jan. 31, 1906, Box 1, DP; Strike Committee Minutes, Dec. 2, 12, Jan. 5, 12, Mar. 9, 16, 23, Apr. 6, 1906, ibid.; Eidlitz and Hulse to Drew, May 1, 1907, Box 2, DP; Farrell to McNamara, Apr. 13, 1906, Box 22, DP; *NYT,* Dec. 8, 1905, Jan. 15, Feb. 25, Mar. 7, 9, 11, 17, Apr. 13, 1906.

55. Strike Committee Minutes, Feb. 7, 23, 26, May 26, 1906, Box 1, DP; Eidlitz and

Hulse to Drew, May 1, 1907, Box 2, DP; *NYT*, Dec. 20, 1905, Jan. 9, 10, Feb. 25, 26, Mar. 7, 8, 11, 25, 27–28, 1906; *Iron Age* 77 (Mar. 1, 1906): 788.

56. Strike Committee Minutes, Dec. 12, 1905, Jan. 1, 22, Mar. 2, 5, 7, May 17, 25 (enclosing Cheney to Garrigues, May 21, 1906), 1906, Box 1, DP; AIA Minutes, Jan. 3, Mar. 7, 1906, ibid.; Ryan to Executive Board, Apr. 11, 1906, Box 22, DP; *NYT*, Dec. 20, 1905, Jan. 15, 1906.

57. George Hagerty to McNamara, Dec. 11, 1905, Feb. 13, Apr. 3, 1906, McNamara to Hagerty, Dec. 13, 1905, McNamara to Ryan, Nov. 29, Dec. 12, 1905, Feb. 27, 1906, Ryan to McNamara, Dec. 13, 1905, E. Allany to McNamara, Apr. 1, 1906, Thomas Dodson to McNamara, Apr. 3, 1906, Box 22, DP.

58. *Iron Trade Review* 39 (Mar. 15, 1906): 1; "List of Depredations," Box 6, DP; "Out-Cleveland," Apr. 4, 1906, Box 4, DP; "C. W. D. A.," Apr. 16, 1906, ibid.; James Doran to Squires, Sanders and Dempsey, May 22, 1911, ibid.

59. Drew, "Strikes and How to Handle Them," *Square Deal* 1 (July 1906): 3–5.

60. Thomas B. O'Connell to Drew, Apr. 10, 1906, enclosing clipping from *Chicago Record Herald*, Box 36, DP.

61. National Association Minutes, Apr. 17, 1906, Box 37A, Walsh Papers; Executive Committee Minutes [May 1906], ibid.; NEA Minutes, Nov. 2, 1906, ibid.; Excerpts, Drew to Mother and Father, May 3, 8, 1906, Box 28, DP; Drew to Dear Sir, May 10, 1906, Box 2, DP.

62. [Drew] to Mitchell, Mar. 31, 1906, Box 14, DP; Drew to Mitchell, Apr. 28, May 16, 1906, ibid.; Drew to Dear Sir, May 10, 1906, Box 2, DP; NEA Minutes, Apr. 17, [May], 1906, Box 37A, Walsh Papers; Strike Committee Minutes, Apr. 20, 27, May 25, 1906, Box 1, DP.

63. Ryan to McNamara, Feb. 6, 1906, McNamara to Farrell, May 5, 1906, Box 22, DP; Strike Committee Minutes, Apr. 30, May 9, 1906, Box 1, DP; Drew to J. K. Mumford, July 22, 1909, Box 18, DP; Minutes of Conference of NEA Executive Committee and AIA [Apr. 30, 1906], Box 37A, Walsh Papers; *Square Deal* 2 (Jan. 1906): 6.

64. Drew to Mitchell, May 16, 1906, Drew to Gentlemen, Sept. 15, 1908, Box 14, DP; Drew to Dear Sir, May 10, 1906, Box 2, DP; unidentified clipping [May 16, 1906], Box 29, DP; Fred W. Cohen to Drew, July 15, 1909, Box 6, DP; Drew to Mumford, July 22, 1909, Box 18, DP; AIA Minutes, May 21, 1906, Box 1, DP; Strike Committee Minutes, May 17, 1906, ibid.; *Bridgemen's Magazine* 9 (May 1909): 263.

65. National Assocation Minutes, Apr. 17, 1906, Box 37A, Walsh Papers; *NEA. What It Is.*

66. [Drew statement], May 9, 1906, Box 12, DP; Drew to Dear Sir, May 10, 1906, Box 2, DP; [*New York Journal*, May 18, 1906], clipping in Box 1, DP; *Iron Age* 77 (May 17, 1906): 1645.

67. McNamara to Ryan, Apr. 30, May 5, 16, 1906, Box 22, DP; McNamara to Ryan, June 21, 1906, Box 23, DP; Minutes of American Federation of Labor Executive Committee, June 18, Nov. 25, 1906, Mar. 18, 1907, Reel 3, American Federation of Labor Records: The Samuel Gompers Era, University of Michigan Library, Ann Arbor, Michigan; American Federation of Labor, *Report of Proceedings of the Twenty-Sixth Annual Convention, Nov. 12–24, 1906* (Washington: Graphic Arts Printing Co., 1906), pp. 93, 221, 227.

68. NEA Executive Committee Minutes, May 25, June 22, 1906, Box 37A, Walsh Papers; Mitchell to Cheney, July 1, 1906, Box 14, DP; Drew to George W. Rouse, May

12, 1913, Box 36, DP; Excerpts, Drew to Mother and Father, May 8, 26, 1906, Box 28, DP; unidentified Louisville newspaper [1906], Scrapbook No. 2, DP.

Chapter 3

1. Minutes of the Meeting of the Executive Committee (hereafter NEA Minutes), Box 37A, Frank P. Walsh Papers, New York Public Library, New York, New York; *National Erectors' Association. What It Is. What It Does.* [1907], p. 8; Box 29, DP; William Haber, *Industrial Relations in the Building Industry* (New York: Arno and New York Times, 1971), p. 4; Clarence E. Bonnett, *Employers' Associations in the United States* (New York: Macmillan Co., 1922), p. 141.

2. *NEA. What It Is.*, pp. 6–8; Report of the Commissioner, May 25, 1917, Box 37A, Walsh Papers; NEA Membership, June 1, 1921, Box 15, DP; Drew to C. Edwin Michael, Oct. 31, 1913, ibid.; [Drew] Statement to Federal Trade Commission. . . , July 21, 1921, Box 17, DP.

3. *NEA. What It Is.,* pp. 5–6, 10; NEA Minutes [May 12], 1906, May 28, 1915, Box 37A, Walsh Papers.

4. *NEA. What It Is.,* p. 6; NEA Minutes, Feb. 16, Nov. 2, 1906, Dec. 20, 1907, Apr. 14, 1908, July 29, 1909, Box 37A, Walsh Papers; Minutes of Finance Committee, May 12, 1906, ibid.

5. Drew to Nathan L. Miller, Aug. 3, 1927, Box 36, DP; Drew to August Ziesing, July 27, 1926, Box 12, DP; Approximate Tonnage Fabricated and Erected during 1913. . . , Box 29, DP; Approximate Tonnage . . . 1914, ibid.; Luke Grant, *The National Erectors' Association and the International Association of Bridge and Structural Ironworkers* (Washington, 1915), p. 75.

6. Grant, Summary of Report on the National Erectors' Association. . . , Oct. 30, 1914, pp. 9–10, Records of the United States Commission on Industrial Relations, in Records of the Department of Labor, RG 174, NARA; Grant, *Erectors' Association,* p. 54; Drew to Kansas City Structural Steel Co., July 25, 1907, Box 9, DP.

7. Drew to E. Gerber, Dec. 7, 1912, Box 14, DP; Drew to C. E. Neudorfer, Apr. 22, 1920, Box 1, DP; Drew to Miller, Aug. 3, 1927, Box 36, DP; Drew, "Structural Steel and Iron Work in New York," Nov. 18, 1919, Box 29, DP; Annual Report of the Open Shop Committee of the NAM, 1931, Series I, Box 251, Archives of the National Association of Manufacturers, Accession 1411, Hagley Museum and Library, Wilmington, Delaware; Grant, *Erectors' Association,* p. 54.

8. The assessment was cut to three cents per ton in 1913 and was yielding about $40,000 a year in 1916. Drew to Kansas City Bridge Co., Feb. 3, 1913, Box 9, DP; Drew to Members, American Erectors' Association, Mar. 20, 1916, Box 1, DP.

9. Drew to Lewis T. Shoemaker, Feb. 17, 1909, Box 12, DP; Gerber to Drew, Dec. 6, 1912, Drew to Gerber, Dec. 7, 1912, Drew to H. H. McClintic, Dec. 9, 1912, Box 14, DP; Memo [1955], Box 15, DP.

10. Drew to McClintic, Jan. 13, 1917, Box 14, DP; James A. Emery to NAM, Jan. 6, 1949, and enclosure, Box 22, DP; Drew to Miller, Apr. 1, 1930, Box 11, DP; J. W. Poushey to C. E. Cheney, Dec. 15, 1916, Box 37A, Walsh Papers; Drew to Members, Dec. 16, 1916, ibid.; Drew Memo for Cheney, Dec. 19, 1916, Exhibit File No. 5, File No. 1-2258-1, Records of the Federal Trade Commission, RG 122, NARA.

11. Drew, "Between Employer and Employee. . . ," *System* 116 (Feb. 1907): 115–17, copy in Box 29, DP; *NEA. What It Is.,* pp. 9–10, 18; Drew to Interstate Engineering Co., Sept. 14, 1907, Box 2, DP; Drew to James M. Carter, Dec. 9, 1914, Box 4, DP.

12. Drew to Gentlemen, Sept. 22, 1906, Box 17, DP; Drew to Gentlemen, Nov. 21, 1906, Box 14, DP; Drew, "Strikes and How to Handle Them," *Square Deal* 1 (July 1906): 3; ibid. 2 (July 1907): 13.

13. Drew, *Some Phases of the Labor Question* (Feb. 2, 1921), p. 4, Box 29, DP; Drew to Walter Gordon Merritt, Oct. 10, 1917, Box 1, DP; Drew to Clarence E. Whitney, Jan. 29, 1918, Box 8, DP; Drew to Raynal C. Bolling, Jan. 5, 1915, Box 20, DP. Cf. Drew, "To Build Open or Closed, Which?" *Square Deal* 6 (Jan. 1910): 401.

14. Drew, "The Labor Trust's Crusade against the Courts," *Square Deal* 2 (Oct. 1906): 16; Drew, "The Political Purpose of Organized Labor," ibid. (Oct. 1908): 15; Drew, "To Build Open or Closed," pp. 400–401; Drew, "Closed Shop Unionism," *Government* 2 (Mar. 1908): 384–88; Drew to Gentlemen, Oct. 26, 1908, Box 14, DP; Drew, "Unions, Collective Bargaining, Compulsory Incorporation and Arbitration," Jan. 31, 1917, Box 29, DP; Drew, "On the Open or Closed Shop," Feb. 26, 1921, ibid.

15. Commission on Industrial Relations, *Industrial Relations. Final Report and Testimony,* 64 Cong., 1 sess., S. Doc. No. 415, 1916, 11:10732; Drew, "Unions, Collective Bargaining."

16. Drew to Frederick J. Koster, Aug. 2, 1917, Box 11, DP.

17. Drew, "Building and the Public," Feb. 16, 1922, Box 29, DP; Drew to Henry C. Hunter, June 7, 1917, Box 16, DP; Drew, "Closed Shop Clauses in Building Contracts," *American Industries* 15 (Mar. 19, 1915): 11.

18. Drew, "The Closed Shop vs. the Building Industry," *Square Deal* 2 (Jan. 1907): 23–26; Drew, "To Build Open or Closed," pp. 399–400; Drew, "The Closed Shop and the Public," *American Industries* 6 (Sept. 15, 1907): 13; Drew to W. F. Dinwiddie, July 16, 1909, Box 12, DP.

19. Drew, "Closed Shop Unionism," *Square Deal* 3 (June 1908): 39; Drew, "To Build Open or Closed," pp. 400–401; Drew, "Closed Shop Clauses," p. 11; Drew to Gentlemen [1910], Box 14, DP; Drew to Henry D. Sharpe, May 17, 1916, Box 37A, Walsh Papers; Drew to Dear Sir, May 17, 1916, George B. Walbridge to Drew, July 12, 1916, Box 18, DP; Drew, "Building and the Public"; Drew, "Labor Trouble on Closed Shop Building Work," Dec. 15, 1931, Box 20, DP.

20. *NEA. What It Is.,* pp. 20–21; Drew, "Closed Shop Industries: An Analysis" [1908], Box 29, DP.; Drew, *Your Agent the Builder* [1920], pp. 3–10, ibid.; Drew, "On the Open or Closed Shop," Feb. 26, 1921, ibid.; Drew, "Building and the Public," ibid.; Drew to Kansas City Structural Steel Co., July 25, 1907, Box 9, DP; Drew to Bolling, Jan. 5, 1915, Box 20, DP; Drew, "Closed Shop and the Public," pp. 13–14; Drew, "Open and Closed Shop in the Structural Iron Industry," *Survey* 35 (Mar. 11, 1916): 703.

21. Drew to Gentlemen, June 20, 1907, Feb. 10, 1911, Box 14, DP; Drew to William H. Sayward, Oct. 15, 1910, Box 11, DP; Drew to S. N. Robinson, Oct. 14, 1907, Box 2, DP; Drew to J. Philip Bird, Box 16, DP; Drew, "Open or Closed Shop," Box 29, DP; Drew, "Closed Shop Clauses," p. 12; Drew, "Labor's Monopoly in Building," *American Industries* 30 (May 19, 1930): 17–19.

22. Drew, "Between Employer and Employee," pp. 111–12, Box 29, DP; Drew to Dinwiddie, July 16, 1909, Box 12, DP.

23. *NEA. What It Is.,* pp. 18–19; Drew to Kansas City Structural Steel Co., July 25, 1907, Drew to H. H. Adams, Apr. 11, 1913, Box 9, DP; Drew to Robinson, Oct. 14, 1907, Box 2, DP; Charles Beum to John J. McNamara, Apr. 17, 1911, Box 26, DP; Drew to Gentlemen, May 14, 1914, Box 14, DP; Grant, *Erectors' Association,* pp. 81–82. Drew claimed that the IABSIW's purpose was to discourage the use of reinforced concrete by making its cost prohibitive. Drew to Gentlemen, May 14, 1914, Box 14, DP.

24. Drew to Adams, Apr. 11, 1913, Box 9, DP; Grant, *Erectors' Association,* pp. 93–94.

25. H. F. Lofland to Drew, Sept. 23, 1907, Box 2, DP; Drew, "Closed Shop Unionism," p. 38. Cf. Drew, "Closed Shop and the Public," p. 14.

26. Jacoby, "Norms and Cycles: The Dynamics of Nonunion Industrial Relations in the United States, 1897–1987," in Katharine G. Abraham and Robert B. McKersie, eds., *New Developments in the Labor Market* (Cambridge, Mass.: MIT Press, 1990), p. 30; Drew to E. R. Cobb, Sept. 30, 1908, Box 6, DP; Drew to C. D. Garretson, June 12, 1916, Box 20, DP; *NEA. What It Is.,* p. 18.

27. Drew to Berlin Construction Co., Oct. 29, 1913, Box 15, DP; Drew to Alvin Johnson, Apr. 3, 1917, Box 17, DP; Drew to W. H. Phillippi, June 23, 1922, Box 4, DP; Drew to Miller, Aug. 3, 1927, Box 36, DP; [Drew], Reply to Morrin statement in opposition to Proposed Code, Oct. 31, 1933, Box 29, DP; Drew to Members, Dec. 16, 1916, Box 37A, Walsh Papers.

28. R. B. Thomas to Drew, May 16, 1929, Clyde MacCornack to Drew, May 22, 1929, Drew to MacCornack, May 24, 1929, Box 10, DP; Drew to H. A. Wagner, Apr. 27, 1921, Box 12, DP.

29. Drew to Gentlemen, Mar. 14, Dec. 16, 1907, Mar. 3, 1909, Box 14, DP; Drew to W. A. Gardner, Apr. 1, 1921, Box 17, DP; Drew to W. Nelson Mayhew, Mar. 12, 1921, Drew to Herbert K. Baer, Mar. 25, 1921, Box 9, DP; Drew to MacCornack, Mar. 9, 1927, Box 12, DP.

30. Drew to Poushey, Apr. 1, 1916, Box 1, DP; Remarks of Walter Drew. . . , Feb. 26, 1915, Box 29, DP; Drew to H. A. Fitch, May 15, 1921, Box 3, DP; Drew to Wagner, Apr. 15, 1921, Box 12, DP; NEA Minutes, June 10, 1916, Box 37A, Walsh Papers; Minutes of NEA Special Meeting, June 20, 1916, ibid.; Drew to Members, Aug. 27, 1919, ibid.; *NYT,* Feb. 26, 1915.

31. Minutes, Meeting of Iron League Erectors' Association (hereafter ILEA Minutes), Dec. 21, 1909, Box 37A, Walsh Papers; NEA Minutes, Dec. 28, 1909, June 10, 1910, Aug. 26, 1919, ibid.; Wagner to NEA, Apr. 26, 1920, ibid.; Wagner to NEA, Apr. 7, 1921, Box 12, DP; Wagner to NEA, Sept. 25, 1931, Box 15, DP; Fred W. Cohen to Drew, July 22, 1910, Box 9, DP; W. N. Kratzer to NEA, May 11, 1929, Box 12, DP.

32. U. S. District Court, District of Indiana, United States vs. Frank M. Ryan, et al., No. 3-Consolidated, No. 24 (Oct. 26, 1912): 3608–9, Box 32, DP; Drew to Cohen, July 25, 1910, Box 9, DP; Drew to J. H. Mueller, Jan. 21, 1916, Box 8, DP; Drew to J. B. Gemberling, Sept. 21, 1932, Box 18, DP.

33. Commission on Industrial Relations, *Industrial Relations,* 11:10766; Frank Ryan to McNamara, Mar. 18, 1907, Box 23, DP; Minutes of NEA General Meeting, May 29, 1914, Box 37A, Walsh Papers; *American Industries* 14 (Dec. 19, 1914): 5; Drew, "Open and Closed Shop," pp. 702–3; Grant, *Erectors' Association,* pp. 78–80.

34. Drew to Members, Apr. 4, 1917, Box 14, DP; Drew, Replies to Questionnaire on Wages. . . , Sept. 30, 1922, Box 29, DP; H. R. Brady to Gentlemen, Jan. 27, 1932, Box 20, DP; Grant, *Erectors' Association,* p. 80; "An Informal History of the Iron Workers" (reprinted from the *Ironworker,* 1971), p. 12, copy in my possession.

35. Drew to Gentlemen, Dec. 14, 1907, Box 28, DP; Drew to Gentlemen, Sept. 15, 1908, Box 14, DP; Drew to Members AIA, Aug. 6, 1909, ibid.; Drew to Belmont Iron Works, July 21, 1915, Box 3, DP; Drew to Mosher Manufacturing Co., Dec. 3, 1919, Box 15, DP; Drew to Bethlehem Fabricators, July 30, 1919, W. S. Hutchinson to Drew, Aug. 3, 1919, Box 3, DP; Excerpts, Drew to Mother and Father, May 8, 1906, Box 28, DP; Drew to A. J. Allen, June 12, 1916, Box 3, DP; James L. DeVou to Brady, July 7, 9,

1920, Brady to DeVou, July 12, 1920, Box 1, DP; Testimony of Eugene F. Fox, Dec. 14, 1920, pp. 3441–50, of Charles H. Kalhorn, Dec. 15, 1920, pp. 3528–32, 3547–48, Exhibit File No. 6, File 12258-1, RG 122; "The Common Welfare," *Survey* 27 (Dec. 30, 1911): 1409.

36. Drew to McClintic-Marshall Construction Co., Aug. 30, 1906, Box 2, DP; Drew to Mosher Manufacturing Co., Dec. 13, 1919, Box 15, DP; Drew to Brady, Apr. 28, 1925, Box 3, DP; Drew to James M. Carter, Dec. 9, 1914, Box 4, DP.

37. Summary Report. . . , Oct. 1914, p. 20, RG 174; Drew to F. W. Hutchings, Aug. 29, 1906, Box 2, DP.

38. AIA Minutes, May 21, 1906, Box 1, DP: Drew to Mosher Steel Construction Co., June 19, 1906, Drew to Jobson and Hooker Construction Co., Sept. 18, 1906, Box 2, DP; Drew to Gentlemen, Mar. 4, 1907, Drew to Members Ornamental Bronze and Iron Masters' Association, Jan. 27, 1909, Drew to Members AIA, Aug. 10, 1909, Box 14, DP; [Drew] Reply to Morrin, Oct. 31, 1933, Box 29, DP; Drew, "Between Employer and Employee," p. 115; Drew, "Closed Shop and the Public," pp. 13–14; Drew, "Strikes against the Open Shop," *Square Deal* 5 (Aug. 1909): 32.

39. *NEA. What It Is.,* pp. 9–10; Drew, "Between Employer and Employee," p. 115; Drew to Dear Sir, May 10, 1906, Drew to Interstate Engineering Co., Sept. 14, 1907, Box 2, DP; Drew to Carter, Dec. 9, 1914, Box 4, DP.

40. AIA Minutes, Aug. 2, 1906, Box 1, DP; Drew to Warren City Tank and Boiler Co., Nov. 14, 1916, ibid.; Drew to Gentlemen, Feb. 4, 1907, Dec. 1, 1908, Jan. 15, 1909, Drew to Members AIA, Aug. 10, 1909, Box 14, DP; Drew to Poushey, Feb. 21, 1917, Box 3, DP; Drew to Belmont Iron Works, July 13, 1921, Box 7, DP; Drew to Members, June 26, 1923, Box 29, DP; NEA Minutes, Sept. 11, Dec. 1, 1908, Box 37A, Walsh Papers; In Re: Investigation of Building Materials . . . Statements of Walter Gordon Merritt and Walter Drew, Jan. 13, 1921, File 1-2258-1, RG 122; *Bridgemen's Magazine* 7 (Nov. 1907): 754.

41. *NYT,* Sept. 13, 1903; Drew to Gentlemen, Apr. 18, Oct. 7, 13, 1908, Box 14, DP; Cheney to Members [ILEA], Jan. 14, 1916, Box 8, DP; Drew to William Becker, Oct. 18, 1917, Box 7, DP; Extracts from Testimony of . . . Cheney. . . , Dec. 16, 17, 1920, pp. 4–5, Box 11, DP; ILEA Minutes, Jan. 13, 1916, Mar. 27, 1917 (Special Meeting), Box 37A, Walsh Papers.

42. AIA Minutes, Aug. 2, 1906, Box 29, DP; Drew to J. H. Greiner, Nov. 20, 1906, Box 2, DP; J. E. Munsey to McNamara, Sept. 21, 1909, Box 24, DP; NEA Minutes, July 24, Sept. 11, 1908, Box 37A, Walsh Papers; *Bridgemen's Magazine* 10 (Oct. 1910): 627; Grant, *Erectors' Association,* pp. 72, 74.

43. Lofland to Drew, Feb. 14, 1907, Drew to Cohen, Feb. 16, 25, 1907, Cohen to Drew, Feb. 18, 1907, Box 2, DP; E. H. Connor to Drew, Aug. 13, 1928, Box 15, DP.

44. Lofland to Drew, Feb. 14, 1907, Drew to Cohen, Feb. 18, 25, 1907, Drew to John Sterling Deans, Feb. 28, 1907, Box 2, DP; Drew to Michael, Nov. 13, 1913, Box 15, DP; Drew to H. B. Hirsh, Mar. 11, 1927, Box 12, DP; NEA Minutes, Mar. 30, 1909, Box 37A, Walsh Papers.

45. Drew to Allen, Feb. 13, 1920, Box 3, DP; McNamara to Harry Jones, Oct. 9, 1908, Box 24, DP; Drew to G. W. Smith, June 22, 1914, Smith to Drew, June 26, 1914, Box 1, DP; Conference, Nov. 1, 1917, File No. 33-756, Records of the Federal Mediation and Conciliation Service, RG 280, NARA; Second Conference, Nov. 5, 1917, ibid.; *Bridgemen's Magazine* 5 (May 1906): 6; Commission on Industrial Relations, *Industrial Relations,* 2:1706.

46. *NEA. What It Is.,* p. 8; Drew to F. J. Lucius, Oct. 26, 1907, Box 2, DP; August

Bussow to McNamara, June 16, 1910, Box 25, DP; McNamara to H. H. Kilbourne, Apr. 6, 1911, Box 26, DP; J. E. McClory to Drew, May 7, 1915, Box 10, DP; Commission on Industrial Relations, *Industrial Relations,* 2:1617.

47. Haber, *Building Industry,* pp. 245–46; Rhodri Jeffreys-Jones, "The Problem of Industrial Violence in the United States" (Ph.D. diss., Cambridge University [1969]), p. 165. For Drew's position, see, for example, Drew to Lucius, Oct. 26, 1907, Box 2, DP; Drew to Gentlemen, Oct. 14, 1907, Box 14, DP; and Drew to J. J. Miller, Dec. 6, 1921, Box 15, DP. See also chapter 2.

48. Strike Committee Minutes, Nov. 22, 1906, Box 1, DP; Drew to Gentlemen, Mar. 23, Oct. 14, Dec. 16, 1907, Mar. 3, 1909, Box 14, DP; Drew to Members AIA, Aug. 6, 1909, ibid.; Drew to Members AIA, Aug. 10, 1909, Box 29, DP; *NEA. What It Is.,* p. 8.

49. ILEA Conference, Jan. 11, 1916, Box 37A, Walsh Papers; ILEA Minutes, Jan. 13, 1916, ibid.; Cheney to Members, Jan. 14, 1916, Box 8, DP; Drew to Gentlemen, Feb. 15, 1916, Box 14, DP; Drew to Richard Kuehn, Feb. 25, 1916, Box 1, DP; Drew to Editor Survey, May 20, 1916, Box 29, DP; Extracts from Cheney Testimony, Dec. 16, 17, 1920, pp. 5–6, Box 11, DP.

50. Drew to Thomas Earle, Dec. 16, 1919, Exhibit File No. 1, File 1-2258-1, RG 122; *Iron Age* 106 (Dec. 23, 1920): 1672.

51. Drew to Wagner, Apr. 4, 1924, Box 14, DP.

52. NEA Minutes, June 19, 1908, Box 37A, Walsh Papers; MacCornack to Drew, June 14, 1924, Box 12, DP; C. W. Brussoek to Drew, Sept. 27, 1920, Exhibit File No. 1, File 1-2258-1, RG 122.

53. Drew to Committee of U.S. Senate, Oct. 28, 1921, Box 11, DP; Drew to Bonnett, July 6, 1922, Box 12, DP.

54. Drew to F. W. Job, May 14, 1912, Drew to Theodore W. Shonts, May 16, 1912, Box 8, DP; Drew to C. J. Smith, Dec. 12, 1910, Box 4, DP; Drew to Roberts, Apr. 21, 1913, Box 3, DP; Drew to McClintic, Feb. 25, 1916, Box 20, DP; Drew to F. P. Lyons, Feb. 21, 1921, Box 11, DP.

55. Drew to G. B. Goff, Aug. 27, Oct. 3, 1906, Drew to Hay Foundry and Iron Works, Sept. 27, 1906, Drew to Levinson and Co., Sept. 27, 1906, Drew to Hinkle Iron Works, Sept. 27, 1906, Box 2, DP; Strike Committee Minutes, Box 1, DP; Lofland to Drew, Nov. 20, 1906, Apr. 20, 1908, Drew to H. W. Lowe, Feb. 13, 19, Apr. 14, 1913, ibid.; Excerpts, Drew to Mother and Father, Aug. 7, 1906, Box 28, DP; "Out-Cleveland . . . ," Apr. 4, 1906, Box 4, DP; Drew to Gentlemen, Mar. 4, 1907, Box 14, DP; Drew to Lucius Engineering Co., July 11, 17, 1912, J. F. Ritter to Drew, May 13, 1915, enclosing—— to Dear Sir, May 10, 1915, Box 11, DP; Drew to Roberts, Apr. 21, 1913, Box 3, DP; Drew to E. W. Krueger, Sept. 16, 1918, Box 4, DP; Autobiography of Robert J. Foster, undated, p. 95, Box 22, DP; P. F. Farrell to McNamara, July 31, 1906, John T. Butler to McNamara, Jan. 21, 1907, Box 23, DP; McNamara to Munsey, Sept. 29, 1909, H. S. Hockin to McNamara, Oct. 13, 1909, Box 24, DP; Beum to McNamara, May 4, 1910, Charles Wachmeister to McNamara, May 23, 1910, Box 25, DP; Poushey to Drew, May 31, 1916, Box 17, DP.

56. Drew to H. S. Sanford, Oct. 28, 1914, Drew to J. A. G. Badorf, Jan. 18, 1915, Box 1, DP; Barrett to Hugh L. Kerwin, Dec. 16, 1920, File 170-1189, RG 280, NARA.

57. Grant, *Erectors' Association,* pp. 100–101; Drew to Gentlemen, Mar. 3, 1909, Box 14, DP.

58. Jacoby, "Norms and Cycles," p. 29; Stuart D. Brandes, *American Welfare Capitalism, 1880–1940* (Chicago: University of Chicago Press, 1976), p. 36 et passim;

Raynal C. Bolling, "The United States Steel Corporation and Labor Conditions," *Annals of the American Academy of Political and Social Science* 42 (July 1912): 38–47; David Brody, *Steelworkers in America: The Nonunion Era* (New York: Harper and Brothers, 1960), pp. 89, 169; *Iron Age* 81 (Jan. 9, 1908): 173.

59. NEA Minutes, Sept. 11, Nov. 24, 1908, Mar. 30, June 10, July 9, 29, Oct. 19, Nov. 1, 1909, Box 37A, Walsh Papers; Drew to Gentlemen, July 22, Sept. 22, 1909, Box 14, DP. Bridgemen received $25 per month for accident and sickness; the accidental death benefit was $125. Comparable benefits for bridgemen holding ordinary policies were $20 and $100.

60. Drew to Gentlemen, Sept 28, 1909, Box 29, DP; Drew to Sayward, Nov. 6, 1909, Box 11, DP; Assistant Commissioner to Dear Sir, Oct. 7, 1909, Box 29, DP.

61. Drew to C. D. Garretson, June 12, 1916, Drew to Lewis H. McLaughlin, Mar. 22, Apr. 30, 1917, Box 20, DP.

62. Drew to E. R. Cobb, Sept. 30, 1908, Box 6, DP. See, for example, NEA to Our Men, Feb. 26, Sept. 15, Oct. 22, 1908, Box 29, DP.

63. Drew to Gentlemen, Oct. 3, 1906, Drew to Members, Nov. 15, 1915, Box 14, DP; George Hagerty to Drew, Mar. 28, 1907, [Apr. 15, 1907], Box 23, DP; "To the Iron Workers of New York and Vicinity . . ." [Nov. 21, 1914], Box 8, DP; C. G. Myers to Drew, July 19, 1915, William J. De Groot to Drew, Oct. 30, Nov. 3, 1915, Drew to De Groot, Nov. 1, 1915, ibid.

64. Worden to Drew, Nov. 26, Dec. 7, 1915, Drew to Worden, Dec. 6, 1915, Box 8, DP.

65. NEA Minutes, June 10, 1916, Box 37A, Walsh Papers; C. A. Wass et al. to McClintic-Marshall Construction Co., May 5, 1916, Poushey to Drew, May 12, 14, 18, 19, 23, 31, June 2, 3, 5, 1916, Drew to Poushey, May 12, 15, 22, June 3, 1916, Drew to Worden, June 1, 1916, Drew to Brady, May 22, 1916, Brady to Drew, May 27, June 1, 2, 1916, Box 20, DP; Resolutions, May 26, 1916, Box 17, DP; Drew to Gentlemen, Aug. 16, 1916, Box 14, DP; *Bridgemen's Magazine* 16 (July 1916): 402, (Sept. 1916): 532–34.

66. Drew to Garretson, June 12, 1916, Drew to McLaughlin, Mar. 22, 1917, Box 20, DP; Drew to Johnson, Apr. 3, 1917, Box 17, DP; Drew to Brady, Apr. 26, 1917, and enclosure, Box 1, DP.

67. *NYT*, July 12–15, 17–20, 25, 27, 28, 1906; Excerpts, Drew to Mother and Father, July 12, 1906, Box 28, DP; Drew to Gentlemen, July 20, 1906, Box 14, DP; Minutes of Arbitration Board Conference Committee, July 12, 1906, Box 2, DP; Eidlitz and Hulse to Drew, May 1, June 6, 1907, Box 2, DP.

68. Ryan to Executive Board, July 24, 1906, Farrell to McNamara, July 31, 1906, Box 23, DP; Drew to Gentlemen, July 20, Oct. 3, 1906, Box 14, DP; Drew to Modern Steel Construction Co., July 19, 1906, Box 2, DP; *Bridgemen's Magazine* 6 (Aug. 1906): 6, 33.

69. Excerpts, Drew to Mother and Father, July 24, 1906, Box 28, DP; Drew to Gentlemen, Oct. 3, 1906, Box 14, DP; AIA Minutes, July 16, 1906, Box 1, DP; Strike Committee Minutes, July 23, 30, 1906, ibid.; AIA to Our Employees, July 25, 1906, ibid.; Ryan to Executive Board, July 24, 1906, Box 23, DP.

70. Excerpts, Drew to Mother and Father, July 24, 1906, Box 28, DP; Drew to Gentlemen [ILEA], Oct. 7, 1908, Box 14, DP; AIA Minutes, Aug. 2, 1906, Box 1, DP; Farrell to McNamara, July 31, 1906, Box 23, DP. Cf. Drew to Jobson and Hooker, Sept. 18, 1906, Box 2, DP.

71. Excerpts, Drew to Mother and Father, July 24, Aug. 7, 1906, Box 28, DP; Drew to Goff, Aug. 27, Oct. 31, 1906, Box 2, DP; Strike Committee Minutes, Aug. 20, 1906, Box 1, DP.

72. Strike Committee Minutes, Aug. 20, Sept. 4, Nov. 22, 1906, Box 1, DP; AIA Minutes, Dec. 12, 1906, ibid.; Drew to Hay Foundry and Iron Works, Sept. 27, 1906, Drew to Levinson and Co., Sept. 27, 1906, Drew to Hinkle Iron Works, Sept. 27, 1906, Box 2, DP; NEA Minutes, Dec. 12, 1906, Box 37A, Walsh Papers.

73. Drew to Gentlemen, Oct. 3, 1906, Box 14, DP; Drew to Lofland, Nov. 23, 1906, Drew to S. P. Mitchell, Nov. 23, 1906, Box 2, DP; AIA Minutes, Dec. 12, 1906, Box 1, DP; NEA Minutes, Nov. 20, 1906, Box 37A, Walsh Papers; *Bridgemen's Magazine* 6 (Nov. 1906): 6.

74. Drew to Gentlemen, Jan. 30, Mar. 4, Apr. 3, May 23, July 23, Sept. 18, 1907, Mar. 3, 1909, Box 14, DP; Drew to Jobson and Hooker, Mar. 1, 1907, Drew to Oscar Daniels, Apr. 4, 1907, Box 2, DP; McNamara to Dear Sir and Brother, Oct. 6, 1907, Box 23, DP; *Bridgemen's Magazine* 7 (May 1907): 254; Grant, *Erectors' Association,* p. 69.

75. *NYT,* Oct. 19, 1907; Drew to Gentlemen, Oct. 14, Nov. 26, 1907, Box 14, DP; McNamara to Dear Sir and Brother, Oct. 16, 1907, Webb to McNamara, June 15, 1908, Box 23, DP; NEA Minutes, Nov. 8, 1907, Box 37A, Walsh Papers; Grant, *Erectors' Association,* p. 70; *Bridgemen's Magazine* 8 (Oct. 1908): 725, 727, 729; Drew, "Strikes against the Open Shop," pp. 31–32.

76. Drew to Gentlemen, Jan. 25, 1910, Sept. 1, 9, Oct. 12, Dec. 15, 1910, Feb. 10, June 6, 1911, Aug. 13, 1912, Feb. 5, June 23, Dec. 16, 1916, Box 14, DP; Drew to W. B. Douglas, Mar. 19, 1914, Box 19, DP; Drew to George W. Geary, June 25, 1915, Box 4, DP; ILEA Minutes, Dec. 21, 1909, Oct. 26, 1910 (Special Meeting), Feb. 9, 1911, May 11, 1916, Box 37A, Walsh Papers; (ILEA) Conference, Jan. 11, 1916, ibid.; NEA Minutes, Oct. 25, 1910, ibid.; *NYT,* Oct. 7, 10, 17, 1911, July 27, 28, 1914, June 20, 22, July 12, 1915, May 11, 1916; *Bridgemen's Magazine* 11 (Dec. 1911): 865–69; ibid. 12 (Jan. 1912): 14, (Feb. 1912): 92; ibid. 13 (Mar. 1913): 259–60; ibid. 14 (Apr. 1914): 204–8; ibid. 16 (July 1916): 390–92, 399, 403, (Oct. 1916): 649–50, 747; Drew, "Conditions in the Structural Erection Industry," *Square Deal* 18 (Mar. 1916): 48.

77. Minutes of NEA General Meeting, May 29, 1914, Box 37A, Walsh Papers; Drew to Gentlemen, Jan. 25, 1910, Box 14, DP; Drew to L. C. Dilks, June 27, 1910, Box 15, DP; Barrett to Kerwin, Dec. 6, 1920, File 170-1189, RG 280. Three additional New York firms had become NEA members by the summer of 1921. [Drew] Statement to Federal Trade Commission, July 21, 1921, Box 7, DP.

78. Drew to Gentlemen, Jan. 30, Mar. 4, Apr. 30, May 23, 1907, June 22, July 28, Dec. 1, 1908, Oct. 12, 1910, Nov. 30, 1914, July 7, 1915, Box 14, DP; Brady to Cheney, Oct. 13, 1914, Box 4, DP; Drew to George Smart, Jan. 29, 1915, Box 1, DP; Lofland to Drew, June 11, 1906, Drew to Greiner, Nov. 20, 1906, Box 2, DP; Drew to W. A. Starrett, Jan. 29, 1909, Drew to W. B. McAllister, Nov. 4, 1914, Box 12, DP; Drew to R. R. Foley, Jan. 27, 1912, John S. Bland to Drew, Apr. 2, 1912, Drew to Bland, Apr. 4, 1912, Box 7, DP; Drew to Mitchell, Jan. 15, 1915, Box 15, DP; Drew to Michael, Jan. 12, 1915, Box 11, DP; NEA General Meeting Minutes, Box 37A, Walsh Papers; *Bridgemen's Magazine* 15 (Feb. 1915): 86, (Mar. 1915): 209.

79. Drew to Gentlemen, Mar. 4, Apr. 3, May 23, July 23, 1907, June 22, 1909, Box 14, DP; NEA Minutes, Nov. 8, 1907, Box 37A, Walsh Papers.

80. Osborn Engineering Co. to McClintic-Marshall Construction Co., July 24, 1909, C. D. Marshall to Drew, July 26, 1909, Drew to McClintic, July 27, 1909, Brady to

Drew, July 31, 1909, Drew to J. B. Bird, Aug. 9, 1909, Box 3, DP; Drew to Gentlemen, Nov. 15, 1909, Box 29, DP.

81. Brady to Drew, Aug. 9, 1909, Drew to Frank J. Farrell, Sept. 15, 1909, E. A. Roberts to Drew, Sept. 15, 22, 29, enclosing [*Cleveland Plain Dealer,* Sept. 15, 1909], Drew to Roberts, Sept. 16, 22, Oct. 1, 1909, Drew to McClintic, Sept. 27, 1909, Drew to Brady, Oct. 20, 1909, Drew to H. W. Lewis, Apr. 23, 1910, Box 3, DP; Drew to Gentlemen, Nov. 1, 1909, Box 14, DP; Drew to Gentlemen, Nov. 15, 1909, Box 29, DP.

82. Drew to Roberts, Apr. 20, 1910, Roberts to Drew, Apr. 22, 1910, Drew to Lewis, Apr. 23, 1910, Brady to Drew, Apr. 23, June 7, 9, 29, 1910, Drew to Brady, June 11, 1910, Box 3, DP.

83. Drew to Roberts, July 8, 1912, Apr. 10, 21, 1913, ibid.; Drew to Wagner, June 7, 1911, Box 9, DP; Drew to McAllister, Nov. 4, 1914, Box 12, DP.

84. NEA Minutes, Apr. 1, 1913, Box 37A, Walsh Papers; Drew to Lowe, Apr. 14, 1913, Box 1, DP; Drew to Berlin Construction Co., Oct. 29, 1913, Box 15, DP; Drew to Gentlemen, May 10, 1913, May 14, 1914, Box 14, DP; Drew to McAllister, Nov. 4, 1914, Box 12, DP; "The Cleveland Situation. . . ," Apr. 1, 1915, Box 4, DP; Drew to Roberts, Mar. 28, 1917, Box 3, DP.

85. NEA General Meeting Minutes, May 19, 1916, Box 37A, Walsh Papers; Building Trades Employers' Association, *Cleveland's Greatest Problem* [1917], pp. 3–7, Box 5, DP.

86. Minutes of the Chicago Federation of Labor, Nov. 4, 1906, Chicago Historical Society, Chicago, Illinois; Excerpts, Drew to Mother and Father, 1906, Box 28, DP; Drew to Lofland, Aug. 6, 1906, Drew to McClintic, Sept. 17, 1906, Drew to Mitchell, Nov. 23, 1906, Drew to Greiner, Nov. 20, 1906, Drew to Frank Barker, Jan. 28, 1907, Box 2, DP; Drew to Mitchell et al., Aug. 27, 1906, Box 14, DP; Drew to Gentlemen, Oct. 3, Nov. 6, 21, 1906, ibid.; Drew to J. K. Mumford, July 22, 1909, Box 18, DP; McNamara Circular Letter #94, Nov. 6, 1906, Ryan to J. H. Barry, Nov. 8, 1906, Box 23, DP.

87. Selig Perlman and Philip Taft, *History of Labor in the United States, 1896–1932* (New York: Macmillan Co., 1935), pp. 139–43; *Bridgemen's Magazine* 10 (Jan. 1910): 29–34; McNamara to E. A. Clancy, Dec. 9, 1909, Box 24, DP; McNamara to Executive Board, Feb. 22, 1910, Box 25, DP.

88. Drew to Gentlemen, Apr. 3, 1907, July 7, 1915, Box 14, DP; Drew to E. W. Krueger, Aug. 24, 1915, Box 9, DP; NEA Minutes, May 19, 1916, Box 37A, Walsh Papers; *Bridgemen's Magazine* 14 (Oct. 1914): 746; ibid. 15 (Jan. 1915): 6, (June 1915): 440, (July 1915): 462, (Sept. 1915): 618.

89. Blodgett to Drew, May 25, 1907, Drew to Blodgett, May 27, 1907, E. H. Connor to Drew, June 6, 1907, Drew to Mitchell, July 21, 1910, Box 9, DP.

90. Drew to Des Moines Bridge Co., Aug. 24, 1910, Drew to Midland Bridge Co., July 20, 1910, A. A. Troem to Drew, July 22, 1910, Drew to Mitchell et al., June 3, July 21, 1910, Drew to Joseph Furber, Aug. 15, 27, 1910, Furber to Drew, Aug. 31, 1910, Drew to Wagner, June 7, 1911, Drew to Connor, Jan. 3, Apr. 3, May 25, June 5, 1911, Connor to Drew, May 3, 1911, ibid.; NEA Minutes, Aug. 9, 1910, Box 37A, Walsh Papers.

91. NEA Minutes, Apr. 5, Sept. 24, 1912, Apr. 1, 1913, Box 37A, Walsh Papers; Drew to Badorf, Apr. 8, 1912, Box 3, DP; Drew to Poushey, Apr. 8, 1912, Drew to Kansas City Bridge Co., Feb. 3, 1913, Drew to Adams, Apr. 11, 17, 23, 1913, Adams to Drew, Apr. 15, 1913, Box 9, DP; Drew to Wagner, Apr. 19, 21, 1913, Box 5, DP.

92. Drew to Missouri Valley Bridge and Iron Co., Apr. 21, 1913, Drew to J. A. Hollinger, Apr. 15, 1913, Box 9, DP.

93. Constitution and By-Laws of the Building Construction Employers' Association of Kansas City, May 6, 1913, ibid.; Drew to Kansas City Bridge Co., June 2, 1913, Badorf to Drew, Sept. 13, 30, 1916, ibid.; Drew to G. H. Williams, June 23, 1913, Box 15, DP; Drew to Gentlemen, May 10, 1913, Box 14, DP; NEA Minutes, May 29, 1913, Box 37A, Walsh Papers.

94. NEA Minutes, June 22, 1906, Box 37A, Walsh Papers; Drew to Gentlemen, July 22, Oct. 3, 1906, Aug. 13, 1912, Box 14, DP; Excerpts, Drew to Mother and Father, 1906, Box 28, DP; Drew to Dear Sir, May 10, 1906, Box 2, DP; Drew to Mumford, July 22, 1909, Box 18, DP; Drew, "Between Employer and Employee," p. 17.

95. *Bridgemen's Magazine* 7 (May 1907): 262–63; *NYT,* Feb. 5, 20, May 20, 21, 30, 1909; Drew to Gentlemen, Jan. 15, 1909, Box 14, DP; *Iron Trade Review* 56 (Apr. 29, 1915): 855; *Square Deal* 16 (June 1915): 478.

96. *Bridgemen's Magazine* 10 (July 1910): 394, (Aug. 1910): 430; ibid. 15 (June 1915: 391, 439, (July 1915): 460, (Aug. 1915): 533; ibid. 16 (June 1916): 330, (Aug. 1916): 402; Drew to Executive Committee, June 29, 1915, Geary to Drew, July 16, 1915, Box 4, DP; Drew to Krueger, Aug. 24, 1915, Box 9, DP; Drew to Gentlemen, Feb. 15, 1916, Box 14, DP.

97. Drew to Kuehn, Jan. 14, 1916, Box 4, DP; Drew to Gentlemen, Feb. 15, Aug. 16, 1916, Box 14, DP; "Structural Erection Industry," p. 48; Chicago Federation of Labor Minutes, Mar. 7, 1915, Chicago Historical Society; Royal E. Montgomery, *Industrial Relations in the Chicago Building Trades* (Chicago: University of Chicago Press, 1927), pp. 46–47, 79–87. Cf. Drew to Geary, July 8, 1915, Box 4, DP. See chapter 1.

98. Commission on Industrial Relations, *Industrial Relations,* 6:5172–73, 5314; Michael Kazin, *Barons of Labor: The San Francisco Building Trades and Union Power in the Progressive Era* (Urbana: University of Illinois Press, 1987), pp. 30, 44; Frederick L. Ryan, *Industrial Relations in the San Francisco Building Trades* (Norman: University of Oklahoma Press, 1936), pp. 43, 103–4, 110, 113; William E. Hague to Johnson, July 25, 1916, Box 17, DP.

99. Robert Lee Knight, *Industrial Relations in the San Francisco Bay Area, 1900–1918* (Berkeley: University of California Press, 1960), p. 121; Kazin, *Barons of Labor,* p. 220; Drew to Gentlemen, Aug. 13, 1912, Box 14, DP; George S. McCallum to Drew, Nov. 22, 1913, Box 19, DP.

100. Knight, *San Francisco Bay Area,* pp. 302–17; Robert H. Frost, *The Mooney Case* (Stanford: Stanford University Press, 1968), pp. 58–60; Kazin, *Barons of Labor,* pp. 237–39; *American Industries* 17 (Dec. 1916): 17; Koster, "The Chamber of Commerce in Industrial Affairs," ibid. (Feb. 1917): 22–23; Drew to Gentlemen, Aug. 16, 1916, Box 14, DP; James A. Emery, "The Story of San Francisco," *Review* 14 (Feb. 1917): 45–55; Stephen C. Levi, "The Battle for the Eight-Hour Day in San Francisco," *California History* 57 (Winter 1978–79): 344–45, 349.

101. Drew to Douglas, Mar. 19, 1914, Drew to Michael, Oct. 20, 1916, Box 19, DP; Report of Commissioner, May 25, 1917, Box 37A, Walsh Papers; Levi, "Eight-Hour Day," pp. 343–44, 348, 350–52; Knight, *San Francisco Bay Area,* pp. 286–87, 301, 320–22, 323.

102. Drew to Constance Meese, Nov. 24, 1916, Box 19, DP; H. M. Webster to NEA, Jan. 22, 1917, Box 11, DP.

103. *Pacific Coast Mechanic* 6 (Nov. 1912): 1067–70, in Box 17, DP; Drew to P. N. Beringer, Mar. 29, 1911, Box 19, DP; Drew to Gentlemen, Apr. 6, 1911, Drew to

Members, Jan. 9, 1913, Box 14, DP; George S. Boudinot to Drew, Jan. 8, 1913, Drew to McClintic, Jan. 24, 1913, Box 17, DP; John Kirby to C. W. Post, June 13, 1911, Box 1, C. W. Post Papers, Bentley Historical Library, Ann Arbor, Michigan; Kazin, *Barons of Labor,* pp. 219–21, 228–29.

104. Drew, "Between Employer and Employee," p. 117; Drew to Gentlemen, Jan. 30, Mar. 4, July 23, Oct. 14, 1907, May 16, July 28, 1908, Jan. 15, Mar. 3, 1909, Box 14, DP; Drew to Douglas, Mar. 19, 1914, Box 19, DP.

105. McNamara to Charles Smith, Jan. 14, 1908, Ed Clark to McNamara, Apr. 5, 1908, McNamara to Clark, Apr. 7, 1908, Webb to McNamara, Mar. 11, 1908, J. T. Butler to McNamara, Apr. 27, 1908, Box 23, DP; William Green to McNamara, July 17, 1908, McNamara to Members, Feb. 26, 1909, Box 24, DP; *Bridgemen's Magazine* 7 (Oct. 1907): 664; ibid. 8 (Oct. 1908): 725–37, 743, 753, 759–60; ibid. 13 (May 1913): 390; Grant, *Erectors' Association,* p. 69; Transcript of Hearing on Code . . . of Structural Steel and Iron Fabricating Industry, Oct. 30, 1933, p. 192, Box 7241, Records of the National Recovery Administration, RG 9, NARA.

106. Leo Wolman, *The Growth of American Trade Unions, 1880–1923* (New York: National Bureau of Economic Research, 1924), pp. 110–11, 131; "The Common Welfare," p. 1410; *Bridgemen's Magazine* 13 (May 1913): 390; ibid. 16 (Oct. 1916): 687; Report of Commissioner, May 25, 1917, Box 37A, Walsh Papers.

107. Grant, *Erectors' Association,* pp. 17–18, 26–27; *Iron Trade Review* 77 (July 23, 1925): 221; Drew to Massilon Bridge Co., Feb. 15, 1915, Box 15, DP; Drew to Ziesing, July 30, 1912, Box 1, DP; Drew to Ferry Heath, Apr. 16, 1930, Box 7, DP; Drew, "Between Employer and Employee," p. 117, Box 29, DP; Drew, "Open and Closed Shop," p. 703.

108. Holt, "Trade Unionism in the British and U.S. Steel Industries, 1880–1914," *Labor History* 8 (Winter 1977): 34.

109. Report of Commissioner, May 25, 1917, Box 37A, Walsh Papers; Drew, "Open and Closed Shop," p. 703; Drew to Whitney, Feb. 28, 1917, Box 8, DP.

Chapter 4

1. On this point, see Luke Grant, *The National Erectors' Association and the International Association of Bridge and Structural Ironworkers* (Washington, 1915), p. 109.

2. Statement of George E. Davis. . . , Oct. 4, 1913, pp. 9–10, 124, Box 6, DP; H. H. McClintic to Drew, Sept. 15, 1906, Box 2, DP; J. J. McCray to Frank E. Ryan, Mar. 14, 1907, Box 23, DP; F. K. Painter to McNamara, May 16, 1910, Charles Becker to McNamara, Aug. 9, 1910, Box 25, DP; Autobiography of Robert J. Foster, undated, pp. 91–92, Box 22, DP; Grant, *Erectors' Association,* pp. 115–17.

3. J. A. Robinson to McNamara, July 29, 1906, P. F. Farrell to McNamara, Aug. 13, 1906, Box 22, DP; Jack [J. T.] Butler to McNamara, Jan. 10, 1907, Charles Smith to McNamara, Feb. 4, 1907, Jan. 13, 1908, McNamara to Smith, Feb. 9, 1907, M. J. Hannon to McNamara, Sept. 30, 1907, Box 23, DP; J. E. Munsey to McNamara, Oct. 16, 1909, P. J. Houlihan to McNamara, Dec. 16, 1908, Box 24, DP; Edward Smythe to McNamara, Mar. 31, 1910, McNamara to Smythe, Apr. 1, 1910, McNamara to William J. Collins, Jan. 7, 1911, Box 25, DP; Ryan to McNamara, Feb. 20, 1911, Box 26, DP; Drew, "Facts Tending to Show. . . ," undated, Box 12, DP; *Bridgemen's Magazine* 8 (Oct. 1908): 710–11.

4. "Assaults Upon Non-Union Foremen and Men" [1912], Box 2, DP; undated list of assaults and dynamitings, Box 6, DP; Subcommittee of Senate Committee on the

Judiciary, *Limiting Federal Injunctions,* 62 Cong., 2 sess., 1912, Part 2, pp. 221–26; Ryan to W. H. Maddox, Aug. 20, 1906, Box 22, DP; Ryan to McNamara, Dec. 11, 1906 (and enclosed clipping), McNamara to Ryan, Mar. 15, 1907, Box 23, DP; Smythe to Ryan, Apr. 28, 1910, Box 25, DP; Brady to Drew, Aug. 8, 1909, Aug. 11, 1910, July 26, 1911, Nov. 26, 1913, Dec. 22, 1915, Box 2, DP; E. A. Roberts to Drew, June 18, 1914, Box 3, DP; Drew to Gentlemen, Dec. 15, 1910, Box 14, DP; Memoranda in Connection with . . . Violence . . . in . . . Cleveland Destrict [Feb. 1918?], Box 5, DP; Foster autobiography, pp. 91–92, Box 22, DP; Grant, *Erectors' Association,* pp. 130–31.

5. Maurice J. Breen to McNamara, Mar. 5, 7, 1907, McCray to McNamara, Mar. 14, 1907, Box 23, DP; Munsey to McNamara, June 9, 13, 16 (and enclosed clippings), Nov. 6, 8, 1909, McNamara to Munsey, Nov. 17, 1909, Box 24, DP; Hannon to McNamara, July 12, 1910, Box 25, DP.

6. Cooley to McNamara, Nov. 17, 21, 23, 1910, Box 25, DP; Cooley to McNamara, Dec. 6, 8, 13, 1910, Harry Jones to McNamara, Jan. 20, 1911, Ryan to McNamara, Feb. 20, 1911, Box 26, DP; U.S. District Court, District of Indiana, United States vs. Frank Ryan, et al. No. 3-Consolidated, No. 43 (Nov. 20, 1912): 11569–70, Box 34, DP; Foster autobiography, pp. 92–93, Box 22, DP.

7. Rhodri Jeffreys-Jones, *Violence and Reform in American History* (New York: New Viewpoints, 1978), p. 68; J. A. G. Badorf, "In Reference to Slattery," June 29, 1909, Box 19, DP; Memoranda in re Thomas Slattery, Oct. 5, 1913, ibid.; Memoranda re Dan Jewart case, n.d., ibid.; [Badorf] to E. F. Sherk, Mar. 18, 1912, Drew to Milliken Brothers, Oct. 27, 1913, Edward W. Booker to C. E. Cheney, Dec. 17, 1917, John E. Rooney to Cheney, Dec. 26, 1917, ibid.

8. Cuyahoga County Common Pleas Court, Robert Elsemore vs. IABSIW, June 25, 1906, Box 3, DP; William J. Boetcker to Badorf, June 8, 9, 1911 (and enclosure), Drew to James A. Emery, Sept. 3, 1912, A. Bentley and Sons to Drew, Sept. 7, 1912, Drew to Elihu Root, Sept. 5, 1912, ibid.; Bordan to International Association, June 4, 1906, Elsemore to International Association, June 4, 1906, Frank Mulholland to McNamara, July 24, 1905, McNamara to Ryan, June 8, 23, Aug. 8, 1906, Feb. 22, 1907, McNamara to Dear Sir and Brother, June 8, 1906, Buchanan to McNamara, June 28, 1906, McNamara to Mulholland, July 26, 1906, Box 22, DP; Decision of Executive Board. . . , June 7, 1906, ibid.; Charles Smith to McNamara, Feb. 8, 9, 1907, A. G. Newcomb to McNamara, Feb. 21, 1907, McNamara to Ryan, Mar. 14, 1907, Box 23, DP; P. J. Smith to McNamara, Dec. 10, 1910, Box 26, DP; Memoranda in Connection with Violence . . . in . . . Cleveland . . . [Feb. 1918?], Box 5, DP; Drew, *Deeds against Words* [1912], Box 29, DP; Drew testimony [1912], Box 29, DP.

9. Excerpts, Drew to Mother and Father, Jan. 22, 1907, Box 28, DP; Drew to [J. J.] Bernet, Jan. 19, 1907, Drew to Alex Laughlin, Jan. 18, 1907, Feb. 27, 1908, H. D. Meskinen to Drew, Jan. 19, 1906 [1907], Feb. 16, 1907, Drew to Franklin W. Barker, Jan. 28, 1907, J. W. Hunter to Drew, Jan. 30, 1907, Brady to Drew, Feb. 16, 1908, Nov. 24, 1910, Box 2, DP; Brady to Drew, Mar. 2, 1908, Box 5, DP; Drew to Gentlemen, Jan. 30, 1907, Feb. 1, 1910, Box 14, DP.

10. Davern to McNamara, Feb. 14, Apr. 19, 1907, McNamara to Davern, Feb. 15, Mar. 18, 1907, McNamara to E. A. Clancy, Feb. 16, 1907, Clancy to McNamara, Mar. 10, 1907, Box 23, DP; Drew to Laughlin, Feb. 16, 1907, Laughlin to Drew, Feb. 13, 24, 1908, [Meskinen] to Drew, Mar. 24, 1907, Charles Taylor to Drew, Feb. 10, 1908, Drew to Taylor, Feb. 11, Apr. 14, 1908, Jan. 31, 1912, Drew to John W. Poushey, Aug. 5, 1909, June 23, July 25, 1910, Drew to Ryle, June 27, July 1, Dec. 31, 1910, Drew to H.

F. Lofland, July 14, 1910, Drew to Roberts, Dec. 2, 1910, Drew to Judson R. Harmon, Dec. 19, 1910, Box 2, DP; Brady to Drew, Dec. 19, 1910, Aug. 26, 1914, Oct. 18, 1915, Drew to John Wilson Hart, July 13, 1910, Jan. 5, 1912, Hart to Drew, Feb. 5, 1912, Paul Kieffer to Drew, Dec. 21, 1912, Oct. 13, 1914, Sept. 9, 1915, Drew to Brady, Oct. 14, 26, 1915, Drew to Thomas Lee Woolwine, Oct. 11, 13, 15, 1915, Woolwine to Drew, Oct. 13, 14, 1915, Box 5, DP; "Shall Davern Be Paid?" [1915?], ibid.; Minutes of the NEA Executive Committee (hereafter NEA Minutes), Mar. 11, 1907, Box 37A, Frank P. Walsh Papers, New York Public Library, New York, New York; Drew to Gentlemen, Feb. 13, 1908, Box 14, DP.

11. E. Brown to Badorf, Nov. 24, 27, 1909, Drew to Edward Hobday, May 29, 1911, Drew to Roberts, Mar. 11, 1910, James A. Johnson to F. W. Cohen, May 22, 24, July 10, 1911, Cohen to Drew, May 26, June 10, 11, 13, July 10, Aug. 10, 1911, Brady to Drew, Apr. 24, May 26, 1909, Aug. 3, 11, 1910, May 1, 16, 24, 26, June 1, 2, 13, 15, 26, 29, Aug. 11, Nov. 6, 1911, June 24, July 1, 29, 1912, Oct. 5, Nov. 26, 28, 1913, Oct. 17, 1914, Jan. 23, Feb. 15, Nov. 15, 1915, Drew to Brady, Nov. 28, 1913, Brady to Badorf, Dec. 11, 1912, H. A. Greene to Drew, Aug. 15, 1911, Box 2, DP; [*Cleveland Plain Dealer,* Nov. 6, 1911], Mar. 13, 1911, clippings in ibid.; [*Cleveland News,* Nov. 26, 1913], clipping in ibid.; "Assaults" [1912], ibid.; Drew to Roberts, June 2, 1913, Box 3, DP; T. B. Van Dorn to Drew, Apr. 27, 1909, Brady to Drew, May 9, 1910, Greene to Brady, Feb. 25, 1908, Box 5, DP; Committee on Labor Disputes, *Violence in Labor Disputes* [June 15, 1915], ibid.; idem., *Second Report,* Jan. 25, 1916, ibid.; Memoranda in Connection with . . . Violence . . . in . . . Cleveland, ibid.; Drew to Gentlemen, Feb. 13, 1908, Drew to H. A. Wagner, Dec. 16, 1914, Box 14, DP; U.S. vs. Ryan, No. 30 [Nov. 2, 1912]: 6010–15, 6015–24, No. 32 (Nov. 6, 1912): 7048–53, No. 43 (Nov. 20, 1912): 10721–50, Box 34, DP; McNamara to H. W. Legleitner, Sept. 18, 1909, Box 24, DP; *Bridgemen's Magazine* 10 (Oct. 1910): 689.

12. NEA Minutes, Feb. 7, 1908, Box 37A, Walsh Papers; Drew to Gentlemen, Feb. 1, 1910, Box 14, DP; Drew to W. J. Springborn [Mar. 2, 1908], Box 5, DP; Committee on Labor Disputes, *Violence,* pp. 3, 6; Drew to Roberts, Mar. 11, 1910, Drew to Jay P. Dawley, Nov. 25, 1910, Drew to Hobday, May 29, 1911, Johnson to Cohen, June 16, 1911, Brady to Drew, June 16, 1911, Drew to Brady, July 12, 1911, Brady to Munson Havens, July 31, 1911 (and enclosure), Box 2, DP; "Operative Special," Jan. 23, 1915, ibid.

13. Butler to McNamara, July 11, 1906, Box 22, DP; Drew to Harmon, Dec. 19, 1910, Drew to Roberts, Apr. 11, 1910, Brady to Drew, May 2, 1911, Drew to Brady, May 31, June 5, 1911, Dec. 31, 1913, Drew to Cohen, Jan. 5, July 13, 1911, Drew to Mitchell, July 6, 1911, Badorf to Drew, July 8, 1911, Drew to Chicago Bridge and Iron Co., July 1, 1911, Drew to Greene, Feb. 26, 1914, Greene to Drew, Mar. 12, 1914, Box 2, DP; Drew to Brady, Feb. 25, 1909, Dec. 19, 1910, Apr. 21, 1913, Brady to Badorf, May 14, 1909, Brady to Drew, July 11, 13, 28, 1911, Drew to Roberts, Apr. 21, 1913, Box 3, DP; T. B. Van Dorn Company to Drew, Jan. 12, Apr. 27, May 8, 1909, Poushey to Drew, Aug. 14, 1909, Drew to Van Dorn Iron Works, Aug. 29, 1910, Drew to Brady, Aug. 29, 1910, Box 5, DP; Drew to J. K. Mumford, July 22, 1909, Box 18, DP; Foster to Drew, Apr. 22, 1913, Box 7, DP.

14. Brady to Drew, July 1, 1911, Feb. 15, 1915, Drew to Mitchell, July 6, 1911, Brady to Havens, July 31, 1911, Box 2, DP; [*Cleveland Plain Dealer,* July 11, 1911], clipping in ibid.; Brady to Drew, Feb. 19, 1910, Aug. 11, 1911, Drew to C. L. McKenzie, Jan. 20, 1910, Havens to Drew, June 12, 27, 1911, Drew to Havens, June 23, 1911, Feb.

26, 1913, Mar. 26, 27, 1915, Drew to Greene, Mar. 29, 1915, Drew to Brady, Mar. 24, 1915, ibid.; Resolution adopted by . . . Cleveland Chamber of Commerce, June 27, 1911, ibid.; Committee on Labor Disputes, *Violence;* idem, *Second Report.*

15. Badorf to Drew, July 8, 1911, Box 3, DP; Cohen to Drew, July 10, 1911, Badorf to Drew, July 11, 1911, Drew to Austin Gavin, July 8, 1911, Gavin to Drew, July 12, 1911, Drew to Cohen, July 6, 13, 1911, McKenzie to Drew, July 7, 1911, Box 2, DP.

16. Drew to Roberts, Mar. 11, 1910, Brady to Drew, May 5, 1911, Van Dorn to Drew, Oct. 6, 1911, Box 2, DP; Brady to Drew, Feb. 19, 1910, Box 5, DP.

17. Cohen to Drew, June 13, July 10, 1911, Box 2, DP; E. A. Gibbs to Drew, Mar. 29, 1915, Box 5, DP.

18. Subcommittee of Senate Committee on the Judiciary, *Federal Injunctions,* Part 2, pp. 206–7; Drew, "National Secret Service. . . ," *Square Deal* 8 (July 1911): 529–30; "List of Depredations," undated, Box 6, DP; Drew to G. L. Peck and John Kirby, Jr., Feb. 3, 1911, Box 18, DP; Charles W. Miller to Attorney General, Feb. 6, 1912, File 15677, Records of the Department of Justice, RG 60, NARA.

19. Drew to C. Edwin Michael, Oct. 31, 1913, Box 15, DP; Drew to Peck and Kirby, Feb. 3, 1911, Box 18, DP; "List of Depredations"; Drew, "National Secret Service," p. 529.

20. *Review* (Mar. 1913): 28; U.S. vs. Ryan et al., No. 35 (Nov. 9, 1912): 8519–22, 8545, 8576–81, No. 44 (Nov. 21, 1912): 11364, Box 34, DP; Drew to Miller, Oct. 21, 1911, File 15677, RG 60; "List of Depredations"; undated list, Box 12, DP; Drew to Peck and Kirby, Feb. 3, 1911, Box 18, DP; Drew to John B. Lewis, Mar. 18, 1914, Box 6, DP; Drew, "National Secret Service," p. 530.

21. Drew to Gentlemen, Feb. 1, 1910, Box 14, DP; Drew to Peck and Kirby, Feb. 3, 1911, Box 18, DP; Drew to William Hilhouse, Apr. 3, 1911, Box 4, DP; Drew to Editor, Harper's Magazine, Nov. 25, 1931, Box 9, DP; Irving Stone to James B. McNamara, Sept. 10, 1940, Box 9, James B. and John J. McNamara Papers, University of Cincinnati Library, Cincinnati, Ohio; Fitch, "The Dynamite Case," *Survey* 29 (Feb. 1913): 612, 615; Grant, *Erectors' Association,* pp. 109–10; Walter V. Woehlke, "Terrorism in America," *Outlook* 100 (Feb. 17, 1912): 361; Taft and Ross, "American Labor Violence," in Ted Robert Gurr and Hugh Davis Graham, eds., *Violence in America* (New York: Bantam Books, 1969), pp. 282, 319, 380.

22. Weed, "Preliminary Report on Violence," Part 1, p. 86; Records of the Commission on Industrial Relations, in Records of the Department of Labor, RG 174, NARA; Louis Adamic, *Dynamite: The Story of Class Violence in America,* rev. ed. (New York: Viking Press, 1934), p. 194; *Indianapolis Star,* Dec. 31, 1912.

23. *Bridgemen's Magazine* 8 (Oct. 1908): 725, 727; U.S. vs. Ryan, No. 38 (Nov. 14, 1912): 9070, No. 47 (Nov. 25, 1912): 12038, Box 34, DP; Drew to F. E. Schmitt, July 17, 1909, Box 18, DP; Drew, "Facts Tending to Show"; Adamic, *Dynamite,* pp. 193–94. See chapter 3 for the local option issue.

24. Subcommittee of Senate Committee on the Judiciary, *Federal Injunctions,* Part 2, p. 204; Drew to Mumford, July 22, 1909, Box 18, DP; Drew to A. M. Blodgett, Apr. 21, 1908, Box 9, DP; Drew to Gentlemen, July 15, 28, 1910, Box 14, DP.

25. Cohen to Drew, July 15, 1909, Box 6, DP; Drew to Peck and Kirby, Feb. 3, 1911, Box 18, DP; Drew to Roberts, Oct. 19, 1911, Box 5, DP; Wagner to Drew, Aug. 24, 1910, Drew to Wagner, Aug. 27, 1911, Box 12, DP; NEA Minutes, Oct. 25, 1910, Mar. 28, 1911, Box 37A, Walsh Papers; McNamara to P. J. Morris, Mar. 11, 1910, Box 25, DP; C. Smith to McNamara, Mar. 7, 1911, Box 26, DP; Drew, "National Secret Service," p. 530; Grant, *Erectors' Association,* p. 123.

26. Drew, "Facts Tending to Show"; Wagner to Drew, Aug. 24, 1910, Box 12, DP; McNamara to W. R. Brown, Aug. 25, 1909, Box 24, DP.

27. Statement of Albert Von Spreckelsen, May 8, 1911, Box 31, DP; undated list, Box 12, DP; U.S. vs. Ryan, No. 20 (Oct. 22, 1912): 2544, Box 33, No. 43 (Nov. 20, 1912): 10964–81, Box 34, DP.

28. "List of Depredations"; Munsey to McNamara, Dec. 24, 1909, Box 24, DP; McNamara to Munsey, Mar. 29, 1910, McNamara Circular to Executive Board, Apr. 14, 1910, Box 25, DP; U.S. vs. Ryan, No. 58 (Nov. 28, 1912): 13148–67, Box 35, DP; Statement of R. H. Johnson, May 18, 1911, Box 30, DP; Subcommittee of Senate Committee on the Judiciary, *Federal Injunctions,* Part 2, pp. 211–12.

29. Subcommittee of Senate Committee on the Judiciary, *Federal Injunctions,* Part 2, p. 208; "List of Depredations"; Painter to McNamara, May 11, 1910, Box 25, DP; A. J. Allen to Drew, Mar. 29, 1911, Box 7, DP; Statement of James Ferry, May 22, 1911, Box 30, DP; Statement of Wallace Marshall, May 5, 1911, ibid.; Marshall to Allen, Mar. 24, 1911, ibid.; Statement of George Caldwell, May 3, 1911, Box 31, DP; Caldwell testimony, undated, ibid.; *Bridgemen's Magazine* 10 (Oct. 1910): 678.

30. U.S. vs. Ryan, No. 45 (Nov. 22, 1912): 11692–93, Box 34, DP; Drew to Gentlemen, Oct. 12, 1910, Box 14, DP; Drew to Roberts, Mar. 27, 1911, Box 3, DP; *American Industries* 10 (Dec. 1909): 59; Leo Wolman, *The Growth of American Trade Unions, 1880–1923* (New York: Bureau of Economic Research, 1924), p. 126; Grant, *Erectors' Association,* pp. 124–26, 138. See chapter 5.

31. U.S. vs. Ryan, No. 4 (Oct. 4, 1912): 802, Box 32, No. 28 (Oct. 31, 1912): 5108, No. 29 (Nov. 1, 1912): 5173–74, No. 36 (Nov. 11, 1912): 8637–38, Box 34, DP; Memorandum, Dec. 24, 1910, Box 4, DP; Memorandum of Evidence, undated, Box 6, DP; August Bussow to McNamara, July 18, Aug. 6, 1907, McNamara to Bussow, July 22, 30, 1907, McNamara to Dear Sir and Brother, Oct. 6, 1907, Webb to McNamara, Oct. 10, 1907, Jan. 14, 1908, McNamara to Ryan, Oct. 12, 22, 1907, Jan. 16, 1908, Ryan to McNamara, Oct. 16, 1907, Webb to Ryan, Oct. 25, 1907, Ryan to Webb, Nov. 7, 1907, Box 23, DP; McNamara to Webb, Aug. 7, 1908, Box 24, DP; *NYT,* Nov. 25, Dec. 5, 1911, Oct. 22, 1912.

32. McNamara to Murray L. Pennell, Mar. 4, 1911, Box 26, DP; Drew to J. A. Hunter (Badorf), Oct. 30, Nov. 23, 1911, Box 3, DP; U.S. vs. Ryan, No. 15 (Oct. 16, 1912): 1529–30, Box 33, No. 40 (Nov. 16, 1912): 9671, 9673–74, 9695–96, No. 47 (Nov. 25, 1912): 12050, Box 34, DP; *NYT,* Apr. 26, Dec. 22, 1911; *Los Angeles Times,* Nov. 12, 1915; William J. Burns, *The Masked War* (New York: George H. Doran Co., 1913), pp. 221–22.

33. William Bernhardt to McNamara, Feb. 15, 1908, Box 23, DP; Munsey to McNamara, Nov. 8, 1909, McNamara to Munsey, Nov. 17, 1909, Box 24, DP; C. L. Schilling to McNamara, Feb. 25, 1911, McNamara to Schilling, Mar. 2, 1911, Box 26, DP.

34. Webb to Ryan, Oct. 25, 1907, Ryan to Webb, Nov. 7, 1907, Ryan to Michael J. Cunnane, June 5, 1908, Box 23, DP; McNamara to John T. Fitzpatrick, Aug. 17, 1910, Box 25, DP.

35. U.S. vs. Ryan, No. 35 (Nov. 9, 1912): 8433–44, No. 36 (Nov. 11, 1912): 8745–46, Box 34, DP; Farrell to McNamara, Feb. 3, 1908 (and enclosed clipping), Webb to McNamara, Mar. 8, 1908 (and enclosed clipping), C. Smith to McNamara, Jan. 13, 1908, Box 23, DP; Cunnane to McNamara, Jan. 29, 1909 (and enclosed clipping), Box 24, DP; McNamara to Legleitner, July 25, 1910, Box 25, DP; Schilling to McNamara, Feb. 25, 1911, Box 26, DP; Memorandum of Evidence, undated, Box 6, DP; undated sheets, Box 17, DP; *Bridgemen's Magazine* 10 (June 1910): 333–34.

36. McNamara to Dear Sir and Brother, Oct 6, 1907, Bernhardt to McNamara, Oct. 22, 1907, Ed Clark to McNamara, Feb. 25, 1908, Box 23, DP; Fred Mooney to McNamara, Aug. 3, 1910, Box 25, DP; "List of Depredations"; *Bridgemen's Magazine* 10 (Oct. 1910): 617–732. For the Slattery resolution (Resolution No. 200, Sept. 19, 1910), see Box 19, DP.

37. McManigal's Extended Statement, undated, Box 30, DP; Hockin to McNamara, Aug. 7, 1907, Box 23, DP; U.S. vs. Ryan, No. 35 (Nov. 9, 1912): 8387–88, 8420, Box 34, DP; *Detroit Free Press,* June 26–28, 1907; Grant, *Erectors' Association,* p. 123. The Extended Statement is a composite of McManigal's confession and his trial testimony. For the 1903 Russel Wheel strike, see Thomas A. Klug, "The Roots of the Open Shop: Employers, Trade Unions, and Craft Labor Markets in Detroit, 1859–1907" (Ph.D. diss., Wayne State University, 1993), pp. 781–82.

38. Statement of George E. Davis, Oct. 4, 1914, pp. 1–8, Box 6, DP; Ryan to Webb, Nov. 7, 1907, Webb to Ryan, Oct. 20, 1907, Box 23, DP.

39. Davis Statement, pp. 12–40, 46–57, Box 6, DP; "List of Depredations"; undated sheets, Box 17, DP.

40. Davis Statement, pp. 27, 57–58, 61–75, Box 6, DP; undated list, ibid.; Drew to Gentlemen, June 22, July 28, Sept. 15, 1908, Box 14, DP; Report of Badorf. . . , June 18, 1908, Box 16, DP; Commonwealth vs. George O'Donnell. . . , Nov. 17–19, 1908, Box 31, DP; John Golden to Ryan, Apr. 28, 1908, Box 23, DP; McNamara to Webb, Aug. 14, 1908, Webb to McNamara, Oct. 14, 1908, Box 24, DP.

41. McManigal's Extended Statement, pp. 8–16, 39, 51, Box 30, DP; Drew to Peck, Aug. 30, 1912, Box 18, DP; "List of Depredations"; Geoffrey Cowan, *The People vs. Clarence Darrow* (New York: Times Books, Random House, 1993), pp. 79–88; Autobiography of James B. McNamara, pp. 118–19, and addendum, pp. 92–96, Robert Cantwell Papers, University of Oregon Library, Eugene, Oregon.

42. McManigal's Extended Statement, pp. 97–102, 134–35, Box 30, DP; U.S. vs. Ryan, No. 36 (Nov. 11, 1912): 8629, No. 38 (Nov. 14, 1912): 8968, Box 34, DP.

43. McManigal's Extended Statement, pp. 147–48, Box 30, DP; *Bridgemen's Magazine* 10 (Aug. 1910): 436; Grace Heilman Stimson, *Rise of the Labor Movement in Los Angeles* (Berkeley: University of California Press, 1935), p. 37; Frederick Palmer, "Otistown of the Open Shop," *Hampton's Magazine* 26 (Jan. 1911): 31, 33.

44. *Los Angeles Times,* Oct. 3–5, 9–11, 13, 1929; Stimson, *Los Angeles,* pp. 104–22, 255–56, 258, 289; Palmer, "Otistown," pp. 35–42.

45. "An Informal History of the Iron Workers" (reprinted from the *Ironworker,* 1971), p. 13, copy in my possession; Palmer, "Otistown," p. 41; *Bridgemen's Magazine* 10 (Oct. 1910): 615; ibid. 11 (Oct. 1911): 754–55; Commission on Industrial Relations, *Industrial Relations. Final Report and Testimony,* 64 Cong., 1 sess., S. Doc. 415, 1916, 6:5569–71, 5625–26, 5629; Stimson, *Los Angeles,* pp. 339–40.

46. Robert Edward Lee Knight, *Industrial Relations in the San Francisco Bay Area, 1900–1918* (Berkeley: University of California Press, 1960), pp. 226–27; Stimson, *Los Angeles,* pp. 290, 314, 334–35, 340–42; *Bridgemen's Magazine* 7 (Oct. 1907): 646; ibid. 8 (Sept. 1908): 541–42; ibid. 10 (Apr. 1910): 230, (Oct. 1910): 615; McNamara to Clancy, Apr. 28, May 26, 1910, Ryan to Albert J. Berres, May 6, 1910, Box 25, DP.

47. *Bridgemen's Magazine* 10 (July 1910): 381, (Oct. 1910): 658; Commission on Industrial Relations, *Industrial Relations,* 6:5551–52; Tveitmoe to McNamara, July 26, 1910, Box 25, DP; *Los Angeles Times,* Oct. 14, 1929; Palmer, "Otistown," p. 39; Robert Gottlieb and Irene Wolt, *Thinking Big: The Story of the Los Angeles Times* (New York: G. P. Putnam's Sons, 1977), pp. 82–83.

48. Clancy to McNamara, June 3, 7, 1910, Hendricks to McNamara, June 11, 1910, McNamara to Berres, Aug. 27, 1910, Box 25, DP; Decision of Executive Board . . . , Aug. 11, 1910, ibid.; *Bridgemen's Magazine* 10 (Aug. 1910): 435–36, (Oct. 1910): 614–15.

49. Hendricks to McNamara, Dec. 9, 1909, Box 24, DP; Clancy to McNamara, June 3, 1910, Ryan to McNamara, June 10, 1910, McNamara to Clancy, June 25, 1910, McNamara to J. H. Barry, July 25, 1910, Barry to McNamara, July 26, 1910, Box 25, DP.

50. *Bridgemen's Magazine* 10 (Aug. 1910): 436, (Oct. 1910): 658–60; Commission on Industrial Relations, *Industrial Relations,* 6:5561–63, 5798–5801, 5807, 5842; Tveitmoe to Ryan, Sept. 3, 1910, Timmons to Ryan, Sept. 3, 1910, Box 25, DP; *Los Angeles Times,* Oct. 14, 1929; Stimson, *Los Angeles,* pp. 341–44; Palmer, "Otistown," p. 41; Adamic, *Dynamite,* pp. 208–9; Irving Stone, *Clarence Darrow for the Defense* (Garden City, N.Y.: Garden City Publishing Co., 1943), pp. 269–70; Lloyd Hustveld, "O. A. Tveitmoe: Labor Leader," *Norwegian-American Studies* 30 (1985): 32–33.

51. Tveitmoe to McNamara, July 26, Aug. 30, 1910, Clancy to McNamara, June 7, 1910, Hendricks to McNamara, June 11, 1910, Berres to McNamara, Aug. 18, 1910, Box 25, DP; *Bridgemen's Magazine* 10 (July 1910): 381–82, (Oct. 1910): 658; ibid. 11 (Oct. 1911): 755–57.

52. Timmons to Ryan, Sept. 3, 1910, Box 25, DP; Statement by William H. Reed, undated, p. 194ff., Box 31, DP; *Bridgemen's Magazine* 10 (Nov. 1910): 739–40; U.S. vs. Ryan, No. 38 (Nov. 14, 1912): 9233–35; Commission on Industrial Relations, *Industrial Relations,* 6:5521; Stimson, *Los Angeles,* pp. 345, 348, 366–68; Gottlieb and Wolt, *Thinking Big,* p. 85. Cf. Palmer, "Otistown," p. 42.

53. Stimson, *Los Angeles,* pp. 375, 381–82; U.S. vs. Ryan, No. 41 (Nov. 18, 1912): 9943–47, 9950–52, Box 34, DP; Burns, *Masked War,* pp. 45–53; Cowan, *Darrow,* p. 87.

54. Michael Kazin, *Barons of Labor: The San Francisco Building Trades and Union Labor in the Progressive Era* (Urbana: University of Illinois Press, 1987), pp. 206–7; U.S. vs. Ryan, No. 38 (Nov. 14, 1912): 9225, Box 34, DP; McManigal, *The National Dynamite Plot* (Los Angeles: Neale Co., 1913), pp. 1, 80–81; *Indianapolis Star,* Dec. 19, 1912; Drew to Oscar Lawler, Apr. 12, 1912, Box 10, DP; Drew to Harry A. Flynn, Dec. 26, 1933, Box 13, DP; Drew to D. H. Creider, May 9, 1911, Box 14, DP; *Iron Trade Review* 54 (Mar. 19, 1914): 53. Cf. U.S. vs. Ryan, No. 46 (Nov. 23, 1912): 11966–67, Box 34, DP; and *Los Angeles Times,* Oct. 16, 1929.

55. McManigal's Extended Statement, pp. 150, 236, 265–66, 271, Box 30, DP; U.S. vs. Ryan, No. 44 (Nov. 21, 1912): 11245, 11357, Box 34, No. 49 (Nov. 27, 1912): 12919–20, Box 35, DP; Munsey to McNamara, May 29, 1909, McNamara to Munsey, June 3, 1909, Box 24, DP; McManigal, *Dynamite Plot,* pp. 79–81; Stimson, *Los Angeles,* pp. 369, 371–72, 376; *Bridgemen's Magazine* 10 (Dec. 1910): 510; *Los Angeles Times,* Oct. 14, 16, 1929; Palmer, "Otistown," p. 42.

56. McManigal's Extended Statement, pp. 328–29, 330, 334–44, 353, 360–61, Box 30, DP; Webb to McNamara, Feb. 22, Mar. 30, 1911, Box 26, DP; Lofland to Drew, Mar. 31, 1911, Box 6, DP; "List of Depredations"; Davis Statement, Oct. 4, 1913, pp. 90–98, 105–7, ibid.; U.S. vs. Ryan, No. 44 (Nov. 21, 1912): 11362, No. 45 (Nov. 22, 1912): 11564, No. 47 (Nov. 25, 1912): 12065–67, Box 34, DP; Burns, *Masked War,* p. 299.

57. Drew to Gentlemen, Apr. 15, 1908, Box 14, DP; U.S. vs. Ryan, No. 28 (Oct. 31, 1912): 4999–5000, Box 34, DP; NEA Minutes, Oct. 2, 1906, Box 37A, Walsh Papers.

58. NEA Minutes, Mar. 1, Apr. 9, Nov. 8, 1907, Apr. 14, May 15, June 19, Sept. 11, 1908, Box 37A, Walsh Papers; Minutes of Meeting of Finance Committee, May 15,

1908, ibid.; Drew to Wagner, Feb. 19, May 16, 1908, Box 12, DP; Lofland to Drew, Apr. 20, June 2, 1908, Box 1, DP; Drew to Lofland, May 1, 1908, Box 6, DP; Drew to Wagner, Aug. 27, 1910, Box 12, DP; Excerpts, Drew to Mother and Father, Jan. 6, 1908, Box 28, DP.

59. Drew to Wagner, May 16, Oct. 12, 1908, Box 12, DP; Drew to Lofland, June 1, 1908, Box 1, DP; Drew to Gentlemen, May 16, 1908, Box 14, DP; NEA Minutes, June 19, 1908, Box 37A, Walsh Papers.

60. NEA Minutes, June 19, Sept. 11, 1908, Box 37A, Walsh Papers; Drew to Gentlemen, July 28, Sept. 15, 1908, Box 14, DP; Drew to Lofland, May 1, June 25, 1908, Drew to Phoenix Bridge Company, June 16, 1908, Drew to William H. Medley, June 18, 19, 24, 1908, Medley to Drew, Aug. 23, 28, 1908, G. C. Ives to Drew, June 20, 1908, Drew to John Sterling Deans, July 1, 7, 8, 1908, James H. Swift to Drew, Sept. 18, 28, 1908, Drew to Swift, Oct. 31, Dec. 8, 1908, Jan. 8, 1909, Badorf to Drew, Sept. 21, 1908, Swift to Badorf, Nov. 21, Dec. 7, 1908, Mar. 23, 1909, Medley to Badorf, Nov. 25, 1908, Box 6, DP; "June 16, 1908," ibid.; Badorf Report, June 18, 1908, ibid.; Thiel Report, June 18, 1908, ibid.

61. Drew to Lofland, June 25, 1908, Box 6, DP; Drew to Wagner, Oct. 12, 1908, Box 12, DP; Drew to Gentlemen, May 16, 1908, Box 14, DP; Drew to Ida M. Tarbell, Apr. 1, 1915, Box 18, DP.

62. Drew to Lofland, June 25, 1908, Box 6, DP; NEA Minutes, July 24, Sept. 1, 1908, Aug. 9, 1910, Box 37A, Walsh Papers.

63. NEA Minutes, Mar. 30, July 9, 29, Oct. 19, 1909, Aug. 9, 1910, Box 37A, Walsh Papers; Drew to Wagner, Oct. 12, 1908, July 7, 1909, Aug. 27, 1910, Drew to E. W. Heyl, Aug. 10, 1910, Box 12, DP; Drew to Wagner, July 12, 1909, McKenzie et al. to S. P. Mitchell et al., June 11, 1909, Drew to Mitchell, June 23, 1909, Box 14, DP; Drew, "National Secret Service," p. 530; *Los Angeles Times,* Nov. 24, 1915.

64. McManigal's Original Confession, pp. 8–9, Box 30, DP; U.S. vs. Ryan, No. 46 (Nov. 23, 1912): 11933–12051, Box 34, No. 51 (Nov. 29, 1912): 13728–57, No. 52 (Nov. 30, 1912): 13874–75, 13900–13907, 13911–12, 13928–30, Box 35, DP; Drew to Emery, June 25, 1912, Box 4, DP; "List of Depredations"; Stimson, *Los Angeles,* pp. 386–87; *Square Deal* 9 (Jan. 1912): 538; *NYT,* Dec. 2, 1911; Subcommittee of Senate Committee on the Judiciary, *Federal Injunctions,* Part 2, p. 207; Burns, *Masked War,* pp. 45–46, 49–53.

65. U.S. vs. Ryan, No. 48 (Nov. 26, 1912): 12935–36, No. 52 (Nov. 30, 1912): 13901–2, 13904–5, Box 35, Nos. 74, 75, (Dec. 25, 26, 1912): 20154–55, Box 36, DP; Hockin to Drew, Mar. 24, 1918, Box 12, ibid.

Chapter 5

1. *NYT,* Oct. 5, 1910; Drew to A. J. Allen, Oct. 31, 1910, Box 6, DP.

2. Minutes of the NEA Executive Committee (hereafter NEA Minutes), Oct. 25, 1910, Jan. 9, 1911, Box 37A, Frank Walsh Papers, New York Public Library, New York, New York; Drew to S. P. Mitchell et al., Jan. 18, Feb. 8, 1911, Box 14, DP. At the October 25 NEA meeting Central District members, including American Bridge and McClintic-Marshall, agreed to contribute their pro rata share of $50–75,000 per year and called for a membership meeting to consider the matter.

3. Drew to Peck and Kirby, Feb. 3, 1911, Box 18, DP; NEA Minutes, Mar. 28, 1911, Box 37A, Walsh Papers.

4. There were eight dynamitings in these three months. See "List of Depredations," undated, Box 6, DP.

5. Drew to Gentlemen, Oct. 12, 1910, Apr. 6, 1911, Box 14, DP; Drew to Peck, Mar. 29, 31, 1911, Box 18, DP.

6. NEA Minutes, Mar. 28, May 3, 1911, Box 37A, Walsh Papers; Minutes of General Meeting, Mar. 28, 1911, ibid.; Drew to Peck, Mar. 29, 1911, Box 18, DP; C. E. Cheney to Gentlemen, Mar. 30, May 4, 1911, Box 29, DP; Mitchell to Drew, May 4, 1911, Box 14, DP.

7. NEA Minutes, Oct. 25, 1910, Jan. 9, 1911, Box 37A, Walsh Papers; Fred W. Cohen to Drew, Oct. 26, 1910, Box 14, DP; Drew, "Facts Tending to Show . . . ," undated, Box 12, DP; Drew to Darius Miller, Oct. 6, 1911, Box 18, DP.

8. Drew to H. H. McClintic, Nov. 10, Dec. 22, 27, 1910, McClintic to Drew, Dec. 23, 1910, Drew to Mitchell and C. L. McKenzie, Dec. 15, 1910, Drew to Mitchell et al., Dec. 15, 1910, Box 5, DP; NEA Minutes, Jan. 9, 1911, Box 37A, Walsh Papers.

9. NEA Minutes, Oct. 25, 1910, Jan. 9, 1911, Box 37A, Walsh Papers; H. F. Lofland to Cheney, Nov. 11, 1910, Drew to McClintic, Nov. 15, 1910, Box 14, DP; Drew to C. J. Smith, Dec. 12, 1910, Drew to H. A. Wagner, Dec. 28, 1910, Drew to Cohen, Jan. 20, 1911, Box 4, DP; Drew to Allen, Oct. 31, 1910, Box 6, DP; Drew, *The Crime of the Century and Its Relation to Politics* (Aug. 1912), p. 14, Box 29, DP; Grace Heilman Stimson, *Rise of the Labor Movement in Los Angeles* (Berkeley: University of California Press, 1955), p. 378. The Peoria clue, actually, helped Burns to determine the responsibility for the *Times* bombing.

10. William J. Burns, *The Masked War* (New York: George H. Doran Co., 1913), pp. 202–4; Commission on Industrial Relations, *Industrial Relations. Final Report and Testimony,* 64 Cong., 1 sess., 1916, S. Doc. 415, 11: 10767–78; Statement of Samuel S. Gerber, p. 181, Statement of Martin J. Hyland, p. 187, Index of Testimony, Box 31, DP; American Federation of Labor, *Report of Proceedings of the Thirty-First Annual Convention, Nov. 13–25, 1911* (New York: Labor Reporter Printing Service, 1911), p. 294; Robert Gottlieb and Irene Wolt, *Thinking Big: The Story of the Los Angeles Times* (New York: G. P. Putnam's Sons, 1977), p. 92; *Indianapolis Star,* Apr. 23, 1911.

11. For the Haywood-Moyer-Pettibone episode, see Melvyn Dubofsky, *We Shall Be All* (Chicago: Quadrangle Books, 1969), pp. 96–100. For the union allegations, see *NYT,* Mar. 24, 1911; AFL, *Proceedings, 1911,* pp. 72, 293; Harry Jones to H. L. Hockin (and enclosed resolution), Apr. 28, 1911, Box 26, DP; Minutes of the Chicago Federation of Labor, May 7, 1911, Chicago Historical Society, Chicago, Illinois; Conference on the McNamara Case, June 25, 1911, Reel 119, American Federation of Labor Records: The Gompers Era, University of Michigan Library, Ann Arbor, Michigan; Ira Kipnis, *The American Socialist Movement, 1897–1912* (New York: Columbia University Press, 1952), pp. 349–51; *Bridgemen's Magazine* 8 (Mar. 1908): 194–95; ibid. 11 (May, 1911): 265; "Informal History of the Iron Workers," p. 21 (reprinted from the *Ironworker,* 1971), copy in my possession; "The Los Angeles Conspiracy against Organized Labor," *International Socialist Review* 11 (Nov. 1910): 262–64; Eugene Debs, "The McNamara Case and the Labor Movement," ibid. 12 (Jan. 1912): 399–400; Herbert Shapiro, "The McNamara Case: A Window on Class Antagonism in the Progressive Era," *Southern California Quarterly* 70 (Spring 1988): 69; Gottlieb and Wolt, *Thinking Big,* p. 104; and Drew to August Ziesing, May 26, 1911, Drew to H. R. Brady, May 26, 1911, Box 4, DP. For the Taylor Arcade case, see chapter 4.

12. Drew to Mother, May 6, 1911, Box 28, DP; Drew to Burns, June 20, 1914, Box 14, DP; Drew to Harris Weinstock, May 18, 1915, Box 20, DP; John M. Lynch and

Frank Duffy to Thomas Marshall, May 31, 1911, Henry Seyfried to Frank L. Mulholland, May 25, 1911, Reel 73, AFL Records; *Bridgemen's Magazine* 11 (May 1911): 260–61, 282, (June 1911): 328–29; AFL, *Proceedings, 1911,* pp. 293–94; Commission on Industrial Relations, *Industrial Relations,* 11:10768; NAM, *Proceedings of the Sixteenth Annual Convention, May 15–17, 1911,* p. 158; *Indianapolis Star,* Apr. 23, 24, 27, 1911.

13. *NYT,* Apr. 25–27, 1911; *Square Deal* 9 (Nov. 1911): 321; Drew to Mother, Apr. 30, May 6, 1911, Box 28, DP; Drew to Dear Sir, May 1, 1911, Box 18, DP; Duffy to Gompers, Apr. 25–27, 1911, Thomas Homan to Duffy, May 3, 1911, Reel 73, AFL Records; U.S. District Court, District of Indiana, United States vs. Frank M. Ryan, et al., No. 3-Consolidated, No. 25 (Oct. 28, 1912): 3776–89, Box 33, No. 28 (Oct. 31, 1912): 4999–5000, Box 34, DP; *Indianapolis Star,* Apr. 25, 27, 1911.

14. Duffy to Gompers, May 6, June 3, 1911, Lynch and Duffy to Marshall, May 31, 1911, Lynch and Duffy to S. L. Shenk, May 31, 1911, Reel 73, AFL Records; Drew to Dear Sir, May 1, 1911, Box 31, DP; Drew to Mother, May 6, 1911, Box 28, DP; document signed by Kirby, May 1, 1911, Box 1, C. W. Post Papers, Bentley Historical Library, Ann Arbor, Michigan.

15. Duffy to Gompers, May 6, 1911, Seyfried to Gompers, June 16, 1911, Reel 73, AFL Records; W. A. Ketcham to Employers' Association, Dec. 27, 1911, Box 7, DP; Drew to Burns, June 20, 1914, Box 4, DP; *NYT,* June 18, July 23, 1911, Jan. 12, 16, 1912; *Bridgemen's Magazine* 11 (May 1911): 272–73, (June 1911): 328–29, (July 1911): 536.

16. I have reconstructed the details of the search from various sources, not all of them in full agreement. See U.S. vs. Ryan, No. 23 (Oct. 25, 1912): 3322, 3324–26, 3337–82, No. 24 (Oct. 26, 1912): 3728, No. 25 (Oct. 28, 1912): 3782–83, 3792, Box 33, DP, No. 27 (Oct. 30, 1912): 4575–78, The Huntington, San Marino, California, No. 52 (Nov. 30, 1912): 13918–22, No. 53 (Dec. 2, 1912): 14286–330, Box 35, No. 66 (Dec. 17, 1912): 18447–52, Box 36, DP; Statement of Harry Graff, p. 182, Hyland statement, p. 187, Index of Testimony, Box 31, DP; Memoranda of Suggestions. . . , with Drew to Ferdinand Winter, Oct. 3, 1911, Box 20, DP; Lynch and Duffy to Shenk, May 3, 1911, Ryan to Members, Apr. 25, 1911, Reel 73, AFL Records; *NYT,* Apr. 23, July 22, 1911; *Bridgemen's Magazine* 11 (May 1911): 263–64, 265; Burns, *Masked War,* pp. 205–7; Autobiography of Robert J. Foster, undated, p. 105, Box 22, DP; *Indianapolis Star,* Apr. 23, 1911; and Geoffrey Cowan, *The People vs. Clarence Darrow* (New York: Times Books, Random House, 1993), pp. 103–6.

17. Burns, *Masked War,* pp. 204–5, 208, 211–12; *NYT,* Apr. 24, 1911; Statement of Patrick Dugan, Apr. 28, 1911, Box 30, DP; Statement of Otto Simon, p. 180, Statement of D. Jones, p. 182a, Hyland statement, p. 187, Index of Testimony, Box 31, DP; U.S. vs. Ryan, No. 23 (Oct. 25, 1912): 3322–24, Box 33, No. 27 (Oct. 30, 1912): 4430–38, 4583–89, 4593, The Huntington, No. 39 (Nov. 15, 1912): 9412–15, Box 34, No. 52 (Nov. 30, 1912): 13925–26, Box 35, DP; *Indianapolis Star,* Apr. 23, 24, 1911; Drew to Mother, May 6, 1911, Box 28, DP; *Square Deal* 9 (Nov. 1, 1911): 321.

18. Drew to D. H. Creider, May 19, 1911, Mitchell to Drew, May 4, 1911, Box 14, DP; Drew to Dear Sir, May 1, 1911, Box 18, DP; NEA Minutes, May 3, 1911, Box 37A, Walsh Papers; E. A. Gibbs to McClintic, May 2, 1911, ibid.; Gompers to Frank Morrison, May 2, 1911, Reel 73, AFL Records; Memorandum on McNamara Case [May 10, 1911], ibid.; Auditing Committee report, Apr. 27, 1912, Reel 74, ibid.; *NYT,* May 1, 1911; *Bridgemen's Magazine* 11 (July 1911): 404–8; Philip Taft, *The A.F. of L. in the Time of Gompers* (New York: Harper and Brothers, 1957), pp. 279–80.

19. [Lofland] to McKenzie, May 6, 1911, McKenzie to Drew, Apr. 27, June 25, 1911, Lofland to Drew, May 6, 1911, J. C. Stewart to Lofland, May 30, 1911, Drew to Raynal C. Bolling, June 1, 1911, Drew to McKenzie, June 26, 1911, Box 18, DP; [Drew] Memorandum for [W. J.] Jackson, May 12, 1911, ibid.

20. [Drew] to Dear Sir, May 1, 1911, ibid.; Drew to Creider, May 19, 1911, Box 14, DP; Drew statement, Aug. 16, 1911, with Kirby to Post, Sept. 6, 1911, Box 1, Post Papers.

21. NEA Minutes, May 16, June 27, 1911, Box 37A, Walsh Papers; Gibbs to Mc-Clintic, May 2, 1911, ibid.; Creider to Cheney, May 9, 1911, Drew to Mitchell, Aug. 22, 1911, Drew to Wagner, Sept. 23, 1913, Secretary to Wagner, Apr. 26, 1912, Box 14, DP; E. P. Rippelyer to Drew, Aug. 1, 1911, Peck to Drew, Aug. 14, 1911, Drew to Peck, Aug. 19, 1911, Aug. 30, 1912, Drew to D. Miller, Aug. 19, 24, 1911, Drew to Julius Kruttschnitt, Oct. 18, 30, 1911, Box 18, DP; Kirby to Post, Sept. 6 (and enclosure), 23, 1911, Box 1, Post Papers; Post to James Emery, Sept. 19, 1911, Box 2, ibid.

22. NEA Minutes, July 18, 1911, Box 37A, Walsh Papers; Badorf to Drew, Aug. 16, Sept. 5, 1911, Box 3, DP; Drew to D. Miller, Oct. 6, 1911, Drew to Peck, Aug. 30, 1912, Box 18, DP; Emery to Post, Oct. 10, 1911, Box 1, Post Papers; Drew statement, Aug. 16, 1911, with Kirby to Post, Sept. 6, 1911, ibid.; A. I. McCormick to Attorney General (hereafter AG), Sept. 20, 1911, File 15677, Records of the Department of Justice, RG 60, NARA; "Oscar Lawler, Los Angeles Attorney," p. 112, Oral History Project, 1962, University of California at Los Angeles, Los Angeles, California.

23. NEA Minutes, May 16, 1911, Box 37A, Walsh Papers; Drew to Burns, May 15, 1911, Drew to Emery, Jan. 29, 1913, Box 4, DP; Drew to Burns, Nov. 24, 1911, Drew to J. A. Hunter (Badorf), Nov. 24, 1911, Box 3, DP; Drew to Mitchell, Oct. 11, 1911, Box 14, ibid.

24. Gibbs to McClintic, May 2, 1911, Box 37A, Walsh Papers; NEA Minutes, May 3, 16, 1911, ibid.; Mitchell to Drew, May 4, 1911, Box 14, DP; Mitchell to Drew, May 8, 1911, Box 12, DP; Drew to Burns, May 18, 1911, Box 4, DP; Drew to Executive Committee, May 19, 1911, Box 6, DP; Badorf to Drew, Aug. 30, 1911, Box 3, DP; *NYT,* Aug. 15, 1911; Stimson, *Los Angeles,* p. 391.

25. Drew to C. Miller, Aug. 19, 1911, Box 18, DP; Badorf to Drew, Aug. 16, 17, 21, 23, 28, 30, Sept. 5, 19, Oct. 5, 1911, Mar. 12, 1913, Box 3, DP; Foster to Drew, Oct. 18, 1911, Box 7, DP; Drew statement, Aug. 16, 1911, Box 1, Post Papers; *NYT,* Apr. 24, Dec. 5, 1911; *Square Deal* 9 (Nov. 1911): 321; *Bridgemen's Magazine* 11 (Oct. 1911): 564. For the witness statements gathered by Badorf, see Boxes 30, 31, DP.

26. Drew to J. E. Munson (Badorf), Aug. 21, 1911, Drew to Allen, Apr. 17, 1916, Box 3, DP; R. Foster to Drew, Sept. 8, 9, 12, 14, 15, 16, 18, 22, Oct. 6, 7, 18, 1911, Drew to R. Foster, Sept. 20, 1911, Box 7, DP; Drew to C. Miller, Oct. 6, 1911, Box 18, ibid.; Drew to Mitchell, Oct. 11, 1911, Box 14, DP; Foster autobiography, pp. 95, 110–11, Box 22, DP; Statement of B. John Cooke, Sept. 9, 1911, Box 30, DP.

27. *NYT,* Apr. 25, 1911; *Bridgemen's Magazine* 11 (May 1911): 264–65; U.S. vs. Ryan, No. 25 (Oct. 28, 1912): 3393–97, 4009–10, 4014, Box 33, No. 53 (Dec. 2, 1912): 14300–14303, Box 35, DP; Hyland statement, p. 187, Index of Testimony, Box 31, ibid.

28. Clifton J. Phillips, *Indiana in Transition: The Emergence of an Industrial Commonwealth, 1880–1920* (Indianapolis: Indiana Historical Bureau, Indiana Historical Society, 1968), pp. 344, 347; Hanch to Drew, Oct. 18, 1911, Box 7, DP; Foster autobiography, p. 106, Box 22, DP.

29. Gibbs to McClintic, May 2, 1911, Box 37A, Walsh Papers; NEA Minutes, May 16, 1911, ibid.; Drew to Dear Sir, May 1, 1911, Box 18, DP; Confidential Note to Mr.

Harding [July 1911], ibid.; Drew to C. Foster, June 27, 1911, Drew to R. Foster, Sept. 22, 1911, Hanch to Drew, Oct. 18, 1911, Box 7, DP; Drew to Winter, Sept. 28, 1911, Box 20, DP; *NYT,* Apr. 28, May 3, 1911.

30. *NYT,* Apr. 25, 28, 1911; Drew to Dear Sir, May 1, 1911, Mitchell to Drew, May 4, 1911, Box 18, DP; C. C. Shirley to Walter Marmon, Feb. 7, 1912, Box 19, DP; Gibbs to McClintic, May 2, 1911, Box 37A, Walsh Papers.

31. Gibbs to McClintic, May 2, 1911, Box 37A, Walsh Papers; Drew to Badorf, May 27, 1911, Badorf to Drew, May 13, 19, 28, 1911, Box 3, DP; Drew to Dear Sir, May 1, 1911, Box 18, DP; R. Foster to Drew, Sept. 2, 13, 14, 17, 26, 27, 30, Oct. 7, 1911, undated, Drew to R. Foster, Oct. 13, 1911, R. Foster to Badorf, July 6, 1911, Drew to Hanch, Sept. 22, Oct. 17, 1911, Hanch to Drew, Sept. 26, 1911, Box 7, DP; Drew to Winter, Aug. 28, 1911, Box 20, DP; Shirley to Drew, July 12, 1911, Shirley to Marmon, Feb. 7, 1912, Box 19, DP; Foster autobiography, p. 106, Box 22, DP; U.S. vs. Ryan, No. 25 (Oct. 28, 1912): 3997–99, Box 33, DP; *NYT,* Apr. 25, Oct. 1, 1911. See the witness statements in Boxes 30, 31, DP.

32. Drew to Mitchell, Jan. 8, 1911, Drew to C. Foster, June 27, 1911, July 2, 1912, C. Foster to Drew June 29, 1911, Hanch to Drew, Sept. 26, 1911, Box 7, DP; Drew to Shirley, July 14, 1911, Box 19, DP; Drew to Badorf, Oct. 11, 1911, Badorf to Drew, Mar. 2, 1913, Box 3, ibid.; *NYT,* June 18, 1911; *Square Deal* 8 (July 1911): 536–37; *NYT,* May 17, 1911.

33. Confidential Note to Harding [July 1911], Box 18, DP; Badorf to Drew, May 19, 1911, Drew to Badorf, July 11, 1911, May 15, 1912, Box 3, DP; R. Foster to Drew, July 20, 1910 [1911], Sept. 23, Oct. 5, 14, 1911, Hanch to Drew, Sept. 26, 1911, Box 7, DP; Foster autobiography, pp. 108–9, Box 22, DP; Statement of John R. Harrington, Feb. 19, 1912, pp. 23–24, Box 30, DP; U.S. vs. Ryan, No. 28 (Oct. 28, 1912): 4002–3, Box 33, DP, No. 27 (Oct. 30, 1912): 4447–53, The Huntington; *NYT,* Apr. 28, 1911.

34. Foster autobiography, pp. 107–10, Box 22, DP; R. Foster to Badorf, July 11, 1910 [1911], July 6, 1911, R. Foster to Cheney, May 17, 1911, R. Foster to Drew, Oct. 1, 7, 1911, undated, C. Foster to Drew, Aug. 10, 1911, Box 7, DP.

35. Hanch to Drew, July 21, Oct. 21, 1911, Drew to Hanch, Sept. 11, 1911, R. Foster to Drew, Oct. 2, 1911, Box 7, DP; Badorf to Drew, July 19, 1911, Drew to Badorf, July 19, 1911, Box 3, DP; Drew to Winter, Oct. 5, 1911, Box 20, DP; Harrington statement, Feb. 19, 1912, p. 22, Box 30, DP.

36. Baker had objected to Shirley's presentation of the motion since he was serving as a deputy prosecutor. Badorf to Drew, July 20, 1911, Box 3, DP.

37. Badorf to Drew, July 20, 1911, ibid.; Winter to Drew, Aug. 30, Sept. 29, Oct. 6, 1911, Drew to Winter, Sept. 7, 28, Oct. 3 (and enclosed Memoranda of Suggestions), 4, 1911, Box 20, DP; Hanch to Drew, July 21, Sept. 8, 1911, Drew to Hanch, Sept. 1, 1911, Foster to Drew, Oct. 5, 1911, Box 7, DP; Drew to D. Miller, Oct. 6, 1911, Box 18, DP; Foster autobiography, p. 112, Box 22, DP; *Square Deal* 9 (Jan. 1912): 522–23.

38. Drew to Mitchell, Oct. 11, 1911, Box 14, DP; Drew to Winter, Oct. 4, 9, 17, 1911, Winter to Drew, Oct. 4, 24, 1911, Drew to Hanch, Oct. 16, 1911, Box 20, DP; Hanch and Drew to C. Foster, Oct. 4, 1911, Hanch to Drew, Oct. 13, 1911, R. Foster to Drew, Oct. 10, 12, 14, 17, 23, 1911, undated, Drew to R. Foster, Oct. 24, 1911, Box 7, DP; Drew to Badorf, Nov. 24, 1911, Box 3, DP; Drew to C. Miller, Oct. 20, 21, 1911, C. Miller to AG, Nov. 6, 1911, Drew to William P. Harr, Oct. 17, 20, 1911, File 15677, RG 60; Motion by Leo Rappaport. . . , Oct. 18, 19, 1911, ibid.; U.S. vs. Ryan, No. 23 (Oct. 25, 1912): 3428–29, Box 33, DP.

39. *Square Deal* 10 (Mar. 1912): 143–44; R. Foster to Drew, Oct. 26, 1911, Box 7,

DP; C. Miller to AG, Nov. 9, 1911, File 15677, RG 60; Hockin to J. McNamara, Oct. 27, 1911, Box 10, James B. and John J. McNamara Papers, University of Cincinnati Library, Cincinnati, Ohio; Foster autobiography, pp. 115–17, Box 22, DP; Foster taped statement [1960], Box 36, DP. There is a slight difference between the two retrospective Foster accounts of the bank story, but they more or less agree in principle.

40. Drew to D. Miller, Oct. 6, 1911, Box 18, DP; R. Foster to Drew, Oct. 26, 1911, Box 7, DP; Diary-like entries, Oct. 27, 1911, ibid.; Drew to Mitchell et al., Oct. 11, 1911, Drew to Executive Committee, Nov. 21, 1911, Box 14, DP; Badorf to Drew, Nov. 30, 1911, Box 3, DP; U.S. vs. Ryan, Nos. 72, 73 (Dec. 24, 25, 1912): 19927–30, Box 36, DP; Edward H. Schmidt to AG, Nov. 7, 1911, C. Miller to AG, Nov. 9, 1911, File 15677, RG 60; *NYT,* Oct. 29, Dec. 3, 1911; *Bridgemen's Magazine* 11 (Dec. 1911): 876–77.

41. Hockin to J. McNamara, Aug. 22, Sept. 30, Oct. 3, 27, Nov. 1, 13, 1911, Box 10, McNamara Papers; Hanch to Drew, Dec. 2, 1911, Box 7, DP; People of California vs. Clarence Darrow, No. 7374 Reporter's Transcript, No. 22 (Mar. 3, 1913): 3655–56, Box 31, DP; *Los Angeles Times* (hereafter *LAT*), Aug. 1, 1912; Alfred Cohn and Joe Chisolm, *"Take the Witness!"* (New York: Frederick M. Stokes Co., 1934), pp. 201–2; Kevin Tierney, *Darrow* (New York: Thomas Y. Crowell, 1979), p. 243; Cowan, *Darrow,* pp. 196–97, 400–404. For various explanations of the McNamara guilty pleas, see Stimson, *Los Angeles,* pp. 402–7; Gottlieb and Wolt, *Thinking Big,* pp. 96, 99–100; Robert Cleland, *California in Our Time (1900–1940)* (New York: Alfred A. Knopf, 1947), p. 84; *Square Deal* 9 (Jan. 1912): 530; *The Autobiography of Lincoln Steffens* (New York: Harcourt, Brace and Co., 1931), pp. 660–89; People vs. Darrow, No. 22, pp. 3689–740, Box 31, DP; *NYT,* Dec 2, 3, 1911; Christopher Connolly, "The Saving of Clarence Darrow," *Collier's* 48 (Dec. 23, 1911): 9–10; Herbert Shapiro, "Lincoln Steffens and the McNamara Case: A Progressive Response to Class Conflict," *American Journal of Economics and Sociology* 38 (Oct. 1980): 399–400; and Cowan, *Darrow,* pp. 249–50, 435–37, 479n.

42. Drew to Fredericks, Nov. 25, 1911, Drew to Hunter (Badorf), Nov. 25, 1911, Box 3, DP; Drew to Fredericks, Dec. 4, 1911, Box 11, DP; People vs. Darrow, No. 22, pp. 3760–66, 3802–3, Box 31, DP; Lawler to Wickersham, Dec. 6, 1911, File 15677, RG 60; Charles Yale Harrison, *Clarence Darrow* (New York: Jonathan Cape and Harrison Smith, 1931), pp. 165–66; *NYT,* Dec. 2–4, 1911. See Gottlieb and Wolt, *Thinking Big,* p. 98, for the allegation that Fredericks had been pressured by the NEA.

43. Graham Adams, Jr., *Age of Industrial Violence, 1910–15* (New York: Columbia University Press, 1966), pp. 17–18; *Bridgemen's Magazine* 12 (Feb. 1912): 256; Emery to Post, Dec. 20, 1911, Box 1, Post Papers; NAM, *Proceedings, 1911,* pp. 158–59; Badorf to Drew, Mar. 21, 1912, Box 3, DP.

44. Drew to Badorf, Oct. 11, 1911, Box 3, DP; Drew to E. Gerber, Dec. 6, 1911, Ziesing to Drew, Dec. 4, 1911, Box 1, DP; Drew to Shirley, July 24, 1911, Box 19, DP; Drew to Winter, Sept. 28, 1911, Box 20, DP; Drew to Hanch, Oct. 16, 1911, Box 7, DP; undated clipping in Drew Scrapbook No. 2, DP; Emery to Post, Oct. 10, 1911, Box 1, Post Papers; *NYT,* Dec. 3, 5, 1911.

45. Memoranda for Conference with AG [Oct. 1911], Box 12, DP; Drew to Winter, Sept. 7, 28, Oct. 2, 3, 9, 1911, Box 20, DP; McCormick to AG, Sept. 20, 1911, Lawler to Wickersham, Sept. 21, 1911, Fredericks to Wickersham, Sept. 21, 1911, Wickersham to McCormick, Sept. 25, 1911, File 15677, RG 60; Transcript of Message. . . , Sept. 28, 1911, ibid.

46. Harr to AG, Sept. 28, 1911, McCormick to AG, Sept. 20, 21, 1911, Harr to McCormick, Sept. 26, 1911, Wickersham to Harr, Sept. 29, 1911, Wickersham to

McCormick, Oct. 10, 1911, Wickersham to Lawler, Oct. 10, 1911, Wickersham to C. Miller, Oct. 9, 1911, File 15677, RG 60; Partial List of Witnesses. . . , undated, ibid.; Transcript of Message. . . , Sept. 28, 1911, ibid.; Wickersham to Drew, Oct. 10, 1911, Drew to Wickersham, Oct. 6, 16, 1911, Badorf to Drew, Oct. 5, 1911, Box 3, DP; Diary-like entries, Oct. 5, 7, 1911, Box 7, DP; Drew to D. Miller, Oct. 6, 1911, Box 18, DP; Drew to Winter, Oct. 2, 3, 4, 6, 9, 1911, Box 20, DP; C. Miller to Drew, Oct. 3, 1911, Box 12, DP; Memoranda for Conference [Oct. 1911], ibid.; Drew to Mitchell et al., Oct. 11, 1911, Box 14, DP.

47. Drew to R. Foster, Oct. 13, 1911, Box 7, DP; C. Miller to Drew, Oct. 13, 1911, Drew to C. Miller, Oct. 16, 1911, Box 12, DP.

48. *NYT,* Oct. 17, 1911; "List of Depredations"; Shapiro, "McNamara Case," pp. 86–91; Cohn and Chisolm, *Witness,* pp. 198–201; Louis Adamic, *Dynamite,* rev. ed. (New York: Viking Press, 1934), p. 244; Otis to Taft, Oct. 12, 1911, Otis to Charles Hilles, Oct. 16, 1911, Reel 410, William Howard Taft Papers, University of Michigan Library; Cowan, *Darrow,* pp. 471–72n.; Lawler to Wickersham, Oct. 23, 1911, File 15677, RG 60; Drew to Kruttschmitt, Oct. 18, 30, 1911, Box 18, DP.

49. Badorf to Drew, Oct. 18, 1911, Drew to Hunter (Badorf), Dec. 5, 1911, Box 3, DP; R. Foster to Drew, Oct. 26, 1911, Box 7, DP; Lawler to Wickersham, Oct. 23, Dec. 5, 9, 12, 1911, Dec 27, 1912, Wickersham to McCormick, Nov. 17, 1911, Wickersham to Lawler, Nov. 18, Dec. 4, 1911, McCormick to AG, Jan. 6, 1912, Harr to Lawler, Dec. 8, 1911, R. P. Stewart to Robert O'Connor, Nov. 2, 1920, File 15677, RG 60; Lawler interview, pp. 121–25, UCLA; Emery to Post, Dec. 8, 1911, Box 1, Post Papers; Adamic, *Dynamite,* p. 244; Stimson, *Los Angeles,* p. 411.

50. Drew to Harr, Oct. 17, 1911, Harr to Drew, Oct. 19, 1911, C. Miller to AG, Oct. 19, 1911, C. Miller to Drew, Oct. 19, 23, 28, 1911, C. Miller to Harr, Oct. 24, 1911, Wickersham to McCormick, Nov. 17, 1911, Wickersham to Lawler, Nov. 18, 1911, File 15677, RG 60; Drew to Mitchell, Oct. 11, 1911, Box 14, DP; Drew to Hanch, Oct. 20, 1911, Hanch to Drew, Oct. 21, 24, 1911, Drew to R. Foster, Oct. 24, 1911, R. Foster to Drew, Oct. 26, 27, 1911, undated, Feb. 19, Mar. 7, 1913, Box 7, DP; Drew to Winter, Oct. 17, 1911, Box 20, DP; Drew to Burns, Nov. 24, 1911, Box 3, DP; Drew to Kruttschnitt, Oct. 30, 1911, Box 18, DP; Drew to Emery, Jan. 29, 1913, Box 4, DP; Foster autobiography, pp. 113–14, Box 22, DP.

51. C. Miller to Kirby, Feb. 12, 1913, Box 4, DP.

52. Drew to Kruttschnitt, Oct. 30, 1911, Box 18, DP; Drew to R. Foster, Oct. 24, 1911, Drew to Hunter (Badorf), Oct. 27, 30, 31, Nov. 23, 1911, Badorf to Drew, Nov. 21, 26, 1911, Drew to Allen, Apr. 17, 1916, Box 3, DP; C. Miller to Drew, Oct. 27, 28, 1911, Drew to Lawler, Dec. 29, 1911, Jan. 30, 1912, Box 12, DP; Drew to Executive Committee, Nov. 21, 1911, Box 14, DP; Brady to Drew, Dec. 18, 1911, Jan. 6, 1912, [Drew] to Brady, Dec. 22, 1911, Box 3, DP; Foster autobiography, p. 127, Box 22, DP; C. Miller to AG, Nov. 6, 1911, File 15677, RG 60; U.S. vs. Ryan, Nov. 19 (Oct. 21, 1912): 2186–256, 2260–387, Box 33, DP.

53. Badorf to Drew, Nov. 21, 26, 29, Dec. 6, 1911, Mar. 2, 1913, Box 3, DP.

54. Drew to Emery, Sept. 30, 1915, Box 4, DP; R. Foster to Drew, Oct. 11, 1912, Box 7, DP; Badorf to Drew, Dec. 6, 8, 1911, Box 3, DP; Drew to Wagner, Dec. 10, 1911, Box 12, DP; Foster autobiography, pp. 123–27, Box 22, DP; U.S. vs. Ryan, No. 26 (Oct. 29, 1912): 4055–64, Box 33, DP, No. 27 (Oct. 30, 1912): 4478–567, The Huntington; C. Miller to AG, Dec. 14, 1911, File 15677, RG 60; *Indianapolis Star,* Oct. 31, 1912.

55. R. Foster to Drew, Oct. 11, 1912, Box 7, DP; Badorf to Drew, Jan. 27, 30, 1912, Box 3, DP; Drew to Lawrence Y. Sherman, Aug. 29, 1916, Box 2, DP; Foster auto-

biography, pp. 133–34, Box 22, DP; U.S. vs. Ryan, No. 23 (Oct. 26, 1912): 3335–36, 3412, 3418, 3422–23, 3447–49, 3459–61, Box 33, DP, No. 27 (Oct. 30, 1912): 4502–9, 4514–15, The Huntington, Nos. 72, 73, (Dec. 24, 25, 1912): 19948–49, Box 36, DP; *NYT*, Feb. 18, 19, 1912.

56. *NYT*, Jan. 28, 1912; R. Foster to Drew, Oct. 11, 1912, Box 7, DP; Badorf to Drew, Jan. 27, 1912, Box 3, DP; Foster autobiography, pp. 134–38, Box 22, DP; U.S. vs. Ryan, No. 23 (Oct. 26, 1912): 3332–34, Box 33, DP; *Bridgemen's Magazine* 12 (Feb. 1912): 91–94.

57. C. Miller to AG, Feb. 8 (and enclosed statement of indictments), Mar. 14, 1912, Drew to Gentlemen, Jan. 20, 1913, File 15677, RG 60; *Bridgemen's Magazine* 12 (Mar. 1912): 165–66; *NYT*, Oct. 2, 1912; *Indianapolis Star*, Oct. 2, 1912; *Review* (Mar. 1913): 26, 36.

58. U.S. vs. Ryan, No. 28 (Oct. 31, 1912): 5071–85, Box 34, DP; Badorf to Drew, May 17, 1912, Box 3, DP; Statement of George E. Davis, Oct. 4, 1914, pp. 118, 123–24, Box 6, DP; Dallas Jones interview with Mrs. Walter Drew, Nov. 14, 15, 1962, p. 1, transcript in my possession.

59. Drew to McClintic, Feb. 26, 1912, Box 12, DP; Badorf to Drew, Apr. 5, 1912, Mar. 12, 1913, Drew to Badorf, Apr. 8, 1912, Box 3, DP.

60. *Review* (Mar. 1913): 29, 37; Drew to Gentlemen, Jan. 20, 1913, File 15677, RG 60; *NYT*, Oct. 4, 1912; John Fitch, "The Dynamite Case," *Survey* 29 (Feb. 1, 1913): 607–17.

61. Miller to Kirby, Feb. 12, 1913, Box 4, DP; R. Foster to Drew, Oct. 11, Nov. 6, 15, 16, 1912, Drew to R. Foster, Nov. 9, 1912, Box 7, DP; Badorf to Drew, Dec. 4, 1912, Box 3, DP; Drew to H. W. Lowe, Dec. 2, 1912, Lowe to Drew, Dec. 3, 1912, Box 1, DP; Fitch, "Dynamite Case," pp. 616–17.

62. U.S. vs. Ryan, Nos. 74–75 (Dec. 25–26, 1912): 20374, Box 36, DP; *Indianapolis Star*, Dec. 18, 20, 21, 23–25, 31, 1912; Drew to Gentlemen, Dec. 6, 1912, Box 14, DP; Drew to Gentlemen, Jan. 20, 1913, File 15677, RG 60; J. E. McClory to Gompers, Jan. 16, 1913, Reel 35, AFL Records; *Bridgemen's Magazine* 13 (Jan. 1913): 16; "Judge Anderson's Remarks . . ." [Dec. 30, 1912], Box 32, DP.

63. *NYT*, Dec. 29, 1912; William L. Putnam to Wickersham, Jan. 1, 1913, File 15677, RG 60; Drew to C. Miller, Dec. 28, 1912, Box 12, DP.

64. W. H. Mackey to AG, Jan. 1, 1912 [1913] (and enclosure), Schmidt to AG, Jan. 7, 1913, J. W. Wilkerson to AG, Jan. 6, 1914, William Wallace, Jr., Memorandum to Todd, Mar. 10, 1914, File 15677, RG 60; C. Miller to Drew, Jan. 6, 1913, Box 12, DP; *Bridgemen's Magazine* 13 (Jan. 1913): 17; *NYT*, Jan. 1, 5, Oct. 30, 1913, Jan. 7, Feb. 25, Mar. 10, 1914; *Ryan et al. vs. U.S.*, 216 Fed Reporter 13 (1914). Cf. Drew to Gentlemen, Mar. 14, 1913, Box 14, DP. See Drew to Wallace, Jan. 15, 1914, File 15677, RG 60, for the misreading of a document by the Circuit Court that Drew believed had led to its decision.

65. Drew to R. Foster, Nov. 17, 1913, Box 6, DP; Badorf to Drew, Nov. 27, 1916, Drew to Badorf, Dec. 6, 1916, Drew to James W. Noel, Jan. 17, 1917, Noel to Drew, Jan. 22, 1917, Box 11, DP; Drew to Mitchell et al., Mar. 3, 1914, Box 14, DP; Drew to J. W. Poushey, Apr. 28, 1913, Box 4, DP; Drew and R. Foster to Edgar K. Wagner, Aug. 25, 1919, Box 12, DP. Fredericks found a job for McManigal as a watchman as late as 1932, a job from which he retired twelve years later. Fredericks to Drew, Mar. 24, 1932, Box 13, DP; Cleland, *California*, p. 87.

66. Wagner to Drew, Jan. 14, Nov. 28, 1913, Drew to McClintic-Marshall, Jan. 22, 1913, H. A. Greene to Drew, Jan. 27, 1913, McClintic to Drew, Jan. 20, 1913, Drew to

Wagner, Apr. 9, 23, Dec. 15, 1913, Drew to Wagner et al., Nov. 25, 1913, Drew to Llewellyn Iron Works, May 12, 1913, Wagner to NEA, Nov. 28, 1913, McKenzie to Drew, Dec. 3, 1913, Drew to McKenzie et al., Dec. 19, 1913, J. Sterling Deans to Drew, Dec. 11, 1913, Drew to Nichols, Dec. 9, 1913, Mar. 3, 1914, Nichols to Drew, Feb. 28, Mar. 11, 19, 1914, Hunsaker and Britt to Harry Chandler, Dec. 27, 1913, Drew to Fredericks, Jan. 15, 1914, Drew to Munson Havens, Feb. 26, 1913, Havens to Drew, Mar. 24, 1913, Box 5, DP; Drew to Edward Hobday, Jan. 25, 1913, Box 2, DP; Drew to O. G. Denman, May 26, 1913, Box 12, DP.

67. Drew to McReynolds, Feb. 5, 1914, B. J. Ramage to Todd, Mar. 1, 1914, File 15677, RG 60.

68. Stimson, *Los Angeles,* pp. 409–15; Darrow to Gompers, July 20, 1911, Reel 73, AFL Records.

69. Drew to Peck, Nov. 9, 1912, Box 18, DP; Drew to Badorf, Feb. 29, 1912, Badorf to Drew, Mar. 2, 1912, Box 3, DP; Foster to Drew, Oct. 11, 1912, Box 7, DP; *NYT,* Mar. 13, 1912; Cohn and Chisolm, *Witness,* p. 212; Cowan, *Darrow,* pp. 298–99. See Lawler to Wickersham, Feb. 24, 1912, File 15677, RG 60, for evidence that the federal prosecutors thought Gompers to be implicated.

70. Lawler to R. Foster, Jan. 26, 1912, Drew to Lawler, Jan. 30, 1912, Lawler to D. M. Parry, Feb. 27, 1912, Box 10, DP; Foster autobiography, pp. 134–35, Box 22, DP; J. B. Davis (R. Foster) to Drew, Feb. 1, 2, 1912, Box 19, DP; *NYT,* Jan. 30, 1912; Irving Stone, *Clarence Darrow for the Defense* (Garden City, N.Y.: Garden City Publishing Co., 1943), p. 321.

71. Davis (R. Foster) to Drew, Mar. 10, 1912, Drew to R. Foster, May 15, 1912, Box 19, DP; Drew to Badorf, June 5, 1912, Box 3, DP; Drew to M. W. Alexander, Mar. 3, 1913, Box 7, DP; Statement by Annie Redhead. . . , Mar. 4, 1912, Box 31, DP; *LAT,* May 28, 29, June 25, 27, 1912; *NYT,* Mar. 13, May 28, June 1, 1912; *Square Deal* 9 (Apr. 1912): 245–46; *Bridgemen's Magazine* 12 (Nov. 1912): 729; Stone, *Darrow,* p. 317; *Indianapolis Star,* Mar. 13, 1912, clipping in Drew Scrapbook No. 2, DP.

72. *LAT,* June 25, 29, Aug. 3, 4, 6, 13, 1912; *NYT,* Aug. 16, 18, 1912, May 9, 1913; *Plea of Clarence Darrow in His Own Defense to the Jury at Los Angeles August, 1912* (Los Angeles: Golden Press, 1912), pp. 41–42; Stimson, *Los Angeles,* pp. 410–13; Arthur Weinberg and Lila Weinberg, *Darrow: Sentimental Rebel* (New York: G. P. Putnam's Sons, 1980), pp. 214–15, 238–39; Harrison, *Darrow,* pp. 196, 201; Adele Rogers St. Johns, *Final Verdict* (Garden City: Doubleday and Co., 1962), pp. 449, 456–57; Cohn and Chisolm, *Witness,* pp. 220–21; Tierney, *Darrow,* pp. 273–74; *Recollections of Hugh Baillie* (New York: Harper and Brothers, 1959), p. 27. In his recently published study of the Darrow bribery charge, Geoffrey Cowan concludes as a historian that the famed attorney was indeed guilty. Cowan, *Darrow,* p. 434.

73. Stimson, *Los Angeles,* pp. 383–84; *NYT,* Feb. 14, 19, 1915.

74. Davis to Drew, Sept. 6, 1913, Drew to C. Miller, Sept. 19, 23, 1913, Drew to R. Foster, Nov. 20, 1913, Box 6, DP; Foster autobiography, p. 199, Box 22, DP; *NYT,* Oct. 3, 4, 1913; Davis Statement, Sept. 12, 13, 1913, Box 31, DP.

75. C. Miller to Drew, Sept. 21, 29, 1913, [Secretary to Badorf, Oct. 2, 1913], Davis Statement, Oct. 4, 1913, Drew to Fredericks, Oct. 8, 1913, R. Foster to Mrs. George E. Davis, Oct. 27, 1913, Davis to Drew, Nov. 13, 1913, July 4, 1914, Drew to R. Foster, Nov. 17, 20, 1913, Drew to Davis, July 6, 1914, Aug. 4, 1923, Brady to Drew, May 8, 1924, Box 6, DP; Money Paid out or advanced by NEA. . . , Oct. 1913–June 1915, ibid.; Memorandum of Evidence, undated, ibid.; Rudolph Tonnings affidavit, Oct. 20, 1913, ibid.; Drew to Wallace, Mar. 21, 1914, Box 12, DP; *NYT,* Oct. 3, 4, 1913.

76. Thomas Lee Woolwine to Drew, Mar. 26, 31, 1915, Drew to Woolwine, Mar. 31, 1915, Noel to Drew, Aug. 16, 31, 1915, Drew to Noel, Aug. 23, 1915, Bessie L. Crocker to Drew, Sept. 14, 1915, E. J. Brennan to Drew, Sept. 15, 1911, Box 11, DP; Drew to Wallace, July 27, 1914, File 15677, RG 60.

77. *LAT,* Nov. 11–Dec. 31, 1915, Jan. 13, 1916.

78. Ibid., Apr. 6, 13, 19–21, 29, May 12, 1913; *NYT,* May 17, Dec. 16, 1916; Stimson, *Los Angeles,* pp. 413–17.

79. *Bridgemen's Magazine* 13 (Mar. 1913): 149, 225; Drew to Brady, Mar. 6, 1913, Box 3, DP; Drew to Luke Grant, Apr. 13, 1915, Box 8, DP; Drew to Samuel Harding Church, Nov. 7, 1919, Box 2, DP; Drew to George S. Kellogg, Sept. 2, 1919, Box 4, DP; Drew to C. G. Conley, Nov. 16, 1933, Box 13, DP; Taft, *A.F. of L.,* pp. 284–85; Stimson, *Los Angeles,* p. 419; Gottlieb and Wolt, *Thinking Big,* p. 104. McNamara was convicted on a charge of "blackmail" and intimidation in September 1925 and sentenced to a five-year prison term and a fine of $1,000 as a result of his effort to unionize some nonunion jobs in the Indianapolis area. Allen to Drew, Oct. 1, 1924, Box 3, DP; *NYT,* Sept. 15, 17, 18, 23, Oct. 3, 1925; *LAT,* Oct. 18, 19, 1929. He was ejected from the union in 1928 for alleged embezzlement. Clipping in scrapbook, Box 16, McNamara Papers.

80. *Iron Trade Review* 54 (Mar. 19, 1914): 532; Subcommittee of Senate Committee on the Judiciary, *Limiting Federal Injunctions,* 62 Cong., 2 sess., 1912, Part 2, p. 202; Drew to Gentlemen, Aug. 13, 1912, Box 14, DP.

Chapter 6

1. Wilson Vance to H. C. Hawk, Dec. 20, 1907, Box 4, C. W. Post Papers, Bentley Historical Library, Ann Arbor, Michigan.

2. Drew to H. A. Wagner, Aug. 22, 1910, Box 12, DP; Drew to G. A. Stafford, June 2, 1913, Box 3, DP; Drew to Berlin Construction Company, Oct. 29, 1913, Drew to Henry Miller, July 3, 1914, Box 15, DP.

3. Drew, "The Closed Shop vs. the Building Industry," *Square Deal* 2 (Jan. 1907): 23; Drew, "Labor Conditions in the Building Trades," *American Industries* 10 (Dec. 1909): 59; Drew, "Closed Shop Clauses in Building Contracts," ibid. 15 (Mar. 1915): 11; Drew to I. H. Scates, Aug. 20, 1912, Box 13, DP; Drew to John Kirby, June 25, 1912, Box 13, DP; Drew to C. E. Whitney, Mar. 11, 1916, Box 8, DP; Drew to Stafford, Mar. 28, 1913, Box 3, DP; Drew to Frank A. Vanderlip, June 8, 1915, in H. M. Gitelman notes on John Henderson Powell, Jr., "The History of the National Industrial Conference Board," in Gitelman's possession.

4. Drew to Citizens' Industrial Association, Apr. 20, 1906, Box 2, DP; Drew to Miller, July 3, 1914, Drew to C. Edwin Michael, Oct. 31, 1913, Box 15, DP; Drew to W. F. Dinwiddie, Feb. 19, 1910, Box 12, DP; Drew, "Between Employer and Employee. . . ," *System* 11 (Feb. 1907): 110–11, 117, Box 29, DP.

5. Drew to Berlin Construction Co., Oct. 29, 1913, Box 15, DP.

6. Minutes of the NEA Executive Committee (hereafter NEA Minutes), Oct. 2, 1906, Box 37A, Frank Walsh Papers, New York Public Library, New York, New York; Drew to Gentlemen, Aug. 28, 1906, Box 15, DP; Drew to Gentlemen (General Contractors), Sept. 22, 1906, Box 17, DP; Drew to Scates, Aug. 20, 1912, Box 13, DP; Drew to L. J. Horowitz, Mar. 12, 1913, Box 12, DP.

7. Scates to Secretary, Aug. 30, 1912, To the Officers and Members. . . , Dec. 11, 1913, Drew to Kirby, Jan. 25, 1912, Drew to Kirby et al., July 3, 1912, Drew to Scates,

Aug. 20, 1912, Jan. 23, 1917, Scates to Drew, Mar. 21, 1913, Jan. 31, 1917, Drew to A. J. Allen, Sept. 29, 1917, Box 13, DP.

8. Drew to Gentlemen, Nov. 15, 1909, and enclosed circular letter, Box 6, DP; Drew to William H. Sayward, Nov. 19, 1909, Box 11, DP; Drew to A. A. Troem, Aug. 19, 1912, Box 9, DP.

9. Earl Constantine to Drew, July 5, 1912, Box 12, DP; Stafford to Drew, May 27, 1913, Drew to Stafford, May 28, June 2, 1913, Drew to Allen, Jan. 21, 29, 1916, Box 3, DP.

10. William C. Pratt, "The Omaha Business Men's Association and the Open Shop," *Nebraska History* 70 (Summer 1989): 172–84; Alvin F. Johnson to Drew, Aug. 24, 1916, Mar. 31, 1917, J. A. G. Badorf to Drew, Aug. 14, 16, 1916, Oct. 3, 1916, Feb. 22, 1917, Johnson to Badorf, Aug. 16, 1916, Drew to Johnson, Aug. 9, Sept. 1, Oct. 9, Nov. 13, 1916, Mar. 21, 27, Apr. 2, 3, 1917, Box 17, DP; Drew to Allen, Apr. 4, 1917, Box 3, DP.

11. NEA Minutes, Nov. 2, 1906, Box 37A, Walsh Papers; Drew to Gentlemen, Nov. 6, 1906, Feb. 5, 1916, Box 14, DP; Drew to Dinwiddie, Feb. 19, 1910, Box 12, DP; Excerpts, Drew to Mother and Father, May 16, 1907, Box 28, DP; Brady to Drew, Nov. 16, 1915, Oct. 7, 1916, H. E. Kurzman to Drew, Feb. 7, 1916, NEA to Charles Kalhorn, Oct. 9, 1916, Box 5, DP.

12. Drew to W. B. McAllister, Nov. 4, 1914, Box 12, DP; Drew to Gentlemen, Nov. 30, 1914, July 7, 1915, Drew to S. P. Mitchell, Aug. 22, Oct. 17, 1911, Box 14, DP; Drew to George Smart, Jan. 29, 1915, Box 1, DP; Drew to Michael, Jan. 12, 1915, Box 11, DP; NEA Minutes, May 28, 1915, Box 37A, Walsh Papers. See chapter 3 for Buffalo and the open shop.

13. Drew to Gentlemen, June 1, July 15, 1910, Box 14, DP; C. E. Whitney to Drew, Oct. 18, 1913, Box 6, DP; Whitney to Drew, Nov. 6, 1916, Box 36, DP; Whitney to Drew, Apr. 7, 1917, Box 8, DP; Drew to Thomas Earle, June 19, 1916, Box 15, DP; Drew to Allen, June 12, 1916, Box 3, DP; Drew to Dear Sir, May 17, 1916, Box 18, DP.

14. Drew to Gentlemen, July 23, Dec. 16, 1907, Box 14, DP; Drew to G. W. Smith, Feb. 20, 1908, Box 6, DP; Drew to George A. Smith, Dec. 2, 1912, Box 12, DP; Excerpts, Drew to Mother and Father, May 16, [June] 1907, Box 28, DP; [Drew], "Open Shop Movement in Washington" [1907], Box 29, DP.

15. Drew to Gentlemen, June 20, 1907, Box 14, DP; C. O. Graham to Dear Sir, June 28, 1907, Box 18, DP; "Open Shop Movement," Box 29, DP; "Open Shop Movement in Washington. Public Letter" [1907], ibid.

16. "Open Shop Movement," Box 29, DP; "Public Letter," ibid.; Drew to Gentlemen, June 20, July 23, Sept. 18, Oct. 14, Dec. 16, 1907, May 16, Sept. 15, 1908, Box 14, DP; Drew to Gentlemen, Sept. 6, Nov. 26, Dec. 14, 16, 1907, Box 29, DP; Excerpts, Drew to Mother and Father, Sept. 13, Oct. 24, Nov. 17, 1907, 1907 (no month), Drew to James A. Miller, Nov. 22, 1907, Box 2, DP; Drew to E. R. Cobb, Sept. 30, 1908, Box 6, DP; *Square Deal* 4 (Oct. 1908): 8–11, 82–83; *Bridgemen's Magazine* 7 (Dec. 1907): 818–19.

17. Drew to Gentlemen, Oct. 14, Dec. 16, 1907, Box 14, DP; G. W. Smith to Drew, Nov. 27, 29, 1907, Secretary to Members and Friends, Mar. 23, 1909, Box 6, DP; Drew, *The Story of Duluth and the Open Shop* [1910], Box 29, DP.

18. Excerpts, Drew to Mother and Father, Dec. 4, 1907, Box 28, DP; Resolution, Dec. 4, 1907, Box 6, DP; H. A. Hall to Drew, Dec. 20, 1907, E. R. Cobb to Drew, Dec. 18, 1907, Cobb to George S. Boudinot, Sept. 25, 1908, Secretary to Members and

Friends, Mar. 23, 1909, ibid.; Drew to Gentlemen, Dec. 16, 1907, Sept. 15, 1908, Box 14, DP; Drew, *Duluth,* Box 29, DP.

19. Cobb to Boudinot, Sept. 25, 1908, Drew to Cobb, Sept. 30, 1908, Drew to Dwight E. Woodridge, Jan. 21, 1908, Secretary to Members and Friends, Mar. 23, 1909, Labor Committee to Duluth Builders' Exchange, May 1, 1909, H. V. Eva to Drew, Oct. 2 [1912], Box 6, DP; Drew to J. K. Mumford, July 22, 1909, Box 18, DP; Fred Mooney to John J. McNamara, July 3, 1910, Box 25, DP; Drew, *Duluth,* Box 29, DP.

20. Vance to Hawk, Dec. 20, 1907, Box 4, Post Papers; *Bridgemen's Magazine* 8 (Apr. 1908): 177.

21. A. D. Schaeffer to Drew, Jan. 5, Feb. 2, 11, 27, 1911, Drew to Schaeffer, Jan. 7, 1911, Drew to William Pratt, Feb. 14, 1911, Drew to F. D. Compau, Feb. 14, Mar. 8, 1911, Drew to Brady, Feb. 14, 1911, Drew to C. W. Post, Feb. 14, 1911, Drew to Acker and Schmidt, Mar. 4, 1911, Schaeffer to Drew, "The Seventh 1911," Box 7, DP; *Gary Evening Post,* Feb. 9, 25, 1911, clippings in ibid.; *Review* (Nov. 1912): 16.

22. Wilmington Employers' Association, Constitution, Apr. 20, 1916, Box 20, DP; Drew to Brady, Apr. 21, 1916, ibid.; Drew to Allen, May 1, 1916, Box 3, DP; Drew to J. H. Mueller, May 13, 1916, Box 6, DP; Drew to Badorf, Sept. 18, 1916, Box 9, DP; Drew to Johnson, Oct. 9, 1916, Box 17, DP; Minutes of the NEA General Meeting, May 19, 1916, Box 37A, Walsh Papers.

23. Drew to Sterling H. Thomas, May 18, 1916, Drew to C. G. Neese, May 22, 1916, Neese to Drew, May 18, June 17, 1916, Drew to C. D. Garretson, June 10, 12, 1916, Drew to Lewis H. McLaughlin, Mar. 22, Apr. 27, 30, 1917, Drew to James E. Stein, Oct. 28, 1919, Apr. 28, 1920, Box 20, DP.

24. NEA Minutes, Mar. 26, May 28, 1915, Box 37A, Walsh Papers; J. W. Poushey to Drew, Oct. 20, 1914, Drew to Smart, Jan. 29, 1915, E. A. Gilbert to Drew, Oct. 19, 1914, and enclosed cards, C. H. Todd to Drew, Aug. 30, 1915, Box 1, DP; Extract from *Boilermakers' Journal,* Sept. 1915, pp. 685–86, ibid.; Drew to Gentlemen, July 7, 1915, Box 14, DP; Commission on Industrial Relations, *Industrial Relations. Final Report and Testimony,* 64 Cong., 1 sess., S. Doc. No. 415, 1916, 11:10750.

25. Petroleum Iron Works to Riter-Conley Manufacturing Company, Oct. 12, 1914, Poushey to Drew, Oct. 18, 26, 27, 1914, Apr. 22, 1916, Drew to H. S. Sanford, Oct. 28, 1914, Jan. 28, 1915, Sanford to Drew, Nov. 28, 1914, Drew to Robert Foster, Jan. 19, 1915, Drew to Poushey, Jan. 18, 1915, George Reeves to Drew, Jan. 23, 1915, Drew to Badorf, Jan. 18, 20, 1915, Box 1, DP; Constitution and By-Laws of the American Erectors' Association, undated, ibid.

26. Drew to Badorf, Jan. 20, 1915, Reeves to Drew, Jan. 23, 29, 1915, Drew to Reeves, Jan. 26, Feb. 23, 1915, Todd to Drew, Mar. 29, Apr. 3, 15, 1915 (and enclosed copy of *Boilermakers' Journal,* Feb. 1915, p. 93), Poushey to Drew, Feb. 15, 27, 1915, Drew to Poushey, Feb. 19, Apr. 1, 1915, Reeves Brothers Co. to Drew, Feb. 19, 1915, Drew to Reeves Brothers, Feb. 20, 1915, Drew to Sanford, Mar. 11, 1915, H. L. Waltham to Poushey, Mar. 30, 1915, ibid.

27. Drew to Todd, May 29, Aug. 27, 1915, Todd to Drew, Apr. 29, Aug. 4, Nov. 11, 1915, Drew to James McKeown, Mar. 5, 1915, Drew to Poushey, Nov. 4, 9, 1915, Apr. 1, 17, June 19, 1916, Poushey to Drew, Mar. 17, Nov. 4, 1916, Drew to Members, AEA, Mar. 20, 1916, Drew to Warren City Tank and Boiler Co., Nov. 14, 1916, Drew to Brady, Nov. 8, 1916, Apr. 26, 1917 (and enclosure), Brady to Drew, Dec. 1, 1916, ibid.; Drew to Poushey, Feb. 21, Mar. 28, 1917, Drew to E. A. Gibbs, June 21, 1916, Jan. 9, 1917, Drew to Brady, Mar. 13, 1917, Brady to Samuel Craig, Mar. 9, 1917, Box 3, DP.

28. Louis B. Perry and Richard S. Perry, *A History of the Los Angeles Labor Movement, 1911–1941* (Berkeley: University of California Press, 1963), pp. 55–65; Graham Adams, Jr., *Age of Industrial Violence, 1910–1915* (New York: Columbia University Press, 1966), pp. 129–36; Selig Perlman and Philip Taft, *History of Labor in the United States* (New York: Macmillan Co., 1935), pp. 370–72; *Square Deal* 9 (Nov. 1911): 323–32; *Railway Age Gazette* 51 (Sept. 1, 1911): 395–96, 444; *Machinists Monthly Journal* 23 (Nov. 1911): 1105, 1151; Commission on Industrial Relations, *Industrial Relations,* 10:9886–88.

29. *NYT,* Mar. 19, 23, 1912; Operative Special, Apr. 11, 1912, Box 19, DP; Kruttschnitt to Drew, Apr. 16, 1912, enclosing T. Fay to Kruttschnitt, Apr. 12, 1912, Drew to H. B. Lowe, Apr. 17, 1912, [Drew] to Charles D. Brooks, Mar. 27, 1912, Drew to Kruttschnitt, Aug. 5, Dec. 31, 1912, ibid.; Drew to Lowe, Mar. 27, 1912, Box 1, DP; Autobiography of Robert J. Foster, undated, pp. 168–69, Box 22, DP; Commission on Industrial Relations, *Industrial Relations,* 10:9957.

30. Drew to Lowe, Mar. 27, 1912, Box 1, DP; Drew to Lowe, Apr. 17, 1912, [Drew] to John Conway (Foster), Mar. 29, Apr. 6, 1912, Drew to Conway, May 15, 1912, Conway to Bird (Drew), Apr. 1, 4, 6, 12, July 1, 1912, Drew to Kruttschnitt, Apr. 17, Aug. 5, Oct. 30, Nov. 14, 29, Dec. 31, 1912, Dave Scanlon (Foster) to Drew, July 1, 3, 1912, Drew to Scanlon, June 28, 1912, Frank Harmon (Foster) to Bird, July 21, 22, 25, Aug. 21, 1912, [Foster] to Bird, July 30, 31, Aug. 5, 1912, Drew to Harmon, Aug. 7, 1912, Foster to Drew, Dec. 31, 1912, Jan. 12, 1913, Box 19, DP; 172 Reports, July 2, 3, 11–17, 1912, ibid.; 186 Reports, July 1, 1912, ibid.; No. 57 Reports, Oct. 16, 23, Nov. 16, 1912, June 10, 13, 1913, ibid.; No. 27 Report, Jan. 13, 1913, ibid.; Drew to Badorf, Mar. 27, 1912, Box 3, DP; Foster autobiography, pp. 170–84, Box 22, DP; Perry and Perry, *Los Angeles,* p. 67.

31. Drew to Gentlemen, Nov. 21, 1906, Box 14, DP; Excerpts, Drew to Mother and Father, Dec. 1906, 1907 (no month), Box 28, DP; Vance to Hawke, Dec. 20, 1907, Box 4, Post Papers; Drew, "Closed Shop vs. Building Industry," pp. 23–26. I have borrowed the term "peak associations" from Howell John Harris, "Getting It Together. . . ," in Sanford M. Jacoby, *Masters to Managers: Historical and Comparative Perspectives on American Employers* (New York: Columbia University Press, 1991), p. 117.

32. Meeting of National Trades Associations, Aug. 19, 1907, Reel 4, Accession 1521, National Association of Manufacturers Microfilm, Hagley Museum and Library, Wilmington, Delaware; NEA Minutes, July 9, Oct. 11, 1907, Box 37A, Walsh Papers; Excerpts, Drew to Mother and Father, Jan. 28, 1908, Box 28, DP.

33. Drew to Gentlemen, Mar. 31, Apr. 6, 1910, Box 14, DP; NAM, *Proceedings of the Fifteenth Annual Convention, May 16–18, 1910,* pp. 283–84.

34. Drew to Wagner, Aug. 22, 1910, Drew to J. W. Schroeder, Dec. 27, 1915; NEA to Citizens' Alliance of Minneapolis, Dec. 31, Box 12, DP; Drew to Mitchell et al., May 19, 1911, Box 6, DP. See chapter 10.

35. Drew to Kirby et al., June 3, 1912, Box 13, DP; Drew to Dear Sir, Sept. 25, 1912, J. B. Bird to Drew, Oct. 19, 1912, Box 7, DP.

36. Allen F. Davis, "The Campaign for the Industrial Relations Commission, 1911–1913," *Mid-America* 45 (Oct. 1913): 212–14; *Survey* 27 (Dec. 30, 1911): 1430–31; *Review* 11 (Dec. 1914): 571–72.

37. Adams, *Industrial Violence,* pp. 34–35, 55–56; Drew to Raynal C. Bolling, Jan. 7, 1913, Badorf to Drew, Nov. 6, 1913, Drew to Walter Gordon Merritt, Dec. 1, 1914, Box 20, DP; Report of Badorf, June 30, 1913, ibid.; undated items, ibid.; "Not for Publication," undated, Box 12, DP; *Review* 11 (Dec. 1914): 572–73.

38. *Iron Trade Review* 55 (Nov. 26, 1914): 1005; Drew to John J. Whirl, July 29, 1914, Emery to Walsh, May 22, 1914, Walsh to Emery, May 29, 1914, Emery to Drew, June 2, 1914, Box 20, DP; Drew to Gentlemen, Nov. 30, 1914, Box 14, DP; *Review* 11 (Dec. 1914): 572.

39. Minutes of the NEA General Meeting, May 29, 1914, Box 37A, Walsh Papers; Minutes of the First Meeting of the Joint Committee. . . , June 24, 1914, Box 12; Drew to Joseph Tumulty, Oct. 16, 1914, Reel 232, Woodrow Wilson Papers, University of Michigan Library, Ann Arbor, Michigan; Drew to George W. Wickersham, July 10, 1914, Box 12, DP; Drew to Whirl, July 29, 1914, Box 20, DP.

40. William H. Barr to Henry B. Joy, July 13, 1914, Drew to Barr et al., July 28, 1914, Drew to Members of Joint Committee, July 7, 1914, Drew to Whirl, July 29, 1914, Drew to Basil Manly, June 8, 1914, Box 20, DP; Drew to G. W. Smith, June 29, 1914, Box 1, DP; Drew to Gentlemen, Nov. 30, 1914, Box 14, DP; "Convention— National Association of Manufacturers, May 25–26, 1915," pp. 39–40, Box 29, DP; Commission on Industrial Relations, *Industrial Relations,* 4:3175–79, 3224–41, 3303– 4, 3356–58, 3393–3408.

41. Drew to Barr et al., July 28, 1914, Box 20, DP; Commission on Industrial Relations, *Industrial Relations,* 6:5176–216, 5487–535, 5566–75.

42. Drew to Whirl, July 29, 1914, Box 20, DP; Commission on Industrial Relations, *Industrial Relations,* 11:10732–68.

43. Eric F. Goldman, *Rendezvous with Destiny* (New York: Alfred A. Knopf, 1952), pp. 170–71; Adams, *Industrial Violence,* p. 209; Drew to Tumulty, Oct. 16, 1914, Reel 232, Wilson Papers; Drew, "The Federal Commission on Industrial Relations," *American Industries* 15 (June 1915): 17–18; "Convention—NAM, 1915," pp. 41–42, Box 29, DP; John R. Commons, *Myself* (New York: Macmillan Co., 1934), pp. 175–77.

44. Walsh to William Marion Reedy, Apr. 17, 1915, Box 34, Walsh Papers; Drew to Walsh, Apr. 5, 1915, Manly to Drew, Apr. 13, 1915, Box 33, ibid.; Adams, *Industrial Violence,* pp. 209–14.

45. Commission on Industrial Relations, *Industrial Relations,* 1:7–8; Drew to Emery, Jan. 15, 1916, Box 22, DP; Adams, *Industrial Violence,* p. 215.

46. Commission on Industrial Relations, *Industrial Relations,* 1:11–269.

47. Grant, *The National Erectors' Association and the International Association of Bridge and Structural Ironworkers* (Washington, 1915), passim; Drew to G. W. Smith, June 29, 1914, Box 1, DP; Drew to Gentlemen, Feb. 15, 1916, Box 14, DP. See Drew, "Open and Closed Shop in the Structural Iron Industry," *Survey* 35 (Mar. 1916): 702–3.

48. H. M. Gitelman, "Management's Crisis of Confidence and the Origin of the National Industrial Conference Board, 1914–1916," *Business History Review* 58 (Summer 1984): 154, 156–57, 158, 162–63; Alexander to Drew, Sept. 29, 1913, Gitelman notes.

49. Alexander, "The First Yama Conference. . . , June 15–17, 1915" (July 18, 1915), copy in my possession; Gitelman, "Crisis of Confidence," p. 165; Drew to G. L. Peck, June 8, 1915, Gitelman notes.

50. Alexander, "The Second Yama Conference. . . , Sept. 18–21, 1915" (undated), Records of the National Industrial Conference Board, Accession 1057, Hagley Museum and Library; Alexander, "The Third Yama Conference. . . , June 2–5, 1916" (undated), ibid., Drew to Vanderlip, Jan. 27, 1917, Gitelman notes; Drew, "National Industrial Conference Board," Feb. 6, 1917, Box 29, DP.

51. Drew, "Conference Board," Box 29, DP; Drew to Vanderlip, Jan. 27, 1917, Gitelman notes; Gitelman, "Being of Two Minds: American Employers Confront the

Labor Problem, 1915–1919," *Labor History* 25 (Winter 1984): 201–2 (for the Drew letter to Lippmann). See chapter 10.

52. Drew to Alexander, Feb. 16, 1917, Gitelman notes; Excerpts, Drew to Mother and Father, June 10, 1906, Box 28, DP; Drew to Gentlemen, May 14, 1908, Box 14, DP; Robert H. Wiebe, *Businessmen and Reform: A Study of the Progressive Movement* (Chicago: Quadrangle Paperbacks, 1968), p. 173.

53. Commission on Industrial Relations, *Industrial Relations,* 11:10743; Drew, "The Labor Trust's Crusade against the Courts," *Square Deal* 2 (Oct. 1906): 15–16; Drew, "Government by Injunction," ibid. (Mar. 1907): 11–14; Drew, "Labor Unions and Socialism," ibid. 3 (Apr. 1908): 10; Drew, "The Political Purpose of Organized Labor," ibid. 4 (Oct. 1908): 15–17; Drew, "A Legal Discussion of the Boycott," ibid. 5 (Sept. 1909): 108; Drew to Sereno E. Payne, June 16, 1908, Box 10, DP; Felix Frankfurter and Nathan Greene, *The Labor Injunction* (New York: Macmillan Co., 1930), pp. 155–56.

54. Subcommittee of Senate Committee on the Judiciary, *Limiting Federal Injunctions,* 62 Cong., 2 sess., 1912, Part 2, 201–26; Drew to Gentlemen, Mar. 25, Aug. 13, Oct. 2, 1912, Mar. 14, 1913, Nov. 30, 1914, Box 14, DP; Drew to Gentlemen, Dec. 6, 1912, Box 29, DP; Drew to Members, Mar. 25, 1912, Drew to Earle, Nov. 6, 1912, Box 10, DP; Drew to Members, June 17, 1912, Box 16, DP; Frankfurter and Greene, *Labor Injunction,* p. 191. See chapter 5.

55. Drew to Members, May 3, 1913, Box 14, DP; Emery to Drew, May 1, 1913, Drew to American Bridge Co., May 8, 1913, Drew to W. P. Hamilton, Jan. 12, 1915, Box 10, DP; *Wall Street Journal,* Jan. 16, 1915, clipping in Box 29, DP; Arther S. Link, *Woodrow Wilson and the Progressive Era, 1910–1917* (New York: Harper and Brothers, 1954), pp. 69–70.

56. Drew to Gentlemen, Feb. 20, 1908, Box 14, DP; Drew to August Ziesing, Feb. 20, 1908, Drew to H. F. Lofland, Feb. 20, 1908, Box 6, DP; Drew, "Labor Unions and Socialism," pp. 10–11; Drew, "Labor Unions and an Eight-Hour Law," *Square Deal* 3 (July 1908): 33–36.

57. Drew to Lofland, Feb. 20, 1908, Drew to J. Sterling Deans, Feb. 27, 1908, Drew to Earle, Feb. 27, 1908, Box 6, DP; Drew to Gentlemen, Feb. 20, 27, Mar. 9, 1908, Box 14, DP; Excerpts, Drew to Mother and Father, Feb. 7–23 [*sic*], 1908, 1908 (no month), Box 28, DP; James W. Van Cleave to Postum Cereal Co., Mar. 11, 1908, Box 1, Post Papers; Subcommittee No. 1, House Committee on Labor, *H.R. 15651. Eight Hours for Labor on Government Work,* 60 Cong., 1908, pp. 127, 150–51, 155, 250. Drew also criticized the Adamson Act as a wage rather than an hours law. Drew, "The Adamson Law," June 11, 1917, Box 29, DP. See chapter 1.

58. Excerpts, Drew to Mother and Father, May 27, 1908, Drew to Gentlemen, June 11, 22, July 28, 1908, Mar. 3, 1909, Box 14, DP; Frank Webb to Frank Ryan, June 2, 1908, Box 23, DP; NEA to Our Men, Sept. 15, Oct. 22, 1908, Box 29, DP; Drew, "Eight-Hour Law," p. 37; Grant, *Erectors' Association,* p. 63.

59. Drew to Gentlemen, Feb. 1, June 10, 1910, Box 14, DP; Wagner to Drew, Aug. 24, 1910, Box 12, DP.

60. Drew to Gentlemen, Nov. 23, 1909, Jan. 25, Apr. 9, 1910, Drew to W. A. Garrigues, Dec. 7, 1909, Box 14, DP; NEA Minutes, Dec. 17, 1909, Mar. 25, 1910, Box 37A, Walsh Papers; NAM, *Proceedings of the Sixteenth Annual Convention, May 15–17, 1911,* pp. 155–57.

61. Drew to A. M. Blodgett, Mar. 31, 1910, Box 15, DP; Drew to Gentlemen, Feb. 24, Mar. 10, 1910, Box 29, DP; Drew to Wagner, Aug. 27, 1910, Box 12, DP; Drew to

Mitchell, Feb. 24, 1911, Box 14, DP; Minutes of NAM Board of Directors Meeting, Feb. 24, 1910, Reel 1, Ser. V, Records of the National Association of Manufacturers, Accession 1411, Hagley Museum and Library; Roy Lubove, *The Struggle for Social Security, 1900–1935* (Cambridge, Mass.: Harvard University Press, 1968), p. 58. Under elective laws, the employer lost his common law defenses if he failed to agree to compensation, but he retained them if the worker refused to elect compensation. Ibid.

62. Robert F. Wesser, "Conflict and Compromise: The Workmen's Compensation Movement in New York," *Labor History* 11 (Summer 1970): 356–60; Drew to Garrigues, Dec. 7, 1909, Drew to Gentlemen, Apr. 12, 1911, Box 14, DP; Drew to Gentlemen, July 9, 26, 1910, C. E. Cheney to Members, Mar. 24, 1911, Box 29, DP; Drew to Wagner, Aug. 27, 1910, Box 12, DP; Drew, "New York Liability Act," *Square Deal* 8 (Feb. 1911): 24–25; Lubove, *Social Security,* pp. 57–58; *Ives* v. *South Buffalo Railway Co.,* 201 NY 271 (1911).

63. Drew to Gentlemen, May 10, 1913, Jan. 30, May 14, June 19, 1914, Box 14, DP; NEA Minutes, Apr. 2, 1914, Box 37A, Walsh Papers; Wesser, "Conflict and Compromise," pp. 369–70; *New York Central Railroad Co.* v. *White,* 243 US 188 (1917).

64. Lubove, *Social Security,* p. 57; Drew to H. H. McClintic et al., Feb. 26, 1913, Box 29, DP; Drew, "Compulsory Invalidity and Old Age Insurance. . . ," 1916, ibid.; Drew to Gentlemen, Mar. 14, 1913, Box 14, DP.

65. Drew, "Compulsory Invalidity."

66. Leo Wolman, *The Growth of American Trade Unions, 1880–1923* (New York: National Bureau of Economic Research, 1924), pp. 33, 110–11.

Chapter 7

1. Drew to Clarence E. Whitney, July 20, 1915, Box 12, DP.

2. *NYT,* July 13, 14, 1915; Drew to Remington Arms Co., July 14, 15, 1915, Drew to Whitney, July 17, 1915, Drew to Spring-Rice, July 17, 1915, Drew to James A. Emery, July 17, 1915, ibid.; Cecilia F. Bucki, "Dilution and Craft Tradition: Bridgeport, Connecticut, Munitions Workers, 1915–1919," *Social Science History* 4 (Feb. 1980): 106, 107.

3. *NYT,* July 16–23, 1915; Drew to Raynal C. Bolling, July 20, 1915, Whitney to Drew, July 22, 1915, Box 12, DP; Bucki, "Dilution and Craft Tradition," pp. 110–11.

4. Drew, "The Workman behind the Army," *Leslie's Weekly* 122 (Mar. 9, 1916): 289, 303, 305; Drew to Editorial Department, Philadelphia Public Ledger, Oct. 8, 1917, Box 18, DP; Drew to E. P. Mitchell, Oct. 24, 1917, Box 12, DP; Drew to Editor, Boston Transcript, Nov. 2, 1917, Box 9, DP; *Iron Trade Review* 61 (Nov. 22, 1917): 1115; *Review* 14 (Nov. 1917): 455; Drew, "War Contracts and the Open Shop," *American Industries* 18 (Dec. 1917): 24.

5. The Council of National Defense, consisting of six cabinet officers, was created in the summer of 1916 to prepare for the possible mobilization of the nation's resources. The Advisory Commission was composed of seven members drawn from the private sector. Valerie Jean Conner, *The National War Labor Board* (Chapel Hill: University of North Carolina Press, 1983), pp. 20–21.

6. "Maintenance of Existing Labor Standards," *Monthly Review of the Bureau of Labor Statistics* 4 (June 1917): 807–9; Dallas L. Jones, "The Wilson Administration and Organized Labor, 1912–1919" (Ph.D. diss., Cornell University, 1955), pp. 325, 341–44; Conner, *Labor Board,* pp. 22–23; Alexander Bing, *War-Time Strikes and Their Adjustment* (New York: Arno and the New York Times, 1971), p. 15.

7. Drew to Emery, Apr. 12, 1917, Drew to William H. Barr, Apr. 16, 1917, H. M. Gitelman notes on John Henderson Powell, Jr., "The History of the National Industrial Conference Board," in Gitelman's possession; Emery to Barr, Apr. 14, 1917, Drew to A. W. Shaw, Apr. 21, 1917, Box 5, DP; Drew to Members, June 1, 1917, Box 14, DP; NICB Minutes of Members' Meetings, May 17, 1917, Ser. 3, Reel 1, Archives of the National Industrial Conference Board, Accession 1057, Hagley Museum and Library, Wilmington, Delaware; NEA Report of the Commissioner, May 25, 1917, Box 37A, Frank P. Walsh Papers, New York Public Library, New York, New York.

8. Drew to Industrial Economist Publishing Co., July 12, 1917, Box 8, DP; Drew to Members, Sept. 20, Oct. 14, 1917, Box 14, DP; Drew, "War Contracts," p. 24; Conner, *Labor Board,* p. 23.

9. Robert Edward Lee Knight, *Industrial Relations in the San Francisco Bay Area, 1900–1918* (Berkeley: University of California Press, 1960), pp. 338–39; Drew to Labor Bureaus, Jan. 8, 1918, Box 12, DP; Drew to Members, Jan. 10, 1918, Box 14, DP; Leonard Philip Krivy, "American Organized Labor and the First World War, 1917–1918 . . ." (Ph.D. diss., New York University, 1965), pp. 184–85.

10. Bing, *War-Time Strikes,* pp. 20–21; P. H. Douglas and F. E. Wolfe, "Labor Administration in the Shipbuilding Industry during War Time," *Journal of Political Economy* 27 (Mar. 1919): 147–49; William John Williams, "Shipbuilding and the Wilson Administration: The Development of Policy, 1914–1917" (Ph.D. diss., University of Washington, 1989), pp. 446–48; Frank Julian Warne, *The Workers at War* (New York: Century Co., 1920), p. 99; *Iron Age* 99 (Jan. 4, 1917): 35.

11. Gordon S. Watkins, *Labor Problems and Labor Administration in the United States during the World War* (Urbana: University of Illinois Press, 1919), pp. 178–95; Douglas and Wolfe, "Shipbuilding Industry," pp. 373–74; Drew to Editor, New York Times, Apr. 28, 1919, Drew to Emery, Apr. 28, 1919, Box 7, DP; B. L. Worden to George E. Oller, Oct. 17, 1917, File 2512-1, Records of the United States Shipping Board, RG 32, NARA.

12. Statement of Thomas Earle, Jan. 13, 1921, Exhibit File No. 3, File 1-2258-1, Records of the Federal Trade Commission, RG 122, NARA; *Iron Age* 100 (Dec. 6, 1917): 1400; Lewis D. Rights to Drew, Dec. 19, 1917, Jan. 5, 1918, Box 19, DP.

13. Secretary to Drew to Rights, Dec. 26, 1917, Rights to Drew, Jan. 18, 21, 1918, Rights to Worden, Jan. 21, 1918, Drew to Rights, Jan. 30, 1918, Box 19, DP; Drew to Members, Jan. 10, 1918, Drew to Gentlemen, Jan. 26, Feb. 21, Mar. 23, 1918, Box 14, DP; Drew to Whitney, Mar. 9, 1918, Box 8, DP.

14. Charles M. Power to Drew, Jan. 18, 1918, Drew to Power, Jan. 29, 1918, Drew to H. D. Sayre, Feb. 6, Mar. 1, 1918, Sayre to Drew, Feb. 9, 1918, Drew to Barr, Feb. 16, 1918, Drew to Charles Piez, Feb. 4, 1918, J. B. Densmore to Drew, Mar. 23, Apr. 6, 1918, Drew to Densmore, Apr. 1, 8, 1918, Box 7, DP; J. W. Schroeder to Drew, Feb. 2, 1918, Box 12, DP.

15. Drew to Emery, Apr. 15, 1918, Mar. 17, Apr. 28, May 26, 1919, Drew to A. C. Marshall, Apr. 15, 1918, Drew to C. C. Mead, Apr. 2, 1919, Drew to Editor, New York Times, Apr. 28, 1919, Drew to Magnus W. Alexander, Feb. 17, 1919, Drew to Dahlman, Feb. 18, 1919, Drew to H. P. Snyder, Feb. 3, 1919, S. P. Mitchell to James W. Good, June 3, 1919, Drew to O. P. Briggs, June 27, 1919, Alexander to Mitchell, May 27, 1919, Box 7, DP; Drew to Members, May 29, 1919, Box 14, DP; Minutes of the NEA Executive Committee (hereafter NEA Minutes), Mar. 15, June 3, 1919, Box 37A, Walsh Papers; *Industry* 1 (Jan. 1, 1919): 4, 5, (June 1919): 1, 9–10; ibid. 2 (Apr. 15, 1920): 3–4; *Detroit Saturday Night,* July 5, 1919; Watkins, *Labor Problems,* pp. 203–4; John

Lombardi, *Labor's Voice in the Cabinet: A History of the Department of Labor . . .* (New York: Columbia University Press, 1942), pp. 193–96, 309–15; Bruce Irving Bustard, "The Human Factor: Labor Administration and Industrial Manpower Mobilization during the First World War" (Ph.D. diss., University of Iowa, 1984), pp. 270–71; Darrell Hevenor Smith, *The United States Employment Service* (Baltimore: John Hopkins University Press, 1923), pp. 46–47; Udo Sautter, *Three Cheers for the Unemployed: Government and Unemployment before the New Deal* (New York: Cambridge University Press, 1991), pp. 164–72, 176–77.

16. Douglas and Wolfe, "Shipbuilding Industry," pp. 369, 373–74; Watkins, *Labor Problems,* pp. 59–61, 67; Bing, *War-Time Strikes,* pp. 20–21; Krivy, "American Organized Labor," pp. 186–87; Minutes NICB Members, Mar. 20, 1918, Ser. III, Accession 1057; Drew to Gentlemen, Feb. 21, 1918, Box 14, DP; Drew to A. J. Allen, Aug. 17, 1918, Box 8, DP; Drew to Emery, Apr. 15, 1918, Emery to Drew, Apr. 20, 1918, Box 12, DP; Drew, "Attitudes of the Structural Iron Workers Union during the War toward Shipyard Work," July 18, 1919, Box 29, DP; J. E. McClory to Gompers, May 8, 1917, Reel 83, American Federation of Labor Records: The Samuel Gompers Era, University of Michigan Library, Ann Arbor, Michigan; *NYT,* Aug. 15, 1918; *Bridgemen's Magazine* 17 (Aug. 1917): 388–89, (Dec. 1917): 642.

17. Bing, *War-Time Strikes,* p. 22; Willard E. Hotchkiss and Henry R. Seager, *History of the Shipbuilding Labor Adjustment Board, 1917 to 1919,* Bureau of Labor Statistics Bulletin No. 283 (Washington: Government Printing Office, 1921), pp. 7–14; Douglas and Wolfe, "Shipbuilding Industry," pp. 369–70; David Palmer, "Organizing the Shipyards: Unionization at New York Ship, Federal Ship, and Fore River, 1898–1945" (Ph.D. diss., Brandeis University, 1989), p. 204; Louis B. Wehle, *Hidden Threads of History* (New York: Macmillan Co., 1953), p. 40; Watkins, *Labor Problems,* pp. 139–41; Krivy, "American Organized Labor," pp. 189, 195.

18. Drew to Members, Oct. 24, 1917, Box 14, DP; Drew to E. P. Mitchell, Oct. 31, 1917, Box 12, DP; Drew to Ferdinand C. Schwedtman, Sept. 4, 1917, Box 7, DP; Drew to Edward N. Hurley, Dec. 14, 1917, File 2512-1, RG 32; Drew to W. L. Capps, Oct. 31, 1917, File 2512-8, ibid.

19. *Iron Age* 100 (Oct. 4, 1917): 804; Memorandum re Strikes on Work of Submarine Boat Corporation . . . , undated, Box 20, DP; Drew to Members AEA, Mar. 19, 1918, Brady to W. W. Boyd, Sept. 11, 1920, Box 1, DP; Drew to Schwedtman, Sept. 4, 1917, Box 7, DP; Drew to Worden, Oct. 15, 1917, Box 16, DP; Drew to Hurley, Oct. 15, 1917, File 2507-1, RG 32; Drew to Worden, Oct. 15, 1917, Drew to Piez, Jan. 3, 1919, File 2512-1, ibid.; *NYT,* Oct. 12, 18, 1917; *Bridgemen's Magazine* 17 (Aug. 1917): 393, (Sept. 1917): 452–76. The union was reinstated by the AFL at its Nov. 1917 convention. Ibid. 18 (Jan. 1918): 8.

20. *NYT,* Oct. 18, 19, Nov. 1, 3, 1917; A. L. Swain to U.S. Shipping Board EFC, Oct. 19, 1917, File 2507-1, RG 32; Board of Business Agents to Admiral Russo, Oct. 29, 1917, File 2512-2, ibid.; Drew to Capps, Oct. 31, 1917, File 2512-8, ibid.; Drew to Paul Cravath, Oct. 25, 1917, Box 12, DP; John R. McQuire to [W. B.] Wilson, Oct. 29, 1917, Greenawalt to Secretary of Labor, Oct. 31, 1917, Henry F. Hilfers to Gompers, Nov. 2, 1917, File No. 33-756, Records of the Federal Mediation and Conciliation Service, RG 280, NARA.

21. Conference, Nov. 1, 1917, File No. 33-756, RG 280; Greenawalt to Secretary of Labor, Nov. 1, 1917, ibid.

22. [*Newark Evening News,* Nov. 2, 1917], clipping in ibid.; Re Lackawanna Bridge Co., Second Conference, Nov. 5, 1917, ibid.; Greenawalt to Secretary of Labor, Nov. 6,

1917, ibid.; Wehle Memorandum to Raymond B. Stevens, Nov. 7, 1917, File 2512-1, RG 32; Alexander to Members of NICB, Oct. 29, 1917, Drew to Editor of New York Sun, Oct. 31, 1917, Box 12, DP; Drew, "Forcing the Closed Shop as a War Measure," *American Industries* 18 (Nov. 1917): 26; *NYT,* Oct. 31, Nov. 9, 1917; *Bridgemen's Magazine* 17 (Dec. 1917): 636–37, 642–43.

23. A. Duncan to EFC, Nov. 12, 1917, Drew to Capps, Nov. 13, 1917, File 2512-8, RG 32; [*Newark Evening News,* Nov. 12, 13, 1917], clippings in File 2512-2, ibid.; [*Newark Ledger,* Nov. 14, 1917], clipping in ibid.; [*Washington Post,* Nov. 13, 1917], clipping in ibid.; Drew to Worden, Dec. 10, 1917, Box 12, DP; Drew to Members, Jan. 10, 1918, Box 14, DP; Memoranda in re Strikes on Work of Submarine Boat Corporation. . . , undated, Box 20, DP; Drew to Emery, Apr. 11, 1918, Emery to Drew, Apr. 20, 1918, Box 12, DP; *Bridgemen's Magazine* 18 (Feb. 1918): 60–61.

24. Drew to Members AEA, Mar. 19, 1918, Box 1, DP; V. Everit Macy to Submarine Boat Corporation, Nov. 20, 1918, L. C. Marshall to Piez, Jan. 3, 1919, and enclosed "Fuller Statement. . . ," Drew to Piez, Jan. 3, 1919, Director General (Piez) to Submarine Boat Corporation, Nov. 20, 1918, File 2512-1, RG 32.

25. Drew to Members, Jan. 10, 1918, Drew to Gentlemen, Feb. 21, 1918, Box 14, DP; Drew to Sayre, Mar. 1, 1918, Box 7, DP; Drew to Earle, Nov. 19, 1917, Box 2, DP; File 33-740, RG 280 (for Fore River strike); *NYT,* Nov. 1, 2, 6, 1917; Palmer, "Organizing the Shipyards," pp. 162–63, 166; Williams, "Shipbuilding and the Wilson Administration,"·p. 499.

26. Drew to Barr, Apr. 16, 1917, Gitelman notes.

27. Clyde Rogers, "Draft History of the Conference Board" [1965], pp. 21–23, Hagley Museum and Library; Minutes of NICB Executive Committee, Sept. 11, 1917, Ser. II, Reel 1, Accession 1057; *National War Labor Board,* Bureau of Labor Statistics Bulletin No. 287 (Washington: Government Printing Office, 1922), pp. 27–28; Conner, *Labor Board,* pp. 25–26; H. M. Gitelman, "Being of Two Minds: American Employers Confront the Labor Problem, 1915–1919," *Labor History* 25 (Winter 1984): 202–4. See chapter 1 for the anthracite ruling.

28. Drew to August Ziesing, Nov. 17, 1917, Box 1, DP; Drew to Cravath, Oct. 25, 1917, Drew to Barr, Oct. 26, 29 (and enclosure), 1917, Drew to Whitney, Oct. 26, 1917, Box 12, DP; Drew Address. . . , Nov. 16, 1917, Box 28, DP; Drew, "Unionization of American Industry as a War Measure," Dec. 11, 1917, Box 29, DP; *Review* 14 (Nov. 1917): 456–57.

29. Conner, *Labor Board,* pp. 27–29; Samuel Gompers, "American Labor Convention in War Time," *American Federationist* 25 (Jan. 1918): 33.

30. *National War Labor Board,* pp. 31–33.

31. Henry F. Pringle, *The Life and Times of William Howard Taft* (New York: Farrar and Rinehart, 1939), 2:917, 919; Lombardi, *Labor's Voice,* pp. 249–50; Jones, "Wilson Administration," pp. 362–63; Drew to Gentlemen, Apr. 13, 1918, Box 14, DP; Drew to Alexander, July 9, 1918, Ser. 5, Box 11, Accession 1057.

32. *National War Labor Board,* pp. 34, 41–42; Conner, *Labor Board,* pp. 30–32.

33. Drew to Alexander, July 9, 1918, Ser. 5, Box 11, Accession 1057; Minutes NICB Members, Oct. 10, 1918, Ser. III, Reel 1, ibid.; Alexander to Taft, Oct. 26, 1918, and enclosure, Reel 199, William Howard Taft Papers, University of Michigan Library; *National War Labor Board,* pp. 52–67; Haggai Hurvitz, "The Meaning of Industrial Conflict in Some Ideologies of the Early 1920s . . ." (Ph.D. diss., Columbia University, 1971), pp. 22–23; Conner, *Labor Board,* pp. 109, 123, 126–27, 136–37, 183; *Iron Age* 102 (Sept. 5, 1918): 584–85, (Nov. 28, 1918): 1323.

34. "Suggestions as to . . . War Labor Board" [Sept. 21, 1918], Box 29, DP; To Our Employees, Aug. 1, 1918, ibid.; Drew, "The Steel Fabricators of the United States," Oct. 21, 1918, Box 19, DP; Drew to Whitney, July 17, 1918, Box 8, DP; Allen to Members and Friends, May 29, 1918, Box 3, DP; NEA to Members, Aug. 23, 1918, Box 14, DP.

35. David Brody, *Steelworkers in America: The Nonunion Era* (New York: Harper and Brothers, 1960), pp. 207, 214–16; *Bridgemen's Magazine* 18 (Oct. 1918): 541–43; Drew to Members, Aug. 1, 1918, Box 14, DP; Drew to William Frew Long, Aug. 5, 1918, Box 12, DP; Drew, "Steel Fabricators."

36. Drew to National and Local Associations, Aug. 14, 1918, enclosing Drew to NWLB, Aug. 13, 1918, Box 16, DP; Drew to Secretaries, Aug. 7, 1918, Box 29, DP; NEA to Members, Aug. 23, 1918, Box 14, DP; Drew to H. H. McClintic, Jan. 18, 1919, Box 19, DP.

37. *Bridgemen's Magazine* 18 (Oct. 1918): 609; Drew to William Bayley Co., Jan. 7, 1919, Drew to McClintic, Jan. 18, 1919, Box 19, DP; Drew to Paul Willis, Sept. 16, 1918, Box 4, DP; Drew to S. E. Roberts, Mar. 8, 1924, Box 15, DP.

38. Drew to Members, Apr. 4, May 1, Oct. 5, 1917, Box 14, DP; Notice, June 18, 1917, ibid.; Drew to Members and Labor Bureaus, Apr. 8, 1918, ibid.; Drew to W. A. Garrigues, May 27, 1918, Box 16, DP; Hiram Oliphant to C. A. Crocker, July 5, 1918, and Exhibit A, Howard Conley to Crocker, July 6, 1918, Docket No. 76, Records of the National War Labor Board, RG 2, NARA; Digest. . . , July 18, 1918, ibid.

39. Minutes of the Special Meeting, June 3, 1918, Box 37A, Walsh Papers; Drew to Paul Starrett, July 3, 1918, Drew to Felix Frankfurter, June 13, 1918, Box 16, DP; Drew to W. Jett Lauck, June 7, 1918, Lauck to Drew, June 10, 1918, Frankfurter to Drew, June 12, 1918, Lauck to Drew and Worden, July 12, 1918, Docket 76, RG 2.

40. Lauck to D. A. Coyle and Thomas Slattery, June 12, 1918, Garrigues to Coyle, June 12, 1918, Coyle to Lauck, June 14, 1918, Lauck to Palmer and Serles, June 14, 1918, Broughton to Lauck, June 16, 1918, Drew to Lauck, June 15, 1918, W. L. Stoddard Memorandum for Lauck, June 20, 1918, Drew to Crocker, July 1, 1918, Crocker to Fuller, July 1, 1918, Conley to Crocker, July 6, 1918, Docket 76, RG 2; Proposed Memorandum of Agreement, undated, ibid.; Digest, ibid.; Memo-Conference, June 18, 1918, Box 16, DP; Conley to Fuller, June 26, 1918, Drew to Crocker, July 8, 1918, ibid.

41. Before the NWLB, Transcript of Record, July 8, 1918, Box 16, DP.

42. Digest, Docket 76, RG 2; Secretary to Drew, Oct. 4, 1918, ibid.; Marshall to Lauck, Oct. 24, 1918, Taft to Marshall, Nov. 7, 1918, Docket No. 58, ibid.; Docket No. 47, Reel 22, Papers of the National War Labor Board, University of Michigan Library; Drew to Taft, Aug. 29, 1918, Reel 197, Taft Papers; "Suggestions as to . . . War Labor Board"; Drew to National War Labor Board, Aug. 13, 1918, Box 16, DP; Drew, "Steel Fabricators," Box 19, DP; Krivy, "Organized Labor," p. 211.

43. "Suspension of the Eight Hour Clause in Contracts," Executive Order, Apr. 28, 1917, Box 6, DP; R. I. Ingalls to Drew, Oct. 29, 1917, Drew to Ingalls, Oct. 31, 1917, Drew to Emery, Oct. 31, 1917, Drew to William F. Richfield, Nov. 19, 1917, Box 12, DP; Drew, "Interpretation of the Eight Hour Law on War Work," Nov. 21, 1917, ibid.; Drew to Emery, Dec. 15, 1917, Box 6, DP; NEA Report of Commissioner, May 25, 1917, Box 37A, Walsh Papers; *American Federationist* 24 (Nov. 1917): 994–95; Conner, *Labor Board,* pp. 90–92.

44. Drew to Jacob Nathan, July 9, 1917, Box 18, DP; Drew to Editor, Boston Transcript, Nov. 2, 1917, Box 9, DP; "The Basic Eight Hour Day," n.d., Box 29, DP. Cf. William DeVoort in *Detroit Saturday Night,* July 27, 1918.

45. Docket No. 58, Reel 22, National War Labor Board Papers; H. L. Kerwin to Harry Jones, Mar. 23, 1918, Charles Bendheim to Kerwin, May 8, 1918, Frederick Davis to Kerwin, June 8, 1918, W. H. Arnold to W. B. Wilson, June 9, 1918, D.C. Bole to Lauck, June 18, 1918, T. A. Rice to Lauck, June 23, 1918, Docket No. 58, RG 2; Davis, Preliminary Report of Commissioner of Conciliation, Apr. 25, 1918, ibid.; Bendheim Preliminary Report. . . , May 11, 1918, ibid.

46. In Re the Issue between the Fort Pitt Bridge Works and Local 214. . . , Brief, undated, Box 29, DP; Adam Wilkinson to Lauck, Aug. 3, 1918, Docket No. 58, RG 2; Local #214 . . . vs. Fort Pitt Bridge Co., Transcript of Proceedings. . . , Aug. 14, 1918, ibid.

47. *NYT,* Sept. 25, 1918; Arnold to Lauck, Sept. 9, 1918, Gilmer Blose to Lauck, Oct. 7, 1918, Secretary to Lauck, Oct. 7, 1918, Secretary to Arnold, Apr. 26, 1919, Docket No. 58, RG 2; Drew to R. R. Woods, June 9, 1919, Exhibit File No. 1, File 1-2258-1, RG 122; Drew to Roberts, Mar. 8, 1924, Box 15, DP; *National War Labor Board,* p. 71.

48. Drew to H. M. O'Blennes, Sept. 27, Oct. 4, 1918, Drew to James E. Stein, Sept. 27, 1918, Drew to John D. Hibbard, Oct. 7, 1918, Drew to Earle, Oct. 15, 1918, Box 6, DP; Drew to Members, Oct. 1, 1918, Box 14, DP; Drew, "Steel Fabricators"; Docket No. 157, Reel 5, Papers of the National War Labor Board; *NWLB Employees Youngstown Foundry Department vs. United Engineering and Foundry Co.,* . . . *Oct 28, 1918,* Box 16, DP; *National War Labor Board,* p. 74.

49. Drew to Members, June 1, 1917, Box 14, DP; Minutes of the Regular Meeting of the AEA, Apr. 5, 1917, Box 1, DP; Drew to Brady, Apr. 26, 1917, Drew to Lauck, Aug. 2, 3, 1918, Drew to Taft, Aug. 19, 1918, Drew to Members AEA, Oct. 15, 1918, Drew to Michael, Oct. 21, 1918, ibid.; Drew to H.A. Fitch, May 15, 1917, Drew to William Graves, June 11, July 13, 1917, Drew to Gentlemen, Apr. 16, 1917, John Poushey to Drew, June 30, Graves to Drew, Apr. 26, 1917, P. Graves to National Refining Co., June 5, 1917, Drew to Poushey, Sept. 7, 1917, Box 3, DP; Drew to Taft, June 12, 1918, Drew to L. A. Osborne, June 26, 1918, Drew to Conley, July 5, 1918, Box 16, DP; Drew to Members (AEA), Oct. 15, 1918, Box 29, DP.

50. *Youngstown Foundry Department vs. United Engineering,* Oct. 28, 1918, Box 16, DP; Memorandum in the Case of . . . Wheeling Mold and Foundry Co. . . , Aug. 6, 1918, Box 29, DP; Drew, *Brief for Rochester Founders, Inc.,* Nov. 21, 1918, ibid.

51. F. H. Munkelt to Chamber of Commerce of the U.S., Sept. 30, 1918, Rights to Worden, Jan. 21, 1918, Munkelt to Fitch, Aug. 19, 1918, Box 19, DP.

52. For the Bridgeport case, see Jeffrey Haydu, *Between Craft and Class: Skilled Workers and Factory Politics in the United States and Britain, 1890–1922* (Berkeley: University of California Press, 1988), pp. 136–37, 183–88; Bucki, "Dilution and Craft Tradition," pp. 110–17; Daniel C. Ernst, "The Lawyers and the Labor Trust: A History of the American Anti-Boycott Association" (Ph.D. diss., Princeton University, 1989), pp. 323–27; Conner, *Labor Board,* pp. 129–34; *National War Labor Board,* pp. 197–208; Drew to Alexander, Aug. 9, 1918, Ser. 5, Box 11, Accession 1057; Drew to Whitney, July 10, 1918, Box 8, DP; and Drew, "Observations on Bridgeport and Smith and Wesson Cases," Sept. 23, 1918, Box 29, DP.

53. Leon Mann to Drew, Aug. 29, 1918, Drew to Frankfurter, Jan. 30, 1919, Box 5, DP.

54. *New York Call,* Sept. 11, 1918, clipping in ibid.; [*New York Tribune,* Sept. 2, 1918], clipping in ibid.; [Drew] to Martin Siegel, undated, [Drew] to E. M. Hopkins, Sept. 13, 1918, [Drew] to Harry Cohen, undated, Cohen to Frankfurter, Oct. 15, 1918,

Drew to Mann, Oct. 30, 1918, Drew to Ripley, Nov. 6, 1918, ibid.; *NYT,* Oct. 29, 30, Nov. 6, Dec. 21, 1918.

55. [*New York Evening World,* Nov. 13, 1918], clipping in Box 5, DP; Joseph Schlossberg to Jacob H. Schiff, undated, Drew to Ripley, Nov. 14, 1918, Drew to Schiff, Dec. 26, 1918, Max H. Friedman to Schiff, Dec. 19, 1918, [Drew] to Cohen, undated, Frankfurter to Drew, Jan. 28, 1919, Drew to Frankfurter, Jan. 30, 1919, Drew to John F. Perkins, Feb. 18, 1921, ibid.; *NYT,* Dec. 21, 1918.

56. *NYT,* Jan. 24, 1919; Drew to Ripley et al., Feb. 4, Mar. 28, 1919, Box 5, DP; United Advisory Board Report, Feb. 14, 1919, ibid.

57. Drew to Badorf, Feb. 18, 22, Mar. 1, 1919, Drew to Mann, Sept. 3, 1919, Box 5, DP; [*New York Record,* Mar. 26, 1919], clipping in ibid.

58. NEA Minutes, May 25, 1917, Box 37A, Walsh Papers; H. H. Anderson to Drew, Sept. 22, 1917, Apr. 12, May 29, Aug. 26, Oct. 31, Nov. 5, 9, 1918, Badorf to Drew, Mar. 30, 1918, Anderson to Members. . . , Aug. 15, 1918, Drew to Anderson, Aug. 24, 1918, Drew to K. L. Strickland, Nov. 4, 1918, Strickland to Drew, Nov. 4, 1918, Box 9, DP. See chapter 3 for the NEA and Kansas City before 1917.

59. Ernst, "Lawyers and the Labor Trust," pp. 132–76.

60. Drew to Ziesing, Oct. 17, 1917, Box 1, DP; Drew to E. Constance Woodward, Sept. 29, 1917, Drew to Whitney, Oct. 3, Nov. 1, 2, 1917, Drew to Alexander, Oct. 4, 1917, Drew to Frank H. Lee, Nov. 11, 1917, Drew to Editor, Danbury News, Oct. 16, 27, 1917, Drew to Industrial Economist, Oct. 19, 1917, Whitney to Lee, Oct. 24, 1917, Whitney to Drew, Nov. 7, 1917, Lee to Drew, Nov. 23, 1917, Feb. 6, 1918, Drew to F. C. Hood, May 6, 1918, Box 5, DP; *NYT,* Oct. 11, 1917; Herbert Janick, "From Union Town to Open Shop: The Decline of the United Hatters of Danbury, Connecticut, 1917–1922," *Connecticut History,* No. 33 (1990): 1–20.

61. Trade Unionism[,] A Constructive Criticism, Oct. 11, 1919, Box 29, DP.

62. Leo Wolman, *The Growth of American Trade Unions, 1880–1923* (New York: National Bureau of Economic Research, 1924), pp. 110–11.

Chapter 8

1. See, for example, Drew, "Structural Steel and Iron Work in New York," Nov. 18, 1919, Box 29, DP.

2. Drew, "Statement to Federal Trade Commission (FTC). . . ," July 21, 1921, Box 11, DP; *Bridgemen's Magazine* 18 (Oct. 1918): 667, 710, (Nov. 1918): 748, 749.

3. Drew, "Structural Steel and Iron Work"; William Simpson, Jr., to George E. Gifford, May 26, 1919, Box 19, DP; Drew and A. S. Roberts, "Situation in the Structural Iron Industry in New York City," Mar. 11, 1920, Box 29, DP; Drew to Thomas Earle, June 25, 1919, Exhibit File No. 1, File 1-2258-1, Records of the Federal Trade Commission, RG 122, NARA; *Bridgemen's Magazine* 19 (May 1919): 232, 236, (Aug. 1919): 408. The St. Louis boycott did not extend to steel fabrication in nonunion shops in the East, which probably killed the small St. Louis fabricators. Statement by Eugene G. Grace, Feb. 5, 1921, Exhibit File No. 3, File 1-2258-1, RG 122.

4. David Brody, *Labor in Crisis: The Steel Strike of 1919* (Philadelphia: J. B. Lippincott Co., 1965), pp. 98–99, 111; *Bridgemen's Magazine* 19 (Nov. 1919): 555; ibid. 20 (Oct. 1920): 545–46, 549.

5. Frank D. Lent Final Report, July 25, 1921, File 1-2258-2-4, RG 122; Drew to Earle, June 25, 1919 (2 letters), Exhibit File No. 1, File 1-2258-1, ibid.

6. Drew to Lackawanna Bridge Co., Aug. 11, 1919, Exhibit File No. 1, File

1-2258-1, ibid.; Minutes of the NEA Executive Committee (hereafter NEA Minutes), Aug. 26, 1919, Box 37A, Frank Walsh Papers, New York Public Library, New York, New York.

7. Secretary to James Emery, Sept. 12, 1919, Box 19, DP; Charles Kalhorn to Drew, Sept. 22, 1919, Box 20, DP; Earle to Executive Committee, Sept. 27, 1919, G. A. Tretter to Earle, Sept. 27, 1919, Clyde MacCornack to Earle, Oct. 2, 1919, Drew to Members NEA and AEA, Oct. 10, 1919, Exhibit File No. 1, File 1-2258-1, RG 122; NEA Minutes, Nov. 13, 1919, Box 37A, Walsh Papers.

8. Earle to Drew, Oct. 27, Nov. 28, 1919, Feb. 18, Mar. 1, 1920, Drew to Earle, Nov. 29, 1919, Exhibit File No. 1, File 1-2258-1, RG 122; Minutes of Meeting of Executive Committee of National Steel Fabricators Association, Dec. 12, 1919, ibid.; [August Ziesing] to J. A. Farrell, May 18, 1920, File 1-2258-2-3, ibid.; Earle to Drew, Feb. 24, 1920, Ziesing to Drew, Dec. 28, 1919, Drew to Ziesing, Dec. 31, 1919, Thomas F. Fulton to J. F. Ritter, Feb. 10, 1920, Box 4, DP; Drew, "FTC Statement"; Drew to H. H. Lewis, Feb. 19, 1921, Box 18, DP; Minutes of the Chicago Federation of Labor, Nov. 2, 1919, Feb. 15, Mar. 21, 1921, Chicago Historical Society, Chicago, Illinois; *Bridgemen's Magazine* 19 (Feb. 1919): 69; ibid. 20 (Mar. 1920): 118, (June 1920): 260, (Oct. 1920): 593.

9. Brody, *Labor in Crisis,* p. 174; *Bridgemen's Magazine* 20 (Oct. 1920): 545–46.

10. *Bridgemen's Magazine* 20 (Feb. 1920): 65–66, (Oct. 1920): 546–47, 745; H. A. Wagner to NEA, July 21, 1919, Box 12, DP; Drew to Members, Aug. 27, 1919, May 5, 1920, Box 14, DP; C. L. McKenzie to Drew, Oct. 13, 1919, G. A. Caffall to Drew, Oct. 17, 1919, Drew to Caffall, Oct. 28, 1919, Drew to MacCornack, Jan. 3, 1920, Earle to Drew, Feb. 16, 1920, Drew to George W. Grant, Mar. 8, 1920, L. F. W. H[ildner] to Earle, Mar. 5, 1920, Drew to Hildner, Mar. 11, 1920, J. J. Brennan to Drew, Apr. 1, 1920, Drew to W. S. Mosher, Sept. 20, 1920, Box 8, DP; NEA, A Statement to Our Open Shop Employees, Mar. 5, 1920, Box 29, DP; Drew to Bethlehem Fabricators, Apr. 22, 1920, Box 20, DP; [ILEA] to Our Employees, Mar. 1, 1920, Box 37A, Walsh Papers; E. F. Zuleger to J. W. Hollenbach, Nov. 3, 1920, Box 64, ibid.; Memorandum on the Open Shop . . . [1920], ibid.; [Ziesing] to Farrell, May 18, 1920, File 1-2258-2-3, RG 122; NEA and ILEA to Our Employees, Mar. 1, 1920, Iron League to Housesmiths and Bridgemen, July 31, 1920, Exhibit File No. 4, File 1-2258-1, ibid.; P. Morrin to Frank Walsh, Aug. 31, 1920, Reel 35, American Federation of Labor Records: The Samuel Gompers Era, University of Michigan Library, Ann Arbor, Michigan.

11. William Haber, *Industrial Relations in the Building Industry* (New York: Arno and New York Times, 1971), pp. 358–59; ILEA v. BTC . . . [Nov. 20, 1919], Box 29, DP; Memorandum [1921], Box 8, DP; Drew, "FTC Statement"; Statements of Walter Gordon Merritt and Walter Drew, Jan. 13, 1921, File 1-2258-1, RG 122; Lent interview with C. G. Norman, June 9, 1921, File 1-2258-2-4, ibid.; Lent Final Report, July 25, 1921, ibid.; Joshua A. Hatfield testimony, Dec. 16, 1920, pp. 3696, 3701, Exhibit File No. 6, File 1-2258-1, ibid. See chapter 2.

12. C. E. Cheney testimony, Dec. 15, 1920, pp. 3593–97, 3603, Exhibit File No. 6, File 1-2258-1, RG 122; Lent interview with Howard Sherwin, Feb. 25, 1921, File 1-2258-2-4, ibid.; Lent Final Report, ibid.; Drew to Richard Kuehn, May 5, 1921, File 1-2258-2-3, ibid.

13. John Hutchinson, *The Imperfect Union: A History of Corruption in America* (New York: E. P. Dutton and Co., 1970), pp. 37–38; Robert Christie, *An Empire in Wood: A History of the Carpenters' Union* (Ithaca: Cornell University Press, 1956), pp. 204–15; Haber, *Building Industry,* p. 383; Drew to Earle, June 25, 1919, Exhibit File No. 1, File 1-2258-1, RG 122; Norman interview, File 1-2258-2-4, ibid.; Lent Final

Report, ibid.; BTEA Circular No. 271, Jan. 10, 1921, ibid.; Joint Legislative Committee on Housing, Minutes of Hearings, Oct. 10, 1920, p. 22, New York Public Library.

14. Cheney to Gentlemen, Nov. 15, 1919, Box 37A, Walsh Papers; Norman interview, File 1-2258-2-4, RG 122; Lent Final Report, July 25, 1921, ibid.; [Drew, U.S. grand jury memorandum, 1921], Box 18, DP; undated document, Box 11, DP; *NYT,* Dec. 31, 1920; *Bridgemen's Magazine* 19 (Nov. 1914): 551.

15. Norman interview, File 1-2258-2-4, RG 122; Minutes of ILEA Special Meeting, Nov. 25, 1919, Box 37A, Walsh Papers; BTEA Circular Letter No. 257, Dec. 19, 1919, ibid.; State of New York, *Intermediate Report of the Joint Legislative Committee on Housing,* Legislative Document No. 60 (Albany: J. Blyon Co., 1922), p. 79; *NYT,* Dec. 3, 1919; *Bridgemen's Magazine* 20 (Feb. 1920): 53.

16. Drew to Earle, June 25, 30, 1919, Drew to Grace, Sept. 22, 1919, Drew to R. P. Hutchinson, Sept. 22, 1919, Exhibit File No. 1, File 1-2258-1, RG 122; Drew to G. W. Smith, June 22, 29, 1914, Box 1, DP. See chapter 3.

17. Secretary of ILEA to Norman, Nov. 11, 1919, File 1-2258-1, President of ILEA to Samuel B. Donnelly, Dec. 5, 1919, Exhibit File No. 2, File 1-2258-1, RG 122; Cheney to Gentlemen, Nov. 15, 1919, Box 37A, Walsh Papers; Minutes of ILEA Special Meeting, Oct 21, 1919, ibid.

18. *NYT,* Dec. 5, 1919; ILEA v. BTC [Nov. 20, 1919], Box 29, DP; Drew, "Structural Steel and Iron Work"; Drew and Roberts, "Structural Iron Industry," Box 29, DP; Drew, "FTC Statement"; [Drew] Memorandum [1921], Box 8, DP; W. L. Garrigues to Grace, Dec. 11, 1919, Exhibit File No. 1, File 1-2258-1, RG 122; Lent interview with Drew, June 2, 1921, File 1-2258-2-3, ibid.

19. ILEA v. BTC [Nov. 20, 1919], Box 29, DP; Drew, "Structural Steel and Iron Work"; Minutes of ILEA Special Meeting, Box 37A, Walsh Papers; To Our Employees, Nov. 28, 1919, ibid.; Member ILEA to All Architects. . . , Nov. 26, 1919, Drew to Earle, Nov. 29, 1919, Drew to George H. Blakeley, Dec. 9, 1919, Exhibit File No. 1, File 1-2258-1, RG 122; Agreement, Nov. 26, 1919, ibid.

20. Minutes of ILEA Regular Meeting, Dec. 11, 1919, Box 37A, Walsh Papers; Minutes of Meeting of Industrial Committee, Dec. 11, 1919, Exhibit File No. 1, File 1-2258-1, RG 122.

21. Drew to Earle, Nov. 29, 1919, Roberts to Members, Dec. 31, 1919, Exhibit File No. 1, File 1-2258-1, RG 122; Minutes of ILEA Regular Meeting, Dec. 11, 1919, Box 37A, Walsh Papers.

22. Drew, "Structural Steel and Iron Work"; Drew to Farrell, Nov. 8, 1919, Drew to Earle, Nov. 3, 1919, Drew to Grace, Nov. 3, 1919, Grace to Drew, Nov. 4, 1919, Cheney to Gentlemen, Nov. 8, 1919, Exhibit File No. 1, File 1-2258-1, RG 122; T. L. L. to Kuehn, Nov. 4, 1919, Kuehn to Gemberling, Nov. 4, 1919, File 1-2258-2-3, ibid.

23. NSFA List of Members, Nov. 20, 1919, Box 64, Walsh Papers; Constitution of NSFA, Nov. 20, 1919, ibid.; NSFA Bulletin No. 4 [Nov. 20, 1919], ibid.; Drew to Editor of World, Feb. 16, 1920, Box 29, DP; Drew to Merritt, Jan. 19, 1921, Box 11, DP; Drew to W. W. Corlett, May 18, 1921, Box 19, DP; George E. Gifford testimony, Dec. 14, 1920, pp. 3456–69, 3474, Exhibit File No. 3, File 1-2258-1, RG 122.

24. Minutes of Meeting of Executive Committee, Dec. 12, 1919, Exhibit File No. 1, File 1-2258-1, RG 122; Drew to Lewis D. Rights, Jan. 5, 1920, ibid.; NSFA Bulletin No. 2, June 7, 1920, ibid.

25. Statement of Thomas Earle, Feb. 19, 1921, Exhibit File No. 3, File 1-2258-1, RG 122; Merritt and Drew Statements, Jan. 13, 1921, File 1-2258-1, ibid.; Lent Final Report, File 1-2258-2-4, ibid.; Drew to John A. Fitch, Jan. 4, 1921, Box 10, DP.

26. Grace to Garrigues, Dec. 15, 1919, Garrigues to Grace, Dec. 11, 1919, Earle to Drew, Nov. 28, Dec. 10, 11, 17, 1919, Drew to Earle, Dec. 11, 12, 1919, Garrigues to Earle, Dec. 13, 18, 1919, Earle to Garrigues, Dec. 17, 1919, Blakeley to Drew, Dec. 17, 1919, Exhibit File No. 1, File 1-2258-1, RG 122; NEA Minutes, Aug. 26, 1919, Box 37A, Walsh Papers.

27. Statements of Thomas Earle and G. H. Blakeley, Jan. 31, 1921, Grace Statement, Feb. 5, 1921, Exhibit File No. 3, File 1-2258-1, RG 122; Harry S. Black testimony, Dec. 14, 1920, pp. 3451–55, Exhibit File No. 6, ibid.; Recommendation of Commissioner [Victor] Murdock, Feb. 1, 1922, File 1-2258-2-4, ibid.

28. *NYT,* Jan. 3, Feb. 26, 29, 1920; Drew and Roberts, "Structural Iron Industry"; Drew to Ziesing, Jan. 9, 1920, Box 4, DP; Minutes of ILEA Regular Meeting, Jan. 8, 1920, Box 37A, Walsh Papers; Roberts to Members ILEA, Jan. 15, 1920, Exhibit File No. 1, File 1-2258-1, RG 122; Roberts to Members ILEA, Feb. 25, 1920, Exhibit File No. 4, ibid.; Minutes of ILEA Special Meetings, Jan. 23, Feb. 7, Apr. 29, 1920, ibid,; Minutes ILEA Regular Meeting, Feb. 13, 1923, ibid.; Drew interview, File 1-2258-2-3, ibid.; Norman interview, File 1-2258-2-4, ibid.

29. *McCord* v. *Thompson Starrett,* 113 NYS (1908); Drew and Roberts to Members, Feb. 4, 1920, Exhibit File No. 1, File 1-2258-1, RG 122; Drew and Roberts, "Structural Iron Industry," Box 29, DP. The New Jersey case was *Lehigh Structural Steel Co. and Donnell Zane Co. Inc.* v. *Atlantic Smelting and Refinery Works, et al.*

30. Notice. . . , Feb. 7, 1920, Box 29, DP; Drew to Dear Sir, Mar. 2, 1920, Box 14, DP; Drew to Brennan, May 7, 1920, Box 8, DP; Drew to Gentlemen, May 28, 1920, Box 4, DP; Drew to Earle, Mar. 2, 10, May 6, 1920 (and enclosure), Roberts to Members, May 27, 1920, Exhibit File No. 1, File 1-2258-1, RG 122; Norman interview, File 1-2258-2-4, ibid.; BTEA Circular No. 260, Apr. 30, 1920, BTEA Circular No. 271, Jan. 10, 1921, ibid.; *NYT,* Apr. 24, 1920; *Bridgemen's Magazine* 20 (May 1920): 217–18, (Aug. 1920): 392, 402; Joint Legislative Committee on Housing, Minutes of Hearings, Oct. 20, 1920, pp. 23–27, New York Public Library.

31. Minutes of ILEA Special Meeting, Apr. 29, 1920, Box 37A, Walsh Papers; Garrigues Papers, undated, Exhibit File No. 1, File 1-2258-1, RG 122; Roberts to Donnelly, May 5, 1920, ibid.; undated document, Box 11, DP.

32. Drew to Gentlemen, May 28, 1920, Box 14, DP; Drew to Earle, May 6, 1920, Exhibit File No. 1, File 1-2258-1, RG 122; Norman interview, File 1-2258-2-4, ibid.

33. Earle and Blakeley statements, Jan. 31, 1921, Statement by Joshua A. Hatfield. . . , Feb. 8, 1921, Exhibit File No. 3, File 1-2258-1, RG 122; [Ziesing] to Farrell, May 18, 1920, File 1-2258-2-3, ibid.; Lent interview with E. A. Gibbs, May 13, 1921, ibid., and C. D. Marshall, File 1-2258-2-2, ibid.

34. Untermeyer remarks, p. 3183, Exhibit File No. 6, File 1-2258-1, ibid.

35. Earle and Blakeley statements, Grace statement, Exhibit File No. 3, File 1-2258-1, ibid.; Lent interview with Blakeley, May 24, 25, 1921, File 1-2258-1, ibid.; Louis Horowitz testimony, Dec. 14, 1920, pp. 3362–79, Eugene G. Grace testimony, Dec. 15, 1920, pp. 3614–43, 3646–47, Exhibit File No. 6, File 1-2258-1, ibid.; Louis J. Horowitz and Boysden Sparks, *The Towers of New York* (New York: Simon and Schuster, 1973), pp. 204–6.

36. Paul Starrett testimony, Dec. 14, 1920, pp. 3343–60, Black Testimony, Dec. 14, 1920, pp. 3451–55, Exhibit File No. 6, File 1-2258-1, RG 122; Earle and Blakeley statements, Grace statement, Exhibit File No. 3, ibid.; Blakeley interview, File 1-2258-1, ibid. Drew claimed that Fuller had disposed of its erection equipment before the 1919 agreement. Drew, "FTC Statement."

37. Affidavit of Timothy J. Tierney, Nov. 4, 1920, Box 64, Walsh Papers; J. R. Buchanan Final Report, Sept. 22, 1920, ibid.

38. Statements of Hatfield, W. W. Corlett, and A. L. Davis, Feb. 8, 1921, Exhibit File No. 3, File 1-2258-1, RG 122; Starrett testimony, p. 3348, Horowitz testimony, pp. 3370–71, Exhibit File No. 6, ibid.; Lent interview with Robert Allen Pendergras, May 6, 1921, File 1-2258-2-2, ibid.; Gibbs interview, Lent interview with Richard Kuehn, May 23, 1921, ibid.; [Ziesing] to Farrell, May 18, 1920, File 1-2258-2-3, ibid.; Drew to Editor the World, Feb. 16, 1920, Box 29, DP.

39. *Bridgemen's Magazine* 20 (Aug. 1920): 402, 404–8; Marion Eucharia Meehan, "Frank Walsh and the American Labor Movement" (Ph.D. diss., New York University, 1962), p. 141.

40. Morrin to Morrison, Jan. 20, Aug. 31, Nov. 2, 1920, Morrison to Morrin, July 14, 1920, Duffy to Morrison, Nov. 27, 1920, Reel 35, AFL Records; Morrin to Kerwin, July 8, 1920, Kerwin to J. J. Barrett, July 9, 1920, Barrett to Kerwin, undated, Barrett to Kerwin, Dec. 6, 1920, File 170-1189, Records of the Federal Mediation and Conciliation Service, RG 280, NARA; Barrett, Preliminary Report of Commissioner of Conciliation, Nov. 27, 1920, ibid.; Lent Final Report, File 1-2258-2-4, RG 122.

41. Horowitz testimony, pp. 3373–74, Grace testimony, pp. 3625, 3633, Exhibit File No. 6, File 1-2258-1, RG 122; Lent interview with C. D. Marshall and C. M. Denise, May 10, 1921, File 1-2258-2-2, ibid.

42. Lent interview with George L. Bingham, Apr. 27, 1921, File 1-2258-2-1, ibid.; Minutes of Meeting of Iron Trade, May 19, 1921, ibid.; Lent interview with Herbert K. Bear, May 3, 1921, John Hohman, May 3, 1921, W. Nelson Mayhew, May 4, 1921, and John L. Wiggins and J. Abbott, May 5, 1921, File 1-2258-2-2, ibid.; Lent interview with W. Nelson Mayhew, File 1-2258-2-3, ibid.; Lent Final Report, File 1-2258-2-4, ibid.; Drew to Joseph M. Steele May 29, 1919, Box 9, DP; NEA Minutes, June 3, 1919, Box 37A, Walsh Papers.

43. Drew to Manufacturers' Association of Philadelphia, May 12, 1919, Drew to Rights, May 14, 1919, Drew to Steele, May 29, 1919, Drew to J. H. Schwake, May 29, 1919, Mayhew to Drew, June 7, 1919, Drew to Mayhew, June 11, 24, 1919, Box 9, DP; Drew to W. B. Douglass, May 31, 1919, Box 7, DP; Drew to Earle, June 25, 1919, Exhibit File No. 1, File 1-2258-1, RG 122; Minutes of Meeting of Iron Trade, May 19, 27, 1919, File 1-2258-2-1, ibid.; Minutes of Meeting of Iron League, June 2, 1919, ibid.; Lent Final Report, File 1-2258-2-4, ibid.; NEA Minutes, June 3, 1919, Box 37A, Walsh Papers.

44. Drew to Dear Sir, Mar. 2, 1920, Drew to Gentlemen, May 28, 1920, Box 14, DP; Drew to Gentlemen, Apr. 5, 25, 1920, Drew to B. T. Mial, Apr. 21, 1920, Box 9, DP; Drew to Gibbs, June 3, 11, 1920, Gibbs to Drew, June 12, 1920, Drew to Mayhew, June 3, July 3, 1920, Box 17, DP; Drew to Earle, Mar. 2, Apr. 27, 1920, Earle to Blakeley, Mar. 9, 1920, Drew to Blakeley, Apr. 19, 1920, Earle to Drew, Apr. 21, May 18, 1920, Mayhew to Drew, June 5, 1920, Mial to Bethlehem Bridge Co., Apr. 23, 1920, Earle to Roberts, June 21, 1920, Roberts to Members, July 9, 20, 1920, Mial to Roberts, Sept. 4, 1920, Exhibit File No. 1, File 1-2258-1, RG 122; Minutes of Iron League Meeting, Apr. 12, 1920, File 1-2258-2-1, ibid.; Lent Final Report, File 1-2258-2-4, ibid,; NEA Minutes, May 28, 1920, Box 37A, Walsh Papers.

45. Roberts to Bethlehem Steel Bridge Corporation, Aug 4, 1920, Bear to Bethlehem Fabricators, Oct. 25, 1920, Drew to Earle, Nov. 3, 1920, Exhibit File No. 1, File 1-2258-1, RG 122; Lent interview with Mike J. Cunnane, Apr. 27, 1921, Drew, Bingham, Olaf Tennessen, Apr. 27, 1921, S. A. Lindstrom, Apr. 27, 1921, Mr. Frank, Apr. 27,

1921, and Lacy Evans, Apr. 28, 1921, File 1-2258-2-1, ibid.; Lent interview with Joseph Steele, May 3, 1921, Bear, Apr. 28, 29, May 3, 1921, Hohman, H. E. Fox, May 4, 1921, F. Roller, May 4, 1921, Mayhew, V. T. Bornet, May 4, 1921, Wiggins and Abbott, and Marshall and Denise, File 1-2258-2-2, ibid.; Lent interview with Bear, Nov. 27, 1921, File 1-2258-2-3, ibid.; Merritt and Drew Statements, File 1-2258-1, ibid.; Lent Final Report, File 1-2258-2-4, ibid. See chapter 9.

46. Joint Legislative Committee, *Intermediate Report,* pp. 1, 6, 256.

47. Ibid., pp. 36–48; Hutchinson, *Imperfect Union,* pp. 38, 40–41; Joint Legislative Committee on Housing, Minutes of Hearings, Oct. 28, 1920, pp. 497–540, New York Public Library, ibid., Part 4, Dec. 6, 1921, p. 4162, University of Michigan Library; *NYT,* Nov. 1, 14, 18, 19, 25, Dec. 15, 1920, Jan. 5, Feb. 4, 13, 1921.

48. Joint Legislative Committee, *Intermediate Report,* pp. 49–52.

49. Ibid., pp. 9, 65–127; *NYT,* Dec. 13, 31, 1920; Ralph P. Taylor, "What the Lockwood Committee Disclosed," *Nation* 113 (July 6, 1921): 13; Affidavit of Theodore Brandle, July 7, 1924, Levering and Garrigues et al. Plaintiff against Paul J. Morrin et al., Box 11, DP; State of New York, *Final Report of the Joint Legislative Committee on Housing,* Legislative Document (1923) (Albany: J. B. Lyon Co., 1923), pp. 12–14; Hutchinson, *Imperfect Union,* pp. 39–40.

50. Walsh to William P. Harvey, Nov. 30, 1920, Untermeyer to John Fitzpatrick, Sept. 20, 1919, Box 9, Walsh Papers; Walsh to B. L. Shinn, Apr. 9, 1921, File 1-2258-2-1, RG 122; Duffy to Morrison, Nov. 27, 1920, Reel 35, AFL Records; Drew to Members, Aug. 1, 1923, Box 14, DP; Emery to Louis Pierson, Dec. 22, 1920, Box 11, DP.

51. Starrett testimony, pp. 3345–54, 3357–60, Horowitz testimony, pp. 3363–79, Grace testimony, p. 3656, Frank McCord testimony, Dec. 14, 1920, pp. 3417–19, Harry W. Lazette et al. testimony, Dec. 15, 1920, pp. 3567–69, Exhibit File No. 6, File 1-2258-1, RG 122; Extracts from Testimony of Charles E. Cheney, Dec. 16, 17, 1920, Box 11, DP.

52. Robert Foster testimony, Dec. 16, 1920, pp. 3209–55, Exhibit File No. 6, File 1-2258-1, RG 122; Cheney testimony, in Structural Steel and Iron Fabricating Industry, Transcript of Hearing, Oct. 30, 1933, pp. 117–33, Box 7241, Records of the National Recovery Administrationn, RG 9, NARA; Drew to Members, Aug. 1, 1923, Box 14, DP; untitled, undated pages, Box 7, DP; Joint Legislative Committee, Minutes of Hearings, Part 4, May 4, 1922, pp. 7106–7, University of Michigan Library; *Bridgemen's Magazine* 21 (Feb. 1921): 87; *NYT,* Dec. 18, 24, 1920, Mar. 31, 1921, Feb. 1, 3, 1922, Jan. 27, 1923.

53. *NYT,* Dec. 17, 18, 1920; *Iron Age* 106 (Dec. 23, 1920): 1673, 1708; Drew to William Butterworth, Dec. 29, 1920, Box 18, DP.

54. Joint Legislative Committee, *Intermediate Report,* pp. 128–30; *NYT,* Dec. 18, 1920; *Bridgemen's Magazine* 21 (Jan. 1921): 25–26, 28.

55. Drew to Untermeyer, Oct. 21, 1920, Box 11, DP; Drew, "FTC Statement," ibid.; Drew to Members, Feb. 16, 1921, ibid.; [Drew, U.S. grand jury memorandum, 1921] Box 8, DP; [Drew] Memorandum [1921], ibid.; Drew to W. F. Hennessey, May 23, 1921, Box 3, DP; Drew to Editor New York Herald, Feb. 15, 1922, Box 29, DP; Drew interview, File 1-2258-2-3, RG 122.

56. [Drew, U.S. grand jury memorandum, 1921], Box 8, DP; [Drew] Memorandum [1920], ibid.; Drew, "FTC Statement"; Drew to Members, Feb. 16, 1921, ibid.; Drew to Members, Aug. 1, 1923, Box 14, DP; Drew interview, File 1-2258-2-3, RG 122; Meehan, "Walsh," p. 142.

57. [Drew] Memorandum [1921], Box 8, DP; Drew to Brennan, May 7, 1920, ibid.;

Minutes of [Iron League] Regular Meeting, May 20, 1920, Exhibit File No. 1, File 1-2258-1, RG 122; Shinn interview with Horowitz, Mar. 8, 1921, File 1-2258-2-1, ibid.; Lent interview with Starrett, Apr. 20, 1921, with John L. Hay, Apr. 22, 1921, ibid.; Lent interview with Gibbs, May 16, 1921, File 1-2258-2-3, ibid.; Untermeyer to Walsh, Dec. 24, 1921, Walsh to Untermeyer, Dec. 29, 1921, Walsh to Basil Manly, Feb. 6, 1922, Box 10, Walsh Papers; Structural Steel Fabricating Industry, Transcript of Hearing, Oct. 30, 1933, pp. 133–34, 192–93, Box 7241, RG 9; Leighton H. Peebles, "History of the Code of Fair Competition for the Structural Steel Fabricating Industry," Oct. 13, 1936, p. 109, Box 7639, ibid.

58. Drew to Untermeyer, Oct. 21, 1920, Box 11, DP; Drew, "FTC Statement"; [Drew, U.S. grand jury Memorandum, 1921], Box 8, DP; Drew to Merritt, Jan. 19, 1921, Drew to Fitch, Jan. 4, 1921, Drew to Ziesing, July 27, 1926, Box 12, DP; Drew interview, June 2, 1921, File 102258-2-3, RG 122.

59. Drew to Fitch, Jan. 4, 1921, Box 10, DP; Drew to NYT, Feb. 1, 1921, Box 29, DP; Drew, "FTC Statement"; [Drew, U.S. grand jury Memorandum, 1921], Box 8, DP; Drew to E. J. McCone, June 29, 1921, Drew to Committee of United States Senate, Oct. 28, 1921, Box 11, DP; *Bridgemen's Magazine* 21 (Mar. 1921): 115, 116. See chapter 3 for NEA espionage after the Indianapolis trial.

60. Drew, "FTC Statement"; Drew to William H. Barr, Dec. 22, 1920, Drew to Editor New York Herald, Feb. 15, 1922, Box 11, DP; Drew to Members, Aug. 1, 1923, Box 14, DP.

61. Shinn to Millard F. Hudson, Jan. 19, 1921, File 1-2258-3, RG 122; Supplemental Report by B. L. Shinn, Aug. 27, 1921, File 1-2258-2-4, ibid.; Drew to Members, Feb. 16, 1921, Drew to Editor of the Times, Nov. 1, 1921, Box 11, DP; Drew to Members, Aug. 6, 1921, Box 14, DP.

62. [Drew, U.S. grand jury Memorandum, 1921], Box 8, DP; [Drew] Memorandum [1921], ibid.; Drew to Members, Feb. 16, 1921, Drew to Ziesing, Feb. 16, 1921, Drew to Committee of United States Senate, Oct. 28, 1921, Box 11, DP; Drew to Members, Aug. 6, 1921, Box 14, DP; Merritt and Drew statements, File 1-2258-1, RG 122; Morrin to Chester M. Wright, June 5, 1924, Reel 35, AFL Records.

63. Shinn Supplemental Report, File 1-2258-2-4, RG 122; Drew to Ziesing, July 27, 1926, Box 12, DP.

64. Shinn Supplemental Report, File 1-2258-2-4, RG 122; Morrin, Petition for Formal Complaint . . . [Nov. 26, 1920], File 1-2258-1, ibid.; Drew, "FTC Statement."

65. Drew to Members, Aug. 1, 1923, Box 14, DP; Walsh to Clarence Darrow, Apr. 22, 1921, Walsh to Morrin, Apr. 29, 1921, Walsh to McNamara, May 3, 1921, Box 10, Walsh Papers.

66. Lent Final Report, File 1-2258-2-4, RG 122.

67. Shinn Supplemental Report, ibid.

68. Board of Review Report, Sept. 12, 1921, ibid.

69. Recommendation of Commissioner Murdock, Feb. 11, 1922, ibid.; FTC Order of Dismissal, July 23, 1923, ibid.

70. Drew to Members, Aug. 1, 1923, Box 14, DP.

71. Untermeyer to McCord, Feb. 5, Dec. 23, 1921, Untermeyer to McCone, June 21, 1921, Box 11, DP; *Greater New York,* Oct. 31, 1921, ibid.; Drew to Ziesing, July 27, 1920, Box 12, DP; [Drew] Memorandum [1921], Box 8, DP; Senate Committee on Education and Labor, *West Virginia Coal Fields. Hearings,* 67 Cong., 1 sess., 1921, pp. 698–701; *NYT,* Oct. 27, 1921.

72. [Drew] Memorandum [1921], Box 8, DP; Drew to McCone, Jan. 21, 1921, Box

15, DP; Drew to McCone, Jan. 23, 1922, Box 18, DP; Drew to Emery, Feb. 12, 1921, Drew to Edwin Allen Stebbins, Feb. 25, 1923, Drew to H. H. Anderson, Feb. 1, 1922, Drew to Committee of U.S. Senate, Oct. 26, 28, 1921, Box 11, DP.

73. For a complete list of the recommended reforms, see Associated Builders of Chicago, *Bulletin,* Jan. 1922, Box 11, DP. See also Joint Legislative Committee, *Intermediate Report,* pp. 53–60.

74. [Drew] Memorandum [1921], Box 18, DP; Drew to Merritt, Jan. 30, 1922, Box 10, DP; Drew to Editor of Times, Nov. 1, 1921, Drew to Anderson, Feb. 1, 1922, Drew to Editor New York Tribune, Feb. 4, 1922, Box 11, DP; Drew to McCone, Jan. 23, 1922, Box 18, DP; *NYT,* Mar. 11, 1922.

75. Haber, *Building Industry,* pp. 364–66; *NYT,* Mar. 11, 1922, Feb. 28, 1923, Feb. 15, 1927; New York Building Trades Situation Information Memorandum. . . , Mar. 23, 1929, Ser. I, Box 251, Records of the National Association of Manufacturers, Accession 1411, Hagley Museum and Library, Wilmington, Delaware; Joint Legislative Committee, *Final Report,* pp. 34, 47–48, 50, 52; *New York World,* Nov. 25, 1929, clipping in Box 29, DP; Hutchinson, *Imperfect Union,* pp. 42–47.

Chapter 9

1. Allen Morton Wakstein, "The Open-Shop Movement, 1919–1933" (Ph.D. diss., University of Illinois, 1961), p. 161; Wakstein, "The Origins of the Open Shop Movement, 1919–1920," *Journal of American History* 51 (Dec. 1964): 460–62.

2. Leo Troy, *Trade Union Membership, 1897–1962* (New York: Columbia University Press [1965]), p. 1; Sumner H. Slichter, "The Current Labor Policies of American Industries," *Quarterly Journal of Economics* 43 (May 1929): 396, 398; Wakstein, "Open-Shop Movement," pp. 34, 37–39; *Iron Age* 106 (Dec. 2, 1920): 1489; Robert K. Murray, *Red Scare* (Minneapolis: University of Minnesota Press, 1955), pp. 105–65; *Detroit Saturday Night,* July 5, 1919, July 10, 1920; Robert L. Friedheim, *The Seattle General Strike* (Seattle: University of Washington Press, 1964), pp. 158–60; Haggai Hurvitz, "The Meaning of Industrial Conflict in Some Ideologies of the 1920's" (Ph.D. diss., Columbia University, 1971), pp. 25–27; NAM, *Proceedings of the Thirtieth Annual Convention, Oct. 26–28, 1925,* p. 76.

3. Wakstein, "Open-Shop Movement," pp. 51–60; Wakstein, "Origins," pp. 462–67, 469–70; A. J. Haun, "Nation Swinging to Open Shop," *Iron Trade Review* 67 (Sept. 23, 1920): 846; Murray, *Red Scare,* pp. 267–68.

4. *Detroit Saturday Night,* July 10, 1920; Wakstein, "Open-Shop Movement," pp. 101–4; Drew to Allen, Oct. 29, 1920, John D. Hibbard to Drew, Nov. 1, 1920, Stephen G. Mason to Drew, Nov. 12, 1920, Allen to Drew, Dec. 6, 1920, Box 7, DP; Drew to Gentlemen, Nov. 30, 1920, Box 29, DP; Minutes of the Open Shop Committee, Nov. 16, 1920, Ser. I, Box 251, Archives of the National Association of Manufacturers, Accession 1411, Hagley Museum and Library, Wilmington, Delaware.

5. Savel Zimand, *The Open Shop Drive* (New York: Bureau of Industrial Research [1921]), pp. 5–6, 19; *Iron Age* 107 (Jan. 20, 1921): 201; George to Drew, Dec. 5, 1921, Drew to George, Dec. 12, 1921, Drew to Allen, Dec. 20, 1921, George to Gentlemen, Mar. 6, 1922, Box 7, DP. The success of the open shop cause in Texas cities led to the formation of the National Open Shop Association, with headquarters in San Antonio. Its purpose was to spread the open shop to cities across the nation, but little more was heard of the organization. *Iron Trade Review* 67 (Aug. 5, 1920): 389.

6. Wakstein, "Open-Shop Movement," pp. 116–17, 119–21, 122–24, 212; Senate

Committee on Education and Labor, *Violations of Free Speech and the Rights of Labor,* 76 Cong., 1 sess., S. Rept. 6, 1939, Part 4, pp. 12–16, 26–27, 138–43; *American Contractor* 5 (Oct. 25, 1924): 29.

7. Wakstein, "Open-Shop Movement," pp. 221–29; Bernstein, *The Lean Years: A History of the American Worker, 1920–1933* (Boston: Houghton Mifflin Co., 1960), p. 97; Minutes of the NAM Board of Directors, Mar. 18, 1928, Ser. V, Reel 1, Accession 1411; Troy, *Trade Union Membership,* p. 1.

8. Bernstein, *Lean Years,* pp. 88, 147; Wakstein, "Open-Shop Movement," pp. 60–75; Jerome L. Toner, *The Closed Shop in American Industry* (Washington: Catholic University of America Press, 1941), p. 79.

9. Drew to Frank Vanderlip, May 29, 1919, Drew to D. E. Felt, July 10, 1919, Box 9, DP; Drew to James Emery, Sept. 15, 1919, Drew to James E. Stein, Sept. 26, 1919, Box 20, DP; Drew to Gentlemen, Nov. 30, 1920, Box 29, DP; Drew, "Some Phases of the Present Industrial Conditions," Dec. 14, 1920, Box 29, DP; Drew, "On the Open or Closed Shop," Feb. 26, 1921, ibid.; Drew to Associated Industries of Detroit, June 25, 1920, Box 6, DP; Philadelphia Chamber of Commerce News Bulletin, Sept. 15, 1920, Box 64, Frank P. Walsh Papers, New York Public Library, New York, New York.

10. *Observations upon Report of Commission on Industrial Relations in Canada by Walter Drew and James Emery,* Sept. 27–28, 1919, Box 29, DP.

11. Drew to John F. Perkins, Jan. 7, 1919, Box 1, DP; Drew to Stein, Oct. 28, 1919, Box 20, DP; Drew, "Some Phases"; Drew, "Open or Closed Shop""; NMTA, "Twenty-Seventh Annual Convention," Apr. 22, 1920, ibid.

12. Drew to Perkins, Jan. 7, 1919, Box 1, DP; Drew to Henry Leland, Nov. 4, 1919, Box 36, DP; Drew to Allen, Oct. 29, 1920, Drew to O. P. Briggs, Dec. 27, 1921, Box 7, DP; Drew, "Some Phases"; Drew, "Open or Closed Shop"; Drew, *Observations,* Box 29, DP; Wakstein, "Open-Shop Movement," pp. 148–61, 187–88.

13. Drew to Stein, Sept. 26, 1919, Box 20, DP; Drew to August Ziesing, July 7, 1926, Box 12, DP.

14. Drew to Felt, July 10, 1919, Box 9, DP; Minutes of the National Industrial Conference Board, Jan. 24, 1918, Ser. III, Reel 1, Accession 1057, Archives of the National Industrial Conference Board, Hagley Museum and Library; Minutes of the NICB Executive Committee, Dec. 12, 1918, Ser. II, Reel 1, ibid.; Chairman (Magnus W. Alexander) to Drew et al., Jan. 29, 1919, Drew to A. F. Bemis, Mar. 18, 1918, Ser. V, Box 11, ibid.; Alexander to Members of Yama Conference, Oct. 19, 1918, enclosed with Alexander to William Howard Taft, Oct. 26, 1918, Series 3, Reel 199, William Howard Taft Papers, University of Michigan Library, Ann Arbor, Michigan.

15. Alexander to W. D. Baldwin, Apr. 7, 1919, Drew to Alexander, May 3, 1919, Drew to Emery, Jan. 19, 1920, Ser. V, Box 11, Accession 1057; Executive Draft of Principles. . . , Apr. 30, 1919, ibid.; Labor Policies Program. . . , Sept. 30, 1919, ibid.; Alexander to Fred A. Jones, May 11, 1920, Box 5, DP. There are various drafts of a labor policies program in Ser. V, Box 11, Accession 1057.

16. *Proceedings of the First Industrial Conference . . . Oct. 6 to 23, 1919* (Washington: Government Printing Office, 1920), p. 4; Drew to Emery, Sept. 15, 1919, Box 22, DP; NICB Minutes, Sept. 18, 1919, Ser. III, Reel 1, Accession 1057.

17. Clyde L. Rogers, "Draft History of the Conference Board [1963]," p. 37, Hagley Museum and Library; Drew to Emery, Jan. 19, 1920, Drew to E. H. Gary, Feb. 6, 1920, Ser. V, Box 11, Accession 1057; NICB Minutes, Oct. 30, 1919, Ser. III, Reel 1, ibid.; Drew to Editor the New York World, Oct. 24, 1919, Box 29, DP; *First Industrial Conference,* pp. 80–83, 108–9, 175; Hurvitz, "Ideology and Industrial Conflict: Presi-

dent Wilson's First Industrial Conference, October 1919," *Labor History* 18 (Fall 1977): 522–24. The conference also failed to agree on any means to resolve the concurrent steel strike.

18. Alexander to Committee. . . , Dec. 22, 1919, Drew to Emery, Jan. 8, 1920, Drew to F. J. Koster, Jan. 14, 1920, Drew to Alexander, Jan. 14, 1920, Ser. V, Box 11, Accession 1057.

19. Suggested Revision by Mr. Drew. . . , Jan. 17, 1920, ibid.; Minutes of Meeting of Committee on Labor Policies Program, Feb. 2, 1920, ibid.; A Statement of Principles Underlying the Employment Relation. . . , Feb. 2, 1920, ibid.

20. Drew to Gary, Feb. 6, 1920, ibid.

21. Philadelphia Chamber of Commerce News Bulletin, Sept. 15, 1920, Box 64, Walsh Papers; *NYT,* Jan. 9, July 31, 1920; *Industry* 2 (Aug. 1, 1920): 12, 13; Drew to H. H. Rice, Aug. 10, 1920, Box 5, DP; Report of the Sub-Committee. . . , Sept. 29, 1920, ibid.; Toner, *Closed Shop,* p. 131.

22. NICB Executive Committee Minutes, Mar. 4, 26, 1930, Ser. II, Reel 1, Accession 1057; NICB Minutes, Mar 18, 1920, Ser. III, Reel 1, ibid.; Alexander to Members, Mar. 22, 1920, Ser. V, Box 11, ibid.; Drew, Comments upon the Tentative Report . . . of the Cleveland Chamber of Commerce, Mar. 23, 1920, Box 12, DP.

23. W. Jett Lauck and Claude Watts, *The Industrial Code* (New York: Funk and Wagnalls, 1922), pp. 326–80; Gary Best, "President Wilson's Second Industrial Conference, 1919–1920," *Labor History* 16 (Fall 1975): 505–20; Hurvitz, "Meaning of Industrial Conflict," pp. 34–35.

24. Alexander to Ogden L. Mills, Apr. 9, 1920, in NICB Minutes, Apr. 15, 1920, Ser. III, Reel 1, Accession 1057; NMTA, "Twenty-Seventh Annual Convention," Apr. 22, 1920, Box 29, DP; Drew to Emery, June 25, 1920, in H. M. Gitelman notes on John Henderson Powell, Jr., "The History of the National Industrial Conference Board," in Gitelman's possession.

25. NICB Minutes, Nov. 18, 1920, Ser. III, Reel 1, Accession 1057; NICB Executive Committee Minutes, Nov. 4, 1920, Mar. 16, 1922, Ser. II, Reel 1, ibid.; Alexander to Members, Oct. 19, Nov. 19, 1920, Ser. V, Box 11, ibid.; Drew to C. S. Ching, Jan. 5, 16, 1925, Drew to Alexander, Feb. 13, 1925, Gitelman notes.

26. NAM, *Proceedings of the Twenty-Fourth Annual Convention, May 19–21, 1919,* p. 36; Emery to Mason, Feb. 12, 1920, Ser. I, Box 251, Accession 1411; NAM Board of Directors Minutes, May 20, July 7, 1920, Ser. V, Reel 1, ibid.; Mason to Drew, July 14, 1920, Box 17, DP; Wakstein, "Origins," pp. 472–73.

27. Minutes of the Open Shop Committee, Sept. 17, Oct. 1, 1920, Box 17, DP; J. B. Bird to Drew, Sept. 21, 1920, ibid.; Mason to Members, Oct. 15, 1920, Ser. I, Box 251, Accession 1411; Drew to Gentlemen, Nov. 30, 1920, Box 29, DP.

28. Drew to Gentlemen, Nov. 30, 1920, Box 29, DP; Sargent to Members, Apr. 9, 1921, Box 17, DP; Open Shop Committee Minutes, Nov. 16, 1920, Feb. 12, Oct. 14, 1921, ibid.; Principles and Recommendations Drawn by the Open Shop Committee, Feb. 12, 1921, Ser. I, Box 251, Accession 1411; NAM Board of Directors Minutes, Feb. 18, 1921, Ser. V, Reel 1, ibid.

29. Open Shop Conference, Oct. 9–10, 1922, Box 17, DP; Open Shop Department, 1921–22, ibid.; Open Shop Committee Minutes, Feb. 14, 1923, ibid.; Sargent to E. A. Holmgreen, Oct. 8, 1923, ibid.; NAM Board of Directors Minutes, Dec. 16–17, 1922, Feb. 16–17, 1923, Ser. V, Reel 1, Accession 1411; NAM, *Proceedings of the Twenty-Eighth Annual Convention, May 14–16, 1923,* p. 200.

30. NAM Board of Directors Minutes, July 12, 1923, Ser. V, Reel 1, Accession 1411.

31. NAM Executive Committee Minutes, Jan. 16, 1926, ibid.; NAM Board of Directors Minutes, June 15, Sept. 15, 1926, Mar. 22, 1927, ibid.; Minutes of Employment Relations Committee, Sept. 14, 1926, and attached proposed NAM Labor Principles. . . , Ser. I, Box 251, ibid.; NAM, *Proceedings of the Thirty-First Annual Convention, Oct. 5–7, 1926*, p. 318; Allen M. Wakstein, "The National Association of Manufacturers and Labor Relations in the 1920s," *Labor History* 10 (Spring 1969): 172–73.

32. Status of the Open Shop [1922], Series I, Box 251, Accession 1411; Open Shop Department, Mar. 30–Sept. 30, 1921, ibid.; Sargent to Holmgreen, Oct. 8, 1923 (and enclosed Report), Sargent to Members, Mar. 29, Apr. 9, 1921 (and enclosed Report), Box 17, DP; Open Shop Department, 1921–22, ibid.

33. Open Shop Committee Minutes, Mar. 18, May 2, 1921, Series I, Box 251, Accession 1411; Sargent to Members Open Shop Committee, May 2, 1921, ibid.; Open Shop Department, Mar. 30–Sept. 30, 1921, Apr. 1–Dec. 31, 1921, ibid.; NAM Board of Directors Minutes, July 18, 1924, Dec. 19, 1930, Ser. V, Reel 1, ibid.; NAM, *Twenty-Eighth Convention*, p. 156; Wakstein, "National Association of Manufacturers," p. 166n.

34. Open Shop Committee Minutes, Feb. 14, Dec. 14, 1923, Apr. 1, 1924, Box 17, DP; Open Shop Committee Minutes, Sept. 10, 1926, Feb. 25, Oct. 4, 1927, Ser. I, Box 251, Accession 1411; NAM Board of Directors Minutes, Feb. 19–20, 1924, Mar. 22, 1927, Ser. V, Reel 1, ibid.; Sargent to Drew, Aug. 26, 1930 (and enclosure), Box 13, DP.

35. Open Shop Department, 1921–22, Box 17, DP; Status of the Open Shop [1922], Ser. I, Box 251, Accession 1411; Sargent, "The Open Shop" [June 1922], ibid.; *Detroit Saturday Night*, Sept. 3, 1921; Wakstein, "Open-Shop Movement," pp. 180–82, 193–95, 231–32; Drew to Clyde MacCornack, Aug. 15, 1927, Box 12, DP.

36. Sargent, "A Practical Test of the Closed Shop" [1924], Ser. I, Box 251, Accession 1411; Analysis of Building, 1921–28, ibid.; Open Shop Bulletin No. 13, May 14, 1926, ibid.; Releases, Apr. 18 [1923], Aug. 8 [1927], ibid.; Sargent to Holmgreen, Apr. 18 [1923], ibid.; Open Shop Department, 1921–22, Box 17, DP; Sargent to Staunton B. Peek, June 22, 1927, ibid.; NAM, *Proceedings of the Thirtieth Annual Convention, Oct. 26–28, 1925*, p. 78; *American Industries* 24 (Aug. 1923): 21–22; *Detroit Saturday Night*, July 26, 1924, July 31, 1926, July 30, 1927, July 28, 1928, July 26, 1930.

37. Drew to Felt, July 10, 1919, Box 9, DP; Drew to Allen, Feb. 24, 1920, Drew to William Frew Long, Nov. 2, 1926, Box 3, DP; Drew to John Corbin, Feb. 6, 1922, Drew to Lauriston Bullard, Oct. 3, 1923, Box 18, DP; Drew to Long, Feb. 23, 1926, Box 6, DP; Drew, *Your Agent the Builder* [1920], Box 29, DP; Drew, "Building and the Public," Feb. 16, 1922, ibid.

38. David Warren Ryder, "The Unions Lose in San Francisco," *American Mercury* 7 (Apr. 1926): 412; Frederick L. Ryan, *Industrial Relations in the San Francisco Building Trades* (Norman: University of Oklahoma Press, 1936), pp. 130, 134–38.

39. Michael Kazin, *Barons of Labor: The San Francisco Building Trades and Union Power in the Progressive Era* (Urbana: University of Illinois Press, 1987), pp. 249–58; Ryan, *San Francisco Building Trades*, pp. 138–57; *NYT*, Apr. 2, 1922; *American Industries* 22 (Oct. 1921): 27.

40. Kazin, *Barons of Labor*, pp. 259–68; Ryan, *San Francisco Building Trades*, pp. 158–69; *Detroit Saturday Night*, Aug. 1, 1925.

41. *Detroit Saturday Night*, Aug. 1, 1925; *NYT*, Apr. 2, June 7, 1922, Jan. 6, June 17, 1923, Apr. 14, 1925; *Iron Age* 115 (Apr. 16, 1925): 1144; *Iron Trade Review* 77 (July 9, 1925): 111; Ryan, *San Francisco Building Trades*, pp. 172–78, 201–2; Walter Galenson, *The United Brotherhood of Carpenters* (Cambridge, Mass.: Harvard University

Press, 1983), p. 205; Kazin, *Barons of Labor,* pp. 271–73; William Haber, *Industrial Relations in the Building Industry* (New York: Arno and New York Times, 1971), pp. 416–24; Ryder, "Unions Lose," pp. 414–16; Albert E. Boynton to Drew, Feb. 9, 1932, Box 13, DP; *Industrial Association of San Francisco* v. *U.S.,* 268 U.S. 64 (1924).

42. *Detroit Saturday Night,* July 31, 1926, July 30, 1927; *NYT,* July 27, 1923, June 6, Aug. 8, Oct. 3, 1926, Jan. 2, 23, 1927; *Bridgemen's Magazine* 29 (July 1929): 421; Haber, *Building Industry,* p. 437; Ryder, "Unions Lose," pp. 416–20; Boynton to Drew, Feb. 9, 1932, Box 13, DP.

43. W. H. George to NEA, June 23, 1921, NEA to George, June 24, 1921, H. R. Brady to George, June 25, 1921, G. W. Bucholz to Drew, July 28, 1921, Secretary to Bucholz, July 29, 1921, Boynton to Drew, May 17, 1930, Box 11, DP.

44. Royal E. Montgomery, *Industrial Relations in the Chicago Building Trades,* (Chicago: University of Chicago Press, 1927), pp. 233–34, 237; Richard Schneirov and Thomas Suhrbur, *Union Brotherhood, Union Town: The History of the Carpenters' Union of Chicago, 1863–1967* (Carbondale: Southern Illinois University Press, 1988), pp. 92, 98–101; *Detroit Saturday Night,* Sept. 2, 1922.

45. *Report of the Illinois State Building Investigation Commission* (Springfield: Illinois State Reporter [1923]), pp. 1–4, 10–16, 34–100; Harold Seidman, *Labor Czars: A History of Labor Racketeering* (New York: Liveright Publishing Co., 1938), p. 94; John Hutchinson, *The Imperfect Union: A History of Corruption in American Trade Unions* (New York: E. P. Dutton and Co., 1970), pp. 58–60.

46. *Decision of . . . Landis, Sept. 7, 1921,* Box 9, DP; Alexander M. Bing, "The Posse Comitatus in Industry. . . , " *Survey* 49 (June 15, 1923): 493–95; *NYT,* Sept. 8, 1921; *Detroit Saturday Night,* Sept. 2, 1922; Schneirov and Suhrbur, *Union Brotherhood,* pp. 101–2; Montgomery, *Chicago Building Trades,* pp. 239–67; Selig Perlman and Philip Taft, *History of Labor in the United States, 1896–1932* (New York: Macmillan Co., 1935), pp. 506–7.

47. Montgomery, *Chicago Building Trades,* pp. 272–78; Schneirov and Suhrbur, *Union Brotherhood,* p. 102; Minutes of the Chicago Federation of Labor, Oct. 2, Dec. 18, 1921, microfilm copy in Chicago Historical Society, Chicago, Illinois; *Detroit Saturday Night,* Sept. 2, 1922; Haber, *Building Industry,* pp. 390–92; Bing, "Posse Comitatus," p. 539.

48. *NYT,* Nov. 24, Dec. 1, 1921; Bing, "Posse Comitatus," pp. 495–96, 538–39; *Detroit Saturday Night,* Sept. 2, 1922, Aug. 1, 1925; Citizens' Committee to Enforce the Landis Award, *The Landis Award . . .* [1927], Box 4, DP; Montgomery, *Chicago Building Trades,* pp. 280–81, 293; Schneirov and Suhrbur, *Union Brotherhood,* pp. 102–3; Haber, *Building Industry,* p. 392; *American Industries* 22 (June 1922): 21–22.

49. *NYT,* Jan. 5, May 11, 12, July 25, 1922; *Detroit Saturday Night,* Sept. 2, 1922; Bing, "Posse Comitatus," p. 496; Edward Nockels to Frank Walsh, Box 11, Walsh Papers; Minutes of Chicago Federation of Labor, Mar. 19, 1922.

50. Thomas Earle to Drew, Sept. 15, 1923, Box 4, DP; Citizens' Committee, *Landis Award,* ibid.; *Year Book of Landis Award Employers' Association. . . ,* Apr. 1, 1932, ibid.; Schneirov and Suhrbur, *Union Brotherhood,* pp. 106–8; Montgomery, *Chicago Building Trades,* pp. 295–304; *Detroit Saturday Night,* July 27, 1929, Aug. 29, 1931; Drew, "Labor's Monopoly in Building," *American Industries* 30 (May 1930): 23; Haber, *Building Industry,* pp. 393–96; Perlman and Taft, *History of Labor,* pp. 508–9.

51. Drew to Donnelley, June 7, 18, 19, 1923, Donnelley to Drew, June 15, 18, 1923, Box 12, DP; Frank C. Chase to Drew, Aug. 14, 1923, Box 4, DP; Pierce E. Wright to

Drew, May 9, 1922, enclosing F. W. Armstrong to John W. Lovett, Apr. 26, 1922, Drew to Wright, May 11, 1922, Box 6, DP.

52. Drew to Armstrong, Aug. 25, 1926, Drew to Members, Sept. 9, 1926, Brady to Drew, May 4, Sept. 15, 1927, Armstrong to Drew, Apr. 13, Aug. 18, 1927, Citizens' Committee to Joshua A. Hatfield, June 6, 1927, Donnelley to Drew, June 6, 1927, Drew to Brady, Aug. 25, 1927, Drew to Elbert A. Gibbs, Sept. 14, 1927, Box 4, DP; Citizens' Committee Release, Sept. 7, 1926, ibid.; Brady statement, Apr. 13, 1927, ibid.; Drew to Hatfield, June 23, 1927, Hatfield to Drew, June 27, 1927 (and enclosure), Drew to Nathan Miller, July 19, 1927, Box 12, DP.

53. H. A. Wagner to J. P. Whitehead, Jan. 29, 1926, Drew to J. E. Sweeney, Aug. 31, 1922, Wright to Brady, May 23, 1922, Wright to Drew, Oct. 12, 1923, Drew to Wright, Oct. 15, 1923, Drew to Members, Mar. 14, 1924, Box 6, DP; Fred A. Jones to Alexander, Apr. 14, 1920, Drew to Jones, May 24, 1920, Drew to Franklin O. Thompson, Apr. 15, 1922, Box 5, DP; Drew to Allen, Feb. 24, 1920, Sept. 16, 1924, Allen to Drew, Dec. 3, 1921, Mar. 3, 1922, Sept. 11, 1924, Allen to Members. . . , Jan. 30, 1922, Box 3, DP; Sweeney to Drew, Dec. 10, 1924, Box 6, DP; Drew to S. E. Roberts, Mar. 8, 1924, Box 15, DP; *Iron Trade Review* 67 (Aug. 26, 1920): 571; Subcommittee of Senate Committee on Education and Labor, *Violations of Free Speech and Rights of Labor,* 75 Cong., 3 sess., 1938, Part 20, p. 9120. For the early development of the open shop in Detroit, see Thomas A. Klug, "The Roots of the Open Shop: Employers, Trade Unions, and Craft Labor Markets in Detroit, 1859–1907" (Ph.D. diss., Wayne State University, 1993), pp. 547–990.

54. Preliminary Report Philadelphia Open Shop Movement [Oct. 30, 1920], File 1-2258-1, Records of the Federal Trade Commission, RG 122, NARA. Cf. Drew to Earle, May 21, 1920, Box 17, DP.

55. Drew to Earle, May 21, June 11, 1920, Box 17; Drew to Sheridan Taylor, May 19, 1920 (and enclosed draft), Taylor to Drew, June 12, 1920, Box 8, DP; [*Philadelphia Public Ledger,* June 10, 1920], clipping in ibid.; *Philadelphia Inquirer,* July 1, 1920, clipping in ibid.; Drew to George L. Peck, July 2, 1920, Box 18, DP; Drew to E. W. Mentel, Nov. 9, 1920, Box 9, DP; Drew to F. C. Hood, Nov. 10, 1920, Box 7, DP; Drew to C. Edwin Michael, Feb. 19, 1926, Box 15, DP. There is a copy of the principles adopted by the Industrial Relations Committee of the Chamber of Commerce in Box 8, DP.

56. Philadelphia Open Shop Movement Report, Nov. 8, 1920, Box 64, Walsh Papers; Minutes of the NEA Executive Committee, July 2, 1920, Box 37A, ibid.; Philadelphia Open Shop Movement, Report of Week Ending Nov. 15, 1920, ibid.; Preliminary Report [Oct. 30, 1920], File 1-2258-1, RG 122; G. S. Stuart to Drew, Sept. 29, 1923, Box 17, DP; Drew to Ziesing, Box 12, DP; Open Shop Bulletin No. 13, May 4, 1926, Ser. I, Box 251, Accession 1411; *Bridgemen's Magazine* 22 (Oct. 1922): 455; ibid. 28 (Oct.–Nov. 1928): 16–17.

57. Drew to Louis J. Horowitz, July 15, 1921, Box 9, DP.

58. Drew to Donnelley, June 7, 1923, Box 12, DP; Drew to Wright, May 11, 1922, Box 6, DP; *Fourth District Finance and Industry,* Feb. 8, 1930, pp. 18–22, 24, Box 29, DP; Drew, "Labor's Monopoly," p. 22; Senate Committee on Education and Labor, *Violations of Free Speech and Rights of Labor,* Report No. 6, Part 4, pp. 29–30.

59. R. C. Marshall, Jr., to Brady, May 9, 1922 (and enclosure), Marshall to Drew, May 9, 12, 1922, Drew to Marshall, May 11, 13, 1922, Box 1, DP; Bulletin No. 1 [Apr. 1922], ibid.; Release, May 14, 1922, ibid.; Frank Freidel, *Franklin D. Roosevelt: The Ordeal* (Boston: Little, Brown and Co., 1954), pp. 153–54.

60. Roosevelt to Drew, May 25, 1922, Marshall to Drew, May 27, 31, 1922, Drew to Marshall, May 29, 1922, Drew to N. J. Kennedy, June 1, 16, 1922, Box 1, DP; Drew to Gentlemen, July 21, 1922, Box 14, DP; *NYT,* June 28, 1922.

61. Drew to Kennedy, June 16, 1922, Sweeney to Drew, June 24, 1922, Drew to Lawrence F. Sherman, June 23 [1922], Drew to Marshall, June 26, 1922, Drew to Ernest Trigg, July 28, 1922, Marshall to Drew, June 29, 1922, Roosevelt to Drew, Aug. 4, May 12, Sept. 18, 1923, Sept. 24, 1924, Drew to S. Wells Utley, Sept. 26, 1936, Box 1, DP; Freidel, *Roosevelt,* p. 155; Haber, *Building Industry,* pp. 485–91.

62. J. M. Bell to Gordon A. Ramsey, Oct. 9, 1923, Drew to Bell, Nov. 17, 21, 1923, Sargent to Drew, July 7, Aug. 25, 1924, Drew to Sargent, July 8, 1924, Sargent to Bell, July 18, 1924, Walter Gordon Merritt to Sargent, Nov. 1, 1924, Box 5, DP; Open Shop Committee Minutes, Feb. 25, 1927, Ser. I, Box 251, Accession 1411.

63. Wagner to NEA, Oct. 7, 1929, Secretary to Wagner, Oct. 9, 1929, Drew to Emery, Mar. 22, 1930, Drew to Ferry Heath, Apr. 16, 1930, Box 7, DP; Drew to Frank Parker, Apr. 9, 1930, Drew to Brady, May 28, 1931, Box 13, DP.

64. Emery to Drew, Mar. 25, 1930, enclosing John Gall Memorandum, Mar. 25, 1930, Drew to Emery, Apr. 12, 1930, Drew to Heath, Apr. 16, 24, 1930, Heath to NEA, Apr. 23, 1930, Box 7, DP. The Independent Building Co. informed Drew that it had been furnishing and erecting steel work for the government "direct" for thirty years. H. R. Hortenstein to Drew, Apr. 10, 1930, ibid.

65. C. S. Garner to Drew, June 29, Aug. 30, 1932, Drew to Garner, July 1, Aug. 31, 1932, Drew to A. J. Post, July 1, 1934, Box 7, DP.

66. Memo re Pittsburgh Post Office Job, July 25, 1932, Box 17, DP; Drew to Emery, Aug. 31, 1932, C. C. Patterson to Drew, Aug. 26, 1932, Drew to Patterson, Aug. 31, Sept. 21, 1932, Brady to Drew, Sept. 21, 1932, R. F. Kennedy to Sargent, Sept. 26, 1932, ibid.; *Pittsburgh Post Gazette,* Sept. 17, 1932, clipping in ibid.; Drew to Gentlemen, Sept. 7, 1932, Box 29, DP.

67. *Greater New York,* May 31, 1920, Box 4, DP; Citizens' Transportation Committee, *The Peril of the Port . . .* [1920], pp. 3–4, Box 29, DP; *NYT,* Apr. 19, May 6, 15, 18, 20, 29, 30, June 6, 1920.

68. *Greater New York,* May 31, 1920, Box 4, DP; *Declaration of Principles. . . ,* May 27, 1920, ibid.; *NYT,* May 6, 8, 15, 26, 28, 1920.

69. William Fellows Morgan to Drew, May 17, 1920, Drew to Morgan, June 3, 1920, John R. Young to Drew, July 3, 1920, Drew to Lewis E. Pierson, June 24, 1920, Drew to Members Iron League Erectors Association, June 25, 1920, Morgan to Commercial and Trade Organizations, Aug. 3, 1920, Box 4, DP; Drew to Gentlemen, July 1, 1920, Box 14, DP; Drew to George Leet, Nov. 10, 1920, Box 18, DP.

70. *NYT,* May 11–13, June 4, 6, 10, 11, 13–15, 20, 23, 24, 28, July 2, 3, 13, 15, 27, 28, Aug. 6, Nov. 10, 1920, Feb. 3, 1921; League for Industrial Rights, "Courts Uphold Rights of Public . . ." [1921], Box 4, DP; Citizens' Transportation Committee, *Peril of Port,* pp. 5–6, 12–13, Box 29, DP; Walter Gordon Merritt, *History of the League for Industrial Rights* (New York: League for Industrial Rights, 1925), pp. 106–8; *Burgess Brothers Co.* v. *Stewart,* 112 Misc. 347 (1921).

71. *NYT,* May 27, 31, June 25, 1920; Drew to C. L. Bardo, July 1, 1920, Drew to Pierson, June 24, 1920, Young to Drew, Aug. 4, 1920, Box 4, DP; unidentified clipping [Aug. 12, 1920], ibid.; [*New York Tribune,* Aug. 18, 1920], clipping in ibid.

72. Colin John Davis, "Bitter Storm: The 1922 National Railroad Shopmen's Strike" (Ph.D. diss., State University of New York at Binghampton, 1988), p. 1; Drew to Renshaw P. Sherer, July 23, 1917, Box 1, DP; Walsh to John J. McNamara, May 3,

1921, Box 9, James B. and John J. McNamara Papers, University of Cincinnati, Cincinnati, Ohio; Drew, "Building and the Public."

73. Davis, "Bitter Storm," p. 4; Walker D. Hines, *War History of American Railroads* (New Haven: Yale University Press, 1928), pp. 152–54; Leo Troy, "Labor Representation on American Railroads," *Labor History* 2 (Fall 1961): pp. 297–99; Leonard A. Lecht, *Experience under Railway Labor Legislation* (New York: Columbia University Press, 1955), p. 32.

74. There were two other adjustment boards, Board No. 1 for train service personnel and Board No. 3 for telegraphers, switchmen, clerks, and maintenance-of-way workers.

75. Hines, *War History,* pp. 155–79; H. D. Wolf, *The Railroad Labor Board* (Chicago: University of Chicago Press, 1927), pp. 17–65; Elwin Wilber Sigmund, "Federal Laws Concerning Railroad Labor Disputes: A Legislative and Legal History, 1877–1934" (Ph.D. diss., University of Illinois, 1961), pp. 95–104; Davis, "Bitter Storm," pp. 86–108.

76. *Statutes at Large of the United States of America,* 41:456–99; Hines, *War History,* pp. 158–59; Lecht, *Railway Labor Legislation,* pp. 36, 40–41; Wolf, *Railroad Labor Board,* p. 103; Sigmund, "Railroad Labor Disputes," p. 103; *Railway Age* 69 (Dec. 30, 1920): 966; ibid. 70 (Jan. 7, 1921): 79–80, (Jan. 14, 1921): 198, (Jan. 21, 1921): 223, (Jan. 28, 1921): 297–99, (Feb. 4, 1921): 317–19.

77. Drew to Gentlemen, Sept. 3, 1920, Box 18, DP.

78. Drew to Gentlemen, Sept. 3, Nov. 16, 1920, ibid.; Drew, "Suggested Statement. . . ," Sept. 9, 1920, ibid.

79. Drew to Editor, American Industries, Sept. 26, 1920, Drew to Gentlemen, Nov. 16, 1920, Emery to Drew, Feb. 18, 1921, enclosing Emery to Atterbury, Feb. 18, 1921, Drew to Emery, Feb. 21, 1921, ibid.; Drew, "Federal Control of Railway Labor," *American Industries* 21 (Oct. 1920): 11.

80. *Statutes at Large,* 41: 469; Wolf, *Railroad Labor Board,* pp. 166–67; Drew to George A. Post, Feb. 8, 1921, Drew to Peck, Apr. 8, 1921, Box 18, DP; *Decisions of the United States Railroad Labor Board. . . , 1920* (Washington: Government Printing Office, 1921), 1:18.

81. Drew to Gentlemen, Sept. 24, 1920, Box 14, DP; Drew to Atterbury, Sept. 2, 24, 1920, Drew to John D. Hibbard, Sept. 24, 1920, Drew to Peck, Oct. 2, 1920, Drew to Emery, Oct. 20, 1920, Drew to Gentlemen, Nov. 16, 1920, Drew to Members, June 27, 1921 (and enclosed Memorandum . . . June 21, 1921), Drew to Leet, Nov. 10, 1920, Drew to William Butterworth, Dec. 29, 1920, Drew to J. A. Campbell, June 28, 1921, Box 18, DP.

82. Davis, "Bitter Storm," pp. 130–37; *Decisions of Labor Board, 1921* (Washington: Government Printing Office, 1922), 2:87–96.

83. Wolf, *Railroad Labor Board,* pp. 295, 302; Davis, "Bitter Storm," pp. 138–39; "Shop Craft Employes: Chronology of Relations. . . ," undated, pp. 69–73, Box B 877, Records of the Pennsylvania Railroad Co., Accession 1807/1810, Hagley Museum and Library.

84. *Decisions of Railroad Labor Board, 1921* (Washington: Government Printing Office, 1922), 2:208–14; Wolf, *Railroad Labor Board,* pp. 303–97; Lecht, *Railway Labor Legislation,* pp. 44–45; *Pennsylvania Railroad Co.* v. *United States Railroad Labor Board,* 261 U.S. 72 (1922). For the position of the Pennsylvania Railroad on the representation question, see Proceedings of the Railroad Labor Board, July 8, 9, 1921, Docket No. 404, Records of the Railroad Labor Board, in Records of the National Mediation Board, RG 13, NARA; and Employe Representation System on the Pennsyl-

vania Railroad System [Sept. 1922], Box 109, W. Jett Lauck Papers, University of Virginia Library, Charlottesville, Virginia.

85. Drew to Peck, July 12, Aug. 2, 1921, Emery to Peck, July 14, 1921, Box 814, Accession 1807/1810; Drew to S. P. Mitchell et al., July 25, 1921, Box 18, DP; The Presentation before the Railroad Labor Board. . . , July 23, 1921, ibid.; Drew to Gentlemen, July 16, 1921, Drew to Members, Aug. 2, 1921, Box 14, DP; Chairman to Emery, July 29, 1921, Docket No. 404, RG 13.

86. Railway Employes' Department, A.F. of L., *The Case of the Railway Shopmen* [1922]; Margaret Gadsby, "Strike of the Railroad Shopmen," *Monthly Labor Review* 15 (Dec. 1922): 1182–90; Davis, "Bitter Storm," pp. 151–73; Wolf, *Railroad Labor Board,* pp. 312–13; B. M. Jewell to Members System Federation No. 90, June 1922, Box 169, Railway Employes' Department Records, Martin P. Catherwood Library, Cornell University, Ithaca, New York.

87. Davis, "Bitter Storm," pp. 55, 296–335; *Detroit Saturday Night,* July 31, 1926, July 27, 1929; Troy, "Labor Representation," pp. 304–5, 306–7, 313–14.

88. Autobiography of Robert J. Foster, undated, pp. 422–50, Box 22, DP; [Foster] to John G. Sargent, Apr. 25, 1927 (and enclosure), Box 27, DP; Scott to G. Warrington, May 18, 1923, Scott to D. J. Collins, June 14, 1923, Scott to Frank Divers, Nov. 24, 1923, Box 109, Railway Employes' Department Records.

89. Foster to Sargent, Apr. 25, 1927, Box 27, DP.

90. Undated document, Box 27, DP; Luhring to Foster, June 9, July 9, Sept. 30, 1927, [Foster] to Sargent, June 30, July 1, 1927, [Foster] to President, July 14, 1927, Box 27, DP.

91. Nathan B. Williams to Emery [July 31, 1928], Drew to Emery, July 31, 1928, Drew to Atterbury, Aug. 2, 1928, Emery to John Edgerton, Aug. 3, 1928, Drew to Federick J. Koster, Aug. 2, 1928, J. M. Manley to Brady, Aug. 3, 1928, N. Sargent to Atterbury, Aug. 5, 1928, Drew to J. M. Bell, Aug. 7, 1928, Drew to Long, Aug. 9, 13, 1928, Drew to Butterworth, Aug. 21, Sept. 24, 1928, Chandler to Koster, Sept. 3, 1928, Box 20, DP; Drew Memorandum, Aug. 1, 1928, ibid.

92. Drew, "The Politicians and the Labor Question" [1928], Box 20, DP.

93. "Federal Prevailing Wage Laws. . . ," May 3, 1932, Box 18, DP; Drew to Brady, Mar. 4, 1932, MacCornack to Drew, Aug. 19, 1932, Drew to MacCornack, Aug. 24, 1932, Drew to Gibbs, Sept. 12, 1932, Drew to Homer D. Sayre, Dec. 21, 1932, Box 18, DP. Cf. Drew to Wagner, Dec. 19, 1932, ibid.

94. Drew to Gentlemen, Feb. 29, 1932, Box 14, DP; Drew to Arthur M. Torrey, Mar. 2, 1932, Box 10, DP; For Release, Mar. 14 [1932], Box 29, DP; Drew to Sayre, Dec. 21, 1932, Box 18, DP.

95. Drew to Michael, Feb. 19, 1926, Box 15, DP.

Chapter 10

1. NEA Membership-Dec. 1, 1920, Box 37A, Frank P. Walsh Papers, New York Public Library, New York, New York; Drew to H. M. Nimmo, June 28, 1922, Box 18, DP.

2. Clarence E. Bonnett, *Employers' Associations in the United States* (New York: Macmillan Co., 1922), pp. 137, 141; Drew to Bonnett, July 6, Aug. 3, 1922, Box 12, DP; Allen Morton Wakstein, "The Open-Shop Movement, 1919–1933" (Ph.D. diss., University of Illinois, 1961), p. 210.

3. Drew to Belmont Iron Works, July 13, 1921, Drew to Andrews, June 26, 1923,

Box 7, DP; Drew to Members, June 26, 1923, Box 14, DP. See chapter 3 for the NEA's tactics to preserve the open shop.

4. Drew to Charles R. Hughes, Box 5, DP. See chapters 3 and 7.

5. Drew to August Ziesing, July 7, 1926, Box 12, DP.

6. Richard Kuehn to C. E. Cheney, Dec. 13, 1920, File 1-2258-1, Exhibit File No. 1, Records of the Federal Trade Commission, RG 122, NARA; Drew to Clyde MacCornack, Sept. 3, 1924, Drew to Ziesing, Aug. 24, 1926, Drew to Nathan Miller, July 19, Aug. 3, 1927, Miller to Drew, July 28, Aug. 4, 1927, Box 12, DP.

7. Drew to Ziesing, July 7, 1926, Drew to H.B. Hirsh, Mar. 11, 1927, Drew to W. A. Garrigues, Mar. 7, 1928, Box 12, DP; Drew to J. L. Kimbrough, June 5, 1926, Drew to C. Edwin Michael, Feb. 19, 1926, Elbert A. Gibbs to Drew, Sept. 8, 1928, Box 15, DP; Drew to Members, Feb. 15, 1926, Box 14, DP; Drew to Wagner, Feb. 1, 1926, Box 6, DP.

8. Drew to Ziesing, Dec. 27, 1926, Garrigues to Drew, May 2, 9, 1928, Drew to Garrigues, May 7, 1928, Box 12, DP; Lewis F. Shoemaker to W. A. Haxard [*sic*], Aug. 12, 1928, Hazard to Drew, Aug. 11, 1928, Box 15, DP; Steel Erection Philadelphia [1930], Box 19, DP; Steel Erection Cleveland [1930], ibid. See chapter 3 for the Shoemaker matter.

9. Drew to Brady, May 28, 1931, Drew to Gibbs, June 1, 11, 1931, Box 12, DP; Drew to Charles F. Abbott, June 11, 1931, Drew to Edward K. Klingelhofer, Nov. 13, 1931, Box 13, DP; Drew to Robert T. Brooks, May 23, 1930, Box 19, DP.

10. Drew to Ferry K. Heath, Apr. 16, 1930, Gibbs to Drew, May 22, 1930, A. S. Miller to Drew, May 27, 1930, Brady to Drew, June 6, 9, 1930, E. H. Perry to Noel Sargent, June 20, 1930, John E. Gross to Sargent, June 20, 1930, H. H. Anderson to Drew, June 25, 1930, Box 19, DP; Steel Erection Chicago, Detroit, Cleveland, Pittsburgh [1930], ibid.; L. M. MacAloon Memorandum. . . , June 27, 1930, ibid.; Brady, Status Structural Iron Rates, Feb. 15, 1932, Box 20, DP; *Bridgemen's Magazine* 33 (Nov., Dec. 1933): 733.

11. *Iron Trade Review* 77 (July 23, 1925): 221; Report of Walter Drew, May 22, 1924, Box 14, DP; Drew to Ziesing, July 7, 1926, Box 12, DP; Drew to Michael, Feb. 19, 1926, Box 15, DP; Drew to Members, Apr. 23, 1927, Box 14, DP; Drew Memorandum, May 6, 1930, Box 13, DP; "An Informal History of the Iron Workers" [1971], p. 28, copy in my possession. Pennsylvania, with about 10 percent of the structural steel erection, was second to New York.

12. *Bridgemen's Magazine* 23 (Apr. 1923): 148–51, (Sept. 1923): 389; ibid. 24 (Jan. 1924): 16, (Apr. 1924): 148, (Oct. 1924): 4, 8–9, 18–21; ibid. 26 (Nov. 1926): 485; "Informal History," p. 23; Morrin to Frank Morrison, Nov. 1, 1921, Reel 35, American Federation of Labor Records: The Samuel Gompers Era, University of Michigan Library, Ann Arbor, Michigan; Circular Letter No. 418, Nov. 11, 1926, ibid.; Drew to Kuehn, Apr. 28, 1924, Box 1, DP.

13. *NYT,* Feb. 12, 1921; *Bridgemen's Magazine* 24 (Oct. 1924): 21; "Informal History," p. 28; Drew to Pierce E. Wright, Apr. 4, 1924, Box 6, DP; Drew to Kuehn, Apr. 28, 1924, Box 1, DP; Drew to Wagner, Apr. 4, 1924, Box 14, DP; Drew Report, May 22, 1924, ibid.; Thomas to Members, Oct. 10, 1923, Box 8, DP. See chapter 3 for the "preferred list" matter.

14. *NYT,* May 1, 2, 8, June 15, 1924; [Drew] to Editor New York Commercial, May 24, 1924, Drew to Editor NYT, June 5, 1924, Box 10, DP; *Bridgemen's Magazine* 24 (June 1924): 236, 243, (July 1924): 286, (Oct. 1924): 21; ibid. (Nov. 1926): 485; *Iron Trade Review* 75 (July 17, 1924): 148.

15. Drew to Brady, May 2, 3, 5, 6, 12, 19, 24, 29, June 2, 12, 17, 1924, Brady to Drew, May 2, 7, 8, 10, 12, 24, June 16, 1924, [Drew] to Brady et al., May 6, 1924, Drew to Andrews, May 2, 1924, Drew to P. Wright, May 5, June 7, 1924, Wright to Drew, May 14, 1924, Bessie L. Crocker to P. Wright, May 7, 8, 1924, Secretary to Brady, May 9, 10, 1924, George W. Ryle to Crocker, May 14, 16, 1924, Brady to John McPartland, May 20, 1924, Drew to E. F. Fox et al., June 17, 1924, To Whom It May Concern, May 3, 1924, Box 20, DP; Iron League of New York General Order No. 2, May 10, 1924, ibid.; Drew Report, May 22, 1924, ibid.; *NYT,* June 5, 1924; *Bridgemen's Magazine* 24 (June 1924): 239.

16. *Bridgemen's Magazine* 24 (June 1924): 236–37, 238, 243, (Oct. 1924): 154, 156–57; Morrin to Chester M. Wright, June 5, 1924, Reel 35, AFL Records; H. H. Anderson to Ryle, May 12, 1924, Brady to Drew, May 12, 1924, P. Wright to Drew, May 14, 1924, Box 20, DP.

17. *Bridgemen's Magazine* 24 (June 1924): 238; Morrin to C. Wright, June 5, 1924, Reel 35, AFL Records; Drew to Brady, May 12, 1924, Box 20, DP; Post and McCord et al. against Patrick [*sic*] J. Morrin et al., Complaint [1924], Box 10, DP; Foster Affidavit, Aug. 3, 1924, ibid.

18. Resolution Adopted. . . , Apr. 10, 1924, Box 8, DP; Iron League General Order No. 2, May 10, 1924, Box 10, DP; Post and McCord Complaint [1924], ibid.; Drew to Brady, May 3, 12, 1924, Drew to P. Wright, May 16, 1924, Box 20, DP; Special Report, Agent X, May 29, 1924, ibid.

19. *Bridgemen's Magazine* 24 (June 1924): 237–38, (July 1924): 283, (Oct. 1924): 24, 155, 171–72; ibid. 26 (Jan. 1926): 12; Morrin to C. Wright, June 5, 1924, Reel 35, AFL Records.

20. New York City required operators of hoisting engines to be licensed, and since most licensed engineers were union members, the Iron League had signed a contract with the union. Post and McCord Complaint [1924], pp. 37–38, Box 10, DP.

21. *NYT,* May 8, 24, 28, June 1, 8, 10, 11, 1924; Drew to Brady, May 9, 12, 1924, Drew to P. Wright, May 16, 1924, Box 20, DP; Drew Report, May 22, 1924, Box 14, DP; Drew to Maxson and Runyon, June 26, 1924, Box 10, DP; Garrigues to Charles D. Marshall, Nov. 24, 1925, Box 9, DP; Morrin to C. Wright, June 15, 1924, Reel 35, AFL Records; *Bridgemen's Magazine* 24 (July 1924): 285; *American Contractor* 5 (July 5, 1924): 25.

22. Walsh to Edward N. Nockels, May 26, 1924, Box 13, Walsh Papers; Post and McCord Complaint [1924], Box 10, DP; Drew to Maxson and Runyon, June 26, 1924, ibid.; Drew Report, May 22, 1924, Box 14, DP; Drew to Thomas, May 28, 1924, Box 20, DP.

23. Maxson and Runyon to Richard P. Lydon, July 20, 1924, Untermeyer to Lydon, July 21, 1924, Box 10, DP; *Bridgemen's Magazine* 24 (Aug. 1924): 322–24, 341–42; *Iron Trade Review* 75 (July 17, 1924): 148; *NYT,* July 8, 9, 1924.

24. *Bridgemen's Magazine* 24 (Aug. 1924): 324–26; *American Contractor* 5 (Aug. 2, 1924): 36–37; *NYT,* July 25, 1924.

25. *Bridgemen's Magazine* 24 (Aug. 1924): 326; Drew to Warren F. Doane, Sept. 24, 1924, Box 10, DP; Drew to Thomas Earle, May 28, 1925, Box 12, DP.

26. Drew to Members, June 30, 1925, Box 29, DP; Drew to T. E. Donnelley, Feb. 7, 1925, Box 20, DP; Levering and Garrigues et al. vs. Paul J. Morrin et al., Equity 31–259, Bill of Complaint [1925], Box 11, DP; *Bridgemen's Magazine* 24 (Sept. 1924): 372–73, (Oct. 1924): 25; ibid. 25 (Feb. 1925): 50–51, (Mar. 1925): 103, (Apr. 1925): 148, 158–59; ibid. 26 (Jan. 1926): 12; ibid. 32 (Sept. 1932): 539–40.

27. Levering and Garrigues vs. Morrin, Bill of Complaint [1925], Box 11, DP; Drew to S. B. Donnelly, Feb. 16, 1925, Drew to Earle, May 28, 1925, Drew to Ziesing, Aug. 22, 27, 1926, Box 12, DP; Thomas to Members Iron League, Nov. 2, 1925, Box 10, DP; [Drew] Reply to Morrin's statement. . . , Oct. 31, 1933, Box 29, DP; *New York Commercial,* Nov. 28, 1925, clipping in ibid.; *NYT,* Mar. 13, 1925, Jan. 19, 1927; *Bridgemen's Magazine* 28 (Oct.–Nov. 1928): 49; ibid. 32 (Sept. 1932): 537–39, 541; Maria Eucharia Meehan, "Frank P. Walsh and the American Labor Movement" (Ph.D. diss., New York University, 1962), pp. 146–47.

28. Minutes of AFL Executive Council, Aug. 11–24, 1924, pp. 46, 97–98, Reel 7, AFL Records; Morrin to William Green, Apr. 17, 1933, Reel 35, ibid.; *Bridgemen's Magazine* 26 (Jan. 1926): 46–47, (Nov. 1926): 184–85; ibid. 28 (Sept. 1928): 589–90, (Oct.–Nov. 1928): 20–21; *Bridgemen and Iron Workers' Magazine* (Jan. 1927), pp. 10–13, (July 1927), p. 6, (Aug. 1929), p. 9; *NYT,* Nov. 10, 1924; Drew to Michael, Feb. 19, 1926, Box 15, DP; A. J. Post to S. P. Mitchell, July 25, 1924, Box 14, DP; Garrigues to Marshall, Nov. 24, 1925, Box 9, DP; Drew to Ziesing, July 7, 1926, Box 12, DP; Thomas to Drew, June 11, 1935, enclosing Thomas to Fiorello La Guardia, June 8, 1935, Box 9, DP. See also *Bridgemen's Magazine* 24 (Oct. 1924): 156–57.

29. Thomas to Mason Builders' Association, Oct. 21, 1926, Box 12, DP; Drew to Ziesing, Nov. 3, 27, 1926, Box 12, DP; Drew Memorandum on Luncheon Meeting, Dec. 13, 1926, Box 16, DP; Report of George O'Dougherty, May 5, 1930, File 60-138-43, Records of the Department of Justice, RG 60, NARA.

30. *NYT,* Mar. 21, 1927, Mar. 28, 1928; Iron League to Members, Mar. 21, 1927, Box 8, DP; Drew to Members, Apr. 23, 1927, Apr. 12, 1928, Box 14, DP; Thomas to Members, Apr. 29, 1927, SSBT to All Structural Ironworkers, Apr. 30, 1927, Box 20, DP; Drew to Merritt Lane, Feb. 27, 1928, Box 11, DP; Thomas to Drew, Mar. 30, 1928, Drew to Emery, July 9, 26, 1928, Box 22, DP.

31. Drew to Miller, Nov. 20, 21, 1929, Box 11, DP; [Drew] Reply to Morrin, Oct. 31, 1933, Box 29, DP; *Bridgemen's Magazine* 32 (Sept. 1932): 541–42.

32. Levering and Garrigues against Morrin, Final Decree [Feb. 14, 1930], Box 11, DP; Expense Iron Workers' Case. . . , July 29, 1924–Apr. 3, 1930, Box 11, DP; Drew to Miller, Apr. 1, 1930, ibid.

33. Drew to MacCornack, Jan. 16, 1930, Drew to Miller, Apr. 1, 1930, Box 11, DP; *Bridgemen's Magazine* 31 (Jan. 1931): 4; ibid. 32 (Sept. 1932): 14; *NYT,* Mar. 28, Apr. 3, May 13, 1930.

34. *NYT,* Mar. 28, 29, Apr. 5, 9, 1930; *Bridgemen's Magazine* 30 (Dec. 1930): 707–8; ibid. 31 (Jan. 1931): 4; Walsh to Edward P. Connor, Apr. 7, 1930, Box 17, Walsh Papers; Charles L. Eidlitz to Smith, Apr. 8, 1930, Box 11, DP; Drew to Frank Parker, Apr. 9, 1930, Box 12, DP; Drew to Franklin Nevius, May 16, 1930, Box 36, DP; Eidlitz Affidavit, Apr. 18, 1930, in U.S. District Court, In the Matter of the Alleged Contempt of Paul Starrett, Paul J. Morrin et al., Apr. 22, 1930, Box 11, DP; *American Plan* 9 (Apr.–May 1930): 15.

35. In the Matter of Alleged Contempt, Apr. 22, 1930, Box 11, DP; MacCornack to Drew, May 7, 1929, Drew to Mitchell et al., Jan. 13, 1931, ibid.; Morrin vs. SSBT, Index Nos. 1280–1931, June 20, 1932, Box 10, DP; Drew to Nevius, May 16, 1930, Box 36, DP; Noel Sargent, "New York City Steel Erection Situation," May 26, 1930, Box 16, DP; Drew to Paul Coddington, Feb. 3, 1931, Box 13, DP; SSBT Resolution, May 8, 1930, Reel 35, AFL Records; To the SSBT, July 2, 1930, ibid.; *NYT,* May 13, June 5, 6, 1930; [*New York Post,* May 17, 1930], clipping in Box 13, DP; *Bridgemen's Magazine* 31 (Jan. 1931): 48; ibid. 32 (Oct. 1932): 12.

36. *Bridgemen's Magazine* 31 (Jan. 1931): 4–5; ibid. 32 (Oct. 1932): 15–24; To the SSBT, July 2, 1930, Reel 35, AFL Records; *NYT,* June 6, July 4, 1930.

37. Drew Memorandum, May 6, 1930, Box 13, DP; Drew to Mitchell, May 6, 1930, Garrigues to Drew, May 13, 1930, Drew to MacCornack, July 7, 1930, Box 11, DP; Sargent, "New York Situation."

38. J. M. Bell to Sargent, June 21, 1930, Paul Eliel to Sargent, June 23, 1930, F. W. Armstrong to Sargent, June 21, 1930, Parker to Sargent, June 24, 1930, J. W. Schroeder to Sargent, June 25, 1930, C. A. Jay to Sargent, June 25, 1930, Gross to Sargent, June 20, 1930, Box 13, DP; Albert E. Boynton to Drew, May 17, June 21, July 7, 1930, Box 11, DP; Brady to Drew, May 22, 1930, Box 19, DP; Sargent, "New York Situation"; *NYT,* June 1, 1930; Industrial Relations Department, 1929–1930, Ser. I, Box 251, Archives of the National Association of Manufacturers, Accession 1411, Hagley Museum and Library, Wilmington, Delaware.

39. Drew to Mitchell, May 24, 1930, Drew to Mitchell et al., July 1, 1930, Box 11, DP; Extract from Minutes of . . . SSBT, July 1, 1930, ibid.; To the SSBT, July 2, 1930, Reel 35, AFL Records; *Bridgemen's Magazine* 30 (Dec. 1930): 707; ibid. 31 (Jan. 1931): 5; *NYT,* July 2, 1930. Post and McCord completed the erection of the structural steel for the Empire State Building. Thomas to NEA, Nov. 11, 1930, Box 12, DP.

40. E. W. Krueger to Wisconsin Bridge and Iron Co., July 7, 1930, Drew to Mitchell et al., July 1, 1930, Drew to MacCornack, July 7, 1930, Drew to Krueger, July 23, 1930, Drew to T. A. Straub, Sept. 29, 1930, Box 11, DP; Extract from Minutes, July 1, 1930, ibid.; Gibbs to Drew, May 22, 1930, Drew to Brooks, May 23, 1930, Box 19, DP; *NYT,* July 2, 1930; *Newark Evening News,* May 19, 1930, clipping in Box 26, DP.

41. Drew to Miller, May 10, 1930, Garrigues to Drew, May 13, 1930, Grace to Drew, May 16, 1930, Emery to J. A. Campbell, May 20, 1930, Drew to Emery, May 21, 1930, Drew to Mitchell, May 24, 1930, Drew to Straub, Sept. 29, 1930, Box 11, DP; Telephone Message, May 20, 1930, ibid.; Sargent to Drew, Aug. 26, 1930, Thomas to NEA, Nov. 11, 1930, Box 12, DP; Thomas to Members, Oct. 10, 1923, Box 8, DP; Sargent, "New York Situation."

42. *NYT,* July 16, 1930, *Bridgemen's Magazine* 31 (Jan. 1931): 6; Thomas to Gibbs, Oct. 6, 1932, Box 11, DP.

43. *Bridgemen's Magazine* 30 (Dec. 1930): 707; ibid. 31 (Jan. 1931): 6–9; ibid. 32 (Sept. 1932): 527, 531; Morrin against SSBT, Index No. 1280–1931, June 14, 1932, Box 11, DP; Crocker to Drew, Jan. 5, 1931, Drew to Bell, Jan. 12, 1931, Drew to Mitchell et al., Jan. 13, 1931, Drew to Coddington, Feb. 3, 1931, Box 11, DP; *Business Week,* Jan. 21, 1931, p. 6; Morrin to John L. Lewis, July 30, 1936, Box 41, W. Jett Lauck Papers, University of Virginia Library, Charlottesville, Virginia.

44. Lane to Thomas, Oct. 1, 1932, Thomas to Gibbs, Oct. 6, 1932, Box 11, DP; *Levering and Garrigues et al.* v. *Morrin et al.,* 61 F(2d) 115 (1932).

45. *Levering and Garrigues* v. *Morrin,* 287 U.S. 590 (1932); 268 U.S. 64 (1924); *Bridgemen's Magazine* 33 (Mar. 1933): 132–37.

46. *Bridgemen's Magazine* 34 (June 1934): 325, 329–35; *NYT,* June 12,1934; *Levering and Garrigues* v. *Morrin,* 71 F(2d) 284 (1934); 293 U.S. 595 (1934); Walsh to Morrin, Apr. 14, 1934, Reel 35, AFL Records.

47. O'Dougherty Report, May 5, 1930, File 60-138-43, RG 60; Drew to O'Brian, Oct. 2, 1930 (and enclosure), ibid.; *Newark Evening News,* Apr. 11, 1930, clipping in ibid.; unidentified clipping [Nov. 1931], ibid.; James Maxwell Fassett Memorandum to O'Brian, Nov. 20, 1930, ibid.; *NYT,* May 8, 1924, Feb. 23, 1928, June 24, 1933; Brandle ["How to Organize the Employer and Employee"], Oct. 3, 1928, Box 26, DP; Amos H.

Radcliffe affidavit, Sept. 4, 1930, ibid.; Statement by Radcliffe, Nov. 29, 1930, ibid.; Statement by Charles Arny, Nov. 29, 1930, ibid.; *Newark Evening News,* May 7, 8, 1930, clippings in ibid.; *Newark Evening News,* Nov. 26, 1930, clipping in Box 16, DP; [*New York Evening Post,* Nov. 12, 1931], clipping in ibid. On March 26, 1927, the IABSOIW's executive board found Brandle guilty of unspecified charges and removed him from his vice presidency in the union. *Bridgemen's Magazine* 27 (Mar.–Apr. 1927): 142–43.

48. Radcliffe affidavit, Sept. 4, 1930, Box 26, DP; Radcliffe Statement, Nov. 29, 1930, ibid.; Arny Statement, Nov. 29, 1930, ibid.; Bernard Bernstein affidavit [1930], ibid.; Certificate of Incorporation. . . , Aug. 22, 1927, ibid.; Drew to O'Brian, Oct. 2, 1930 (and enclosure), File 60-138-43, RG 60.

49. O'Dougherty Report, May 18, 1930, File 60-138-43, RG 60; Franklin J. Lunding Memorandum for the Chief Examiner, May 17, 1930, File 1-5697-1, Records of the Federal Trade Commission, RG 122, NARA; Radcliffe affidavit, Sept. 4, 1932, Box 26, DP; Radcliffe Statement, Nov. 29, 1930, ibid.; Arny Statement, Nov. 29, 1930, ibid.; Bernstein affidavit [1930], ibid.; *NYT,* Feb. 23, 1928.

50. Fassett Memorandum for O'Brian, Nov. 20, 1930, File 160-38-43, RG 60; O'Dougherty Report, May 18, 1930, ibid.; Drew to O'Brian, Oct. 2, 1930 (and enclosure), ibid.; Lunding Memorandum. . . , May 17, 1930, File 1-5697-1, RG 122; Brandle ["How to Organize"], Oct. 3, 1928, Box 26, DP; Drew to Marshall, Sept. 30, 1930, ibid.; Foster interview with Charles Selbach, Nov. 29, 1930, ibid.; Bernstein affidavit [1930], ibid.; Radcliffe Statement, Nov. 29, 1930, ibid.; Arny Statement, Nov. 29, 1930, ibid.; *Newark Evening News,* May 8, June 25, 1930, clippings in ibid.; *Newark Evening News,* Mar. 3, 1931, clipping in Box 16, DP; Autobiography of Robert J. Foster, undated, pp. 478–81, 485, 488–89, Box 22, DP; Harold Seidman, *Labor Czars* (New York: Liveright Publishing Co., 1938), pp. 150–51.

51. Fassett Memoranda to O'Brian, Apr. 6, Dec. 12, 1930, File 60-138-43, RG 60; O'Dougherty Reports, May 5, Dec. 18, 1930, ibid.; Interview with S. Fassler, Dec. 19, 1930, Box 26; Foster Interview with Nat Lasher, Dec. 11, 1930, ibid.; John C. Sample Statement, Dec. 31, 1930, ibid.; Bernstein affidavit [1930], ibid.; Statement by Gustave Wickstrand, Dec. 30, 1930, ibid.; Foster Investigation. . . , Apr. 3, 1930, ibid.; *Newark Evening News,* June 5, 1930, clipping in ibid.; [Drew] In re Alleged Combination [1930], Box 16, DP.

52. George P. Alt and Fassett Memorandum for O'Brian, Apr. 16, 1930, File 60-138-43, RG 60; O'Dougherty Report, May 5, 1930, ibid.; T. G. Melvin Reports, Aug. 20, Oct. 13, 1930, ibid.; Fassett to O'Brian, Mar. 5, 1931, ibid.; Fassett Memoranda to O'Brian, May 27, 1930, Feb. 19, Mar. 13, 1931, ibid.; O'Brian Memorandum for the Files, Aug. 28, 1931, Mar. 31, 1932 (both dates given), ibid.; Lewis J. Dundin to Foster, May 16, 1930, Box 26, DP; [Foster] report, undated, ibid.; R. A. Pendergrass to Drew, May 27, 1930, Box 19, DP; Drew to Thomas Farnam, May 2, 1931, Box 13, DP; Drew to M. Benson, Sept. 7, 1932, Box 8, DP; [*Newark Evening News,* Mar. 21, 26, Apr. 2, 4, 19, May 15, 26, 1930], clippings in Box 26, DP.

53. *Newark Evening News,* Oct. 9, 10, 12, 1930, clippings in File 60-138-43, RG 60; A Suffering Tradesman to William D. Mitchell, Apr. 3, 1932, ibid.; *Newark Evening News,* Feb. 9, Aug. 8, 1931, Mar. 28, 1932, clippings in Box 16, DP; [*Newark Evening News,* Feb. 10, 13, 1931], ibid.; *NYT,* Nov. 20, 1930, Mar. 24, 30, 1932; Foster Investigation. . . , Mar. 16, 1930, Box 26, DP; Arny Statement, Nov. 29, 1930, ibid.; [Drew] document, Oct. 31, 1933, Box 6, DP; Foster autobiography, pp. 535, 539–40, Box 22, DP.

54. *NYT,* Nov. 20, 1930, Mar. 24, 30, 1932; *Newark Evening News,* Nov. 19, 1930, Feb. 9, 1931, Mar. 28, 1932, clippings in Box 16, DP; [*Newark Evening News,* Feb. 10, 1931], clipping in ibid.; [Drew] document, Oct. 31, 1933, Box 6, ibid.

55. Fassett Memorandum for O'Brian, Nov. 20, 1930, File 60-138-43, RG 60; Selbach interview, Nov. 29, 1930, Box 26, DP; Foster autobiography, pp. 483–84, Box 22, DP; *Newark Evening News,* June 3, 1930, clipping in Box 26, DP; [*Newark Evening News,* July 2, 1930], clipping in Box 16, DP.

56. Foster autobiography, p. 475, Box 22, DP; Thomas to Lane, Feb. 20, 1930, Box 16, DP; Statement by Walter Drew, May 27, 1930, Box 13, DP; Drew to O'Brian, Sept. 15, 1930, Box 29, DP; Drew to C. M. Benson, Sept. 7, 1932, Box 26, DP; Pendergrass to Drew, May 27, 1930, Box 19, DP; O'Dougherty Report, May 5, 1930, File 60-138-43, RG 60.

57. Pendergrass to Drew, May 27, 1930, Box 19, DP; MacCornack to Drew, June 3, 1930, Box 16, DP; O'Dougherty Report, Jan. 13, 1931, File 60-138-43, RG 60; Fassett Memorandum to O'Brian, Feb. 19, 1931, ibid.; Melvin Report, Mar. 31, 1931, ibid.; O'Brian Memorandum for the Files, Mar. 31, 1932, ibid.

58. Foster autobiography, pp. 495–509, Box 22, DP; Radcliffe Statement, Nov. 29, 1930, Box 26, DP; Drew to Members, July 30, 31, 1931 (and enclosed Statement by American Bridge, McClintic-Marshall, Phoenix Bridge, July 30, 1931), Drew to Mac-Cornack, Nov. 18, 1931, Box 16, DP; Drew to Benson, Sept. 7, 1932, Box 8, DP; Suffering Tradesman to Mitchell, Apr. 3, 1932, File 160-38-43, RG 60; Subcommittee of the Senate Committee on Education and Labor, *Violations of Free Speech and the Rights of Labor,* 75 Cong., 1 sess., 1937, Part 7, pp. 2353, 2360–66, 2372–73, 2376–78, 2381–93, 2403–5; Senate Committee on Education and Labor, *Violations,* 76 Cong., 1 sess., 1939, S. Rept. 6, Part 4, pp. 25–26; *NYT,* Mar. 1, 3, 9, 12, Apr. 1, 14, 16, 22, June 25, Dec. 8, 1932; *Jersey Journal,* Dec. 9, 1932, clipping in Box 26, DP; Dayton Dana McKean, *The Boss: The Hague Machine in Action* (Boston: Houghton Mifflin Co., 1940), p. 186.

59. Subcommittee of Senate Committee on Education and Labor, *Violations,* 76 Cong., 1 sess., Part 7, p. 2394; McKean, *The Boss,* pp. 185–87; Seidman, *Labor Czars,* pp. 154–55; John Hutchinson, *The Imperfect Union: A History of Corruption in American Trade Unions* (New York: E. P. Dutton Co., 1970), pp. 50–51; *NYT,* Dec. 15, 1932; Drew to Benson, Sept. 7, 1932, Box 8, DP. The La Follette Committee provided the $2 million figure for the job. Seidman placed the cost at $16 million.

60. David H. Sibbett Memorandum for the Chief Examiner, Sept. 7, 1929, File 1-5697-1, RG 122; Lunding Summary Memorandum, Dec. 28, 1929, ibid.; Lunding Memorandum for Chief Examiner, May 17, 1930, ibid.; H. L. Anderson Memorandum for the Commission, May 19, 1930, ibid.; John B. Wilson Memorandum for the Chief Examiner, May 10, 1934, ibid.; Alt and Fassett Memorandum for O'Brian, Apr. 16, 1930, File 60-138-43, RG 60; Drew to Charles F. Abbott, June 11, 1931, Box 13, DP; Drew to William E. Humphrey, May 25, 1931, Humphrey to Drew, May 28, 1931, Box 26, DP.

61. Daily Report of Conference (Antitrust Division), Apr. 16, 1930, File 60-138-43, RG 60; Alt and Fassett Memorandum for O'Brian, Apr. 16, 1930, ibid.; O'Brian to FTC, May 6, 1930, ibid.; Fassett Memorandum for O'Brian, May 22, 1930, ibid.

62. Alt Memorandum for O'Brian, May 28, 1930, ibid.; Fassett Memoranda for O'Brian, Sept. 6, Nov. 30, Dec. 3, 1930, ibid.; Mitchell Memorandum for O'Brian, Nov. 4, 1930, ibid.; Daily Report. . . , Nov. 21, 24, 1930, ibid.; Fassett to O'Brian, Sept. 12, 1930, Drew to O'Brian, Sept. 15, Oct. 2, 1930, O'Brian to Drew, Nov. 6, 1930, Drew to

Fassett, Nov. 11, 1930, Foster to Fassett, Dec. 1, 1930, Foster to O'Brian, Dec. 4, 1930, ibid.; Drew to Marshall, Sept. 30, 1930, Drew to Mitchell, Oct. 2, 1930, Box 26, DP.

63. Fassett Memorandum for O'Brian, Dec. 12, 1930, File 60-138-43, RG 60; Foster to O'Brian, Jan. 12, 1931, O'Brian to Foster, Jan. 16, 1931, Drew to O'Brian, Feb. 24, 1931, ibid.

64. O'Brian Memorandum for the Files, Mar. 31, 1932, ibid.; Fassett Memorandum for O'Brian, Dec. 12, 1930, ibid.; O'Dougherty Report, May 5, 1930, ibid.; Melvin Report, Aug. 26, 1930, ibid.; Russell Hardy Memoranda for O'Brian, Mar. 10, 1931, Apr. 2, 1932, ibid.; Lunding Memorandum for Chief Examiner, May 17, 1930, File 1-5697-1, RG 122; Drew to O'Brian, Feb. 24, 1931, Box 16, DP; Memoranda re Jersey Situation [Oct. 1930], Box 29, DP.

65. O'Brian Memorandum for the Files, Mar. 31, 1932, File 60-138-43, RG 60; Fassett Memorandum for Hardy, Jan. 27, 1933, ibid.; Arnold Memorandum for Bennett Crain, Dec. 15, 1939, Arnold to John Henry Lewin, Dec. 15, 1939, ibid. For the 1939 Arnold probe, see Sidney Fine, *Frank Murphy: The Washington Years* (Ann Arbor: University of Michigan Press, 1984), pp. 49–54.

66. William H. McHugh to Chief Intelligence Unit, Bureau of Internal Revenue, Sept. 20, 1930, File 5-48-115, RG 60; E.C. Crouter Memorandum for [G. A.] Youngquist, Nov. 12, 1931, ibid.; Philip Forman to Attorney General, Apr. 13, 1932, ibid.; Youngquist to Forman, Mar. 9, 1931, Forman to Attorney General, Apr. 5, 1932, File 5-48-116, ibid.; Fassett Memorandum for O'Brian, Mar. 13, 18, 1931, File 60-138-43, RG 60; *Newark Evening News,* Nov. 26, 1930, clipping in Box 16, DP; *NYT,* Mar. 19, 1930, Feb. 19, Mar. 28, Oct. 4, 1931, Apr. 24, 1932.

67. Fassett Memorandum for O'Brian, July 8, 1932, File 60-138-43, RG 60; *Bridgemen's Magazine* 33 (June 1933): 333, ibid. 36 (Oct. 1936): 42–44; Drew to Members, June 30, 1933, Box 14, DP; [Drew] document, Oct. 31, 1933, Box 6, DP; *NYT,* July 15, 16, Dec. 13, 1932, Mar. 2, June 24, 1933, Mar. 1, May 9, 22, 1934; Seidman, *Labor Czars,* pp. 154, 155; Hutchinson, *Imperfect Union,* p. 51.

68. Thomas to W. R. Mason, Feb. 7, 1931, Box 12, DP; Drew to Members, Oct. 6, 1931, Drew to Hirsh, July 13, 1932, Box 14, DP; Brady to Members, June 22, 1932, Box 20, DP; unidentified and undated notes, Box 28, DP; *NYT,* Jan. 9, 1933; National Recovery Administration, Code of Fair Competition for Structural Steel and Iron Fabricating Industry, Transcript of Hearing, Appendix, pp. 130–32, Box 7241, Records of the National Recovery Administration, RG 9, NARA; Dallas Jones interview with Mrs. Walter Drew, Nov. 12, 1962, p. 5, transcript in my possession. The managers of the NEA's Philadelphia, Buffalo, and Milwaukee labor bureaus were kept on when the bureaus were closed and were paid a monthly retainer. Drew to Hirsh, July 13, 1932, Box 14, DP.

69. *Bridgemen's Magazine* 28 (Oct.–Nov. 1928): 111; ibid. 32 (Oct. 1932): 111–12; ibid. 33 (Nov.–Dec. 1933): 733, 737; United States Bureau of the Census, *Sixteenth Census of the United States: 1940, Population, Comparative Occupation Statistics, 1870 to 1940* (Washington: U.S. Government Printing Office, 1943), p. 106.

Chapter 11

1. Drew to Members, Apr. 21, 1933, Box 14, DP; Drew to Members, Apr. 26, 1933, Box 10, DP; Drew to E. A. Gibbs, Apr. 20, 1933, Drew to J. M. Bell, May 2, 1933, Box 13, DP; Drew to Dana Jones, May 4, 1933, Drew to Long, May 5, 1933, Drew to Clyde

MacCornack, May 24, 1933, Box 16, DP; Drew to James Emery, May 6, 1933, Box 15, DP.

2. Drew to H. A. Wagner, May 25, July 14, 1933, Drew to Charles F. Abbott, June 14, 1933, Drew to Members, June 30, 1933, Aug. 10, 17, 1934, Box 14, DP; Drew to H. B. Hirsh, Nov. 23, 1933, Box 13, DP; Meeting of Employment Relations Committee, Sept. 10, 1934, Ser. V, Box 1, Archives of the National Association of Manufacturers, Accession 1411, Hagley Museum and Library, Wilmington, Delaware.

3. Drew to W. N. Kratzer, July 14, 1933, Box 13, DP.

4. Morrin to Walsh, May 31, 1933, Box 20, Frank P. Walsh Papers, New York Public Library, New York, New York; [W. Jett] Lauck to Morrin, June 18, Dec. 13, 1933, Morrin to Lauck, July 7, 1933, Box 41, W. Jett Lauck Papers, University of Virginia Library, Charlottesville, Virginia; Leighton H. Peebles, "History of the Code of Fair Competition for the Structural Steel and Iron Fabricating Industry," Oct. 13, 1936, pp. 20–36, Box 7639, Records of the National Recovery Administration, RG 9, NARA; Membership . . . in SSBEA, Oct. 11, 1933, Box 5462, ibid.; SSBEA Membership, Nov. 1, 1933, ibid.; *Bridgemen's Magazine* 36 (Oct. 1936): 170.

5. *Iron Age* 136 (July 18, 1935): 48; Gibbs to Drew, June 16, 1933, Box 16, DP; Drew to Members, Aug. 10, 17, 1934, Box 14, DP; Drew to E. W. Krueger, Aug. 17, 1934, Box 13, DP; Dan M. Gayton to Morrin, June 11, 1934, Box 41, Lauck Papers; Paul Coddington to Franklin D. Roosevelt, Oct. 1, 1932, [Michael E. Sherman] to H. L. Kerwin, undated, File 176-1978, Records of the Federal Mediation and Conciliation Service, RG 280, NARA; Bell to Drew, Sept. 6, 1934, enclosing Settlement of Strike as Proposed by Worden-Allen Co., undated, Box 19, DP. The Milwaukee Bridge Co., after a brief strike, came to terms with the union on August 2 and resigned from the NEA. See Chicago Regional File 338, Records of the National Labor Relations Board, RG 25, NARA, and Drew to Bell, Aug. 31, 1934, Box 19, DP.

6. Transcript of Proceedings. . . , Aug. 16, 1934, Box 19, DP; Secretary to Noel Sargent, Aug. 31, 1934, Bell to Drew, Sept. 6, 14, Oct. 2, Nov. 15 (enclosing Milwaukee Employers' Council Bulletin No. 22, Nov. 12, 1934), 1934, Drew to Bell, Sept. 18, 1934, Drew to Gordon Hostetter, Jan. 22, 1935, Box 19, DP; Drew to Members, Nov. 20, 1934, Box 14, DP.

7. Bell to Drew, Sept. 14, Dec. 17, 1934, Drew to Bell, Sept. 18, 1934, Box 19, DP.

8. Sherman to Kerwin, Nov. 2, 11, 1934, File 176-1978, RG 280; Agreement for Strike Settlement at Lakeside Bridge and Steel Co., Nov. 10, 1934, ibid.; Agreement for Strike Settlement at Worden-Allen Co., Nov. 8, 1934, Chicago Regional File 356, RG 25; Bell to Drew, Dec. 8, 1934, and enclosed clippings, Box 19, DP; Drew to Members, Dec. 15, 1934, Box 14, DP.

9. Drew to Members, Nov. 20, 1934, Box 14, DP; Drew to Bell, Nov. 21, 1934, Drew to Hostetter, Jan. 18, 1935, Box 19, DP.

10. Drew to Members, Jan. 20, July 19, 1934, Box 14, DP; Drew to Bell, Jan. 2, 1935, Box 19, DP; Drew affidavit, June 1934, Box 8, DP; [Roberts B. Thomas] Memorandum. . . , June 14, 1934, ibid.

11. *NYT,* Apr. 6, 1935; [Walsh] to Morrin, Mar. 13, 1935, Morrin to Walsh, Apr. 8, 1935, Box 41, Lauck Papers; Thomas to Lindsay Rogers, Apr. 16, 1935, Box 13, Drew to B. T. Mial, Aug. 9, 1935, Thomas to Drew, June 11, 1935, enclosing Thomas to Fiorello LaGuardia, June 8, 1935, Box 9, DP; John McKenzie to Iron League, June 11, 1935, Thomas to McKenzie, June 15, 1935, Box 8, DP; Thomas Report on the New York Erection Labor Situation, Jan. 8, 1936, Box 9, DP.

12. William H. Kelley to Supervising Engineer, Aug. 2, 1935, Harry Watts to Kelley,

Aug. 7, 1935, Charles H. Probert Memorandum to Branscombe, Aug. 10, 1935, Kelley to District Engineer, Sept. 12, 1935, Records of the Public Buildings Service, RG 121, NARA; Valentine G. Schneible to Frances Perkins, Sept. 28, 1935, T. J. Williams to Kerwin, Oct. 4, 16, 1935, File 182-265, RG 280; Thomas to Rogers, Apr. 16, 1935, Box 13, DP; Thomas Report, Jan. 8, 1936, Box 9, DP; Annual Report of New York Labor Situation, July 9, 1936, Box 8, DP; *NYT,* Aug. 3, 1935; *Bridgemen's Magazine* 36 (Oct. 1936): 55–57. See chapter 10.

13. *Bridgemen's Magazine* 36 (Oct. 1936): 82–84; Irving Bernstein, *A Caring Society: The New Deal, the Worker, and the Great Depression* (Boston: Houghton Mifflin Co., 1985), p. 173.

14. Wagner to Drew, Sept. 18, 1933, Drew to Members, Sept. 22, Oct. 6, 1933, Jan. 11, 1935, Drew to Ickes, Sept. 25, 1933, Box 14, DP.

15. Public Works Administration, *America Builds* (Washington: Government Printing Office, 1939), p. 86; Drew to Members, Sept. 5 (enclosing NAM Release, Sept. 2, 1933), 22, 25, Oct. 6, 1933, Box 14, DP; Drew affidavit, June 1934, Box 8, DP; Thomas to Rogers, Apr. 16, 1935, Box 13, DP; Secretary to John C. Gall, Aug. 31, 1934, Box 20, DP; Drew to E.W. Krueger, Jan. 28, 1935, Drew to Emery, Jan. 28, 1935, Box 4, DP.

16. *Iron Trade Review* 71 (Nov. 30, 1922): 1498; Code Analysis Division to Control Division, Sept. 18, 1933, Box 5455, RG 9; Peebles, "Code of Fair Competition," pp. 6–7.

17. AISC Annual Report, Sept. 30, 1933, Box 5461, RG 9; Thomas to Robert T. Brooks, June 27, 1933, C. Edwin Michael to Drew, June 30, 1933, Drew to Conley, June 29, 1933, Box 16, DP; Bessie L. Crocker note, Aug. 25, 1933, Box 14, DP.

18. *Iron Trade Review* 86 (Jan. 30, 1930): 52; Michael to Drew, June 30, 1933, Box 16, DP; RMG [Gates] Memorandum, Dec. 7, 1933, Box 5453, RG 9; Memo to [L. C.] Marshall, Nov. 8, 1934, Box 12, Leon Henderson Papers, Franklin D. Roosevelt Library, Hyde Park, New York.

19. Thomas to Brooks, June 27, 1933, Michael to Drew, June 30, 1933, Drew to Conley, July 6, 12, 13, 14, 19, 1933, Conley to Drew, July 1, 7, 14, 18, 1933, Michael to Conley, July 18, 1933, Box 16, DP.

20. Drew to Conley, July 13, 1933, ibid.; *Iron Trade Review* 93 (Oct. 23, 1933): 15; Code of Fair Competition Structural Steel and Iron Fabricating Industry, Sept. 5, 1933, Box 5454, RG 9; Code Analysis Division to Control Division, Sept. 18, 1933, Box 5456, ibid.; Structural Steel and Iron Fabricating Industry, Transcript of Hearing, Oct. 30, 1933, pp. 10–13, Box 7241, ibid.; John Kennedy Ohl, *Hugh S. Johnson and the New Deal* (DeKalb: Northern Illinois University Press, 1985), pp. 120–21.

21. There is a copy of the code in Transcript of Hearing, Oct. 30, 1933, pp. 5–67, Box 7241, RG 9.

22. Code Analysis Division to Control Division, Sept. 18, 1933, Box 5456, ibid.; Transcript of Hearing, pp. 91, 141, Box 7241, ibid.; *Iron Trade Review* 94 (May 28, 1934): 12.

23. *Bridgemen's Magazine* 33 (Nov.–Dec. 1933): 645–47, 649; Morrin to Lauck, Box 41, Lauck Papers; E. H. Handy to NRA, Oct. 12, 1933, Box 5457, RG 9; Peebles, "Code of Fair Competition," p. 2; Morrin to Johnson, Oct. 11, 1933, Box 5459, RG 9.

24. Transcript of Hearing, Oct. 30, 1933, pp. 69–70, 77–82, 86–91, 133–34, 136–44, Box 7241, RG 9.

25. Ibid., pp. 146–53, 169–71, 177–93; *Bridgemen's Magazine* 36 (Oct. 1936): 99. There is a copy of the SSBEA code in Transcript of Hearing, Appendix, pp. 1–22, Box 7241, RG 9.

26. Memorandum, Jan. 17, 1934, Box 5461, RG 9; Peter A. Stone to Walter G. Hooks, May 14, 1934, ibid.; Report of Conference, Sept. 27, 1934, ibid.; AISC . . . Memorandum. . . , Nov. 6, 1933, Box 5454, ibid.; Conley to Barton W. Murray, Nov. 17, 1933, Box 5457, ibid.; Peebles, "Code of Fair Competition," pp. 102–4; Ruth W. Ayres Memorandum. . . , Nov. 25, 1934, Box 5455, RG 9; Statement by Labor Advisory Board, Dec. 7, 1934, Box 5453, ibid.; Gates to Sidney Hillman, Dec. 22, 1934, ibid.

27. AISC Memorandum, Nov. 6, 1933, Box 5454, ibid.; Reply of P. J. Morrin, Nov. 16, 1933, Box 5457, ibid.; Code Conferences, Feb. 7, 9, 10, 15, 16, 19, 27, 1934, Box 5461, ibid.; Ayres Memorandum, Nov. 25, 1934, Box 5455, ibid.; Statement by Labor Advisory Board, Dec. 7, 1934, Box 5453, ibid.; Gates to Hillman, Dec. 22, 1934, ibid.; Peebles, "Code of Fair Competition," pp. 107–9; *Bridgemen's Magazine* 33 (Nov.–Dec. 1933): 724–25, 728–29, 731–34, 737.

28. Peebles, "Code of Fair Competition," pp. 26, 27; Gates to Hillman, Dec. 22, 1934, Box 5453, RG 9; Ayres Memorandum, Nov. 25, 1934, Box 5455, ibid.; *Bridgemen's Magazine* 34 (Jan. 1934): 3–5; ibid. 36 (Oct. 1936): 107–8; National Recovery Administration, *Codes of Fair Competition* (Washington: Government Printing Office, 1934), 5:655–67.

29. Code Conference, Mar. 14, 1934, Box 369, Lauck Papers; Hearing on Code of . . . Structural Steel and Iron Fabricating Industry, Mar. 15, 1934, Box 7241, RG 9.

30. Stone to Hooks, May 14, 1934, Box 5461, RG 9; Code Conference, Apr. 20, 1934, ibid.; Legal Division to Hooks, May 10, 1934, Labor Advisory Board to Hooks, May 12, 1934, Box 5453, ibid.; Minutes of Meeting. . . , May 2, 1934, Box 5462, ibid.; Re Steel Erection, May 16, 1934, Box 5457, ibid.; Peebles, "Code of Fair Competition," pp. 39–41, 46–47, 63–64.

31. National Recovery Administration, *Codes of Fair Competition* (Washington: Government Printing Office, 1934), 13:47–88; Chairman Code Committee to Johnson, July 18, 1934, Memo to Marshall, Nov. 8, 1934, Box 12, Henderson Papers; AISC Release, Oct. 26, 1934, Box 5453, RG 9; Walter White to W. P. Witherow, Apr. 11, 1935, Box 5456, ibid.; [Michael] Memo to Marshall, Nov. 8, 1934, Box 5460, ibid.; *Steel* 95 (July 23, 1934): 10.

32. Peebles, "Code of Fair Competition," pp. 60–61, 78, 95, 101; White to Blackwell Smith, Oct. 5, 1934, Box 5460, RG 9; Hooks to Administrator, Aug. 16, 1934, Box 5455, ibid.; Report of Conference, Sept. 27, 1934, Box 5461, ibid.; Committee on the . . . Code Problem to Advisory Council, Dec. 3, 1934, ibid.; Ayres Memorandum, Nov. 8, 1934, Box 5455, ibid.; Gates to Hillman, Dec. 22, 1934, Box 5453, ibid.; Code. . . , Mar. 13, 1935, Box 5454, ibid.; B. R. Value et al., Report on the March 13, 1935 Draft. . . , Apr. 3, 1935, Box 5456, ibid.; Memorandum, Apr. 12, 1935, ibid.; White to Witherow, Apr. 11, 1935, ibid.; Memo to Marshall, Nov. 8, 1934, Box 12, Henderson Papers; [Lauck] to Morrin, Mar. 13, 1935, Morrin to Walsh, Apr. 8, 1935, Box 41, Lauck Papers.

33. *Steel* 95 (Oct. 29, 1934): 10; Legal Division to Robert N. Campbell, Apr. 4, 1935, Box 5453, RG 9; Labor Advisory Board to Campbell, Mar. 22, 1935, Campbell to NIRB, Apr. 6, 1935, Box 5456, ibid.; Marshall to Campbell, Apr. 18, 1935, Box 5460, ibid.; 295 U.S. 495 (1935); Anthony J. Badger, *The New Deal* (New York: Noonday Press, 1989), p. 93.

34. *Bridgemen's Magazine* 36 (Oct. 1936): 103.

35. Drew to Members, Mar. 17, 1934, Box 14, DP.

36. The Wagner-Connery . . . Bill, Statement in opposition by Walter Drew, Apr. 5,

1934, Box 16, DP; Drew to David Walsh, Mar. 29, Apr. 7, 1934, Drew to J. M. Taylor, May 10, 1934, Drew to J. D. Fredericks, May 10, 1934, Drew to Henry D. Sayre, Apr. 23, 1934, Drew to Louis Howe, Apr. 20, 1934, Box 16, DP; Drew to Members of U.S. Senate, May 31, 1934, Box 14, DP.

37. Drew to Hubert Rice, Jan. 2, 1935, Box 13, DP; Drew to Members, Mar. 25, 1935, Box 14, DP.

38. Drew to Members, Mar. 25, 1935, Drew to Brann and Stuart, Mar. 11, 1941, Box 14, DP; United States Senate Committee on Education and Labor, *Violations of Free Speech and the Rights of Labor,* 76 Cong., 1 sess., S. Rept. 6, Part 4, pp. 7–9.

39. Drew to Members, Apr. 23, 1937, MacCornack to Drew, May 4, 1937, Drew to MacCornack, May 12, 1937, Box 14, DP; Thomas to Drew, Apr. 19, 1937, Box 16, DP; 301 U.S. 1 (1937).

40. Walter Galenson, *The CIO Challenge to the AFL* (Cambridge, Mass.: Harvard University Press, 1960), p. 93; *Steel* 100 (Apr. 26, 1937): 24; *Bridgemen's Magazine* 37 (Mar. 1937): 131–39, (Apr. 1937): 193, (July 1937): 356; *NYT,* Apr. 20, 1937; Dallas Jones interview with Harry Smedley, Nov. 1, 1962, pp. 1–2, with Clyde MacCornack, Dec. 12, 1962, pp. 5–6, transcripts in my possession; "International Association of Bridge, Structural and Ornamental Iron Workers," reprinted from "The Builders" (1983), p. 177, in my possession; Leo Troy, *Trade Union Membership, 1897–1962* (New York: Columbia University Press [1965]), table A-1.

41. Thomas to Members, May 21, 1937, Box 8, DP; Memorandum, June 1937, Box 9, DP; MacCornack to Drew, July 16, 1937, Box 14, DP.

42. Drew to George W. Ryle, Dec. 20, 1938, Drew to Members, Dec. 30, 1938, Box 7, DP; Drew to MacCornack, Mar. 20, 1939, Secretary to Brooks, Apr. 12, 1939, NEA to Lawrence M.C. Smith, Box 13, DP; Drew to H. R. Brady, June 27, 1940, Drew to Hirsh, Sept. 27, 1940, Secretary to MacCornack, May 23, 1941, Box 14, DP.

43. "International Association of Bridge, Structural and Ornamental Iron Workers," pp. 177–78 (copy in my possession); Robert Gottlieb and Irene Wolt, *Thinking Big: The Story of the Los Angeles Times* (New York: G. P. Putnam's Sons, 1977), p. 104.

44. MacCornack to Drew, Feb. 13, 1945, Feb. 17, 1947, Box 14, DP; Crocker to Members, Sept. 4, 1951, F. A. Strouce to MacCornack, Feb. 6, 1952, MacCornack to Conley, Feb. 12, 1952, MacCornack to Heyl and Patterson, Oct. 25, 1955, Drew to Hoyt A. Moore, Jan. 6, 1956, Box 15, DP; MacCornack interview, p. 4.

45. Minutes of Employment Relations Committee, May 20, 1937, Ser. V, Box 1, Accession 1411; Drew to Members of Congress, July 20, 1936, Box 14, DP; Drew to Members of Congress, Nov. 26, 1946, Drew to Lewis Guenther, Nov. 3, 1949, Drew to Henry T. Taylor, Dec. 23, 1949, Drew to Ben Hibbs, May 5, 1954, Box 13, DP; Drew to A. L. Reimer, May 22, 1950, Drew to Moore, June 6, 1956, Box 15, DP; Drew tape [1952], Box 36, DP; Harry A. Millis and Emily Clark Brown, *From the Wagner Act to Taft-Hartley* (Chicago: University of Chicago Press, 1950), pp. 496–513.

46. Millis and Brown, *Wagner Act to Taft-Hartley,* pp. 317, 326–30; Drew to John Paul, June 9, 1954, Drew to Lester A. Hunt, Apr. 25, 1956, Box 13, DP; Drew to Moore, June 6, 1956, Box 15, DP.

47. MacCornack to Executive Committee, Jan. 26, 1954, Crocker Memorandum to Drew, May 19, 1954, Crocker to MacCornack, Jan. 26, 1956, MacCornack to Members and Past Members, July 11, 1956, Drew to Moore, June 6, 1956, Box 15, DP; Drew to Hostetter, May 23, 1956, Box 8, DP; MacCornack interview, pp. 4–5.

48. Memo [1955], Box 15, DP; Josephine Foster to Katherine King, May 29, 1957,

Box 13, DP; MacCornack interview, p. 5; Jones interview with J. Foster, Nov. 12, 1962, p. 4, transcript in my possession.

49. On this point, see Sanford M. Jacoby, "American Exceptionalism Revisited: The Importance of Management," in Jacoby, ed., *Masters to Managers* (New York: Columbia University Press, 1991), pp. 177, 187, 189, 197–200.

50. Michael Goldfarb, *The Decline of Organized Labor in the United States* (Chicago: University of Chicago Press, 1987), pp. 191–92.

51. Phone Conversations with Eric Waterman, Nov. 1992, and Joseph R. LaRocca, Dec. 8, 1992; LaRocca to Fine, Feb. 3, 1993, and enclosed "The National Steel Erectors Today," in my possession.

Bibliography

Manuscript and Archival Collections

Bentley Historical Library, Ann Arbor, Michigan
    Walter Drew Papers
    C. W. Post Papers
Chicago Historical Society, Chicago, Illinois
    Minutes of the Chicago Federation of Labor, 1903–1922 (microfilm copy)
Franklin D. Roosevelt Library, Hyde Park, New York
    Leon Henderson Papers
Grand Rapids Public Library, Grand Rapids, Michigan
    Records of the Citizens Alliance of Grand Rapids
Hagley Museum and Library, Wilmington, Delaware
    Records of the National Association of Manufacturers, 1895–1913, microfilm
        copy, Accession 1521
    Archives of the National Association of Manufacturers, Accession 1411
    Archives of the National Industrial Conference Board, Accession 1057
    Records of the Pennsylvania Railroad Company, Accession 1807/1810
Martin P. Catherwood Library, Cornell University, Ithaca, New York
    Railway Employees' Department, American Federation of Labor, Records
National Archives and Records Administration, Washington, D.C.
    Records of the National War Labor Board, Record Group 2
    Records of the National Recovery Administration, Record Group 9
    Records of the Railroad Labor Board, in Records of the National Mediation
        Board, Record Group 13
    Records of the National Labor Relations Board (Chicago Regional File), Record
        Group 25
    Records of the United States Shipping Board, Record Group 32
    Records of the Department of Justice, Record Group 60
    Records of the Public Buildings Service, Record Group 121
    Records of the Federal Trade Commission, Record Group 122
    Records of the Commission on Industrial Relations, in General Records of the
        Department of Labor, Record Group 174
    Records of the Federal Mediation and Conciliation Service, Record Group 280
New York Public Library, New York, New York
    Papers of Marc Eidlitz and Sons
    Frank P. Walsh Papers

University of Cincinnati Library, Cincinnati, Ohio
    James B. and John J. McNamara Papers
University of Michigan Library, Ann Arbor, Michigan (microfilm copies)
    American Federation of Labor Records: The Samuel Gompers Era
    Papers of the National War Labor Board
    William Howard Taft Papers
    Woodrow Wilson Papers
University of Oregon Library, Eugene, Oregon
    Robert Cantwell Papers
University of Virginia Library, Charlottesville, Virginia
    W. Jett Lauck Papers

United States Government Documents

Chaney, Lucien W., and Hugh S. Hanna. *The Safety Movement in the Iron and Steel Industry, 1907–1913.* Bureau of Labor Statistics Bulletin No. 234. Washington: Government Printing Office, 1918.
Commission on Industrial Relations. *Industrial Relations. Final Report and Testimony.* 64 Cong., 1 sess., 1916. S. Doc. No. 415. 11 vols.
"Decisions of the Railroad Labor Board: The Pennsylvania Railroad Cases." *Monthly Labor Review* 17 (Aug. 1923): 428–35.
Decisions of the United States Railroad Labor Board, with Addenda and Interpretations, 1921–1925. 6 vols. Washington: Government Printing Office, 1921–26.
Gadsby, Margaret. "Strike of the Railroad Shopmen." *Monthly Labor Review* 15 (Dec. 1922): 1171–91.
Hotchkiss, Willard E., and Henry R. Seager. *History of the Shipbuilding Labor Adjustment Board.* Bureau of Labor Statistics Bulletin No. 283. Washington: Government Printing Office, 1921.
"Maintenance of Existing Labor Standards." *Monthly Review of the Bureau of Labor Statistics* 4 (June 1917): 807–9.
National Recovery Administration. *Codes of Fair Competition.* Vols. 5, 13. Washington: Government Printing Office, 1934.
National War Labor Board: A History. . . . Bureau of Labor Statistics Bulletin No. 287. Washington: Government Printing Office, 1922.
Proceedings of the First Industrial Conference (Called by the President) October 6 to 23, 1919. Washington: Government Printing Office, 1920.
Public Works Administration. *America Builds.* Washington: Government Printing Office, 1939.
Report on Conditions of Employment in the Iron and Steel Industry. 62 Cong., 1 sess., 1913. S. Doc. No. 110. 4 vols.
"Report on Conditions of the Building Industry in New York." *Monthly Labor Review* 15 (Sept. 1922): 645–48.
"Structural Ironworkers—New York City." *Monthly Labor Review* 17 (Aug. 1923): 427–30.
U.S. Congress. House. Committee on Investigation of United States Steel Corporation. *Hearings.* 62 Cong., 2 sess., 1911–12. 8 vols.
U.S. Congress. House. Subcommittee No. 1, Committee on Labor. *HR 15651. Eight Hours for Laborers on Government Work. Hearings.* 60 Cong., 1908.

U.S. Congress. Senate. Committee on Education and Labor. *Violations of Free Speech and the Rights of Labor.* 76 Cong., 1 sess., 1939, S. Rept. 6, pt. 4; 77 Cong., 1 sess., 1941, S. Rept. 151, pt. 4.

U.S. Congress. Senate. Subcommittee of the Senate Committee on Education and Labor. *Violations of Free Speech and the Rights of Labor. Hearings.* 75 Cong., 1 sess., 1937, pt. 7; 75 Cong., 3 sess., 1938, pts. 17–18, 20–21; 76 Cong., 1 sess., 1939, pt. 35.

U.S. Congress. Senate. Committee on Education and Labor. *West Virginia Coal Fields. Hearings.* 67 Cong., 1 sess., 1921. 2 vols.

U.S. Congress. Senate. Subcommittee of the Senate Committee on the Judiciary. *Limiting Federal Injunctions. Hearings.* 62 Cong., 1 sess., 1912, pts. 1 and 2.

————. *Maintenance of a Lobby to Influence Legislation. Hearings.* 63 Cong., 1 sess., 1913. 4 vols. and Appendix, 4 vols.

Winslow, Charles. *Conciliation and Arbitration in the Building Trades of Greater New York.* Bureau of Labor Statistics Bulletin No. 124. Washington: Government Printing Office, 1913.

State Government Documents

Illinois General Assembly. *Report of the Illinois Building Investigation Commission Authorized by the 52d General Assembly, 1921.* 53rd General Assembly, 1923.

State of New York. *Intermediate Report of the Joint Legislative Committee on Housing.* Legislative Document (1922) No. 60, 1922.

————. *Final Report of the Joint Legislative Committee on Housing.* Legislative Document (1923), 1923.

Interviews

Dallas L. Jones interviews (transcripts in my possession) with
    Alice Dickson, Nov. 13, 1962
    Mrs. Walter Drew, Nov. 12, 14, 15, 1962
    Josephine Foster, Nov. 12, 1962
    Lynn Franklin, Dec. 11, 1962
    Earl Harding, Nov. 13, 1962
    Clyde MacCornack, Dec. 12, 1962
    Noel Sargent, Nov. 15, 1962
    M. Harry Smedley, Nov. 14, 1962
    Fred Taylor, Nov. 14, 1962
Oscar Lawler, Los Angeles Attorney. History Project, University of California, Los Angeles, 1962.
Joseph R. LaRocca, Dec. 18, 1992 (phone conversation).
Eric Waterman, Nov. 1992 (phone conversation).

Newspapers

Detroit Saturday Night, 1915–31.
Indianapolis Star, Apr. 1911, Oct. to Dec. 1912.
Los Angeles Times, 1911–13, 1915–16, Oct. 1929.
New York Times, 1903–37.

Periodicals

American Contractor, 1923–24.
American Industries, 1902–30.
Bridgemen and Iron Workers Magazine, 1926–29.
Bridgemen's Magazine, 1901–37.
Industry (became *Industrial Progress* in 1922), 1918–24.
Iron Age, 1903–37.
Iron Trade Review (became *Steel* in 1930), 1903–37.
Machinists' Monthly Journal, 1911–15, 1920–23.
Railway Age, 1919–24.
Railway Age Gazette, 1911–12.
Railway Carmen's Journal, 1911–15.
Review (became *Open Shop Review* in 1919 and *Shop Review* in 1928), 1909–32.
Square Deal, 1905–16.

Doctoral Dissertations

Bustard, Bruce. "The Human Factor: Labor Administration and Industrial Mobilization during the First World War." University of Iowa, 1984.

Davis, Colin John. "Bitter Storm: The 1922 National Railroad Shopmen's Strike." State University of New York at Binghampton, 1988.

Ernst, Daniel Robinson. "The Lawyers and the Labor Trust: A History of the American Anti-Boycott Association." Princeton University, 1989.

Hurvitz, Haggai. "The Meaning of Industrial Conflict in Some Ideologies of the Early 1920's: The AFL, Organized Employers and Herbert Hoover." Columbia University, 1971.

Jeffreys-Jones, Rhodri. "The Problem of Industrial Violence in the United States, 1899–1909." Cambridge University [1969].

Jones, Dallas L. "The Wilson Administration and Organized Labor, 1912–1919." Cornell University, 1955.

Klug, Thomas A. "The Roots of the Open Shop: Employers, Trade Unions, and Craft Labor Markets in Detroit, 1859–1907." Wayne State University, 1993.

Meehan, Maria Eucharia. "Frank P. Walsh and the American Labor Movement." New York University, 1962.

Palmer, David. "Organizing the Shipyards: Unionization at New York Ship, Federal Ship, and Fore River, 1898–1945." Brandeis University, 1989.

Scheinberg, Stephen J. "The Development of Corporation Labor Policy, 1900–1940." University of Wisconsin, 1966.

Shapiro, Herbert. "Lincoln Steffens: The Evolution of an American Radical." University of Rochester, 1964.

Sigmund, Elwin Wilber. "Federal Laws Concerning Railroad Labor Disputes: A Legislative and Legal History, 1877–1934." University of Illinois, 1961.

Wakstein, Allen Morton. "The Open-Shop Movement, 1919–1933." University of Illinois, 1961.

Williams, William John. "Shipbuilding and the Wilson Administration: The Development of Labor Policy, 1914–1917." University of Washington, 1989.

Other Unpublished Material

Alexander, Magnus W. "The First Yama Conference on National Industrial Efficiency, June 5 to June 7, 1915." 1915 (copy in Conference Board).
———. "The Second Yama Conference on National Industrial Efficiency, September 18 to 21, 1915." [1915] (copy in Hagley Museum and Library).
———. "The Third Yama Conference on National Industrial Efficiency, July 2 to 5, 1916." [1916] (copy in Hagley Museum and Library).
Gitelman, H. M., notes on John Henderson Powell, Jr., "The History of the National Industrial Conference Board" (in Gitelman's possession).
[New York] Joint Legislative Committee on Housing, Minutes of Hearings, Oct. 20–Nov. 11, 1920 (copy in New York Public Library).
———. Minutes of Hearings, May 18–June 3, 1922 (copy in University of Michigan Library).
Rogers, Clyde L. "Draft History of the Conference Board." [1965] (copy in Hagley Museum and Library).

Published Books, Articles, and Proceedings

Adamic, Louis. *Dynamite: The Story of Class Violence in America.* Rev. ed. New York: Viking Press, 1934.
Adams, Graham, Jr. *Age of Industrial Violence, 1910–1915.* New York: Columbia University Press, 1966.
Adams, T. S. "Violence in Labor Disputes." *Publications of the American Economics Association,* 3d. Ser. 7 (1906): 176–206.
American Federation of Labor. *Proceedings of the Annual Conventions.* 1906, 1911, 1917.
Badger, Anthony. *The New Deal.* New York: Noonday Press, 1989.
Baillie, Hugh. *High Tension: The Recollections of Hugh Baillie.* New York: Harper and Brothers, 1959.
Baker, Ray Stannard. "Parker and Roosevelt on Labor." *McClure's Magazine* 24 (Nov. 1904): 41–52.
———. "Trust's New Tool—the Labor Boss." *McClure's Magazine* 22 (Nov. 1903): 30–43.
Barnett, George E. "Growth of Labor Organizations in the United States, 1897–1914." *Quarterly Journal of Economics* 30 (Aug. 1916): 780–95.
Berman, Edward. *Labor Disputes and the Presidents of the United States.* New York: Longman's, Green and Co., 1924.
Bernstein, Irving. *A Caring Society: The New Deal, the Worker, and the Great Depression.* Boston: Houghton Mifflin Co., 1985.
———. *The Lean Years: A History of the American Worker, 1920–1933.* Boston: Houghton Mifflin Co., 1960.
Best, Gary. "President Wilson's Second Industrial Conference, 1919–20." *Labor History* 16 (Fall 1975): 505–20.
Bing, Alexander M. "The Posse Commitatus in Industry." *Survey* 49 (Jan. 15, 1923): 493–96+.
———. *War-time Strikes and Their Adjustment.* New York: Arno and the New York Times, 1971.
Bolling, Raynal C. "The United States Steel Corporation and Labor Conditions." *Annals of the American Academy of Political and Social Science* 42 (July 1912): 38–47.

Bonnett, Clarence E. *Employers' Associations in the United States.* New York: Macmillan Co., 1922.

Brandes, Stuart D. *American Welfare Capitalism, 1880–1940.* Chicago: University of Chicago Press, 1976.

Brody, David. *Labor in Crisis: The Steel Strike of 1919.* Philadelphia: J. B. Lippencott Co., 1965.

———. *Steelworkers in America: The Nonunion Era.* New York: Harper and Brothers, 1960.

Brooks, Robert R. R. *As Steel Goes.* New Haven: Yale University Press, 1940.

Bucki, Cecelia F. "Dilution and Craft Tradition: Bridgeport, Connecticut, Munitions Workers, 1915–1919." *Social Science History* 4 (Feb. 1980): 105–23.

Bullard, F. Lauriston. "Labor Unions at the Danger Line: Considerations of the Public Safety." *Atlantic Monthly* 132 (Dec. 1923): 721–31.

Burns, William J. *The Masked War.* New York: George H. Doran Co., 1913.

Charles, Searle F. *Minister of Relief: Harry Hopkins and the New Deal.* Syracuse: Syracuse University Press, 1963.

Chenery, William L., and John A. Fitch. "The Untermeyer Revelations." *Survey* 45 (Jan. 1, 1921): 491–95.

Christie, Robert A. *Empire in Wood: A History of the Carpenters' Union.* Ithaca: Cornell University Press, 1956.

Clarkin, Franklin. "The Daily Walk of the Walking Delegate." *Century Magazine* 67 (Dec. 1903): 298–304.

Cleland, Robert. *California in Our Time (1900–1940).* New York: Alfred A. Knopf, 1947.

Cohn, Alfred, and Joe Chisholm. *"Take the Witness!"* New York: Frederick A. Stokes, 1934.

"The Common Welfare." *Survey* 27 (Dec. 30, 1911): 1407–12.

Commons, John R. "Causes of the Union Shop Policy." *Publications of the American Economics Association,* 3d Ser. 6 (1905): 140–59.

———. *Myself.* New York: Macmillan Co., 1934.

———, ed. *Trade Unionism and Labor Problems.* Boston: Ginn and Co., 1905.

Condit, Carl W. *The Rise of the Skyscraper.* Chicago: University of Chicago Press, 1952.

Conner, Valerie Jean. *The National War Labor Board.* Chapel Hill: University of North Carolina Press, 1983.

Connolly, Christopher. "The Saving of Clarence Darrow." *Collier's* 48 (Dec. 23, 1910): 9–10.

Cowan, Geoffrey. *The People v. Clarence Darrow.* New York: Times Books, Random House: 1993.

Craig, E. M. "Building Conditions in Chicago." *American Contractor* 44 (Jan. 6–Dec. 22, 1923): 24–25 et passim.

Cross, Ira B. *A History of the Labor Movement in California.* Berkeley: University of California Press, 1935.

Darrow, Clarence. *The Story of My Life.* New York: Charles Scribner's Sons, 1932.

Davis, Allen F. "The Campaign for the Industrial Relations Commission, 1911–1913." *Mid-America* 45 (Oct. 1963): 211–29.

Debs, Eugene V. "The McNamara Case and the Labor Movement." *International Socialist Review* 12 (Jan. 1912): 397–401.

Donnelly, Samuel B. "The Trade Agreement in the Building Trades." *Annals of the American Academy of Political and Social Science* 27 (May 1906): 48–54.

Douglas, P. H., and F. E. Wolfe. "Labor Administration in the Shipbuilding Industry during War Time." *Journal of Political Economy* 27 (Mar. 1919): 145–87, (May 1919): 362–96.

Drew, Walter. "The Closed Shop and the Public." *American Industries* 6 (Sept. 15, 1907): 13–14.

———. "Closed Shop Clauses in Building Contracts." *American Industries* 15 (Mar. 1915): 11–12.

———. "Closed Shop Unionism." *Government* 2 (Mar. 1908): 384–88.

———. "The Closed Shop vs. the Building Industry." *Square Deal* 2 (Jan. 1907): 23–26.

———. "Conditions in the Structural Erection Industry." *Square Deal* 18 (Mar. 1916): 47–49.

———. "The Federal Commission on Industrial Relations." *American Industries* 15 (June 1915): 17–18.

———. "The Federal Industrial Relations Commission Report." *American Industries* 15 (Jan. 1915): 15–17.

———. "Federal Control of Railway Labor." *American Industries* 21 (Oct. 1920): 10–12.

———. "Forcing the Closed Shop as a War Measure." *American Industries* 18 (Nov. 1917): 26.

———. "Government by Injunction." *Square Deal* 2 (Dec. 1906): 11–14.

———. "Labor Conditions in the Building Trades." *American Industries* 10 (Dec. 1909): 59.

———. "The Labor Trust's Crusade against the Courts." *Square Deal* 2 (Oct. 1906): 15–16.

———. "Labor Unions and an Eight Hour Law." *Square Deal* 3 (July 1908): 33–38.

———. "Labor Unions and Socialism." *Square Deal* 3 (Apr. 1908): 9–12.

———. "Labor's Monopoly in Building." *American Industries* 30 (May 1930): 16–24.

———. "National Secret Service Is Now Proposed for Protection." *Square Deal* 8 (July 1911): 529-31.

———. "New York Liability Act." *Square Deal* 8 (Feb. 1911): 24–25.

———. "Open and Closed Shop in the Structural Iron Industry." *Survey* 35 (Mar. 11, 1916): 702–3.

———. "The Political Purpose of Organized Labor." *Square Deal* 4 (Oct. 1908): 13–18.

———. "The Strike, the Lockout, and the Neutral Citizen." *American Industries* 17 (Mar. 1917): 32–33.

———. "Strikes against the Open Shop." *Square Deal* 5 (Aug. 1909): 312–33.

———. "Strikes and How to Handle Them." *Square Deal* 1 (July 1906): 3–5.

———. "To Build Open or Closed, Which?" *Square Deal* 6 (June 1910): 399–405.

———. "The Union and the Law: Some Legal Phases of the Labor Question." *Square Deal* 1 (May 1906): 21–24.

———. "War Contracts and the Open Shop." *American Industries* 18 (Dec. 1917): 24.

———. "The Workman behind the Army." *Leslie's Weekly* 122 (Mar. 9, 1916): 289+.

Dubofsky, Melvyn. *We Shall Be All: A History of the Industrial Workers of the World.* Chicago: Quadrangle Books, 1969.

Emery, James A. "The Story of San Francisco." *Review* 14 (Feb. 1917): 45–55.

Fine, Sidney. *Frank Murphy: The Washington Years.* Ann Arbor: University of Michigan Press, 1984.

————. "The National Erectors' Association and the Dynamiters." *Labor History* 32 (Winter 1991): 5–41.

Fitch, John A. *The Causes of Industrial Unrest.* New York: Harper and Brothers, 1924.

————. "The Dynamite Case." *Survey* 29 (Feb. 1, 1913): 607–17.

Foner, Philip S. *History of the Labor Movement in the United States.* Vol. 3. New York: International Publishers, 1964.

"Forty Years a Daredevil." *Literary Digest* 85 (May 30, 1925): 38–45.

Frankfurter, Felix, and Nathan Greene. *The Labor Injunction.* New York: Macmillan Co., 1930.

Franklin, Fabian. "Social Workers and Labor Violence." *Survey* 29 (Feb. 1, 1913): 618–21.

Freidel, Frank. *Franklin D. Roosevelt: The Ordeal.* Boston: Little, Brown and Co., 1954.

Friedheim, Robert L. *The Seattle General Strike.* Seattle: University of Washington Press, 1964.

Frost, Richard H. *The Mooney Case.* Stanford: Stanford University Press, 1968.

Galenson, Walter. *The CIO Challenge to the AFL.* Cambridge, Mass.: Harvard University Press, 1960.

————. *The United Brotherhood of Carpenters.* Cambridge, Mass.: Harvard University Press, 1983.

Garraty, John A. "The United States Steel Corporation versus Labor: The Early Years." *Labor History* 1 (Winter 1960): 3–38.

Gitelman, H. M. "Being of Two Minds: American Employers Confront the Labor Problem, 1915–1919." *Labor History* 25 (Spring 1984): 188–216.

————. "Management's Crisis of Confidence and the Origin of the National Industrial Conference Board, 1914–1916." *Business History Review* 58 (Summer 1984): 153–77.

————. "Perspectives on American Industrial Violence." *Business History Review* 47 (Spring 1973): 1–23.

Goldfarb, Michael. *The Decline of Organized Labor in the United States.* Chicago: University of Chicago Press, 1987.

Gompers, Samuel. "American Labor Union Convention in War Time." *American Federalist* 25 (Jan. 1918): 29–39.

————. "The McNamara Case." *American Federationist* 18 (June 1911): 433–50.

————. "The Organized Assault against the Rights and Leaders of the American Workingmen." *McClure's Magazine* 38 (Feb. 1912): 371–76.

————. *Seventy Years of Life and Labour.* 2 vols. London: Hurst and Blackett [1925].

"Gompers and Burns on Unionism and Dynamite." *McClure's Magazine* 38 (Feb. 1912): 363–76.

Gottlieb, Robert, and Irene Wolt. *Thinking Big: The Story of the Los Angeles Times.* New York: G. P. Putnam's Sons, 1977.

Grant, Luke. *The National Erectors' Association and the International Association of Bridge and Structural Ironworkers.* Washington, 1915.

————. "The Walking Delegate." *Outlook* 84 (Nov. 10, 1906): 615–21.

Green, Marguerite. *The National Civic Federation and the American Labor Movement, 1900–1925.* Washington: Catholic University of America Press, 1956.

Haber, William. *Industrial Relations in the Building Industry.* New York: Arno and New York Times, 1971.

Harrison, Charles Yale. *Clarence Darrow.* New York: Jonathan Cape and Harrison Smith, 1931.

Haydu, Jeffrey. *Between Craft and Class: Skilled Workers and Factory Politics in the United States and Britain.* Berkeley: University of California Press, 1988.

———. "Employers, Unions, and American Exceptionalism: Pre–World War I Open Shops in the Machine Trades in Comparative Perspective." *International Review of Social History* 33 (1988): 25–41.

Hines, Walker D. *War History of American Railroads.* New Haven: Yale University Press, 1928.

Hoagland, H. E. "Closed Shop versus Open Shop." *American Economic Review* 8 (Dec. 1918): 752–62.

Hollander, Jacob H., and George E. Barnett, eds. *Studies in American Trade Unionism.* New York: Henry Holt and Co., 1912.

Holt, James. "Trade Unionism in the British and U.S. Steel Industries, 1880–1914: A Comparative Study." *Labor History* 18 (Winter 1977): 5–35.

Horowitz, Louis J., and Boyden Sparks. *The Towers of New York: The Memoirs of a Master Builder.* New York: Simon and Schuster, 1937.

Hurvitz, Haggai. "Ideology and Industrial Conflict: President Wilson's First Industrial Conference of October 1919." *Labor History* 18 (Fall 1977): 509–24.

Hustveldt, Lloyd. "O. A. Tvietmoe: Labor Leader." *Norwegian American Studies* 30 (1985): 3–54.

Hutchinson, John. *The Imperfect Union: A History of Corruption in American Trade Unions.* New York: E. P. Dutton and Co., 1970.

"An Informal History of the Iron Workers" (Reprinted from the *Ironworker,* 1971).

Jackson, Robert Max. *The Formation of Craft Labor Markets.* Orlando: Academic Press, 1984.

Jacoby, Sanford M. "Norms and Cycles: The Dynamics of Nonunion Industrial Relations in the United States, 1897–1987." In Katharine G. Abraham and Robert McKersie, eds. *New Developments in Human Resources and Labor Markets.* Cambridge, Mass.: MIT Press, 1990.

———, ed. *Masters to Managers: Historical and Comparative Perspectives on American Employers.* New York: Columbia University Press, 1991.

Janick, Herbert. "From Union Town to Open Shop: The Decline of the United Hatters of Danbury, Connecticut, 1917–1922." *Connecticut History* 31 (1990): 1–20.

Jeffreys-Jones, Rhodri. *Violence and Reform in American History.* New York: Academic Viewpoints, 1978.

Jewell, B. M. "The Railway Strike: Strikers' Viewpoint." *New York Times Current History* 17 (Nov. 1922): 202–7.

Kazin, Michael. *Barons of Labor: The San Francisco Building Trades and Union Power in the Progressive Era.* Urbana: University of Illinois Press, 1987.

Keith, John. "The New Union of Employers." *Harper's Weekly* 48 (Jan. 23, 1904): 130–33.

Kipnis, Ira. *The American Socialist Movement, 1897–1912.* New York: Columbia University Press, 1952.

Klug, Thomas. "Employers' Strategies in the Detroit Labor Market." In Nelson Lichtenstein and Stephen Meyer, eds. *On the Line: Essays on the History of Auto Work.* Urbana: University of Illinois Press, 1989.

Knight, Robert Edward Lee. *Industrial Relations in the San Francisco Bay Area, 1900–1918.* Berkeley: University of California Press, 1960.

Koster, Frederick J. "The Chamber of Commerce in Industrial Affairs." *American Industries* 17 (Feb. 1917): 22–23.

"Larger Bearings of the McNamara Case." *Survey* 27 (Dec. 30, 1911): 1413–29.

Lauck, W. Jett, and Claude S. Watts. *The Industrial Code*. New York: Funk and Wagnalls, 1922.

Lecht, Leonard A. *Experience under Railway Labor Legislation*. New York: Columbia University Press, 1955.

Levi, Stephen C. "The Battle for the Eight-Hour Day in San Francisco." *California History* 57 (Winter 1978–79): 342–53.

Link, Arthur S. *Woodrow Wilson and the Progressive Era, 1910–1917*. New York: Harper and Brothers, 1954.

Lombardi, John. *Labor's Voice in the Cabinet: A History of the Department of Labor from its Origin to 1921*. New York: Columbia University Press, 1942.

Lorwin, Lewis L. *The American Federation of Labor*. Washington: Brookings Institution, 1933.

Lubove, Roy. *The Struggle for Social Security, 1900–1935*. Cambridge, Mass.: Harvard University Press, 1968.

McFarlane, Peter Clark. "What Is the Matter with Los Angeles?" *Collier's* 48 (Dec. 2, 1911): 28, 30–31.

McKean, Dayton David. *The Boss: The Hague Machine in Action*. Boston: Houghton Mifflin Co., 1940.

McLaughlin, Doris. "The Second Battle of Battle Creek: The Open Shop Movement in the Early Twentieth Century." *Labor History* 14 (Summer 1973): 323–39.

McManigal, Ortie E. *The National Dynamite Plot*. Los Angeles: Neale Co., 1913.

Marcosson, Isaac F. "The Fight for the Open Shop." *World's Work* 11 (Dec. 1905): 6955–65.

Merritt, Walter Gordon. *History of the League for Industrial Rights*. New York: League for Industrial Rights, 1925.

Millis, Harry A., and Emily Clark Brown. *From the Wagner Act to Taft-Hartley*. Chicago: University of Chicago Press, 1950.

Montgomery, David. *The Fall of the House of Labor: The Workplace, the State, and American Labor Activism, 1865–1925*. New York: Cambridge University Press, 1987.

———. *Workers' Control in America*. Cambridge, England: Cambridge University Press, 1979.

Montgomery, Royal E. *Industrial Relations in the Chicago Building Trades*. Chicago: University of Chicago Press, 1927.

———. "Jurisdictional Disputes." *Journal of Political Economy* 35 (Feb. 1927): 91–113.

Murray, Robert K. *Red Scare*. Minneapolis: University of Minnesota Press, 1955.

National Association of Manufacturers. *Open Shop Encyclopedia for Debaters*. . . . [New York]: National Association of Manufacturers, 1921.

———. *Proceedings of the Annual Conventions*. 1903–1928.

Ohl, John Kennedy. *Hugh S. Johnson and the New Deal*. (DeKalb: Northern Illinois University Press, 1985.

Palmer, Frederick. "Otistown of the Open Shop." *Hampton's Magazine* 26 (Jan. 1911): 29–44.

Perlman, Mark. *The Machinists*. Cambridge, Mass.: Harvard University Press, 1961.

Perlman, Selig, and Philip Taft. *History of Labor in the United States, 1896–1932.* New York: Macmillan Co., 1935.

Perry, Louis B., and Richard S. Perry. *A History of the Los Angeles Labor Movement, 1911–1941.* Berkeley: University of California Press, 1963.

"Petition to the President for a Federal Commission on Industrial Relations." *Survey* 27 (Dec. 30, 1911): 1430–31.

Phillips, Clifton J. *Indiana in Transition: The Emergence of an Industrial Commonwealth, 1880–1920.* Indianapolis: Indiana Historical Bureau and Indiana Historical Society, 1968.

Pickering, Ruth. "Newark and the War Labor Board." *Nation* 107 (Oct. 26, 1918): 484–85.

Plea of Clarence Darrow in His Own Defense to the Jury at Los Angeles August, 1912. Los Angeles: Golden Press, 1912.

Poole, Ernest. "Cowboys in the Skies." *Everybody's* 19 (Nov. 1908): 641–53.

Pratt, William C. "The Omaha Business Men's Association and the Open Shop, 1903–1909." *Nebraska History* 70 (Summer 1989): 172–83.

Pringle, Henry F. *The Life and Times of William Howard Taft.* 2 vols. New York: Farrar and Rinehart, 1939.

Railway Employes' Department, American Federation of Labor. *The Case of the Railway Shopmen* [1922].

Ramirez, Bruno. *When Workers Fight: The Politics of Industrial Relations in the Progressive Era, 1898–1916.* Westport, Conn.: Greenwood Press, 1978.

Robinson, Jesse. *The Amalgamated Association of Iron, Steel and Tin Workers.* Baltimore: Johns Hopkins Press, 1920.

Rotsch, Melvin M. "Building with Steel and Concrete." In Melvin Kranzberg and Carroll W. Pursell, Jr., eds. *Technology and Western Civilization.* Vol. 2. New York: Oxford University Press, 1967.

Ryan, Frederick L. *Industrial Relations in the San Francisco Building Trades.* Norman: University of Oklahoma Press, 1936.

Ryder, David Warren. "The Unions Lose in San Francisco." *American Mercury* 7 (Apr. 1926): 412–17.

St. Johns, Adela Rogers. *Final Verdict.* Garden City, N.Y.: Doubleday and Co., 1962.

Sautter, Udo. *Three Cheers for the Unemployed: Government and Unemployment before the New Deal.* New York: Columbia University Press, 1991.

Schneirov, Richard, and Thomas J. Suhrbur. *Union Brotherhood, Union Town: The History of the Carpenters' Union of Chicago, 1863–1987.* Carbondale: Southern Illinois University Press, 1988.

Scott, Leroy. *The Walking Delegate.* Upper Saddle River, N.J.: Literature House, 1969.

Seidman, Harold. *Labor Czars: A History of Labor Racketeering.* New York: Liveright Publishing Co., 1938.

Shapiro, Herbert. "Lincoln Steffens and the McNamara Case: A Progressive Response to Class Conflict." *American Journal of Economics and Sociology* 39 (Oct. 1980): 397–412.

———. "The McNamara Case: A Crisis of the Progressive Era." *Southern California Quarterly* 59 (Fall 1977): 271–87.

———. "The McNamara Case: A Window on Class Antagonism in the Progressive Era." *Southern California Quarterly* 70 (Spring 1988): 69–95.

Shaw, Frank L. *The Building Trades.* Cleveland: Survey Committee of the Cleveland Foundation, 1916.

"Ships and Organized Labor." *New Republic* 14 (Mar. 2, 1918): 132–33.

Slichter, Sumner H. "The Current Labor Policies of American Industries." *Quarterly Journal of Economics* 43 (May 1929): 393–435.

Smith, Darrell Hevenor. *The United States Employment Service.* Baltimore: Johns Hopkins University Press, 1923.

Soule, George. "The Building Scandal." *Nation* 111 (Nov. 17, 1920): 560–61.

Staley, Eugene. *History of the Illinois Federation of Labor.* Chicago: University of Chicago Press, 1930.

Stecker, Margaret Loomis. "The National Founders' Association." *Quarterly Journal of Economics* 30 (Feb. 1916): 352–86.

Steffens, Lincoln. *Autobiography of Lincoln Steffens.* New York: Harcourt D. Brace and Co., 1931.

Steigerwalt, Albert K. *The National Association of Manufacturers, 1895–1914.* Ann Arbor: Bureau of Business Research, Graduate School of Business Administration, 1964.

Stimson, Grace Heilman. *Rise of the Labor Movement in Los Angeles.* Berkeley: University of California Press, 1955.

Stockton, Frank T. *The Closed Shop in American Trade Unions.* Baltimore: Johns Hopkins University Studies, 1911.

Stone, Irving. *Clarence Darrow for the Defense.* New York: Garden City Publishing Co., 1943.

Taft, Philip. *The A.F. of L. in the Time of Gompers.* New York: Harper and Brothers, 1957.

Taft, Philip, and Philip Ross. "American Labor Violence: Its Cause, Character, and Outcome." In Hugh Davis Graham and Ted Robert Gurr. *Violence in America: Historical and Comparative Prospectives.* New York: Bantam Books, 1969.

Taylor, Albion Guilford. *Labor Policies of the National Association of Manufacturers.* Urbana: University of Illinois, 1928.

Taylor, Ralph B. "What the Lockwood Committee Disclosed." *Nation* 113 (July 6, 1921): 12–14.

Tierney, Kevin. *Darrow.* New York: Thomas Y. Crowell, 1979.

Toner, Jerome L. *The Closed Shop in the American Labor Movement.* Washington: Catholic University of America Press, 1941.

Troy, Leo. "Labor Representation on American Railroads." *Labor History* 2 (Fall 1961): 295–322.

———. *Trade Union Membership, 1897–1962.* New York: Columbia University Press [1965].

Ulman, Lloyd. "Who Wanted Collective Bargaining in the First Place?" In Industrial Relations Research Association, *Proceedings of the Thirty-Ninth Annual Meeting (December 28–30, 1986).* [New York, 1986].

Unionist. "The Los Angeles Conspiracy against Organized Labor." *International Socialist Review* 11 (Nov. 1910): 260–66.

Wakstein, Allen M. "The National Association of Manufacturers and Labor Relations in the 1920s." *Labor History* 10 (Spring 1969): 163–76.

———. "The Origins of the Open-Shop Movement, 1919–1920." *Journal of American History* 51 (Dec. 1964): 460–75.

Walling, William English. "The Building Trades Employers and the Unions." *World's Work* 6 (Aug. 1903): 3790–94.

Warne, Frank Julian. *The Workers at War.* New York: Century Co., 1920.

Watkins, Gordon S. *Labor Problems and Labor Administration in the United States during the World War.* Urbana: University of Illinois, 1919.

Watts, Sarah Lyon. *Order against Chaos: Business Culture and Labor Ideology in America, 1880–1915.* New York: Greenwood Press, 1991.

Wehle, Louis B. *Hidden Threads of History.* New York: Macmillan Co., 1953.

Weinberg, Arthur, and Lila Weinberg. *Clarence Darrow: A Sentimental Rebel.* New York: G. P. Putnam's Sons, 1980.

Wesser, Robert F. "Conflict and Compromise: The Workmen's Compensation Movement in New York, 1890–1913." *Labor History* 11 (Summer 1971): 345–72.

Whitney, Nathaniel Ruggles. *Jurisdiction in American Building-Trades Unions.* Baltimore: Johns Hopkins University Press, 1914.

Wiebe, Robert H. *Businessmen and Reform: A Study of the Progressive Movement.* Cambridge, Mass.: Harvard University Press, 1962.

Willoughby, William Franklin. "Employers' Associations for Dealing with Labor in the United States." *Quarterly Journal of Economics* 20 (Nov. 1905): 110–50.

Woehlke, Walter V. "The End of the Dynamite Case—'Guilty.'" *Outlook* 99 (Dec. 16, 1911): 903–8.

———. "Terrorism in America." *Outlook* 100 (Feb. 17, 1912): 359–67.

Wolf, H. D. *The Railroad Labor Board.* Chicago: University of Chicago Press, 1927.

Wolman, Leo. *Ebb and Flow in Trade Unionism.* New York: National Bureau of Economic Research, 1936.

———. *The Growth of American Trade Unions, 1880–1923.* New York: National Bureau of Economic Research, 1924.

Zimand, Savel. *The Open Shop Drive.* New York: Bureau of Industrial Research [1921].

Index

strike, 52, 132–33, 199, 214, 220, 222; on the IABSOIW, 53, 159, 289n.23; on employer responsibility, 54, 56, 138, 146, 202, 205, 208, 211; on wages, 54–56, 57, 66; on employment bureaus, 57, 58; and foremen, 58–59, 139, 235–36; and subcontracts, 59; and denial of steel, 59–60; and 1906 strike, 60; and preference for nonunionists, 60–61, 61–62, 70, 139, 194; and "yellow dog" contracts, 61, 138, 236; and espionage, 62–63, 68, 99–100, 100–102, 106, 107, 112, 124, 139, 191, 194; on detective companies, 62, 101, 107; and Foster, 63, 140, 153, 191, 194, 220, 230, 251, 252; and American Erectors' Association, 63, 138–39, 169; and accident insurance, 64–65; and welfare capitalism, 64–65; and employee representation, 65, 66, 134, 138, 205, 208; and notices to workers, 65; and dual unions, 65–66; and Buffalo, 70, 134; and Philadelphia, 70, 187, 188–89, 194, 220–21, 237; and Cleveland, 70–72, 126, 221; and Gary (Indiana), 72–73, 137; and Illinois Steel, 72–73; and Milwaukee, 73; and Kansas City, 73–75, 172; and San Francisco, 76, 77, 78, 143, 144, 216; on condition of NEA, 80; and slugging, 82–86; and dynamiting, 88, 98, 99–102, 105–7, 110–11, 126, 139; and Sherman Antitrust Act, 105, 106–7, 126; and possible IABSOIW damage suits, 106–7, 125–26; and W. Burns, 107, 112; and arrest and extradition of John J. McNamara, 107–9, 144; arrest of, 109; and search of IABSOIW headquarters, 109–10; and prosecution of McNamaras, 111–13; and Indianapolis evidence, 113–15, 116; and federal prosecution of dynamiters, 115, 116, 118–23, 124, 125, 126–27, 254; and McNamaras' guilty pleas, 117, 118; and sentencing of McNamaras, 118; alleged plot against, 122, 123, 127; and NEA witnesses, 125; and Darrow trials, 126–28; and Davis confession, 128; and Schmidt trial, 128; and AFL and IABSOIW reaction to dynamite cases, 129; view of NEA of, 131; use of dynamite trials by, 129, 165, 181, 196; and anti-injunction legislation, 129, 142, 144, 147–48, 165, 181, 196, 231, 232; view of construction industry of, 131–32, 141, 213–14, 221; view of general contractors of, 132–33, 137–38, 214, 221; and Business Men's Association of Omaha, 133–34, 172; and Pittsburgh, 134,

223–24; and Hartford, 134; and Washington, D.C., 135–36, 141; and Duluth, 136–37; IABSOIW on, 137; and Wilmington, 137–38; and Harriman lines strike, 139–41; and National Council for Industrial Defense, 141, 142, 147–48; and National Association of Manufacturers, 141–42, 149, 150, 210–13, 258, 271, 272; and National Industrial Conference Board, 141, 146–47, 161, 162, 206–9; and National Open Shop Publicity Bureau, 141–42; and Joint Committee of Associated Employers, 142, 146; and Commission on Industrial Relations, 142–46; and Walsh, 143, 144, 165, 240; and eight-hour day, 147, 148–49, 167–69; and workmen's compensation, 147, 149–51; and World War I, 151, 153, 154, 155, 156–57, 158–61, 161–62, 163–65, 166–71, 231; and Remington Arms strike, 153–54; and Steel Fabricators of the United States, 157, 165, 169; and United States Employment Service, 157; and Lackawanna Bridge Company, 158–61; definition of right to organize by, 164, 204; and steel workers organizing campaign, 165, 169, 175; and Danbury, 172–73; and 1919–20 steel boycott, 176–77, 180, 183–84, 185, 188, 192–93, 194, 196, 328n.36; and 1919–20 steel strike, 177; and National Steel Fabricators Association, 183, 194; and Lockwood Committee, 190, 192, 194, 198–99; and Department of Justice steel probe, 195; and Federal Trade Commission steel probe, 196; on effort to dissolve NEA and Iron League Erectors' Association, 197–98; and Untermeyer, 198–99; opposition of to open shop federations, 202; and 1920s open shop movement, 204–6; effort of to define a postwar national labor policy, 206–9; and President's Industrial Conference, 106–7; and United States Chamber of Commerce, 208; and President's Second Industrial Conference, 209; and Open Shop Committee and Department, 210–13; and Detroit, 219; and Dallas, 219; and Indianapolis, 220; and American Construction Council, 222; and public construction, 222–24, 232; and Citizens' Transportation Committee, 224–25, 228; and railroad shopcrafts dispute, 226–31; and union label issue, 231–32; on politicians and the open shop, 231–32; and Davis-Bacon Act, 232; and Norris-La Guardia Act, 232; and

223; and Pennsylvania Railroad, 229; and
Davis-Bacon Act, 232; and Black Thirty-
Hour bill, 257
National Association of (Manufacturers) and
Erectors of Structural Steel: principles of,
24–25; and 1903 strike, 25–26; renewal of
1903 agreements by, 27–28; and 1905 and
1906 strikes, 32, 33; and open shop, 33–34
National Association of Steel Fabricators,
192
National Building Trades Employers' Asso-
ciation, 21
National Civic Federation, 1, 10, 26, 55
National Committee for Organizing Iron and
Steel Workers, 165, 175, 176
National Construction Planning and Adjust-
ment Board, 266
National Council for Industrial Defense, 9,
143, 148, 269; and National Association of
Manufacturers, 7–8, 10; and Citizens' Industrial Association of America, 8–9; and
NEA, 141; and Drew, 141, 142, 147–48
National Erectors' Association, 53, 198; and
United States Steel, 1, 50, 51, 107, 108, 111,
232, 236, 246; nature of, 11; origins of, 23;
and American Bridge, 24, 48, 49–50, 236,
271; naming of, 34; and open shop, 34–35,
36–37, 45–46, 47, 50, 54, 60–61, 62, 64, 66,
69, 73–74, 76, 134, 141, 191, 201, 210; and
costs issue, 34–35, 53–54, 111, 137, 146,
181, 191, 213; selection of commissioner by,
35, 46; and National Association of Manufacturers, 35, 141–42, 150; organizational
problems of, 35–36; funding of and assessments, 35, 48, 49–50, 101, 106, 111–12,
132, 270–71, 288n.8, 304n.2; in New York,
43, 44–45, 46, 47, 48, 55, 56, 60–61, 65,
67–70, 78, 79, 99, 150, 175, 178–79, 182,
190, 235, 236, 237, 241–42, 245, 246, 271,
294n.77; and general contractors, 35, 132,
237; employment bureaus of, 44, 45, 50, 57,
66, 68, 70, 72, 73, 73–74, 156, 160, 169,
178, 235, 238, 256, 270, 294n.77, 347n.68;
in Chicago, 44–45, 75–76, 79, 219; and Allied Iron Associations, 44, 46, 47, 68–69;
Principles and Working Rules of, 45; wage
policy and wages of, 45, 51, 54–57, 66, 70,
146, 236, 255–56, 261; membership of, 47,
48–49, 57, 70, 73, 73–74, 76, 83, 90, 95,
131, 147, 176, 178–79, 182, 235, 236–37,
241, 242, 245, 262, 270–71, 294n.77,
348n.5; governance of, 47–48; and fabricators, 48–49, 79; as open shop defender of the
shops and mills, 49, 79, 175, 265, 268, 272;

role of, 50; and guard service, 50, 58, 85, 88;
discouragement of unionism by, 54; and
IABSOIW, 56, 57, 78, 79, 80, 81, 87, 108,
126; in Pittsburgh, 56, 57, 63, 66, 70, 72, 79;
in Chicago, 57, 75–76, 79, 219; in Cleveland, 57, 70–72, 79, 83–86, 219; and strikebreakers, 57; employees of, 58, 61–62, 78,
79; and foremen, 58–59, 64; subcontracting
policy of, 59, 236–37; denial of steel by, 59–
60, 160, 240, 265; preference of for nonunionists, 60–62, 178, 187, 236; espionage
by, 62–63, 85, 88, 99–100, 100–102, 106,
107, 112, 116, 191, 194; and Foster, 63, 191,
194, 230; and welfare capitalism, 63–64;
and accident insurance, 64–65, 293n.59; and
workmen's compensation, 64, 149–51; notices to workers by, 65; and dual unions, 65–
66, 79; and employee representation, 66; in
Buffalo, 70, 79; in Gary, 72–73; in Kansas
City, 73–75, 172; in Milwaukee, 73, 79, in
San Francisco, 76, 78, 79, 216; success of
open shop policy of, 78–80; in Hartford, 79;
steel tonnage erected by, 79, 132, 223, 235,
236, 237, 242, 256; and slugging, 83–86, 99;
and dynamiting, 86, 87, 88, 90, 99–102,
105–7, 124, 129, 139, 143; and 1910 Los
Angeles strike, 96; and prosecution of
McNamaras, 111–13; and Indianapolis evidence, 113, 115, 117; and federal prosecution of dynamiters, 114, 115, 121, 123–24,
125; and sentencing and guilty pleas of
McNamaras, 118, 140; and McManigal,
125; and Darrow trials, 126–28; and Davis,
128; and Schmidt trial, 128; Drew view of,
131; and building trades unions, 131, 132;
and Omaha, 133; and American Erectors'
Association, 138, 139; and railroad shopmen's strike, 140; and National Council for
Industrial Defense, 141; and Commission on
Industrial Relations, 143; and legislation,
147, 151; and eight-hour day, 148–49, 168–
69; and World War I, 155, 156, 156–57, 158,
160, 162, 167, 168–69; and steel workers organizing campaign, 165, 175; and Steel Fabricators of the United States, 169; and
Philadelphia, 175, 188; and 1919–20 steel
strike, 177; and open shop locals, 178; and
National Steel Fabricators Association, 182,
183; and 1919–20 steel boycott, 186, 194;
and Lockwood Committee, 190, 191, 192,
198; and Department of Justice steel probe,
195; and Federal Trade Commission steel
probe, 195–96, 197; and Untermeyer, 198–
99; and National Industrial Conference

O'Donnell, George. *See* Davis, George E.
Old Dominion Transportation Company, 225
Omaha: closed and open shop in, 133–34;
Business Men's Association of Omaha in,
133–34, 172
Open shop, 21; and Anthracite Coal Strike
Commission, 2, 4, 161; definition of, 2, 4,
54, 182, 191, 192, 194, 198, 203, 207–8,
225, 271; in Dayton, 2; and National Association of Manufacturers, 3–4, 210–13;
and Citizens' Industrial Association of
America, 5, 7, 9; in Battle Creek, 6; and
United States Steel, 10–11, 25, 48, 49, 51,
73, 149, 150, 176, 182, 209, 220; and
American Bridge Company, 23, 33, 44, 49,
54; in New York, 28, 33, 40, 69–70, 79,
179, 180–81, 182, 237, 242, 243–44, 261;
and construction cost issue, 33–34, 52–53,
53–54, 73, 74, 111, 137, 146, 181, 191,
213; and general contractors, 34, 49, 132,
176; and NEA, 36–37, 45, 46, 47, 50, 54–
56, 60–61, 64, 66, 69, 73–74, 76, 78–81,
141, 210; in Grand Rapids, 37; and Drew,
38, 43, 45, 46, 47, 49, 50–51, 53–54, 78,
146, 147, 153, 154, 164–65, 170, 188,
194, 203, 206, 207–8, 220, 222, 231–32,
242, 269, 271, 272; in Los Angeles, 53,
94, 220, 237; in Detroit, 53, 219; and employment bureaus, 57–58; and foremen,
58, 59, 61, 139, 235–36; in Buffalo, 70,
90, 134, 165, 176–77, 237; in Pittsburgh,
70, 134; in Philadelphia, 70, 187, 220, 221,
237; in Cleveland, 71, 72, 221; in Kansas
City, 73, 172; in San Francisco, 77, 78,
215–16, 237, 247; degree of in structural
steel erection, 79, 132, 233, 235, 236, 237,
242, 256, 270; in Milwaukee, 90, 237, 259;
and slugging, 81–82, 84, 85–86; and
dynamiting, 90, 106, 118, 125, 129; and
employer associations, 105; and the building trades, 132; in Omaha, 133; in Columbus, 134; in New England, 134; in
Hartford, 134, 172; in Washington, D.C.,
135–36, 137; in Duluth, 136–37; in Gary,
137; in Wilmington, 137–38; and American Erectors' Association, 138, 139; on
Harriman lines, 141; in construction industry, 141; and Commission on Industrial Relations, 142, 143, 145; and National
Industrial Conference Board, 147, 206,
207–8, 210; and workmen's compensation,
149; and World War I, 153, 155, 156, 158,
161, 162, 163, 164–65, 166, 169, 170,
172–73; and Lackawanna Bridge Com-

pany, 158; in Bridgeport, 169, 170; and
National Steel Fabricators Association,
183; and Bethlehem Steel, 186, 191; and
1919–20 steel boycott, 188–89; Untermeyer on, 198; in the 1920s, 201–3, 213,
236; in Indianapolis, 202; and American
Plan, 203; and President's Industrial Conference, 207–8; and United States Chamber of Commerce, 207–8; in Chicago,
218–19; in Dallas, 219, 237; and public
construction, 222, 223; and Citizens'
Transportation Committee, 225; and Pennsylvania Railroad, 227; and railroad shopcrafts, 228; and union label, 231–32; and
Norris–La Guardia Act, 232; in Minneapolis, 237; in St. Paul, 237; in Seattle,
237; and National Industrial Recovery Act,
237; in New Jersey, 252; and structural
steel and steel codes, 263, 264, 265, 268;
demise of in structural steel erection, 269–
70; and right-to-work movement, 271
Ornamental ironworkers, 11
Oscar Daniels Company, 42
Otis, Harrison Gray, 94, 97, 108, 112, 119,
144, 230

Page, George T., 229
Panama Canal, 99
Panama-Pacific International Exposition, 78
Pan-American Bridge Company, 89, 91
Parks, Samuel, 18, 19–20, 23, 26–27, 40, 52,
82
Parry, David McLean, 3–4, 4–5, 111, 118
Parry Manufacturing Company, 3
Pearre bill, 148
Peck, G. L., 105, 106
Pelham (New York), 93
Pennsylvania: structural steel erection in,
341n.11
Pennsylvania Railroad Company: and slug-
ging, 83; and dynamiting, 105; and open
shop, 227; and railroad shopcrafts dispute,
227, 228–29, 230, 231; and Drew, 229;
and New Jersey, 251–52
Pennsylvania Steel Company, 48; and the
open shop, 33, 34; and Blackwell's Island
Bridge, 44–45, 88; and subcontracts, 59;
and espionage, 63; and slugging, 84, 85, 86
Peoria, 91, 92, 114, 305n.9
Peoria and Pekin Union Railway Company,
89, 102, 107, 115
Pettibone, George, 108
Philadelphia: IABSOIW in, 28, 91; open
shop in, 70, 187, 188–89, 220, 221, 237;

Heritage University Library
3240 Fort Road
Toppenish, WA 98948